Lecture Notes in Computer Science　2563

Edited by G. Goos, J. Hartmanis, and J. van Leeuwen

Springer

Berlin
Heidelberg
New York
Barcelona
Hong Kong
London
Milan
Paris
Tokyo

Yannis Manolopoulos   Skevos Evripidou
Antonis C. Kakas (Eds.)

Advances
in Informatics

8th Panhellenic Conference on Informatics, PCI 2001
Nicosia, Cyprus, November 8-10, 2001
Revised Selected Papers

 Springer

Series Editors

Gerhard Goos, Karlsruhe University, Germany
Juris Hartmanis, Cornell University, NY, USA
Jan van Leeuwen, Utrecht University, The Netherlands

Volume Editors

Yannis Manolopoulos
Aristotle University, Dept. of Informatics
54006 Thessaloniki, Greece
E-mail: manolopo@csd.auth.gr

Skevos Evripidou
Antonis C. Kakas
University of Cyprus, Dept. of Computer Science
P.O. Box 20537, 1678 Nicosia, Cyprus
E-mail:{skevos/antonis}@ucy.ac.cy

Cataloging-in-Publication Data applied for

A catalog record for this book is available from the Library of Congress

Bibliographic information published by Die Deutsche Bibliothek
Die Deutsche Bibliothek lists this publication in the Deutsche Nationalbibliografie;
detailed bibliographic data is available in the Internet at <http://dnb.ddb.de>.

CR Subject Classification (1998): H.2, D.2, I.2, I.4, C.2, K.3, E.1, F.2, H.5.2-3

ISSN 0302-9743
ISBN 3-540-3-540-07544-5 Springer-Verlag Berlin Heidelberg New York

Springer-Verlag Berlin Heidelberg New York
a member of BertelsmannSpringer Science+Business Media GmbH

http://www.springer.de

© Springer-Verlag Berlin Heidelberg 2003
Printed in Germany

Typesetting: Camera-ready by author, data conversion by DA-TeX Gerd Blumenstein
Printed on acid-free paper   SPIN 10871835   06/3142   5 4 3 2 1 0

Preface

The Panhellenic Conference on Informatics (PCI) was founded by the Greek Computer Society (EPY) in the early 1980s with the first event taking place in Athens in 1984. The conference has now been established as a biennial meeting of high importance for the Greek academic and industrial informatics communities, while recently the conference has been very successful in attracting significant international participation.

Usually, the 8th PCI was organized in Nicosia, the capital of Cyprus, during 8–10 November 2001, in cooperation with the Cyprus Computer Society (CCS), the University of Cyprus, and the Cyprus Telecommunications Authority (CYTA). The most important factor in the decision to hold the 8th PCI in Cyprus was the aim of strengthening the existing ties between Greece and Cyprus in the academic and industrial sectors of information technology. This is particularly important in view of the imminent accession of Cyprus to the European Union.

The main aim of the 8th PCI was twofold:

- The presentation of the most recent research work in the field of informatics carried out in Greece, Cyprus and by the Greek Diaspora, and
- The further promotion of information and communication technologies in Greece and Cyprus, in the broad perspective of the Information Society.

In particular, the wider conference comprised the following:

- Twenty-three scientific sessions for refereed original research or case-study academic papers,
- Seven workshops of two sessions each, where non-refereed papers on applications areas of information technology were presented in a more informal setting,
- Three distinguished keynote speakers from government and academia,
- A panel on the information Society with panelists from academia and industry,
- An exhibition of products and services related to information and telecommunication technologies, and
- An industrial track where sponsors were given the opportunity to present their solutions and technologies to a professional audience.

The two-volume proceedings of the conference included 104 refereed research and case-study papers accepted for presentation. Over 90% of the papers were reviewed by at least 3 referees in order to ensure a careful and fair selection of accepted papers. The 8th PCI event was therefore a very successful one in terms of the quality of contributions, program diversity, conference selectivity, and the caliber of the invited keynote speakers. For this reason, the organizers decided to publish a compendium of selected papers out of the 104 published in the conference proceedings. The present volume contains 31 selected papers that have been elaborated and extended by their authors and reviewed for a second time by two referees for each paper. We believe that this competitive procedure is a guarantee of the high quality of the outcome.

During the selection process special emphasis was given to papers that deal with advances in new directions in informatics. The Internet and the World Wide Web have not only transformed informatics but they also have affected most aspects of human life, from access to information to the way we do business and the way we entertain ourselves. Thus from the pool of the best rated papers of the conference some emphasis was given towards papers that have a higher degree of relevance to the Internet and the WWW. The 31 papers in this special issue are organized into eight sections as follows:

- **Databases**, dealing with issues related to: access methods and query processing for spatial databases, the design of OLAP servers, the use of materialized views for data warehouses and the Web, extensions of SQL for spatiotemporal environments and enhancements to the two-phase commit protocol.
- **Data Mining and Intelligent Systems**, covering topics of: belief revision in the context of knowledge representation, efficient maintenance of discovered schemas for semistructured data, new clustering methods for pharmaceutical applications, adaptive classification of Web documents based on user interests, data management and mining of seismic data, and the utilization of fuzzy cognitive maps as a support system for political decision making.
- **E-learning**, including a contribution proposing an architecture for an open learning management system using state-of-the-art software engineering techniques and a contribution on the use of a knowledge-based approach to organizing and accessing educational resources.
- **Human-Computer Interaction**, investigating issues related to: website evaluation under a usability-based perspective, a conceptual framework for studying interaction in online environments with an emphasis on learning environments, as well as statistical analysis and a comparison of the accessibility ratings for different domain categories for Cyprus-related websites.
- **Image Processing**, with papers on: an information-hiding method based on the 3-coloring problem that can be used for proving copyright ownership of digital objects, an experimental evaluation of the Monte/Carlo algorithm for singular value decomposition, and a face image synthesis system.
- **Networks and Systems**, with contributions on: a methodology for building communicating X-machines from existing standalone X-machine models, task allocation onto and execution of MPI applications on parallel architectures, communication issues for data-driven multithreading mobility, and QoS provisioning in IPv6 DECT networks.
- **Software and Languages**, which contains three contributions dealing with: high-level timed Petri Net temporal verification of real-time multiprocessor applications, architectural and application issues of a Greek morphological lexicon, and design patterns and roles in the context of behavioural evolution.

– **Theoretical Issues**, containing four papers focusing on: a new randomized data structure for the 1.5-dimensional range query problem, acceptor definable counting classes, the stability behaviour of the FIFO protocol in the adversarial queuing model, and a formal proof that k-splay fails to achieve base-k logN behavior.

We thank Springer-Verlag for accepting to publish this volume and for helping us make it a reality. We anticipate that this support will help in increasing further the quality of the PCI conference and we hope that this collaboration will continue in the future. Finally, the papers of this volume would not have met the desired standard of high quality without the invaluable help of the referees, all of whom we thank very much.

February 2003   Yannis Manolopoulos
                                                             Skevos Evripidou
                                                             Antonis C. Kakas

Reviewers

Andreas Andreou, University of Cyprus
Nikolaos Avouris, University of Patras
Panagiotis Bozanis, University of Thessaly
Vassilis Christofides, University of Crete
Stavros Dimitriadis, Aristotle University of Thessaloniki
Petros Drineas, Yale University
George Eleftherakis, City Liberal Studies Thessaloniki
George Evangelidis, University of Macedonia, Thessaloniki
George Hassapis, Aristotle University of Thessaloniki
Yannis Ioannidis, National and Kapodistrian University of Athens
Dimitrios Katsaros, Aristotle University of Thessaloniki
Petros Kefalas, City Liberal Studies Thessaloniki
Evangelos Kehris, City Liberal Studies Thessaloniki
Constantine Kotropoulos, Aristotle University, Thessaloniki
Nectarios Koziris, National Technical University of Athens
Evangellos Markatos, University of Crete
Pericles Mitkas, Aristotle University of Thessaloniki
Costas Mourlas, University of Athens
Alexandros Nanopoulos, Aristotle University of Thessaloniki
George Papadimitriou, Aristotle University of Thessaloniki
Nikolaos Papaspyrou, National Technical University of Athens
Iraklis Paraskakis, City Liberal Studies Thessaloniki
Andreas Pitsillides, University of Cyprus
Simos Retalis, University of Cyprus
Dimitrios Sampson, Inst. of Telecom and Informatics Thessaloniki
Paul Spirakis, University of Patras
Ioannis Stamelos, Aristotle University of Thessaloniki
Yannis Stavrakas, NCSR Democritos, Athens
Yannis Theodoridis, University of Piraeus
Athanasios Tsakalidis, University of Patras
Michael Vassilakopoulos, Higher TEI of Thessaloniki
Panos Vassiliadis, University of Ioannina
Michael Vazyrgiannis, Athens University of Economics and Business
Ioannis Vlahavas, Aristotle University of Thessaloniki
Stathis Zachos, National Technical University of Athens

Table of Contents

Processing Distance-Based Queries in Multidimensional Data Spaces Using R-trees

Antonio Corral[1][*], Joaquin Cañadas[1], and Michael Vassilakopoulos[2]

[1] Department of Languages and Computation, University of Almeria
04120 Almeria, Spain
acorral,jjcanada@ual.es
[2] Department of Information Technology
Technological Educational Institute of Thessaloniki
P.O. BOX 14561, 541 01, Greece
vasilako@it.teithe.gr

Abstract. In modern database applications the similarity, or dissimilarity of data objects is examined by performing distance-based queries (DBQs) on multidimensional data. The R-tree and its variations are commonly cited multidimensional access methods. In this paper, we investigate the performance of the most representative distance-based queries in multidimensional data spaces, where the point datasets are indexed by tree-like structures belonging to the R-tree family. In order to perform the K-nearest neighbor query (K-NNQ) and the K-closest pair query (K-CPQ), non-incremental recursive branch-and-bound algorithms are employed. The K-CPQ is shown to be a very expensive query for datasets of high cardinalities that becomes even more costly as the dimensionality increases. We also give ϵ-approximate versions of DBQ algorithms that can be performed faster than the exact ones, at the expense of introducing a distance relative error of the result. Experimentation with synthetic multidimensional point datasets, following Uniform and Gaussian distributions, reveals that the best index structure for K-NNQ is the X-tree. However, for K-CPQ, the R*-tree outperforms the X-tree in respect to the response time and the number of disk accesses, when an LRU buffer is used. Moreover, the application of the ϵ-approximate technique on the recursive K-CPQ algorithm leads to acceptable approximations of the result quickly, although the tradeoff between cost and accuracy cannot be easily controlled by the users.

1 Introduction

Large sets of multidimensional data are used in modern applications such as multimedia databases [12], medical images databases [21], CAD [18], metric databases [2], etc. In such applications, complex objects are stored. To support distance-based queries (DBQ), multidimensional feature vectors are extracted

---

[*] The author has been partially supported by the Spanish CICYT (project TIC 2002-03968).

Y. Manolopoulos et al. (Eds.): PCI 2001, LNCS 2563, pp. 1–18, 2003.

from the objects and organized in multidimensional indices. The most important property of this feature transformation is that these feature vectors correspond to points in the Euclidean multidimensional space. We need to calculate the distance between them for obtaining the similarity or dissimilarity of the original objects in the underlying application.

The distance between two points is measured using some metric function over the multidimensional data space. We can use the Euclidean distance for expressing the concepts of "neighborhood" and "closeness". The concept of "neighborhood" is related to the discovery of all the multidimensional points that are "near" to a given query point. The δ-distance range query and the K-nearest neighbors query are included in this category. The concept of "closeness" is related to the discovery of all pairs of multidimensional points that are "close" to each other. The δ-distance join query and the K-closest pairs query are included in this category.

Usually, distance-based queries are executed using some kind of multidimensional index structure [13] such as the R-trees, since the result can be found in logarithmic time, applying pruning techniques. The multidimensional access methods belonging to the R-tree family (the R-tree [14], the R*-tree [4] and particularly the X-tree [5]) are considered a good choice for indexing multidimensional point datasets in order to perform nearest neighbor queries. The branch-and-bound algorithms for DBQs employ distance metrics and pruning heuristics based on the MBR characteristics in the multidimensional Euclidean space, in order to reduce the searching space.

The main objective of this paper is to study the performance of the K-nearest neighbor and the K-closest pairs queries in multidimensional data spaces, where both point datasets are indexed by tree-like structures belonging to the R-tree family. To the authors knowledge, this paper and its successor [8] are the first research efforts in the literature that study performance of distance join queries for more than one tree structures and dimensionality of data larger than 2. We compare the results of exact recursive algorithms, applied in different kinds trees, in terms of the I/O activity and the response time.[1] We also test ϵ-approximate versions of the algorithms using the average relative distance error (ARDE) with respect to the exact solutions as a metric of the accuracy of the result. Experimental results are presented for several dimensionalities, numbers of elements in the result and fixed cardinalities of multidimensional point datasets following Uniform and Gaussian distributions in each dimension. Based on these experimental results, we draw conclusions about the behavior of these multidimensional access methods over these kinds of queries.

The paper is organized as follows. In Section 2, we review the literature (distance-based queries on multidimensional data spaces) and motivate the research reported here. In Section 3, a brief description of the R-tree family, and the definitions of the most representative distance-based queries are presented. In Section 4, recursive branch-and-bound algorithms based on metrics and pruning heuristics over MBRs for answering K-NNQs and K-CPQs are examined.

---

[1] A preliminary version of such a comparison appears in [10].

In Section 5, we discuss the ϵ-approximate versions of the K-NNQ and K-CPQ algorithms. Moreover, in Section 6, a comparative performance study of these algorithms is reported. Finally, in the last section, conclusions on the contribution of this paper and future work are summarized.

2   Related Work and Motivation

For the completness of presentation, Fig. 1 demonstrates examples of the distance-based queries that we study. In the left part of the figure, a set of 2-dimensional points organized according to an R-tree structure (MBR-based index) is depicted. Suppose that we want to find the three nearest neighbors (3-NNs) of the query point q. It is easy to see that the 3-NNs of q are p_{11}, p_8 and p_4. On the other hand, in the right part of the figure, two different sets of 2-dimensional points (organized according to two different R-tree structures, one depicted with non-colored MBRs and another depicted with shaded MBRs) are shown. It is again easy to see that the three closest pairs of points (3-CPs) of the two sets are (p_8, q_8), (p_{11}, q_{10}) and (p_4, q_6).

Numerous algorithms exist for answering distance-based queries. Most of these algorithms are focused in the K-nearest neighbors query (K-NNQ) over a multidimensional access method.

In [24] a branch-and-bound algorithm for K-NNQ using R-trees was proposed. It traverses the index in a depth-first traversal manner using recursion. K must be fixed in advance, giving rise to a non-incremental approach. In [6], this recursive algorithm was enhanced with respect to the pruning heuristics. On the other hand, in [17] an incremental algorithm for K-NNQ using R-trees (K must not be fixed in advance) was proposed, based on work for PMR-Quadtrees [15]. This algorithm employs a best-bound (best-first) searching strategy with a priority queue.

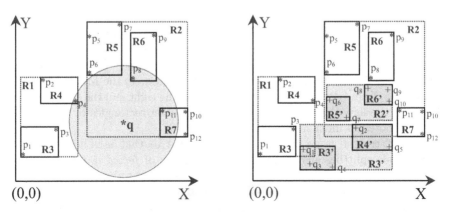

Fig. 1. Examples of a K-NNQ (left) and a K-CPQ (right)

For K-CPQs in spatial databases using R-trees, [9, 16, 25] are the only references in the literature. In [16], an incremental and iterative algorithm based on priority queues is presented for solving the distance join query and its extension for Semi-distance join query. The techniques proposed in [16] are enhanced in [25] by using adaptive multi-stage techniques, plane-sweep algorithm [23] and other improvements based on sweeping axis and sweeping direction, for K-distance join and incremental distance join. In [9], non-incremental recursive and iterative branch-and-bound algorithms are presented for solving the K-CPQ.

All the previous efforts about distance-based queries are mainly focused over only one multidimensional tree-like structure ("neighborhood" queries). Moreover, research involving more than one R-trees has been only presented for 2-dimensional data (points in 2-dimensional Euclidean space). Thus, here our objective is to investigate the behavior of DBQs, in particular, K-CPQ, over two multidimensional point datasets that are indexed by tree-like structures belonging to the R-tree family (that are widely used in spatial databases) and to present related approximate algorithms based on the ϵ-approximate technique. The successor of this paper [8], extending this study, presents three more approximation techniques (α-allowance, N-consider and M-consider) and studies experimentally their efficiency, their accuracy and especially the ability that each technique provides for tuning the trade-off between cost and accuracy.

3   The R-tree Family and Distance-Based Queries

3.1   The R-tree Family

R-trees [14] are hierarchical, height balanced multidimensional data structures, used for the dynamic organization of d-dimensional objects that are represented by d-dimensional MBRs. R-trees obey the following rules. Leaves reside on the same level and contain pairs of the form (R, O), where R is the MBR contains (spatially) the object determined by the identifier O. Internal nodes contain pairs of the form (R, P), where P is a pointer to a child of the node and R is the MBR covering (spatially) the rectangles stored in this child. Also, internal nodes correspond to MBRs covering (spatially) the MBR of their children. An R-tree of class (m, M) has the characteristic that every node, except possibly for the root, contains between m and M pairs, where $m \leq \lceil M/2 \rceil$. If the root is not a leaf, it contains at least two pairs. In the R-tree, the MBRs of siblings can overlap. Figure 2 depicts some rectangles on the right and the corresponding R-tree on the left. Dotted lines denote the bounding rectangles of the subtrees that are rooted in inner nodes.

The R*-tree [4] is an enhancement of the R-tree that uses a more sophisticated node-splitting algorithm and the technique of *forced reinsertion*. First, rather than just considering the area, the node-splitting algorithm in R*-trees also minimizes the perimeter and overlap enlargement of the MBRs. Second, an overflowed node is not split immediately, but a portion of entries of the node is reinserted from the top of the R*-tree (forced reinsertion). With these two enhancements, the R*-tree generally outperforms R-tree.

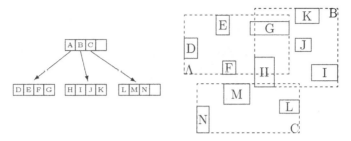

Fig. 2. An example of an R-tree

The X-tree [5] avoids splits that could result in a high degree of overlap of bounding rectangles in the internal nodes of the R*-tree. Experiments showed that the overlap of MBRs increases significantly for high dimensional data, resulting in performance deterioration of the R*-tree. Instead of allowing splits that produce high degree of overlaps, the nodes in the X-tree are extended to a larger than the usual node size, resulting in the so-called *supernodes*. In order to find a suitable split, the X-tree also maintains the history of the previous split. The main objective of the overlap-minimizing split and *supernodes* is to keep the internal nodes as hierarchical as possible, and at the same time to avoid splits in the internal nodes that would result in a high overlap. Thus, a balance between overlap (that deteriorates performance) and large supernodes (that result to a linear scan) is considered using a constant value (MAX_OVERLAP). Experiments in [5] showed that X-tree improves the performance of point query and nearest neighbor queries in comparison to the R*-tree and the TV-tree [22]. In the literature, it is commonly accepted that the X-tree is one of the most efficient tree-like structure for nearest neighbor search in high-dimensional vector spaces.

3.2   Distance-Based Queries

We assume a point dataset P in the d-dimensional data space D^d and a metric distance function $dist$ for a pair of points, i.e. $dist : P \times P \rightarrow \Re^+$. The function $dist$ satisfies the non-negativity, identity, symmetry and Δ-inequality conditions.

In general, $dist$ is called L_t-distance (L_t), L_t-metric, or Minkowski distance between two points, $p = (p_1, p_2, \ldots, p_d)$ and $q = (q_1, q_2, \ldots, q_d)$, in the d-dimensional data space, and it is defined as follows:

$$L_t(p, q) = \left(\sum_{i=1}^{d} \mid p_i - q_i \mid^t \right)^{1/t}, \quad \text{if} \quad 1 \leq t < \infty$$

$$L_\infty(p, q) = \max_{1 \leq i \leq d} \mid p_i - q_i \mid, \quad \text{if} \quad t = \infty$$

For $t = 2$ we have the Euclidean distance and for $t = 1$ the Manhattan distance. They are the most known L_t-metrics. Often, the Euclidean distance is used as the distance function but, depending on the application, other distance functions may be more appropriate.

The d-dimensional Euclidean space, E^d, is the pair (D^d, L_2). That is, the d-dimensional Euclidean space is the d-dimensional data space, D^d, with the Euclidean distance (in the following we will use d instead of L_2).

The most representative DBQs can be divided into two groups: "neighborhood" queries and "closeness" queries. In the first category, we can find the δ-distance range query and the K-nearest neighbors query (the K-furthest neighbors query is a variant). And in the second one, we have the δ-distance join query and the K-closest pairs query (the K-furthest pairs query is an extension).

Definition. δ-distance range query
Let P be a point dataset $(P \neq \emptyset)$ in E^d. Then, the result of the δ-distance range query with respect to a query point q and two positive values, $\delta_1, \delta_2 \in \Re^+ \; \delta_1 \leq \delta_2$, is the dataset δ-DRQ$(P, q, \delta_1, \delta_2)$ which contains all the points $(p_i \in P)$ that fall on the distance range defined by $[\delta_1, \delta_2]$ with respect to the query point q:

$$\delta\text{-DRQ}(P, q, \delta_1, \delta_2) = \{p_i \in P : \delta_1 \leq d(p_i, q) \leq \delta_2\}$$

Definition. K-nearest neighbors query
Let P be a point dataset $(P \neq \emptyset)$ in E^d. Then, the result of the K-nearest neighbors query with respect to a query point q is the dataset K-NNQ(P, q, K) which contains all the ordered sequences of K $(1 \leq K \leq |P|)$ different points of P, with the K smallest distances from q:

$$K\text{-NNQ}(P, q, K) = \{(p_1, p_2, \ldots, p_K) \in P^K : p_i \neq p_j \; i \neq j \; 1 \leq i, j \leq K \text{ and}$$
$$\forall p_i \in P - \{p_1, p_2, \ldots, p_K\}, \; d(p_1, q) \leq d(p_2, q) \leq \ldots \leq d(p_K, q) \leq d(p_i, q)\}$$

Definition. δ-distance join query
Let P and Q be two point datasets $(P \neq \emptyset$ and $Q \neq \emptyset)$ in E^d. Then, the result of the δ-distance join query is the dataset δ-DJQ$(P, Q, \delta_1, \delta_2)$ which contains all the possible pairs of points that can be formed by choosing one point of P and one point of Q, having a distance between δ_1 and δ_2, such that $\delta_1, \delta_2 \in \Re^+$ and $\delta_1 \leq \delta_2$:

$$\delta\text{-DJQ}(P, Q, \delta_1, \delta_2) = \{(p_i, q_j) \in P \times Q : \delta_1 \leq d(p_i, q_j) \leq \delta_2\}$$

The result of the δ-distance join query contains all possible pairs of points (from two points datasets) having a distance in the range $[\delta_1, \delta_2]$. The high-dimensional similarity join [20], where two point sets of a high-dimensional vector space are combined such that the result contains all the point pairs which distance does not exceed a given distance τ, is a particular case of δ-distance join query where $\delta_1 = 0$ and $\delta_2 = \tau$.

Definition. K-closest pairs query
Let P and Q be two point datasets $(P \neq \emptyset$ and $Q \neq \emptyset)$ in E^d. Then, the result of the K-closest pairs query is a dataset K-CPQ(P, Q, K) which contains all the

ordered sequences of K $(1 \leq K \leq |P| \cdot |Q|)$ different pairs of points of $P \times Q$, with the K smallest distances between all possible pairs of points that can be formed by choosing one point of P and one point of Q:

$$K\text{-CPQ}(P, Q, K) =$$
$$\{((p_1, q_1), (p_2, q_2), \ldots, (p_K, q_K)) \in (P \times Q)^K :$$
$$(p_i, q_i) \neq (p_j, q_j) \ i \neq j \ 1 \leq i, j \leq K \text{ and}$$
$$\forall(p_i, q_j) \in P \times Q - \{(p_1, q_1), (p_2, q_2), \ldots, (p_K, q_K)\},$$
$$d(p_1, q_1) \leq d(p_2, q_2) \leq \ldots \leq d(p_K, q_K) \leq d(p_i, q_j)\}$$

Usually, DBQs are executed using some kind of multidimensional index structures such as R-trees. If we assume that the point datasets are indexed on any tree-like structure belonging to the R-tree family, then the main objective while answering these types of queries is to reduce the search space. In [9], a generalization of the function that calculates the minimum distance between points and MBRs (MINMINDIST) was presented. We can apply this distance function to pairs of any kind of elements (MBRs or points) stored in R-trees during the computation of branch-and-bound algorithms based on a pruning heuristic for DBQs ("neighborhood " or "closeness" queries). MINMINDIST(M_1, M_2) calculates the minimum distance between two MBRs M_1 and M_2. If any of the two (both) MBRs degenerates (degenerate) to a point (two points), then we obtain the minimum distance between a point and an MBR [24] (between two points).

Definition. MINMINDIST(M_1, M_2)
Let two MBRs $M_1 = (a, b)$ and $M_2 = (c, d)$, in E^d, where $a = (a_1, a_2, \ldots, a_d)$ and $b = (b_1, b_2, \ldots, b_d)$ such that $a_i \leq b_i, 1 \leq i \leq d$ and $c = (c_1, c_2, \ldots, c_d)$ and $d = (d_1, d_2, \ldots, d_d)$ such that $c_i \leq d_i, 1 \leq i \leq d$. We define MINMINDIST($M_1$, M_2) as follows:

$$\text{MINMINDIST}(M_1, M_2) = \sqrt{\sum_{i=1}^{d} y_i^2}, \quad \text{such that} \quad y_i = \begin{cases} c_i - b_i, & \text{if } c_i > b_i \\ a_i - d_i, & \text{if } a_i > d_i \\ 0, & \text{otherwise} \end{cases}$$

The general pruning heuristic for DBQs over R-trees is the following: "if MINMINDIST(M_1, M_2) $> z$, then the pair of MBRs (M_1, M_2) will be discarded", where z is the distance value of the K-th nearest neighbor (K-NNQ), or the K-th closest pair (K-CPQ) that has been found so far.

4   Algorithms for Distance-Based Queries

According to the definition of K-NNQ (K-CPQ) the related result, in general, consists of a number of ordered sequences of K points (pairs of points). The algorithms that we present in the following, discover one of these sequences (although, it is rather straightforward to be modified to discover all the sequences).

In order to design branch-and-bound algorithms for processing K-NNQ or K-CPQ in a non-incremental way (K must be fixed in advance), an extra data structure that holds the K nearest neighbors or the K closest pairs is necessary. This data structure is organized as a maximum binary heap (called K-heap) and holds points (K-NNQ) or pairs of points (K-CPQ) according to their distance (the K points or pairs of points with the smallest distance processed so far). For example, for K-CPQ, the pair of points with the largest distance resides on top of the K-heap (we will prune the unnecessary branches using this distance value). Initially, the K-heap is empty and the distance of the K-th closest pair equals infinity. The pairs of points discovered at the leaf level are inserted in the K-heap until it gets full. Then, when a new pair of points is discovered at the leaf level, if its distance is smaller than the top of the K-heap, the top is deleted and this new pair is inserted in the K-heap (updating the K-th closest pair).

For the "neighborhood" queries, most of the algorithms are focused in K-NNQ [24, 6, 17]. The recursive and non-incremental branch-and-bound algorithm (following a depth-first traversal) for processing the K-NNQ between a set of points P stored in an R-tree (R_P) and a query point q can be described by the following steps [24][2] (z is the distance value of the K-th nearest neighbor found so far; at the beginning $z = \infty$):

KNNQ1 Start from the root of the R-tree.

KNNQ2 If you access an internal node, then calculate MINMINDIST between q and each possible MBR, sort them in ascending order of MINMINDIST. Following this order, propagate downwards recursively only for those MBRs having MINMINDIST $\leq z$.

KNNQ3 If you access a leaf node, then calculate MINMINDIST between q and each possible point stored in the node. If this distance is smaller than or equal to z, then remove the root of the K-heap and insert the new point, updating this structure and z.

The adaptation of the algorithm from K-NNQ to the δ-DRQ is quite easy. For the non-incremental alternative, we have to consider three modifications:

- for internal nodes, if MINMINDIST$(M, q) > \delta_2$, then the MBR M will be pruned. This means that δ_2 will be used as a prunning distance instead of the distance value of the K-th nearest neighbor that have been found so far (z);
- for leaf nodes, the point in the distance range $[\delta_1, \delta_2]$ is selected, and
- the result of the query must not be in sorted order. Therefore, the K-heap is unnecessary.

For the "closeness" queries, we are going to extend the recursive algorithm of [9] for two multidimensional point datasets (P and Q) that are indexed in two tree-like structures belonging to the R-tree family (R_P and R_Q). The recursive

---

[2] The descriptions of algorithms in this section also appear in [8].

and non-incremental branch-and-bound algorithm (with a synchronous traversal, following a depth-first search strategy) for processing the K-CPQ between two sets of points (P and Q) stored in two R-trees (R_P and R_Q) with the same height can be described by the following steps [9] (z is the distance value of the K-th closest pair found so far; at the beginning $z = \infty$):

KCPQ1 Start from the roots of the two R-trees.

KCPQ2 If you access a pair of internal nodes, then calculate MINMINDIST for each possible pair of MBRs. Propagate downwards recursively only for those pairs having MINMINDIST $\leq z$.

KCPQ3 If you access two leaves, then calculate MINMINDIST of each possible pair of points. If this distance is smaller than or equal to z, then remove the root of the K-heap and insert the new pair, updating this structure and z.

The main advantage of the recursive algorithms is that they transform the global problem in smaller local ones at each tree level, and over every subproblem we can apply pruning heuristics for reducing the search space (branch-and-bound). Moreover, for improving the I/O and CPU cost of this algorithm, two techniques were presented in [9] for the case that two internal nodes are accessed. The first improvement aims at reducing the number of I/O operations, and consists in sorting the pairs of MBRs in ascending order of MINMINDIST, while obeying this order when propagating downwards recursively. The second improvement aims at reducing the CPU cost and applies the distance-based plane-sweep technique [23]. With this technique we avoid to process all possible combinations of pairs of MBRs, or points from two internal or leaf nodes, respectively.

The adaptation of the branch-and-bound algorithm from K-CPQ to the δ-DJQ is very similar to the one of "neighborhood" queries. For the non-incremental alternatives, we have also to consider three modifications:

– for internal nodes, if MINMINDIST(M_1, M_2)$>\delta_2$, then the pair of MBRs (M_1, M_2) will be pruned. This means that δ_2 will be used as a prunning distance instead of the distance value of the K-th closest pair that has been found so far;
– for leaf nodes, the pair of points in the distance range [δ_1, δ_2] is selected, and
– the result of the query must not be in sorted order. Therefore, the K-heap is unnecessary.

5   Approximate Algorithms

The previous recursive algorithms for K-NNQ and K-CPQ lead to exact solutions of these queries. However, in practical situations and high-dimensional data spaces, the user may be willing to sacrifice algorithm accuracy for improving performance. In the following, we describe the ϵ-approximate technique [1, 7], which leads to a result worse than the exact one by at most ϵ. More formally, given any positive real ϵ ($\epsilon > 0$) as maximum relative distance error to be tolerated, the result of a DBQ (K-NNQ or K-CPQ) is $(1 + \epsilon)$-approximate if the distance of its i-th item is within relative error ϵ (or a factor $(1 + \epsilon)$) of the distance of the i-th item of the exact result of the same DBQ, $1 \leq i \leq K$. For example, an $(1 + \epsilon)$-approximate answer to the K-CPQ is an ordered sequence of K distinct pairs of points $((p'_1, q'_1), (p'_2, q'_2), \ldots, (p'_K, q'_K)) \in (P \times Q)^K$, such that (p'_i, q'_i) is the $(1 + \epsilon)$-approximate closest pair of the i-th closest pair (p_i, q_i) of the exact result $((p_1, q_1), (p_2, q_2), \ldots, (p_K, q_K)) \in (P \times Q)^K$, that is $(d(p'_i, q'_i) - d(p_i, q_i))/d(p_i, q_i) \leq \epsilon, 1 \leq i \leq K$.

When the pruning heuristic is applied on a branch-and-bound algorithm over R-trees, an item X is discarded if $\text{MINMINDIST}(X) > z/(1 + \epsilon) \Leftrightarrow \text{MINMINDIST}(X) + (\text{MINMINDIST}(X) * \epsilon) > z \Leftrightarrow \text{MINMINDIST}(X) > z - (\text{MINMINDIST}(X) * \epsilon)$. The decrease of z depends on the value of MINMINDIST(X) multiplied by ϵ (an unbounded positive real). Note that for $\epsilon = 0$, the ϵ-approximate algorithm behaves as an exact algorithm and leads to the precise solution. The recursive and non-incremental ϵ-approximate branch-and-bound algorithm (following a depth-first traversal) for processing the K-CPQ (the ϵ-approximate version of the K-NNQ algorithm is very similar to the K-CPQ ϵ-approximate algorithm) between two sets of points (P and Q) indexed in two R-trees (R_P and R_Q) with the same height can be described by the following steps (AKCPQ) (z is the distance value of the K-th closest pair found so far and at the beginning $z = \infty$):

AKCPQ1 Start from the roots of the two R-trees.

AKCPQ2 If you access a pair of internal nodes, then calculate MINMINDIST for each possible pair of MBRs. Propagate downwards recursively only for those pairs having MINMINDIST $\leq z/(1 + \epsilon)$.

AKCPQ3 If you access two leaves, then calculate MINMINDIST of each possible pair of points. If this distance is smaller than or equal to z, then remove the root of the K-heap and insert the new pair, updating this structure and z.

There are many other approximation methods to apply in branch-and-bound algorithms for reporting approximate results quickly. For example, (1) to replace the complete distance computations in high-dimensional spaces by partial distance computations in a space with much lower dimensionality, choosing the more representative dimensions (relaxation method); (2) to extend the MBRs on the R-tree leaf nodes by a given distance in each dimension before computing the distance functions; (3) during the processing of the algorithm, to select randomly a number of candidates for searching (internal nodes), or for the result (leaf nodes) and report the best solutions obtained from such trials (random search method); etc. However, in this paper, we only focus on the well-known ϵ-approximate technique as search space reduction method over tree-like structures as an approximation technique embedded in recursive and non-incremental branch-and-bound algorithms for DBQs.

6 Experimentation

This section provides the experimental results that aim at measuring and evaluating the behavior of the exact and ϵ-approximate recursive branch-and-bound algorithms for K-NNQ and K-CPQ using R*-trees and X-trees (MAX_OVER-LAP = 0.2) for synthetic point datasets following Uniform and Gaussian distributions. The values in each dimension were randomly generated in the range [0, 1] with either Uniform and Gaussian distributions. For the Gaussian distribution, the mean and the standard deviation were 0.5 and 0.1 respectively. The datasets cardinality was equal to 100000, K was varying from 1 to 100000 (for a more detailed study K was equal to 100), there was a global LRU buffer (256 pages) and several dimensions (d = 2, 5, 10, 15, 20 and 25) were tested. The query points for K-NNQ were generated randomly in the space of the data points stored in the indexes.

All experiments ran on a Linux workstation with a Pentium III 450 MHz processor, 128 MB of main memory and several GB of secondary storage, using the *gcc* compiler. The index page size was 4Kb, and the fan-out decreased when the dimensionality increased ($m = 0.4*M$). We are going to compare the performance of the recursive exact and approximate algorithms based on the total response time (seconds), I/O activity (disk accesses) and the average relative distance error of the solutions of the ϵ-approximate algorithm (AKCPQ) with respect to the exact results. The construction of indexes was not taken into account for the response time.

From the results of the Table 1, which follow the same trends to the results of Table 1 that appears in [8] and refers to data following Uniform distribution, it is apparent that the X-tree is the most appropriate index structure for the K-NNQ

Table 1. Performance of the exact DBQs (K-NNQ and K-CPQ, K = 100) on R*-trees and X-trees indexing synthetic high-dimensional points following Gaussian distribution, in terms of the number of disk accesses (I/O) and response time (seconds)

	K-NNQ (I/O)		K-CPQ (I/O)		K-NNQ (sec)		K-CPQ (sec)	
Dim	R*-tree	X-tree	R*-tree	X-tree	R*-tree	X-tree	R*-tree	X-tree
2	10	7	1744	1980	0.01	0.01	2.77	2.88
5	139	116	16056	11021	0.18	0.04	76.11	3.91
10	2880	2799	233620	5788971	1.52	1.48	4537.21	4583.12
15	4281	4582	762683	13285752	1.92	2.13	13225.52	14164.36
20	5520	5582	1287559	23041829	3.26	3.02	24993.17	25099.45
25	6300	6972	1404989	38246555	2.92	3.61	31463.36	31682.73

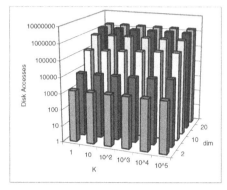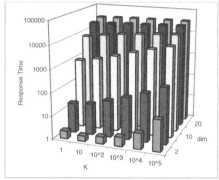

Fig. 3. Disk accesses and response time (in seconds) of the exact K-CPQ recursive algorithm indexing Uniform data, as a function of K and the dimensionality

(this is in accordance to the results of [5] for Uniform distributions), although for the Gaussian data the R*-tree is slightly better than the X-tree in high dimensions (e.g. $d = 15$ and $d = 25$). On the other hand, the results with respect to the K-CPQ show that the R*-tree is a better index structure than the X-tree regardless of the data distribution (primarily, due to the presence of supernodes in the X-trees that increase the number of backtracks at internal nodes, decreasing the search performance). The main objective of the R*-tree is to minimize the overlap between nodes at the same tree level (the less the overlap, the smaller the probability to follow multiple search paths). Therefore, the overlap plays an important role in K-CPQs and the R*-tree relies on it to obtain better performance for this DBQ. If we compare the results for K-CPQs with respect to the I/O activity and the response time, we can conclude that this query becomes extremely expensive as the dimensionality increases, in particular for values larger than 5, and we are going to focus on such dimensions. Therefore, the use of approximate branch-and-bound algorithms based on the ϵ-approximate technique is justified for the K-CPQ, since they aim at obtaining acceptable results quickly.

Figure 3 (log scale) shows that the number of R*-tree nodes fetched from disk (left part) and the response time (right part) of each dimension get higher as K increases. Moreover, in the left part of this figure, it is shown that the increment of I/O cost between two K values K_1 and K_2 ($K_1 \leq K_2$) decreases when the dimensionality increases. For example, if we consider the dimensions 10, 15, 20 and 25, the increment of I/O cost between $K_1 = 100$ and $K_2 = 100000$ is a 34%, 2%, 0.01% and 0%, respectively; for instance, the number of disk accesses for $d = 15$ is only a 2% cheaper for $K_1 = 100$ than for $K_2 = 100000$. The same behavior can be observed in the right part of the Fig. 3 for the response time, although the increment of this metric is greater for low dimensions. For example, the increment of the response time for all considered dimensions ($d = 2, 5, 10, 15, 20$ and 25) is a 91%, 86%, 74%, 29%, 13% and 3%, respectively, faster for $K_1 = 100$ than

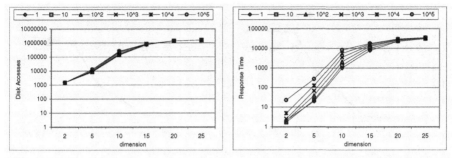

Fig. 4. Performance (log scale) of the exact K-CPQ on R*-trees, in terms of I/O activity (disk accesses) and response time (in seconds), for all K values and over all considered dimensions

for $K_2 = 100000$ (or equivalently, the algorithm is 11.37, 6.99, 3.91, 1.41, 1.15, 1.03 times faster for $K_1 = 100$ than for $K_2 = 100000$). We can also observe this interesting behavior more clearly in the charts of Fig. 4 (log scale), where the performance gap between two K values in increasing order gets smaller as the dimensionality increases and this performance gap is greater for the response time than for the disk accesses. Moreover, this gap is almost negligible for high dimensions (e.g. $d = 25$) with respect to the I/O activity and very small for the response time.

In Fig. 5, we can observe for R*-trees that the number of disk accesses tends to be the same for all K values when the dimensionality is high (e.g. $d = 15$ and $d = 20$), although the response time increases continuously. An explanation of this behavior with respect to the I/O activity can be primarily related to the existence of a global LRU buffer and the reduction of the R*-tree node fan-out when the dimensionality increases. On the other hand, the increase of response time is mainly due to the computation of MINMINDIST distance metric in the high-dimensional data spaces and this is an important drawback when

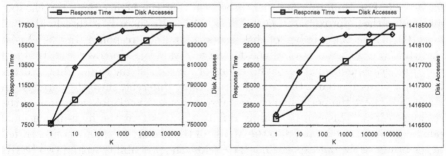

Fig. 5. Response time (in seconds) versus I/O activity (disk accesses) for the exact K-CPQ on R*-trees, as a function of K for dimensions $d = 15$ (left) and $d = 20$ (right)

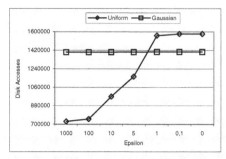
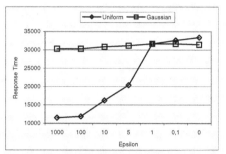

Fig. 6. Performance of the K-CPQ approximate algorithm (AKCPQ) on R*-trees indexing Uniform and Gaussian data ($K = 100$ and $d = 25$), in terms of the number of disk accesses (left) and response time (right)

we want to manage higher dimensions (the performance with respect to the response time degrades as the number of dimensions increases). In order to obtain acceptable response times in high dimensional data spaces, algorithms that obtain approximate solutions should be used.

The ϵ-approximate technique is a well-known approximate method for reporting approximate results quickly for DBQs within a maximum relative distance error ϵ ($\epsilon > 0$). For approximate K-NNQ using this approximate technique, an exhaustive study can be found in [1, 7]. Here, we are going to focus on the study of this distance-based approximate technique applied to the recursive K-CPQ algorithm, where $d = 25$ and $K = 100$, taking different values for ϵ: 0 (exact), 0.1, 1, 5, 10, 100 and 1000. Moreover, in order to establish a representative comparison, apart from using the I/O activity and the response time, we are going to consider the average relative distance error (ARDE). In order to obtain ARDE, we have to calculate the exact result off-line, then apply the ϵ-approximate algorithm (AKCPQ) and compute the average relative error for all K items in the result (exact and approximate). Figure 6 illustrates the I/O activity (left) and the response time (right) of the experiments for K-CPQ using the ϵ-approximate algorithm on R*-trees indexing Uniform and Gaussian data for $d = 25$. For Uniform data, it can be seen that the higher the ϵ the cheaper and faster the approximate algorithm is, although there is a threshold when $\epsilon \geq 100$, where the number of disk accesses and the response time is almost the same (i.e. no gain is obtained for large ϵ values). Moreover, the trend of the two performance metrics as functions of ϵ is almost the same. On the other hand, for Gaussian data, the behavior is notably different, since the variation of ϵ does not affect the performance metrics (only just a negligible variation of the response time). This can be mainly due to the fact that the high-dimensional points of two datasets (and also the MBRs of the two R*-trees) are concentrated in the center of the data space $[0, 1]^d$; therefore the probability to find two MBRs with MINMINDIST equal to 0 is very high and the ϵ parameter in the modified

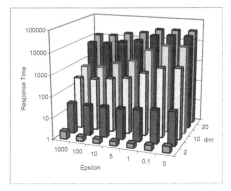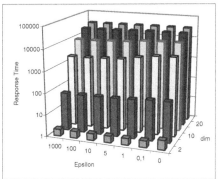

Fig. 7. Response time (in seconds in log scale) of the K-CPQ algorithm ($K =$ 100) using the ϵ-approximate technique for Uniform (left) and Gaussian (right) data distributions, as a function of ϵ (Epsilon) and the dimensionality.

pruning heuristic ($\mathrm{MINMINDIST}(X) + (\epsilon * \mathrm{MINMINDIST}(X)) > z$) does not intervene in the pruning.

In Fig. 7, we compare the response time of the ϵ-approximate algorithm for the two data distributions, Uniform (left) and Gaussian (right), as a function of the ϵ values and the dimensionality. For both types of synthetic datasets, the response time increases notably with the increase of dimensionality. In general, the K-CPQ for Gaussian datasets is more expensive than for Uniform ones, except for higher dimensions (20 and 25) and small ϵ values (0 and 0.1). Also, we can observe and highlight the particular behavior of the ϵ-approximate K-CPQ algorithm over Gaussian data: for a given dimension, the increase of the total response time of the algorithm is almost negligible with the increase of ϵ.

Intuitively, one could say that the higher the ϵ is, the faster the approximate algorithm is expected to execute. However, this is not always true (see the results of Gaussian data) and the accuracy of the result is very difficult to control. In Fig. 8, we can see that ration of ARDE over ϵ varies from 0.0 to 0.009 for Uniform data (left) and from 0.0 to 0.0006 for Gaussian data (right). Apparently, this effect is not positive, since the users cannot easily adjust the accuracy (ARDE) of the result by ϵ (an unbounded parameter). Moreover, this performance deterioration with the increase of dimension is mainly due to the reduction of the variance of the distance between points, which is responsible of the *dimensionality curse* [3]. From this figure, we can also conclude that the ϵ-approximate technique is affected by the *dimensionality curse*, since it is a distance-based approximate method and can become unpractical when the dimensionality is very high, regardless of the ϵ values. Therefore, the ϵ-approximate technique applied to the K-CPQ over index structures, like R*-trees, is not a good enough approximate technique and we should find other approximate methods that do not depend on distances (e.g. characteristics of the indexes, time constraints, etc.).

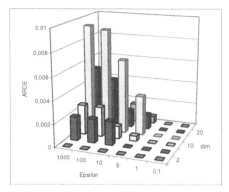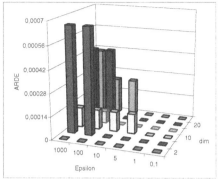

Fig. 8. ARDE (average relative distance error) of the K-CPQ algorithm ($K =$ 100) using the ϵ-approximate technique for Uniform (left) and Gaussian (right) data distributions, as a function of ϵ (Epsilon) and the dimensionality

7   Conclusions and Future Work

In this paper we investigate the performance of the most representative DBQs (K-NNQ and K-CPQ) in multidimensional data spaces, where the point datasets are indexed by tree-like structures belonging to the R-tree family (R*-tree and X-tree). We employ recursive branch-and-bound algorithms (based on pruning heuristics) in a non-incremental way in order to answer K-NNQs and K-CPQs. From our experiments with synthetic and random multidimensional point datasets, under Uniform and Gaussian data distributions, it is revealed that the best index structure for K-NNQs is the X-tree. However, for K-CPQs, the R*-tree outperforms the X-tree with respect to the response time and the number of disk accesses, when an LRU buffer is used. Whatever the index structure, the cost of K-CPQs in I/O activity and response time is very high. Therefore, in order to obtain acceptable response times in high-dimensional data spaces, algorithms that report approximate solutions should be used. In this research line, we have also presented the ϵ-approximate technique in the recursive branch-and-bound algorithm for K-CPQ on R*-trees. Moreover, we have investigated by experimentation the performance of the exact and approximate algorithms in high-dimensional data spaces for K-CPQ (the most expense DBQ). The most important conclusions drawn from our experimental study are the following: (1) the ϵ-approximate technique exhibits a good performance when the user is interested in a high quality of the result, but this approximate technique is affected by the *dimensionality curse* (it is a distance-based approximate method) and requires significant time when employed; and (2) it is very difficult for the users to adjust the search and find a trade-off between cost and quality of the result when the ϵ-approximate technique is employed; hence, alternative approximate methods should be examined.

Future research may include:

- the adaptation of the recursive K-CPQ (exact and approximate) algorithms to other new index structures such as the A-tree [26] and the SR-tree [19],
- the adaptation of the iterative algorithms for K-NNQ [17] and K-CPQ [9], studying its performance in high-dimensionality spaces,
- use of other approximate techniques that do not depend on distances as *anytime algorithms* [11], and
- consideration of real high-dimensional point datasets from real color images, CAD, etc. for further experimentation.

Acknowledgments

We would like to thank Mr. Jordi Rodriguez for his help on the implementation of the X-trees.

References

[1] S. Arya, D. M. Mount, N. S. Netanyahu, R. Silverman and A. Y. Wu: "An Optimal Algorithm for Approximate Nearest Neighbor Searching Fixed Dimensions", *Journal of the ACM*, Vol.45, No.6, pp.891-923, 1998. 9, 14

[2] B. Braunmuller, M. Ester, H. P. Kriegel and J. Sander: "Efficiently Supporting Multiple Similarity Queries for Mining in Metric Databases", *Proceedings ICDE Conference*, pp.256-267, 2000. 1

[3] K. S. Beyer, J. Goldstein, R. Ramakrishnan and U. Shaft: "When Is "Nearest Neighbor" Meaningful?", *Proceedings 7th ICDT Conference*, pp.217-235, 1999. 15

[4] N. Beckmann, H. P. Kriegel, R. Schneider and B. Seeger: "The R*-tree: and Efficient and Robust Access Method for Points and Rectangles", *Proceedings 1990 ACM SIGMOD Conference*, pp.322-331, 1990. 2, 4

[5] S. Berchtold, D. Kiem and H. P. Kriegel: "The X-tree: An Index Structure for High-Dimensional Data", *Proceedings 22nd VLDB Conference*, pp.28-39, 1996. 2, 5, 12

[6] K. L. Cheung and A. W. Fu: "Enhanced Nearest Neighbour Search on the R-tree", *ACM SIGMOD Record*, Vol.27, No.3, pp.16-21, 1998. 3, 8

[7] P. Ciaccia and M. Patella; "PAC Nearest Neighbor Queries: Approximate and Controlled Search in High-Dimensional and Metric Spaces", *Proceedings ICDE Conference*, pp. 244-255, San Diego, CA, 2000. 9, 14

[8] A. Corral, J. Cañadas and M. Vassilakopoulos: "Approximate Algorithms for Distance-Based Queries in High-Dimensional Data Spaces Using R-Trees", *Proceedings 6th ADBIS Conference*, pp. 163-176, 2002. 2, 4, 8, 11

[9] A. Corral, Y. Manolopoulos, Y. Theodoridis and M. Vassilakopoulos: "Closest Pair Queries in Spatial Databases", *Proceedings 2000 ACM SIGMOD Conference*, pp.189-200, 2000. 4, 7, 8, 9, 17

[10] A. Corral, J. Rodriguez and M. Vassilakopoulos: "Distance-Based Queries in Multidimensional Data Spaces using R-trees", *Proceedings 8th Panhellenic Conference on Informatics*, Vol.I, pp.237-246, Nicosia, Cyprus, 2001. 2

[11] T. Dean and M. S. Boddy: "An Analysis of Time-Dependent Planning", *Proceedings AAAI Conference*, pp.49-54, St. Paul, MN, 1988. 17

[12] C. Faloutsos, R. Barber, M. Flickner, J. Hafner, W. Niblack, D. Petkovic, and W. Equitz: "Efficient and Effective Querying by Image Content", *Journal of Intelligent Information Systems*, Vol.3, No.3-4, pp.231-262, 1994. 1

[13] V. Gaede and O. Gunther: "Multidimensional Access Methods", *ACM Computing Surveys*, Vol.30, No.2, pp.170-231, 1998. 2

[14] A. Guttman: "R-trees: A Dynamic Index Structure for Spatial Searching", *Proceedings 1984 ACM SIGMOD Conference*, pp.47-57, 1984. 2, 4

[15] G. R. Hjaltason and H. Samet: "Ranking in Spatial Databases", *Proceedings 4th SSD Conference*, pp.83-95, 1995. 3

[16] G. R. Hjaltason and H. Samet: "Incremental Distance Join Algorithms for Spatial Databases", *Proceedings 1998 ACM SIGMOD Conference*, pp.237-248, 1998. 4

[17] G. R. Hjaltason and H. Samet: "Distance Browsing in Spatial Databases", *ACM Transactions on Database Systems*, Vol.24, No.2, pp.265-318, 1999. 3, 8, 17

[18] H. V. Jagadish: "A Retrieval Technique for Similar Shapes", *Proceedings 1991 ACM SIGMOD Conference*, pp.208-217, 1991. 1

[19] N. Katayama and S. Satoh: "The SR-tree: An Index Structure for High-Dimensional Nearest Neighbor Queries", *Proceedings 1997 ACM SIGMOD Conference*, pp.369-380, 1997. 17

[20] N. Koudas and K. C. Sevcik: "High Dimensional Similarity Joins: Algorithms and Performance Evaluation", *Proceedings ICDE Conference*, pp. 466-475, Orlando, FL, 1998. 6

[21] F. Korn, N. Sidiropoulos, C. Faloutsos, C. Siegel and Z. Protopapas: "Fast Nearest Neighbor Search in Medical Images Databases", *Proceedings 22nd VLDB Conference*, pp.215-226, 1996. 1

[22] K. I. Lin, H. V. Jagadish and C. Faloutsos: "The TV-tree: an Index Structure for High-Dimensional Data", *The VLDB Journal*, Vol.3, No.4, pp.517-542, 1994. 5

[23] F. P. Preparata and M. I. Shamos: *"Computational Geometry: an Introduction"*, Springer, 1985. 4, 9

[24] N. Roussopoulos, S. Kelley and F. Vincent: "Nearest Neighbor Queries", *Proceedings 1995 ACM SIGMOD Conference*, pp.71-79, 1995. 3, 7, 8

[25] H. Shin, B. Moon and S. Lee: "Adaptive Multi-Stage Distance Join Processing", *Proceedings 2000 ACM SIGMOD Conference*, pp.343-354, 2000. 4

[26] Y. Sakurai, M. Yoshikawa, S. Uemura and H. Kojima: "The A-tree: An Index Structure for High-Dimensional Spaces Using Relative Approximation", *Proceedings 26th VLDB Conference*, pp.516-526, 2000. 17

A Simple, Compact and Dynamic Partition Scheme Based on Co-centric Spheres

Dimitris G. Kapopoulos and Michael Hatzopoulos

Department of Informatics and Telecommunications
University of Athens, 157 71 Ilisia, Athens, Greece
{dkapo,mike}@di.uoa.gr

Abstract. This paper describes the MB-tree, a symmetric data structure for the organization of multidimensional points. The proposed structure is based on a new partition scheme that divides the data space into co-centric partitions in an 'onion'-like manner and ensures that partitions that are spatially successive in a multidimensional space are also successive in terms of their storage. Each partition is characterized from a distance from a fixed point and the resultant structure is k-d-cut, adaptable and brickwall. It has very efficient point search and adapts nicely to dynamic data spaces with high frequency of insertions and deletions and to non-uniformly distributed data. The organization is an extension of B-trees in order to index multidimensional data when the data space is metric. The indexing mechanism is organized as a B^+-tree and compared to similar approaches the size of the index is minimum. Although the MB-tree has a simple structure, its performance compares to the one of other more complex indexes. We present the partition scheme and the index, describe its dynamic behavior, examine algorithms for several types of queries and provide experimental results.

1 Introduction

Dealing with large amounts of multidimensional data efficiently implies the adoption of effective, as simple as possible, indexing schemes in order to save disk accesses, whilst maintaining reasonable use of available space. As B-trees are efficient data structures for indexing only one-dimensional data, many other data structures have been proposed for the management of multidimensional data. A survey of these methods can be found in [1,5,6,16,17].

Among other data structures we note the k-d-B-trees [15] and the grid file [12] because they have been used as the starting point for the development of many other indexing methods as well as have served a variety of applications. k-d-B-trees divide a k-dimensional data space into smaller k-dimensional regions that are organized into trees similar to B-trees. On the other hand, grid files divide a data space into a grid structure by splitting each dimension into several non-uniformly spaced intervals. G-trees [8,10] that combine the features of both B-trees and grid files, are based on

Y. Manolopoulos et al. (Eds.): PCI 2001, LNCS 2563, pp. 19-31, 2003.

the BD-tree [3,4] and the z-ordering [13,14]. Another data structure similar to the BD-tree is the BANG file [6].

Some multidimensional access methods, like the SS-tree [19], the M-tree [2] and the Slim-tree [18] employ bounding *spheres* for the shape of regions and take advantage of the characteristics of metric spaces.

We present the *MB-tree*, a data structure that uses a partition scheme that divides a k-dimensional space in spherical co-centric partitions in an 'onion'-like manner. The structure uses the properties of metric spaces; it is independent of the data distribution and accelerates the update operations. Moreover, it requires minimum space because for a partition it has need of the storage of a real number only. The MB-tree performs a linearization of the k-dimensional space. The location of a point in a multidimensional data space is determined by its distance from a fixed point. In fact, it is this distance that defines an ordering of the multidimensional data. The search for the partition that does (or does not) contain this point is conducted through an index that is organized as a B^+-tree.

The rest of the paper is organized as follows: Section 2 presents the partition scheme and the structure of the MB-tree. Section 3 discusses the dynamic behavior of the MB-tree and gives algorithms for insertion and deletion. Section 4 deals with searching algorithms. Section 5 gives experimental results and Section 6 concludes this work with a summary and hints for future research.

2   The MB-Tree

In order to organise a data space S through the MB-tree, S must be considered as a *metric space* $M = (S,d)$, where d is a *metric* or *distance function*. Distance functions are used in access methods that aim to facilitate content-based retrieval applications [2,16]. A distance function has the properties of symmetry, non-negativity and triangle inequality. That is, for every x, y in S there is a real number $d(x,y)$, called the distance of x from y, such that:

$$d(x, y) = d(y, x) \tag{1}$$

$$d(x, x) = 0 \ \wedge \ d(x, y) > 0, \quad \forall x \neq y. \tag{2}$$

$$d(x, y) \leq d(x, z) + d(z, y), \quad \forall z \in S. \tag{3}$$

The k-dimensional space S^k of the MB-tree is a subset of the Euclidean space R^k, $k \geq 1$. We associate the *norm* of the difference of two points as the distance function for this space i.e.,

$$d(x, y) = |x - y|, \quad \forall x, y \in R^k \tag{4}$$

We have

$$|x - y| = \left(\sum_{j=1}^{k} (x_j - y_j)^2 \right)^{\frac{1}{2}}, \quad \forall x, y \in R^k \tag{5}$$

We assume that the data in each dimension are bounded i.e., for each point $x = (x_1, x_2, ..., x_k)$ of S^k we have that $l_{c_j} \le x_j \le h_{c_j}$, $1 \le j \le k$, where $l_c = (l_{c_1}, l_{c_2}, ..., l_{c_k})$ and $h_c = (h_{c_1}, h_{c_2}, ..., h_{c_k})$ are the leftmost and rightmost points of S^k.

Throughout this paper we use the word sphere for hyper-sphere. A *closed sphere* $\overline{S}(cp, r)$ and an *open sphere* $S(cp, r)$ with central point cp and radius r in S^k, are defined as follows

$$\overline{S}(cp, r) = \left\{ x \in S^k : d(x, cp) \le r \right\} \tag{6}$$

$$S(cp, r) = \left\{ x \in S^k : d(x, cp) < r \right\} \tag{7}$$

A *partition P* imposed by the MB-tree is an area of S^k that is defined as the complement of an open sphere $S(cp, r_s)$ to a co-centric closed sphere $\overline{S}(cp, r)$. We have

$$P = \overline{S}(cp, r) - S(cp, r_s) \tag{8}$$

We use the notation r_s for the radius that resides on the left of r and it is the closest to it. That is, there does not exist radius rr in the MB-tree such that $r_s < rr < r$. If r is the smallest radius, then we define $r_s = 0$. The similar notation r_b is used for the radius that resides on the right of r and is the closest to it. That is, there does not exist radius rr in the MB-tree such that $r < rr < r_b$. If r is the maximum radius, then r_b does not exist. We choose the point l_c to be the central point of the spheres.

There is a one to one correspondence between the partitions of the MB-tree and physical data blocks. The MB-tree adapts well to dynamic environments and excludes the possibility for empty partitions to exist.

Figure 1(a) shows the insertion of data in the first partition P_1 of a two-dimensional space S^2. This partition is created from the radii $r_1 = d(cp, h_c)$ and $r_0 = r_{s_1} = 0$. It is

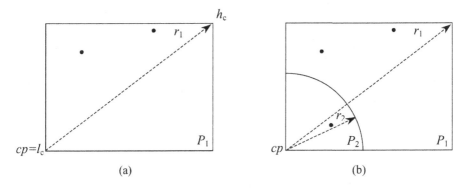

(a)   (b)

Fig. 1. The first split in a two-dimensional space

$$P_1 = \overline{S_1}(cp,r_1) - S_0(cp,r_0) = \overline{S_1}(cp,r_1) \equiv S^2 \tag{9}$$

Figure 1(b) shows how P_1 is split when it overflows. For simplicity we assume that the data block capacity is $BC = 2$.

A split of a full partition P_i is triggered by the insertion of a new point. The parent partition P_i is replaced by its children partitions P_i and P_i'. The first child accepts the notation of his parent, as its external sphere has the same radius with that of its parent. We can sort the new point and the old points of the parent partition by distance. Afterwards, we distribute them equally in the old parent data block (first child) and in a new block (second child) by the proper selection of a new radius r_i'. We define r_i' as the half of the sum of the distances that are in the positions $\lceil BC/2 \rceil$ and $\lceil BC/2 \rceil + 1$ of the sorted list. It is $r_{s_i} < r_i' < r_i$ and the new partitions P_i and P_i' are

$$P_i = \overline{S_i}(cp,r_i) - S_i'(cp,r_i') \tag{10}$$

$$P_i' = \overline{S_i'}(cp,r_i') - S_{s_i}(cp,r_{s_i}) \tag{11}$$

The points of the first $\lceil BC/2 \rceil$ positions correspond to P_i', whereas P_i accepts the remaining points. Data blocks are written on disk and the index is updated with the new radius r_i'. Based on the above, the new partitions P_1 and P_2 of Figure 1(b) are

$$P_1 = \overline{S_1}(cp,r_1) - S_2(cp,r_2) \tag{12}$$

$$P_2 = \overline{S_2}(cp,r_2) - S_0(cp,r_0) = \overline{S_2}(cp,r_2) \tag{13}$$

Figure 2(a) and Figure 2(b) are examples of further partitions.

The radii that correspond to the partitions of the MB-tree are stored in a B^+-tree. We use links from right to left in its leaf level. This will facilitate sequential processing when we search for the remaining answers, after the first match.

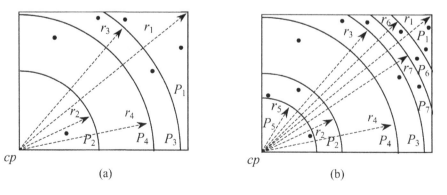

Fig. 2. Further partitions in a two-dimensional space

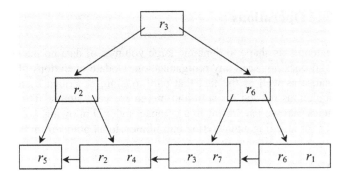

Fig. 3. The MB-tree for the partitions of Figure 2(b)

Partitions that are spatially successive in the data space are also successive in the leaf level of the tree. Figure 3 depicts the MB-tree that corresponds to the partitions of Figure 2(b). To facilitate presentation we assume again that $BC = 2$.

An entry in a leaf level of the MB-tree is a pair (r_i, pr_i) of a radius (float) and an address (pointer) of a data block. The size of the pair is 8 bytes long, assuming 4 bytes per field. pr_i, $i \geq 1$, corresponds to the block of $P_i = \overline{S_i}(cp, r_i) - S_{s_i}(cp, r_{s_i})$. Internal nodes consist of radii and addresses of nodes of lower levels.

The drawback of the MB-tree has to do with the fact that points far away from each other in a multidimensional space may be stored in the same partition. This has a negative effect on query performance as it may increase the number of partitions that are overlapped by a range query. This drawback is annihilated in the Arc-tree [] by the adoption of a more complex partition scheme.

The MB-tree preserves symmetry as it arranges partitions around a starting point. This makes the method particularly suitable for applications where distance queries that involve this point are concerned. Until now, we have used as this point, the leftmost point of the data space. This is not a restrictive constraint. A starting point may be any point of special interest. For example, in astronomic applications where the earth is considered the center of the universe, and distance queries from it are of special interest, the starting point could be the center of the data space.

Figure 4 shows partitions in a two-dimensional space with uniform distribution. The starting point of the organization is the center of the data space.

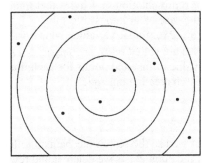

Fig. 4. Partitions in a two-dimensional space with uniform distribution

3   Update Operations

The MB-tree adapts its shape to dynamic large volumes of data no matter what their distribution and does not need any reorganization. Update operations of the MB-tree are rapid because as well as the fact that partitions are described by a real number only, the calculations needed for split and merge are very simple. The splitting and merging policies that we use, result in a compact index. Following, we will describe the procedures for inserting and deleting multidimensional points from the MB-tree.

3.1   Insertion

To insert a point p in the file, we first compute its distance $d(cp,p)$ from the point cp. Then, we search the index for the partition P_i where p should be inserted. This means that for the searched radius r_i and its forgoing radius r_{s_i} must be

$$r_{s_i} < d(cp,p) \le r_i \qquad (14)$$

If $p = cp$, then r_i is the first radius of the leaf level. The data block with address pr_i is transferred into main memory and if there is space we insert p and write the block back on disk. If the block is full we have a case of overflow and we split the block, as described in the previous section.

Alternatively, before splitting and creating a new block, we can check if there is space in the next or the previous partition. If this is the case, then we can avoid the creation of the new block. For example, if there is space in the previous partition P_{s_i} then we can increase its radius r_{s_i} in order to include at least one point of P_i. Afterwards, we update the MB-tree and the data blocks. There is no need to store any meta-information regarding splitting.

If the attributes of two points are integers or real numbers, then the calculation of their distance is obvious. For strings we use an algorithm that transforms them to unsigned long integers. Thus, distance calculations are arithmetic for all data types. There is a slight possibility two different strings to be transformed to the same long integer. The likelihood of an impossible partition split due to the mapping of all data points to the same point is remote. The greater the number of dimensions, the smaller the possibility. Another rare case of an impossible split may occur when r_i and r_{s_i} are successive, as far as their representation to 4 bytes real numbers is concerned. Overflow data blocks handle the case of an impossible split.

In the MB-tree there are $2*k$ global variables whose values are based on the inserted data. These variables are called $minv_i$ and $maxv_i$, $1 \le i \le k$ and denote the minimum and the maximum value of inserted points for each dimension. The use of these values may restrict the search area in range queries.

3.2   Deletion

For the deletion of a point we use the search mechanism to locate the block where the point should be stored. If the point exists we delete it and rewrite the block on disk.

In order to have blocks filled over a threshold we use a technique similar to the one used in B-trees. If P_i underflows after the deletion, which means that its block is left with less than $\lceil BC/2 \rceil$ points, we first check if the previous or the next partition has no more than $\lceil (BC+1)/2 \rceil$ data. If it is true, it is possible to merge two blocks. We can merge the underflow block P_i with P_{s_i} or with P_{b_i} by moving all data in one block. If we merge P_{s_i} with P_i the two partitions are replaced with one with radius r_i and the MB-tree is updated accordingly. In a similar way we treat the case when P_i is merged with P_{b_i}. If P_i underflows and P_{s_i} as well as P_{b_i} has more than $\lceil (BC+1)/2 \rceil$ data, we choose between P_{s_i} and P_{b_i} the partition with the maximum number of data. If this is P_{s_i}, we distribute equally the points of P_i and P_{s_i} into these partitions and update the radius of P_{s_i} in the MB-tree. The same technique can be used for the block that corresponds to partition P_{b_i}.

The above policy plus the one that distributes points equally in a split, guarantee that the MB-tree achieves a minimum space utilization of 50%.

4   Search

In this Section we examine how several types of queries are processed using the MB-tree.

An *exact match query* finds if a point p exists in data. In order to answer this query, we compute the distance $d(cp,p)$ and traverse downwards the index to find the partition of p. Afterwards, we access the data block of the partition. Hence, the required number of accesses is

$$h + \frac{1}{BC*U} + 1 \approx h + 1 \qquad (15)$$

where h is the height of the MB-tree and U the utilization of nodes. The approximation of the above formulae is quite restrictive because the block capacity of nodes is high, due to the small size of records, and their utilization around $ln2$, as partition numbers are organized in a B^+-tree.

A *range query* is equivalent to a hyper-rectangle RQ in the data space. The number of corners of RQ in a k-dimensional space is at most 2^k. Let $c_j(RQ)$, $1 \leq j \leq 2^k$, be the corners of RQ. If $l_c(RQ)$ and $h_c(RQ)$ are the leftmost and rightmost corners of the range query, respectively then

$$d\left(cp, l_{c_i}(RQ)\right) \leq d\left(cp, c_{ji}(RQ)\right) \leq d\left(cp, h_{c_i}(RQ)\right) \ \forall \ j, i, \ 1 \leq j \leq 2^k \wedge 1 \leq i \leq k \qquad (16)$$

In order to answer a range query, we search for the radii with value greater than or equal to the radius of the partition of $l_c(RQ)$ and less than or equal to the radius of the partition of $h_c(RQ)$.

To facilitate range queries, we take into account the variables $maxv_i$ and $minv_i$. Actually, we make the following replacements that restrict the area of the query.

$$l_{c_i}(RQ) = \min v_i, \quad \text{if } l_{c_i}(RQ) < \min v_i$$
$$h_{c_i}(RQ) = \max v_i, \quad \text{if } h_{c_i}(RQ) > \max v_i \tag{17}$$

Figure 5 shows a range query RQ for the data space of Figure 2(b). RQ overlaps with the partitions P_5, P_2 and P_4. Due to the use of $minv_1$, shown with the dash line, the region of RQ is restricted and the overlap is reduced to the partitions P_2 and P_4. Only the blocks of these two partitions are examined for qualified data.

The procedure to answer a *partial match query* is similar to that of a range query, as the set of partial match queries is a subset of the range queries. If i, $1 \leq i \leq k$, is a dimension that participates in a partial match query with free value, then the upper and lower corners of RQ, as concerns this dimension, have values $maxv_i$ and $minv_i$, respectively.

We will now examine some *similarity* queries. These queries are important in metric spaces and their goal is to retrieve data whose similarity has been decided through the use of the distance function. Two basic types of these queries are 'similarity range' or 'window query' and 'n-nearest neighbors query'. To facilitate our presentation let rsq_{min} and rsq_{max} be the minimum and the maximum radius, respectively of the partitions that overlap with a similarity query. In order to answer such a query, the radii belonging to the interval $[rsq_{min}, rsq_{max}]$ have to be accessed.

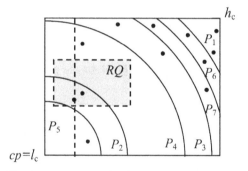

Fig. 5. A range query for the partitions of Figure 2(b)

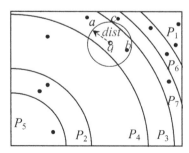

Fig. 6. A similarity range query for the partitions of Figure 2(b)

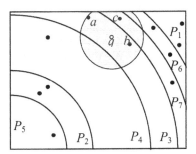

Fig. 7. *n*-nearest neighbor query for the partitions of Figure 2(b)

A *similarity range query SRQ(q,dist)*, selects the points *p* for which it is $d(q,p) \leq dist$, where *dist* is a real number. In this type of query, rsq_{min} is the radius of the MB-tree that is the first greater than or equal to the value $d(cp,q) - dist$. In addition, rsq_{max} is the radius of the MB-tree tree that is the first greater than or equal to the value $d(cp,q) + dist$. If such a radius does not exist, then $rsq_{max} = d(cp,h_c)$. To find the addresses of data blocks we search the index in the range $[rsq_{min}, rsq_{max}]$. Points in these data blocks are examined for qualification.

In Figure 6 we can see a similarity range query for the partitions of Figure 2(b). For the query *SRQ(q,dist)* we have $rsq_{min}=r_4$, $rsq_{max}=r_7$ and the answer is the point *b*.

An *n-nearest neighbors query NNQ(q,n)* where *n* integer, $1 \leq n$, selects the *n* data points with the shortest distance from *q*. We use a two dimensional list to hold the searched points and their distances from *q*. First, we examine the entries of the partition P_i of *q* and it follows the alternate examination of partitions that reside on the left and right of P_i. If the number of points in the list is lower than *n*, then the current examined point is inserted in the list. Otherwise, the point is inserted if its distance is lower than a distance of an already existing point in the list. The new point replaces the point with the maximum distance.

The radius rsq_{min} resides on the left of r_i and is the closest one to it and such that the value $(d(cp,q) - rsq_{min_s})$ be greater than all the distances of the points of the full list. If this condition is not an issue, then rsq_{min} is the smaller radius of the MB-tree. The radius rsq_{max} resides on the right of r_i and is the closest one to it and such that the value $(rsq_{max} - d(cp,q))$ be greater than all the distances of the points of the full list. If this is not valid, then rsq_{max} is the bigger radius of the MB-tree.

In Figure 7 we show the nearest neighbor query *NNQ(q,3)* for our running example. We have $rsq_{min} = r_4$, $rsq_{max} = r_6$ and qualified points *a*, *b* and *c*.

5   Experimental Results

In this Section we provide experimental results on the performance of MB-tree and compare them to the corresponding performance of G-tree [10].

G-trees [8],[10] are efficient multidimensional point structures. They have the ability to adapt their shape to high dynamic data spaces and to non-uniformly distributed data. G-trees divide the data space into a grid of variable size partitions. These partitions are stored in a B-tree-like organization. Only non-empty partitions, which span the data space, are stored.

Our implementation was made in C and the performance comparison on a SUN4u Sparc Ultra 5/10 under SunOS 5.8. We used separate files for the indexes and the data.

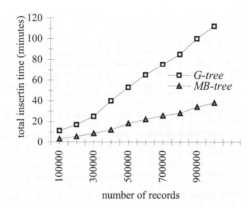

Fig. 8. Total insertion time.

We present experiments with four dimensions, all included in the index and attribute size of 4 bytes. We used 1 Kbytes page size. We use as the starting point, the leftmost point of the data space. The data followed the normal distribution with mean value 0 and standard deviation $5*10^6$. We chose to present our experiments with data following the normal distribution because it approximates other distributions well and also it is common in real world measurements. Similar experiments with other distributions showed that results depend slightly upon the nature of the distribution from which the data is drawn. The range of inserted records was $[10^5,10^6]$ and the step of increment 10^5.

Figure 8 shows the total insertion time in minutes versus the number of records. We repeated the insertion procedure three times in a dedicated machine. We present the average insertion times. The insertion time of MB-tree is 0.34 of the corresponding time of G-tree in a volume of 10^6 records. This is justified by the fact that in the MB-tree the partition of an inserted record is determined using a very simple calculation.

Figure 9 shows the heights of the trees versus the number of records. As we can see, both trees have short heights, which grow slowly.

Figure 10 shows the space requirements of the two indexes in Kbytes compared with the number of records. As shown in this figure, the MB-tree needs smaller storage space than the G-tree to organize its data.

Figure 11 depicts the average number of disk block accesses versus the distance from the center of similarity range queries. The distance was $dist = 10^3 \div 10^4$, the number of records 10^6 and the average value derived from 100 queries with the same distance. This figure shows that the disk accesses required by the MB-tree are fewer than the ones required by the G-tree.

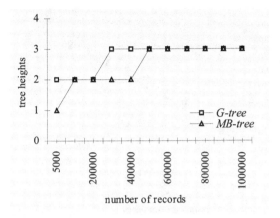

Fig. 9. Tree heights

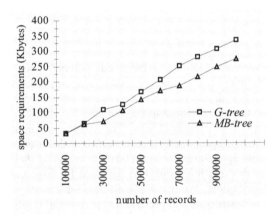

Fig. 10. Space requirements

On the above grounds, we believe that the MB-tree, although its simple partition scheme, is comparable to other more complex indexes.

At this point, we refer to the paper [11]. This work presents a new method for the estimation of the sphere radius in an *n*-nearest neighbour query. The method transforms the above type of query into a range query. Experimental results presented in this paper show a substantial reduction in the number of disk block accesses and seek time. The method is based on fractal dimensionality and sampling. The estimation error of the method is below of 14%. For applications where estimation errors are not allowed and the used index is paged, the authors suggest an algorithm that gives an upper limit for the sphere radius. The estimation error of this algorithm is below 1%.

As the above techniques are applicable to any paged index, we believe that their adoption by the MB-tree may contribute to its efficiency.

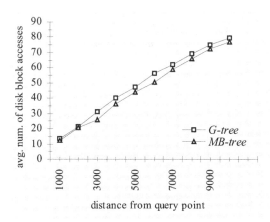

Fig. 11. Average number of disk block accesses per similarity range queries

6   Summary

In this paper, we presented the MB-tree, a balanced, symmetric, compact and dynamic index structure for multidimensional point data. The proposed structure uses a new simple partition scheme that divides the data space into co-centric spheres. It makes a linearization of the k-dimensional space, excludes the storage of empty partitions and ensures a minimum utilization of 50%. The MB-tree combines the features of distance functions of metric spaces and B-trees. Partitions that are spatially successive in a multidimensional space are also successive in terms of their storage. The MB-tree is k-d-cut, adaptable and brickwall. It is designed for large volumes of data, no matter what the distribution. We gave algorithms for inserting deleting and searching data from the new structure and presented experimental results.

We believe that the compact size of the MB-tree in conjunction with its robust update and search operations will promote it to a valuable index. In addition, the simple partition scheme of the MB-tree may become the base for the development of new multidimensional access methods. On-going research includes algorithms for the proper selection of the starting point based on data distribution and the extension of the MB-tree in order to handle complex geometric objects efficiently.

References

[1]   Boehm C., Berchtold S. and Keim D.A.: "Searching in High-Dimensional Spaces: Index Structures for Improving the Performance of Multimedia Databases", ACM Computing Surveys, Vol.33, No.3, pp. 322-373, 2001.

[2]   Ciaccia P., Patella M. and Zezula P.: "M-tree: an Efficient Access Method for Similarity Search in Metric Spaces", Proceedings 23rd VLDB Conference, pp. 426-435, 1997.

[3]   Dandamundi S. and Sorenson P.: "An empirical performance comparison of some variations of the k-d-tree and BD-tree", International Journal of Computer and Information Sciences, Vol.14, pp. 135-159, 1985.

[4]   Dandamundi S. and Sorenson P.: "Algorithms for BD-trees", Software Practice and Experience, Vol. 16, No.12, pp. 1077-1096, 1986.

[5]   Faloutsos C.: "Searching Multimedia Databases by Content", Kluwer, Boston, 1996.

[6]   Freeston M.: "The BANG file: a New Kind of Grid File", Proceedings 1987 ACM SIGMOD Conference, pp. 260-269, 1987.

[7]   Gaede V. and Gunther O.: "Multidimensional Access Methods", ACM Computing Surveys, Vol. 30, No.2, pp. 170-231, 1998.

[8]   Kapopoulos D.G. and Hatzopoulos M.: "The Gr-Tree: the Use of Active Regions in G-Trees", Proceedings 3rd ADBIS Conference, pp. 141-155, 1999.

[9]   Kapopoulos D.G. and Hatzopoulos M.: "The Arc-Tree: a Novel Symmetric Access Method for Multidimensional Data", Proceedings 5th ADBIS Conference, pp. 294-307, 2001.

[10]   Kumar A.: "G-Tree: A New Data Structure for Organizing Multidimensional Data", IEEE Transactions on Knowledge and Data Engineering, Vol.6, No.2, pp. 341-347, 1994.

[11]   Lang C. and Singh A.: "A Framework for Accelerating High–dimensional NN-queries", Technical Report TRCS01-04, University of California, Santa Barbara, 2002.

[12]   Nievergelt J., Hintenberger H. and Sevcik K.C.: "The Grid File: an Adaptable, Symmetric Multikey File Structure", ACM Transactions Database Systems, Vol. 9, No.1, pp. 38-71, 1984.

[13]   Orenstein J. and Merrett T.: "A Class of Data Structures for Associative Searching", Proceedings 3rd ACM PODS Symposium, pp. 181-190, 1984.

[14]   Orenstein J.: "Spatial Query Processing in an Object-Oriented Database System", Proceedings 1986 ACM SIGMOD Conference, pp. 326-336, 1986.

[15]   Robinson J.T.: "The K-D-B-tree: A Search Structure for Large Multidimensional Dynamic Indexes", Proceedings 1981 ACM SIGMOD Conference, pp. 10-18, 1981.

[16]   Samet H.: "Spatial Databases", Proceedings 23rd VLDB Conference, pp. 63-129, 1997.

[17]   Manolopoulos Y., Theodoridis Y. and Tsotras V. J.: "Advanced Database Indexing", Kluwer, Boston, 1999.

[18]   Traina C., Traina A., Seeger B. and Faloutsos C.: "Slim-Trees: High Performance Metric Trees Minimizing Overlap Between Nodes", Proceedings 7th EDBT Conference, 2000.

[19]   White D. and Jain R.: "Similarity Indexing with the SS-tree", Proceedings 12th ICDE Conference, pp. 516-523, 1996.

Design of the ERATOSTHENES OLAP Server

Nikos Karayannidis, Aris Tsois, Panos Vassiliadis, and Timos Sellis

Institute of Communication and Computer Systems and
National Technical University of Athens
Zographou 15773 Athens, Hellas
{nikos,atsois,pvassil,timos}@dblab.ece.ntua.gr

Abstract. On-Line Analytical Processing (OLAP) is a trend in data-base technology, based on the multidimensional view of data and is an indispensable component of the so-called *business intelligence* technology. The systems that realize this technology are called *OLAP servers* and are among the most high-priced products in software industry today [24]. The aim of this paper is twofold: (a) to describe the core levels of an OLAP system's architecture and to present design choices and reasoning for each one of them, and (b) to present the specific design decisions that we made for a prototype under development at NTUA, ERATOSTHENES. The paper describes in detail the most important decisions taken regarding the basic layers of the server component of ERATOSTHENES.

1 Introduction

On-Line Analytical Processing (OLAP) is a trend in database technology, based on the multi-dimensional view of data. The focus of OLAP servers is to provide multidimensional analysis of the underlying information. To achieve this goal, these tools employ multidimensional models for the storage and presentation of data. The goal of this paper is to present what is our understanding of the basic architecture of an OLAP system and discuss requirements and design choices. The perspective that we take is the one of the technology provider: we focus on the internals of an OLAP system, rather than the external behavior of the system. Moreover we present specific design choices for the architecture of an OLAP system that we develop at NTUA. ERATOSTHENES is an internal project of the database group at NTUA and aims to provide OLAP facilities to the end-user through optimized data structures and query processing techniques.

This paper is essentially divided in two parts. In the first part (section 2) we present the basic levels of the architecture of an OLAP system and discuss requirements. In the second part (sections 3), we present the architecture of ERATOSTHENES. Also, in this part we discuss specific design choices for the storage layer (section 4) as well as for the processing and optimization layer (section 5).

Y. Manolopoulos et al. (Eds.): PCI 2001, LNCS 2563, pp. 32–49, 2003.

2 Entities, Models and Requirements for an OLAP System

The core of the multidimensional paradigm is the fact that information is conceptually considered to be defined in terms of a multidimensional space. The axes of the multidimensional space are called *dimensions* and their points determine functionally the value of the points of the multidimensional space, called *measures*. Imagine for example an international publishing company, with traveling salesmen, selling books and CD's to other bookstores all over the world. The dimensions of our example are `arrival date`, `departure date` (when the salesman arrives/leaves the store), `product`, `location` and `salesman`. The functionally dependent measures are `Sales`, `PercentChange`. The combination of a set of dimensions and a set of measures produces a *cube* (or *hypercube*).

The multidimensional space is also characterized from the fact that each dimension comprises several levels of consolidation. The combination of these levels produces one or more *hierarchies* for each dimension. For example, the `location` hierarchy can comprise the levels `city`, `province`, `country` and `continent`. The values of each level in the hierarchy are related to the values of other levels (e.g., "Athens", which is a value at the `city` level, is related to the value "Europe" at the `continent` level). The combination of the multidimensional space of a cube with the dimension hierarchies produces a *multi-level multidimensional space*.

The overall architecture of an OLAP system comprises an hierarchy of basically three data models: the *physical model*, the *logical model* and the *presentation model*. The central logical cube model defines the concept of a cube and its corresponding operations. The physical model deals with how the cubes are stored or indexed for efficient access. The presentation model is concerned with grouping several logical cubes, defined as parts of one (or more) underlying cube(s), in one presentation entity. The mapping between these levels ensures independence and this is achieved through the use of the intermediate logical model. In the sequel, we will try to give a brief description of what we think each of these levels should cover. The following also comprise the models setting the framework of ERATOSTHENES.

2.1 Presentation Model

Presentation models are essentially an extension to the classical *conceptual-logical-physical* hierarchy of database models [22]. The presentation model is similar to a report definition language and it extends a logical or a conceptual model. Through the presentation model the user can define how the results should be visualized. This is achieved by defining complex views and visualization strategies. There are many reasons for which these models are an essential need in OLAP systems.

First, practice in the field of multidimensional databases is concentrating on models of representation; for example, Microsoft has already issued a commercial standard for multidimensional databases, where the presentation issues are a big part of it [16]. Moreover, data visualization is presently a quickly evolving field, and has proved its power in presenting vast amounts of data to the user [13, 1]. Finally, since analysis of data is the basic requirement for an OLAP system, the presentation model is of greater significance than in traditional RDBMS's. It is obvious that the more powerful the presentation model is, the greater analysis power is supplied to the end user.

Apart from the industrial proposal of Microsoft, previous proposals already exist in the literature, with the *tape model* [7] being the most prominent one. One invaluable feature that should accompany a presentation model is a declarative query language. The benefits of declarative query languages are best demonstrated by the success of SQL in relational systems. We will not argue more on the subject, but simply note that in the case of OLAP systems a powerful query language enables the possibility of providing the user with complex reports, created from several cubes (or actually subsets of existing cubes).

2.2   Logical Model

The logical model is the center of any DBMS and an OLAP DBMS could not escape this rule. Apart from the requirement for *data independence*, which is actually the reason for the existence of a logical model, there are some extra requirements for the logical model of an OLAP DBMS:

Logical Operations that Abstract the Specialized Processing: The logical model must provide a set of operations (e.g., a set of algebraic operations) that on the one hand abstract the specialized processing entailed in OLAP and on the other hand that are powerful enough to capture all the usual operations performed from an OLAP system. Moreover, even if not directly covered, *sequences of operations* such as `roll-up`, `drill-down`, `select` etc., should be enabled through these operations. Algebraic expressions should be derived directly from the declarative query language of the presentation model.

Support for "Rich" Dimensions: It is impossible to do anything interesting in OLAP, (e.g., run a complex report, which will reveal some hidden trends in your business) with a poor dimension consisting of only a few attributes. Clearly, all analysis power of OLAP lies in the dimensions. All queries are defined through the dimension attributes and thus the richer is the set of attributes that characterizes a dimension, the more analysis opportunities you have. However, keeping a large list of attributes for each dimension still is not enough. There must be support for defining various dependencies between different attributes, such as hierarchical relationships, or other functional dependencies. Thus, we come to the next requirement, which is:

Meta-information that Captures the Complexity of the Data Space: There must be support for storing meta-information that will capture all the dependencies between different attributes, as well as the specific role of each object (e.g., a dimension, a cube, a hierarchy level and so on). This will enable specialized processing and optimization of user queries.

2.3   Physical Model

The physical model provides the structures which will be used for the storage of cubes. Conceptually, we can think of cube data as *cells* of a multidimensional array. However, the underlying physical schema could be anything; even something radically different from the array perspective, e.g. conventional relations. The physical data independence mentioned earlier, dictates that changes in the physical schema do not impose any changes to the logical schema.

In the literature there are several proposals for cube storage and indexing structures [20]. Moreover, commercial products rely on their own proprietary techniques for dealing with the same problem [6]. We believe that there is a number of crucial requirements particular to OLAP cubes, that should be the main focus of physical schema design. In particular, the system should satisfy the following requirements:

Minimum Response Time for Ad-hoc Queries: With the term *"ad hoc"* we refer to queries that are not known in advance, in contrast to *report queries* that are known a-priori and therefore the administrator can optimize the DBMS specifically for these, e.g., by precomputing and materializing their result. Ad-hoc star queries represent the majority of OLAP queries, since they capture the essense of true *"on-line analysis"*.

Efficient Navigation in the Multi-Level Multidimensional Space: User queries are defined in terms of dimensions and hierarchy levels, therefore the underlying physical organization must provide "access paths" to the data that are "hierarchy aware" and enable fast access to data through all kind of combinations of different hierarchy levels.

Efficient Range Queries with Respect to all Dimension Levels: The majority of OLAP operations involves some form of a range query. Therefore, there is a need for efficient handling of range queries along any of the levels of a cube.

Coping with Cube Sparseness: According to [4], 20% of a typical cube contains real data but our experiences from real-world data have revealed cube densities of less that 0.1%. Therefore, cubes are inherently very sparse. Moreover, empty cells tend to be clustered, rather than randomly distributed in the multidimensional space [19]. It is imperative for the physical organization to efficiently cope with this issue.

Efficient Updating: OLAP databases are mostly read-only and batch updates occur at regular intervals. Still the volume of data is such that full reconstruction of a cube may prove prohibitive w.r.t the available time window. Thus, the physical organization of data must allow such bulk updates to be performed *incrementally*.

3   The Architecture of the ERATOSTHENES OLAP System

ERATOSTHENES is a specialized DBMS for OLAP cubes. The components of ERATOSTHENES cover the whole spectrum of an OLAP system, starting from

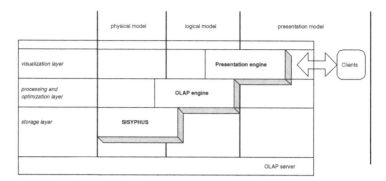

Fig. 1. The layers of the ERATOSTHENES architecture

the visualization of multidimensional data at the user-end, down to the efficient physical storage of cubes on disk. In this paper we focus on the server part of ERATOSTHENES. The architecture of the OLAP server consists of three major layers: the *storage layer*, the *processing layer* and the *visualization layer*. Each of these layers contain a major component of the OLAP server. Figure 1 presents the major components of the ERATOSTHENES OLAP server aligned along these three layers. Also, the intersection of the server components with the aforementioned models of an OLAP system is depicted.

At the back end lies the *storage engine* (in the so-called *storage layer*), which is responsible for the efficient access to the stored data. The cube storage manager used by ERATOSTHENES, is called SISYPHUS [11] and has been implemented on top of the SHORE Storage Manager (SSM)[9]. SISYPHUS includes modules responsible for file management, buffer management, locking management and provides appropriate access methods to the stored data.

The *OLAP engine* component lies at the *processing and optimization layer* and is responsible for all processing tasks. It is responsible for the compilation of queries expressed in terms of the logical model, the optimization of the execution plans using knowledge about the logical and physical organization of data, and the efficient execution of these plans through data retrieval offered by SISYPHUS.

Finally, the *presentation engine* is responsible for the initial parsing of the client requests and for the compilation of the final output as required. The client requests are expressed in terms of the presentation model. The presentation engine transforms each such request into the appropriate queries to the OLAP engine. The presentation engine is also responsible for the on-demand retrieval of the results from the OLAP engine and the proper combination and formatting of these results according to the specifications given by the client request. The results are then properly delivered to the client side through the interfaces of the presentation engine.

In the sequel, we will describe in more detail the first two layers of the ERATOSTHENES architecture, which essentially comprise the driving force of the OLAP server.

4   Designing the Storage Layer

In this section we will describe the major design choices regarding the storage layer of the ERATOSTHENES architecture. Ideally, this layer implements the necessary storage base and deals with all the subtleties of the physical organization of the data. Therefore, conceptually it belongs to the physical model of an OLAP system described in subsection 2.3.

In ERATOSTHENES we have adopted a physical organization whose primary goal is to achieve maximum physical clustering of the cube data according to the dimension hierarchies. The incentive for this decision lies in the fact that the majority of cube data accesses are guided by restrictions on the hierarchies. Multidimensional data structures that cluster data hierarchically are a new trend in OLAP technology that has exhibited very promising results [15, 11, 12]. In the sequel we will outline the adopted physical organization and also present other aspects of the design of the storage management services of ERATOSTHENES.

Cube data in ERATOSTHENES are organized in a chunk-based file organization that achieves hierarchical clustering. *Chunking* is not a new concept in the relevant literature. Several works exploit chunks; to our knowledge, the first paper to introduce the notion of the chunk was [21]. Very simply put, a chunk is a sub-cube within a cube with the same dimensionality as the encompassing cube. A chunk is created by defining distinct ranges of members along each dimension of the cube. In other words, by applying chunking to the cube we essentially perform a kind of grouping of data. It has been observed [21, 5] that chunks provide excellent clustering of cells, which results in less I/O cost when reading data from a disk and also better caching, if a chunk is used as a caching unit.

Chunks can be of uniform size [21, 2] or of variable size [5]. Our approach of chunking deals with variable size chunks. Each chunk represents a semantic subset of the cube. The semantics are drawn from the parent-child relationships of the dimension members along aggregation paths on each dimension. A similar approach has been adopted in [5] for caching OLAP query results.

A chunk-oriented file organization destined for a storage base for OLAP cubes, apart from clustering the data effectively, also has to provide the following services:

Storage Allocation: It has to store chunks into the storage-unit (in our case this unit is called a *bucket* and equals the size of a disk page) provided by the underlying file system.

Chunk Addressing: A single chunk must be addressable from other modules. This means that an identifier must be assigned to each chunk. Moreover, an efficient access path must exist via that identifier.

Enumeration: There must be a fast way to get from one chunk to the "next" one. However, in a multi-dimensional multi-level space, "next" can have many interpretations, since there are many dimensions to follow and many levels to drill-down or to roll-up.

Data Point Location Addressing: Cube data points should be made accessible via their location in the multi-dimensional multi-level space.

Data Sparseness Management: Space allocated should not be wasteful and must handle efficiently the native sparseness of cube data.

Maintenance: Although transaction oriented workloads are not expected in OLAP environments, the system must be able to support at least periodic incremental loads in a batch form.

These have been amongst the most important requirements when designing the storage layer. In order to provide the above services and also accomplish a hierarchical clustering of the cube data, dimension values are assigned a special key called a *hierarchical surrogate key*, or simply *h-surrogate*, which is unique for each dimension value. Assignment of system-generated surrogate keys is something very common in data warehousing practice, since surrogate keys provide a level of independence from the keys of the tables in the source systems [14]. In our case, surrogate keys are defined over the levels of the hierarchy of a dimension and are essentially the means to achieve hierarchical clustering of the cube data.

The main idea is that an h-surrogate value for a specific dimension table tuple is constructed as a combination of encoded values of the hierarchical attributes of the tuple. For example, if h_1, h_2, h_3 are the hierarchical attributes of a dimension table from the most detailed level to the most aggregated one, then the h-surrogates for this dimension table will be represented by the values $oc_a(h_3)/oc_b(h_2)/oc_c(h_1)$, where the functions $oc_i(i = a, b, c)$ define a numbering scheme for each hierarchy level and assign some *order-code* to each hierarchical attribute value. Obviously the h-surrogate attribute of a dimension table is a key for this table since it determines all hierarchical attributes, which in turn determine functionally all feature attributes (i.e., other non-hierarchical attributes that characterize a hierarchical attribute, e.g., the "color" of a product item (see also subsection 5.1)). The h-surrogate should be a system assigned and maintained attribute, and typically should be made transparent to the user.

In Figure 2(a) we depict an example of a **STORE** dimension consisting of a hierarchy path of four levels. We call the most detailed level the *grain level*

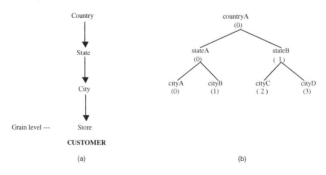

Fig. 2. (a) An example of a hierarchy path of a dimension. (b) An h-surrogate denotes the whole path of a member in a specific level hierarchy

of the dimension. The *h-surrogate* of a member (also called a *member-code*) is constructed by the order codes of all its ancestor members along the hierarchy path, separated by dots. For example, the member code of `cityC` along the hierarchy path of Figure 2(b) is 0.1.2.

The chunk-based file organization in **ERATOSTHENES** exploits h-surrogates by recursively chunking the cube along the levels of the dimension hierarchies. The chunking process begins from the most aggregated levels (coarser chunks) and descends down to the grain level (finer chunks). Therefore, chunks at different *chunking depths* are produced, which correspond to different aggregation levels of the cube data space . The order-code ranges along each dimension that a specific chunk covers, are defined from the parent-child relationship of the dimension members. For example, if a 2-dimensional chunk is defined by the dimension members with h-surrogates: 1.2 and 0.5; and the corresponding "children" order-codes cover the ranges 1.2.[5..12] and 0.5.[9..20], then this chunk will cover the [5..12] × [9..20] rectangular region at the specific depth (i.e., aggregation level) of the cube data space.

This *hierarchical chunking* results in a data structure consisting of a hierarchy of chunks, with intermediate nodes playing the role of *directory chunks*, which guide the access to the leaf-level *data chunks*. An example of such a *"chunk-tree"* for a 2-dimensional cube is depicted in Figure 3.

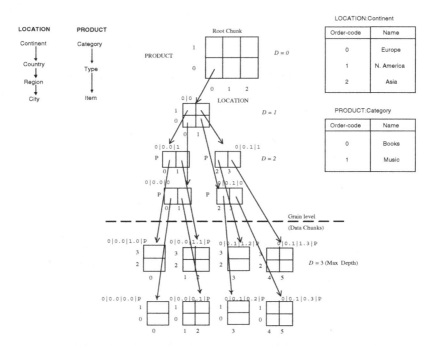

Fig. 3. The whole sub-tree up to the data chunks under chunk 0|0

In Figure 3, the topmost chunk is called the *root-chunk*. We can see the directory chunks containing "pointer" entries that lead to larger depth directory chunks and finally to data chunks. If we interleave the member codes of the level members that define a chunk, then we get a code that we call *chunk-id*. This is a unique identifier for a chunk within a cube in ERATOSTHENES. Moreover, this identifier depicts the whole path of a particular chunk. In Figure 3 we note the corresponding chunk-id above each chunk. For example, if we consider the chunk defined from the level members with h-surrogates $LOCATION : 0.0$ and $PRODUCT : 0.1$, for an interleaving order $ord = (LOCATION, PRODUCT)$ (major-to-minor from left-to-right), its chunk-id is $0|0.0|1$, with the "|" character acting as a dimension separator. This id describes the fact that this is a chunk at depth $\mathcal{D} = 2$ and it is defined within chunk $0|0$ at $\mathcal{D} = 1$ (parent chunk).

Hierarchical clustering of data is achieved by a special chunk-to-bucket allocation algorithm that tries to store in the same bucket as many chunks of the same family (i.e., sub-tree) as possible. The incentive here lies in the hierarchical nature of OLAP query loads. By imposing this "hierarchical clustering" of data, we aim at improving query response time by reducing page accesses significantly. For example, the sub-tree hanging from the root-chunk in Figure 3, at the leaf level contains all the sales figures corresponding to the continent "Europe" (order code 0) and to the product category "Books" (order code 0). By storing this tree into a single bucket, we can answer all queries containing hierarchical restrictions on the combination "Books" and "Europe" and on any children-members of these two, with just a single I/O operation. A more detailed presentation of the file organization of ERATOSTHENES is beyond the scope of this article; the interested reader may find more details in [11].

Recapitulating, we can say that the adopted physical organization has been designed in order to provide clustering of data according to the dimension hierarchies and in order to fulfill certain storage management requirements, as these were listed above. Hierarchical clustering is achieved by imposing a chunking based on the dimension hierarchies and by allocating the produced chunks into buckets according to these hierarchies. Chunk addressing, as well as enumeration and navigation in the multidimensional and multi-level cube data space is achieved by the assigned chunk-ids and a set of basic access operations (such as move_to(), get_next(), roll_up() and drill_down()). Data sparseness management is achieved by allocating chunks *only for non-empty sub-tress* and by applying a compression scheme to data chunks based on the use of bitmaps [11]. Finally, incremental batch updates are supported. In most of the cases the advent of some new data (e.g., the sales of the last day) correspond to append-only operations in a few buckets containing a specific "family" of chunks [11].

We wish to close this subsection with a comment for the alerted reader. The chunk-oriented file organization is based on a single hierarchy path from each dimension. We call this path the *primary path* of the dimension. Data will be physically clustered according to the dimensions' primary paths. However, a dimension might have more than one hierarchical paths. Since queries based on primary paths are likely to be favored in terms of response time, it is crucial for the designer to decide on the paths that will play the role of the primary paths based on the query workload. In other words, the path (per dimension) where the majority of queries impose their restrictions should be identified as the primary path. Naturally, the only way to favor more than one path (per dimension) in clustering is to maintain redundant copies of the cube [21], or to treat different hierarchy paths as separate dimensions [15], thus increasing the cube dimensionality.

5 Designing the Processing and Optimization Layer

In the core architecture of ERATOSTHENES, above the storage layer lies the processing and optimization layer. This layer is independent from the underlying storage layer in the sense that any storage organization that exploits h-surrogates (e.g., [15, 11]) can be used as a basis for the performed processing. In this section we will present the basic design of the processing services of ERATOSTHENES. In particular, we will identify the target set of queries and present the major processing steps in terms of abstract operators. Then, we will go further by outlining the query optimization services offered by our system.

5.1 An Abstract Processing Plan for Star Queries

The data model assumed in this layer is the well-known *star schema* [3]. In this model the cube is represented by a central (and usually very large) fact table, which is surrounded by several dimension tables that link to the former with $1 : N$ foreign-key relationships. We emphasize again that in this layer the only assumption regarding the physical organization of the data is that the fact table is stored in a structure that enables hierarchical clustering through the use of h-surrogates (see section 4).

Dimension tables consist of *hierarchical attributes* $h_1, h_2, \ldots, h_k$ that form a classification hierarchy; e.g., h_1 is classified by the values of h_2, which is further classified by h_3, and so on. A dimension table may also contain other attributes that we call *feature attributes f*. These are descriptive attributes and are semantically different from hierarchical attributes in that they cannot participate in a dimension hierarchy. Feature attributes contain additional information about a number of hierarchical attributes and are always functionally dependent on one (or more) hierarchical attribute. For example, population could be a feature attribute dependent on the region attribute of dimension LOCATION.

The star-schema of Figure 4, is a star schema where the dimension tables have been hierarchically encoded. This schema consists of N dimensions stored in the dimension tables $D_1, \ldots, D_N$. Each dimension is logically structured in a hierarchy. The hierarchy elements for dimension D_i are $h_1, h_2, \ldots, h_{k_i}$ (h_1 being the most detailed level). Each dimension table D_i may also include a set of feature attributes $f_1, f_2, \ldots, f_{l_i}$ that characterize one or more hierarchical attributes. In Figure 4 we depict h_1, i.e., the most detailed level in each hierarchy as the primary key of each dimension table. In Figure 4 we can also see the h-surrogate

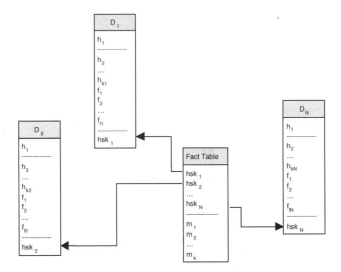

Fig. 4. Star schema with flat dimension tables

attribute (hsk_i), which is an alternate key for each table $D_i(i = 1, \ldots, N)$. The fact table contains the measure attributes $(m_1, m_2, \ldots, m_k)$ and the reference to the h-surrogate of each dimension $(hsk_1, hsk_2, \ldots, hsk_N)$. All measure values refer to the most detailed level of the hierarchy of each dimension.

OLAP queries typically include restrictions on multiple dimension tables that trigger restrictions on the (usually very large) fact table. This is known as a *star join* [17]. In this paper, we use the term *star query* to refer to flat SQL queries, defined over a single star schema, that include a star join. In particular, we are interested in *ad hoc star queries* (see section 2).

In [12], an abstract processing plan for the evaluation of star-queries over hierarchically clustered fact tables was presented. We will briefly discuss this plan here. Essentially, the evaluation of a star query is a 3-step process:

Identify and Retrieve Fact Table Data: The processing begins with the evaluation of the restrictions on the individual dimension tables. This step performed on a hierarchically encoded dimension table will result in a set of h-surrogates that will be used in order to access the corresponding fact table data. Due to the hierarchical nature of the h-surrogate this set can be represented by a number of h-surrogate intervals called the *h-surrogate specification*. Using the notation of [11], an interval can for example have the form $v_3/v_2/*$, where v_3, v_2 are specific values of the h_3 and h_2 hierarchical attributes of the dimension in question. The symbol "*" means all the values of the h_1 attribute in the dimension tuples that have $h_3 = v_3$ and $h_2 = v_2$. In the case of a `DATE` dimension, the h-surrogate specification could be $1999/January/*$ to allow for any day in this month. Due to the assigned order-codes (see section 4) the qualified h-surrogate have consecutive order

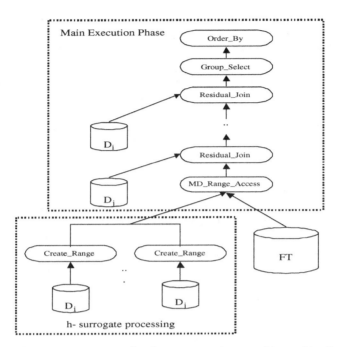

Fig. 5. The abstract processing plan for star-queries over hierarchically clustered OLAP cubes

codes, therefore we can use the term *range* to denote the h-surrogate specification arising from the evaluation of the restriction on a single dimension. Once the h-surrogate ranges are produced, then the corresponding fact table data must be retrieved. This could be simply called *"the evaluation of the star-join"*. However, due to the underlying multidimensional structure, which physically organizes the fact table data, this so-called "join" is transformed to one or more simple *multidimensonal range queries*. The actual processing depends on the specific data structure (see [15, 11] for more details).

Perform Residual Joins: The tuples resulting from the fact table contain the h-surrogates, the measures and the dimension table primary keys. At this stage, there might be a need for joining these tuples with a number of dimension tables in order to retrieve certain hierarchical and/or feature attributes that the user wants to have in the final result and might also be needed for the grouping operation. We call these joins *residual joins*.

Perform Grouping and Ordering: Finally, the resulting tuples may be grouped and aggregated and the groups further filtered and ordered for delivering the result to the user.

The abstract processing plan comprising of the above phases is illustrated in Figure 5. This plan is abstract in the sense that it does not determine specific algorithms for each processing step: it just defines the processing that needs to be done. That is why it is expressed in terms of *abstract operators* (or *logical operators*), which in turn can be mapped to a number of alternative *physical operators* that correspond to specific implementations.

As can be seen from the figure, the plan is logically divided in two main processing phases: *the hierarchical surrogate key processing (HSKP) phase* which corresponds to the first processing step mentioned earlier, and the *main execution phase (MEP)* corresponding to the other two steps.

We will briefly describe now the operators appearing in Figure 5: The operator **Create_Range** is responsible for evaluating the restrictions on each dimension table. This evaluation will result in an h-surrogate specification (set of ranges) for each dimension. **MD_Range_Access** receives as input the h-surrogate specifications from the **Create_Range** operators and performs a set of range queries on the underlying multidimensional structure that holds the fact table data. Apart from the selection of data points that fall into the desired ranges, this operator can perform further filtering based on predicates on the measure values and projection (without duplicate elimination) of fact table attributes. **Residual_Join** is a join on a key-foreign key equality condition among a dimension table and the tuples originating from the **MD_Range_Access** operator. This way, each incoming fact table record is joined with at most one dimension table record. The join is performed in order to enrich the fact table records with the required dimension table attributes. **Group_Select** performs grouping and aggregation on the resulting tuples while filtering out unwanted groups and finally, **Order_By** simply sorts the tuples in the required output order.

5.2   Query Optimization in ERATOSTHENES

In this subsection we will briefly describe the optimization framework of the processing layer in **ERATOSTHENES**. The optimization engine of our system consists of a *rule-based optimizer* enhanced with a specialized *cost model*. We have to clarify here that as a first approach our optimization efforts have concentrated solely on speeding up star-queries executed within our abstract processing plan framework presented earlier. Therefore, the following discussion does not cover traditional optimization techniques applied generally to SQL queries.

The rule optimizer of **ERATOSTHENES** consists of *implementation rules* and *heuristic optimization rules* (or simply *heuristic rules*). An *implementation rule* provides a mapping between a single abstract operator (see subsection 5.1) and a set of *physical operators* in the form of an *operator tree* [8] bound with some condition. The key observation here is that a single abstract operator can have many different implementations. The decision of which implementation is applicable is governed by the *rule condition*. This condition generally depends on the physical design of the data (i.e., physical organizations used, existence of secondary indexes, etc.) and on the form of the processed query. Note that these conditions merely say *when a specific implementation can be applied*, and not when such an application will lead to an optimal execution.

For example, in Figure 6, we depict two (out of many possible) implementations regarding the **Create_Range** abstract operator. On the left-side we de-

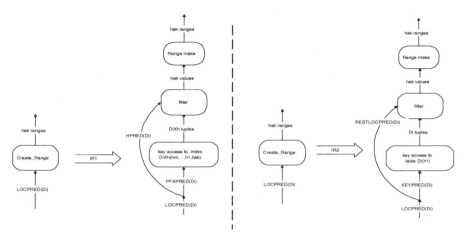

Fig. 6. The abstract processing plan for star-queries over hierarchically clustered OLAP cubes

pict the processing steps included in an implementation rule, called IR_1. With $locpred(D_i)$ we denote the *local predicate* on dimension table D_i. This is a restriction involving only a single dimension table and its evaluation will yield the h-surrogate specification (see subsection 5.1) for each dimension. In this rule we assume the existence of a secondary index on each dimension table D_i with the following composite key: $h_m, h_{m-1}, \ldots, h_1, hsk_i$, where $h_k(k = 1, \ldots, m)$ are hierarchical attributes forming a hierarchy path (h_m corresponding to the most aggregated level and h_1 corresponding to the most detailed level; and hsk_i being the h-surrogate attribute). We denote this index as $D_i X h$.

Initially, we use a condition on the search key of $D_i X h$, contained within $locpred(D_i)$, to descend the B^+tree index. In particular we assume that $locpred(D_i)$ is expressed as:

$$locpred(D_i) = pfxpred(D_i) \wedge hpred(D_i)$$

The first predicate matches the $D_i X h$ key and thus used to descend the tree; the second is empty or it contains restrictions on hierarchical attributes only. Each tuple at the leaves that qualifies is further evaluated against $hpred(D_i)$. Finally, the hsk_i attribute is projected and all other attributes are discarded. The condition for the application of this rule is the existence of a prefix match in the local predicate as well as the absence of any feature attribute restriction. It is obvious that the latter would entail an access to the real D_i tuples and not just to the index entries.

On the right side of Figure 6, we depict another example of an implementation rule, named IR_2. In this case we have assumed that the primary organization of any dimension table D_i is a B^+tree with h_1 being the search key. In IR_2, we access directly the D_i table. This rule exploits the local predicate's key match (included in $keypred(D_i)$) in order to descend the B^+tree representing dimension table D_i. As before, the final step includes the filtering of D_i tuples and projection of hsk_i values. The condition for applying IR_2 is the existence of a restriction on the key of D_i, i.e. attribute h_1.

The application of a series of implementation rules on an abstract processing plan will yield an execution plan. However, for a specific abstract plan there might exist many potential combinations of implementation rules to apply. In this case, we can use some *heuristic rules* to help us decide, which implementation rule to apply.

For example, assume that we know that the local predicate on a dimension table D_i consists of a hierarchical prefix restriction and that it does not include restrictions on any feature attribute. In this case, both of the aforementioned rules (IR_1 and IR_2) can be applied. However, IR_1 can lead to a more efficient execution, since it accesses only the secondary index's tuples, in order to evaluate the local predicate, without the need to retrieve the actual D_i tuples. Naturally, the index contains smaller entries, therefore more hsk_i values reside in each disk page and thus less I/O's will be performed. This leads to the definition of a simple heuristic rule stating that:

> *If a hierarchical prefix restriction exists on the local predicate for a dimension D_i and there is no feature attribute restriction, then apply implementation rule IR_1.*

Unfortunately, even with the use of heuristic rules ambiguity is not always resolved. Imagine a query where only hierarchical restrictions (i.e., no feature attribute restriction exist) are posed on a dimension D_i but these do not form a hierarchical prefix restriction; however, the hierarchical attribute h_1 (i.e., the most detailed in the hierarchy) is restricted with a predicate of the form $h_1 < c$, where c is some constant . In this case, it is not clear whether an access directly to the D_i B^+tree with the h_1 predicate as a search condition is always better than a full-scan on the secondary index D_iXh and then subsequent filtering. For example, if we have a non-selective h_1 restriction, then the latter implementation could be a better alternative.

Situations like the above are clearly *cost-based decisions*. Thus, we recognized from the very early stages that there is a need for estimating the cost of implementation rules. To this end, we have developed a cost-model [23] pertaining to the specific operations in our abstract processing plan and to the underlying implementation alternatives. This model consists of analytic formulae, which estimate for each operator its execution cost as well as the size of its output. Whenever, there is ambiguity as to which implementation rule to apply, at a specific part of the processing plan, the appropriate cost functions are invoked and the lowest cost rule is selected.

Our cost formulae are based on several parameters that describe the data distribution. While testing the cost model with queries and data from a real-world application, it was clear that certain assumptions for these parameters where unacceptable in terms of required accuracy. For example, the *value independence assumption*, where it is assumed that there are no correlations between different dimension values, is simply wrong, and leads to erroneous cost estimations. Therefore we have concluded that an efficient cost optimizer for OLAP must include structures that approximate the data distribution of the cube.

There are many successful approaches in the literature [18, 10, 25] for approximating multidimensional data distributions. However, our experiments have shown that this is not enough. What is needed in order to have accurate cost estimations for star-query execution plans, is a multidimensional data distribution approximation method, which *incorporates hierarchies*. Accurate answers on questions like:

> *How many data points in the most detailed level fall into the region defined by level A of dimension D_1, level B from dimension D_2 and level C from dimension D_3?*

are essential for producing accurate cost estimations and unfortunately cannot be answered by the current multidimensional statistics techniques. To this end, our research efforts are directed toward incorporating into our cost optimizer multidimensional data distribution approximation techniques that are *hierarchy-aware*.

6   Conclusions

In this paper, we have presented requirements and design choices for OLAP systems. The aim of the paper has been twofold: on the one hand, we have provided a description of what comprises the core models of an OLAP system architecture, and on the other hand we presented the specific design decisions that we made for a prototype under development at NTUA, ERATOSTHENES.

In particular, we have described requirements for each model and have presented in more detail the design of the storage layer, and the processing and optimization layer of the server part of ERATOSTHENES. At this point, we would like to synopsize the key design choices regarding these two layers in correspondence to the requirements set in section 2.

Minimum Response Time for Ad-hoc Queries: We cluster cube data hierarchically and apply processing and optimization techniques specific to the most common queries in an OLAP workload.

"Hierarchy-aware" Navigation: Our physical organization provides a set of access operations, which provide navigation in the multi-level multidimensional data space and thus integrate smoothly with the processing layer.

Fast Range Queries w.r.t. All Dimension Levels: Our physical organization exploits a natively multidimensional data structure. Moreover the intermediate nodes (directory chunks, see section 4) are created according to the dimension hierarchy boundaries and therefore can lead to the appropriate range of detailed data, no matter on what level a restriction is imposed.

Handling Cube Sparseness: Sparse regions are detected during the initial loading phase and no allocation of space is made for empty regions. Moreover a compression scheme is adopted in order to handle sparse data chunks [11].

Efficient Updating: Our physical organization supports incremental updating in batch mode, which is the most common maintenance operation in an OLAP environment. Moreover it supports a *"data purging"* operation, where old data are removed along the time dimension and archived, and new ones are appended (e.g., the oldest year is removed in order to insert a new "current year") [11].

Operations that Abstract the Specialized Processing Entailed:
We have defined an abstract processing plan (see subsection 5.1, also [12] for a more detailed presentation) that captures the specialized processing steps, when a typical star query is executed over a hierarchically clustered OLAP cube.

Support for "Rich" Dimensions and Relative Meta-Information:
Dimensions in ERATOSTHENES consist of both hierarchical and feature attributes. There is no restriction on the number of hierarchy paths (although one path per dimension is used for clustering the cube data) and on the number of feature attributes that describe one or more hierarchical attributes. Moreover, we record the functional dependencies of feature attributes from specific hierarchical attributes and exploit this information during query optimization.

As future work we plan to (a) fully implement a first version of ERATOSTHENES, (b) work on query and update optimization, and (c) evaluate experimentally our storage framework. Finally, we would like to investigate the use of ERATOSTHENES in other domains where multidimensional data with hierarchies play an important role, e.g., XML documents or other hierarchically structured data.

Acknowledgements

This research has been partially funded by the European Union's Information Society Technologies Programme (IST) under project EDITH (IST-1999-20722).

References

[1] P. A. Bernstein, M. L. Brodie, S. Ceri, D. J. DeWitt, M. J. Franklin, H. Garcia-Molina, J. Gray, G. Held, J. M. Hellerstein, H. V. Jagadish, M. Lesk, D. Maier, J. F. Naughton, H. Pirahesh, M. Stonebraker, and J. D. Ullman. The Asilomar Report on Database Research. *ACM SIGMOD Record*, 27(4):74–80, 1998. 34

[2] C.-Y. Chan and Y. Ioannidis. Hierarchical Cubes for Range-Sum Queries. In *Proceedings 25th VLDB Conference*, pages 675–686, September 1999. 37

[3] S. Chaudhuri and U. Dayal. An overview of data warehousing and olap technology. *ACM SIGMOD Record*, 26(1):65–74, 1997. 41

[4] G. Colliat. OLAP relational and multidimensional database systems. *ACM SIGMOD Record*, 25(3):74–80, September 1996. 35

[5] P. Deshpande, K. Ramasamy, A. Shukla, and J. F. Naughton. Caching Multidimensional Queries Using Chunks. In *Proceedings 1998 ACM SIGMOD Conference*, pages 259–270, 1998. 37

[6] R. J. Earle. Arbor software corporation u.s. patent #5359724, October 1994. http://www.arborsoft.com. 35

[7] M. Gebhardt, M Jarke, and S. Jacobs. A Toolkit for Negotiation Support Interfaces to Multidimensional Data. In *Proceedings 1997 ACM SIGMOD Conference*, pages 348–356, 1997. 34

[8] G. Graefe. Query evaluation techniques for large databases. *ACM Computing Surveys*, 25(2), 1993. 44

[9] The Shore Project Group. The Shore Storage Manager Programming Interface, 1997. Available at: http://www.cs.wisc.edu/shore/doc/ssmapi/ssmapi.html. 36

[10] D. Gunopulos, G. Kollios, V. J. Tsotras, and C. Domeniconi. Approximating multi-dimensional aggregate range queries over real attributes. In *Proceedings 2000 ACM SIGMOD Conference*, pages 463–474, 2000. 47

[11] N. Karayannidis and T. Sellis. SISYPHUS: The Implementation of a Chunk-Based Storage Manager for OLAP Data Cubes. *Data and Knowledege Engineering*, 2003. 36, 37, 40, 41, 42, 43, 47, 48

[12] N. Karayannidis, A. Tsois, T. Sellis, R. Pieringer, V. Markl, F. Ramsak, R. Fenk, K. Elhardt, and R. Bayer. Star-Queries on Hierarchically-Clustered Fact-Tables. In *Proceedings 28th VLDB Conference*, August 2002. 37, 42, 48

[13] D. A. Keim. Visual Data Mining. In *Tutorials in 23rd VLDB Conference*, 1997. 34

[14] R. Kimball. *The Data Warehouse Toolkit*. John Wiley & Sons, 1st edition, 1996. 38

[15] V. Markl, F. Ramsak, and R. Bayer. Improving OLAP Performance by Multidimensional Hierarchical Clustering. In *Proceedings 1999 IDEAS Symposium*, pages 165–177, 1999. 37, 41, 43

[16] Microsoft. OLEDB for OLAP, February 1998. Available at: http://www.microsoft.com/data/oledb/olap/. 34

[17] P. E. O'Neil and G. Graefe. Multi-table joins through bitmapped join indices. *ACM SIGMOD Record*, 24(3):8–11, 1995. 42

[18] V. Poosala and Y. E. Ioannidis. Selectivity estimation without the attribute value independence assumption. In *Proceeding 23rd VLDB Conference*, pages 486–495, 1997. 47

[19] The OLAP Report. Database Explosion, 1999. Available at: http://www.olapreport.com/DatabaseExplosion.htm. 35

[20] S. Sarawagi. Indexing olap data. *IEEE Data Engineering Bulletin*, 20(1):36–43, 1997. 35

[21] S. Sarawagi and M. Stonebraker. Efficient Organization of Large Multidimensional Arrays. In *Proceedings 11th IEEE ICDE Conference*, pages 328–336, 1994. 37, 41

[22] D. Tsichritzis and A. Klug. The ANSI/X3/SPARC DBMS framework report of the study group on database management systems. *Information Systems*, 3(3):173–191, 1978. 33

[23] A. Tsois, N. Karayannidis, T. K. Sellis, and D. Theodoratos. Cost-based optimization of aggregation star queries on hierarchically clustered data warehouses. In *Proceedings 4th DMDW Workshop*, 2002. 46

[24] P. Vassiliadis. Gulliver in the land of data warehousing: practical experiences and observations of a researcher. In *Proceedings 2nd DMDW Workshop*, 2000. 32

[25] J. S. Vitter, M. Wang, and B. R. Iyer. Data Cube Approximation and Histograms via Wavelets. In *Proceedings 7th CIKM Conference*, pages 96–104, 1998. 47

Spatio-temporal SQL[*]

Spatio-temporal SQL[*]

José R. Rios Viqueira[1] and Nikos A. Lorentzos[2]

[1] Computation Department, University of A Corunia
Castro de Elvinia S/N, A Corunia, Spain
joserios@mail2.udc.es
[2] Informatics Laboratory, Agricultural University of Athens
Iera Odos 75, GR 11855 Athens, Greece
lorentzos@aua.gr

Abstract. An extension of SQL is formalized for the management of spatio-temporal data, i.e. of spatial data that evolves with respect to time. The syntax and semantics of the extension is fully consistent with SQL. The formalism is very general, in that the extension can be applied to any kind of data, either temporal or spatial or conventional.

1 Introduction

In recent years a lot of research has been undertaken for the management of temporal [12] and spatial [4, 8, 10, 15] data. More recently, however, a further research effort can be identified for the management of spatio-temporal data, i.e. of spatial data that evolves with respect to time [1, 2, 3, 7, 9, 11, 13, 14, 16].

Such a formal extension of SQL is described in the present paper. One of its major characteristics is that spatial, temporal and spatio-temporal data are handled in a uniform way. This has been achieved by the generalization of two research efforts, one for the management of temporal data [5] and another for the management of spatial data [6]. This is also witnessed by the fact that except the fundamental operations of the relational model only two new had to be defined, *Unfold* and *Fold*. Based on these operations, some more can be defined, which can be applied to either temporal or spatial or spatio-temporal data. The SQL extension is minimal and, as should be obvious from the above discussion, it is defined in terms of relational algebra operations.

The remainder sections are organized as follows: In Section 2 a *quantum-based* formalism is provided that allows the definition of time and space data types. Both time and space are considered as discrete. Relational algebra operations are formalized in Section 3. The SQL extension is defined in Section 4. The advantages of the formalism, comparison with other approaches and further research are discussed in the last section.

---

[*] This work has been supported by the European Union, TMR Project CHOROCHRONOS (FMRX-CT96-0056).

Y. Manolopoulos et al. (Eds.): PCI 2001, LNCS 2563, pp. 50–63, 2003.
© Springer-Verlag Berlin Heidelberg 2003

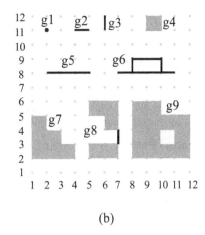

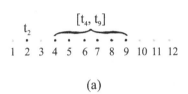

(a)   (b)

Fig. 1. Examples of quanta and spatial objects

2   Time and Space Data Types

In this section data types for time and space are formalized.

2.1   Formalism for Time Data Types

A *discrete 1-dimensional (1-d) space* is defined as a nonempty, finite, totally ordered set $I_n = \{1, 2, ..., n\}$, $n > 0$, whose elements are called *(1-d) points*. Figure 1(a) shows a (1-d) space for $n = 12$. If p, q are two points of I_n, then a *period* [p, q] over I_n is defined as the set $[p, q] = \{i \mid i \in I_n, p \leq i \leq q\}$.

Quanta and Types for Time. Based on the previous definitions, if the elements of I_n are replaced by a set of generic *time elements* $\{t_1, t_2, ..., t_n\}$, the following two *discrete generic types for time* can be obtained [5]:

- $T = \{t_1, t_2, ..., t_n\}$, whose elements are called *(time) instants* or *quanta of time*. Element t_2 in Figure 1(a) is one such instant.
- PERIOD(T), whose elements are called *time periods* over T. Element $[t_4, t_9]$ in Figure 1(a) is one such period.

Temporal Connectivity. By definition, T is totally ordered. Taking this into consideration, it is defined that a set P of instants *is connected* iff it matches the period $[min(t_i \in P), max(t_i \in P)]$.

2.2   Formalism for Space Data Types

A *discrete 2-dimensional (2-d) space* is defined as a nonempty, finite set I_m^2, where $I_m = \{1, 2, ..., m\}$, $m > 0$. The elements of I_m^2 are called *(2-d spatial) points*. If $p \equiv (i, j)$ is such point, then

$p_N \equiv (i, j+1)$,
$p_S \equiv (i, j-1)$,
$p_E \equiv (i+1, j)$ and
$p_W \equiv (i-1, j)$

are the *neighbors* of p. Points p, p_E, $p_{NE} \equiv (i+1, j+1)$ and p_N are called *corner* points. Figure 1(b) shows such a 2-d space for m = 12. Based on these, the following three types of *spatial quanta* are now defined.

Quantum Point. It is any set {p}, where p is a 2-d spatial point. The set of all quantum points is denoted by Q_{POINT}. An example of a pure quantum point is g1 = {(2, 11)} in Figure 1(b).

Quantum Line. Let {p}, {q} ∈ Q_{POINT} be two neighbor points, one of which is to the east of the other (i.e. the coordinates of one of them are (i, j) whereas those of the other are (i+1, j)). Then the set

$$ql_{p,q} \equiv \{(x, y) \in R^2 \mid i \leq x \leq i+1 \wedge y = j \}$$

is called a *pure horizontal quantum line*. Similarly, if one of them is to the north of the other (i.e. the coordinates of one of them are (i, j) whereas those of the other are (i, j+1)) then

$$ql_{p,q} \equiv \{(x, y) \in R^2 \mid x = i \wedge j \leq y \leq j+1\}$$

is called a pure vertical quantum line. Finally, *pure quantum line* is called any pure horizontal or any pure vertical quantum line.

As can be deduced from the definition, $ql_{p,q} = ql_{q,p}$. As is also obvious, a *pure quantum line* consists of an infinite number of R^2 elements. A *pure quantum line* can geometrically be interpreted as a line segment whose *end points* are {p}, {q} ∈ Q_{POINT}. Examples of pure quantum lines are g2 = $ql_{(4, 11), (5, 11)}$ and g3 = $ql_{(6, 11), (6, 12)}$ in Figure 1(b).

If Q_{PL} denotes the set of all *pure quantum lines* then

$$Q_{LINE} \equiv Q_{PL} \cup Q_{POINT}$$

is called *the set of all quantum lines*. Since $Q_{POINT} \subset Q_{LINE}$, every element in Q_{POINT} is also called a *degenerate quantum line* (*quantum line degenerated to a point*).

Quantum Surface. Let {p}, {q}, {r}, {s} ∈ Q_{POINT} be a clockwise or a counter-clockwise order of four corner points (i.e. their coordinates are (i, j), (i+1, j) (i+1, j+1) and (i, j+1)). Then

$$qs_{p,q,r,s} \equiv \{(x, y) \in R^2 \mid i \leq x \leq i+1 \wedge j \leq y \leq j+1 \}$$

is called a pure quantum surface. By definition, $qs_{p,q,r,s}$, $qs_{q,r,s,p}$, $qs_{s,r,q,p}$ etc are equivalent notations of the same *pure quantum surface*. It is also true that a *pure quantum surface* consists of an infinite number of R^2 elements. A *pure quantum surface* can geometrically be interpreted as a square whose *corners* are the points {p}, {q}, {r}, {s} ∈ Q_{POINT} and whose *sides* are the four quantum lines $ql_{p,q}$, $ql_{q,r}$, $ql_{r,s}$, and $ql_{s,p}$. An example of a pure quantum surface is g4 = $qs_{(9, 11),(10, 11),(10, 12),(9, 12)}$ in Figure 1(b).

If Q_{PS} denotes the set of all *pure quantum surfaces* then

$$Q_{SURFACE} = Q_{PS} \cup Q_{LINE}$$

is called *the set of all quantum surfaces*. Since $Q_{LINE} \subset Q_{SURFACE}$, every element in Q_{LINE} is called a *degenerate quantum surface*. More precisely, if $q \in Q_{SURFACE}$ and it is also true that:

- $q \in Q_{LINE} - Q_{POINT}$ then q is a quantum surface degenerated to a quantum line.
- $q \in Q_{POINT}$ then q is a quantum surface degenerated to a quantum point.

Quanta. Any element in $Q_{SURFACE}$ is called (*spatial*) *quantum*.

Quantum Set. A set $S \subset R^2$ is a *quantum set* iff $S = \bigcup_i q_i$, where each q_i is a spatial quantum.

Spatial Connectivity. A quantum set $S \subset R^2$ is *connected* iff for every pair of points x, y $\in$ S there exists a sequence of spatial quanta $q_1, q_2, ..., q_n \subseteq S$ that satisfies the following two properties:

1. $x \in q_1$ and $y \in q_n$.
2. $q_i \cap q_{i+1} \neq \emptyset$ for $i = 1, 2, ..., n-1$.

Spatial Data Types. Based on the above definitions, a set of *space data types* are now defined. In particular, a non-empty, connected quantum set $g = \bigcup_i q_i$ is defined to be of a (*2-d spatial*)

- POINT type iff $q_i \in Q_{POINT}$.
- PLINE type iff $q_i \in Q_{PL}$.
- *LINE* type iff $q_i \in Q_{LINE}$.
- *PSURFACE* type iff $q_i \in Q_{PS}$.
- *SURFACE* type iff $q_i \in Q_{SURFACE}$.

An element of the above types is called, respectively, a (*2-d spatial*) *point, pure line, line, pure surface* and *surface*. An element of any of these types is called a *spatial* or *geo object*. Some examples in Figure 1(b) are the following:

- Point: g1 = {(2, 11)}
- Pure lines: g6 (consisting of the union of eight quantum lines), g5, g3, g2.
- Lines: Any of the pure lines, g1 (degenerate line or line degenerated to a point).
- Pure surfaces: g7 (consisting of the union of six quantum surfaces), g9 (surface with a *hole*), g4.
- Surfaces: Any of the pure surfaces, g8 (hybrid surface), g6, g5, g3, g2 (degenerate surfaces or surfaces degenerated to lines), g1 (degenerate surface or surface degenerated to a point).

From the above it follows that:

- LINE = PLINE $\cup$ POINT and
- SURFACE $\supset$ PSURFACE $\cup$ LINE.

3   Relational Formalism

Based on the previous section, it is now shown how spatio-temporal data can be modeled in relational structures.

3.1   Spatio-temporal Data Structures

A relation is defined in the known way, except that now one or more of its attributes can be of a time or of a space type (Figure 2). Moreover, Figure 2(a) gives an example of HYDRO, a *spatio-temporal* relation recording the evolution of a spatial object, Morpheas, with respect to time. Indeed, from the geometric interpretation of the values recorded in attribute Shape, it can be seen that during [d11, d20] Morpheas was a spring. Next, during [d21, d40], [d41, d60], and [d61, d90] it became, respectively, a river, a river flowing into a small lake and a big lake.

Two more examples of spatio-temporal relations are depicted in Figure 3. Specifically, LAND_USE records the evolution of land use with respect to time. The plots of these lands are given in the same figure. Note that the lifespan of object g3 (last tuple of LAND_USE) is [d31, d50]. However, two plots of this object are given, one during [d31, d40] and another for [d41, d50]. This discipline is followed in the sequel for other objects too, for ease of presentation, as will be realized later. Similarly, LAND_PARCEL is used to record the owner and the shape of various land parcels during various periods of time.

In the sequel, R(**A**, T, G) denotes a relation, where **A** consists of one or more attributes of any type, T is an attribute of some time type and G is an attribute of some space type. Moreover, TG denotes an attribute of either a time or of a space type, exclusively.

HYDRO

Name	Time	Shape
Morpheas	[d11, d20]	g1
Morpheas	[d21, d40]	g2
Morpheas	[d41, d60]	g3
Morpheas	[d61, d90]	g4

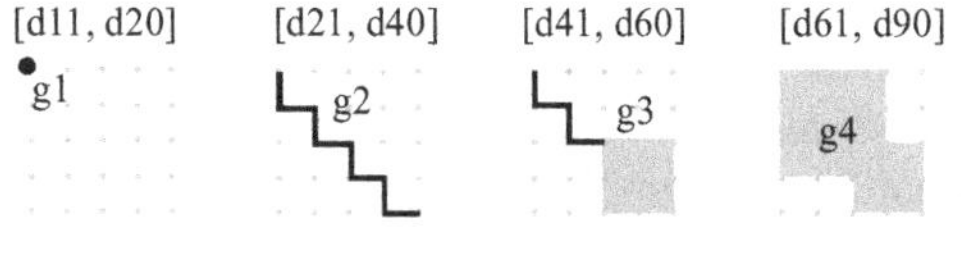

(a) Spatio-temporal relation normalized on space and time.

HYDRO1

Name	Time	Shape
Morpheas	[d11, d20]	g5
Morpheas	[d21, d40]	g6
Morpheas	[d21, d60]	g7
Morpheas	[d41, d90]	g8
Morpheas	[d61, d90]	g9

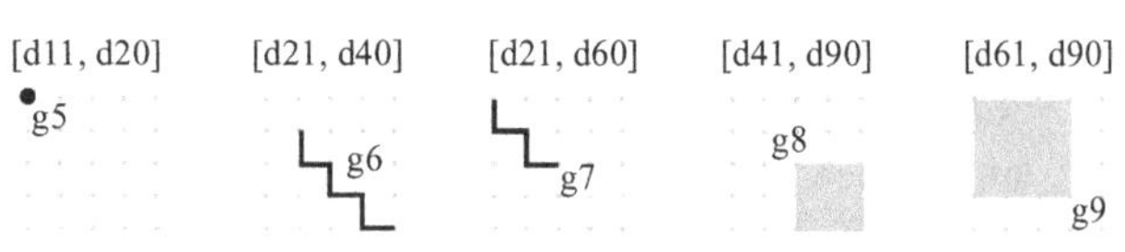

(b) Non-normalized spatio-temporal relation.

Fig. 2. Examples of spatio-temporal relations and their geometric interpretation

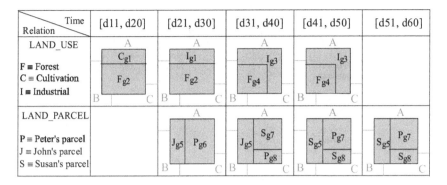

Time \ Relation	[d11, d20]	[d21, d30]	[d31, d40]	[d41, d50]	[d51, d60]
LAND_USE F ≡ Forest C ≡ Cultivation I ≡ Industrial	C_{g1} F_{g2}	I_{g1} F_{g2}	I_{g3} F_{g4}	I_{g3} F_{g4}	
LAND_PARCEL P ≡ Peter's parcel J ≡ John's parcel S ≡ Susan's parcel		J_{g5} P_{g6}	J_{g5} S_{g7} P_{g8}	S_{g5} P_{g7} S_{g8}	S_{g5} P_{g7} S_{g8}

LAND_USE

Luse	Time	Shape
Cultivation	[d11, d20]	g1
Forest	[d11, d30]	g2
Forest	[d31, d50]	g4
Industrial	[d21, d30]	g1
Industrial	[d31, d50]	g3

LAND_PARCEL

Pid	Powner	Time	Shape
p1	Peter	[d21, d30]	g6
p1	Peter	[d31, d40]	g8
p1	Susan	[d41, d60]	g8
p2	John	[d21, d40]	g5
p2	Susan	[d41, d60]	g5
p3	Susan	[d31, d40]	g7
p3	Peter	[d41, d60]	g7

Fig. 3. Spatio-temporal relations and their geometric interpretation

3.2   Relational Algebra Operations

The model incorporates the well-known relational operations, *Union, Except, Project, Cartesian Product, Select, Intersect, Join* etc. For the remainder operations, it is pre-liminarily defined that $set(x) \equiv \{x\}$ if x is not a set and $set(x) \equiv x$ otherwise. Based on this, the remainder operations are the following.

Unfold. When applied to a relation R(A, TG) on attribute TG, each tuple (a, tg) of R is decomposed into a set of tuples (a, q_i) in the result relation, where q_i is a quantum, subset of tg. Formally, U = *Unfold*[TG](R) consists of the tuples

$\{(a, q_i) \mid q_i$ is a quantum $\wedge\ set(q_i) \subseteq set(tg) \wedge (a, tg) \in R\}$.

As an example, if HYDRO is the relation in Figure 2(a) then

T1 = *Unfold*[Time](HYDRO)

is the relation in Figure 4(a). Similarly, Figure 4(b) shows part of the result of

T2 = *Unfold*[Shape](T1),

in particular the set of tuples obtained from tuple (Morpheas, d60, g3) in T1. Note that some of the quanta recorded in attribute Shape of T2 are quantum points, some others are quantum lines and the remainders are quantum surfaces. Each of these quanta is a subset of the spatial object g3 whose geometry can be seen in Figure 2(a).

T1

Name	Time	Shape
Morpheas	d11	g1
...	...	...
Morpheas	d20	g1
Morpheas	d21	g2
...	...	...
Morpheas	d40	g2
Morpheas	d41	g3
...	...	...
Morpheas	d60	g3
Morpheas	d61	g4
...	...	...
Morpheas	d90	g4

(a) *Unfold*[Time](HYDRO)

T2

Name	Time	Shape
Morpheas	d60	$q3_1$
Morpheas	d60	$q3_2$
Morpheas	d60	$q3_3$
.	.	.
.	.	.
.	.	.
Morpheas	d60	$q3_n$

* $\{q3_1, ..., q3_n\}$ denotes the
set of quanta contained in g3

(b) *Unfold*[Shape](T1)

Fig. 4. Examples of operation *Unfold*

Fold. It is the converse of *Unfold*. In particular, when *Fold* is applied to a relation R(A, TG) on attribute TG, a set of tuples {(a, tg_i)} in R returns one tuple (a, tg) in the result relation, where tg is connected, composed from all the tg_i. Formally, the relation

F = *Fold*[TG](R)

consists of the tuples

$$\{(a, \ tg = \bigcup_{i=1}^{n} set(tg_i) \ ) \ | \ (tg \ is \ connected) \wedge ((a, tg_i) \in R, i = 1, 2, ..., n) \wedge$$
$$(\not\exists (a, tg_{n+1}) \in R \ such \ that \ set(tg) \cup set(tg_{n+1}) \ is \ connected)\}$$

As an example, the relations in figure 4 satisfy

T1 = *Fold*[Shape](T2).

Also,

Fold[Time](T1)

returns HYDRO in Figure 2(a).

The above operations can be generalized as follows:

Unfold[TG_1, TG_2, ..., TG_n](R) ≡ *Unfold*[TG_n](...(*Unfold*[TG_2](*Unfold*[TG_1](R))))
Fold[TG_1, TG_2, ..., TG_n](R) ≡ *Fold*[TG_n](...(*Fold*[TG_2](*Fold*[TG_1](R)))).

As an example, HYDRO in Figure 2(a) and T2 in Figure 4(b) satisfy

T2 = *Unfold*[Shape, Time](HYDRO) and

HYDRO = *Fold*[Shape, Time](T2).

4   Spatio-Temporal SQL Extension

Based on the previous section, we now formalize the spatio-temporal extension to SQL. Keywords are given in bold.

4.1   Data Types

The SQL extension supports, in addition, the types for time and space that have been defined in Section 2. Predicates and functions for these types are also supported, though not presented here.

4.2   Data Query Expressions

<reformat clause>. For an informal description of this extension, consider relation HYDRO in Figure 2(a) and the query

SELECT   Name, Time, Shape
FROM   HYDRO
REFORMAT AS UNFOLD Time

Assume also that S is the relation returned by the first two lines. Due to the last line, which is a <reformat clause>, operation *Unfold*[Time](S) is next executed, yielding a relation whose content matches T1 in Figure 4(a).

As should be obvious, the keyword UNFOLD may be followed by a list of more than one attribute. Assuming for example that the first two lines of

SELECT   Name, Time, Shape
FROM   HYDRO
REFORMAT AS UNFOLD Time, Shape

return a relation S then, in a similar manner, the above query is equivalent to *Unfold*[Time, Shape](S) and yields a relation whose content matches that of T2 in Figure 4(b). One major importance of *Unfold* is that it enables defining subsequent SQL extensions of practical interest, as will be seen later. As opposed to this, the practical importance of applying a *Fold* operation, in place of an *Unfold*, is straightforward. Assume, for an example, that the first two lines of

SELECT   Name, Time, Shape
FROM   T2
REFORMAT AS FOLD Shape, Time

return a relation S. Then the above query is equivalent to *Fold*[Time, Shape](S) and yields a relation whose content matches that of HYDRO in Figure 2(a). More generally, a <reformat clause > may consist of a sequence of *Unfold* and *Fold* expressions, such as

'REFORMAT AS UNFOLD G1, T1 FOLD G2, T2 UNFOLD G3'.

<normalize clause>. To demonstrate this extension by an example, consider HYDRO1 in Figure 2(b) and the query

SELECT   Name, Time, Shape
FROM   HYDRO1
NORMALIZE ON Shape, Time

The last line is a <normalize clause >. Generally, if **TG** is a list of attributes, the expression

'NORMALIZE ON TG'

is defined as a shorthand for

'REFORMAT AS UNFOLD TG FOLD TG'.

The above query yields a relation whose content matches that of HYDRO in Figure 2(a).

This specific example demonstrates some aspects of the spatio-temporal functionality of the extension. In particular, it is firstly noticed that relation HYDRO1 in Figure 2(b) contains *redundant* data. As an example, consider its fourth tuple and the geometric interpretation of object g8. It is then noted that during the period [d61, d90] (which is a sub-period of the lifespan of g8), object g8 contains the top left quantum surface. From the geometric interpretation of object g9, it is noted that during [d61, d90] this quantum surface is also contained in object g9. A similar observation applies to objects g6, g7 for the period [d21, g40]. Hence, a piece of surface has been recorded redundantly in two distinct tuples during [d61, d90]. Contrary to these observations, the relation obtained by the above query does not contain redundant data.

Secondly, as can be seen from the geometric interpretation in Figure 2(a), the use of the specific <normalize clause > enabled retrieve the geometric evolution of Morpheas with respect to time. Hence, the proposed syntax enables *eliminating redundant data* and retrieving *the evolution of a spatial object with respect to time*.

Similarly with the <reformat clause>, a <normalize clause> may also be applied to only space or to only time attributes. Considering for example LAND_PARCEL in Figure 3, the following statements

SELECT	Time, Shape
FROM	LAND_PARCEL
WHERE	Powner = 'Susan'
NORMALIZE ON Shape	

SELECT	Powner, Time, Shape
FROM	LAND_PARCEL
WHERE	Powner = 'Susan'
NORMALIZE ON Shape	

return relations whose content matches, respectively, that of relations S1 and S2 in Figure 5.

As a final note, the extension allows for a <reformat clause> to be followed by a <normalize clause>. Formally, if <select> denotes the SQL expression

SELECT-FROM-WHERE-GROUP BY-HAVING

then the extended syntax, <extended select>, is defined as follows.

<extended select> ::=	<select> [<reformat clause>][<normalize clause>]
<reformat clause > ::=	**REFORMAT AS** <reformat item>
<reformat item> ::=	**UNFOLD** <reformat column list> [<reformat item>]
	| **FOLD** <reformat column list> [<reformat item>]
<normalize clause > ::=	**NORMALIZE ON** <reformat column list>

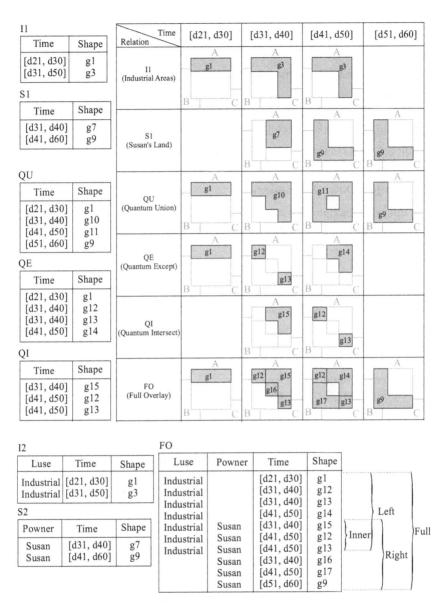

Fig. 5. Examples of extended SQL operations and their geometric interpretation

where <reformat column list> is a subset of the attributes that appear after the key-word SELECT in <select>. In terms of functionality, the result is computed as follows.

Assume that <select> yields a relation R_0. If a <reformat clause > is present, then the UNFOLD and FOLD operations that follow this clause are executed in the order they appear. Each of them is applied to the previously returned relation R_{i-1} and yields a new one, R_i. In particular,

'**UNFOLD** <reformat column list>' ('**FOLD** <reformat column list>')

is applied to R_{i-1} and its result matches that of the relational algebra expression

Unfold[<reformat column list>](R_{i-1}) (*Fold*[<reformat column list>](R_{i-1})).

Similarly, if a <normalize clause > is present, then 'NORMALIZE ON <reformat column list>' is applied to R_n, the relation returned by the previous operation and yields a result which is functionally equivalent to the relational algebra expression

Fold[<reformat column list>](*Unfold*[<reformat column list>](R_n)).

4.3   Non-join Query Expressions

For an informal description of an extension to the UNION operation of SQL, consider relations LAND_USE (Figure 3) and S1 (Figure 5) and the query

SELECT	Time, Shape
FROM	LAND_USE
WHERE	Luse = 'Industrial'
UNION EXPANDING (Shape, Time)	
SELECT	Time, Shape
FROM	S1

The result of the first (second) of the above query expressions matches that of relation I1 (S1) in Figure 5. If the extension 'EXPANDING(Shape, Time)' were missing, the above query would return the ordinary union of relations I1 and S1. Due to this extension, however, the final result is equivalent to that obtained by the relational algebra expression

Fold[Shape, Time](*Unfold*[Shape, Time](I1) *Union Unfold*[Shape, Time](S1))

and matches the content of relation QU in Figure 5. By the geometric interpretation of QU, it can be seen that the proposed syntax enables retrieving *the evolution of the spatial union of objects with respect to time*.

If UNION is now replaced by EXCEPT (INTERSECT) in the above query then relation QE (QI) in Figure 5 is obtained. By the geometric interpretation of this relation it can be seen that the proposed syntax enables retrieving *the evolution of the spatial difference (intersection) of objects with respect to time*.

Formally therefore, the relevant SQL syntax has been extended as follows

<uei>	::=	<query exp 1>
		NONJOINOP [**EXPANDING** (<reformat column list>)]
		<query exp 2>
NONJOINOP	::=	**UNION | EXCEPT | INTERSECT**

where <query exp 1> and <query exp 2> return two union-compatible relations and <reformat column list> is a sub-list of the attributes of <query exp 1>. (Note that any of <query exp 1> and <query exp 2> may include either a <reformat clause> or a <normalize clause>.) If the expression in square brackets is present then the result obtained is functionally equivalent with that of the relational algebra expression

EMP	
Ename	Dcod
John	d1
Peter	d2

DEP	
Dcod	Dname
d2	Sales
d3	Personnel

F		
Ename	Dcod	Dname
John	d1	
Peter	d2	Sales
	d3	Personnel

Fig. 6. Example of an SQL Full Join operation

Fold[<reformat column list>](*Unfold*[<reformat column list>](<query exp 1>)
NONJOINOP
Unfold[<reformat column list>](<query exp 2>))

4.4   Join Query Expressions

As a preliminary step, to define another SQL extension, it is first recalled that if EMP and DEP are the relations in Figure 6, then the SQL query

SELECT   Ename, Dcod
FROM   EMP
FULL JOIN
SELECT   Dcod, Dname
FROM   DEP
USING (Dcod)

returns a relation whose content matches that of F in the same figure. Based on this, it is now defined that

<table ref 1>
FULL OVERLAY (<reformat column list>)
<table ref 2>

is a shorthand for the SQL expression

SELECT *
FROM   **(SELECT * FROM** < table ref 1>
REFORMAT AS UNFOLD <reformat column list>)
FULL JOIN
(SELECT * FROM < table ref 2>
REFORMAT AS UNFOLD <reformat column list>)
USING (<reformat column list>)
REFORMAT AS FOLD <reformat column list>

As an example, consider relations LAND_USE (Figure 3) and S2 (Figure 5) and the query

SELECT   Luse, Time, Shape
FROM   LAND_USE
WHERE   Luse = 'Industrial'
FULL OVERLAY (Shape, Time)
SELECT   Powner, Time, Shape
FROM   S2

The first (second) table reference returns a relation whose content matches that of I2 (S2) in Figure 5. Next, *Full Overlay* is applied to them, yielding relation FO in the same Figure. As can be seen from the geometric interpretation of the content of FO, also shown in Figure 5, the operation enables retrieving *the evolution of the overlay of spatial objects with respect to time*.

5   Conclusions

An extension to SQL for the management of spatio-temporal data has been formalized. The advantages of the proposed model can be summarized as follows:

-   All the algebraic operations are closed. As a side effect, the algebra is not many-sorted.
-   As opposed to [3, 13, 14], it can be applied uniformly to temporal, conventional and interval data [5], spatial data [6], n-dimensional spatial and spatio-temporal data as well as to relations of practical interest with arbitrarily many time attributes [5] and arbitrarily many space attributes.
-   It has also been identified that certain operations, originally defined solely for the management of spatial data [6] are also of practical interest for the handling of temporal or conventional data.
-   As opposed to other approaches [3], the model is also close to human intuition. For example, a line or a surface consists of an infinite number of 2-d points, a line is treated as a degenerate surface and a point is treated as either a degenerate line or as a degenerate surface. Due to this, it is estimated that the model is also user-friendly.
-   Regarding the management of spatial data, it has been identified that a *map* matches the geometric representation of relations that contain spatial data.
-   Regarding the SQL extension, the syntax is minimal and fully consistent with SQL.
-   Finally, we are not aware of any model based on temporal and spatial quanta.

Efficient storage structures, optimization techniques and implementation issues were outside the scope of the present paper. These are topics of further research.

References

[1]   L. Becker, A. Voigtmann and K.H. Hinrichs: "Temporal Support for Geo-data in Object-oriented Databases", *Springer LNCS* Vol.1134, pp.79-93, 1996.
[2]   S. Grumbach, P. Rigaux and L. Segoufin: "Spatio-temporal Data Handling with Constraints", *Proceedings 6th ACM-GIS Symposium, pp.*106–111, 1998.
[3]   R.H. Güting, M.H .Böhlen, M. Erwig, C.S .Jensen, N.A. Lorentzos, M. Schneider and M. Vazirgiannis: "A Foundation for Representing and Querying Moving Objects", *ACM Transactions on Database Systems,* Vol.25, No.1, pp.1–42, 2000.

[4]   R. Laurini and D. Thompson: *"Fundamentals of Spatial Information Systems"*, Academic Press, New York, 1992.

[5]   N.A. Lorentzos and Y.G. Mitsopoulos: "SQL Extension for Interval Data", *IEEE Transactions on Knowledge and Data Engineering*, Vol.9, No.3, pp.480–499, 1997.

[6]   N.A. Lorentzos, N. Tryfona and J.R. Rios Viqueira: "Relational Algebra for Spatial Data Management", *Proceedings Workshop Integrated Spatial Databases. Digital Images and GIS (ISD)*, pp.192–208, 2000.

[7]   J. Moreira, C. Ribeiro and J.-M. Saglio: "Representation and Manipulation of Moving Points: an Extended Data Model for Location Estimation", *Cartography and Geographic Information Science, Special Issue on Dealing with Time*, Vol.26, No.2, pp.109–123, 1999.

[8]   P. Rigaux, M. Scholl and A. Voisard: *"Spatial Databases: with Application to GIS"*, Morgan Kaufmann, 2001.

[9]   T. Sellis: "Research Issues in Spatio-temporal Database Systems", *Proceedings 6th SSD Symposium*, pp.5–11, 1999.

[10]   S. Shekhar, S. Chawla, S. Ravada, A. Fetterer, X. Liu, and C.-T. Lu: "Spatial Databases: Accomplishments and Research Needs", *IEEE Transactions on Knowledge and Data Engineering*, Vol.11, No.1, pp.45–55, 1999.

[11]   A. Sistla, O. Wolfton, S. Chamberlain and S. Dao: "Modeling and Querying Moving Objects", *Proceedings 13th IEEE ICDEE Conference,* pp.422–433, 1997.

[12]   A. Tansel, J. Clifford, S. Gadia, S. Jajodia, A. Segev and R. Snodgrass: *"Temporal Databases: Theory, Design, and Implementation"*, Benjamin/Cummings, 1993.

[13]   N. Tryfona and T. Hadzilacos: "Logical Data Modelling of Spatio-temporal Applications: Definitions and a Model", *Proceedings 1998 IDEAS Symposium*, pp.14–23, 1998.

[14]   M.F. Worboys: "A Unified Model for Spatial and Temporal Information", *The Computer Journal,* Vol.37, No.1, pp.27–34, 1994.

[15]   M.F .Worboys: *"GIS: a Computing Perspective"*, Taylor&Francis, 1995.

[16]   T.-S. Yeh and B. de Cambray: "Managing Highly Variable Spatio-temporal Data", *Proceedings 6th Australiasian Database Conference*, pp.221–230, 1995.

The Opsis Project: Materialized Views for Data Warehouses and the Web

Nick Roussopoulos[1], Yannis Kotidis[2*],
Alexandros Labrinidis[3*], and Yannis Sismanis[1]

[1] Department of Computer Science, University of Maryland
Maryland, College Park, MD 20742, USA
{nick,isis}@cs.umd.edu
[2] AT&T Labs Research
180 Park Ave, P.O. Box 971, Florham Park, NJ 07932, USA
kotidis@research.att.com
[3] Department of Computer Science, University of Pittsburgh
Pittsburgh, PA 15260, USA
labrinid@cs.pitt.edu

Abstract. The real world we live in is mostly perceived through an incredibly large collection of views generated by humans, machines, and other systems. This is the view reality. The Opsis project concentrates its efforts on dealing with the multifaceted form and complexity of data views including data projection views, aggregate views, summary views (synopses) and finally web views. In particular, Opsis deals with the generation, the storage organization (Cubetrees), the efficient run-time management (Dynamat) of materialized views for Data Warehouse systems and for web servers with dynamic content (WebViews).

1 Introduction

Most of the data stored and used today is in the form of *materialized views*, generated from several possibly distributed and loosely coupled source databases. These views are sorted and organized appropriately in order to rapidly answer various types of queries. The relational model is typically used to define each view and each definition serves a dual purpose, first as a specification technique and second as an execution plan for the derivation of the view data.

The importance of the "algebraic closedness" of the relational model has not been recognized enough in its 30 years of existence. Although a lot of energy has been consumed on dogmatizing on the "relational purity", on its interface simplicity, on its mathematical foundation, etc., there has not been a single paper with a central focus on the importance of relational views, their versatility, and their yet-to-be exploited potential.

Materialized views are approximately 10 years younger than the relational model. Early papers that foresaw their importance include [32, 31, 9, 28] and

---

* Work performed while the author was with the Department of Computer Science, University of Maryland, College Park.

Y. Manolopoulos et al. (Eds.): PCI 2001, LNCS 2563, pp. 64–81, 2003.

[35, 44, 38, 37]. During this period, materialized views were considered by top relationalists as the "Pandora's box". It took another 6-7 years before it was realized how useful and versatile they were. Then, a flurry of papers rehashed the earlier results and almost brought the research on materialized views to extinction. But, materialized views were too important and research continues as of today.

Relational views have several forms:

- *pure program:* an unmaterialized view is a program specification, "the intention", that generates data. Query modification [41] and compiled queries [4] were the first techniques exploiting views– their basic difference is that the first is used as a macro that does not get optimized until run-time, while the second stores optimized execution plans. Such a view form is a pure program with no extensional attachments. Each time the view program is invoked, it generates (materializes) the data at a cost that is roughly the same for each invocation.

- *derived data:* a materialized view is "the extension" of the pure program form and has the characteristics of data like any other relational data. Thus, it can be further queried to build *views-on-views* or collectively grouped [26] to build *super-views*. The derivation operations are attached to materialized views. These procedural attachments along with some "delta" relational algebra are used to perform incremental updates on the extension.

- *pure data:* when materialized views are converted to snapshots, the derivation procedure is detached and the views become pure data that is not maintainable (pure data is at the opposite end of the spectrum from pure program).

- *pure index:* view indexes [32] and ViewCaches [33] illustrate this flavor of views. Their extension has only pointers to the underlying data which are dereferenced when the values are needed. Like all indexing schemes, the importance of indexes lies in their organization, which facilitates easy manipulation of pointers and efficient single-pass dereferencing, and thus avoids thrashing.

- *hybrid data & index:* a partially materialized view [5] stores some attributes as data while the rest are referenced through pointers. This form combines data and indexes. B-trees, Join indexes [45], star-indexes [42] and most of the other indexing schemes belong to this category, with appropriate schema mapping for translating pointers to record field values. Note that in this form, the data values are drawn directly from the underlying relations and no transformation to these values is required[1].

- *OLAP aggregate/indexing:* a data cube [12] is a set of materialized or indexed views [14, 29, 20]. They correspond to projections of the multidimensional space data to lesser dimensionality subspaces and store aggregate values in it.

---

[1] This is how the indexed form is almost exclusively used although there is no intrinsic reason for not applying a transformation function, other than the identity one, to the underlying values before indexing them- e.g., calibrate the values before entered in a B-tree.

In this form, the data values are aggregated from a collection of underlying relation values. Summary tables and Star Schemas [42] belong in this form (the latter belongs here as much as in the previous category).

– *WebViews:* HTML fragments or entire web pages that are automatically created from base data, typically stored in a DBMS [23, 24]. Similarly to traditional database views, WebViews can be in two forms: *virtual* or *materialized*. Virtual WebViews are computed dynamically on-demand, whereas materialized WebViews are precomputed. In the virtual case, the cost to compute the WebView increases the time it takes the web server to service the access request, which we will refer to as the *query response time*. On the other hand, in the materialized case, every update to base data leads to an update to the WebView, which increases the server load. Having a WebView materialized can potentially give significantly lower query response times, compared to the virtual approach. However, it may also lead to performance degradation, if the update workload is too high.

Each of these forms is used by some component of a relational system. Having a unified view of all forms of relational views is important in recognizing commonalities, re-using implementation techniques, and discovering potential uses not yet exploited. The Opsis project [1] has focused on developing storage and update techniques for all forms of materialized views. We have been particularly careful with the efficient implementation and scalability of these methods. We have architected, designed, implemented, and tested giant-scale materialized view engines for the demands of todays abundance of connectivity and data collection.

In this paper we briefly present that current status of our work and the paper is organized as follows. In the next section we describe the Cubetree Data Model, a storage abstraction for the data cube, and also present a compact representation for it using packed R-trees [30]. In Section 3, we present our algorithm for bulk incremental updates of the data cube. Section 4 has a brief outline of *DynaMat*, a view management system that materializes results from incoming aggregate queries as views and exploits them for future reuse. In Section 5 we explore the materialization policies for WebViews and present results from experiments on an industrial-strength prototype. Section 6 discusses the Quality of Service and Quality of Data considerations for WebViews. Finally, we conclude in Section 7.

2   A Storage Abstraction for OLAP Aggregate Views

Consider the relation $R(A, B, C, Q)$ where A, B, and C are the *grouping attributes* that we would like to compute the cube for the *measure attribute* Q. We represent the grouping attributes A, B, and C on the three axes of $AxBxC$ and then map each tuple $T(a, b, c, q)$ of R using the values a,b,c for coordinates and the value q as the content of the data point $T(a, b, c)$. We now project all the data points on all subspaces of $AxBxC$ and aggregate their content. We assume that each domain of R has been extended to include a special value (zero in

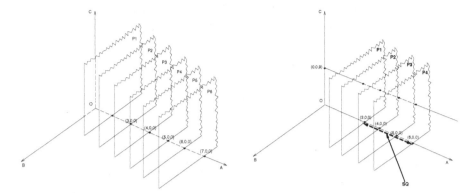

Fig. 1. Group by A projections   **Fig. 2.** Querying the Cube

this example) on which we do the projections. Furthermore, the content of each projection can hold a collection of values computed by multiple aggregate functions such as *sum()*, *count()*, *avg()*, etc. A projection on a subspace D^K with dimension $K <= N$, where N is the number of grouping attributes, represents the *group by* of all those attributes that correspond to D^K. The aggregate values of D^K are stored in the intersection points between D^K and the orthogonal $(N - K)$-dimensional hyper-planes that correspond to the remaining dimensions not included in D^K. For example, the projection planes $P1, P2,...$ parallel to plane BxC shown in Figure 1, correspond to group by A and their aggregated values are stored in the content of their intersection point with axis A. Similarly, the projections that correspond to the group by A, B values are lines perpendicular to the AxB plane and the content of their intersection with AxB stores the aggregated values of all data points lying on these lines. The origin $O(0, 0, ..., 0)$ is used to store the (super)-aggregate value obtained by no grouping at all. We call this the *Cubetree Data Model* (CDM).

In CDM, we map cube and relational queries into multi-dimensional range queries. For example, a query to find all the group by A values for A between 3 and 6 would be formulated as a range query $[(3, 0, 0) < A < (6, 0, 0)]$ shown by the bold-dashed line SQ in Figure 2. If now we would like to find out the percent contribution (multidimensional ratio) of $C = 9$ to these group by A values, we obtain the intersection points of line $C = 9$ with planes $P1$, $P2$, etc. and the content of them is divided by the corresponding aggregates on A.

Clearly, different combinations of relational, 1-dimensional or multi-dimen/-sional storage structures can be used to realize the CDM. For example, the whole CDM can be realized by just a conventional relational storage [12] with no indexing capability for the cube. Another possibility, would be to realize CDM by an R-tree [16], or a combination of relational structures, R-trees and B-trees [7]. Since most of the indexing techniques are hierarchical, without loss of generality, we assume that the CDM is a tree-like (forest-like) structure that we refer to as the *Cubetree* of R. Clearly, query performance mainly depends on the clustering of the data and projection points of CDM.

3   Bulk Incremental Updates

Perhaps the most critical issue in data warehouse environments is the time to generate and/or refresh its derived data from the raw data. This is especially critical because the off-line window for computing the cube and its indexes has shrank due to the international operations of the organizations.

The proposed *bulk incremental update* computation is split into a *sort phase* where an update increment dR of relation R is sorted, and a *merge-pack phase* where the old Cubetree is packed together with the updates:

$$cubetree(R \cup dR) = \text{Merge-Pack}(cubetree(R), \text{sort}(dR))$$

Sorting could be the dominant cost factor in the above incremental computation, but it can be parallelized and/or confined to a quantity that can be controlled by appropriate schedules for refreshing the cube. Note that dR contains any combination of relation insertions, deletions, and updates. For the cube, they are all equivalent because they all correspond to a write of all projection points with their content adjusted by appropriate arithmetic expressions.

3.1   The Merge-Packing Algorithm

Random record-at-a-time insertions are not only very slow because of the continuous reorganization of the space, but also destroy data clustering in all multidimensional indexing schemes. *Packed R-trees*, introduced in [30], avoid these problems by first sorting the objects in some desirable order and then *bulk loading* the R-tree from the sorted file and *packing* the nodes to capacity. This *sort-pack* method achieves excellent clustering and significantly reduces the *overlap* and *dead space* (i.e. space that contains no data points).

The proposed *Merge-Packing* algorithm uses packed R-trees for realizing the Cubetree. The bulk incremental update procedure includes two phases. In the first *sorting* phase, the cube is computed for the updates dR. We assume that a tuple in dR has the following structure:

$$< v_1, v_2, \dots, v_N, q >$$

where v_j, denotes the value on dimension $j, j=1, \dots, N$ and q is the *measure* attribute. The generalization where more measure attributes are provided is straightforward. For aggregate functions that are *Self Maintainable* [25] like *count()* and *sum()* this representation of the increment allows all possible modifications to the data (insertions, deletions, updates), without having to access the original relation R. For example, a deletion can be expressed by simply negating the measure attribute q when computing the *sum()* function. A modification is also handled by first doing a deletion and then an insertion. However

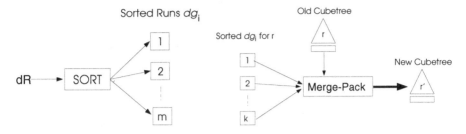

Fig. 3. The Sort Phase   **Fig. 4.** The Merge-Pack Phase

for functions like *min()*, *max()* we would have to access the base data, unless only insertions are allowed.

This first step is shown in Figure 3. The sort procedure reads dR and creates a sorted run dg_i for each group by in the Cube. The format of a typical tuple in dg_i is:

$$< v_1^i, v_2^i, \ldots, v_{m_i}^i, agr_1, \ldots, agr_k >$$

where $v_j^i, j = 1, \ldots, m_i$, denotes the values of each dimension in that group by. For a specified point in this m_i-dimensional space $agr_1, \ldots, agr_k$ hold the aggregated values. In order to be able to merge dg_i with the existing aggregates that are stored within the Cubetrees, the data within each update increment dg_i are being sorted in the same order as the data within the Cubetrees. For example, if all points of group by ABC are stored in the $A \to B \to C$ order, then the same sort order is being used for the new projections from the deltas.

During a second *merge-pack phase* the old Cubetrees are packed together with the updates. The old Cubetrees are now just another run that has to be merged with the new data. Figure 4 depicts this process. For each Cubetree r, all increments dg_i that are stored in that Cubetree are opened and merge-packed with r to create a new instance of the index. In this way the old Cubetree remains available for queries during maintenance, thus eliminating query down time.

The Merge-Packing algorithm reads and processes input data from the old Cubetrees and the deltas. This task requires *merging* the incoming input streams, updating the aggregate functions of the merged points and generating processed (full) Cubetree pages. Whenever a new Cubetree page is produced it can be safely written to the disk. Because we use new storage, the actual writing can be performed asynchronously from the input process. This corresponds to a simple producer-consumer schema that we exploit using two concurrent threads. The *producer* thread processes data from the input streams and generates ready-to-store Cubetree data pages. These pages are actually written to disk by a second *consumer* thread. In this way most data input and manipulation overhead is overlapped with the creation of the new Cubetree.

Table 1. View description for the Grocery Dataset

Gross revenue & cost by:	#dimensions	#tuples
state	1	49
store, state	2	2,000
product, store, date	3	36,345,005
product, store, year, month	4	30,174,476
product, store, year, quarter	4	28,169,173
product, store, year	3	25,370,245
product, customer, store, pay method, trans-start, trans-end	6	40,526,195
Total	–	160,587,143

An important feature of the Merge-Packing algorithm is that it generates only sequential I/O, as the old Cubetrees and deltas are scanned sequentially.[2] Similarly, the consuming thread writes new Cubetree pages sequentially. As a result, Merge-Packing utilizes most of the I/O bandwidth of the disk subsystem as demonstrated in our experiments.

3.2   Creation/Maintenance Measurements for a Grocery Demo Dataset

We used a synthetically generated grocery demo dataset that models super-market transactions. The data warehouse is organized according to the star schema [19] organization. There is a single *fact table* `sales` that includes 11 dimension attributes and two real (4-byte) measure attributes, namely `revenue` and `cost`.[3] We pre-computed seven aggregate views and stored them within Cubetrees. These views aggregate data over attributes chosen from the dataset and compute the *sum()* aggregate for both measures. Table 1 describes the stored views, while Table 2 describes the grouping attributes used.

The hardware platform used for this experiment was a 360MHz Ultra SPARC 60 with two SCSI 18GB Seagate Cheetah hard drives. We sorted the data using the architecture of Figure 3. There are numerous optimizations that we could have exploited for speeding up this phase. Since sorting and computation of Data Cube aggregates is a well studied problem [2, 11, 36, 27] we implemented this part using a simple quick-sort algorithm. Table 3 shows the time for the initial load of the Cubetrees and the time for each bulk-incremental update with a year's and five month's worth of data. The corresponding sizes for each update increment dR are also given.

For sorting and packing we utilized both Seagate Cheetah disks i.e. reading the input from one disk and packing the Cubetrees in the other. The size of the

---

[2] This is achieved be maintaining pointers among the data leaves of the tree during the packing process.

[3] A more detailed description of the dataset as well as an online demo are available at http://opsis.umiacs.umd.edu:8080.

Table 2. Attributes used in the Grocery Demo

Attribute	Type	Domain
product_id	int	1-10,000
customer_id	int	1-100,000
store_id	int	1-2,000
pay_method	char(6)	ATM, Cash, Check, Credit
state	char(2)	AK-WY
date	int	900101-991231
year	int	90-99
quarter	int	1-4
month	int	1-12
trans_start	char(5)	00:00-23:59
trans_end	char(5)	00:00-23:59
revenue	float	-
cost	float	-

Table 3. Initial Bulk-load and Bulk-incremental Updates

Transactions	Ins+Upds	Total Rows	Sort Time	Pack Time	Cubetrees [GB]	Packing rate [GB/h]
1/1/90-12/31/97	127,702,708	127,702,708	3h 04m 30s	5m 51s	2.92	29.95
1/1/98-12/31/98	22,468,605	143,216,789	13m 52s	7m 54s	3.41	25.95
1/1/99-5/31/99	26,027,692	160,587,143	10m 11s	8m 53s	3.83	25.88

views for the initial creation was 2.92GB and the packing phase was completed in less than 6 minutes. This corresponds to a packing rate (speed) of 29.95GB/h or 8.52MB/sec. Using a simple program that writes dummy pages to the disk we measured the effective maximum disk write-bandwidth of our hardware platform to be 12.6 MB/secs. Thus, our packing algorithm attains roughly 68% of the raw serial disk write rate. The remaining bandwidth is lost due to the necessary processing of the input. The second and third lines of the table show the performance during bulk-incremental updates. The effective disk packing rate that we got for updates was slightly slower, at about 26GB/h. This is because we only used two disks, storing the input data (updates) in the first and the Cubetrees in the second. Therefore, during updates both the old and the new-version of the Cubetrees were on the same disk sharing its I/O bandwidth.

4   Dynamic Management of Aggregate Views

Disk space and creation/maintenance overhead will not allow us to materialize all interesting group-bys of the data cube. The view selection problem consists of finding those group-bys that minimize query response time, see [32, 17, 6] and [15, 14, 39, 40, 18, 43] under a resource constraint (typically disk space) and store them as materialized views. Most view selection algorithms also take as

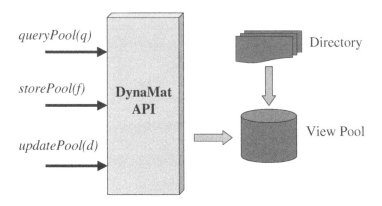

Fig. 5. DynaMat Overview

input some description of the workload (e.g. frequency counts for each group-by) and return a set of views that fit in the available disk space and best optimize query performance.

This static selection of views however, contradicts the dynamic nature of decision support analysis. Especially for ad-hoc queries where the expert user is looking for interesting trends in the dataset, the query pattern is difficult to predict. Furthermore, as query patterns and data trends change overtime and as the data warehouse is evolving with respect to new business requirements that continuously emerge, even the most fine-tuned selection of views that we might have obtained at some point, will very quickly become outdated. In addition, the maintenance window, the disk space restrictions and other important functional parameters of the system also change. For example, an unexpected large volume of daily updates will throw the selected set of views as not update-able unless some of these views are discarded.

Another inherent drawback of a static view selection scheme is that the system has no way of tuning a wrong selection by re-using results of queries that couldn't be answered by the materialized set. Notice that although OLAP queries take an enormous amount of disk I/O and CPU processing time to be completed, their output is often quite small as they summarize the underlying data. Moreover, during *roll—up* operations [12] the data is examined at a progressively coarser granularity and future queries are likely to be computable from previous results without accessing the base tables at all.

In [22, 21] we introduced DynaMat, a dynamic view management system for data warehouses (Figure 5). DynaMat manages a dedicated disk space that we call the *View Pool*, in which previously computed aggregates are stored. DynaMat manages the collection of materialized views under two different modes of operation. The first is the "on-line" mode during which user queries are posed through a *queryPool()* API call. DynaMat determines whether or not aggregates stored in the View Pool can be used in a cost-effective manner to answer the new query, in comparison to running the same query against the detailed records in the data warehouse. This is achieved by probing the query-optimizer and getting an estimate of the execution cost of the query at the data warehouse. Our model exploits dependencies among materialized aggregates of different levels of aggregation using an indexing structure. This way, a more detailed aggregate is used to answer queries of coarser granularity, like for instance when computing the monthly sales out of the available daily aggregates. Whenever a new query result is computed, it is fed back to DynaMat through the *storePool()* call. DynaMat uses a specialized admission/replacement strategy that exploits spatio-temporal locality in the user access pattern, but also takes into account the computational dependencies of the stored query results.

Periodically, updates received from the data sources get shipped to the data warehouse and the View Pool gets refreshed. During updates, DynaMat switches to an "off-line" mode in which queries are not permitted. The maximum length of the update phase is specified by the administrator. Updates are introduced through an *updatePool()* function call, which defines a data source that holds the update increment. This can be a log-file, a regular table or a virtual view over multiple tables. Different update policies are implemented, depending on the types of updates, the properties of the data sources and the aggregate functions that are computed by the query results. From DynaMat's point of view the goal is to select and update the most useful fragments within the update time constraint. Notice that this is not equivalent to updating as many fragments as possible, although often both yield similar results.

5   WebView Materialization

WebViews are HTML fragments that are automatically created from based data, which are typically stored in a DBMS. For example, a search at an online book-store for books by a particular author returns a WebView that is generated dynamically; a query on a cinema server generates a WebView that lists the current playing times for a particular movie; a request for the current sports scores at a newspaper site returns a WebView which is generated on the fly. Except for generating web pages as a result of a specific query, WebViews can also be used to produce multiple versions (*views*) of the same data, for example, translating the contents of a web page in multiple languages automatically[4]. Finally, an emerging need in this area is for the ability to support *multiple web devices*, especially browsers with limited display or bandwidth capabilities, such as cellular phones or networked PDAs.

Although there are a few web servers that support arbitrary queries on their base data, most web applications "publish" a relatively small set of *predefined* or *parameterized* WebViews, which are to be generated automatically through DBMS queries. A weather web server, for example, would most probably report current weather information and forecast for an area based on a ZIP code, or

---

[4] Google recently announced a similar service. Details at:
   http://www.google.com/machine_translation.html

a city/state combination. Given that weather web pages can be very popular and that the update rate for weather information is not high, materializing such WebViews would most likely improve performance. In general, WebViews that are a result of arbitrary queries, are not expected to be shared, and hence need not be considered for materialization. This category would include, for example, WebViews that were generated as a result of a query on a search engine. On the other hand, predefined or parameterized WebViews can be popular and thus should be considered for materialization in order to improve the web server's performance.

Personalized WebViews [8] can also be considered for materialization, if first they are decomposed into a *hierarchy* of WebViews. Take for example a personalized newspaper. It can have a selection of news categories (only metro, international news), a localized weather forecast (for Washington, DC) and a horoscope page (for Scorpio). Although this particular combination might be unique or unpopular, if we decompose the page into four WebViews, one for metro news, one for international news, one for the weather and one for the horoscope, then these WebViews can be accessed frequently enough to merit materialization.

5.1 WebView Derivation Path

In this section we give an overview of the derivation path for each WebView. First, a set of base tables, the *sources*, is queried, and, then, the query results, the *view*, are formatted into an HTML page, the *WebView*. Figure 6 illustrates how WebView derivation works for the summary pages of a web server with stock information. In order, for example, to generate the WebView for the biggest losers, we start from the base table with all the stocks (Figure 6a - the source), and issue a query to get the ones with the biggest decrease (Figure 6b - the view) and, then, format the query results into HTML (Figure 6c - the WebView).

name	curr	prev	diff	volume
AMZN	76	79	-3	8.06M
AOL	111	115	-4	13.29M
EBAY	138	141	-3	2.16M
IBM	107	107	0	8.81M
IFMX	6	6	0	1.42M
LU	60	61	-1	10.98M
MSFT	88	90	-2	23.49M
ORCL	45	46	-1	9.19M
T	43	44	-1	5.97M
YHOO	171	173	-2	7.10M

name	curr	prev	diff
AOL	111	115	-4
EBAY	138	141	-3
AMZN	76	79	-3

```
<html><head>
<title>Biggest Losers</title>
</head><body>
<h1>Biggest Losers</h1><p>

<table>
<tr><td> name <td> curr <td> diff
<tr><td> AOL <td> 111 <td> -4
<tr><td> EBAY <td> 141 <td> -3
<tr><td> AMZN <td> 76 <td> -3
</table>

Last update on Oct 15, 13:16:05
</body></html>
```

    (a) source   (b) view   (c) WebView

Fig. 6. Derivation path for the stock server example

Although in the above example the WebView corresponds to an entire HTML web page, in the general case WebViews correspond to *HTML fragments* and can be defined over a hierarchy of views or WebViews (exactly like relational views). Finally, all WebViews have the same derivation path regardless of the materialization policy. What is different among the various materialization policies is whether any intermediate results will be cached and if so, where they will be cached.

5.2   WebView Materialization Policies

We explore three materialization policies: virtual, materialized inside the DBMS and materialized at the web server.

In the *virtual* policy (`virt` for short), everything is computed on the fly. To produce a WebView we would need to query the DBMS and format the results in HTML. Since nothing is being cached under the virtual policy, whenever there is an update on the base tables that produce the WebView, we only need to update the base tables.

In the *materialized inside the DBMS* policy (`mat-db` for short), we save the results of the SQL query that is used to generate the WebView. To produce the WebView, we would need to access the stored results and format them in HTML. The main difference of WebView materialization from web caching is that, in the materialization case, the stored query results need to be kept up to date all the time. This leads to an immediate refresh of the materialized views inside the DBMS with every update to the base tables they are derived from.

In the *materialized at the web server* policy (`mat-web` for short), we do not need to query the DBMS or perform any further formatting in order to satisfy user requests. We simply have to read the WebView from the disk, where a fresh version is expected to be stored. This means that on every update to one of the base tables that produce the WebView, we have to refresh the WebView (or recompute it, if it cannot be incrementally refreshed) and save it as a file for the web server to read.

5.3   The Selection Problem

The choice of materialization policy for each WebView has a big impact on the overall performance. For example, a WebView that is costly to compute and has very few updates, should be materialized to speed up access requests. On the other hand, a WebView that can be computed fast and has much more updates than accesses, should not be materialized, since materialization would mean more work than necessary. We define the WebView selection problem as following:

> *For every WebView at the server, select the materialization strategy (virtual, materialized inside the DBMS, materialized at the web server),* which **minimizes the average query response time** *on the clients. We assume that there is no storage constraint.*

The assumption that there is no storage constraint is not unrealistic, since storage means disk space (and not main memory) for both materialization policies (inside the DBMS or at the web server) and also WebViews are expected to be relatively small. With the average web page at 30KB [3], a single 50GB hard disk for example could hold approximately 1.5 million pages. In this work, we also assume a no staleness requirement, i.e. the WebViews must always be up to date.

The decision whether to materialize a WebView or not, is similar to the problem of selecting which views to materialize in a data warehouse [13, 15, 34], known as the *view selection problem*. There are, however, many substantial differences. First of all, the multi-tiered architecture of typical database-backed web servers raises the question of *where* to materialize a WebView. Secondly, updates are performed *online* at web servers, as opposed to data warehouses which are usually off-line during updates. Finally, although both problems aim at decreasing query response times, warehouse views are materialized in order to speed up the execution of a few, long analytical (OLAP) queries, whereas WebViews are materialized to avoid repeated execution of many small OLTP-style queries.

In [24] we considered the full spectrum of materialization choices for Web-Views in a database-backed web server. We compared them analytically using a detailed cost model that accounts for both the inherent parallelism in multitasking systems and also for the fact that updates on the base data are to be done concurrently with the accesses. We have implemented all flavors of WebView materialization on an industrial strength database-backed web server and ran extensive experiments. We then compared the various materialization choices quantitatively. In the next section, we present a few of the results of our experiments.

5.4   Experiments

We performed extensive experiments on an industrial-strength system, based on the Apache web server and Informix, running on a SUN UltraSparc-5 with 320MB of memory and a 3.6GB hard disk. We used a pool of 22 SUN Ultra-1 workstations as clients. Due to space constraints we only present two experiments, the rest can be found in [24].

In the first set of experiments, we varied the incoming access request rate from 10 requests per second to 50 requests per second and measured the average query response time under the three different materialization policies: virtual (virt), materialized inside the DBMS (mat-db) and materialized at the web server (mat-web). A load of 50 requests per second corresponds to a rather "heavy" web server load of 4.3 million hits per day for dynamically generated pages. For comparison, our department's web server (http://www.cs.umd.edu) gets about 125,000 hits per day for mostly static content or 1.5 requests per second. The incoming update rate was 5 updates/sec for all experiments.

In Figure 7 we report the average query response time per WebView as they were measured at the web server. We immediately notice that the mat-web

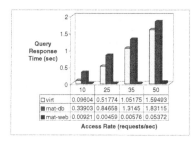

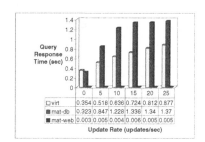

Fig. 7. Scaling up the access rate   **Fig. 8.** Scaling up the update rate

policy has average query response times that are consistently at least an order of magnitude (10 - 230 times) less than those of the `virt` or `mat-db` policies. This was expected, as the `mat-web` policy, in order to service a request, simply reads a file from disk (even if the updater process is running in the background, constantly updating this file), whereas under the `virt`, `mat-db` policies we have to compute a query at the DBMS for every request (even if the WebView is materialized inside the DBMS, we still have to access it). Furthermore, since the web processes are "lighter" than the processes in the DBMS, the `mat-web` policy scales better than the other two.

In the second set of experiments, we varied the incoming update rate from 0 to 25 updates/sec, while the access request rate was set at 25 accesses/sec. In Figure 8 we plot the average query response times for this experiment under the three materialization policies. Our first observation is that the average query response time remains practically unchanged for the `mat-web` policy despite the updates, because the updates are performed in the background. The second observation is that the `mat-db` policy is performing significantly worse than the `virt` policy in the presence of updates. This is explained by the fact that updates under the `mat-db` policy lead to extra work at the DBMS in order for the materialized views to be kept up to date. On the other hand, since the view generation queries are not expensive, the gain from precomputing is negligible compared to the cost of accessing the stored results inside the DBMS. As a result, the `virt` policy gives 56% - 93% faster query response times compared to the `mat-db` policy in the presence of updates.

6   Measuring Quality

Caching of static web pages [10] is known to improve the *Quality of Service* (QoS) for user requests, since it improves the average query response time. For dynamic content however, web caching does not provide any freshness guarantees on the cached data. Servicing user requests fast is of paramount importance only if the data is fresh and correct, otherwise it may be more harmful than slow or

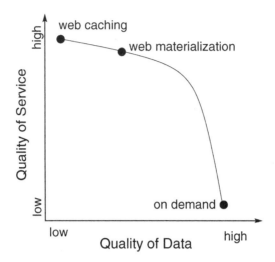

Fig. 9. Considering both QoS and QoD

even no data service. In general, when measuring the Quality of a system that uses materialized views, we need to evaluate both QoS and the *Quality of Data* (QoD), or how "fresh" the served data are. Figure 9 illustrates the effects of QoS and QoD in two orthogonal axes. Web caching improves QoS dramatically, but completely ignores QoD of the cached data. On the other hand, when QoD is very important, web servers rely on computing constantly changing web data on-demand . This achieves near-perfect QoD, but seriously impedes performance or leads to server melt-downs. WebView Materialization [23, 24, 46] aims at bridging this gap, since it prolongs the QoS benefits of caching using amortization and incremental update algorithms on the cached data. This improves the QoD at a small degradation in QoS.

In a perfect system, all data served would be on the right upper corner, which offers the highest QoS and QoD. However, depending on the rates of updates and for different classes of data, this may not be possible. In our work we try to provide the best trade-off between QoS and QoD based on the user/application requirements and the incoming workload.

7   Conclusions

In this paper we concentrated on the most important feature of the relational database model: *materialized views*. We focused on their usage on data ware-housing and Web servers, with emphasis on updateability, performance, and scalability.

Specifically, we presented the Cubetree Data Model, a storage abstraction for the data cube. Cubetrees maintain the view records internally sorted (using packed R-trees) and allow bulk incremental updates through an efficient merge-packing algorithm. We briefly described DynaMat, a dynamic view management system that manages collections of materialized aggregate views based on user workload and available system resources (disk space, update cost). Finally, we explored the materialization policies for WebViews, presented experimental results from an industrial-strength prototype and discussed the Quality of Service and Quality of Data considerations for WebViews.

There is another area which could not be addressed in this limited space. It has to do with the delivery of views and their updates, data streaming, continuous evolution, and mobile users of them. These are all areas of active research [1] and we expect that materialized views and the techniques discussed in this paper will play a major role in providing solutions to these problems.

References

[1] http://www.cs.umd.edu/projects/opsis. 66, 79
[2] S. Agrawal, R. Agrawal, P. Deshpande, A. Gupta, J. Naughton, R. Ramakrishnan, and S. Sarawagi. On the Computation of Multidimensional Aggregates. In *Proceedings 22nd VLDB Conference*, pages 506–521, Bombay, India, August 1996. 70
[3] Martin F. Arlitt and Carey Williamson. "Internet Web Servers: Workload Characterization and Performance Implications". *IEEE/ACM Transactions on Networking*, 5(5), October 1997. 76
[4] M.M. Astrahan et al. System R: Relational Approach to Database Management. *ACM Transactions on Database Systems*, 1(2):97–137, June 1976. 65
[5] Lars Baekgraard and Nick Roussopoulos. "Efficient Refreshment of Data Warehouse Views". Technical Report CS-TR-3642, Dept. of Computer Science, Univ of Maryland, College Park, MD, May 1996. 65
[6] E. Baralis, S. Paraboschi, and E. Teniente. Materialized View Selection in a Multidimensional Database. In *Proceedings 23rd VLDB Conference*, pages 156–165, Athens, Greece, August 1997. 71
[7] R. Bayer and E. McCreight. Organization and Maintenance of Large Ordered Indexes. *Acta Informatica*, 1(3):173–189, 1972. 67
[8] Phil Bernstein, Michael Brodie, Stefano Ceri, David DeWitt, Mike Franklin, Hector Garcia-Molina, Jim Gray, Jerry Held, Joe Hellerstein, H. V. Jagadish, Michael Lesk, Dave Maier, Jeff Naughton, Hamid Pirahesh, Mike Stonebraker, and Jeff Ullman. "The Asilomar Report on Database Research". *ACM SIGMOD Record*, 27(4), December 1998. 74
[9] José A. Blakeley, Per Åke Larson, and Frank Wm. Tompa. "Efficiently Updating Materialized Views". In *Proceedings ACM SIGMOD Conference*, pages 61–71, Washington, DC, May 1986. 64
[10] Lee Breslau, Pei Cao, Li Fan, Graham Phillips, and Scott Shenker. "Web Caching and Zipf-like Distributions: Evidence and Implications". In *Proceedings IEEE INFOCOM'99*, New York, NY, March 1999. 77
[11] P.M. Deshpande, S. Agrawal, J.F. Naughton, and R. Ramakrishnan. Computation of Multidimensional Aggregates. Technical report, 1314, University of Wisconsin, Madison, 1996. 70

[12] J. Gray, A. Bosworth, A. Layman, and H. Piramish. Data Cube: A Relational Aggregation Operator Generalizing Group-By, Cross-Tab, and Sub-Totals. In *Proceedings 12th IEEE ICDE Conference*, pages 152–159, New Orleans, February 1996. 65, 67, 72

[13] Ashish Gupta and Inderpal Singh Mumick. "Maintenance of Materialized Views: Problems, Techniques, and Applications". *IEEE Data Engineering Bulletin*, 18(2):3–18, June 1995. 76

[14] H. Gupta, V. Harinarayan, A. Rajaraman, and J. Ullman. Index Selection for OLAP. In *Proceedings IEEE ICDE Conference*, pages 208–219, Burmingham, UK, April 1997. 65, 71

[15] Himanshu Gupta. "Selection of Views to Materialize in a Data Warehouse". In *Proceedings 6th ICDT Conference*, pages 98–112, Delphi, Greece, January 1997. 71, 76

[16] A. Guttman. R-Trees: A Dynamic Index Structure for Spatial Searching. In *Proceedings ACM SIGMOD Conference*, pages 47–57, Boston, MA, June 1984. 67

[17] V. Harinarayan, A. Rajaraman, and J. Ullman. Implementing Data Cubes Efficiently. In *Proceedings ACM SIGMOD Conference*, pages 205–216, Montreal, Canada, June 1996. 71

[18] H. J. Karloff and M. Mihail. On the Complexity of the View-Selection Problem. In *Proceedings 18th ACM PODS Symposium*, pages 167–173, Philadelphia, PA, May 1999. 71

[19] R. Kimball. *The Data Warehouse Toolkit*. John Wiley & Sons, 1996. 70

[20] Y. Kotidis and N. Roussopoulos. An Alternative Storage Organization for ROLAP Aggregate Views Based on Cubetrees. In *Proceedings ACM SIGMOD Conference*, pages 249–258, Seattle, WA, June 1998. 65

[21] Y. Kotidis and N. Roussopoulos. A case for Dynamic View Management. *ACM Transaction on Database Systems 26(4)*, pages 388–423, 2001. 72

[22] Yannis Kotidis and Nick Roussopoulos. DynaMat: A Dynamic View Management System for Data Warehouses. In *Proceedings ACM SIGMOD Conference*, pages 371–382, Philadelphia, PA, June 1999. 72

[23] Alexandros Labrinidis and Nick Roussopoulos. "On the Materialization of Web-Views". In *Proceedings ACM SIGMOD Workshop on the Web and Databases (WebDB'99)*, Philadelphia, PA, June 1999. 66, 78

[24] Alexandros Labrinidis and Nick Roussopoulos. "WebView Materialization". In *Proceedings ACM SIGMOD Conference*, Dallas, TX, May 2000. 66, 76, 78

[25] I. S. Mumick, D. Quass, and B. S. Mumick. Maintenance of Data Cubes and Summary Tables in a Warehouse. In *Proceedings ACM SIGMOD Conference*, pages 100–111, Tucson, AZ, May 1997. 68

[26] Y. Papakonstantinou. Computing a Query as a Union of Disjoint Horizontal Fragments. Technical report, University of Maryland, College Park, MD, 1994. Working Paper, Department of Computer Science. 65

[27] K.A. Ross and D. Srivastava. Fast Computation of Sparse Datacubes. In *Proceedings 23rd VLDB Conference*, pages 116–125, Athens, Greece, Augoust 1997. 70

[28] N. Roussopoulos and Y. Kang. Preliminary Design of ADMS±: A Workstation–Mainframe Integrated Architecture. In *Proceedings 12th VLDB Conference*, August 1986. 64

[29] N. Roussopoulos, Y. Kotidis, and M. Roussopoulos. Cubetree: Organization of and Bulk Incremental Updates on the Data Cube. In *Proceedings ACM SIGMOD Conference*, pages 89–99, Tucson, AZ, May 1997. 65

[30] N. Roussopoulos and D. Leifker. Direct Spatial Search on Pictorial Databases Using Packed R-trees. In *Proceedings 1985 ACM SIGMOD Conference*, pages 17–31, Austin, 1985. 66, 68

[31] Nick Roussopoulos. "The Logical Access Path Schema of a Database". *IEEE Transactions on Software Engineering*, 8(6):563–573, November 1982. 64

[32] Nick Roussopoulos. "View Indexing in Relational Databases". *ACM Transactions on Database Systems*, 7(2):258–290, June 1982. 64, 65, 71

[33] Nick Roussopoulos. "An Incremental Access Method for ViewCache: Concept, Algorithms, and Cost Analysis". *ACM Transactions on Database Systems*, 16(3):535–563, September 1991. 65

[34] Nick Roussopoulos. "Materialized Views and Data Warehouses". *ACM SIGMOD Record*, 27(1), March 1998. 76

[35] Nick Roussopoulos and Hyunchul Kang. "Principles and Techniques in the Design of ADMS ±". *IEEE Computer*, pages 19–25, December 1986. 65

[36] S. Sarawagi, R. Agrawal, and A. Gupta. On Computing the Data Cube. Technical report, RJ10026, IBM Almaden Research Center, San Jose, CA, 1996. 70

[37] A. Segev and J. Park. Maintaining Materialized Views in Distributed Databases. In *Proceedings 5th IEEE ICDE Conference*, pages 262–270, Los Angeles, CA, 1989. IEEE. 65

[38] Timos Sellis. "Intelligent caching and indexing techniques for relational database systems". *Information Systems*, 13(2), 1988. 65

[39] A. Shukla, P.M. Deshpande, and J.F. Naughton. Materialized View Selection for Multidimensional Datasets. In *Proceedings 24th VLDB Conference*, pages 488–499, New York, NY, August 1998. 71

[40] J. R. Smith, C. Li, V. Castelli, and A. Jhingran. Dynamic Assembly of Views in Data Cubes. In *Proceedings ACM PODS Symposium*, pages 274–283, Seattle, WA, June 1998. 71

[41] Michael Stonebraker. "Implementation of Integrity Constraints and Views by Query Modification". In *Proceedings ACM SIGMOD Conference*, pages 65–78, San Jose, CA, May 1975. 65

[42] Red Brick Systems. "Star Schemas and STARjoin Technology". White Paper, 1996. 65, 66

[43] D. Theodoratos, S. Ligoudiastianos, and T.K. Sellis. View Selection for Designing the Global Data Warehouse. In *Data and Knowledge Engineering 39(3)*, pages 219–240, 2001. 71

[44] F. Tompa and J. Blakeley. Maintaining Materialized Views Without Accessing Base Data. *Information Systems*, 13(4):393–406, 1988. 65

[45] Patrick Valduriez. "Join Indices". *ACM Transactions on Database Systems*, 12(2):218–246, June 1987. 65

[46] Khaled Yagoub, Daniela Florescu, Valerie Issarny, and Patrick Valduriez. "Caching Strategies for Data-Intensive Web Sites". In *Proceedings 26th VLDB Conference*, Cairo, Egypt, September 2000. 78

Two-Phase Commit Processing
with Restructured Commit Tree

George Samaras[1*], George K. Kyrou[1,2**], and Panos K. Chrysanthis[2**]

[1] Department of Computer Science, University of Cyprus
Nicosia, Cyprus
`{cssamara,kyrou}@cs.ucy.ac.cy`
[2] Department of Computer Science, University of Pittsburgh
Pittsburgh, PA 15260, USA
`panos@cs.pitt.edu`

Abstract. Extensive research has been carried out in search for an efficient atomic commit protocol and many optimizations have been suggested to improve the basic two-phase commit protocol, either for the normal or failure case. Of these optimizations, the read-only optimization is the best known and most widely used, whereas the flattening-of-the-commit-tree optimization is the most recent one proposed for Internet transactions. In this paper, we study in depth the combined use of these two optimizations and show the limitations of the flattening-of-the-commit-tree method in committing large trees. Further, we propose a new restructuring method of the commit tree and show using simulation that it performs better than flattening method even when dealing with large trees.

Keywords: Atomic Commit Protocols, Commit Optimizations, Distributed Transaction Processing

1 Introduction

A transaction provides reliability guarantees for accessing shared data and is traditionally defined so as to provide the properties of *atomicity, consistency, isolation, and durability* (ACID) [8]. In order to ensure the atomicity of distributed transactions that access data stored at multiple sites, an *atomic commit protocol* (ACP) needs to be followed by all sites participating in a transaction's execution to agree on the transaction's final outcome despite of program, site and communication failures. That is, an ACP ensures that a distributed transaction is either *committed* and all its effects become persistent across all sites, or *aborted* and all its effects are obliterated as if the transaction had never executed at any

---

* This work was supported in part by the European IST project DBGlobe, IST-2001-32645.
** This work was supported in part by the National Science Foundation under grant IIS-9812532.

site. The *two-phase commit protocol* (2PC) is the first proposed and simplest ACP [7, 14].

It has been found that commit processing consumes a substantial amount of a transaction's execution time [22]. This is attributed to the following three factors:

Message Complexity, that is the number of messages that are needed to be exchanged among the sites participating in the execution of a transaction in order to reach a consistent decision regarding the final status of the transaction. This captures the cost of delays due to network traffic and congestion.

Log Complexity, that is the amount of information that needs to be recorded at each participant site in order to achieve resilience to failures. Log complexity considers the required number of *non-forced* log records, which are written into the log buffer in main memory, and the *forced* log records, which are written into the log on a disk (stable storage) that sustains system failures. Typically, however, log complexity is expressed only in terms of forced log writes because during forced log writes, the commit processing is suspended until the log record is guaranteed to be on stable storage. Thus, this captures the cost due to I/O delays.

Time Complexity, that is the number of *rounds* or *sequential exchanges* of messages that are required in order for a decision to reach the participants. This captures the cost due to propagation and network latencies.

An increase to any one of these factors, it will increase the delay in making the final decision to commit a transaction and consequently will increase the transaction response time. Further, any delay in making and propagating the final decision to commit a transaction, it delays the release of resources which in turn decreases the level of concurrency and adversely affects the overall performance of a distributed transaction processing system. For these reasons, extensive research has been carried out over the years to reduce message, log and time complexities in an effort to optimize 2PC, improving both response time and system throughput during normal processing or during recovery from failures.

These research efforts resulted in a number of 2PC variants and new atomic commit protocols [16, 13, 24, 21, 10, 19, 15, 5, 1, 4] and an even greater number of commit optimizations for different environments [20, 6]. Of these optimizations, the *read-only* optimization is the best known and most widely used, whereas the *flattening-of-the-commit-tree* optimization is the most recent one originally proposed in [20] for *Internet transactions*, distributed across sites in a wide area network. Interestingly, the performance effects on transaction processing when combining some of these optimizations have not been studied in depth.

In this paper, we concentrate on the combined use of read-only and flattening-of-the-commit-tree optimizations. We show using simulation how the flattening-of-the-commit-tree optimization improves distributed commit processing by minimizing propagation latencies and allowing forced log writes to be performed in parallel. A major shortfall of the flattening method when dealing with large trees is identified and investigated both analytically and quantitatively. This shortcoming is unnecessarily exacerbated when dealing with partially read-only transactions. During our attempt to combine flattening of the commit tree with the read-only optimization, we develop a new restructuring method which we call *restructuring-the-commit-tree around update participants* (RCT-UP). RCT-UP avoids the disadvantages of the flattening method while at the same time retains (and in some cases improves) the performance benefits of the flattening method and read-only optimization. Based on simulation results, we show that RCT-UP provides an overall superior performance.

The paper is organized as follows. In the next section, we provide a brief introduction to distributed transaction processing and in Section 3, we describe our assumed system model and the simulator which we use to support our analysis and evaluation of the commit optimizations examined in the remaining of the paper. In Section 4, we discuss the basic 2PC and the read-only optimization and in Section 5, we examine 2PC in the context of multi-level commit trees. In Section 6, we introduce and evaluate the flattening-of-the-commit-tree 2PC optimization, whereas we discuss its inefficiencies in Section 7. Also in Section 7 we propose and evaluate a new restructuring method that exploits read-only participants. In Section 8, we present our final conclusions.

2   Distributed Transaction Concepts

A distributed system consists of a set of computing nodes linked by a communication network. The nodes cooperate with each other in order to carry out a distributed computation or a network application. For the purpose of cooperation, the nodes communicate by exchanging messages via the network.

In a distributed environment, transactions are particularly useful to support consistent access to data resources such as databases or files [8], stored at different sites. A transaction consists of a set of operations that perform a particular logical task, generally making changes to shared data resources. These data access operations are executed within processes and can invoke additional data operations that may initiate other processes at the local site or different sites. Thus, while a transaction executes, processes may be dynamically created at remote sites (or even locally) in response to the data access requirements imposed by the transaction.

In general, a distributed transaction is associated with a tree of processes, called *execution tree* that is created as the transaction executes, capturing the parent-child relationship among the processes (Figure 1). At the root of the tree is the process at the site at which the transaction is initiated. For example, in the Client-Server model as Figure 1 shows, the root is the process at the client site. The execution tree may grow as new sites are accessed by the transaction and sub-trees may disappear as a result of the application logic or because of site or communication link failure.

When all the operations of a distributed transaction complete their execution, the process at the root of the tree becomes the *coordinator* for committing

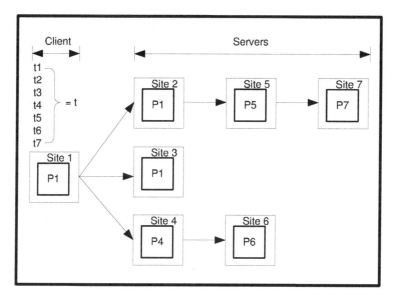

Fig. 1. A process tree within the Client-Server model

the transaction and initiates an atomic commit protocol such as 2PC. Typically, the interactions between the coordinator of the transaction and any process have to go through all the intermediate processes that have caused the creation of a process. That is, a parent-child relationship in the execution tree implies a coordinator-subordinate relationship for executing the commit protocol. Consequently, the *commit protocol tree* is the same as the execution tree.

3   System and Simulation Model

In order to evaluate reliably the performance of the optimizations studied in this paper, we have developed a realistic simulator of a distributed transaction processing system. Our simulator is based on a synchronous discrete event simulation model and implemented in Object Pascal of Delphi 5 [11].

The simulator has been built to effectively capture not only distributed commit processing at the participating sites but also the communication processing as well. By modeling the details of the network infrastructure, our simulator is capable to simulate multi-level commit trees of any depth. In this respect, our simulator is different from the ones used in [18, 12] which are limited to flat, two-level, execution and commit trees.

The high-level components of the simulator, as in real systems, are the computing nodes, the communication links and routers (Figure 2).

Each computing node consists of a *transaction manager* (TM), a *log manager* (LM), a *communication manager* (CM) and a *storage manager* (SM). The transaction manager is responsible for handling requests to initiate new transactions .

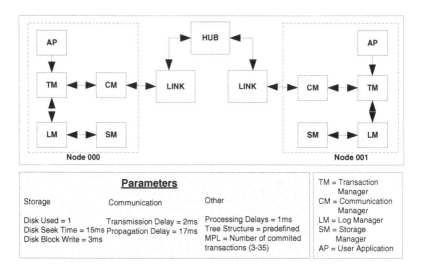

Fig. 2. Simulation Model

and requests to initiate and coordinate the commitment of transactions. The log manager processes any log request. For forced log writes that require disk access, the log manager invokes the storage manager to handle it. The disk read/write delay is achieved using a queue, while the blocking/unblocking of transaction processes through callback routines. Finally, the communication manager is responsible for queuing out-going messages and redirecting incoming messages to the transaction manager.

All of these components share a single processing unit (CPU) except from the storage manager which encapsulates the hard disk drive and controller and thus can function independently. The various commit protocols and optimizations are coded in special classes called protocol handlers[1] which are assigned to transaction processes that are executed by the transaction manager in a round-robin fashion. All components are built so that their full functionality is emulated as closely as possible. The parameters used, closely resemble those of a real world system (see Figure 2).

Simulating the network infrastructure precisely, was also a very important requirement so that we could capture not only the transmission and propagation delays of communication networks, but also the queuing delays when a link is highly utilized. All links support full-duplex communication, hence they implement two separate queues. Message routing is accomplished, with a routing device. For all experiments presented in this paper, we have used only one switching hub.

---

[1] The protocol handler is probably the most complex class in our simulator. It is built around a state machine with states and event handlers implementing all the transaction commit states and actions.

Also, in all the experiments discussed in the paper, we have not considered data processing that takes place before commit processing. Although this would have a significant effect on the overall system performance, we do not expect data processing to affect the relative performance between the various 2PC optimizations and in particular the ones under evaluation in this paper.[2]

In all the experiments, we have measured the transaction throughput, which is the total number of committed transactions per unit time by varying the multiprogramming levels (MPLs). The MPL represents the total number of transactions executing at any given site and at any given point in time (since the system operates at full capacity). Specifically, commit processing is initiated when an application (AP)[3] at a node triggers a new transaction. In response the transaction manager spawns a new process and associates it with a protocol handler to execute the request. Based on a predetermined commit tree it also informs all the participating nodes that a new transaction has been initiated. When the process is given CPU time to execute, it will initiate the commit protocol by executing the proper actions of the protocol handler.

4   The Two-Phase Commit Protocol and Read-Only Transactions

In this section, we discuss the details of the *two-phase commit* protocol (2PC) in the context of two-level commit trees and its read-only optimization.

4.1   Basic Two-Phase Commit

The basic 2PC [7, 14] assumes a two-level execution tree where the root process spawns all the (leaf) processes. Consequently, it assumes a two-level, or depth 1, commit tree with the coordinator being the root and all the participants being at the leaf nodes.

As its name implies, 2PC involves two phases: a *voting* (or prepare) phase and a *decision* phase (Figure 3). During the voting phase, it is determined whether or not a transaction can be committed at all participating sites, whereas, during the decision phase, the coordinator decides either to commit or abort the transaction and all participants apply the decision. To provide fault-tolerance the protocol records its progress in logs at the coordinator and participating sites.

The Voting Phase: During the voting phase, the coordinator requests via the "prepare" message that all participants in a transaction agree to make the transaction's changes to data permanent. When a participant receives a "prepare" message, it votes Yes if it is prepared to commit the transaction. A participant

---

[2] For one-phase commit protocols such as Early Prepare (EP) [23], Implicit-Yes Vote (IYV) [1] and Coordinator Log (CL) [24] that require part of commit processing to be performed during data processing, data processing is essential.

[3] The application is also responsible for maintaining the MPL level at each coordinator node.

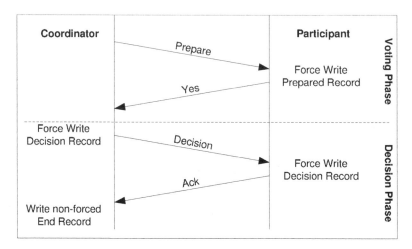

Fig. 3. Simple Two-Phase Commit Processing

becomes *prepared to commit* a transaction after making sure that the transaction can be committed locally and force writing a Prepared log record that will enable it to resume the execution of the protocol after a site failure. If a participant has voted *Yes*, it can no longer unilaterally decide to abort or commit the transaction and it is considered blocked until it receives the final decision from the coordinator.

If a participant cannot prepare itself (that is, if it cannot guarantee that it can commit the transaction), it must abort the transaction and respond to the prepare request with the *No* vote.

The Decision Phase: When the coordinator has received a positive vote (i.e., *Yes* vote) from all of the participants, it decides to commit the transaction and force-writes a Commit log record. Logging the commit decision ensures that even in case that the coordinator fails, when it becomes available after restart, the transaction can still commit successfully. If any of the participants has voted *No*, the coordinator decides to abort the transaction and force-writes an Abort log record. After the coordinator has forced written a Commit (or Abort) log record, it sends a *"Commit"* (or *"Abort"*) message to all the voted *Yes* participants.

When a participant receives the final decision, it complies with the decision, force-writes a Commit (or Abort) log record to indicate that the transaction is committed (or aborted), releases all resources held on behalf of the transaction, and returns an acknowledgment (namely the *"Ack"* message) to the coordinator. The coordinator discards any information that it keeps in main memory regarding the transaction when it receives acknowledgments from all the participants and forgets the transaction.

From the above it follows that, during normal processing the cost to commit or abort a transaction executing at n sites is the same. The log complexity of 2PC amounts to **2n-1** force log writes (one forced write at the coordinator's site and two at each of the n-1 participants), and the message complexity to **3(n-1)** messages. The time complexity of 2PC is **3** rounds, the first one corresponds to the sending of the "prepare" requests, second one to the sending of votes, and the last one to the sending of the decision messages. We have not included in the message and time complexities the **n-1** acknowledgement messages and their corresponding round because these messages are used for bookkeeping purposes after the transaction has been committed or aborted.

4.2   Read-Only Optimization

Traditionally, a transaction is called *read-only* if all its operations are reads. On the other hand, a transaction is called *partially read-only* if some of its participants have executed writes as well. Otherwise, a transaction is called an *update* transaction.

Similarly, participants in the execution of a transaction can be distinguished into *read-only* participants, if they have performed only read operations on behalf of the transaction, and *update* participants, if they have performed at least one write operation on behalf of the transaction.

For a read-only participant in the execution of a transaction, it does not matter whether the transaction is finally committed or aborted since it has not modified any data at the participant. Hence, the coordinator of a read-only participant can exclude that participant from the second phase of commit processing, saving both in number of messages and forced log records. This is accomplished by having the read-only participant vote *Read-Only* when it receives the "prepare" message from its coordinator [16]. Then, without writing any log records, the participant releases all the resources held by the transaction.

In the case of a read-only transaction in which all participants are read-only, committing the transaction will require **0** forced-write log records and **2n-1** messages and have time complexity of **1**. Given that read-only transactions are the majority in any general database system, the read-only optimization can be considered one of the most significant optimizations. In fact, the performance gains allowed by the read-only optimization for both read-only and partially read-only transactions provided the argument in favor of the *Presumed Abort* protocol (PrA) (PrA is a variation of the 2PC [16]) to become the current choice of commit protocol in the OSI/TP standard [17] and other commercial systems.

5   Committing Multi-level Transactions

In the general case, distributed transactions can be associated with a multi-level execution tree of any depth greater than 1. At commit time, 2PC adopts the same multi-level tree as the commit tree to propagate the coordination messages, making no assumption regarding any knowledge about the participating sites.

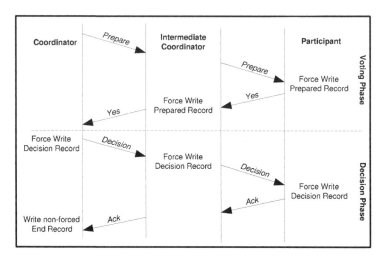

Fig. 4. Two-phase commit with intermediate/cascaded coordinator

Specifically, each intermediate participant or *cascaded coordinator* propagates the various 2PC coordination messages down and up the transaction tree in a sequential manner, level by level. This is illustrated in Figure 4.

For example, consider the distributed transaction tree of depth 3, shown in Figure 5(a) in which all participants agree to commit the transaction. When the application finishes its processing, it issues commit to the Transaction Manager (TM) at site TP-0. TM-0[4] initiates the 2PC protocol and sends prepare to TM-1. Having subordinate transaction managers, TM-1 cascades (propagates) the "prepare" message to TM-2 and waits for its reply. Siqmilarly, TM-2 cascades the "prepare" message to TM-3 and wait for its reply. After TM-3 receives the "prepare" message, it force-writes a Prepared log record and responds with a *Yes* vote to its immediate cascaded coordinator, TM-2. When TM-2 (and similarly any subsequent cascaded coordinator) receives the vote from all its subordinates, it force-writes a Prepared log record and replies to its immediate coordinator. Finally, when TM-0, the coordinator at the root receives the votes, it initiates the decision phase. The decision phase follows an analogous scenario.

This sequencing of the "prepare" and "decision" message implies that:

- A leaf participant will not receive the prepare message sent by the root coordinator until that message has been processed by all the intermediate, cascaded coordinators.
- An intermediate coordinator will not force-write a Prepared log record until it has received the responses from all its subordinates.
- A leaf participant will not force-write a commit log record until the commit message has been processed by all the intermediate coordinators.

---

[4] From this point forward, we refer to the transaction manager of side TP-i as TM-i.

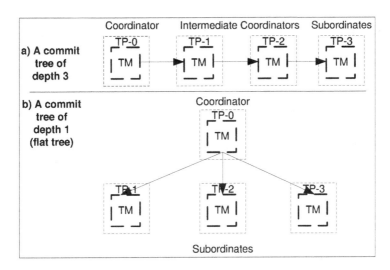

Fig. 5. A commit tree of depth 3 and its flattened counterpart

– An intermediate coordinator can not acknowledge commitment to its coordinator until all acknowledgements from its subordinates are received, delaying the return to the application and the processing of another transaction.

For a transaction tree of depth three, as in our example, the vote message will arrive to the coordinator after three times the cost of receiving, processing and re-sending the prepare message and force writing a Prepared log record! The same applies for the "commit" and "Ack" message.

6   Flattening of the Commit Tree Optimization

It is clear that the serialization of the 2PC messages as well as of the forced log writes in multi-level commit trees increases the duration of commit processing as the tree depth grows. This serialization of messages/log writes is unavoidable in the general case in which the coordinator does not know all the participating sites in the execution of a transaction.

However, an alternative scheme that eliminates the sequencing of messages is feasible in communication protocols where a round trip is required before commit processing. Remote Procedure Calls (RPC) or message-based protocols where each request must receive a reply, are examples of such communication protocols. With these protocols, during the execution of the transaction, the identity of the participating TMs can be returned to the (root) coordinator when the child replies to its parent. Gaining knowledge of the execution tree enables the coordinator to communicate with all the participants directly. As a result a multi-level execution tree is *flatten* or transformed into a 2-level commit tree during commit processing [20].

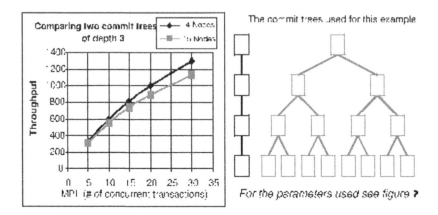

Fig. 6. Demonstrating the depth domination over the number of nodes when measuring the performance of 2PC processing. For the parameters used see Figure 7

For example, by flattening the transaction execution tree of Figure 5(a), transforming it into the commit tree as shown in Figure 5(b), the root coordinator sends coordination messages directly to, and receives messages directly from, any participant. This eliminates the cascading coordinators and avoids the propagation delays (i.e., extra rounds of messages) due to cascading coordinators. By executing the prepare and decision phases in parallel across all participants, this optimization not only avoids the serial processing of messages, which significantly reduces time complexity, but also allows forced log writes to be performed in parallel, which significantly reduce the maximum duration of each phase. As illustrated below, the compound effect of the reduction in time complexity and phase duration is so significant on performance gains that makes this optimization as important as the read-only one for committing distributed transactions with deep execution trees.

6.1   Performance Analysis

Let M be the average time cost for transmitting a message, L the average time cost of force-writing a log record and P the average time needed for processing a particular event. For the commit tree in Figure 5(a), the minimum time to successfully commit a transaction is approximately $(3*3M+2*3L+L)P$. In general, for a balanced commit tree of depth D the minimum time required for processing commitment is $(3*DM+2*DL+L)P$; the formula is solely based on the fact that for a balanced commit tree, commit processing (i.e., sending the various messages and force-writing different log records) is done at each level in parallel (see in Figure 6 the performance of two balanced trees of the same depth). The multipliers $3*$ accounts for the number of messages and $2*$ for the number of

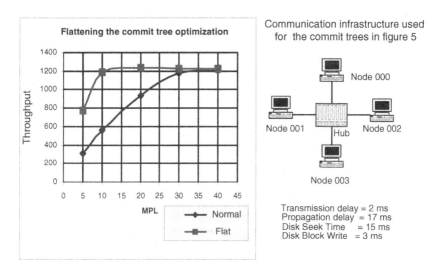

Fig. 7. Simulation results for the normal and flat commit trees of Figure 6

forced log writes required by the basic 2PC protocol. This clearly shows that the cost is dominated by the depth and not as much by the number of participants.

For the flattened commit tree of Figure 5(b) (and any commit tree of depth 1) the time cost is only $(3*M+2*L+L)P$. This is so because the cost of sending the various messages downstream is eliminated and the various force-writes are now done in parallel across all the participants - transmitting the messages (namely the "prepare" and "commit" messages) in parallel involves only minor transmission delay[5]. Based on this, the formula is transformed into $(3M+3L)P+2(N-1)Td$, where Td is the transmission delay and N the total number of participants. This is a considerable improvement. In general, the performance of a flattened tree is (theoretically) almost D times better than the performance of its counterpart of depth D.

Our simulation experiments produced similar results. Figure 7 shows the simulation results for the example trees in Figure 5. The deviation from our estimate can be attributed to the transmission delay. The upper bound throughput value ($\sim$1200), on which both lines converge is the maximum system throughput. At that point, the communication-link of the coordinator is 100% utilized. Similarly, an upper bound system throughput can be imposed by the storage subsystem. This is merely dependent on the performance characteristics of the hard drives and of course, the maximum number of force-writes executed by an individual system.

---

[5] As we will see later this is not the case for large trees.

6.2   System and Communication Requirements

A limitation of the flattening-the-commit-tree optimization is that in some distributed systems, security policies of the participating nodes may not permit direct communication with the coordinator. Protocols that support security features that prohibit any-to-any connectivity cannot use this optimization without additional protocols to handle the case where a partner cannot directly connect with the commit coordinator.

Another limitation is that a reply message is required so that the identity of all the partners is known to the coordinator before the voting phase of the 2PC protocol. Protocols that do not require replies, such as conversational protocols (for example, IBM's LU6.2 [9]), may not know the identities of all participants. These protocols save time by not requiring a reply to every request. For those protocols, it is possible to flatten the tree during the decision phase, by returning the identity of each subordinate to the coordinator during the reply to the "prepare" message, that is, as part of the vote message.

7   Restructuring – A New Approach

Flattening the tree can shorten the commit processing significantly at the cost of requiring extra processing on behalf of the coordinator. This is not much of a problem when transactions involve only a small number of participants or when the network infrastructure supports multicasting. However, when this is not the case, as with the TCP/IP communication protocol, sending commit messages to a great number of participants might lead to the following drawbacks:

– Because of transmission delays, a participant may actually receive a "prepare" or "decision" message later than what would normally have received (i.e., without flattening).
– Communication from and to the coordinator is overloaded, effectively reducing the overall system throughput.

To make these observations more profound consider the flattened commit tree of Figure 8(b). For this tree, during the prepare phase the coordinator (P0) needs to exchange with its subordinates eight messages. Consequently, the last subordinate receives the "prepare" message with an additional delay equal to at least seven times the transmission delay of the "prepare" message. *Note that the computer system hosting the coordinating process P0 is connected to the communication network through a single line* (Figure 7). In order to send eight messages, the hardware (i.e., the network card) requires eight times the cost (transmission delay) of sending one message. If the networking protocol used requires acknowledgment of message reception (round-trip protocols), the cost becomes even greater.

Regardless of the networking protocol used, for large commit trees, consisting of large number of participants or for high volume transaction-systems, the cost of exchanging a huge number of messages can decrease the performance of 2PC

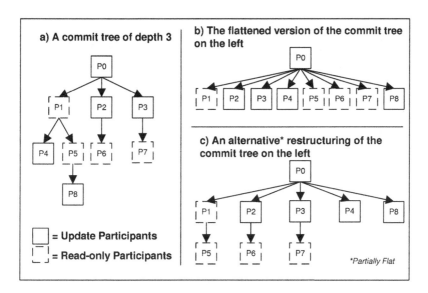

Fig. 8. Flattening and an alternative Restructuring based on read-only status

dramatically. In fact, our simulation results confirmed that for large trees, certain non-flat structures might perform better than the flat structure! For example, for a one-level tree with sixteen[6] subordinates and a transmission delay of *3ms* the two-level, non-flat commit tree performs better than its flattened counterpart (Figure 9). The performance degradation of the flattened tree is attributed to the transmission delay, which is exacerbated by the communication burden placed on the coordinator. When running more than five concurrent transactions (MPL 5) the coordinator's communication link is 100% utilized. This case, however, represents a non-typical scenario. It is worth noting that the number is not chosen at random but is derived with the aid of the previous formulas[7].

7.1   Restructuring around Update Participants (RCT-UP)

The above drawback can be avoided by taking advantage of read-only participants that can be eliminated from the second phase of commit processing. Instead of flattening the commit tree completely and having the coordinator to send prepare to *all* participants, we can restructure[8] the tree in such a way so

---

[6] We used a large transmission delay to show the inefficiency of the flat tree for a small number of participants to ease the simulation. For a smaller transmission delay ($<$ 0.5ms) which is the normal for Ethernet networks, a larger number of participants would be needed for the performance of the flattened tree to significantly degrade.

[7] The number of intermediate participants must be greater than $P*(2M+L)(D-1)/Td$.

[8] From this point forward, we use the term *restructuring* to refer to the partial flattening of the commit tree. The authors of this paper consider flattening a specific form of restructuring.

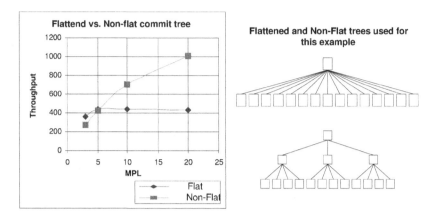

Fig. 9. Demonstrating the performance collapsing of the flattened commit tree

that the coordinator needs to directly send messages to the update participants that actually modified data and have to force-write log records.

To accomplish this, *only* participants that modify data notify the coordinator of their identity. This can be done in a manner similar as in the *unsolicited update-vote* optimization where when a participant executes the first update operation on behalf of a transaction, it notifies the transaction's coordinator [3, 4]. They also notify their intermediate coordinator (if they have one) so that during the voting phase the intermediate coordinator can exclude these participants from its subordinates. This has the notion of removing update nodes and even sub-trees from the bottom of the commit tree and connecting them directly to the root (i.e., the coordinator). A useful observation is that at the end of the data processing, in the transformed commit tree, all nodes that have depth greater than one are read-only. Figure 8(c) (and Figure 10(3)) illustrates this algorithm. For this tree, only processes P4 and P8 need to be restructured.

Clearly, our proposed new *restructuring of the commit tree around the update participants* (RCT-UP) technique is better than the flattening optimization as it relieves the communication from and to the coordinator, enhancing its multiprogramming efficiency (i.e., the ability to run many transactions concurrently). In addition, since read-only participants can be excluded from the second phase of 2PC processing, not flattening them does not affect the performance of 2PC processing. Recall that each immediate subordinate (of the coordinator) in this restructuring method *"knows"* that all its subordinates are read-only. Therefore, all immediate subordinates can force-write a Prepared log record and respond to the coordinator *before* sending any messages to their subordinates. Of course, this is a divergence from the standard 2PC, but that is the case with almost all optimizations. On the other hand, we can just send them a *read-only* message [3] and forget about them.

Figure 10 demonstrates the performance effects of the RCT-UP optimization. The least performing structure is the normal, non-flat tree (Figure 10(1)).

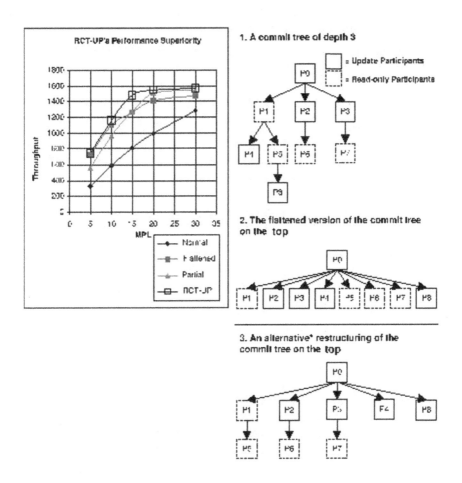

Fig. 10. Simulation results for the commit trees of Figure 8 (reproduced for clarity)

An improvement in performance is demonstrated by the restructured tree (Figure 10(3)), so that all update participants communicate directly with the coordinator. The interesting observation though is the performance of the flattened tree (Figure 10(2)). Although initially it has a very high throughput, after MPL 15 it proves inadequate compared to the *partially flat* structure, that is RCT-UP with no prior knowledge of read-only participants. This, as we have already explained, is attributed to the transmission delay. In both cases (flattened and partially flattened) no prior knowledge of read-only participants has been assumed and hence they have used traditional read-only optimization. However, when we take advantage of the existence of read-only participants, the performance gains in the case of RCT-UP are significant. From this, the advantage of the RCT-UP optimization is evident.

8   Conclusions

The *flattening-of-the-commit-tree* optimization has been proposed to enhance the performance of distributed transactions in wide area networks but without any systematic analysis of its performance. In this paper, we presented such a detailed evaluation both analytically and quantitatively using simulation. We demonstrated how it improves distributed commit processing by minimizing propagation delays and by allowing log writes to be performed in parallel. A major shortfall of flattening when dealing with large transaction trees has been also identified. It was shown that this deficiency, attributed to the transmission delay and message congestion, is exacerbated when dealing with partially read-only transactions.

To effectively remedy this problem we proposed a new restructuring method, which we call *restructuring-the-commit-tree-around-update-participants* (RCT-UP), that avoids the disadvantages of flattening while at the same time improving upon its advantages. Based on simulation results, we showed that RCT-UP, which in essence is a combination of the flattening-of-the-commit-tree and the read-only optimization provides an overall superior performance.

References

[1] Al-Houmaily Y. J. and Chrysanthis P. K.: "An Atomic Commit Protocol for Gigabit-Networked Distributed Database Systems", *The Journal of Systems Architecture*, Vol.46, No.9, pp.809-833, 2000. 83, 87

[2] Al-Houmaily Y. J. and Chrysanthis P. K.: "Atomicity with Incompatible Presumptions", *Proceedings 8th ACM PODS Symposium*, pp.306-315, 1999.

[3] Al-Houmaily Y. J., Chrysanthis P. K. and Levitan S. P.: "Enhancing the Performance of Presumed Commit Protocol", *Proceedings 12th ACM SAC Symposium*, pp.131-133, 1997. 96

[4] Al-Houmaily Y. J., Chrysanthis P. K. and Levitan S. P.: "An Argument in Favor of Presumed Commit Protocol", *Proceedings 13th IEEE ICDE Conference*, pp.255-265, 1997. 83, 96

[5] Al-Houmaily Y. J. and Chrysanthis P. K.: "Dealing with Incompatible Presumptions of Commit Protocols in Multidatabase Systems", *Proceedings 11th ACM SAC Symposium*, pp.186-195, 1996. 83

[6] Chrysanthis P. K., Samaras G. and Al-Houmaily Y. J.: "Recovery and Performance of Atomic Commit Protocols in Distributed Database Systems", In *Recovery in Database Management Systems*, V. Kumar and M. Hsu (eds.), pp.370-416, Prentice Hall, 1998. 83

[7] Gray J. N.: "Notes on Data Base Operating Systems", In *Operating Systems - an Advanced Course*, R. Bayer, R. Graham, and G. Seegmuller (eds.), LNCS, Vol.60, Springer-Verlag, 1978. 83, 87

[8] Gray J. N. and Reuter A.: *Transaction Processing: Concepts and Techniques*. Morgan Kaufman, 1993. 82, 84

[9] IBM Database System DB2, Version 3, Document Number SC30-3084-5, IBM, 1994. 94

[10] IBM Systems Network Architecture. SYNC Point Services Architecture Reference, Document Number SC31-8134, 1994. 83

[11] Kyrou G. and Samaras G.: "A Graphical Simulator of Distributed Commit Protocols", Internet Site: http://ada.cs.ucy.ac.cy/~cssamara/ 85

[12] Liu M., Agrawal D. and El Abbadi A.: "The Performance of Two-Phase Commit Protocols in the Presence of Site Failures", *Proceedings 24th Symposium on Fault-Tolerant Computing*, 1994. 85

[13] Lampson B. and Lomet D.: "A New Presumed Commit Optimization for Two Phase Commit"", *Proceedings 19th VLDB Conference*, pp.630-640, 1993. 83

[14] Lampson B. W.: "Atomic Transactions", In *Distributed Systems: Architecture and Implementation - an Advanced Course*, B. W. Lampson (ed.), LNCS, Vol.105, Springer-Verlag, pp.246-265, 1981. 83, 87

[15] Mohan C., Britton K., Citron A. and Samaras G.: "Generalized Presumed Abort: Marrying Presumed Abort and SNA's LU6.2 Commit Protocols", *Proceedings Workshop on Advance Transaction Models and Architectures (ATMA96)*, 1996. 83

[16] Mohan C., Lindsay B. and Obermarck R.: "Transaction Management in the R* Distributed Data Base Management System", *ACM Transactions on Database Systems*, Vol.11, No.4, pp.378-396, 1986. 83, 89

[17] Information Technology - Open Systems Interconnection - Distributed Transaction Processing - Part 1: OSI TP Model; Part 2: OSI TP Service, ISO/IEC JTC 1/SC 21 N, 1992. 89

[18] Gupta R., Haritsa J. and Ramamritham K.: "Revisiting Commit Processing in Distributed Database Systems", *Proceedings ACM SIGMOD Conference*, pp.486-497, 1997. 85

[19] Raz Y.: "The Dynamic Two-Phase Commitment Protocol", *Proceedings 5th Conference on Information Systems and Data Management*, 1995. 83

[20] Samaras G., Britton K., Citron A. and Mohan C.:"Commit Processing Optimizations in the Commercial Distributed Environment", *Distributed and Parallel Databases Journal*, Vol.3, No.4, pp.325-361, 1995. 83, 91

[21] Samaras G., Britton K., Citron A. and Mohan C.: "Enhancing SNA's LU6.2 Sync Point to Include Presumed Abort Protocol", IBM Technical Report TR29.1751, IBM Research Triangle Park, 1993. 83

[22] Spiro P., Joshi A., Rengarajan T. K.: "Designing an Optimized Transaction Commit Protocol", *Digital Technical Journal*, Vol.3, No.1, Winter 1991. 83

[23] Stamos J. W. and Cristian F.: "A Low-Cost Atomic Commit Protocol", *Proceedings 9th Symposium on Reliable Distributed Systems*, pp.66-75, 1990. 87

[24] Stamos J. W. and Cristian F.: "Coordinator Log Transaction Execution Protocol", *Distributed and Parallel Databases Journal*, Vol.1, No.4, pp.383-408, 1993. 83, 87

On the Use of Matrices for Belief Revision

Giorgos Flouris and Dimitris Plexousakis

Institute of Computer Science, FO.R.T.H.
P.O. Box 1385, GR 71110, Heraklion, Greece
{fgeo,dp}@ics.forth.gr

Abstract. A most crucial problem in knowledge representation is the revision of knowledge when new, possibly contradictory, information is obtained (belief revision). In this paper, this problem is addressed for propositional knowledge bases. A new, more expressive representation of propositional expressions is introduced, which uses 2-dimensional complex matrices to store knowledge. The increased expressiveness of this representation can be exploited for devising a solution to the problem of belief revision. A simple method for belief revision is proposed, and the new problems and opportunities arising for query answering under this new representation are addressed. Finally, some results regarding matrices are presented as well as their connection with logic.

1 Introduction

The problem of revising beliefs is the problem of maintaining a knowledge base (KB) so that the information contained in it is as accurate as possible in the face of changes in the modelled world and incomplete (or even faulty) information. This problem is greatly interwoven with the representation of knowledge; before deciding on a proper belief revision method, we should choose a proper knowledge representation scheme [2, 15].

The updating methods of knowledge are by no means obvious, even when we are concerned with the intuitive processes only. Let us consider the simple example of knowing facts α and $\alpha \rightarrow b$. One obvious implication of our knowledge is b (by *modus ponens*), which could be inserted into our KB as a new fact. Let us now consider the negation of b ($\neg b$) entering into the base as a new piece of knowledge (revision). This contradicts our previous assumption that b is true, forcing us to give up some (or all) of our previous beliefs or end up with an inconsistent KB. Alternatively, we could reject the revision as non-valid. Even in this trivial example, the approach to be taken is not at all clear. Extra-logical factors should be taken into account, like the source and reliability of each piece of information or some kind of bias towards or against revisions.

Such problems have been addressed by philosophers, computer scientists, logicians and others, in an effort to provide an intuitively correct method of revising beliefs. In this paper, we introduce a new representation of propositional expressions using complex matrices. Based on it, we devise an elegant solution to the problem of belief revision and explore some of its properties, as well as its relation with proposed algorithms from the literature.

Y. Manolopoulos et al. (Eds.): PCI 2001, LNCS 2563, pp. 100–117, 2003.

2   Matrices and Knowledge Representation

Our method for addressing the problem of belief revision uses a special function named *Table Transformation* (*TT*) function, which transforms an expression of any finite propositional language into a complex matrix. The power of this representation stems from the concept of *Reliability Factor* (*RF*), which is a real number indicating the level of confidence in a belief.

We will first describe how the RF assignment is made on atoms. In any formula, say p, an atom of the language, say α, can occur either as a positive (α) or as a negative literal ($\neg\alpha$); alternatively, it may not occur at all. If α does appear in p, its occurrence indicates belief in the atom itself (α) or its negation ($\neg\alpha$), or, equivalently, our confidence that, in the real world, α is true or false respectively; RF indicates the level of this belief. RF is a real number, attached to all atoms' truth and all atoms' falsehood and may be positive, negative or zero. Using RF, all knowledge related to one occurrence of a given atom in a given proposition can be expressed using a pair of real numbers (x, y), representing the RFs of the atom's truth and falsehood respectively.

By using the well known isomorphism of the set $\mathcal{R}^2$ to the set of complex numbers $\mathcal{C}$, we can equivalently express an atom's knowledge using the complex number $z = x + yi$. This number will be referred to as the atom's knowledge, or the number attached to the atom, and we will use atoms and complex numbers interchangeably. The pair of RFs could be equivalently used (or any other system that pairs numbers), but the more compact form of complex numbers gives us more flexibility and allows us to directly use the operations studied for complex numbers and matrices.

The complex number so defined can express a variety of information for each atom, depending on the real and imaginary part of $z = x + yi \in \mathcal{C}$. If $x = 0$, we know nothing about the truth of the respective atom. In a different case, the sign of x indicates whether we believe ($x > 0$) or not ($x < 0$) the atom's truth, while its absolute value indicates the level of trust/distrust. Similar comments apply for y and the atom's falsehood.

It must be noted that distrust in one proposition is not equivalent to believing that proposition's negation, as far as belief revision is concerned. Disbelieving (negative RF) refers to retraction of knowledge. For example, retracting α (ie disbelieving α) from $\alpha \wedge b$ should result in b while revising the same KB with $\neg\alpha$ would lead to inconsistency, which should be remedied somehow to get an "acceptable" KB. Thus, a negative RF attached to the truth of an atom is not equivalent to a positive RF attached to its falsehood (and vice-versa). In older works of the authors, like [6], RF was a non-negative real number, thus unable to express disbelief; the current definition is more powerful.

By combining different values (sign and absolute value) of x and y we can express different types of knowledge regarding the atom. If $x = y = 0$, we have no knowledge on the atom's state, so we must accept both the atom's affirmation or negation as there is no reason to disallow any of the two. This case may occur when the atom does not appear in the proposition at hand. If one of x, y is 0, we know nothing about the truth (if $x = 0$) or falsehood (if $y = 0$) of the atom, so our knowledge must rely on the non-zero element. Such numbers are assigned to literals; a positive literal indicates no knowledge regarding the atom's falsehood, so $y = 0$; similarly, for a negative literal, $x = 0$. On the other hand, if both $x > 0$ and $y > 0$, then we believe in both the atom's affirmation and negation. This implies a contradiction whose intensity is a function of x and y; by comparing x and y the prevailing belief can be determined. If both $x < 0$ and $y < 0$ the same comments apply, for disbelieving (instead of believing). Finally, if $x > 0$ and $y < 0$, then the negative value of y enhances our initial impression that the atom must be true in the real world. The same comments apply if $x < 0$ and $y > 0$, but for the atom's falsehood. All the above apply in different degrees depending on the absolute values of x and y, and imply a significant ability regarding our power of expressiveness and a great improvement over the classical method of representation using propositional expressions.

In order to expand these thoughts to include arbitrary propositions and define TT, we need to integrate knowledge from different atoms. Initially we restrict ourselves in formulas in Disjunctive Normal Form (DNF). For the transformation, each atom of the language is assigned to one column of the matrix, and there are as many lines in the matrix as the number of disjuncts in the DNF of the formula. Each element of the matrix is the complex number that expresses the knowledge regarding the respective atom (column) in the respective disjunct (line).

We show the transformation of the expression $p = (\alpha \wedge b \wedge \neg c) \vee (\alpha \wedge \neg b \wedge d) \vee (c \wedge e)$ into its respective matrix. We suppose that language L consists of 5 atoms, namely α, b, c, d and e, so the matrix has 5 columns. The expression is in DNF, having 3 disjuncts, so the number of lines in the matrix is 3. As far as the elements of the matrix are concerned, the procedure is the following: an element has the value of 1 if the respective atom in the respective disjunct appears as a positive atom; if negative the value is i; if the atom does not appear at all, then the value of the element is 0. The application of these rules on the expression p results in the first matrix shown below. If information regarding the elements' RFs is available, it can be accommodated as in the second matrix:

$$\begin{pmatrix} \alpha \wedge b \wedge \neg c \\ \alpha \wedge \neg b \wedge d \\ c \wedge e \end{pmatrix} \implies \begin{bmatrix} 1 & 1 & i & 0 & 0 \\ 1 & i & 0 & 1 & 0 \\ 0 & 0 & 1 & 0 & 1 \end{bmatrix} \overset{RF}{\implies} \begin{bmatrix} 1 & 2 & i & 0 & 0 \\ 3 & 2i & 0 & 4 & 0 \\ 0 & 0 & 5.5 & 0 & 2 \end{bmatrix}$$

To transform a matrix back to a logical expression, we must "decode" the information contained in each element of the matrix. This procedure is called *Inverse Table Transformation (TTI)*. Due to the inherent inability of propositional logic to express disbelief, elements implying disbelief in a fact (having negative RF) are mapped into the negation of the fact, despite the difference in semantics. Similarly, since any RF ("intensity") data cannot be expressed in logic, it is ignored during the transformation.

The above simple definition of TT captures the intuition that will be used throughout this paper to describe our belief revision scheme. It is used to transform a formula p into a matrix P, including RF information (if available) in a very compact form. TT causes no loss of information, making matrices an attractive alternative for knowledge representation. Each line of P represents a different clause in p, or a different possible state of the world represented by p. For this reason, we will sometimes refer to lines as *possible world states*. Each element of P represents information regarding one atom in one possible world state. Each line is actually an ordered tuple of such information for one such state. The ordering of lines in the matrix is simply a syntactic convenience, as a different ordering would make no difference as far as the knowledge contained in the matrix is concerned.

In our attempt to expand this representation to propositions not in DNF we will encounter some problems making the above informal definition a special easy case and forcing us to change it somewhat. However, these issues are irrelevant as far as the knowledge representation and belief revision problems are concerned, so we postpone their discussion until a later point (see definition 7, section 5).

3   Matrices and Belief Revision

In order to use this transformation in belief revision we will initially assume that both the knowledge and the revision are represented by matrices. In other words, we assume that we already have a general method of transforming the abstract notion of "real world knowledge" to a specific weighted matrix that represents it. Intuitively, this is easy to do, using the method described in the previous section.

For the moment, we will additionally assume that both the base K and the revision matrix M have only one line, so they both represent only one possible state of the world. In this special case, the revision will be defined as the *addition* of the two matrices, because the inclusion of matrix M in our knowledge increases our trust in all the information that M carries, effectively increasing our reliance in each atom and/or its negation. This adjustment may or may not be enough to force us to change our beliefs. In general, when we believe something with reliability x and a new piece of knowledge confirms this belief, coming from a source with reliability y, then the intuitively expected result of the revision should be the same belief with reliability $x + y$. This is the notion behind defining the revision as the addition of the two matrices. One can verify that the operation of addition is intuitively correct even in cases where x and/or y are negative numbers, or when they refer to contradicting data (one implying α and the other $\neg\alpha$ for some atom α). For example, let $K = \begin{bmatrix} i & 3 & 0 \end{bmatrix}$, $M = \begin{bmatrix} 3 & 2 & 1 \end{bmatrix}$. Using the TTI function we can verify that the matrices represent the expressions $K = \neg\alpha \wedge b$ (base) and $M = \alpha \wedge b \wedge c$ (revision). The matrices also show the reliability per atom in each proposition. In this case, a's negation ($\neg\alpha$) is believed with an RF of 1 in K, but M should force us to abandon this belief as α is believed with an RF of 3 in M. In b, there is no contradiction between K and M; however this revision should increase our confidence in the truth of b. Finally, in c, we know now that c is true, with a reliance of 1; we had no knowledge regarding c before.

The resulting matrix is K' where the symbol "$\bullet$" stands for the operation of revision: $K' = K \bullet M = \begin{bmatrix} i\ 3\ 0 \end{bmatrix} + \begin{bmatrix} 3\ 2\ 1 \end{bmatrix} = \begin{bmatrix} 3+i\ 5\ 1 \end{bmatrix}$.

The proposition related (via the TTI function) to the resulting matrix is: $F \wedge b \wedge c \cong F$, because the first element $(3 + i)$ implies a contradiction. This is not generally acceptable, as such a KB contains no useful information. The result should be $a \wedge b \wedge c$, as showed by the previous analysis. We will deal with this problem in the next section (which is in fact not a problem at all!).

In the general case where one (or both) of the matrices contain more than one line, each line represents one possible state of the world. In order to be sure that the real world will be represented by a line in the resulting matrix, we must add (revise) each line of K with each line of M, creating one line per pair in the resulting matrix K'. Let us see one example:

$$K = \begin{bmatrix} 1 & 2 \\ 0 & 5i \end{bmatrix}, M = \begin{bmatrix} i & 3 \\ 2i & 3i \end{bmatrix}, K \bullet M = \begin{bmatrix} 1+i & 5 \\ 1+2i & 2+3i \\ i & 3+5i \\ 2i & 8i \end{bmatrix}$$

4   Queries and Contradictions

Any given matrix has no intuitive meaning for a user, because finding the knowledge contained in a large KB matrix is not a trivial operation. More importantly, the user is normally not allowed nor interested to see the whole KB, but wishes to execute queries for finding specific information. To reply to a user query, we must transform the KB matrix back into a proposition expressing the knowledge contained in it. TTI is inadequate because there are cases (as the one above) when the result of a revision is a matrix corresponding via TTI to the logical constant F; equivalently, the KB related to the matrix via TTI is inconsistent. To overcome this problem, we will perform some pre-processing on the KB matrix before applying TTI, in order to remove the parts of the matrix that cause the contradictions and that contain data not properly describing the real world.

Before defining such a function, we notice that not all lines of a matrix properly model the real world, so a selection has to be made. One may argue that contradictory lines represent contradictory world states, so they contain false information and they could as well be deleted. This is the policy followed by the TTI function, as shown in the previous example. However, this is not entirely true. A single faulty revision may create a contradiction in an otherwise correct line, so we must be careful before discarding a contradictory line as non-true. On the other hand, even a non-contradictory line could be too far from the real world. The absence of contradictions indicates that nothing that overrules this line has been known up to now; still, we cannot be sure that the line properly describes the modelled world. Therefore, our policy is to keep the matrix as-is and to let inconsistency stay in the KB, even if some (or all) lines are contradictory.

One possible way to materialize these requirements is described in [7]. In order to estimate the proximity of a line to the real world, a function named *Line*

Reliability (*RL*) is used, depending on the *Element Reliability* (*RE*) function. RE is a function that calculates our reliance in the truth of the information that one element carries. This quantity is a real number having nothing to do with the truth or falsity of the respective atom; it expresses our estimation on whether the information carried by the element corresponds to this atom's truth value in the real world. Similarly, RL is a function that uses RE in order to estimate the proximity of the line's information to the real world. For a KB matrix A, RE returns a matrix B in which all elements of A have been replaced by their reliability, a real number. RL produces a column matrix C composed of real numbers, in which each element represents the reliability of the respective line.

Given the estimation provided by the RL function, we should select the lines that are sufficiently close to the real world (according to our estimations, as usual). This selection is made by a function named *Line Selection* function (*LS*), which returns a set S of indices, corresponding to the selected lines of the original matrix. This set is used by the *Submatrix Selection* function (*MS*) to produce a new matrix $D = MS(A, S) = MS(A, LS(C))$, which is a submatrix of the original matrix, according to our selection.

In order to remove the contradictions possibly appearing in the selected lines, the *Matrix Normalization* function (*MN*) is used to transform each element to its normalized (non-contradictory) counterpart. To decide whether to believe in the truth or falsity of the atom (instead of both or neither, which is the source of the contradiction), we compare the RF of the real and imaginary part of the element by subtracting them. MN returns a new matrix $E = MN(D)$.

This procedure ensures that there will be no contradictions in the matrix that resulted by the selection implied by the LS function. This final matrix (E) expresses the (consistent) KB that will be used in queries. It contains the most reliable lines of our KB, which have been normalized in order to extract the information contained in the contradictory elements. At this point, we can eventually apply the TTI function to get the (satisfiable) logical expression p related to matrix A, corresponding to the knowledge store in the KB.

The whole process (function) of transforming a matrix to a proposition for the needs of queries will be denoted by QT (*Query Transformation*), so $p = QT(A)$. It is clear by the analysis above that QT is in fact a composite function, being composed of six functions. The first three (RE, RL, LS) are not clearly defined, because we claim that a reasonable definition of such functions is application-dependent. Arguments for this claim, as well as its importance, will be provided in section 6. The final three functions (MS, MN, TTI), will be formally defined in the next section and express the process of extracting information out of (possibly contradictory) elements. Finally, we stress that the QT operation does not actually change the matrix; it temporarily transforms it to a logical expression for the needs of queries. The next revision will be executed upon the original matrix and the whole process of query transformation should be repeated after the revision to calculate the new related proposition.

5   Formal Framework

With the introduction of the QT function, we completed the description of the framework we propose for representing and revising knowledge. Summarizing our method, we can say that it consists of the following three parts:

1. *Knowledge Representation*: express the knowledge represented by the logical propositions of the input into matrices and encode the reliability information, if available, into the matrix elements, transforming our knowledge into the more expressive and convenient form of the matrix representation.
2. *Knowledge Revision*: whenever any new data is introduced (revision), apply the belief revision algorithm to accommodate the new knowledge.
3. *Knowledge Query*: apply the QT function upon the matrix representing the KB to extract the KB's information, in order to reply to user queries.

In this section we provide a formal framework for the procedures informally described in previous sections. Proofs are omitted due to lack of space, but they can be found in [7]. At first, some notational conventions should be introduced. We denote by $\mathcal{C}^{(+)}$ the set of complex numbers whose real and imaginary part are both non-negative. For matrices, we define $\mathcal{C}^{m \times n}$ to be the set of $m \times n$ matrices whose elements are complex numbers, and $\mathcal{C}^{* \times n}$ the union of $\mathcal{C}^{m \times n}$ for all $m \in \mathcal{N}^*$. Analogously, we define the sets $\mathcal{C}^{(+)m \times n}$ and $\mathcal{C}^{(+)* \times n}$. We will use the usual notation for addition / multiplication of matrices, and the multiplication of a number with a matrix. We define the operation of *juxtaposition* as follows:

Definition 1. *Let $A, B \in \mathcal{C}^{* \times n}$. The juxtaposition of A and B, denoted by $A|B$, is the matrix that results by placing the lines of B below the lines of A.*

We also define a partitioning on $\mathcal{C}$ as follows:

Definition 2. *Let $z = x + yi \in \mathcal{C}$. Then:*

- *z is called positive iff $x \geq 0$, $y \leq 0$. Such numbers (forming set $\mathcal{C}_+$) denote trust in the truth and distrust in the falsehood of the atom (positive literal).*
- *z is called negative iff $x \leq 0$, $y \geq 0$. Such numbers (forming set $\mathcal{C}_-$) denote distrust in the truth and trust in the falsehood of the atom (negative literal).*
- *z is called contradictory iff $x \cdot y > 0$ (so $x > 0$ and $y > 0$ or $x < 0$ and $y < 0$). Such numbers (forming set $\mathcal{C}_*$) denote trust or distrust in both the atom's truth and falsehood. Both these cases are invalid (contradictory), because an atom can be either true or false, but not both or neither.*
- *z is called zero iff $z = 0$ (forming set $\mathcal{C}_0$). In this case, $x = y = 0$, so z is both positive and negative and denotes lack of knowledge regarding both the atom and its negation; we have no reason to accept or discard the truth or falsehood of the atom, so we have to accept both.*

We get that: $\mathcal{C}_0 = \{0\}, \mathcal{C}_+ \cap \mathcal{C}_- = \mathcal{C}_0, \mathcal{C}_+ \cap \mathcal{C}_* = \emptyset, \mathcal{C}_- \cap \mathcal{C}_* = \emptyset, \mathcal{C}_- \cup \mathcal{C}_+ \cup \mathcal{C}_* = \mathcal{C}$.

Definition 3. *We define the following matrices:*

- *The k-atom:* $A_k = [0 \ldots 0 \ 1 \ 0 \ldots 0] \in \mathcal{C}^{1 \times n}$, *where the element 1 is in the k-th column.*
- *The generalized k-atom:* $A_k(z) = z \cdot A_k \in \mathcal{C}^{1 \times n}$, *for some* $z \in \mathcal{C}$.
- *The n-true matrix:* $T_n = [0 \ldots 0] \in \mathcal{C}^{1 \times n}$.
- *The n-false matrix:* $F_n = [1 + i \ldots 1 + i] \in \mathcal{C}^{1 \times n}$.

Definition 4. *We define the truth constants* $F = 0 \in \mathcal{C}$ *and* $T = 1 \in \mathcal{C}$. *Any sequence* $I \in \{0, 1\}^n$ *is called an interpretation of space* $\mathcal{C}^{* \times n}$, *forming set* $I(n)$. *Let* $I = (\alpha_1, \ldots, \alpha_n) \in I(n)$, $A \in \mathcal{C}^{1 \times n}$ *such that:* $A = \Sigma_{j=1}^n A_j(a_j + (1 - a_j) \cdot i)$. *A is called an interpretation matrix of space* $\mathcal{C}^{* \times n}$.

Notice that there is a direct mapping between logical interpretations, interpretations and interpretation matrices. Moreover, the number $z = \alpha_j + (1 - \alpha_j) \cdot i$ can be either $z = 1$ (for $\alpha_j = 1$) or $z = i$ (for $\alpha_j = 0$). Therefore, an interpretation matrix is a matrix of the set $\mathcal{C}^{1 \times n}$, whose elements are from the set $\{1, i\}$.

Definition 5. *Let* $I = (\alpha_1, \ldots, \alpha_n) \in I(n)$, $A \in \mathcal{C}^{1 \times n}$. *A is satisfied by I iff there exist* $z_1, \ldots, z_n \in \mathcal{C}^{(+)} : A = \Sigma_{j=1}^n A_j((2 \cdot a_j - 1) \cdot \overline{z_j})$, *where* $\overline{z_j}$ *is the conjugate complex of* $z_j \in \mathcal{C}^{(+)}$. *If* $A \in \mathcal{C}^{m \times n}$ *such that* $A = A^{(1)} | \ldots | A^{(m)}$, $A^{(j)} \in \mathcal{C}^{1 \times n}, j = 1, \ldots, m$, *then we say that A is satisfied by I iff there exists* $j \in \{1, \ldots, m\}$ *such that* $A^{(j)}$ *is satisfied by I. The set of interpretations satisfying A, called the set of models of A, will be denoted by* $mod(A)$.

Notice that $(2 \cdot \alpha_j - 1) \in \{-1, 1\}$ and $x_j = (2 \cdot \alpha_j - 1) \cdot \overline{z_j} \in \mathcal{C}_+$ iff $\alpha_j = 1$ and $x_j \in \mathcal{C}_-$ iff $\alpha_j = 0$. Numbers z_j represent RF; interpretation matrices, having elements in $\{1, i\}$ lack "intensity" information, whereas a matrix may be weighted with RF information. To calculate $mod(A)$, two easier, contructive methods can be devised:

Proposition 1. *Let* $A = \begin{bmatrix} w_{jk} \end{bmatrix} \in \mathcal{C}^{m \times n}$. *Then* $mod(A) = \bigcup_{j=1}^m (I_{j1} \times \ldots \times I_{jn})$, *where for any* $j \in \{1, \ldots, m\}, k \in \{1, \ldots, n\}$:

- $I_{jk} = \{0\}$ *iff* $w_{jk} \in \mathcal{C}_- \backslash \mathcal{C}_+ = \mathcal{C}_- \backslash \mathcal{C}_0$
- $I_{jk} = \{1\}$ *iff* $w_{jk} \in \mathcal{C}_+ \backslash \mathcal{C}_- = \mathcal{C}_+ \backslash \mathcal{C}_0$
- $I_{jk} = \{0, 1\}$ *iff* $w_{jk} \in \mathcal{C}_0$
- $I_{jk} = \emptyset$ *iff* $w_{jk} \in \mathcal{C}_*$

Furthermore, $mod(A) = \bigcup_{j=1}^m \bigcap_{k=1}^n mod(A_k(w_{jk}))$.

The latter result indicates a close connection between juxtaposition and addition of matrices to union and intersection between models, respectively. Juxtaposition is closely related to the union of models:

Proposition 2. *Let* $A, B \in \mathcal{C}^{* \times n}$. *Then* $mod(A|B) = mod(A) \cup mod(B)$.

Unfortunately, the connection between addition and intersection is not so straightforward. We explore their relation in [7]. In order to define TT, we need operations on matrices emulating the usual operations of propositional logic:

Definition 6. *We define 3 classes of functions in $C^{*\times n}$, denoted by $\mathcal{F}_\vee$, $\mathcal{F}_\wedge$ and $\mathcal{F}_\neg$, called the classes of disjunction, conjunction and negation functions:*

- *A function $f_\vee : (C^{*\times n})^2 \to C^{*\times n}$ is said to belong in $\mathcal{F}_\vee$ iff for any $A, B \in C^{*\times n}$, $mod(f_\vee(A, B)) = mod(A) \cup mod(B)$. We use $A \vee B$ to denote $f_\vee(A, B)$.*
- *A function $f_\wedge : (C^{*\times n})^2 \to C^{*\times n}$ is said to belong in $\mathcal{F}_\wedge$ iff for any $A, B \in C^{*\times n}$, $mod(f_\wedge(A, B)) = mod(A) \cap mod(B)$. We use $A \wedge B$ to denote $f_\wedge(A, B)$.*
- *A function $f_\neg : C^{*\times n} \to C^{*\times n}$ is said to belong in $\mathcal{F}_\neg$ iff for any $A \in C^{*\times n}$, $mod(f_\neg(A)) = I(n) \backslash mod(A)$. We use $\neg A$ to denote $f_\neg(A)$.*

The space $C^{*\times n}$, equipped with functions $\vee \in \mathcal{F}_\vee$, $\wedge \in \mathcal{F}_\wedge$, $\neg \in \mathcal{F}_\neg$, is called a logically complete matrix space of dimension n and is denoted by $(C^{*\times n}, \vee, \wedge, \neg)$.

No further restrictions are set on the selection of operators $\vee$, $\wedge$, $\neg$ and different selections imply different logically complete spaces. The same discipline can be used to define additional operators (like $\to$), if necessary, but the above are enough for the main definition of this section:

Definition 7. *Assume $(C^{*\times n}, \vee, \wedge, \neg)$ and L a finite propositional language. We denote by α_j the atoms of the language and by A_j the atoms of $C^{*\times n}$. We define the Table Transformation function, $TT : L^* \to C^{*\times n}$, recursively, as follows:*

- $TT(T) = T_n$, $TT(F) = F_n$
- *For any $j \in \{1, \ldots, n\} : TT(\alpha_j) = A_j$*
- $TT(p\theta q) = TT(p)\theta TT(q)$, *for any $p, q \in L^*, \theta \in \{\wedge, \vee\}$*
- $TT(\neg p) = \neg TT(p)$, *for any $p \in L^*$*

Similarly, for $j \in \{1, \ldots, n\}, z \in C$, we define the Inverse Table Transformation function, $TTI : C^{*\times n} \to L^*$, recursively, as follows:

- $TTI(A_j(z)) = \alpha_j$, *iff $z \in C_+ \backslash C_- = C_+ \backslash C_0$*
- $TTI(A_j(z)) = \neg\alpha_j$, *iff $z \in C_- \backslash C_+ = C_- \backslash C_0$*
- $TTI(A_j(z)) = T$, *iff $z \in C_0$*
- $TTI(A_j(z)) = F$, *iff $z \in C_*$*

For $m \in \mathcal{N}^*$, $A = [z_{kj}] \in C^{m \times n}$, $TTI(A) = \bigvee_{k=1}^{m}(\bigwedge_{j=1}^{n} TTI(A_j(z_{kj})))$.

The transformations above have a very important property:

Proposition 3. *For any proposition $p \in L^*$ and any matrix $P \in C^{*\times n}$ it holds that $mod(p) = mod(TT(p))$ and $mod(P) = mod(TTI(P))$.*

The above proposition shows that the transformation of a matrix to a logical expression and vice-versa does not cause any loss of (logical) information, as any interpretation that satisfies a given matrix satisfies its respective logical expression (via the TTI function) and vice-versa (via the TT function). This is true as far as logic is concerned; if RF information is available, TTI may cause information loss, in knowledge representation terms. Moreover, notice that the above proposition holds regardless of the selection of the operations $\vee$, $\wedge$, $\neg$.

We have already stressed the fact that matrices' elements can have negative real and/or imaginary parts. Such numbers indicate lack of confidence to a given literal and/or its negation, so they do not give direct information on the truth or falsity of a literal; instead, they indirectly imply its truth or falsity by specifying distrust in its falsity or truth respectively. Such kind of knowledge will be denoted by the term *negative knowledge* contrary to elements with non-negative parts (real and imaginary), which will be referred to as *positive knowledge*. The distinction is justified by the fact that logic can only express positive knowledge. Negative knowledge is only useful as far as knowledge representation is concerned, and its importance will be set forth in the next section.

By restricting ourselves to positive knowledge, it becomes easier to define operations like $\wedge, \neg$. For a specific selection of operators, for positive knowledge and for propositions in DNF, the simple informal definition of TT given in section 2 coincides with the operation given by definition 7 (see [7]). TT, as defined in definition 7 is only important as a theoretical construction, showing the relation between matrices and logic; it will also allow us to prove some results (e.g. proposition 4). TT cannot express the additional reliability information that we may have, nor can it express negative knowledge. This seriously reduces our expressive abilities. Furthermore, this approach requires the explicit definition of the propositional operations. However, it has no real intuitive meaning to define such operations in the general case, though possible; remember that negative knowledge cannot be expressed in propositional logic. All we need is their existence, to support definition 7.

Having completed the formalization of our knowledge representation scheme and its relation with propositional logic, we can now proceed to the definition of our revision scheme:

Definition 8. *Let $A, B \in \mathcal{C}^{*\times n}$, where $A = A^{(1)}|\ldots|A^{(k)}$, $B = B^{(1)}|\ldots|B^{(m)}$, for some $k, m \in \mathcal{N}^*$, $A^{(j)} \in \mathcal{C}^{1\times n}$, $j \in \{1,\ldots,k\}$ and $B^{(j)} \in \mathcal{C}^{1\times n}$, $j \in \{1,\ldots,m\}$. We define the operation of revision, denoted by $\bullet$, between those two matrices as follows: $A\bullet B = |_{h=1,j=1}^{h=k,j=m}(A^{(h)} + B^{(j)})$.*

It is easy to verify that this definition concurs with the informal description of the revision operator of section 3. It has been proved in [7] that, for positive knowledge: $mod(A\bullet B) = mod(A) \cap mod(B)$.

Definition 9. *We define the submatrix selection function $MS : \mathcal{C}^{*\times n} \times P(\mathcal{N}^*) \to \mathcal{C}^{*\times n}$. For $k \in \mathcal{N}^*$, $A \in \mathcal{C}^{k\times n}$, $S \subseteq \mathrm{N}^*$, such that $A = A^{(1)}|\ldots|A^{(k)}$, $A^{(j)} \in \mathcal{C}^{1\times n}$, $j \in \{1,\ldots,k\}$, we define:*

- *$MS(A, S) = A$, iff $S = \emptyset$ or there exists $m \in S$ such that $m > k$,*
- *$MS(A, S) = |_{j\in S}A^{(j)}$, otherwise*

We define the matrix normalization function $MN : \mathcal{C}^{*\times n} \to \mathcal{C}^{*\times n}$ such that for $A = [a_{ij}] \in \mathcal{C}^{k\times n}$: $MN(A) = [Re(a_{ij}) - Im(a_{ij})] \in \mathcal{C}^{k\times n}$.

The above functions are used in the third part of our method, namely the querying of the knowledge in the KB. The MS function returns a submatrix of A which consists of some of the lines of A, those whose indexes belong to the set S. Some abnormal cases have been included in the above definition for completeness, but they will not appear in this application. The MN function is used to remove any contradictions from the matrix, by comparing (subtracting) the real and imaginary part of a_{ij}. TTI is the final step to transforming a matrix to its respective logical expression. The first three functions of the QT (RE, RL, LS) will not be explicitly defined for the reasons set forth in the next section.

6   Comments, Properties and Results

In this section, we will discuss some of the problems and considerations researchers have to face when dealing with the problem of belief revision, as well as how our method deals with these problems.

One such problem is the representation of knowledge. In our framework, the abstract term "knowledge" (or "belief") will refer to any propositional formula over a finite language L along with its reliability information, or, equivalently, by the matrix that represents this information. So, a KB is a single matrix, constituting a compact knowledge representation scheme. This matrix contains all the information of the past revisions in an encoded fashion. A world state is an interpretation and the real world that we are trying to model is actually one such state which may change through time. Each revision describes the world partially by denoting a set of acceptable states (interpretations), namely those that it satisfies.

Another primary consideration regarding belief revision is the concurrence of the results with human intuition. Unfortunately, it is not absolutely clear how humans revise their beliefs, despite several efforts in the area. One example of disagreement is the representation of knowledge in the human brain. In [9] two general types of theories concerning this representation are described: *foundation* and *coherence* theories. According to foundational theorists, only some beliefs (called *foundational*, or *reasons*) can stand by themselves; the rest are derived from the most basic (foundational) beliefs. On the other hand, coherence theorists believe that each piece of knowledge has an independent standing and needs no justification, as long as it does not contradict with other beliefs. Experiments [9] have shown that the human brain actually uses the coherence paradigm, by showing that people tend to ignore causality relationships once a belief has been accepted as a fact, even if it has been accepted solely by deduction from other beliefs. There has been considerable controversy [9, 10] on the experiments' results based on the argument that humans do not actually *ignore* the causality relationships, but *forget* them.

The approach (foundational or coherence) chosen greatly influences the algorithms considered. Foundational KBs need to store the reasons for beliefs, whereas KBs based on the coherence paradigm need to store the set of beliefs, without any reason information. Reasons should be taken into account when revising a KB only under the foundational approach. In any case, the set of beliefs of any KB includes the derived beliefs, which, in general, may be too many or even infinitely many. It has been proposed in [11, 18] that instead of the whole set of beliefs (*belief set*), a small number of propositions could be stored (*belief base*), enough to reproduce the whole set via deduction. The use of belief bases does not necessarily force us to use the foundational paradigm; the causality relationships possibly implied by the selection of a belief base may or may not be used, depending on the approach. The use of belief bases gives rise to the problem of the selection of a proper belief base, as there may be several for any given belief set. Different selections become critical under the foundational approach, but are irrelevant under the coherence paradigm. An example of belief base selection appears in [3, 4] where a single proposition is used as the KB.

In this work, we adopt Nebel's proposition [18] for the selection of the belief base where the contents of the KB are the individual revisions, each of them expressing an observation, experiment, rule etc regarding a domain of interest. In principle, knowledge is derived from our observations about the world, so this is the best way to describe our knowledge. As in any belief base, the knowledge of the KB consists of these revisions as well as their logical consequences, but the selection of the belief base just described implies that this approach follows the foundational paradigm. The foundational approach is generally viewed as being more compatible with common sense [9].

There are cases when a revision contradicts previous ones or their consequences. In such cases, at least one of the previous revisions (old knowledge) or the new revision itself is usually modified or discarded altogether in order for the KB to remain consistent. This is generally done while revising the KB, but, in our method, contradictions are resolved at query time using QT (see also [14] for a similar approach). In most cases, the removal of contradictions is done following Dalal's Principle of Primacy of New Information, which states that the revision is more reliable than the KB, so it is the KB that should be adapted to accomodate the revision [3]. Despite the fact that a revision represents the latest information about the world and can be *usually* assumed correct, the new data may come from a noisy or otherwise unreliable source, so it should not be *always* assumed correct.

This problem is overcome in our method by the use of the RF and the MN function. In queries, given that the respective line is selected (by the LS function), the information with the largest RF will be kept, regardless of whether it resulted from the last revision or the old data. This is concurrent with human intuition, as our beliefs, eventually, are unaffected by the order information is received. This fact additionally allows us to perform KB merging in a straightforward way. The important problem of data rejection in contradicting revisions is also solved in the same way (using the QT function). Rejection is only temporary, for the needs of queries, and depends on the RF and the functions RE and RL, being minimal with respect to these quantities. The notion of minimality depends on the LS function selection.

Some of the most important results of our method originate from the inexplicit definition of the RE, RL and LS functions. These functions determine the lines to be used for queries, because they select the "important" lines of a matrix.

The best selection is application-dependent. To see this, one could try to determine which of the (contradictory) elements 1+3i and 100+300i is more reliable (less contradictory). Many would argue that both elements are equally reliable, as the belief ratio of truth to falsehood of the atom is the same. Others would disagree, on the argument that the removal of the contradiction in 100+300i requires greater changes in the KB than in 1+3i. In any case, the RE function will determine that. In an application where data is generally obtained through noisy channels, the contradiction in 1+3i is likely to have occurred due to some random noise (error) of the input; on the other hand, 100+300i is less likely so, statistically, therefore it could be safely assumed that this element implies a real contradiction. In an environment where the world often changes dynamically, the contradiction in both elements may be due to information received in a previous state of the world; thus, they can be assumed equally reliable as they have the same belief ratio. In some other application where decisions are based on subjective opinions, instead of facts, the fact that the number 100+300i implies a bigger sample may force us to consider it more reliable than 1+3i.

The effect of the element reliability on the overall reliability of a line (RL parameter), as well as our tolerance in contradictory lines and the number of lines selected for use in a query (LS parameter) depends mainly on the reliability of the input devices. In a medical application, where the input devices are most reliable, even small contradictions should be "fatal" for the line that they appear in; contradictions in such a sensitive application should be unacceptable, unless there is no other choice. This is not the case in applications with often dynamic changes of the world's state or with noisy input channels.

Moreover, the ability to freely define RE, RL and LS functions provides a considerable flexibility in the extraction of the knowledge in a matrix. This flexibility allows relating the result of any given revision (and any given matrix) to several different propositions; as far as the user is concerned, this is equivalent to supplying different belief revision algorithms. Consequently, our framework provides a whole class of belief revision algorithms and the problem of finding a good such algorithm is reduced to the problem of finding a good way to extract the information from a matrix. The search for some interesting members of this class of algorithms is an ongoing work, but it has already been proven that Dalal's algorithm [3, 4], gives the same results as our method for a specific parameter selection, as shown by the following proposition:

Proposition 4. *Let $p, q \in L^*$ be two satisfiable propositional expressions in DNF and let r be the revision of p with q under Dalal's algorithm $(r = p \bullet^D q)$. Moreover, let $P \in C^{(+)* \times n}$ the matrix related to p via the TT function, using an RF of 1 for all atoms $(P = TT(p))$, $Q \in C^{(+)* \times n}$ the matrix related to q via the TT function, using an RF of 2 for all atoms $(Q = 2 \cdot TT(q))$ and $R \in C^{(+)* \times n}$ the matrix resulting by the revision of P with Q under our framework $(R = P \bullet Q)$. Under these RF selections, there exist selections for the functions RE, RL and LS such that the resulting propositional expression (to be used in queries) is logically equivalent to the expression r as defined above, that is: $QT(R) \cong r$.*

The phrasing of the above proposition implies the important fact that the selection of the RFs of a matrix's elements has great effects on the result of a revision. Its proof, as well as the definition of one possible set of RE, RL and LS functions that satisfy it, is given in [7].

One effort to formalize the concurrence of the results of belief revision with human intuition was made by Alchourron, Gärdenfors and Makinson in a series of papers [1, 8, 17]. Unlike other researchers, they receded from the search of any specific algorithm and attempted to formalize the notion of revision. As a result, a set of widely accepted properties of belief revision algorithms was introduced, in the form of postulates expressed as a set of logical propositions (named AGM postulates after the authors' initials). Using these postulates, a series of important theoretical results were proved and a series of other works were inspired. Nebel in [18], investigated generalizations of these postulates into the knowledge level. In [13], a different theoretical foundation of revision functions was proposed by reformulating the AGM postulates in terms of formulas and an elegant representation based on orderings of belief sets was provided. In the same paper, Dalal's algorithm was proven to satisfy all 8 AGM postulates; this implies that there exist parameters under which our method satisfies the AGM postulates for revision.

One of the most peculiar problems in belief revision is the fact that the result of a revision may not only depend on the data itself but on its source as well. Let us suppose that there are two lamps, A and B, in a room and we know that exactly one of them is on. Our knowledge can be represented by the proposition: $(\alpha \wedge \neg b) \vee (\neg \alpha \wedge b)$. If we make the observation that lamp A is on, we should revise our KB with the proposition α and the intuitively correct result for the revision is the proposition $\alpha \wedge \neg b$, as we know now that B is off. On the other hand, if a robot is sent into the room in order to turn lamp A on, then we would again have to revise with α. The proper intuitive result of this revision is the proposition α in this case, as we know nothing about the state of lamp B; it could have been on or off before sending the robot in the room (and stayed so). This example shows that even identical (not just equivalent) KBs can give different intuitively correct results with identical revisions!

In order to overcome the problem, two different types of "knowledge change" have been defined in [12], namely *revision* and *update*. Revision is used when new information about a static world is obtained. This is the first case of our example where the observation did not change the state of A and B. A revision is performed when the source of the data is an observation regarding the world. Update is used when the world dynamically changes and we have to record that change. In the second case of our example, the robot changed the state of lamp A, thus the state of the world being modeled. Therefore, the result of an update must be different. An update is performed when the reason of change is an action, instead of an observation. An excellent study on the problem may be found in [12], where a new set of postulates, adequate for update, is presented.

An important novelty of our scheme is the introduction of negative knowledge. The disbelief expressed by such type of knowledge cannot be expressed in propositional logic, so this is a direct improvement of our expressive abilities over the conventional knowledge representation schemes. Using negative knowledge we are able to deal with the above operations (revision, update, contraction, erasure) in terms of revision only, by changing the revision matrix's RF in such a way as to signify the operations' different nature.

We will see how this is possible with an example, which will also show the dominating effect of the RF selection and negative knowledge on the result of a revision as well as the power of parameterization. The reliability of an element $x + yi$ will be defined as $|x - y|$, ie the difference between its true and false part. The reliability of a line will be defined as the sum of the reliabilities of all its elements and LS will select the lines with maximum reliability.

Revisiting the above example with the lamps, we could express our knowledge using the proposition: $p = (\neg\alpha \wedge b) \vee (\alpha \wedge \neg b)$. When we conclude (through observation) that A is on, the proposition representing the revision is $q = \alpha$. By assigning an RF of 1 on all atoms of the KB and an RF of $x > 0$ on the revision we get: $P = \begin{bmatrix} i & 1 \\ 1 & i \end{bmatrix}, Q = \begin{bmatrix} x & 0 \end{bmatrix}, P' = P \bullet Q = \begin{bmatrix} x+i & 1 \\ 1+x & i \end{bmatrix}$.

Note that the first line contains a contradictory element $(x + i)$, whereas the second contains no contradictions. Using the parameterization above, we get reliabilities of $|x - 1| + 1$ for the first line and $|x + 1| + 1$ for the second. For all $x > 0$ it holds that $|x - 1| + 1 < |x + 1| + 1$, thus LS will only select the second line. Upon applying MS function, P' matrix will be mapped to $P'' = [1 + x \ i]$ (containing only the second line of P'). Applying the MN function will have no effect on P'', as there are no contradictions to resolve, thus the respective proposition of P' is: $QT(P') = \alpha \wedge \neg b$, as expected. Alternatively, the RL function could be defined as the minimum over the reliabilities of all elements in the line (only the least reliable element of the line is considered in the calculation). In this case, for $x \geq 2$ both lines would have equal reliability (equal to 1), so the LS function would select them both. Thus, for this selection of the RL function, the RF of Q is crucial; for $x \geq 2$ we get $QT(P') = (\alpha \wedge b) \vee (\alpha \wedge \neg b) \cong \alpha$, whereas for $0 < x < 2$ we get $QT(P') = \alpha \wedge \neg b$.

A more intuitively correct approach for the LS function would be to select the non-contradictory lines only; if there are no such lines, then we go on by selecting the most reliable contradictory ones, as before. It can be verified that in this case, the result would have been $QT(P') = \alpha \wedge \neg b$, regardless of the selection of the parameters RE, RL or x.

Continuing this example, notice that if we had sent a robot into the room with the order "turn lamp A on", then we should *update* (not revise) p with $q = \alpha$. Matrix $Q' = [1 - i \ 0]$, corresponds to the same information as Q, because $TTI(Q') = \alpha = TTI(Q)$. However, Q' includes some disbelief in the negation of α because the imaginary part of $1 - i$ is negative (-1). Thus, Q' has been enhanced in such a way as to contain the additional information that the action of the robot voids the previous state of A, if A was off, because the dynamic change indicated by the update renders any previous knowledge on the world irrelevant. The revision of P with Q' under our scheme gives: $P' = \begin{bmatrix} 1 & 1 \\ 2-i & i \end{bmatrix}$.

The important point here is that there are no contradictory lines in P', therefore, by using the rational LS function previously described (regardless of the RE and RL selection), we would select both lines of P', so $QT(P') = (\alpha \wedge b) \vee (\alpha \wedge \neg b) \cong \alpha$. This is the expected result of an *update*!

Update and revision are used to add knowledge to a KB. Essentially, new data enhances our knowledge about the domain of interest. In some cases though, we wish to remove knowledge from the KB. This operation is called *contraction* and it is dual to revision. It has been argued [8, 17] that it is intuitively simpler to deal with contraction instead of revision. We could also define the operation of *erasure* which is dual to update. For the class of revision schemes that satisfy the AGM postulates, it has been proven that revision and contraction can be defined in terms of each other. Similar results apply for the update/erasure schemes that satisfy the postulates for update/erasure defined in [12].

We notice that using negative information we can also get a contraction operation, by revising with matrix $-M$ whenever we want to contract M. Similar considerations can lead to the integration of the operation of erasure as well. This fact eliminates the need for additional operators, as they can all be defined in terms of revision. Moreover, we can perform partial operations, by, for example, contracting knowledge regarding some atoms and revising others (or any other combination), a property not available in conventional revision schemes.

Another important consideration in belief revision is the problem of *iterated revisions*. All the algorithms described so far work well with one revision, but there are sequences of revisions which give counter-intuitive results if we process each one individually. The main problem regarding these algorithms is the fact that the belief base is not properly selected after each revision, because the algorithms are only concerned with the result of the revision and do not keep information regarding the previous KB states. This can cause the loss of valuable information as far as future revisions are concerned. One proposed solution to this problem is to process the sequence of revisions as a whole [5, 16].

In our method, iterated revisions are inherently supported. Each line in the KB matrix contains the additive information over all revisions (for a certain combination of lines) regarding the truth and falsehood of each atom in the world. By not removing any lines from the KB, we lose no data regarding past revisions, because all world states are kept. Such states may be useful in future revisions.

An example will show this fact. Suppose the propositions: $p_1 = \alpha \leftrightarrow b$, $p_2 = \alpha \leftrightarrow c$, and $p_3 = b \leftrightarrow c$, with a reliability of 1, as well as the proposition $p_4 = \alpha \leftrightarrow (\neg b)$ with a reliability of 2. It is easily verified that the intuitively correct result for the revisions $p_1 \bullet p_2$ and $p_1 \bullet p_3$ is $\alpha \leftrightarrow b \leftrightarrow c$. If we subsequently revise with p_4, the intuitively correct result is different in each case. Specifically, given the increased reliability of p_4, we should have $(p_1 \bullet p_2) \bullet p_4 = \alpha \leftrightarrow (\neg b) \leftrightarrow c$ and $(p_1 \bullet p_3) \bullet p_4 = (\neg \alpha) \leftrightarrow b \leftrightarrow c$. Most revision schemes (e.g., Dalal's [3, 4]) would give $(p_1 \bullet p_2) \bullet p_4 = (p_1 \bullet p_3) \bullet p_4 = \alpha \leftrightarrow (\neg b)$, thus losing all information regarding c. This happens because Dalal's algorithm does not support iterated revisions.

Let us assume that the reliability of $x+yi$ is $|x-y|$, that of a line is the sum of the element reliabilities and LS is the function described in the previous example. It is easy to verify that, under this parameterization, our revision operator gives the intuitively correct results for $p_1 \bullet p_2$, $p_1 \bullet p_3$, $(p_1 \bullet p_2) \bullet p_4$ and $(p_1 \bullet p_3) \bullet p_4$. The additional information that is needed in order to do the second revision correctly is "hidden" in the contradictory lines of the first revision in both cases. These are ignored when answering queries after the first revision, but they play an important role in the formulation of the result of the second revision. If such lines were permanently discarded after the first revision, we would get the same (incorrect) result as Dalal's operator. A detailed proof of these facts is omitted due to lack of space.

Unfortunately, there is an annoying fact about the above method; the number of lines in a KB is exponential with respect to the number of revisions performed, making the KB matrix too large to be manageable. We propose the technique of *abruption*, a procedure that permanently prunes lines from the KB. The selection of the lines to be removed could be made using functions similar to the RE, RL and LS functions. However, we should bear in mind that such removal always implies loss of knowledge; thus, the use of abruption is a trade-off between knowledge integrity and processing speed and should be carefully designed to prune lines that are too far from the real world to ever affect the result of QT. The effect of abruption upon the complexity and the correctness of the revision algorithm varies from case to case and is another application-specific parameter for which no universally defined function can work satisfactorily.

7   Conclusions and Future Work

In this paper, we used an innovative representation of propositional expressions to address the problem of belief revision. The approach was proven fruitful, resulting in a very flexible and general-purpose method of revising beliefs. The introduction of RF and the quantitative nature of the representation introduce an increased expressiveness, allowing the use of features not normally available, like negative knowledge or the integration of "knowledge change" operators.

We believe that much more work needs to be done in order to fully exploit this representation's capabilities. The behavior of our algorithm under different parameter selections (RE, RL and LS functions, RF selection, abruption effects etc) is only partially explored. Such a study may reveal interesting connections between our method and existing approaches, such as the general conditions under which the AGM postulates are satisfied. It would also allow us to formulate some general, formal methods regarding the integration of operators that was informally described above. Finally, knowledge representation issues could be addressed under the light of this new representation.

References

[1] Alchourron C., Gärdenfors P. and Makinson D.: "On the Logic of Theory Change: Partial Meet Contraction and Revision Functions", *The Journal of Symbolic Logic*, Vol.50, pp.510-530, 1985. 113

[2] Bertino E., Catania B. and Zarri G. P.: "*Intelligent Database Systems*", ACM Press, 2001. 100

[3] Dalal M.: "Investigations Into a Theory of Knowledge Base Revision: Preliminary Report", *Proceedings 7th National Conference on Artificial Intelligence*, pp.475-479, 1988. 111, 112, 115

[4] Dalal M.: "Updates in Propositional Databases", Technical Report, DCS-TR-222, Department of Computer Science, Rutgers University, February 1988. 111, 112, 115

[5] Darwiche A. and Pearl J.: "On the Logic of Iterated Belief Revision", *Artificial Intelligence*, Vol.89, No.1-2, pp.1-29, 1997. 115

[6] Flouris G. and Plexousakis D.: "Belief Revision in Propositional Knowledge Bases", *Proceedings 8th Panhellenic Conference on Informatics*, Nicosia, Cyprus, November 2001. 101

[7] Flouris G. and Plexousakis D.: "Belief Revision using Table Transformation", Technical Report TR-290, ICS-FORTH, July 2001. 104, 106, 107, 109, 113

[8] Gärdenfors P.: "Belief Revision: An introduction", pp.1-20 in "*Belief Revision*", by P. Gärdenfors (ed.), Cambridge University Press, 1992. 113, 115

[9] Gärdenfors P.: "The Dynamics of Knowledge and Belief: Foundational vs. Coherence Theories", *Revue Internationale de Philosophie*, Vol.44, pp.24-46. Reprinted in "*Knowledge, Belief and Strategic Interaction*", by Bicchieri and M. L. dalla Chiara (eds.), Cambridge University Press, Cambridge, pp.377-396, 1992. 110, 111

[10] Harman G.: "*Change in View: Principles of Reasoning*", Bradford Books, MIT Press, Cambridge, MA, 1986. 110

[11] Hansson S. O.: "In Defense of Base Contraction", *Synthese*, Vol.91, pp.239-245, 1992. 111

[12] Katsuno H. and Mendelzon A.: "On the Difference Between Updating a Logical Database and Revising it", in "*Belief Revision*", by Gärdenfors P. (ed.), Cambridge University Press, 1992. 113, 115

[13] Katsuno H. and Mendelzon A.: "Propositional Knowledge Base Revision and Minimal Change", KRR-TR-90-3, Technical Reports on Knowledge Representation and Reasoning, University of Toronto, March 1990. 113

[14] Konieczny S. and Marquis P.: "Three-valued Logics for Inconsistency Handling", *Proceedings 8th European Conference in Artificial Intelligence (JELIA02)*, 2002. 111

[15] Levesque H. J. and Lakemeyer G.: "*The Logic of Knowledge Bases*", MIT Press, 2000. 100

[16] Liberatore P.: "The Complexity of Iterated Belief Revision", *Proceedings 6th ICDT Conference*, pp.276-290, 1997. 115

[17] Makinson D.: "How to Give it up: a Survey of some Formal Aspects of the Logic of Theory Change", *Synthese*, Vol.62, pp.347-363, 1985. 113, 115

[18] Nebel B.: "A Knowledge Level Analysis of Belief Revision", *Proceedings 1st International Conference on Principles of Knowledge Representation and Reasoning*, pp.301-311, 1989. 111, 113

Efficiently Maintaining Structural Associations of Semistructured Data

Dimitrios Katsaros

Department of Informatics, Aristotle University of Thessaloniki
Thessaloniki, 54124, Greece
dkatsaro@csd.auth.gr

Abstract. Semistructured data arise frequently in the Web or in data integration systems. Semistructured objects describing the same type of information have similar but not identical structure. Finding the common schema of a collection of semistructured objects is a very important task and due to the huge volume of such data encountered, data mining techniques have been employed. Maintenance of the discovered schema in case of updates, i.e., addition of new objects, is also a very important issue. In this paper, we study the problem of maintaining the discovered schema in the case of the addition of new objects. We use the notion of "negative borders" introduced in the context of mining association rules in order to efficiently find the new schema when objects are added to the database. We present experimental results that show the improved efficiency achieved by the proposed algorithm.

1 Introduction

Much of the information that is available on-line, is semistructured [1]. Documents like XML, BibTex, HTML and data encountered in biological applications are examples of such information. The intrinsic characteristic of semistructured data is that they do not have a rigid structure, either because the data source does not force any structure on them (e.g., the Web) or because the data are acquired from various heterogeneous information sources (e.g., in applications that use business-to-business product catalogs, data from multiple suppliers – each with its own schema – must be integrated, so that buyers can query them).

It is quite common that semistructured objects representing the same sort of information have similar, though not identical, structure. An example of semistructured objects is depicted in Figure 1, where a portion of semistructured "fish" objects, maintained by the "Catalogue of Life" database (found in URL http://www.sp2000.org), is illustrated.

Finding the common schema of a large collection of semistructured objects is very important for a number of applications, such as querying/browsing information sources, building indexes, storage in relational or object oriented database systems, query processing (regular path expressions), clustering documents based on their common structure, building wrappers.

Y. Manolopoulos et al. (Eds.): PCI 2001, LNCS 2563, pp. 118–132, 2003.

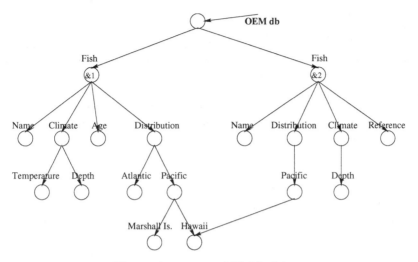

Fig. 1. A portion of "fish" objects

Semistructured schema discovery is a challenging task, mainly for two reasons. The first is the huge volume of data and the second is their irregularity. Several approaches targeting at this goal have been done [8, 14, 13, 10] to name a few. Due to the huge amount of data to be processed, the primary requirement for the algorithm employed is its scalability, both in terms of input and output data. The algorithm presented by Wang and Liu in [13], *WL* in the sequel, meets this requirement. Its objective is to discover all "typical" structures (substructures) that occur in a minimum number of objects specified by the user. *WL* is based on the association rule discovery [2] paradigm.

When insertions take place into the collection (i.e., an "increment" database is added into the "regular" database), which is a very frequent situation in the Web, then the set of the aforementioned "typical" structures may change. Thus, arises the need to maintain the set of discovered structures.

1.1 Motivation

The only work addressing this issue is that reported in [15], which presents the algorithm *ZJZT*. They adopt the FUp [4] algorithm, that was proposed for the maintenance of the discovered large itemsets from a transaction database. In each iteration, *ZJZT* makes a scan over the whole updated database. The increment database is scanned first and the results are used to guide the mining of the regular database. The number of iterations is k, where k is the size of the largest (in terms of the number of path expressions it contains) *tree expression* (the definition of tree expression is presented in Section 2).

Incremental schema maintenance for semistructured data as addressed by *ZJZT*, suffers from two main drawbacks. The first is that the employed algorithm is inefficient, since it requires at least as many passes over the database as the "size" of the longest *j-sequence*. Even in the case that the new results are merely a subset of the old results, that is, the updates do not modify the schema, their algorithm will make the same constant number of passes over the database. The second is that their method cannot provide the mining results for the increment database itself. These results are important in order to discover temporal changes in the schema and drive decisions regarding storage issues [5]. So, we employ the notion of *negative borders* [3, 6, 9, 11] in order to efficiently deal with the problem of efficient incremental schema maintenance for semistructured data.

1.2   Contributions

In this paper, we deal with the problem of how to efficiently maintain the discovered schema (structural associations) of a collection of semistructured objects in the case of insertions of new objects into the collection. We utilize the notion of *negative borders* [7] and devise the $DeltaSSD$ algorithm, which is an adaptation of the *Delta* algorithm [9], in order to efficiently find the new schema of the collection.

We present a performance evaluation of $DeltaSSD$ and a comparison with existing algorithms using synthetic data. The experiments show that $DeltaSSD$ incurs the least number of database scans among all algorithms, which indicates its superiority.

The rest of this paper is organized as follows: Section 2 defines the problem of the incremental maintenance of semistructured schema. Section 3 presents the proposed algorithm $DeltaSSD$. Section 4 presents the experimental results and finally, Section 5 contains the conclusions.

2   Incremental Schema Mining

For our convenience, we recall some definitions from [13] and some features of the *WL* and *ZJZT* algorithms.

2.1   Overview of the *WL* Algorithm

We adopt the *Object Exchange Model* [1] for the representation of semistructured objects, where each object is identified by a unique identifier $\&a$ and its value $val(\&a)$. Its value may be *atomic* (e.g., integer, string), a *list* $\langle l_1 : \&a_1, l_2 : \&a_2, \cdots, l_n : \&a_n \rangle$ or a *bag* $\{l_1 : \&a_1, l_2 : \&a_2, \cdots, l_n : \&a_n\}^1$, where each l_i identifies a label. For the incremental schema maintenance problem (to be defined shortly after) the user must specify some objects, called *transaction objects* and denoted as $\top$, whose common structure we are interested in identifying (e.g., in Figure 1 the transaction objects are the fish objects $\&1$ and $\&2$).

---

[1] Order does matter in a list but it does not in a bag. We deal only with nodes of list type, since our target is ordered semistructured data (e.g., XML).

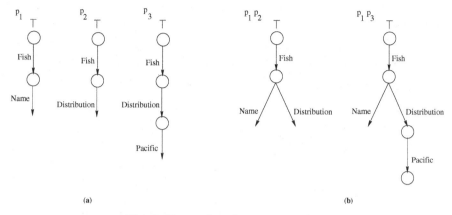

Fig. 2. Examples of tree expressions

Definition 1 (Tree Expressions). *Consider an acyclic OEM graph. For any label l, let l^* denote either l or the wild-card label ?, which matches any label.*

1. *The nil structure $\perp$ (that denotes containment of no label at all) is a tree-expression.*
2. *Suppose that te_i are tree expressions of objects a_i, $1 \leq i \leq p$. If $val(\&a) = \langle l_1 : \&a_1, l_2 : \&a_2, \cdots, l_p : \&a_p \rangle$ and $\langle i_1, i_2, \cdots, i_q \rangle$ is a subsequence of $\langle 1, \cdots, p \rangle$ $q > 0$, then $\langle l_{i_1}^* : te_{i_1}, \cdots, l_{i_q}^* : te_{i_q} \rangle$ is a tree-expression of object a.*

Therefore, a tree expression represents a partial structure of the corresponding object. A *k-tree-expression* is a tree-expression containing exactly k leaf nodes. Hence, a 1-tree-expression is the familiar notion of a *path expression*. Figure 2(a) shows three 1-tree expressions, p_1, p_2, p_3. Each k-tree-expression can be constructed by a sequence of k paths $(p_1, p_2, \cdots, p_k)$, called *k-sequence*, where no p_i is a prefix of another. For example, Figure 2(b) illustrates two 2-tree expressions. In the same example, we see that we can not combine the 1-tree expressions p_2 and p_3 to form a 2-tree expression, since the former is prefix of the latter.

In order to account for the fact that some children have repeating outgoing labels, *WL* introduced superscripts for these labels. Hence, for each label l in $val(\&a)$, l^i represents the i-th occurrence of label l in $val(\&a)$. Consequently, a k-tree-expression can be constructed by a k-sequence $(p_1, p_2, \cdots, p_k)$, each p_i of the form $[\top, l_{j_1}^1, \cdots, l_{j_n}^n, \perp]$. Although Definition 1 holds for acyclic graphs, in [13] cyclic OEM graphs are mapped to acyclic ones by treating each reference to an ancestor (that creates the cycle) as a reference to a terminating leaf node. In this case, the leaf obtains a label which corresponds to the distance of the leaf from its ancestor (i.e., the number of intermediate nodes). For this reason, henceforth, we consider only acyclic OEM graphs. Additionally, *WL* replicates each node that has more than one ancestors. The result of the above transformation is that each object is equivalently represented by a tree structure.

Definition 2 (Weaker than). *The nil structure $\perp$ is weaker than every tree-expression.*

1. *Tree-expression $\langle l_1 : te_1, l_2 : te_2, \cdots, l_n : te_n \rangle$ is weaker than tree-expression $\langle l'_1 : te'_1, l'_2 : te'_2, \cdots, l'_m : te'_m \rangle$ if for $1 \leq i \leq n$, te_i is weaker than some te_{j_i}, where either $l'_{j_i} = l_i$ or $l_i = ?$ and $\langle j_1, j_2, \cdots, j_n \rangle$ is a subsequence of $\langle 1, 2, \cdots, m \rangle$.*
2. *Tree-expression te is weaker than identifier &a if te is weaker than val(&a).*

This definition captures the fact that a tree-expression te_1 is weaker than another tree-expression te_2 if all information regarding labels, ordering and nesting present in te_1 is also present in te_2. Intuitively, by considering the paradigm of association rules [2], the notion of tree expression (Definition 1) is the analogous of the *itemset* of a transaction and the notion of weaker-than relationship (Definition 2) corresponds to the *containment* of an itemset by a transaction (or by another itemset).

The target of *WL* is to discover all tree expressions that appear in a percentage of the total number of the transaction objects. This percentage is defined by the user and it is called minimum support, *MINSUP*.

WL works in phases. In each phase, it makes a pass over the transaction database. Firstly, it determines the frequent path expressions, that is, frequent 1-tree-expressions. Then it makes several iterations. At the k-th ($k \geq 1$) iteration *WL* constructs a set of candidate $(k+1)$-tree-expressions using the frequent k-sequences and applying some pruning criteria. This set is a superset of the actual frequent $(k+1)$-tree-expressions. Then, it determines the support of the candidates by scanning over the database of transaction objects.

2.2 Problem Definition

We describe below the problem of incremental semistructured schema maintenance in the case that new objects are added into the database.

Definition 3 (Incremental Schema Maintenance). *Consider a collection of transaction objects in an OEM graph and a minimum support threshold MINSUP. Let this collection be named db (regular database). Suppose that we have found the frequent (or large) tree expressions for db, that is, the tree expressions which have support greater than or equal to MINSUP. Suppose that a number of new objects is added into the collection. Let the collection of these objects be named idb (increment database). The incremental schema maintenance problem is to discover all tree expressions which have support in $db \cup idb$ greater than or equal to MINSUP.*

When insertions into a database take place, then some large tree expressions can become small in the updated database (called "losers"), whereas some small tree expressions can become large (called "winners").

ZJZT is based on the idea that instead of ignoring the old large tree expressions, and re-running *WL* on the updated database, *the information from the old large tree expressions can be reused.*

ZJZT works in several passes. In the k-th phase ($k \geq 1$), it scans the increment and recognizes which of the old large k-tree expressions remain large and which become "losers". In the same scan, it discovers the k-tree expressions, which are large in the increment and do not belong to the set of the old large k-tree expressions. These are the candidates to become large k-tree expressions in the updated database. Their support is checked by scanning the regular database. A more detailed description of *ZJZT* can be found in [4, 15].

3 The *DeltaSSD* Algorithm

3.1 The Notion of the *Negative Border*

It is obvious that scanning the regular database many times, as *ZJZT* does, can be time-consuming and in some cases useless, if the large tree expressions of the updated database are merely a subset of the large tree expressions of the regular database. So, [11, 6, 3] considered *using not only the large tree expressions of the regular database, but the candidates that failed to become large in the regular database*, as well. These candidates are called the *negative border* [12].

Below we give the formal definition of the *negative border* of a set of tree expressions.

Definition 4 ([7]). *Let the collection of all possible 1-tree expressions be denoted as R. Given a collection of $S \subseteq \mathcal{P}(R)$ of tree expressions,[2] closed with respect to the "weaker than" relation, the negative border Bd^- of S consists of the minimal tree expressions $X \subseteq R$ not in S.*

The collection of all frequent tree expressions is closed with respect to the "weaker than" relationship (Theorem 3.1 [13]). The collection of all candidate tree expressions that were not frequent is the negative border of the collection of the frequent tree expressions.

3.2 The *DeltaSSD* Algorithm

The proposed algorithm utilizes negative borders in order to avoid scanning multiple times the database for the discovery of the new large tree expressions. It differs from [11, 6, 3] in the way it computes the negative border closure. It adopts a hybrid approach between the one layer at a time followed by [6, 3] and the full closure followed by [11]. In summary, after mining the regular database, *DeltaSSD* keeps the support of the large tree expressions along with the support of their negative border. Having this information, it process the increment database in order to discover if there are any tree expressions that moved from the negative border to the set of the new large tree expressions. If there are such tree expressions, then it computes the new negative border. If there are tree expressions with unknown support in the new negative border and

---

[2] The "power-set" $\mathcal{P}(R)$ includes only "natural" and "near-natural" tree expressions (see [13]).

Table 1. Symbols

Symbol	Explanation
db, idb, DB $(= db \cup idb)$	regular, increment and updated database
L^{db}, L^{idb}, L^{DB}	frequent tree expressions of db, idb and DB
N^{db}, N^{idb}, N^{DB}	negative border of db, idb and DB
TE^{db}	$L^{db} \cup N^{db}$
L, N	$L^{DB} \cap (L^{db} \cup N^{db})$, Negative border of L
$SupportOf(set, \ database)$	updates the support count of the tree expressions in set w.r.t. the $database$
$NB(set)$	computes the negative border of the set
$LargeOf(set, \ database)$	returns the tree expressions in set which have support count above MINSUP in the $database$

are large in the increment database, then $\mathcal{D}eltaSSD$ scans the regular database, in order to find their support.

The description of the $\mathcal{D}eltaSSD$ requires the notation presented in Table 1.

First Scan of the Increment. Firstly, the support of the tree expressions which belong to L^{db} and N^{db} is updated with respect to the increment database. It is possible that some tree expressions of L^{db} may become small and some others of N^{db} may become large. Let the resulting large tree expressions be denoted as L and the remaining $(L^{db} \cup N^{db}) - L$ tree expressions as *Small*. If no tree expressions that belonged to N^{db} become large, then the algorithm terminates. This is the case that the new results are a subset of the old results and the proposed algorithm is optimal in that it makes only a single scan over the increment database. This is valid due to the following theorem [11]:

Theorem 1. *Let s be a tree-expression such that $s \notin L^{db}$ and $s \in L^{DB}$. Then, there exists a tree-expression t such that t is "weaker than" s, $t \in N^{db}$ and $t \in L^{DB}$. That is, some "component" tree-expression of s moved from N^{db} to L^{DB}.*

Second Scan of the Increment. If some tree expressions do move from N^{db} to L, then we compute the negative border N of L. The negative border is computed using the routine presented in [13], which generates the k-sequences from the $k-1$ sequences. Tree expressions in N with unknown counts are stored in a set N^u. Only the tree expressions in N^u and their extensions may be large. If N^u is empty, then the algorithm terminates. Any element of N^u that is not large in db cannot be large in $db \cup idb$ [4]. Moreover, none of its extensions can be large (antimonotonicity property [2]). So, a second scan over the increment is made in order to find the support counts of N^u.

Third Scan of the Increment. Then, we compute the negative border closure of L and store them in a set C. After removing from C the tree expressions that belong to $L \cup N^u$ for which the support is known, we compute the support counts of the remaining tree expressions in the increment database.

First Scan of the Regular Database. The locally large in idb tree expressions, say $ScanDB$, of the closure must be verified in db, as well, so a scan over the regular database is performed. In the same scan, we compute the support counts of the negative border of $L \cup ScanDB$, since from this set and from $Small$ we will get the actual negative border of the large tree expressions of $db \cup idb$. After that scan the large tree expressions from $ScanDB$ and the tree expressions in L comprise the new set of the large tree expressions in $db \cup idb$.

Table 2. The $\mathcal{D}eltaSSD$ algorithm

$\mathcal{D}eltaSSD$ $(db, idb, L^{db}, N^{db})$
$//db$: the regular database, idb: the increment database
$//L^{db}, N^{db}$: the large tree expressions of db and their negative border, respectively.

$BEGIN$
1        $SupportOf(TE^{db}, idb)$ //First scan over the increment.
2        $L = LargeOf(TE^{db}, DB)$
3        $Small = TE^{db} - L$
4        $if\ (L == L^{db})$ //New results alike the old ones.
                $RETURN(L^{db}, N^{db})$
5        $N = NB(L)$
6        $if\ (N \subseteq Small)$
                $RETURN(L, N)$
7        $N^u = N - Small$
8        $SupportOf(N^u, idb)$ //Second scan over the increment.
9        $C = LargeOf(N^u)$
10       $Small^{idb} = N^u - C$
11       $if\ (|C|)$
12            $C = C \cup L$
13            $repeat$ //Compute the negative border closure.
14                 $C = C \cup NB(C)$
15                 $C = C - (Small \cup Small^{idb})$
16            $until\ (C\ does\ not\ grow)$
17            $C = C - (L \cup N^u)$
18            $if\ (|C|)\ then\ SupportOf(C, idb)$ //Third scan over the increment.
19       $ScanDB = LargeOf(C \cup N^u, idb)$
20       $N' = NB(L \cup ScanDB) - Small$
21       $SupportOf(N' \cup ScanDB,\ db)$ //First scan over the regular.
22       $L^{DB} = L \cup LargeOf(ScanDB, DB)$
23       $N^{DB} = NB(L^{DB})$
END

Table 3. The regular and increment database

db		idb	
1)	a, b	1)	a, b, c
2)	a, b	2)	a, b, c, d
3)	a, c	3)	a, d, g
4)	b, c		
5)	c, d		
6)	a, d, f		
7)	a, d, g		
8)	b, f, g		
9)	a, c, i		

3.3   Mining Results for the Increment

Executing the above algorithm results in computing $L^{db \cup idb}$ and $N^{db \cup idb}$ and their support. We also need the complete mining results for the increment database idb, that is, L^{idb} and N^{idb} and their support. We describe how this can be achieved without additional cost, but during the three passes over the increment database. After the first pass, we know the support of the tree-expressions belonging to $L^{db \cup idb}$ and $N^{db \cup idb}$ in the increment itself. From these, we identify the frequent ones and compute their negative border. If some tree-expressions belonging to the negative border are not in $L^{db \cup idb} \cup N^{db \cup idb}$ we compute their support during the second pass over the increment. Then the negative border closure of the resulting (frequent in idb) tree-expressions is computed. If there are new tree-expressions, which belong to the closure and whose support in idb is not known, then their support is computed in the third pass over the increment.

Example 1. We give a short example of the execution of the $\mathcal{D}eltaSSD$. For the sake of simplicity, we present the example using flat itemsets and the set containment relationship instead of tree expressions and the weaker than relationship. Suppose that all the possible "items" are the following $R = \{a, b, c, d, f, g, i\}$. Let the regular database be comprised by nine transactions and the increment database be comprised by three transactions. The databases are presented in Table 3. Let the support threshold be 33.3%. Thus, an item(set) is large in the regular database, if it appears in at least three transactions out of the nine.

We can confirm that the frequent "items" in the regular database db are the following $L^{db} = \{a, b, c, d\}$. Thus, their negative border, which is comprised by the itemsets that failed to become large, is $N^{db} = \{f, g, i, ab, ac, ad, bc, bd, cd\}$. The steps of the $\mathcal{D}eltaSSD$ proceed as shown in Table 4.

Table 4. An example execution of the $\mathcal{D}eltaSSD$ algorithm

---

$\mathcal{D}eltaSSD\ (db, idb, L^{db}, N^{db})$
Input: $L^{db} = \{a, b, c, d\}$ and $N^{db} = \{f, g, i, ab, ac, ad, bc, bd, cd\}$

BEGIN

1	count support of $(L^{db} \cup N^{db} = \{a, b, c, d, f, g, i, ab, ac, ad, bc, bd, cd\})$ in idb
2	$L = \text{LargeOf}(L^{db} \cup N^{db})$ in $DB \implies L = \{a, b, c, d, ab, ac, ad\}$
3	$Small = (L^{db} \cup N^{db}) - L \implies Small = \{f, g, i, bc, bd, cd\}$
4	$L \neq L^{db}$
5	$N = \text{NegativeBorderOf}(L) \implies N = \{f, g, i, bc, bd, cd, abc, abd, acd\}$
6	$N \subsetneq Small$
7	$N^u = N - Small \implies N^u = \{abc, abd, acd\}$
8	count support of $(N^u = \{abc, abd, acd\})$ in idb
9	$C = \text{LargeOf}(N^u)$ in $idb \implies C = \{abc, abd, acd\}$
10	$Small^{idb} = N^u - C \implies Small^{idb} = \emptyset$
11	$C \neq \emptyset$ thus
12	$\quad C = C \cup L \implies C = \{a, b, c, d, ab, ac, ad, abc, abd, acd\}$
13	$\quad repeat$ //Compute the negative border closure.
14	$\quad\quad C = C \cup \text{NegativeBorderOf}(C)$
15	$\quad\quad C = C - (Small \cup Small^{idb})$
16	$\quad until\ (C$ does not grow)
	$\quad$ Finally: $C = \{a, b, c, d, ab, ac, ad, abc, abd, acd, abcd\}$
17	$\quad C = C - (L \cup N^u) \implies C = \{abcd\}$
18	$\quad C \neq \emptyset$ thus
	$\quad\quad$ count support of $(C = \{abcd\})$ in idb
19	$ScanDB = \text{LargeOf}\ (C \cup N^u)$ in $idb \implies ScanDB = \{abc, abd, acd, abcd\}$
20	$N' = \text{NegativeBorderOf}(L \cup ScanDB) - Small \implies N' = \emptyset$
21	count support of $(N' \cup ScanDB = \{abc, abd, acd, abcd\})$ in db
22	$L^{DB} = L \cup \text{LargeOf}(ScanDB)$ in $DB \implies L^{DB} = \{a, b, c, d, ab, ac, ad\}$
23	$N^{DB} = \text{NegativeBorderOf}(L^{DB}) \implies N^{DB} = \{f, g, i, bc, bd, cd\}$

END

---

4   Experiments

We conducted experiments in order to evaluate the efficiency of the proposed approach $\mathcal{D}eltaSSD$ with respect to $ZJZT$, and also with respect to WL, that is, re-running Wang's algorithm on the whole updated database.

4.1   Generation of Synthetic Workloads

We generated acyclic transaction objects, whose nodes have list semantics. Each workload is a set of transaction objects. The method used to generate synthetic transaction objects is based on [2, 13] with some modifications noted below.

Each transaction object is a hierarchy of objects. *Atomic* objects, located at level 0, are the objects having no descendants. The *height* (or *level*) of an object is the length of the longest path from that object to a descendant atomic object. All transaction objects are at the same level m, which is the *maximal nesting level*. Each object is recognized by an identifier. The number of identifiers for objects of level i is N_i. Each object is assigned one (*incoming*) label, which represents a "role" for that object. Any object i that has as subobject an object j, will be connected to j through an edge labelled with the label of object j. All transaction objects have the same incoming label.

Objects belonging to the same level are assigned labels drawn from a set, different for each level i, with cardinality equal to L_i. We treat each object serially and draw a label using a self-similar distribution. This power law provides the means to select some labels ("roles"), more frequently than others. A parameter of this distribution determines the skewness of the distribution ranging from uniform to highly skewed. In our experiments, we set this parameter equal to 0.36 to account for a small bias.

The number of the subobject references of an object at level i is uniformly distributed with mean equal to T_i. The selection of subobjects models the fact that some structures appear in common in many objects. To achieve this, we used the notion of *potentially large sets* [2]. Thus, subobject references for an object at level i are not completely random, but instead are drawn from a pool of *potentially large sets*. If the *maximum nesting level* equals m, then this pool is comprised by $m - 1$ portions, namely $\Gamma_1, \Gamma_2, \ldots, \Gamma_{m-1}$. Each Γ_i is comprised by sets of level-i identifiers. The average size of such a set is I_i. More details regarding these sets can be found in [2]. The construction of the objects is a bottom-up process. Starting from level-2, we must construct N_2 objects. For each object, we first choose the number of its subobject references (its size) and then pick several potential large sets from Γ_1 until its size is reached. Recursively, we construct the level-3 objects and so on. For any object belonging to any level, say level $i > 2$, we obligatorily choose one potentially large set from Γ_{i-1} and then we choose the rest of the potentially large sets equiprobably from all $\Gamma_j, 1 \leq j < i$.

Thus, a generated data set in which transaction objects are at level m will be represented as: $\langle L_1, N_1, I_1, P_1 \rangle$, $\langle L_2, N_2, T_2, I_2, P_2 \rangle, \ldots, \langle N_m, T_m \rangle$. [3] Table 5 presents the notation for the generation of synthetic data.

The way we create the increment is a straightforward extension of the technique used to synthesize the database. In order to do a comparison on a database of size $|db|$ with an increment of size $|idb|$, we first generate a database of size $|db + idb|$ and then the first $|db|$ transactions are stored in the regular database and the rest $|idb|$ are stored in the increment database. This method will produce data that are identically distributed in both db and idb and was followed in [4, 9], as well.

---

[3] Remember that $T_1 = 0$, $L_m = 1$ and that there is no Γ_m.

Table 5. Notation used for the generation of synthetic data

Symbol	Explanation
L_i	Number of level-i labels
N_i	Number of level-i object identifiers
T_i	Average size of $val(o)$ for level-i identifiers o
I_i	Average size of potentially large sets in Γ_i
P_i	Number of potentially large sets in Γ_i
m	maximal nesting level

4.2   Experimental Results

For all the experiments reported below, we used the following dataset comprised by 30000 transaction objects: $\langle 100, 5000, 3, 100 \rangle$, $\langle 500, 500, 8, 3, 400 \rangle$, $\langle 3000, 8 \rangle$.

We used as performance measure the number of passes over the whole database $db \cup idb$. For an algorithm, which makes α passes over the regular database and β passes over the increment database, the number of passes is estimated as $\frac{\alpha * |db| + \beta * |idb|}{|db| + |idb|}$, where $|db|$ and $|idb|$ is the number of transactions of the regular and the increment database, respectively.

Varying the Support Threshold. Our first experiment aimed at comparing the performance of the algorithms for various support thresholds and the results are depicted in Figure 3. We observe that $DeltaSSD$ performs much better than the rest of the algorithms and makes on the average (almost) only one pass over the whole database. For higher support thresholds, it performs even better, because it does not scan the regular database, but scans once or twice the increment database. $ZJZT$ and WL perform 4 full scans, because the number of passes depends on the number of leaves of the tree expression with the largest number of leaves.

Varying the Increment Size. Our second experiment aimed at evaluating the performance of the algorithms for various increment sized. The results are depicted in Figure 4. We notice that $ZJZT$ and WL make the same constant number of scans for the reason explained earlier, whereas the number of scans performed by $DeltaSSD$ increases slightly with the increment size, as a function of the increment size and the number of candidate tree expressions that move from the negative border to the set of the large tree expressions, imposing a scan over the regular database.

Comparison of $ZJZT$ and WL. Since both $ZJZT$ and WL perform the same number of scans over the database, we further investigated their performance by comparing the number of node comparisons they make during the tree matching

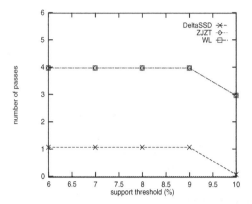

Fig. 3. Database passes with varying support threshold (10% increment)

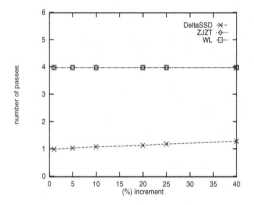

Fig. 4. Database passes with varying increment size (8% support)

operation (involved in the computation of the *weaker than* relationship). This measure is independent on any particular implementation and reflects the CPU time cost of the algorithms. The results are depicted in Figure 5.[4]

We can observe that with increasing support the performance gap between *ZJZT* and *WL* broadens, because higher support means fewer candidate tree expressions and even fewer large tree expressions and thus smaller number of tree matchings.

Increment sizes impacts also the performance of the algorithms. Larger increment means that more new candidates arise in the increment and thus larger number of tree matchings in order to count their support both in the increment and in the regular database. Thus, the number of comparisons made by

---

[4] The right graph presents the ratio of the number of node comparisons made by *ZJZT* to the number of comparisons made by *WL*.

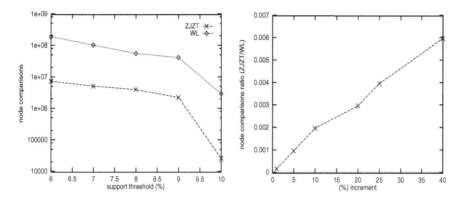

Fig. 5. *Left* Varying support (10% increment), *Right* Varying increment size (8% support)

ZJZT increases with respect to *WL* (larger ratio, as depicted in the right part of Figure 5).

The results clearly indicate the superiority of the *DeltaSSD* algorithm, which performs the smaller number of scans over the database. The *ZJZT* algorithm performs the same number of scans with *WL*. This is expected, since the number of scans depends on the size (in terms of the number of path expressions it contains) of the largest *tree-expression*. But, *ZJZT* is much better than *WL* for low and large support thresholds and small increment sizes, whereas their performance gap narrows for moderate support thresholds and large increment sizes.

5   Conclusions

As the amount of on-line semistructured data grows very fast, arises the need to efficiently maintain their "schema". We have considered the problem of incrementally mining structural associations from semistructured data. We exploited the previous mining results, that is, knowledge of the *tree-expressions* that were frequent in the previous database along with their negative border, in order to efficiently identify the frequent *tree-expressions* in the updated database.

We presented the *DeltaSSD* algorithm, which guarantees efficiency by ensuring that at most three passes over the increment database and one pass over the original database will be conducted for any data set. Moreover, in the cases where the new "schema" is a subset of the old, *DeltaSSD* is optimal in the sense that it will make only one scan over the increment database.

Using synthetic data, we conducted experiments in order to assess its performance and compared it with the *WL* and *ZJZT* algorithms. Our experiments showed that for a variety of increment sizes and support thresholds,

$\mathcal{D}eltaSSD$ performs much better than its competitors making (almost) only one scan over the whole database.

In summary, $\mathcal{D}eltaSSD$ is a practical, robust and efficient algorithm for the incremental maintenance of structural associations of semistructured data.

References

[1] S. Abiteboul. Querying semistructured data. In *Proceedings 6th ICDT Conference*, pages 1–18, 1997. 118, 120

[2] R. Agrawal and R. Srikant. Fast algorithms for mining association rules in large databases. In *Proceedings 20th VLDB Conference*, pages 487–499, 1994. 119, 122, 124, 127, 128

[3] Y. Aumann, R. Feldman, O. Liphstat, and H. Mannila. Borders: an efficient algorithm for association generation in dynamic databases. *Journal of Intelligent Information Systems*, 12(1):61–73, 1999. 120, 123

[4] D. Cheung, J. Han, V. Ng, and C. Wong. Maintenance of discovered association rules in large databases: An incremental updating technique. In *Proceedings 12th IEEE ICDE Conference*, pages 106–114, 1996. 119, 123, 124, 128

[5] A. Deutsch, M. Fernandez, and D. Suciu. Storing semistructured data with STORED. In *Proceedings ACM SIGMOD Conference*, pages 431–442, 1999. 120

[6] R. Feldman, Y. Aumann, A. Amir, and H. Mannila. Efficient algorithms for discovering frequent sets in incremental databases. In *Proceedings ACM DMKD Workshop*, 1997. 120, 123

[7] H Mannila and H. Toivonen. Levelwise search and borders of theories in knowledge discovery. *Data Mining and Knowledge Discovery*, 1(3):241–258, 1997. 120, 123

[8] S. Nestorov, S. Abiteboul, and R. Motwani. Extracting schema from semistructured data. In *Proceedings ACM SIGMOD Conference*, pages 295–306, 1998. 119

[9] V. Pudi and J. Haritsa. Quantifying the utility of the past in mining large databases. *Information Systems*, 25(5):323–343, 2000. 120, 128

[10] A. Rajaraman and J. Ullman. Querying Websites using compact skeletons. In *Proceedings 20th ACM PODS Symposium*, 2001. 119

[11] S. Thomas, S. Bodagala, K. Alsabti, and S. Ranka. An efficient algorithm for the incremental updation of association rules in large databases. In *Proceedings KDD Conference*, pages 263–266, 1997. 120, 123, 124

[12] H. Toivonen. Sampling large databases for association rules. In *Proceedings 22nd VLDB Conference*, pages 134–145, 1996. 123

[13] K. Wang and H. Liu. Discovering structural association of semistructured data. *IEEE Transactions on Knowledge and Data Engineering*, 12(3):353–371, 2000. 119, 120, 121, 123, 124, 127

[14] Q. Y. Wang, J. X. Yu, and K.-F. Wong. Approximate graph schema extraction for semi-structured data. In *Proceedings 7th EDBT Conference*, pages 302–316, 2000. 119

[15] A. Zhou, Jinwen, S. Zhou, and Z. Tian. Incremental mining of schema for semistructured data. In *Proceedings Pasific-Asia Conference on Knowledge Discovery and Data Mining (PAKDD)*, pages 159–168, 1999. 119, 123

Identification of Lead Compounds in Pharmaceutical Data Using Data Mining Techniques

Christodoulos A. Nicolaou

Bioreason, Inc.
150 Washington Ave., Suite 220, Santa Fe, NM 87501, USA
christos.nicolaou@bioreason.com

Abstract. As the use of High-Throughput Screening (HTS) systems becomes more routine in the drug discovery process, there is an increasing need for fast and reliable analysis of the massive amounts of resulting biological data. At the forefront of the methods used for analyzing HTS data is cluster analysis. It is used in this context to find natural groups in the data, thereby revealing families of compounds that exhibit increased activity towards a specific biological target. Scientists in this area have traditionally used a number of clustering algorithms, distance (similarity) measures, and compound representation methods. We first discuss the nature of chemical and biological data and how it adversely impacts the current analysis methodology. We emphasize the inability of widely used methods to discover the chemical families in a pharmaceutical dataset and point out specific problems occurring when one attempts to apply these common clustering and other statistical methods on chemical data. We then introduce a new, data-mining algorithm that employs a newly proposed clustering method and expert knowledge to accommodate user requests and produce chemically sensible results. This new, chemically aware algorithm employs molecular structure to find true chemical structural families of compounds in pharmaceutical data, while at the same time accommodates the multi-domain nature of chemical compounds.

1   Introduction

The necessity for the introduction and wide use of automation in the modern drug discovery process is a well-known and accepted fact [1]. The overwhelming complexity of the drug discovery process, the increased complication of both targets and corporate libraries and the higher market demands require advancements in the process to make it more efficient and effective. In this respect automation could be particularly useful in eliminating current bottlenecks, improving the quality of the results, reducing the time and cost of the process and thus, increasing the overall throughput.

In the past decade the pharmaceutical industry placed emphasis on automating the screening and synthesis of compounds. As a result, High-Throughput Screening

Y. Manolopoulos et al. (Eds.): PCI 2001, LNCS 2563, pp. 133–146, 2003.

(HTS) and Combinatorial Chemistry are currently the norm rather than the exception in the process. However, automation of these two steps of the drug discovery process resulted in the creation of new bottlenecks further downstream. One such bottleneck is proving to be the task of analyzing thoroughly and effectively the screening datasets produced, commonly made of 100's of thousands of results. As a consequence the overall throughput increase of the drug discovery process is not nearly as much as expected.

Automating the analysis of screening data produced by HTS systems is a formidable task. HTS datasets are comprised of large amounts of complex and noisy data. This type of data poses a serious challenge to most of the widely used computational algorithms and tools. In addition, the analysis needs to be of high quality and accuracy due to the importance of the decisions based on its results. Wrong decisions at this crucial step can lead to a tremendous waste of resources, increased costs, and a significantly longer time for the completion of the drug discovery cycle [2].

In the next sections we discuss some observations on the nature of chemical data and the current methods of analysis employed by the pharmaceutical industry. To this end we investigate the impact of those observations on a traditional clustering process. Further, we introduce a data-mining algorithm designed for thorough analysis and knowledge extraction from HTS datasets and discuss the results of its application on the NCI-AIDS dataset. Our conclusions and notes on future work complete this paper.

2   Analyzing Chemical and Biological Data

2.1   Multi-domain Nature of the Data

We contend that chemical compounds are intrinsically multi-domain data. A molecule can contain multiple chemically significant domains and thus be a member of more than one chemical family [3]. Figure 1, shows a compound that is a member of the chemical families of biphenyls, alkanes and benzylics among others. A clustering process is usually considered successful if it places this compound in a cluster related to any one of these families. However, this outcome is only partially correct since the molecule is a member of other families as well, and not indicating so may lead to false conclusions.

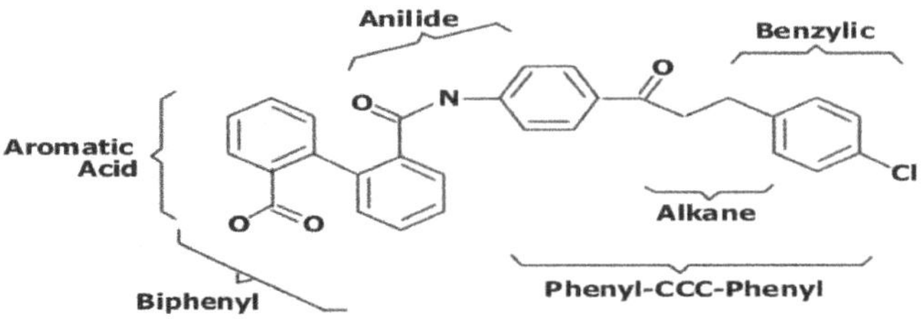

Fig. 1. A multi-domain compound

2.2   Chemical Compounds Representations

Chemical compounds are often represented in the form of binary strings -bit vectors-such as Daylight fingerprints or MACCS keys [4, 5]. Such binary string representations are calculated with the use of a predefined list of molecular fragments. Each bit of the binary string represents a fragment defined in the list used. A bit is set to 1 if the molecule contains the corresponding molecular fragment of the list used and 0 if it does not.

The application of the above method results in a vector representation of a molecule suitable for numerical analysis. A whole set of molecules is transformed into a set of vectors which can then be analyzed in a number of ways including clustering and classification methods as well as various distance and similarity measures.

Despite the simplicity and obvious benefits of this category of molecular representations there exist a number of disadvantages as well. Principal among others, the transformation of a molecular graph into a binary vector is accompanied by a significant loss of information about the exact topology of the molecule and the relation among molecular fragments represented by bits. In addition, the enormous size of chemical space poses a significant challenge to the ability of any predefined list of molecular fragments to capture all potentially interesting parts of a molecule.

3   Clustering Background

Clustering can be defined as the process of grouping data points into sets based on measurements of their similarity. This process is founded on the assumption that highly similar data points have much in common, whereas highly dissimilar data points share very little, if anything. Thus, clustering becomes far easier when the dataset under investigation consists of data points that fall into sets of well-defined, clearly distinct clusters, each containing highly similar data points.

Often, however, this is not the case. Clusters are not distinct and share individual data points. This happens when data points contain a set of roughly equivalent features that are characteristic of more than one clusters of the dataset. In the latter case appropriate clustering algorithms could be used to allow clusters to overlap, such that patterns can belong to more than one cluster [3].

Traditional clustering methodology often ignores the multi-domain data problem and attempts to partition the data points into clusters even if by doing so multi-domain patterns are forced into only one of the clusters to which they belong. For example, the molecule in Figure 1 was placed in a cluster with all other biphenic acids by an application of the widely used Wards hierarchical clustering algorithm. The molecule was absent from the clusters representing the alkanes and benzylics and therefore a user interested in one of the latter chemical families would have no direct way of finding out about the association with this compound.

Fuzzy clustering algorithms [6] are a more recent development in cluster analysis designed specifically to address the multi-domain data problem from a probabilistic standpoint. These algorithms take into account the multi-domain nature of data by assigning to each pattern probabilities of membership in each cluster. Clusters become fuzzy -or overlapping- since they may contain a number of the same compounds (even though, with differing degrees of probability for each compound). The effect of fuzzy clustering is to enable the clustering process to find more families of compounds in a data set and populate each discovered family with the compounds in the dataset that are members of that family [1].

Generalized Pyramidal Clustering (GPC) is an alternative to traditional fuzzy clustering. GPC is a multi-domain, hierarchical agglomerative approach, where patterns can have membership in more than one cluster. This is analogous to fuzzy clustering without the notion of probability of membership. The algorithm exploits the multi-domain nature of data to find and better populate the natural clusters present in the data while following a procedure closely related to the widely used hierarchical agglomerative clustering algorithms [3].

4   Clustering Chemical Data

As mentioned previously, at the forefront of the methods used for analyzing HTS data is cluster analysis. It is used in this context to find natural groups in the data, thereby revealing families of compounds that exhibit increased activity towards a specific biological target. Engels et. al. [7], and Willett et. al. [8] have proposed HTS lead discovery algorithms involving the usage of clustering processes. Clustering often requires a methodology whereby several clustering algorithms, measures, and data representations are explored, depending on the knowledge of the domain and the data dependencies. Clustering compound data is no different in this respect. Martin and Brown [9] and Wild and Blankley [10] have explored in depth the usage of various clustering algorithms and data representations for screening data analysis.

The efficacy of clustering methodologies is in general data dependent, so it comes as no surprise that there is no definitive clustering methodology with respect to clustering compound data. One problem that makes clustering compound data difficult is the multi-domain nature of individual compounds and compound classes. Namely, features or properties of groups of compounds overlap. The problem of multi-dimensionality is further confounded by the use of bit string representations, which result in significant information loss. The use of bit string representation results in the drastic reduction of the range and accuracy of distance and similarity values among molecular vectors obtained with the use of measures such as the Euclidean and the Tanimoto. In fact, the measurements obtained are only approximations that do not reflect the actual similarity between molecules. The ties in proximity problem described in [11, 12] is a natural consequence of the above methodology. In this context, the more traditional partitioning of the data found in most clustering algorithms will not suffice [3].

Our focus here is on employing GPC, a more appropriate clustering approach for processing chemical data represented by fingerprints, as part of a new data mining algorithm designed to extract knowledge interesting to medicinal chemists from large HTS datasets.

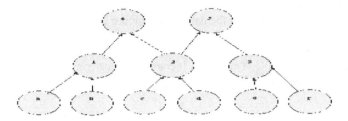

Fig. 2. A section of a cluster hierarchy produced by a GPC process. Cluster 2 is equidistant to clusters 1 and 3 and therefore merged with both

4.1   The Generalized Pyramidal Clustering (GPC) Algorithm

Pyramidal clustering [13] is a form of agglomerative hierarchical clustering that is dual domain, and maintains a partial ordering at each level of the hierarchy. Our algorithm is a generalization of this structure where no effort is expended towards maintaining a partial ordering at each level of the hierarchy and the multi-domain nature of patterns is supported in full. The goal of GPC is to place patterns in all the appropriate clusters. To achieve this goal the algorithm uses a modified version of the agglomerative clustering approach. This approach detects and employs compounds that belong to multiple clusters to achieve "fuzzification"/overlap of the clusters.

GPC starts by computing the distances between all individual compounds. It then merges the two closest compounds into a cluster and computes the distance of the new cluster to all non-merged compounds. At each consecutive step it merges the pair of compounds or clusters that have the least distance between them and computes the distance of the newly created cluster to all non-merged individual compounds and clusters formed during previous steps. The merging rules available in our current implementation are the commonly used Wards, Group-Average, Complete-Link and Single-Link. The novelty of GPC is found in the way it treats compounds or clusters that are equidistant, else involved in ambiguous α-ties [1]. While traditional methods ignore this situation GPC takes advantage of it by "cloning" the compound or cluster responsible for the tie and merging it as many times needed for all pair-wise merges to take place. The result of this cloning and merging process is to place the patterns responsible for α-ties in more than one cluster at the same level and thus produce overlapping clusters. The above process continues until only one cluster is left and no more merges can be performed. The output of GPC is a cluster hierarchy where each cluster at the bottom contains a single compound and the cluster on top contains all the compounds in the dataset [3]. Figure 2 shows an example of a cluster hierarchy fragment that the GPC algorithm might produce. Note that cluster 2 is equidistant to clusters 1, 3 and therefore merged with both following the cloning-and-merging facility of GPC. Traditional hierarchical clustering algorithms, like Wards, would have forced cluster 2 to merge with one of the two clusters in an arbitrary way.

5   LeadPyramid:
The Proposed Screening Data Analysis Algorithm

In order to capture expertise on screening data analysis, human experts assigned with the task of identifying leads in screening data were interviewed and consulted repeatedly. These experts were also involved in the process of defining the specifications during the design and implementation of the proposed screening data analysis system. The majority of them outlined a three step analysis process:

- Organize screening data in structural families of chemical compounds
- Look for Structure-Activity Relationships (SAR)
- Combine information to make hypotheses about which compounds to screen next, what would make compounds more or less active and what are the mechanisms of action that active compounds share [2]

5.1   Organizing Compounds in Structural Families

Organizing compounds in groups, or clusters, based on representations of their chemical structure or biological characteristics is a subject well researched [9, 10, 14]. However, organizing compounds in chemical families based on common structural characteristics, e.g., chemical substructures or scaffolds, goes a step beyond.

PhyloGenetic-Like Trees (PGLT) are data structures designed to represent the chemical family characteristics of the compounds in a dataset in a hierarchical manner. These trees are constructed from a given screening dataset to organize molecules into structurally similar groups/families, and to characterize those families with one or more substructures that all the compounds in the structural family share. Figure 3 shows a structural family of compounds. Each PGLT is constructed based on the active compounds in the dataset and thus produces the set of structural families that are biologically interesting for the specific assay. The branches of the tree are extended level by level thus capturing finer and finer levels of detail about the family characteristics.

The construction of a PGLT is performed via the LeadPyramid (LP) algorithm [15]. The steps of the algorithm are as following:

1. Divide the screening dataset in two subsets, the actives and the inactives by using a user defined activity threshold.

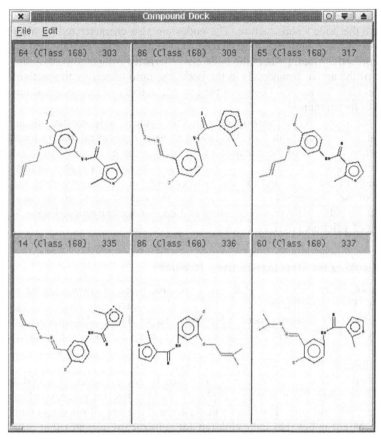

Fig. 3. A chemical family of compounds. The black part of the molecules is the maximum substructure they have in common

2. Represent the active chemical data using fragment-based bit vectors.
3. Cluster active chemical data using GPC and their vector representations.
4. Compute the Maximum-Common-Substructure (MCS) of the compounds in each cluster produced by the GPC clustering process
5. Prune the cluster tree by removing or hiding clusters/nodes that do not form structurally homogeneous chemical families. Structural homogeneity of the clusters is computed by:

   - Comparing the MCS of the cluster to the set of compounds in the cluster. In its simplest form MCS-based structural homogeneity is defined to be the ratio of the number of atoms in an MCS to the average number of atoms in the molecules used to compute it.
   - Computing the homogeneity of the cluster molecules. Commonly the methods used are based on the average value of all pair-wise similarities of the compound vectors. For the computation of the similarities the popular tanimoto measure is often used [1,10,11]

After construction, the nodes of the tree are populated with inactive compounds that share the node's substructure. The nodes are also characterized by means of the properties of the compounds they contain via the application of statistical and expert driven methods. Among others the node characteristics computed contain the average activity of the active compounds in the node, the ratio of actives to inactives and the statistical significance level between the average activity of the node and the average activity of its parent node.

The main goal for organizing data in this manner is to capture all significant chemical information from an HTS dataset in natural chemical family lineage. This organization helps focus the attention of the user on the interesting and relevant parts of chemistry space for the particular assay. The association of highly similar inactive compounds in each node and the ability to compute or import properties and characteristics of the compounds in each node make this data structure an excellent launching point for subsequent post-processing and knowledge extraction. Figure 4 shows a fragment of a fictional PGLT.

5.2   Looking for Structure-Activity Relations

Structure-Activity Relations (SAR) are a valuable piece of knowledge for medicinal chemists. They describe the relation of chemical structures/molecular fragments to measured activity against a specific biological target. Thus, SAR information enables chemists to identify potency increasing or decreasing chemical substructures, which they then attempt to combine, eliminate, improve, or optimize in a variety of ways in order to increase the biological activity of compounds.

The step of SAR identification is facilitated by the existence of a PGLT. In this context it is reduced to a thorough exploration of the tree for potency enhancing and decreasing substructures. The hierarchical nature of the tree allows direct comparisons between parent nodes and their children for substructure changes that resulted in a significant increase or decrease of activity. For example, in Figure 4, note the differences in mean activity and percentage of actives between nodes 1 and 11. This difference justifies the assumption that the addition of the NN fragment in node 11 to the MCS of its parent, node 1, constitutes a biologically significant action. Similarly, the nature of the tree allows easy comparisons among sibling nodes for better understanding of the effect that different substructure substitutions have on the parent family scaffold.

5.3   Extracting Knowledge

The construction and exploration of a PGLT results in a significant amount of information about the chemical families of interest and the SAR present. All this information is used to prioritize the chemical families for follow-up studies. The prioritization is performed by a knowledge-based system containing expert-rules defined in close cooperation with human experts. Classes with a higher potential for increasing potency, with SAR, may be given higher priority. Classes with minimal SAR may be given lower priority. Indications for potential false positive and false negative screening results are also available.

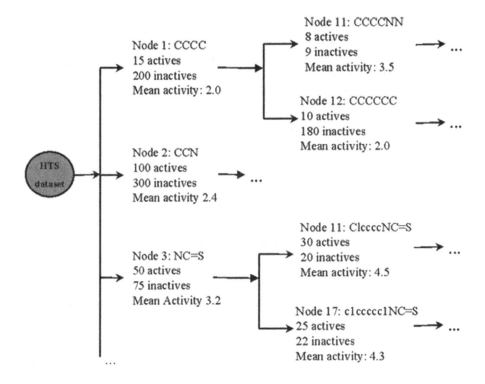

Fig. 4. A fragment of a fictional PGLT. Nodes of the tree fragment are shown to contain the substructure defining the node (in Smiles language notation), the number of active and inactive compounds sharing that substructure and the mean activity of all the compounds in the node. A typical PGLT node contains additional properties obtained via the application of statistical and expert driven methods on the characteristics of the compounds it contains. Note the differences in mean activity and percentage of actives between nodes 1 and 11. In a real setting the explanation to these differences would be related to the addition of the NN fragment in node 11 to the MCS of its parent node 1

6   Empirical Results

For the purposes of this paper, we chose to use the NCI-AIDS dataset comprising of 33255 compounds. A total of 453 drug-like compounds were shown to have activity against the AIDS virus while 32802 compounds were either inactive or not drug-like [16]. The compounds in the dataset were represented by BR-MACCS keys [3], a set of 157 fragment-based substructure keys. BR-MACCS keys are a slightly modified version of the public MACCS keys [5].

Table 1. Comparison of NCI-AIDS analysis with Wards and GPC-Wards. This version of the dataset contained 453 drug-like compounds

Clustering Method	Wards	GPC-Wards
Method type	Partitional	Multi-domain
Cluster Hierarchy Size (nodes #)	905	946
Average Compound Duplication	0	0.09

6.1   Clustering Analysis of an HTS Dataset

Our first set of experiments focused on comparing a traditional, partitional clustering algorithm with its GPC version [3]. We chose to use Wards, since it is considered one of the best hierarchical clustering algorithms and is widely used in the chemoinformatics literature [9, 10]. The analysis of the NCI-AIDS dataset was then performed in two ways. First, we used the Wards method to cluster the dataset. Following we used the Wards-GPC algorithm. For all runs, we used BR-MACCS keys and the Euclidean distance. Table 1 reveals the main differences among the two runs.

The results showed that the clustering analysis of the NCI-AIDS with the GPC version of Wards produces a number of novel findings over the traditional version of Wards. Multi-domain compounds, taking advantage of the nature of GPC found their way into multiple clusters. This freedom of placement of multi-domain compounds had a significant impact in two ways. First, a number of small under-represented classes that could not be discovered using the traditional version of Wards were revealed as nodes, mostly at the lower levels of the GPC cluster hierarchy, and occasionally at the higher levels as well. In contrast, when using normal Wards, the compounds of these classes were commonly merged into other, bigger classes.

Second, the allowed overlap resulted in an increased total number of compounds in a number of classes, and thus better representation of the chemical families described by those classes. Even though the traditional Wards algorithm had detected these classes they only contained a subset of the compounds of the dataset they should. As an example, Figure 5 shows two classes of compounds found by the GPC algorithm. With traditional Wards, the first compound would have been a member of only one of the clusters shown. Consequently, the relation between that compound and the family represented by the second cluster could not be detected. Overall, the use of GPC succeeded in revealing the multi-domain property of the compounds in the NCI-AIDS dataset, and thereby the discovery of relations among compounds that would not have been found with traditional algorithms [3].

6.2   HTS Dataset Analysis Using LeadPyramid

The second part of our experimental section was devoted to the evaluation of the results produced by the application of the LP algorithm on the HIV-AIDS dataset. The evaluation was performed by medicinal chemists and focused on the scientific validation of the results produced and the evaluation of the usefulness of the results' content.

Scientific Validation of the Results Produced by the LP Algorithm

Our experts found several known chemical classes in the results produced by the LP algorithm application. A total of twenty-seven chemical classes were formed by the analysis of the HIV-AIDS data. As expected, known chemical families like the pyrimidine nucleosides and the AZTs, were featured prominently in the results' list. Furthermore a number of small, underrepresented in the dataset classes were found. This observation is especially important since most algorithms used by the chemoinformatics community have significant problems in detecting underrepresented chemical families.

In addition to the identification of known chemical families several pieces of SAR information were also detected. Of very important nature is the ability of the algorithm to not only provide SAR information related to potency enhancing features or substructures but also information related to potency decreasing features. This is feasible since the algorithm proceeds to populate the chemical families detected using the active subset of the compounds with all inactive compounds in the dataset that share the MCS associated with that family. In comparison, current methods do not use the inactive part of a dataset -usually containing more than 98% of the total compounds screened- in any way and thus neglect the majority of information HTS processes produce and negative SAR information present. However, the LP analysis seemed to weight nitrogen groups too heavily, thus chemical families such as the biaryl sulfones were not coalesced into one cluster. Rather they were found in a few distinct, smaller classes that were made of compounds with additional chemical substructures in common. This can be attributed partly to the limitations of the predefined list of substructures used to generate the bit-vectors of the chemical compounds. The choice of a more descriptive list of substructures, or better, a customized to the dataset list would likely remove this problem to a considerable degree. However, it is worth remembering that the characteristic described above could be safely attributed to the nature of the data analyzed, especially the distribution of the attributes of the molecular vectors used to describe the patterns, and the dependency of any data driven algorithm on the data examined.

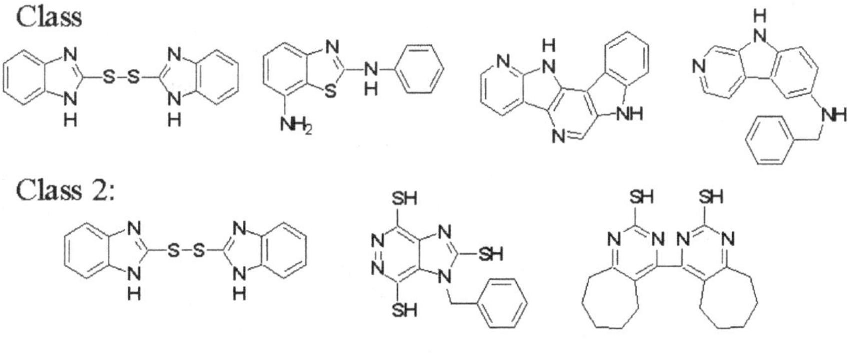

Fig. 5. An example of overlapping classes discovered using GPC. The first compound of the two classes is identical and happens to be a member of both class 1, a collection of compounds with multicyclic nitrogenous heteroaromatic rings and class 2, a collection of compounds with heteroaromatic rings with two nitrogen atoms and a sulfur attached to the central carbon

Evaluation of the Results' Content

The results of a screening dataset analysis with the LP algorithm produce more information than simple clustering analyses on the same dataset. In addition to clusters of similar compounds LP provides information such as the maximum common substructure and the homogeneity/diversity of the compounds in each cluster, and the relations among the clusters of compounds available through the inspection of the PGLT. Such information was found to be of great value to the users since it enabled them to focus on the clusters of compounds that made chemical sense (e.g. formed structurally homogeneous chemical families) and eliminate from consideration a significant amount of irrelevant or low priority information. With the overlay of biological information, such as activity, on the chemical families/nodes of the PGLT, chemists found it easier to associate chemical substructures (e.g. the MCS of each node) to the desirable biological behavior of compounds. The pruning of the analysis results (e.g. the PGLT) during the last phase of the LP algorithm execution, although by no means perfect, managed to cut down the size of the cluster hierarchy by removing clusters of compounds that were too structurally diverse to be of interest to medicinal chemists. This further facilitated the task of our users and allowed faster extraction of valuable pieces of pharmaceutical information.

In general, the results of the LP analysis compared favorably with those produced by other techniques both with respect to the discovery of what is known to be true about the dataset and when taking into account the ease of interpretation of the analyses results.

7   Conclusions

Informed and rapid decision making is highly desirable in the modern drug discovery process. In the case of analyzing HTS datasets, inherently large, complex and noisy, the current, human expert driven process is facing serious problems. As a result a significant amount of information generated by the screening process is neglected and the time required for the analysis has increased. A way of alleviating this problem is to employ automated data analysis methods that perform a number of tasks currently assigned to human experts. Such systems can emulate the data analysis process of humans, apply that process without biases on the screening dataset in short periods of time and scale up to large amounts of data with relative ease.

In order to enable thorough analysis of HTS datasets we designed and implemented LP, a new algorithm, in close cooperation with screening data analysis experts. The algorithm aims in finding chemical families of compounds that are of biological interest and are likely to contain information useful for lead compound identification and drug development. The algorithm employs the GPC clustering method to construct a phylogenetic-like tree that represents chemical families and relations among them in a natural lineage form. GPC, a recent development in the clustering community accommodates the multi-domain nature of compounds to find more families of compounds and to better populate the detected families with the appropriate compounds from the dataset. Further, LP employs maximum common substructure and structural homogeneity assessment methods to analyze and remove from consideration clusters of compounds that have low likelihood of forming a chemical family. In this manner a notable increase in the density of the information content of the results is achieved. The lack of low information content results and the use of a presentation format that makes chemical sense enable human analysts to proceed to a rapid interpretation and assessment of the most interesting and promising chemical families.

With the help of the proposed algorithm human experts, while always in full control of the data analysis process, are freed from a number of tasks that can be performed by an automated system. Consequently they can invest more time in exploring the knowledge extracted in the form of chemical families and related information, including SAR and structural homogeneity, and make important decisions quicker and with more confidence.

8   Future Work

In our current research we chose to use one of the most popular clustering algorithms in the chemoinformatics area to create the PGLT data structure needed for thorough chemical data organization. We are currently exploring other ways of creating this data structure that do not rely on the use of predefined lists of molecular fragments. Rather, they learn the important chemical substructures from the dataset under investigation. In addition we are working on methods that take into account the need for high structural similarity of the clusters of compounds produced during the formation of the PGLT instead of creating the data structure and then pruning it to leave only the clusters that contain structurally similar compounds.

Acknowledgements

The author would like to thank Drs. Susan Y. Tamura and Terence K. Brunck, of Bioreason, Inc. for insightful discussions, comments and suggestions.

References

[1]   MacCuish J.D., Nicolaou C.A. and MacCuish N.J.: "Ties in Proximity and Clustering Compounds", *J. Chem. Inf. Comput. Sci.*, Vol.41, No.1, pp.134-146, 2001.

[2]   Nicolaou C.A.: "Automated Lead Discovery and Development in HTS Datasets", *JALA*, Vol.6, No.2, pp.60-63, 2001.

[3]   Nicolaou C.A., MacCuish J.D. and Tamura S.Y.: "A New Multi-domain Clustering Algorithm for Lead Discovery that Exploits Ties in Proximities", *Proceedings 13th European Symposium on Quantitative Structure-Activity Relationships*, September, 2000.

[4]   Daylight Chemical Information Systems: URL http://www.daylight.com/.

[5]   MDL Information Systems, Inc.: URL http://www.mdli.com/.

[6]   Xie X.L. and Beni G.: "A Validity Measure for Fuzzy Clustering", *IEEE Transactions on Pattern Analysis and Machine Intelligence*, Vol.13, No.8, pp.841-847, 2001.

[7]   Engels M.F., Thielemans T., Verbinnen D., Tollenacre J. and Verbeeck R.: "CerBeruS: a System Supporting the Sequential Screening Process", *J. Chem. Inf. Comput. Sci.*, Vol.40, No.2. pp.241-245. 2000.

[8]   Willett P., Winterman V. and Bawden D.: "Implementation of Non-hierarchic Cluster Analysis Methods in Chemical Information Systems: Selection of Compounds for Biological Testing and Clustering of Substructure Search Output", *J. Chem. Inf. Comput. Sci.*, Vol.26, pp.109-118, 1986.

[9]   Brown R.D. and Martin Y.C.: "Use of Structure-activity Data to Compare Structure-based Clustering Methods and Descriptors for Use in Compound Selection", *J. Chem. Inf. Comput. Sci.*, Vol.36, pp.572-584, 1996.

[10]   Wild D.J. and Blankley C.J.: "Comparison of 2d Fingerprint Types and Hierarchy Level Selection Methods for Structural Grouping Using Wards Clustering", *J. Chem. Inf. Comput. Sci.*, Vol.40, pp.155-162, 2000.

[11]   Godden J., Xue L. and Bajorath J.: "Combinatorial Preferences Affect Molecular Similarity/diversity Calculations Using Binary Fingerprints and Tanimoto Coefficients", *J. Chem. Inf. Comput. Sci.*, Vol.40, pp.163-166, 2000.

[12]   Flower D.R.: "On the Properties of Bit String-based Measures of Chemical Similarity", *J. Chem. Inf. Comput. Sci.*, Vol.38, pp.379-386, 1998.

[13]   Bertrand P.: "Structural Properties of Pyramidal Clustering", *DIMACS Series in Discrete Mathematics and Theoretical Computer Science*, Vol.19, pp.35-53, 1995.

[14]   Barnard J.M. and Downs G.M.: "Clustering of Chemical Structures on the Basis of Two-dimensional Similarity Measures", *J. Chem. Inf. Comput. Sci.*, Vol.32, No.6, pp.644-649, 1992.

[15]   MacCuish J.D. and Nicolaou C.A.: "Method and System for Artificial Intelligence Directed Lead Discovery Through Multi-Domain Agglomerative Clustering. Application for a United States Patent", MBHB Case No. 99,832. Assignee: Bioreason Inc.

[16]   National Cancer Institute. Bethesda, MD, USA. URL http://ww.nci.nih.gov/.

Adaptive Classification of Web Documents to Users Interests

George Potamias[1,2]

[1] Institute of Computer Science
Foundation for Research & Technology - Hellas (FORTH)
711 10 Heraklion, Crete, Greece
[2] Dept. of Computer Science, University of Crete
714 09 Heraklion, Crete, Greece

Abstract. Current Web search engines are not able to adapt their operations to the evolving needs, interests and preferences of the users. To cope with this problem we developed a system able to classify HTML (or, XML) documents into user pre-specified categories of interests. The system processes the user profile and a set of representative documents- for each category of interest, and produces a classification schema- presented as a set of *representative* category vectors. The classification schema is then utilized in order to classify new incoming Web documents to one (or, more) of the pre-specified categories of interest. The system offers the users the ability to modify and enrich his/her profile depending on his/her current search needs and interests. In this respect the *adaptive* and *personalized* delivery of Web-based information is achieved. Experimental results on an indicative collection of Web-pages show the reliability and effectiveness of our approach.

1   Introduction

Throughout the world, information and communications technologies are generating a new industrial revolution. It is a revolution based on information with the explosive growth of the World Wide Web (Web) to provide millions of end-users access to ever-increasing volumes of information.

Current Web search engines offer effective ways to access and retrieve huge amounts of information. At the same time they proved to be inadequate to locate the "right" information- that is, the information that matches at a high degree of relevance the user's interests and preferences. In fact, all currently available search tools suffer either from poor precision (i.e., too many irrelevant documents) or, from poor recall (i.e., too little of the Web is covered by well-categorized directories). In most of the cases few of the results are *"valuable"* to a user (see [2, 3]), resulting into the "lost in the information cyberspace" situation. Which documents are valuable depends on the *context* of the query [11].

In other words, the underlying representation and matching operations should be able to capture and model the users preferences and (evolving) needs, and offer *adaptive* search and retrieval operations. Therefore, the need to put

Y. Manolopoulos et al. (Eds.): PCI 2001, LNCS 2563, pp. 147–158, 2003.

some intelligence into search-engines, which on one hand will be able to integrate and adapt the available information, and on the other to present it in a coherent and cohesive way, seems inevitable [17].

Text classification or, *categorization* research aims towards the automated assignment of 'natural' text references (i.e., texts written in natural language) to a set of two or more predefined categories based on their *content*. It differs from the traditional text-retrieval operations which aims to sort texts into two classes: those that the user would like to retrieve and see (the relevant documents), and those they would like not to see (the non-relevant documents) [12]. Furthermore, text-categorization is fundamental in *text-mining* operations where, the basic task is to extract useful and comprehensive knowledge from huge collections of texts [19].

The automated classification of Web pages requires the solution of two problems, which are typical of the machine learning field [6]: (i) the definition of a representative language for HTML/ XML pages, and (ii) the construction of a classifier that is able to categorize new Web pages on the basis of their representation.

There are several different approaches to manage the proliferation of the amount of information published in the Web. To cope with this problem, an important amount of research and development work is devoted in the development of *intelligent agents* used to locate and retrieve information in the Web. For example in [1], an adaptive agent is presented that can bring back Web pages of user's interest daily. Another approach is systems known as *browsing assistants*. Examples of such systems are *InfoFinder* [10] and *Amalthaea* [14]. Moreover, systems to filter information coming from the Web have been developed-*SIFT* [20] and *Pefna* [9] are examples of such systems. The *CMU World Wide Knowledge Base* project, presents another effort towards classification of Web documents that utilizes a mixture of information retrieval and machine learning techniques [5].

In order to cope with the aforementioned problems and needs we developed a system for the automatic classification of Web-documents (i.e., semi-structured HTML or XML documents) according to users' personal interests and preferences. The approach is based on *adaptive filtering* operations and offers *personalized classification* of Web documents. The system utilizes techniques from the *Information Retrieval* [18] and *Machine Learning* [13], disciplines.

In the next section the outline of our approach is presented. In section 3, the user profiling operations and the underlying Web-document parsing and representation schemas are presented. In section 4 the Web-documents classification process is described accompanied with the underlying pattern matching functions and metrics. In section 5 we present experimental results on an indicative set of pre-classified Web-documents. Last section states the basic conclusions of our work, and points to future research and development aspects.

2   The Approach

The fundamental operations of the system are based on appropriate representation schemas for devising user-profiles, document matching metrics, and respective classification functions.

- *Representation.* We rely on the well-known vector-space representation model [18]. Each Web-document is represented by a *text binary vector (TBV)*, where *bin* '1' is used to represent the occurrence of an index term in the document, and '0' its absence. The entries in the vector keep the pre-specified appearance of the index terms in the declared user-profile; in that sense it is an ordered vector.
- *User profiling.* The user profile is composed by a set of user-declared *categories* of *interest* each one described by a set of user-specified *key-words* or, *key-phrases* (i.e., the *index terms*). The users may adjust their profiles according to their evolving needs, interests and preferences (the implemented Perl-based system offers a set of respective tools for that).
- *Training and representative category-vectors.* Utilizing techniques from information retrieval, a *weight* for each index term is computed. The weight represents the *importance* or, the *representative-power* of an index term in describing the categories. The weights are computed according to a pre-selected set of *training* Web documents. The final outcome of the training process is a set of *class relevant weighted vectors*, each one presenting a *representative vector* for each category.
- *Classification and prioritization.* Each binary-vector is matched against each of the class relevant vectors. The matching process is realized by the introduction of specially devised *similarity-metrics*. The final outcome is the classification of new incoming Web-documents to the category with which they exhibit the *highest* similarity. Furthermore, for each of the classified documents a *priority index* is computed to indicate the degree with which each document belongs to each category. Moreover, the Web-documents that exhibit similarity-indices lower than a user-specified threshold are considered as of *no-relevance* to the specified Web inquiry.
- *Exploiting tagging information.* In the course of similarity matching we exploit the *structure* of the Web-document (i.e., its tagging information) by assigning a *special weight to the index terms that occur within pre-specified tags.* The users may adjust the type of tags they want to focus-on and the weights to assign. In this way, the system is capable to capture and model the dynamically changing interests and preferences of the users and so, to achieve *personalized delivery* of related Web-based information.

In figure 1, the components and the flow of operations of the overall *personalised* "Web Documents Classification" system, are shown.

3   User Profiling and Representation Schemas

User Profiling. User profiles are modelled by a set of declared categories of interest each one described by a set of pre-specified *index terms* (*representative*

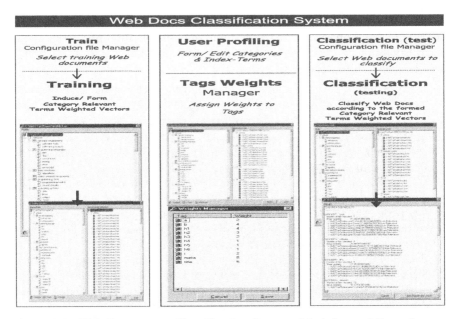

Fig. 1. The Web Documents Classification System: Modules and flow of operations

keywords or, key-phrases). Each index term is accompanied by a set of *synonyms*. A useful utilization of synonyms is for *multi-lingual* text collections where, the basic reference term in one language is declared and its potential translations follow as synonyms. Here we have to note that the devise of the controlled vocabulary (categories, their names and the respective index terms) is in the full responsibility of the user. Of course, automated (or, semi-automated) methods could be utilized in order to assess the importance of the words that appear in a collection of text references and then, select (by applying an appropriate threshold mechanism) the most informative of them (see [7, 15]). The format of a user profile is shown in figure 2.

Parsing. Each Web-document, training or testing (i.e., new incoming document), is *parsed*. The parser identifies the index terms (and their synonyms) defined in the user profile. The outcome is a *Text Binary Vector*- TBV.

The system's parser utilizes the *stemming* techniques of Porter's algorithm [16], with the inclusion of specially defined grammar. After stemming a *pattern* is constructed for each of the terms. Then, the patterns are matched instead of the terms themselves. If a pattern matches, the corresponding index term is supposed to be identified. However the use of stemming may cause additional problems. For example, consider the term 'DOS' (i.e., the operating system). A casual stemming would produce the stem 'DO' for this term. A pattern for this term would be one that matches every word starting with 'do' or, 'DO'- consider

```
<CATEGORY-1-name>
term-11-name-string [synonym-111-string, synonym-112-string ...]
term-12-name-string [synonym-121-string, synonym-122-string ...]
............. other categories .............
<CATEGORY-c-name>
term-c1-name-string [synonym-c11-string, synonym-c12-string ...]
term-c2-name-string [synonym-c21-string, synonym-c22-string ...]
```

Fig. 2. Format of a user profile

how many words start with these two sub-strings. To avoid such situations we permit users to input terms in the profile that will be tested for exact matching. This is achieved by the introduction of appropriate rules for forming and parsing respective *regular expressions*, and *quoting* the respective terms.

Text Binary Vectors. For each parsed document t, a corresponding *Text Binary Vector*, TBV_t is formed. Suppose that in the user profile there are c categories, each one described with C_c number of terms. Then, TBV_t is a vector of $m = c \times C_c$ places (= the total number of terms in the user profile). The TBV is an *ordered* vector in the sense that, the entries in the vector keep the order of the categories and the appearance of their respective index terms in the user profile. Every entry in the TBV will be "1" if the corresponding term occurs (identified) in the document or, "0" if the corresponding term does <u>not</u> occur (was not identified) in the document. The $TBVs$ constructed during the training procedure have one more place than the total number of the terms in the user profile. The extra place holds the name of the category into which the document is assigned.

3.1   Category Relevant Terms Weighted Vectors

Each category is linked with a set of *representative* Web-documents, the *training* set. The outcome of the training process is a set of *Category Relevant Weighted Vectors*- CRWV each one corresponding to a respective category. The entries in each CRWV represent the *importance* (or, the *weight*) that each index term posses in describing the respective category and discriminating between the categories.

Consider a term v and a category c. The *importance* of term v for category c is computed by formula 1 below.

$$W_{c,v} = \log \left\{ \frac{(N_{c,v} + 0.5) \times [(N - N_v) - (N_c - N_{c,v}) + 0.5]}{(N_v - N_{c,v} + 0.5) \times (N_c - N_{c,v} + 0.5)} \right\} \qquad (1)$$

where, N: the number of training documents; N_c: the number of training documents for category c; $N_{c,v}$: the number of training documents for category c with term v present; and N_v: the number of training documents for all categories with term v present (the 0.5 entries are used in order to avoid indeterminate forms of the formula).

The above weighting metric is the so-called *term-precision* metric, one of the most known formulas in information and text retrieval research [21]. Its utility comes from the fact that it takes advantage of the information that concerns *relevant* and *non-relevant* documents. This is the reason why we do not utilize the well-known *tf/idf* (term frequency / inverse-document-frequency) term weighting formula [18], which refers just to the collection of documents with no relevance-related entries. In our case, relevant are the Web-documents that are assigned to a specific category, all others being considered as non-relevant.

4   Classification of Web Documents

The formed CRWVs are utilized to classify new and unseen Web-documents. Each Web-document under classification is also represented by a TBV, which is of the same form as the ones formed to represent training documents. The only difference is the extra place holding the assigned category which is now empty.

The *similarity* between a Web-document and a category of interest is computed as the *inner product* of the document's TBV and the respective CRWVs. Consider a document t; its corresponding vector $TBV_t = < v_1, v_2, \ldots v_k >$, $v_i \in \{0, 1\}$, and a category c declared in the user profile with its corresponding $\mathrm{crwv}(c) = < W_{c,v_1}, W_{c,v_2}, \ldots W_{c,v_k} >$, where W_{c,v_i} is the importance of term v_i for category c. Then, the similarity between document t and category c is computed by formula 2 below.

$$similarity\,(t, c) = \sum_{i=1}^{k} v_i \times W_{c,v_i} \tag{2}$$

4.1   Exploiting HTML/XML Structure

A novelty of our approach is the exploitation of the structure of HTML/XML documents to compute *more reliable* and *pragmatic* weights for the index terms. It is quite possible that an HTML/XML *tag* will contain a term. Depending on the formatting, a term found in a Web document may be assigned an *extra* importance apart from the one computed by formula 1, above. Consider for example the term 'software' which is identified as part of a Web-document's title (i.e., within the $< title >$ tag) of a training document which is assigned to category 'science'. Consider also the term 'disk' identified as part of a paragraph of the same document. Suppose that both of these terms are defined in the user profile. Then it is natural to assume that 'software' is more important than 'disk' for category 'science', because the term appears in the title, and titles possess more descriptive power for the document they appear.

Our system permits users to define *weights* for the HTML/XML tags. Once a tag weight is defined, the importance, $W_{c,v}$ of a term v, is *multiplied by the tag's weight* iff *the term is contained within the tag*. It is possible that a term will be contained in more than one tag. In this case the weight assigned to the term is the *greatest of all the weights of the tags containing it.*

Assume that $tw(v_i)$ is the tag-related weight computed for term v (during parsing of the document and identification of the term within specific tags). Then, the similarity metric becomes:

$$similarity(t, c) = \sum_{i=1}^{k} v_i \times W_{c,v_i} \times tw(v_i) \qquad (3)$$

Ordering and Prioritizing Web-documents. Once a set of Web documents has been classified we compute the *mean similarity* for each category of interest (for all documents classified to the category). Consider a number of m documents $t_1, t_2..., t_m$ classified to category c. The mean similarity for category c is computed by the following formula:

$$mean\_similarity\,(c) = \frac{\sum\limits_{i=1}^{m} similarity\,(t_i, c)}{m} \qquad (4)$$

A classified HTML document is considered as of *high-relevance* to the category classified to, if its similarity with this category is greater than the category's mean similarity. Otherwise it is considered as being of *low-relevance* or, of *no-relevance* if its similarity index with all the categories is below a pre-specified threshold).

5 Experimental Results

We evaluated the system through a series of experiments using a manually-constructed user profile, and a set of 208 Web-pages. The documents used for the evaluation of the system were collected using various Web search engines (Yahoo and Altavista). The pre-classification of Web pages to specific categories relied on the respective search-engines' classification hierarchy. Five- (5) categories of interest were investigated with a total of 208 documents: *Human Computer Interaction - hci*: 27 documents; *Information Systems - infosys*: 52 documents; *Communication Networks - network*: 49 documents; *Software - software*: 39 documents; and *Sports - sport*: 41 documents (see Appendix). The evaluation was performed conducting a series of *V-fold cross-validation* experiments (for $V = 10$).

We conducted experiments exploiting tagging information referring to tags: $< h1 >, < h2 >, < a >, < b >, < i >, < title >$, and $< meta >$. In particular, we run the system on three different combinations of tags and weight-assignment to them; see table 1, above, for the names and the specifics of each experimental run. For each of the runs a respective *learning-curve* was formed. All the learning-curves are shown in figure 3.

Table 1. Specifics of the performed experiments

Experiment →	NW	MT	ALL
Tags ↓	equal weights ~no-weighting	<meta> <title>	all tags
$< h1 >$	1	1	5
$< h2 >$	1	1	5
$< a >$	1	1	5
$< b >$	1	1	5
$< i >$	1	1	5
$< title >$	1	5	5
$< meta >$	1	5	5

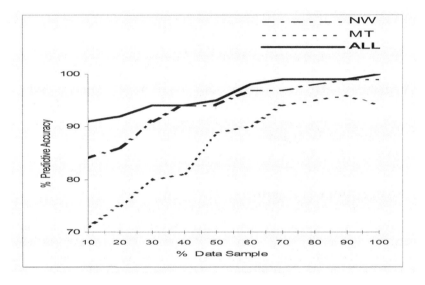

Fig. 3. Learning curves for the performed experiments

5.1   Discussion

<u>ALL</u>. The performance of the system, when the information about <u>all</u> the focused tags is utilized (all tags are given the highest weight [=5]), is very-good. It starts from a predictive accuracy level of $\sim 91\%$ (when just 10% of the documents are provided) and reaches the highest accuracy level, *100%* when all the documents are provided. The basic finding concerns the fact that the performance remains more-or-less stable, and outperforms the respective NW and MT results. The results show the power of tagging-information exploitation when Web-documents classification tasks are considered, and in-a-way it proves the reliability of our approach.

NW. The performance of the system when no-tagging information is utilized (i.e., all weights are set equal to 1), is quite good. The predictive accuracy level starts from about *84%* (on 10% of the Web-documents available) and reaches a level of *99%* when all data are available. It reaches a high-accurate level of about *95%* when about half of the data are available ($\sim$ 50-60%). The high-accurate results should be attributed to the term-precision formula used to weight the index terms. The 'right' pre-classification of training and testing documents is also a factor influencing the performance. Here, it is worthwhile to notice that the right selection and 'correct' pre-classification of training documents is crucial. The system offers to the user the ability to revise/ refine his/her collections in order to devise a 'correct' set of representative documents.

MT. The performance of the system when the $< meta >$ and $< title >$ tag information is exploited (i.e., terms within these tags are assigned the highest weight, i.e., 5) starts from a predictive accuracy of about 71% and reaches its highest accuracy level, $\sim$95%, when about 90% of the data are available. The performance should be considered as inferior to the NW and ALL experiments. This should be attributed to the fact that only about half of the available Web-documents in the collection have $< title >$ or, $< meta >$ tags in their source. So, more documents should be provided in order to reach higher accuracy levels.

Statistical Significance. Applying a paired one-tail t-test statistic on the V-fold accuracy results for ALL vs. NW, a significance difference on the $P > 99\%$ level was observed. The same test for ALL vs. MT, resulted in an observed significance difference on the $P > 95\%$ level. These results indicate the reliability and effectiveness of the presented Web documents classification approach.

We should also note that the use of Porter's *stemming* algorithm [16], and the use of regular expressions (for the stemming process) contributed to the overall performance. Moreover, the incorporation of *relevance-feedback* operations [4, 8], in order to induce and acquire better term-weights, would potentially yield even better results.

6   Conclusion and Future Work

The vast quantity of information that is disposed by means of the Web has turned into a difficult and some times painful process the location and acquisition of information by the users. Although the search engines of the Web offer several facilities for the location of information in the network, the techniques used for the indexing of the latter and for the expression of further queries, are proved to be too deficient to cover the evolving needs and interests of the users.

In this paper a system was presented, which aims towards the automated classification of HTML/XML documents in users' pre-specified categories of interest. The system combines techniques and methods from the areas of information retrieval and machine learning. Also a graphical user interface was designed for the evaluation and demonstration of the system (a Perl-based application). Apart from the basic filtering functions that have to perform, the system through its interface offers a number of management operations, which are used to adapt its functionality. Experimental results showed the reliability and effectiveness of our approach.

The implemented system could be quite easily re-configured and adapted to serve the need of classifying different types of semi-structured documents, other than HTML, e.g., emails, news or, XML. The user may simply call the *'tag-manager'* of the system in order to add/ delete tags, and define/ revise their weights.

Our future research and development plans are moving towards three directions: (a) experimentation with large-scale benchmark document collections (e.g., REUTERS, TREC; preliminary results on the REUTERS collection and for various classification tasks produce encouraging results) in order to test the effectiveness and scalability of the system; (b) re-configuration and adaptation of the system to other types of documents and experimentation with respective document collections (emails, news, etc); (c) development and inclusion of modules that offer and support automatic user-profiling and relevance-feedback services.

References

[1] Balabanovic M., Shoham Y. and Yun Y.: "An adaptive Agent for Automated Web Browsing", *Journal on Intelligent and Cooperative Information Systems*, Vol.6, No.4, pp.127-158, 1992. 148

[2] Barry C. L.: "User-Defined Relevance Criteria: an Exploratory Study", *Journal of the American Society for Information Science*, Vol.45, No.3, pp.149-159, 1994. 147

[3] Barry C. L. and Schamber L.: "Users' Criteria for Relevance Evaluation: a Cross-Situational Comparison", *Information Processing and Management*, Vol.34, No.2/3, pp.219-236, 1998. 147

[4] Chang C. H. and Hsu C. C.: "Enabling Concept-Based Relevance Feedback for Information Retrieve on the World Wide Web", *IEEE Transaction on Knowledge and Data Engineering*, Special issue on Web Technologies, Vol.11, No.4, pp.595-609, 1999. 155

[5] Craven M., DiPasquo D., Freitag D., McCallum A., Mitchell T., Nigam K. and Slattery S.: "Learning to Construct Knowledge Bases from the World Wide Web", *Artificial Intelligence*, Vol.118, No.1-2, pp.69-113, 2000. 148

[6] Esposito F., Malerba D., Di Pace L. and Leo P.: "WebClass: an Intermediary for the Classification of HTML Pages", Demo paper for AI*IA '99, Bologna, Italy, 1999. 148

[7] Fawcett T. and Provost F.: "Combining Data Mining and Machine Learning for Effective User Profiling", *Proceedings 2nd KDDM Conference*, pp.8-13, 1996. 150

[8] Harman D.: "Relevance Feedback Revisited", *Proceedings 15th ACM SIGIR Conference*, pp.1-10, 1992. 155

[9] Kilander F.: "IntFilter Home Page - K2LAB", Department of Computer Sciences, Stockholm University, Sweden, 1996. Available from: http://www.dsv.su.se/~fk/if_Doc/IntFilter.html. 148

[10] Krulwich B.: "InfoFinder Internet. Andersen Consulting's Center for Strategic Technology Research", 1996. Available from: http://www.ac.com/cstar/hsil/agents/framedef_if.html. 148

[11] Lawrence S.: "Context in Web Search", *IEEE Data Engineering Bulletin*, Vol.23, No.3, pp.25-32, 2000. 147

[12] Lewis D. D.: "An Evaluation of Phrasal and Clustered Representation on a Text Categorization Task", *Proceedings 15th ACM SIGIR Conference*, Compenhagen, Denmark, pp.37-50, 1992. 148

[13] Mitchell T.: *"Machine Learning"*, McGraw Hill, 1997. 148

[14] Moukas A.: "Amalthaea: Information Discovery and Filtering Using a Multi-agent Evolving Ecosystem", *Proceedings Conference on the Practical Application on Intelligent Agents and Multi-Agent Technology*, London, UK, 1996. Available from: http://moux.www.media.mit.edu/people/moux/ papers/ PAAM96/. 148

[15] Pazzani M. and Billsus D.: "Learning and Revising User Profiles: the Identification of Interesting Web Sites", *Machine Learning*, Vol.27, pp.313-331, 1997. 150

[16] Porter M. F.: "An Algorithm for Suffix Stripping", *Program*, Vol.14, No.3, pp.130-137, 1980. 150, 155

[17] Quek C. Y.: "Classification of World Wide Web Documents", Senior Honors Thesis. School of Computer Science, CMU, 1997. Available from: http:// www.cs.cmu.edu/afs/cs.cmu.edu/project/theo-11/www/wwkb/choon-thesis.html. 148

[18] Salton G. and McGill M. J.: *"Introduction to Modern Information Retrieval"*, McGraw-Hill, New York, 1983. 148, 149, 152

[19] Text-Mining: "Text Mining: Foundations, Techniques and Applications", *Proceedings IJCAI'99 Workshop*, Stockholm, Sweden, 1999. 148

[20] Yan T. and Garcia-Molina H.: "SIFT - a tool for Wide Area Information Dissemination", *Proceedings 1995 USENIX Technical Conference*, pp.177-186, 1995. Available from: ftp://db.stanford.edu/pub/sift/sift.ps. 148

[21] Yu C. T., Lam K. and Salton G.: "Term Weighting in Information Retrieval Using the Term Precision Model", *Journal of the Association for Computing Machinery*, Vol.29, No.1, pp.152-170, 1982. 152

Appendix

User Profile: Categories and Their Index Terms

< software >

software engineering [software tools, software products]
programming languages [perl, "lisp", visual basic, prolog, java, javascript]
data structures [algorithms]
object oriented programming
programming tools [programming toolkit, visual studio]
operating systems [unix, linux, solaris, "X11, "DOS", "X windows"]
microsoft ["windows 95", "windows 98", "windows NT"]
programs [debugging, compile, run, script, applet]
files [source files, binary file, "ASCII"]
license agreement [freeware, shareware]

< information systems >

information systems
heterogeneous information sources [heterogeneous databases, heterogeneous data sources]

information retrieval [information access, information integration, text retrieval, "data
    mining", information gathering, Information Browsing, information processing]
databases [data bases, knowledge bases, data source, information source]
knowledge discovery [knowledge representation, information discovery]
mediator [warpper]
relational databases [object-oriented databases, object database]
metadata
query ['queries', thesaurus, query processing]
query languages [SQL, OQL, MySQL, JDBC]
data base vendors [sybase, oracle, ingress, gemstone, postgreSQL]
digital library

< hci >

human computer interaction [human-computer interaction, "hci", user interfaces,
    human computer interface,human-computer interface, human machine interface,
    human-machine interface, user interfaces for all, UI4ALL]
computer graphics [multimedia, graphical user interface, "GUI", "UI"]
user modeling [human factors]
ergonomics [usability, usability test]
user interface software tools [Tk/Tcl, xview, motif]
user interface design [interface design and evaluation interface evaluation]

< networks >

networks [WAN, LAN, ethernet, ATM, intranet]
ISDN [BISDN]
"OSI model"
ip address [hosts, host name, hostname, domain name, "DNS", "DNS server"]
network protocols [aloha, "X.25", TCP/IP, TCP, IP, UDP, PPP, SLIP, SNMP, SMTP,
    OSPF, 'NFS']
browsing [ftp, internet navigation]
telnet
internet providers [internet service provider, forthnet, "hellas on line", "compuling",
    "america on line", aol, dial up]

< sport >

sports
basketball ["NBA", "CBA", Jordan, Chicago Bulls, rebound]
football ["FIFA", World cup, football association, soccer, Panathinaikos, Pele,
    Olympiakos]
tennis [table tennis]
hockey ["NFL"]
volley [volleyball, beach volleyball]
baseball
softball
athletics
olympic games [olympics, gymnastics]

Seismo-Surfer: A Prototype for Collecting, Querying, and Mining Seismic Data

Yannis Theodoridis

Department of Informatics
University of Piraeus
GR-18534 Piraeus, Greece
ytheod@unipi.gr

Abstract. Earthquake phenomena constitute a rich source of information over the years. Typically, the frequency of earthquakes worldwide is one every second. Collecting and querying seismic data is a procedure useful for local authorities in order to keep citizens informed as well as for specialized scientists, such as seismologists, physicists etc., in order to study the phenomenon in its detail. A seismic data management system should meet certain requirements implied by the nature of seismic data. This kind of data is not solely characterized by alphanumeric attributes but also from a spatial and a temporal dimension (the epicenter and the time of earthquake realization, for example). Moreover, visualizing areas of interest, monitoring seismicity, finding hidden regularities or irregularities, and assisting to the understanding of regional historic seismic profiles are essential capabilities of such a system. Thus, a spatiotemporal database system, a set of data analysis and knowledge discovery techniques and a user-friendly visualization interface, compose the Seismo-Surfer, a prototype that, further to the above, aims to integrate seismic data repositories available over the WWW.

1 Introduction

Since the ancient years, humans have been feeling, recording and studying earthquake phenomena. Taking into account that at least one earthquake of magnitude $M < 3$ ($M > 3$) occurs every one second (every ten minutes, respectively) worldwide, the seismic data collection is huge and, unfortunately, ever increasing. Scientists, such as seismologists and physicists, record this information in order to describe and study tectonic activity. For a certain time period, tectonic activity can be described by recording geographic information, i.e. epicenter and disaster areas, together with attributes like magnitude, depth, etc.

Desirable components of a seismic data management application include tools for quick and easy data exploration and inspection, algorithms for generating historic profiles of specific geographic areas and time periods, techniques providing the association of seismic data with other geophysical parameters of interest such as soil profile, geographic and perhaps specialized maps (e.g. topological and climatological) for the presentation of data to the user and, topline, visualization components supporting sophisticated user interaction.

Y. Manolopoulos et al. (Eds.): PCI 2001, LNCS 2563, pp. 159–171, 2003.
© Springer-Verlag Berlin Heidelberg 2003

In particular, we distinguish three user profiles that such an application should support:

- Researchers of geophysical sciences, who could, for example, be interested in constructing and visualizing seismic profiles of certain regions during specific time periods or in discovering regions of similar seismic behavior.
- Key personnel in public administration, usually asking for information such as distances between epicenters and other geographical entities like schools and heavy industries.
- Citizens (web surfers), who are interested in general about the phenomenon, and might query the system for seismic properties of general interest, e.g. for finding all epicenters of earthquakes in distance no more than 50Km from Athens.

Management of seismic data, due to their spatiotemporal nature, demands more than a relational or an object-relational Database Management System (DBMS) and a Geographical Information System (GIS) on top of the DBMS. Recent advances in the areas of non-traditional Databases, Knowledge Discovery in Databases (KDD) and Data Visualization allow better approaches for the efficient storage, retrieval and analysis of seismic data. For example, commercial DBMS's have been already providing tools for the management of spatial (2D, 3D, 4D) data, see e.g. [14], while KDD techniques have shown their potential through a wide range of applications. Additionally, several research prototypes have applied these technologies and have utilized certain benefits.

Our proposal, called SEISMO-SURFER[1], consists not only of a spatiotemporal DBMS, but also of a data mining module and a graphical interface with GIS features. The development of this prototype aims to the better understanding of seismic phenomena and of the relationships between seismic parameters themselves or between those and other factors like subsoil properties, weather conditions during earthquake realization etc. We envisage that SEISMO-SURFER could be a useful tool for geophysical scientists who would be mostly interested in high level concepts rather than in plain collections of raw observational data.

Moreover, it is our intention to face the challenge of exploiting the available seismic data repositories over the web. Assuming that the user would periodically, but not very frequently, check these repositories for newly available data, load them into the local database (namely, in a batch update fashion) and taking into consideration the very large size and heterogeneity of these repositories, it seems natural to extend the database of the tool with a Data Warehouse (DW) for storing aggregate information about remote data.

The rest of the paper is organized as follows. In the next section we survey available technologies and research trends that we argue a so-called Seismic Data Management and Mining System (SDMMS) should take into consideration. Section 3 presents such an SDMMS, the SEISMO-SURFER prototype under development, and describes its architecture, functionality and current status of implementation. In section 4, we discuss related work and present several research

---

[1] General information is available at
http://thalis.cs.unipi.gr/~ytheod/software/seismo/.

prototypes developed for the management of spatiotemporal and geophysical data. Finally, section 5 concludes with directions for future work.

2 Requirements for Management and Mining of Seismic Data

A combination of three state-of-the-art database technologies is required for the efficient handling of seismic data, namely, spatiotemporal databases, data warehouses and data mining techniques.

2.1 Spatiotemporal Databases

Modelling the real world for seismic data applications requires the use of spatiotemporal concepts like snapshots, changes of objects and maps, motion and phenomena [16]. In particular, we are concerned with the following concepts:

- *Spatial objects in time points.* It is a simple spatiotemporal concept where we record spatial objects in time points, or, in other words, we take snapshots of them. This concept is used, for example, when we are dealing with records including position (latitude and longitude of earthquake epicenter) and time of earthquake realization together with attributes like magnitude, depth of epicenter, and so on.
- *Spatial objects in time intervals.* This could be the case when we intend to capture the evolution of spatial objects over time, for example when, additionally to the attributes mentioned previously, we are interested in recording the duration of an earthquake and how certain parameters of the phenomenon vary throughout the time interval of its duration.
- *Layers in time points.* Layers correspond to thematic maps showing the spatial distribution of certain attributes in the database. The combination of layers and time points results into snapshots of a layer. For example, this kind of modelling is used when we are interested in magnitude thematic maps of earthquakes realized during a specific day inside a specific area.
- *Layers in time intervals.* This is the most complex spatiotemporal concept we are interested in for the modelling of earthquake phenomena. For example, modelling the whole sequence of earthquakes, including the smaller in magnitude that precede or follow the main earthquake, uses the notion of layers in time intervals.

It is clear that we are mostly interested in the spatiotemporal attributes of earthquake data. For example, typical queries that involve the spatial and the temporal dimension of data are the following:

- *Find the ten epicenters of earthquakes realized during the past four months, which reside more closely to a given location.*
- *Find all epicenters of earthquakes residing in a certain region, with a magnitude $M > 5$ and a realization time in the past four months.*

- *(Assuming multiple layers of information, e.g. corresponding to main cities' coordinates and population) find the five strongest quakes occurred in a distance of less than 100Km from cities of population over 1 million during the 20th century.*

In order to support the above data models and queries, novel data types [4] have been proposed in the literature. Seismic data are multi-dimensional and, as a consequence, require different techniques for their efficient storage and retrieval than those traditionally used for alphanumeric information. A great deal of effort has been also spent for the development of efficient Spatial Access Methods (SAM) and some (R-trees, Quadtrees) have been integrated into commercial DBMS's (Oracle, Informix, DB2). Recently, SAMs that take the dimension of time into consideration have been also proposed [15, 9, 20]

2.2   Data Warehouses

Additional to the spatiotemporal DBMS, for the reasons stated in section 1, a data warehouse approach can be adopted for the integration of the available sources of seismic data over the Web and the utilization of on-line analytical processing (OLAP) technology. A data warehouse is usually defined as a subject-oriented, integrated, time-variant, nonvolatile collection of data in support of management decision making process [5]. We illustrate the benefits obtained by such an approach with two examples of operations supported by spatial data warehouse and OLAP technologies:

- A user may ask to view part of the historical seismic profile, i.e. the ten most destructive quakes in the past twenty years, over Europe, and, moreover, he/she can easily view the same information over Greece (more detailed view, formally a *drill-down* operation) or worldwide (more summarized view, formally a *roll-up* operation).
- Given the existence of multiple thematic maps, perhaps one for quake magnitude and one for another, non-geophysical parameter such as the resulting · damage, they could be overlayed for the exploration of possible relationships, such as finding regions of high, though non-destructive, seismicity and vice versa.

A data warehouse is based on a multidimensional data model which views data in the form of a data cube [1]. A data cube allows data to be modelled and viewed in multiple dimensions and is typically implemented by adopting a star schema model, where the data warehouse contains a *fact table* related with a set of *dimensional tables*, e.g. *quake(quake id, quake type, ...)*, *geography(geography id, region, country, continent)* and *time(time id, date, month, year, century)*. Fact table contains measures on seismic data, such as *number of earthquakes*, and keys to each of the related dimension tables (figure 1). Especially for seismic data, where multidimensional information is involved in the dimensional tables as well as in the fact table, spatial data cubes are also of interest [19].

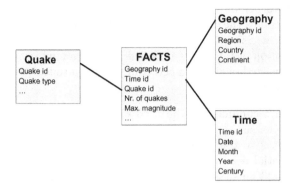

Fig. 1. A possible star schema for an SDMMS

Further to the operations of roll-up and drill-down described above, typical data cube operations include *slice* and *dice*, for selecting parts of a data cube by imposing conditions on one or more cube dimensions, respectively, and *pivot*, which provides alternative presentations of the data to the user.

2.3   Data Mining

The integration of data analysis and mining techniques into an SDMMS ultimately aims to the discovery of interesting, implicit and previously unknown knowledge. We study the integration of three basic techniques for this purpose: methods for finding association rules, clustering algorithms and classification methods. Recently, there have been proposals that expand the application of knowledge discovery methods on multidimensional data [10, 11].

- Association rules have are implications of the form $A \Rightarrow B$, $A \subset J$, $B \subset J$ where A, B and J are sets of items and are characterized by two numbers, s, which is called *support* of the rule and expresses the probability that a transaction in a database contains both A and B, and c, which is called *confidence* of the rule and expresses the conditional probability that a transaction containing A also contains B. For example, an association rule could be that during a specific time period, earthquakes of $M > 4$ (itemset A) occurred in a certain region in Greece (itemset B), with confidence 10% and support 80%.
- Clustering algorithms [8, 5] group sets of objects into classes of similar objects. Possible applications on seismic data could be for the purpose of finding densely populated regions according to the Euclidean distance between the epicenters, and, hence, locating regions of high seismic frequency or dividing the area of a country into a set of seismicity zones (e.g. low / medium / high seismic load) .
- Data classification is a two-step process [5]. In the first step a classification model is built using a *training data set* consisting of database tuples that

it is known to belong in a certain class (or, in many cases, an attribute of the tuples denotes the corresponding class) and a proper supervised learning method, e.g. decision trees [5]. In the second step, this model is used for the classification of tuples not included in the training set. For example, we could classify earthquake data according to magnitude, location of epicenter or their combination.

Visualization techniques can be used either for the purpose of presenting query results or for assisting the user in the formulation of queries and allowing visual feedback to the Knowledge Discovery in Databases (KDD) process. For example, spatial regions can be selected graphically and queries concerning these regions could be subsequently formulated or the selection of variables on which classification will be performed could be decided after the examination of a parallel coordinate plot [7]. Furthermore, visual interaction tools allow quick and easy inspection of spatiotemporal relationships as well as evaluation and interpretation of data mining results.

Widely used visualization techniques include the usage of geographic maps for the visualization of the spatial and temporal distribution of data attributes, clusters and classes and tree views, scatter plots and various types of charts for the visualization of mining results. Examples of mining results visualization include, among others, tree-views for the results of the application of a decision tree learning algorithm and scatter plots for the visualization of relationships between variables of association rules.

3   The SEISMO-SURFER Prototype

For an SDMMS following the above requirements, we propose the architecture presented in figure 2. A number of filters perform Extract-Transform-Load (ETL) operations for integrating data from external data sources (e.g. web sites) into the local database. Hence, a new filter has to be implemented into SEISMO-SURFER each time we would like to connect a new source. The purpose of the data load manager is twofold: (i) it loads filtered data into the local database and (ii) it calculates aggregations and cube operations and updates the data warehouse.

The visual data selector module allows the selection of subsets of data, e.g. by visually zooming into an area of interest or by setting constraints on the values of desirable attributes (figure 3), and the selection of the abstraction level at which the data are studied, e.g. by performing DW operations like drill-down, roll-up etc.

On the other hand, the data mining module includes a set of data mining algorithms providing the main functionality, i.e. classification, association rules and clustering (figure 4). Both off-the-shelf algorithms provided together with the DBMS and from scratch implementations of novel techniques can be exploited.

After the user has selected the data of interest, either by posing queries or after performing a data mining task on the selected data, a data visualization

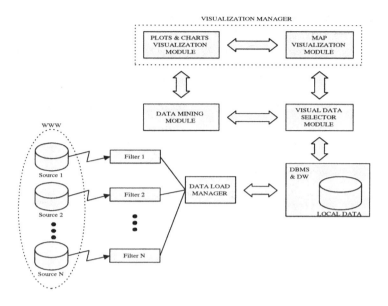

Fig. 2. The SEISMO-SURFER architecture

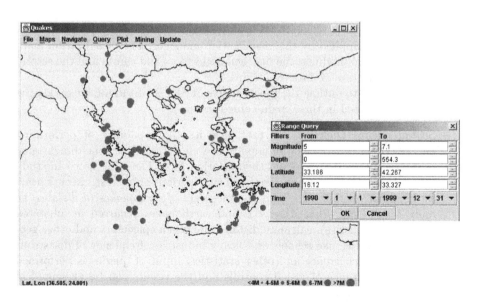

Fig. 3. Screen-shot of our prototype illustrating the spatial distribution of earth-quake epicenters in Greece during 90's, corresponding to $M_L \geq 5$

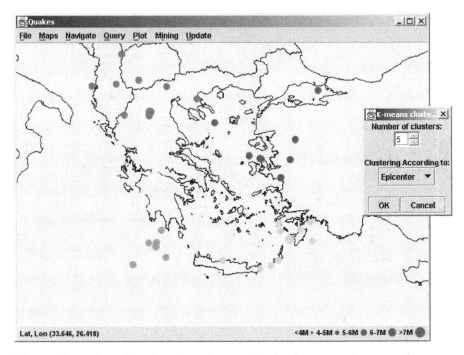

Fig. 4. Clustering of earthquake epicenters in the Aegean and surrounding area using the k-means algorithm. Five clusters are visualized, composing the well known to seismologists "Hellenic arc"

technique can be applied by the visualization manager. The visualization manager consists of two modules; the first generates plots and charts and the second performs visualization of data over maps.

In an attempt to outline the functionality of SEISMO-SURFER, we divide the operations supported in three main categories:

– *Spatiotemporal Queries.* The tool provides the capability of performing queries concerning the spatiotemporal as well as traditional one-dimensional properties of seismic data and their relationships. Thus, the user can study seismicity and by isolating regions and time periods of interest, execute nearest neighbor queries (e.g. *"find all epicenters of earthquakes in distance no more than 50Km from Athens"*), find earthquakes occurred in inhabited areas (range queries), calculate distances between epicenters and other geographical entities like schools and heavy industries, frequency of disastrous earthquakes occurrence and other statistics. Input of queries is performed with the assistance of visual controls and the results can be presented in form of tables or charts and over maps.
– *Data Cube Operations.* The prototype can deal with the very large size of the observational data sets by supporting summarized views of data in different

levels of abstraction of the spatial (e.g. province, country, continent), temporal (e.g. month, year, ten year period) or any other dimension characterizing the data.

— *Remote data sources management functionality.* The proposed architecture provides a flexible implementation framework. For example, as an option, only summaries of seismic data could be stored locally and in case the user requests a detailed data view which is not available, additional data can be loaded, from the remote (web) source, on demand.

— *Simple Mining Operations.* By means of clustering, classification and association rules, SEISMO-SURFER provides capabilities of constructing seismic profiles of certain areas and time periods, of discovering regions of similar seismic behavior, of detecting time recurrent phenomena and of relating seismic parameters between themselves and to information like damages, population of areas, proximity of epicenter to cities etc.

— *Phenomena extraction.* The data mining module is also used for the automatic extraction of semantics from stored data, such as the characterization of the mainshock and possible intensive aftershocks in shock sequences (for example, see figure 5, where M_L values, i.e. the local magnitudes[2] of a shock sequence, are depicted). Moreover, one could search for similar sequences of earthquake magnitudes in time or in space, i.e. time-patterns that occurred in several places or space-patterns that occurred in several time periods.

Furthermore, by providing links between them, the two visualization modules can be used in parallel. For example, rules could be presented in the form of a chart in one window, while, in another window, a map could be showing the spatial distribution of the data for which these rules hold true.

Currently, the prototype is at an early stage of development. In particular:

— Two remote sources have been integrated: one from the Institute of Geodynamics, National Observatory of Athens, with earthquakes in Greece since 1964 and one for recent earthquakes worldwide from the US Geological Survey[3]. Users can check for newly arrived data and, if they exist, the database is updated accordingly.

— Queries are formulated using visual controls for setting conditions on both the alphanumeric and spatiotemporal attributes of data, retrieving and visually presenting qualifying items.

— A data mining algorithm for clustering epicenters, the well known k-means, has been implemented and integrated into the system.

— Basic map functionality (zoom in/out and shift operations) is also provided, while pairs of attributes of the earthquakes whose epicenters are shown on the map can be further explored by means of 2D plots.

---

[2] M_L (local magnitude), developed by Richter in 1935, is only one of earthquake magnitude scales used by seismologists. Other scales also include M_S (surface wave magnitude) and M_W (moment magnitude). For a discussion on these and other scales, see http://www.seismo.berkeley.edu/seismo/faq/magnitude.html.

[3] Available at http://www.gein.noa.gr/services/cat.html and http://neic.usgs.gov/neis/bulletin/, respectively.

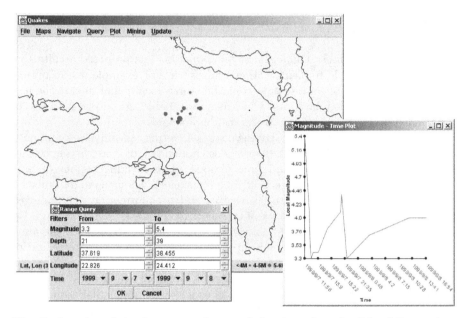

Fig. 5. A series of shocks occurred on and the day after the 7th of September 1999 in Athens, Greece. The greatest peak refers to the disastrous mainshock of local magnitude $M_L = 5.4$, while it is clear that at least one intensive aftershock followed a few hours later

Next stages of development include the implementation of more sophisticated visualization techniques, of more data mining algorithms, of the data warehouse and of more filters for the integration of other web data sources. The underlying database technology used is a modern Object-Relational DBMS, namely Oracle *9i*. For our selection, we considered two issues: first, the special data types, predicates and advanced indexing mechanisms for spatial data incorporated (R-trees and Quadtrees), allowing integration of the models described in section 2 into the database system, and, second, the off-the-shelf data mining algorithms included in this version (naive bayes and decision trees for classification, association rules, clustering using k-means). The data warehouse is also planned to be implemented by taking advantage of the ready to use functionality provided by Oracle *9i*, including support for constructing data cubes, for performing aggregation queries etc.

4   Related Work

Taking into consideration the availability of massive spatiotemporal data sets, the need for high level management, analysis and mining has already been recognized by several researchers as shown by the development of several research prototypes. In the sequel, we briefly describe the purpose and functionality of the most important, to our knowledge so far, that have appeared in the literature. We distinguish two categories of interest. The first includes prototypes that perform one or more of the operations of managing, mining and visualizing either spatial or spatiotemporal data, while the second includes relevant prototypes - applications for scientific and geophysical data.

Geo-miner [6] is a data mining system for spatial data that includes modules for mining (rules, classifications, clusters), for spatial data cube construction and for spatial OLAP. These modules are accompanied with a geo-mining query language and visualization tools.

In [2], the building of an integrated KDD environment for spatial data is proposed, based on the prototypes Kepler, for data mining, and Descartes, for interactive visual analysis. This work is primarily focused on visualization techniques that increase the effectiveness of the KDD process by means of sophisticated user interaction.

In [3], five case studies are presented in order to bring up critical issues and to show the potential contribution of applying data mining techniques for scientific data while application prototypes for several scientific fields (SKICAT for determining whether observed sky objects are stars or galaxies, JarTool for searching for features of interest on the surface of planets, a system for mining bio-sequence databases, Quakefinder for detecting tectonic activity from satellite data and CONQUEST for the analysis of atmospheric data) are presented. This study is mainly concerned with the issues of dealing with the very large size of observational data sets and of how KDD techniques can be used for extracting phenomena on high conceptual level from the low-level data.

Finally, commonGIS [12] is a web-based system for the visualization and analysis of spatially-related statistical data based on the previously mentioned Descartes prototype and on a geo-spatial database. CommonGIS has been used for the construction of a database of earthquake events registered within the European Countries between 500 AC and 1984 DC.

We intend to combine some interesting functionalities of the above systems and integrate them into SEISMO-SURFER. What most distinguishes our prototype from related work is that it proposes a integrated environment for managing and mining spatial data and for the exploitation of heterogeneous data sources.

5 Conclusion

In this paper, we have proposed a novel SDMMS architecture, described its functionality and outlined the potential benefits, by providing extended examples, for potential users: researchers of geophysical sciences, key personnel in public administration as well as people who are just interested on querying or viewing seismic data (web surfers). Main issues discussed include spatiotemporal concepts necessary for the modelling of seismic activity and for efficient storage and retrieval of seismic data, KDD and DW technologies for dealing with the very large amount of available seismic parameters observations and for their effective analysis, and visualization techniques that empower the user to fully exploit the capabilities of an SDMMS by linking it with KDD operations.

Additionally, we have presented SEISMO-SURFER, an SDMMS prototype under development, which fulfills the requirements of the proposed SDMMS architecture. Current implementation includes the functionalities of (a) importing data from a remote web source into the local database, (b) asking queries on both the alphanumeric and the spatiotemporal attributes of data, (c) clustering spatial attributes, such as epicenters, and (d) providing map operations (zoom in/out, shift) and 2D plots. Next development stages include, among others, the data warehouse facility, more data mining algorithms, and filters for new remote data sources.

The current version of SEISMO-SURFER is available at desktop mode. Apart from the above mentioned further development issues, future steps include a web interface, a generator of tectonic activity scenarios and simulator in the line of the GSTD generator for spatiotemporal data [21], as well as a study of how KDD techniques can be applied on seismic data. For example, the exploitation of already proposed clustering algorithms satisfying the special requirement of spatial databases [17, 18] could also be a task for future work.

Acknowledgements

The author wishes to thank the anonymous referees for their comments. This work was partially supported by Directorate-General Environment of the European Commission under grant PEADAB (Post EArthquake Damage and usability Assessment of Buildings)

References

[1] S. Agarwal, R. Agrawal, P. Deshpande, A. Gupta, J. Naughton, R. Ramakrishnan and S. Sarawagi: "On the Computation of Multidimensional Aggregates", *Proceedings 22nd VLDB Conference*, pp.506-521, Bombay, India, September 1996. 162

[2] G. Andrienko and N. Andrienko: "Knowledge-based Visualization to Support Spatial Data Mining", *Proceedings 3rd Symposium on Intelligent Data Analysis*, pp.149-160, Amsterdam, The Netherlands, August 1999. 169

[3] U. Fayyad, D. Haussler and P. Stolorz: "KDD for Science Data Analysis: Issues and examples", *Proceedings 2nd Conference on Knowledge Discovery and Data Mining*, pp.50-56, Portland, OR, 1996. 169

[4] R. Guting, M. Bohlen, M. Erwig, C. Jensen, N. Lorentzos, M. Schneiderand and M. Vazirgiannis: "A Foundation for Representing and Quering Moving Objects", *ACM Transactions on Database Systems*, Vol.25, No.1, pp.1-42, March 2000. 162

[5] J. Han and M. Kamber: "*Data Mining: Concepts and Techniques*", Morgan Kaufmann, 2000. 162, 163, 164

[6] J. Han, K. Koperski, and N. Stefanovic: "GeoMiner: a System Prototype for Spatial Data Mining", *Proceedings ACM SIGMOD Conference*, pp.553-556, Tucson, AZ, May 1997. 169

[7] A. Inselberg: "Multidimensional Detective", *Proceedings IEEE Visualization Conference*, pp.100-107, Phoenix, AZ, October 1997. 164

[8] A. Jain, M. Murty and P. Flynn: "Data Clustering: a Review", *ACM Computing Surveys*, Vol.31, No.3. pp.264-323, September 1999. 163

[9] G. Kollios, V. J. Tsotras, D. Gunopulos, A. Delis and M. Hadjieleftheriou: "Indexing Animated Objects Using Spatiotemporal Access Methods", *IEEE Transactions on Knowledge and Data Engineering*, Vol.13, No.5. pp.758-777, September/October 2001. 162

[10] K. Koperski and J. Han: "Discovery of Spatial Association Rules in Geographic Information Databases", *Proceedings 4th SSD Symposium*, pp.47-66, Portland, Maine, August 1995. 163

[11] K. Koperski, J. Han and J. Adhikary: "Mining Knowledge in Geographical Data", *Communications of the ACM*, Vol.26, No.1. pp.65-74, March 1998. 163

[12] U. Kretschmer and E. Roccatagliata: "CommonGIS: a European Project for an Easy Access to Geo-data", *Proceedings 2nd European GIS Education Seminar (EUGISES)*, Budapest, Hungary, September 2000. 169

[13] M. Nascimento and J. Silva: "Towards Historical R-trees", *Proceedings ACM SAC Symposium*, pp.235-240, Atlanta, GA, February/March 1998.

[14] Oracle Corporation. Oracle R Locator - Location-based Services for Oracle 9i. Oracle Technology Network data sheet, 2002. Available at: http://otn.oracle.com/products/oracle9i/datasheets/spatial/9iR2_locator_ds.html. 160

[15] D. Pfoser, C. Jensen and Y. Theodoridis: "Novel Approaches in Query Processing for Moving Object Trajectories", *Proceedings 26th VLDB Conference*, pp.395-406, Cairo, Egypt, September 2000. 162

[16] D. Pfoser and N. Tryfona: "Requirements, Definitions, and Notations for Spatiotemporal Application Environments", *Proceedings 6th ACM-GIS Symposium*, pp.124-130, Washington, DC, November 1998. 161

[17] J. Sander, M. Ester, H.-P. Kriegel X. Xu: "A Density-Based Algorithm in Spatial Databases: the Algorithm DBSCAN and its Applications", *Data Mining and Knowledge Discovery*, pp.169-194, 1998. 170

[18] C. Sheikholeslami, S. Chatterjee A. Zhang: "WaveCluster: a-MultiResolution Clustering Approach for Very Large Spatial Database", *Proceedings 24th VLDB Conference*, New York, NY, 1998. 170

[19] N. Stefanovic, J. Han and K. Koperski: "Object-Based Selective Materialization for Efficient Implementation of Spatial Data Cubes", *IEEE Transactions on Knowledge and Data Engineering*, Vol.12, pp.6, pp.938-958, November/December 2000. 162

[20] Y. Tao and D. Papadias: "MV3R-Tree: a Spatio-Temporal Access Method for Timestamp and Interval Queries", *Proceedings 27th VLDB Conference*, pp.431-440, Roma, Italy, September 2001. 162

[21] Y. Theodoridis and M. Nascimento: "Spatiotemporal Datasets on the WWW", *ACM SIGMOD Record*, Vol.29, No.3, pp,.39-43, September 2000. 170

[22] Y. Theodoridis, M. Vazirgiannis and T. Sellis: "Spatio-temporal Indexing for Large Multimedia Applications", *Proceedings 3rd IEEE Conference on Multimedia Computing and Systems*, pp.441–448, Hiroshima, Japan, 1996.

Using Fuzzy Cognitive Maps
as a Decision Support System for Political Decisions

Athanasios K. Tsadiras[1], Ilias Kouskouvelis[2], and Konstantinos G. Margaritis[1]

[1] Department of Applied Informatics
[2] Department of International & European
Economic & Political Studies University of Macedonia
Egnatias 156, P.O.Box 1591, Thessaloniki 54006, Greece

Abstract. In this paper we use Fuzzy Cognitive Maps (FCMs), a well-established Artificial Intelligence technique that incorporates ideas from Artificial Neural Networks and Fuzzy Logic, to create a dynamic model of the Former Yugoslavian Republic of Macedonia (FYROM) Crisis in March 2001. FCMs create models as collections of concepts and the various causal relations that exist between these concepts. The decision capabilities of the FCM structure are examined and presented using a model that is developed based on the beliefs of a domain expert. The model is first examined statically using graph theory techniques to identify the vicious or the virtuous cycles of the decision process. The model is also tested dynamically thought simulations, in order to support political analysts and decision makers to their political decisions concerning the crisis. Scenarios are introduced and predictions are made by viewing dynamically the consequences of the corresponding actions.

1   Introduction to Fuzzy Cognitive Maps

International Relations theory has long been concerned with Decision-Making, negotiations and crisis management [1]. Cognitive Map (CM) models were introduced by Axelrod in the late 1970s and were widely used for Political Analysis and Decision Making in International Relations [2]. The structural and decision potentials of such models were studied and the explanation and prediction capabilities were identified [2,3]. The introduction of Fuzzy Logic gave new representing capabilities to CMs and led to the development of Fuzzy Cognitive Maps by Kosko in the late 1980s [4,5]. The use of fuzzy logic allows the representation both of the type (positive or negative) of the causal relationships that exist among the concepts of the model but also of the degree of the causal relationship.

FCMs models are created as collections of concepts and the various causal relationships that exist between these concepts. The concepts are represented by nodes and the causal relationships by directed arcs between the nodes. Each arc is accompanied by a weight that defines the degree of the causal relation between the two nodes.

Y. Manolopoulos et al. (Eds.): PCI 2001, LNCS 2563, pp. 172-182, 2003.

The sign of the weight determines the positive or negative causal relation between the two concepts-nodes. An example of FCM is given in figure 1, showing the causal relationships that were identified in Henry A. Kinssinger's essay "Starting Out in the Direction of Middle East Peace" in *Los Angeles Times* 1982 and presented in [6].

In FCMs, although the degree of the causal relationships could be represented by a number in the interval [-1,1], each concept, in a binary manner, could be either activated or not activated. In 1997, Certainty Neuron Fuzzy Cognitive Maps (CNFCMs) were introduced [7], providing additional fuzzification to FCMs, by allowing each concept's activation to be activated just to a degree. The aggregation of the influences that each concept receives from other concepts is handled by function $f_M()$ that was used in MYCIN Expert System [8,9] for certainty factors' handling. The dynamical behaviour and the characteristics of this function are studied in [10]. Certainty Neurons are defined as artificial neurons that use this function as their threshold function [11]. Using such neurons, the updating function of CNFCMs as a dynamic evolving system is the following:

$$A_i^{t+1} = f_M (A_i^t , S_i^t)- d_i\ A_i^t \tag{1}$$

where, A_i^{t+1} is the activation level of concept C_i at time step t+1, $S_i^t = \sum_j w_{ji}A_j^t$ is

the sum of the weight influences that concept C_i receives at time step t from all other concepts, d_i is a decay factor and

$$f_M(A_i^t,S_i^t)=\begin{cases} A_i^t+S_i^t(1-A_i^t)=A_i^t+S_i^t-S_i^tA_i^t & if\ A_i^t \geq 0,\ S_i^t \geq 0 \\ A_i^t+S_i^t(1+A_i^t)=A_i^t+S_i^t+S_i^tA_i^t & if\ A_i^t <0,\ S_i^t <0 \quad |A_i^t|,|S_i^t|\leq 1 \\ (A_i^t+S_i^t)/(1-\min(|A_i^t|,|S_i^t|)) & otherwise \end{cases} \tag{2}$$

is the function that was used for the aggregation of certainty factors to the MYCIN expert system.

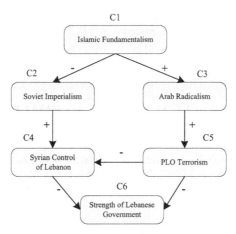

Fig.1. Henry Kissinger's FCM [6]

2   The FYROM Crisis

FYROM is one of the states created after the 1991 breakdown of the Yugoslav Federation. It is composed by two ethnic groups: Slavs and Albanians (estimated between 25 and 40%).

In the first days of March 2001 the Albanian insurgents initiated their open military and political actions against FYROM and its government, in the area neighbouring FYROM's borders with Kosovo. The actions were spread to some of FYROM's main cities, particularly where the majority of the population is Albanian. The Albanian insurgents demanded better political and economic standing for Albanians in the country. Behind that, the dream of "Great Albania" or "Great Independent Kosovo" could be hidden, especially when the political future of Kosovo is still uncertain. It was argued by politicians and international relations experts in the press that such a conflict to a new country as FYROM could cause multiple stability problems and affect the general stability of the whole Balkan region [12,13,14]. Under these conditions, voices were raised asking the international community to interfere.

FYROM's government admitted that it underestimated the power and the problems that Albanian insurgents could cause to the country and asked for better patrolling by KFOR of the borders between Kosovo and FYROM in order to reduce possible assistance by Kosovo Albanians to insurgents. FYROM's neighboring countries such as Greece and Bulgaria expressed voiced concern for a domino phenomenon, spreading war to their territories. Greece has undertaken contacts for a NATO and EU involvement seeking a peaceful settlement of the conflict. European Union countries, the USA, NATO, and even Albania stated their position that the current borders of FYROM should remain stable and gave political support to FYROM's government against Albanian insurgents.

FYROM's government for resolving the conflict, among other things, had to take into consideration the following two basic questions:

a)   Will better political and economic standing of FYROM's Albanians cause the decrease of their demands or this will cause the increase of their demands, asking even for complete independence from FYROM?
b)   Are Albanian insurgents supported by other third parties and to what degree? How these parties would react if FYROM asks and gets military support from other countries?

3   Development of FCM Model for FYROM Crisis

The reliability of an FCM model depends on whether its construction method follows rules that ensure its reliability. There are two main methods for the construction of FCMs :

a)   The Documentary Coding method [15], which involves the systematic encoding of documents that present the assertions of a specific person for the specific topic.
b)   The Questionnaire method [16,17] which involves interviews and filling in of questionnaires by domain experts.

Instability in FYROM will cause and to what degree to the following:	Very Big		Big		Moderate		Small		Very Small		No
Political support from NATO											
Financial Support from Greece											
Appeasement from FYROM's government											
......											
Numerical weights	1	0.9	0.8	0.7	0.6	0.5	0.4	0.3	0.2	0.1	0

Fig.2. Part of the questionnaire concerning FYROM crisis

For our case we used the second method, interviewing and also supplying with questionnaires a domain expert. The domain expert was a faculty member of the Department of International & European, Economic & Political Studies of the University of Macedonia. During the interviews, the concepts that should be included in the model were identified. In questionnaires the causal relationship that exist between these concepts were defined by the expert, accompanied by the degree to which a concept influence each other concept. The format of the questionnaire is given in Figure 2.

The expert had to fill in with + or – whether he believed that there is a positive or negative causal relationship between the concepts. The degree of these causal relationships was captured by allowing the expert to fill in the sign in one of the fields "Very Big", "Big", "Moderate", "Small", "Very Small". These linguistic values could be transformed into numerical weights by assigning weights from the interval [0,1] according to the way that is shown in figure 2. If according to his believe there is no causal relationship, the field "none" could be checked. After studying the questionnaires and taking the weights identified by expert, the model presented in figure 3 was developed. In figure 3, only the signs of the arcs-causal relationships are shown. The weights of the arcs are given in Appendix A. The model created is studied both statically and dynamically.

4   Static Analysis

The static analysis of the model is based on studying the characteristics of the weighted directed graph that represent the model, using graph theory techniques. The most important feature that should be studied is that of the feed back cycles that exist in the graph. Each cycle is accompanied by a sign, identified by multiplying the signs of the arcs that participate in the cycle. Positive cycles behaviour is that of amplifying any initial change, leading to a constant increase in case an increase is introduced to the system. This is why they are also called deviation amplifying cycles [18], augmenting cycles [17] or vicious cycles [19], [18], [20]. An example of a positive/vicious cycle is that of C1(Albanians insurgents actions in FYROM) ⇨ C5 (Instability in FYROM) ⇨ C14 (Military support from Greece) ⇨ C3 (Support to Albanian insurgents from other third parties) ⇨ C1(Albanian insurgents actions in FYROM). Through this cycle the "Instability of FYROM" will constantly increase.

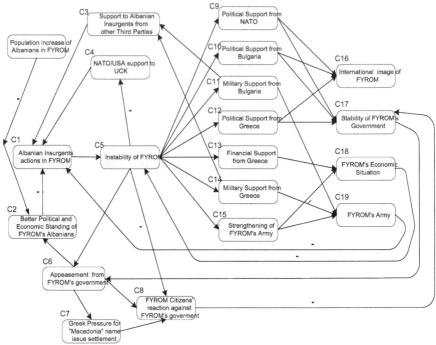

Fig.3. FYROM's crisis FCM model

Negative cycles on the other hand, counteract any initial change. This means that they lead to decrease in the case where an increase is introduced in the cycle. Negative cycles are also called deviation counteracting cycles [18], inhibiting cycles [17] or virtuous cycles [19], [18], [20]. An example of a negative/virtuous cycle is that of C1 (Albanian insurgents actions in FYROM) ⇨ C5 (Instability in FYROM) ⇨ C14 (Military support from Greece) ⇨ C19 (FYROM's Army) ⇨(-) C1 (Albanian insurgents actions in FYROM). Through this cycle the "Instability of FYROM" will constantly decrease. The model of Figure 3 is rich of cycles. All cycles appear in Table I

In Table I the signs of the cycles are shown for two scenarios. In scenario #1, the weight w21 that connects Concept 2 ("Better Political and Economic Standing of FYROM's Albanians") to Concept 1 ("Albanian insurgents' actions in FYROM") is negative. This means that if FYROM's government measures provide better political and economic standing to FYROM's Albanian population, there will be a decrease of Albanian insurgents' actions. In this case the FCM model has eleven negative (deviation counteracting) cycles and three positive (deviation amplifying) cycles, showing a preference towards moderation.

In scenario #2, the weight w21 is positive, meaning that if FYROM's government measurements provide better political and economic standing to FYROM's Albanians, there will be an increase of Albanian insurgents' actions, asking for even more. In this case the FCM model has seven negative (deviation counteracting) cycles and seven positive (deviation amplifying) cycles, showing strong interactions among the concepts of the model and instability. Four cycles changed sign if compared with scenario #1 and they appear shadowed in Table I. All fourteen cycles exist concurrently in domain expert's mind. Which of the cycles will prevail is difficult to know even for model with much less cycles. Additionally, it is difficult to make scenarios, predictions and draw conclusions, having all these cycles in mind. For this reason, dynamical analysis and simulations are required.

Table 1.

	Cycles	Scenario #1 (w21 : negative)	Scenario #2 (w21 : positive)
1	C5 ⇨C9 ⇨ C17 ⇨ C6 ⇨ C2 ⇨ C1 ⇨ C5	-	+
2	C5 ⇨C10 ⇨ C17 ⇨ C6 ⇨ C2 ⇨ C1 ⇨ C5	-	+
3	C5 ⇨C12 ⇨ C17 ⇨ C6 ⇨ C2 ⇨ C1 ⇨ C5	-	+
4	C5 ⇨C11 ⇨ C19 ⇨ C1 ⇨ C5	-	-
5	C5 ⇨C14 ⇨ C19 ⇨ C1 ⇨ C5	-	-
6	C5 ⇨C15 ⇨ C19 ⇨ C1 ⇨ C5	-	-
7	C5 ⇨C13 ⇨ C18 ⇨ C5	-	-
8	C5 ⇨C15 ⇨ C18 ⇨ C5	+	+
9	C5 ⇨ C6 ⇨ C2 ⇨ C1 ⇨ C5	-	+
10	C5 ⇨ C4 ⇨ C1 ⇨ C5	-	-
11	C5 ⇨ C11 ⇨ C3 ⇨ C1 ⇨ C5	+	+
12	C5 ⇨ C14 ⇨ C3 ⇨ C1 ⇨ C5	+	+
13	C17 ⇨ C6 ⇨ C7 ⇨ C8 ⇨ C17	-	-
14	C17 ⇨ C6 ⇨ C8 ⇨ C17	-	-

5   Dynamical Analysis

After some indications for stability or instability that were found from the static analysis of the model, conclusions will be drawn by simulating. The model of figure 3 was simulated using the CNFCM technique that was mentioned in section 1. Initially the weight w21 was set to a negative value (scenario #1 of Table I). The initial values of the activation levels of all the concepts in the model were determined by the domain expert. The concepts of the system were left free to interact and the nineteen concepts of the system reach equilibrium at zero after almost 250 iterations. The transition of the system to equilibrium is shown in fig 4.

The study of the transition phase of the FYROM's crisis CNFCM has shown that the strength of the negative cycles that counteracted any cause of instability in FYROM was such that led to equilibrium at zero. The support (political, financial and military) that FYROM received from third parties (NATO, Greece, Bulgaria) gave stability to FYROM's government, strengthened its economic situation, and through the actions of FYROM's army the actions Albanian insurgents were ceased. Furthermore FYROM's government took measures for better political and economic standing of FYROM's Albanians. In this way, part of the demands of the Albanians were satisfied, limiting the support of FYROM's Albanians to Albanian insurgents. The support of other third parties to Albanian insurgents did not manage to maintain insurgents' actions.

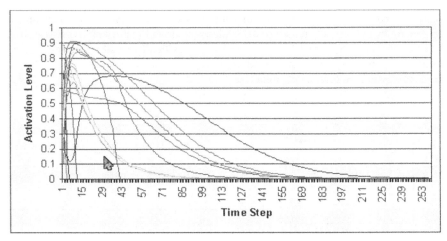

Fig.4. Transition phase of FYROM's crisis CNFCM. System stabilizes at zero (scenario #1: w21 is negative)

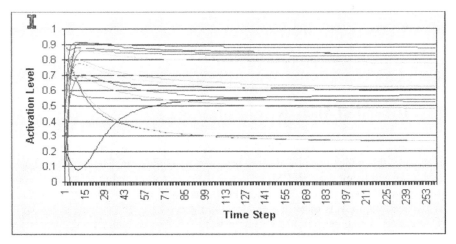

Fig.5. Transition phase of FYROM's crisis CNFCM. System stabilizes at no zero (scenario #2: w21 is positive)

The second scenario that was suggested by the expert and introduced to the system is that of scenario #2, where weight w21 is positive, meaning that actions from FY-ROM's government towards better political and economic standing of FYROM's Albanians will be taken as a proof that violence did its work and so Albanians will ask for even more rights. Simulation of this scenario, using the CNFCM technique, give the results of Figure 5.

Now the dynamic behaviour of the system is different. The system reaches once again equilibrium but not at zero. On the contrary, all concepts have an activation level in the interval [0,1] that represent the degree of each concept's activation. The equilibrium point, with the activation levels of all concepts at equilibrium, is given in

Appendix B. It should be noticed that the system stabilizes with FYROM being instable. Concept "Instability of FYROM" has an activation level 0.259 that means there is some instability despite the measures that FYROM's government takes and the support that FYROM receives from NATO, Greece and Bulgaria. The main reason for this is that the support to FYROM's government from Greece and Bulgaria causes other third part countries to support Albanian insurgents. Furthermore, the increase of the population of Albanians in FYROM is another reason for constant instability, as indicated by the expert. This constant instability will change when some concepts or causal relationships of the model are affected by a factor external to the model.

Another suggested scenario was introduced to the model, testing the stability of the system according to the degree of the support that Albanian insurgents receive from other countries. In this third scenario, as in scenario #2, the weight w21 is positive, but now the support that Albanian insurgents receive from other countries is less (weight w31 changed from 0.5 to 0.2). The transition phase of the simulation of this third scenario is given in figure 6. Like scenario #1, the system reaches equilibrium at zero, meaning that Albanian insurgents actions in FYROM are ceased. This means that even if, when FYROM's government gives rights to Albanians and FYROM's Albanians ask for more, the battles of Albanian insurgents will cease if they are not well supported by other third parties.

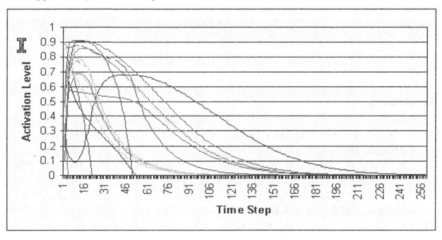

Fig.6. Transition phase of FYROM's crisis CNFCM. System stabilizes at zero (scenario #3: w21 is positive, w31 decreased to 0.2)

6   Summary – Conclusions

Using the FCM method, a model was created for FYROM's crisis in March 2001, based on the opinion of a domain expert. The model was examined statically and the signs of model's fourteen cycles were identified. Using the CNFCM technique for simulations, three scenarios were introduced to the model. Through the study of the simulations, the conclusions that were drawn and concern the FYROM crisis are the following:

The model predicted a different outcome of the crisis, depending on :

a)   whether providing of better political and economic standing for FYROM's Albanians by FYROM's government will cause decrease of Albanian insurgents' actions (since their demands are even partly satisfied, FYROM's Albanian citizens do not support any more actions by insurgents) or increase of Albanian insurgents' actions (since they see that violence had an effect and so they ask for more).

b)   the degree to which other third parties support Albanian insurgents, especially when FYROM gets support by countries such as Greece, Bulgaria or by NATO.

So before any decision is taken, a good estimation of these factors is vital for making the right decisions. Apart from just making estimations of these factors, in a more drastic manner, measurements can be taken to affect these key factors for the crisis outcome. In this way political decisions can be taken and supported by a CNFCM model.

In this study, CNFCM technique was found capable of providing decision makers and political analysts with a decision support system. The CNFCM flexible structure proved suitable for making political decisions in fuzzy and uncertain situations like political crisis. Predictions can be made and scenarios can be introduced and tested through simulations. The important key for the success of an FCM model remains the validity of the knowledge that is extracted from domain experts and is used for the creation of the model.

References

[1]   I. Kouskouvelis: "*Decision Making, Crisis, Negotiation*" (in greek), Papazisis, Atrhens, 1997.

[2]   R. Axelrod: "*Structure of Decision. The Cognitive Maps of Political Elites*", Princeton University Press, Princeton, NJ, 1976.

[3]   J. A. Hart: "Cognitive Maps of Three Latin American Policy Makers", *World Politics*, Vol.30, pp.115-140, 1977.

[4]   B. Kosko: "Fuzzy Cognitive Maps," *International Journal of Man-Machine Studies*, Vol.24, pp.65-75, 1986.

[5]   B. Kosko: "*Neural Networks and Fuzzy Systems*", Prentice Hall, 1992.

[6]   B. Kosko: "*Fuzzy Thinking. the New Science of Fuzzy Logic*", Harper Collins, London, 1994.

[7]   A. K. Tsadiras and K.G. Margaritis: "Cognitive Mapping and the Certainty Neuron Fuzzy Cognitive Maps", *Information Sciences*, Vol.101, pp.109-130, 1997.

[8]   E. H. Shortliffe: "*Computer-based Medical Consultations:MYCIN*", Elsevier, New York, 1976.

[9]   B. G. Buchanan and E.H. Shortliffe: "Rule-Based Expert Systems. The MYCIN Experiments of the Stanford Heuristic Programming Project", Addison-Wesley, Reading, MA, 1984.

[10] A. K. Tsadiras and K.G. Margaritis: "The MYCIN Certainty Factor Handling Function as Uninorm Operator and its Use as Threshold Function in Artificial Neurons", *Fuzzy Set and Systems*, Vol.93, pp.263-274, 1998.

[11] A. K. Tsadiras and K.G. Margaritis: "Using Certainty Neurons in Fuzzy Cognitive Maps", *Neural Network World*, Vol.6, pp.719-728, 1996.

[12] S. Kouzinopoulos: "The Crisis in FYROM and the Dream of `Great Kosovo'", Macedonian Press Agency, March 2001. Available at: http://philippos.mpa.gr/gr/other/crisis/

[13] Newspaper Macedonia: "Crisis in FYROM", 18 March 2001.

[14] L. Branson: "It's only a Lull in Balkans Drama. Act II: The Fight for Greater Albania", *Washington Post*, 15 April 2001, pp. B02.

[15] M. T. Wrightson: "The Documentary Coding Method", in "*Structure of Decision. The Cognitive Maps of Political Elites*", R. Axelrod (ed.), pp.291-332, Princeton University Press, Princeton, NJ, 1976.

[16] F. R. Roberts: "Strategy for the Energy Crisis: the Case of Commuter Transportation Policy", in "*Structure of Decision. The Cognitive Maps of Political Elites*", R. Axelrod (ed.), pp.142-179, Princeton University Press, Princeton, NJ, 1976.

[17] F. S. Roberts: "Weighted Digraph Models for the Assessment of Energy Use and Air Pollution in Transportation Systems", *Environment and Planning*, Vol.7, pp.703-724, 1975.

[18] M. Masuch: "Vicious Circles in Organizations", *Administrative Science Quarterly*, Vol.30, pp.14-33, 1985.

[19] A. Ramaprasad and E. Poon: "A Computer Interactive Technique for Mapping Influence Diagrams (MIND)", *Strategic Management Journal*, Vol.6, pp.377-392, 1985.

[20] M. G. Bougon: "Congregate Cognitive Maps: a Unified Dynamic Theory of Organization and Strategy", *Journal of Management Studies*, Vol.29, pp.369-389, 1992.

Appendix A – Weights of Causal Relationships between Concepts

	C1	C2	C3	C4	C5	C6	C7	C8	C9	C10	C11	C12	C13	C14	C15	C16	C17	C18	C19
C1	0	-0.8	0.5	0.7	0	0	0	0	0	0	0	0	0	0	0	0	0	0	-0.9
C2	0	0	0	0	0	0.8	0	0	0	0	0	0	0	0	0	0	0	0	0
C3	0	0	0	0	0	0	0	0	0	0	0.5	0	0	0.8	0	0	0	0	0
C4	0	0	0	0	-0.9	0	0	0	0	0	0	0	0	0	0	0	0	0	0
C5	0.9	0	0	0	0	0	0	0	0	0	0	0	0	0	0	0	0	-0.6	0
C6	0	0	0	0	0.7	0	0	0	0	0	0	0	0	0	0	0	0.7	0	0
C7	0	0	0	0	0	0.2	0	0	0	0	0	0	0	0	0	0	0	0	0
C8	0	0	0	0	-0.5	0	0.6	0	0	0	0	0	0	0	0	0	0	0	0
C9	0	0	0	0	0.6	0	0	0	0	0	0	0	0	0	0	0	0	0	0
C10	0	0	0	0	0.8	0	0	0	0	0	0	0	0	0	0	0	0	0	0
C11	0	0	0	0	0.2	0	0	0	0	0	0	0	0	0	0	0	0	0	0
C12	0	0	0	0	0.9	0	0	0	0	0	0	0	0	0	0	0	0	0	0
C13	0	0	0	0	0.5	0	0	0	0	0	0	0	0	0	0	0	0	0	0
C14	0	0	0	0	0.2	0	0	0	0	0	0	0	0	0	0	0	0	0	0
C15	0	0	0	0	0.9	0	0	0	0	0	0	0	0	0	0	0	0	0	0
C16	0	0	0	0	0	0	0	-0.8	0.9	0.2	0	0.4	0	0	0	0	0	0	0
C17	0	0	0	0	0	0	0	0	0.8	0.5	0	0.8	0	0	0	0	0	0	0
C18	0	0	0	0	0	0	0	0	0	0	0	0	0.5	0	0.7	0	0	0	0
C19	0	0	0	0	0	0	0	0	0	0	0.7	0	0	0.7	0.7	0	0	0	0

Appendix B – Equilibrium Point of scenario #2

	C1	C2	C3	C4	C5	C6	C7	C8	C9	C10	C11	C12	C13	C14	C15	C16	C17	C18	C19
Activation Level	0.604	0.777	0.777	0	0.259	0.841	0.537	0.570	0.517	0.588	0.588	0.617	0.472	0.263	0.617	0.851	0.837	0.821	0.876

An Architecture
for Open Learning Management Systems

Paris Avgeriou[1], Simos Retalis[2], and Manolis Skordalakis[1]

[1] Software Engineering Lab, Department of Electrical & Computer Engineering
National Technical University of Athens, Zografu, Athens, 15780 Greece
{pavger,skordala}@softlab.ntua.gr
[2] Department of Computer Science, University of Cyprus
75 Kallipoleos St., P.O. Box 20537, 1678 Nicosia, Cyprus
retal@softlab.ntua.gr

Abstract. There exists an urgent demand on defining architectures for Learning Management Systems, so that high-level frameworks for understanding these systems can be discovered, and quality attributes like portability, interoperability, reusability and modifiability can be achieved. In this paper we propose a prototype architecture aimed to engineer Open Learning Management Systems, that professes state-of-the-art software engineering techniques such as layered structure and component-based nature. Our work is based upon standards and practices from international standardization bodies, on the empirical results of designing, developing and evaluating Learning Management Systems and on the practices of well-established software engineering techniques.

1 Introduction

Governments, authorities and organizations comprehend the potential of the Internet to transform the educational experience and envisage a knowledge-based future where acquiring and acting on knowledge is the primary operation of all life-long learners. In order to realize this vision, the use of Learning Technology Systems (LTS) is being exponentially augmented and broadened to cover all fields of the new economy demands. *Learning Technology Systems (LTS)* are learning, education and training systems that are supported by the Information Technology [1]. Examples of such systems are computer-based training systems, intelligent tutoring systems, Web-based Instructional Systems and so on.

Web-based Instructional Systems (WbISs) are LTSs that are based on the state-of-the-art Internet and WWW technologies in order to provide education and training following the open and distance learning paradigm. WbISs are comprised of three parts: *human resources* (students, professors, tutors, administrators etc.), *learning resources* (e-book, course notes etc.), and *technological infrastructure* (hardware, software, networks). A major part of the technological infrastructure of WbISs is the *Learning Management System (LMS)*. LMSs are software systems that synthesize the

Y. Manolopoulos et al. (Eds.): PCI 2001, LNCS 2563, pp. 183-200, 2003.

functionality of computer-mediated communications software (e-mail, bulletin boards, newsgroups etc.) and on-line methods of delivering courseware (e.g. the WWW) [2]. An LMS is a middleware that acts and interfaces between the low-level infrastructure of the Internet and the WWW from the one side and the customized domain-specific learning education and training systems on the other side.

LMSs have been established as the basic infrastructure for supporting the technology-based, open and distance-learning process in an easy-to-use, pedagogically correct and cost-efficient manner. LMSs have been used for educational and training purposes, not only because they have been advertised as the state of the art learning technology, but also because they have substantial benefits to offer. In specific, they alleviate the constraints of time and place of learning; they grant multiple media delivery methods through hypermedia; they allow several synchronous and asynchronous communication facilities; they provide an excellent degree of flexibility concerning the way of learning; they support advanced interactivity between tutors and learners and they grant one-stop maintenance and reusability of resources [3, 4].

LMSs that are in use today are either commercial products (e.g. WebCT, Blackboard, Intralearn), or customized software systems that serve the instructional purposes of particular organizations. The design and development of LMSs though, is largely focused on satisfying certain *functional* requirements, such as the creation and distribution of on-line learning material, the communication and collaboration between the various actors, the management of institutional information systems and so on. On the contrary, the *quality* requirements of LMSs are usually overlooked and underestimated. This naturally results in inefficient systems of poor software, pedagogical and business quality. Problems that typically occur in these cases are: bad performance which is usually frustrating for the users; poor usability, that adds a cognitive overload to the user; increased cost for purchasing and maintaining the systems; poor customizability and modifiability; limited portability and reusability of learning resources and components; restricted intercpcrability between LMSs.

The question that arises is how can these deficiencies be remedied, how can the quality attributes be incorporated into the LMSs being engineered? Quality attributes in a software system depend profoundly on its architecture and are an immediate outcome of it [5, 6, 7, 8]. Therefore the support for qualities should be designed *into the architecture* of the system [7, 8, 9]. These principles have only recently been widely accepted and adopted and have lead to a research trend into defining software architectures that support quality attributes. Furthermore some of this effort is focused not only in developing but in standardizing software architectures LMSs, in order to provide a more systematic development process for these systems and achieve the aforementioned goals. At present there is an increasing interest in defining such architectures, from academic research teams (e.g. the Open Knowledge Initiative project http://web.mit.edu/oki/), from the corporate world (e.g. Sun Microsystems, see [9] and [10]), and from standardization bodies (e.g. the IEEE LTSC Learning Technology Systems Architecture, [http://ltsc.ieee.org/wg1/]). This paper describes a similar effort of defining a layered component-based architecture for LMSs and primarily aims at the incorporation of quality attributes into the LMS under construction. The ultimate goal is to build truly *Open* Learning Management Systems, that conform to the definition of *Open Systems* given by the Reference Model of Open Distributed Processing (RM-ODP) [12]: "Open systems are systems that are designed to enable portability of the software, and to allow other software entities to interoperate with it across dissimilar software and systems, whether or not the software entities are on the same computer or reside on different computers."

The structure of the paper is as follows: In section 2 we provide the theoretical background of the proposed architecture in terms of the context of LMSs, i.e. Web-based Instructional Systems and Learning Technology Systems. Section 3 deals with the description of the architecture per se. Section 4 contains conclusions about the added value of our approach and future plans.

2   Business Systems Are Supported by LMSs

As aforementioned we consider Learning Management Systems to be a part of one of the three components of Web-based Instructional Systems, and in particular the technological infrastructure. In order to comprehend the nature and characteristics of LMSs, we need to put things into perspective and take into account the context of LMSs, i.e. the WbIS and the LTS. Learning Technology Systems, and their specializations, like WbIS, can be considered as *business systems* that are supported by special *software systems*, like LMSs, which automate some of the business processes [13]. The reason for studying the generic category of LTSs is that there is a lot of work being done on the standardization of LTS architectures, and the development of LMSs can benefit from basing its foundations on such a strong and commonly accepted background.

We thus adopt a three-fold approach: we see LMSs as part of WbISs and the latter as children of LTSs, as illustrated in Figure 1. The profit of this approach is that the LTS refined into a WbIS can provide the business case for the LMS under development and can act as the business model in the architecture-centric approach of an LMS engineering process. This, in turn, provides the following advantages [7]:

1. The LMS become an integrated part of the overall business supporting the business and enhancing the work and the results.
2. The LMS and the business systems integrate easily with each other and can share and exchange information.
3. The LMS are easier to update and modify as dictated by changes in the business model. This in turn reduces the cost of maintaining the LMS and of continuously updating the business processes.
4. Business logic can be reused in several systems.

2.1   The LTS and WbIS Business Systems

The largest effort on developing an LTS architecture has been carried out in the IEEE P1484.1 Learning Technology Systems Architecture (LTSA) working group, which has developed a tentative and rather stable working standard. The LTSA describes a high-level system architecture and layering for learning technology systems, and identifies the objectives of human activities and computer processes and their involved categories of knowledge. These are all encompassed into 5 layers, where each layer is a refinement of the concepts in the above layer.

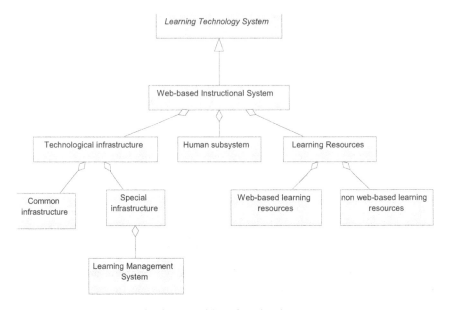

Fig. 1. The decomposition of a WbIS into components

Out of the five refinement layers of architecture specified in the LTSA, only layer 3 (system components) is normative in this Standard. Layer 1, *"Learner and Environment Interactions"* addresses the learner's acquisition, transfer, exchange, formulation, discovery, etc. of knowledge and/or information through interaction with the environment. Layer 2, *"Human-Centered and Pervasive Features"* addresses the human aspects of learning technology systems in terms of human-specific strengths and weaknesses. Layer 3, *"System Components"* describes the component-based architecture, as identified in human-centered and pervasive features. Layer 4, *"Stakeholder Perspectives and Priorities"* describes learning technology systems from a variety of perspectives by reference to subsets of the system components layer. Layer 5, *"Operational Components and Interoperability — codings, APIs, protocols"* describes the generic "plug-n-play" (interoperable) components and interfaces of an information technology-based learning technology architecture, as identified in the stakeholder perspectives. The added value derived from the abstraction-implementation layers, is that the five layers represent five independent areas of technical analysis, which makes it easier to discuss each layer independently of the others.

LTSs are applied in a plethora of domains for learning education and training purposes. A very popular domain of LTS application is web-based open and distance learning. There are currently no standards for architecting and building systems in this particular domain, so we will present a prototype architecture of *Web-based Instructional Systems (WbISs)* that has derived from experience on instructional design and has been mostly influenced by the LTSA. According to this architecture, WbISs are comprised of:

- *The human subsystem*, which describes the roles, in as much detail as possible, for each kind of human agent involved in the instructional process [14].

- *The learning resources subsystem,* which is divided into web-based learning resources and non web-based learning resources. The former is perceived as a mosaic of online learning resources. Such learning resources can be course notes, slideware, study guides, self-assessment questionnaires, communication archives, learning material used for communication purposes, etc. The latter is comprised of digital or non-digital learning resources that are <u>not</u> deployed on the WWW like textbooks, papers, audio/video cassettes, CDs, DVDs, etc.
- *The technological infrastructure subsystem,* which is divided into common and special. An instructional system basically makes use of services from *common infrastructure*, which is a set of *learning places*, that support student learning in general (e.g. laboratories, networking facilities, etc.). However, in order to best support the instructional process, *special infrastructure* should be created (e.g. multimedia conferencing systems, state of the art hardware and software components etc.), which will provide services unique to a particular instructional problem. [13]. A most significant part of the special infrastructure is the LMS.

The decomposition of a WbIS using the UML notation is depicted in Figure 1 shown above.

2.2   Overview of LMS

Systems exist and have certain meaning and purpose within certain business contexts. Now that we have identified LTSs and WbISs, we can define LMSs, so that the latter will make sense in the bounds of the former.

A vast number of Learning Management Systems (e.g. WebCT, Blackboard, LearningSpace, Centra, TopClass) that provide integrated services, exist nowadays [2, 10]. Such systems offer different services and capabilities regarding organization and distribution of learning content, course management, student assessment, communication and collaboration tools, administration of instructional institutions and so forth. They offer different features and address different needs and concerns as far as pedagogy, open learning and instructional design are concerned. Consequently instructional designers that are called upon to solve a specific instructional problem with explicit needs and requirements must choose a specific LMS that fits closer to the above problem. In particular, the people involved in the decision-making process concerning instructional design and organization of educational institutions would use a Learning Management System in order to:

- Create, operate and administrate an on-line course.
- Support the collaboration between students and provide motivation and resources for team building [15].
- Create and deliver questions and tests for student assessment.
- Organize educational, financial and human resources.
- Administer virtual, distributed classes where the students are geographically scattered and communicate via the Internet.

These diverse usage scenarios of LMS, correspond to different categories of Learning Technology Systems, which are respectively the following:

General Systems, which have a number of tools for creating and managing courses and do not give emphasis to any particular set of features. We call these systems 'general' and not, for example 'Course Management', because they provide a plethora of features that span many assorted areas, in order to provide fully functional on-line courses, such as communication tools, administration tools, etc. These systems are also called **Learning Portals** and **Course Management Systems**.

Learning Content Management Systems, which deal with creating, storing, assembling, managing and delivering hypermedia learning content. Often these systems provide metadata management tools so that learning material is accompanied by appropriate metadata [16].

Collaborative Learning Support Systems, which emphasize on team building, student group management and providing the synchronous and asynchronous collaboration tools to support the aforementioned activities.

Question and Test Authoring and Management Systems, which facilitate the design and authoring of quizzes and tests, which are published on the WWW and taken on-line. They provide tools for test creation and their on-line delivery, automatic grading, results manipulation and report generation.

People and Institute Resource Management Systems, which deal with human resources and financial management. These systems are also called **Student Administration Systems**.

Virtual Classrooms, which establish a virtual space for live interaction between all the participants in the learning process, i.e. instructors, tutors and students.

The LMS that can be classified in each one of the above categories support a number of **features**, or tools or capabilities in order to carry out certain tasks. These features do not discretely belong to only one LMS category but can be shared by several categories. These features can be classified into certain groups, namely [17]:

Course Management, which contains features for the creation, customisation, administration and monitoring of courses.

Class Management, which contains features for user management, team building, projects assignments etc.

Communication Tools, which contains features for synchronous and asynchronous communication such as e-mail, chat, discussion fora, audio/video-conferencing, announcements and synchronous collaborative facilities (desktop, file and application sharing, whiteboard).

Student Tools, which provide features to support students into managing and studying the learning resources, such as private & public annotations, highlights, bookmarks, off-line studying, log of personal history, search engines through metadata etc.

Content Management, which provide features for content storing, authoring and delivery, file management, import and export of content chunks etc.

Assessment Tools, which provides features for managing on-line quizzes and tests, project deliverables, self-assessment exercises, status of student participation in active learning and so on.

School-Management, which provide features for managing records, absences, grades, student registrations, personal data of students, financial administration etc.

All these groups of features will be supported in the architecture, presented in the next section. This architecture is meant to be generic enough to embrace the different categories of LMS, and therefore it does not delve into specific details of single LMS.

3   The Architecture

The proposed architecture is a result of a prototype **architecting process** that is characterized of five important key aspects: it is founded on the higher-level architecture of IEEE P1484.1 Learning Technology Systems Architecture [http://ltsc.ieee.org/]; it uses a prototype architecture of a Web-based Instructional System [18] to build a complete business model and refine and constrain the requirements for the LMS; it adopts and customizes a big part of the well-established, software engineering process, the Rational Unified Process (RUP) [9, 19]; it uses the widely-adopted Unified Modeling Language [20, 21] to describe the architecture; and it is fundamentally and inherently component-based. The latter is justified by the fact that great emphasis has been put, not only in providing a pure component-based process, that generates solely components and connectors, but also in identifying the appropriate binding technologies for implementing and integrating the various components. Further study of the architecting process can be found at [22].

In order to describe the architecture for an LMS we need to base our work on a commonly accepted definition of the concept of software architecture. Unfortunately the software architecture community has not reached consensus on a common definition for the term of software architecture, given that the whole discipline is still considered very immature [7]. A rather broadly-used academic definition is the one given in [23]: "Abstractly, software architecture involves the description of elements from which systems are built, interactions among those elements, patterns that guide their composition, and constraints on these patterns". A similar definition from the IEEE Recommended Practice for Architectural Description of Software-Intensive Systems [24] is: "The fundamental organization of a system embodied in its components, their relationships to each other, and to the environment, and the principles guiding its design and evolution." We will adopt these definitions and attempt to refine them so as to *describe* the LMS architecture in terms of the RUP, which has been used as the basis for the architecting process. Therefore in compliance to the above definitions and according to [9, 19, 25], the *architectural description* should contain the following:

- The views (i.e. the most important or architecturally significant modeling elements) of the 5 models described in the RUP (use case model, analysis model, design model, deployment model, implementation model). This set of views corresponds with the classic *"4+1 views"* described in [26].

- The quality requirements that are desirable for the system and must be supported by the architecture. The requirements might or might not be described by use cases.
- A brief description of the platform, the legacy systems, the commercial software, the architecture patterns to be used.

For reasons of clarity and completeness, it is noted that the above list is not exhaustive, meaning that the RUP mentions other items that can also be included in the architectural description. On the other hand, the process is flexible enough to allow the architect to choose what he or she wants to take account of the particular system under development. For the purposes of this paper and for the final goal, i.e. the definition of the LMS architecture we will suffice to say that the above description is comprehensive enough.

3.1   The Architectural Description

The first and most sizeable part of the architectural description is the views of the 5 models dictated by the RUP. It is obvious that it is neither meaningful nor practical to illustrate even a small representative sample of the numerous diagrams produced in the 5 models. Instead, we will emphasize certain points, that will provide a minimum basis for demonstrating the LMS architecture, such as: a first level decomposition of the system; an exemplar second-level decomposition of one subsystem; how component interfaces are specified; platform and implementation decisions; the architectural patterns and the commercial software used.

The first-level decomposition of the Learning Management System is performed by specifying the very coarse-grained discrete subsystems in the design model, as they have derived from the use case and analysis model. It is noted that throughout the paper, the words 'component' and 'subsystem' are used interchangeably to denote pieces of the system that comply with the definition given in [6]: "A software component is a unit of composition with contractually specified interfaces and explicit context dependencies only. A software component can be deployed independently and is subject to composition by third parties." The decomposition is combined with the enforcement of the "Layered Systems" architecture pattern [23, 27, 28], which helps organize the subsystems hierarchically into layers, in the sense that subsystems in one layer can only reference subsystems on the same level or below. The communication between subsystems that reside in different layers is achieved through clearly defined interfaces and the set of subsystems in each layer can be conceptualized as implementing a virtual machine [28]. The most widely known examples of this kind of architectural style are layered communication protocols such as the ISO/OSI, or operating systems such as some of the X Window System protocols.

The RUP utilizes the aforementioned architectural pattern by defining four layers in order to organize the subsystems in the design model. According to the RUP, a *layer* is a set of subsystems that share the same degree of generality and interface volatility. The four layers used to describe the architectural structure of a software system are [9]:

- *Application-specific:* A layer enclosing the subsystems that are application-specific and are not meant to be reused in different applications. This is the top layer, so its subsystems are not shared by other subsystems.
- *Application-general:* A layer comprised of the subsystems that are not specific to a single application but can be re-used for many different applications within the same domain or business.
- *Middleware:* A layer offering reusable building blocks (packages or subsystems) for utility frameworks and platform-independent services for things like distributed object computing and interoperability in heterogeneous environments, e.g. Object Request Brokers, platform-neutral frameworks for creating GUIs.
- *System software:* A layer containing the software for the computing and networking infrastructure, such as operating systems, DBMS, interface to specific hardware, e.g. TCP/IP.

The proposed layered architecture for an LMS is depicted in Figure 2, which is a first-level decomposition in the design model. This diagram, besides identifying all first-level subsystems and organizing them into layers, also defines dependencies between them, which are realized through well-specified interfaces. The list of subsystems contained in this diagram, although not exhaustive, highlights the most important of these subsystems.

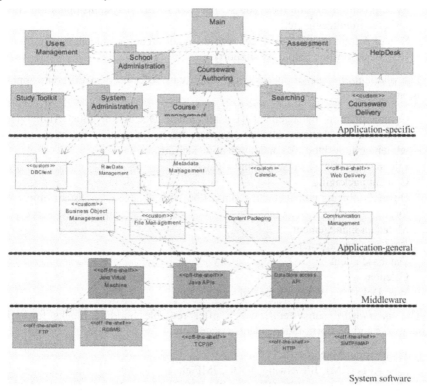

Fig. 2. The layered architecture of the component-based LMS

The *application-specific* sub-systems of the layered architecture, which are the top-level components of the application, are:

1. Main subsystem (master component that initializes and launches everything else)
2. User management (registration in system, in courses and in groups, groups creation, authentication, access control with different views, student tracking, student profile management)
3. Courseware authoring (web page editing, design templates)
4. Courseware delivery (WWW server and client, delivery of hypermedia pages concerning e-book, glossary, index, calendar, course description etc., personalization per user)
5. Assessment (on-line quiz or exam, project deliverables, self-assessment exercises)
6. Searching (applies to all learning objects through metadata)
7. Course management (creation, customization, administration and monitoring of courses)
8. Study toolkit (private & public annotations, highlights, bookmarks, print out, off-line studying, notepad, log of personal history, adaptive navigation and presentation, intelligent tutoring systems)
9. System Administration (new course, back up, security, systems operation check, resource monitoring etc.)
10. School Administration (absences records, grades records, student registrations)
11. Help desk (on-line help, user support)

The *application-general* subsystems, which can be re-used in different applications, are:

1. Communication management (E-mail, Chat, Discussion fora, Audio/video-conferencing, Announcements, Synchronous collaborative facilities such as whiteboard, desktop, file and application sharing)
2. File management (FTP server and client)
3. Content packaging
4. Business objects management (connection with database, persistent object factory)
5. Metadata management
6. Raw data management
7. Database client
8. Calendar
9. Web Delivery (WWW client and server)

The *middleware* subsystems, which offer reusable building blocks for utility frameworks and platform-independent services, are:

1. Java Virtual Machine
2. Java APIs (RMI, JFC/Swing, JDBC, JMF etc.)
3. Data Store Access API (JDBC API, JDBC driver, DB access through RMI, Connection pooling)

The *system-software layer* subsystems, which contains the software for the computing and networking infrastructure, are the TCP/IP, HTTP, FTP, SMTP/IMAP protocols and an RDBMS.

These subsystems are further elaborated by identifying their contents, which are design classes, use-case realizations, interfaces and other design subsystems (recursively). For example the decomposition of the "Data Store Access API" into its design sub-systems is depicted in Figure 3. This specific subsystem is comprised of the JDBC API, which is the Java API for Open Database Connectivity, the JDBC driver of the database used, a component that performs connection pooling to the database, and a component that offers access to the database through the Java Remote Method Invocation API. This decomposition must continue hierarchically until we reach the 'tree leaves', i.e. the design classes. It is noted that the relationships between the subsystems are UML *dependencies* and are simply meant to denote that one subsystem *uses* another.

Furthermore, for each subsystem an interface must be specified so that the provided and the required operations are well defined. The *provided* operations are the ones that a specific subsystem offers to the other subsystems, the way a subsystem is used. The *required* operations state the functions that a subsystem expects from other subsystems, so that it can execute its functionality. A very simple example of an interface, with provided operations only, is depicted in Figure 4, where the aforementioned "Data Base access through RMI" subsystem's provided operations are shown. The SQLConnector class implements the RemoteSQLConnector interface, in order to connect to the database through RMI and perform SQL queries and updates, and handles ResultSetLite objects that contain the queries results. The signatures of the operations of the two classes and the interface are visible, and thus can be utilized in the design of other subsystems that interoperate with this one. As it will be shown later (Section 3.2), this formal form of interface specification is of paramount importance to the component nature of the architecture and yields significant advantages for the quality attributes of the system.

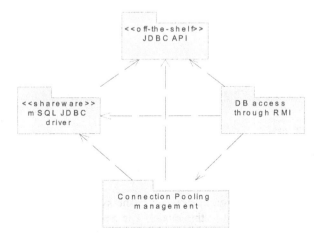

Fig. 3. The decomposition of the Data Store Access API into its design sub-systems

After the five views of the system have been completed, the core of the architecture is complete and is comprised of:

- the most significant functional requirements;
- nonfunctional requirements that are specific to architecturally significant use-cases;
- the most important design classes and their organization into packages and sub-systems, and the organization of these packages and subsystems into layers;
- some use case realizations;
- an overview of the implementation model and its organization in terms of components into packages and layers;
- a description of the tasks (process and threads) involved, their interactions and configurations, and the allocation of design objects and classes to tasks;
- the description of the various physical nodes and the allocation of tasks (from the Process View) to the physical nodes.

The next part of the component-based architecture concerns platform and implementation decisions, so that the architecture is completed, and the development team is assisted in implementing it into a physical system. In the architecture described in this paper, we propose certain implementation technologies and platforms that we consider to be the most suitable for a component-based system. These technologies implement the component-based paradigm using object-oriented techniques, specifically the Unified Modeling Language, and the Java, C++ and VBA programming languages. The application of these technologies results in components implemented as JavaBeans or Microsoft Component Objects. The component development process, comprised of such technologies, is depicted in Figure 5.

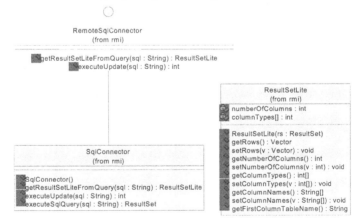

Fig. 4. The interface of the "DB Access through RMI" subsystem specified in UML

The artifacts from the design model, that is sub-systems with UML-defined interfaces are provided as an input to this model. The next step is to transform the UML interfaces into the implementation platform, in our case either Java or Microsoft technologies. This forward engineering process can be easily automated with CASE tools such as Rational Rose [http://www.rational.com/rose] or Control Center [http://www.togethersoft.com/products/controlcenter/index.jsp], that generate abstract code from UML models. It is noted that we have included both Java and Microsoft, as alternative implementation platforms, for reasons of completeness, since they are the state-of-the-art component technologies. It is up to the development team to make the choice between them. For the architectural prototype presented in the next sub-section we have chosen the Java platform.

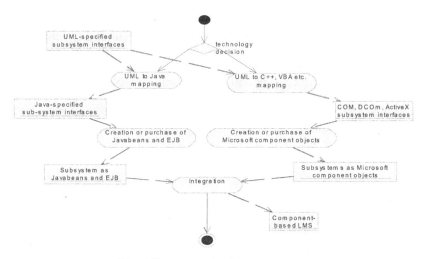

Fig. 5. Component development process

After the component interfaces are concretely defined in the programming language, they can either be constructed from scratch, or acquired from existing implementations and possibly modified to exactly fit their interfaces. The result is the implementation of the sub-systems as JavaBeans or Enterprise JavaBeans (EJB), which is the Java form of components, or, as Microsoft component objects (COM/DCOM objects, ActiveX controls etc.). The possible re-use of components is one of the areas where the component-based approach thrives. The final step is to integrate the components through an integration and testing process into the final outcome, i.e. the LMS.

Additional issues related to the architecture description, such as the legacy systems, the commercial software, the architectural patterns to be used etc. are also quite important and are outlined as following. In the proposed architecture there are no legacy systems since, the whole prototype system is being developed from scratch. As far as the commercial systems, we have adopted several of them such as the mySQL RDBMS [http://www.mysql.com] and the Resin Web Server and Servlets engine [http://www.caucho.com], the Sun 1.3.1 Java Run Time Environment, as well as some outsourced java packages such as mySQL JDBC driver, the Java Media Framework API, etc. The architectural patterns that have been used, as seen in the catalogue composed in [23, 27, 28] include: the *layered* style as aforementioned; the *Client-Server* style has been used extensively, especially in the communication management components; the *Model-View-Controller* style in the GUI design, which is inherent in all Java Swing UI components; the *blackboard* style in the mechanisms that access the database in various ways; the *Virtual Machine* and the *object-oriented* style which are both a result of the implementation in Java; the *event systems* style for notification of GUI components about the change of state of persistent objects.

The final concerns that need to be addressed in this architectural description are the desirable qualities of the architecture, also known as nonfunctional requirements. Software architectures can be evaluated according to specific criteria and are designed to fulfill certain quality attributes [5, 8, 28]. It is noted that no quality can be maximized in a system without sacrificing some other quality or qualities, instead there is always a trade-off while choosing on supporting the different quality attributes [5, 8, 28]. We have decided to evaluate the architecture using two techniques: by evaluating the architectural prototype, and by informally assessing the architecture itself using our architectural experience combined and supporting it with the appropriate line of reasoning. Even though the evaluation results are out of the scope of this paper, we will only mention here the quality criteria that we have adopted from [28] and used in our research: performance, security, availability, functionality, usability, modifiability, portability, integrability, interoperability, reusability, testability, time to market, cost, projected lifetime of the system and targeted market.

3.2   The Architectural Prototype

An architecture is a visual, holistic view of the system, but it is only an abstraction. In order to evaluate the architecture in terms of the quality attributes it promotes, we must build it. Therefore, the software architecture must be accompanied with an **architectural prototype** that implements the most important design decisions sufficiently to validate them - that is to test and measure them [5, 8, 19]. The architectural prototype is the most important artifact associated with the architecture itself, which illustrates the architectural decisions and help us evolve and stabilize the architecture. In order to assess and validate the proposed architecture, a prototype was engineered that implements the main architectural elements. The prototype LMS is named "Athena" and Figure 6 depicts some of its tools in action. There was the option of choosing a platform, Java or Microsoft-based as already shown in Figure 5. Our choice was the Java platform because it is an open technology, rather than proprietary, and based on a Virtual Machine, thus promoting portability. The specific technologies used are applets, servlets, Java Beans, Enterprise Java Beans, Java Server Pages, as well as the JFC/Swing, RMI, JDBC, 2D Graphics, JMF and JAF Java APIs. The eXtensible Markup Language (XML) was used as the default language for the representation of data that were not stored in the database.

The decision on implementing the prototype was to emphasize on the implementation of the majority of the components, and not on providing the full functionality of them. About 75% of the total number of components have been implemented or acquired and put into operation, even though some of them do not offer the complete functionality prescribed in the system design. More specifically and with reference to the layered architecture illustrated above, the components that were acquired from third parties are: WWW Server and servlet engine (Resin), WWW browser (Internet Explorer), FTP Server, Mail Server, RDBMS (mySQL), Audio/Video Conferencing client (MS Netmeeting), Sun Java Run Time Environment. In addition the components that were implemented from scratch are: Main Subsystem, User Management,

Courseware Authoring, Course Management, Searching, Assessment, Help Desk, Data Base client, Raw Data Management, Business Objects Management, FTP client, Metadata Management, Calendar, Communication System (E-mail client, Chat server and client, Whiteboard server and client, Announcements tool), Data Store Access API.

Finally there was an attempt on adopting international standards within the various components in order to promote interoperability of LMSs and portability of the learning resources. For that purpose we have developed the metadata management component conforming to the IEEE LTSC Learning Object Metadata working standard [16]. We have also implemented the assessment component in order to adopt the IMS Question and Testing Interoperability Standard [29]. Unfortunately most of these standards have not finalized just yet, but the aim of adopting them at such an early stage was to explore the feasibility of implementing them into our components. Furthermore, as it will be shown later, the system has been designed with the quality of modifiability in mind, and therefore changes in future versions of the standards should be easy to incorporate.

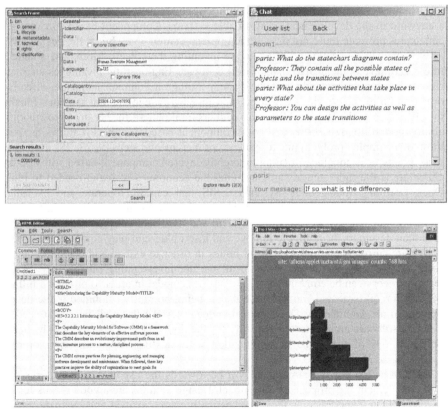

Fig. 6. Screenshots of the architectural prototype

4   Conclusions and Future Work

We have portrayed a layered component-based architecture for an LMS, which uses the IEEE P1484.1 LTSA and a prototype WbIS architecture as a business model, adopts the architecting practices of the Unified Software Development Process and grants special emphasis on enforcing a component-based nature in it. Each one of these key concepts adds special value to the proposed architecture.

It has been strongly supported that an architecture-centric development process professes numerous advantages [5, 9, 20]. In general, the purpose of developing software architecture is to discover high-level frameworks for understanding certain kinds of systems, their subsystems, and their interactions with related systems. In other words, an architecture isn't a blueprint for designing a single system, but a framework for designing a range of systems over time, thus achieving adaptability, and for the analysis and comparison of these systems [1]. Furthermore, an all-important necessity for an LMS is interoperability and portability, which is a fundamental feature of component-based architectures and is achieved by identifying critical component interfaces in the system 's architecture. Portability of components also leads to reusability, a keyword in the development of affordable systems. Component-based software architectures promote reuse not only at the implementation level, but at the design level as well, thus saving time and effort of 're-inventing the wheel'. Moreover, architecture-based development offers significant Software Engineering advantages such as: risk mitigation, understanding of the system through a common language, effective organization of the development effort, and making change-tolerant systems. Finally the utilization of the 'Layered Systems' architectural pattern further promotes modifiability, portability, reusability and good component-based design as it allows the partition of a complex problem into a sequence of incremental steps [9, 23, 28]. Based on these points, it is concluded that an inherently layered component-based software architecture is the right step towards bringing the economies of scale, needed to build Open Learning Management Systems: LMS that can interoperate and exchange learning material, student data, course information; LMS that can be ported to any platform, independently of operating system and hardware configuration; LMSs that give their designers the ability to remove and insert plug-and-play components at will.

We are currently examining several issues in order to extend and elaborate on the work presented in this paper. First of all we are investigating on the way, that a learning theory can be combined with the business model in order to provide a full set of system requirements. Another issue that is being currently examined is the development of an Architecture Description Language (ADL) that will be customized to describe software architectures especially for the domain of LMSs, and will be based on extensions of the UML in combination with existing ADLs and development methods [30, 31, 32].

Moreover, the new research steps will be towards the use of design patterns that will complement the proposed WbIS model. Design patterns are a good means for recording design experience as they systematically name, explain and evaluate important and recurrent designs in software systems [33]. They describe problems that occur repeatedly, and describe the core of the solution to these problems, in such a way that we can use this solution many times in different contexts and applications. Looking at known uses of a particular pattern, we can see how successful designers solve recurrent problems. In some cases, it is possible to give structure to simple patterns to develop a pattern language: a partially ordered set of related patterns that work together in the context of certain application domain. This work will be in line with the research efforts that are being performed by [34, 35, 36].

References

[1]   IEEE Learning Technology Standards Committee (LTSC), Draft Standard for Learning Technology Systems Architecture (LTSA), Draft 9, November 2001, http://ltsc.ieee.org/

[2]   Oleg S. and Liber B.: "*A Framework of Pedagogical Evaluation of Virtual Learning Environments*", 1999. Available at http://www.jtap.ac.uk/reports/htm/jtap-041.html

[3]   McCormack C. and Jones J.D.: "*Building a Web-based Education System*", Wiley, 1997.

[4]   Lowe D. and Hall W.: "Hypermedia & the Web: an Engineering Approach", Wiley, 1999.

[5]   Bosch J.: "Design and Use of Software Architectures", Addison-Wesley, 2000.

[6]   Szyperski C.: "Component Software – beyond Object-Oriented Programming", ACM Press, 1999.

[7]   Eriksson H. and Penker M.: "Business Modeling with UML - Business Patterns at Work", Wiley, 2000.

[8]   Clements P., Kazman R. and Clein M.: "*Evaluating Software Architecture*", Addison-Wesley, 2002.

[9]   Jacobson I., Booch G. and Rumbaugh J.: "*The Unified Software Development Process*", Addison-Wesley, 1999.

[10]   Sun Microsystems: "Understanding Distance Learning Architectures", White Paper, 1999.

[11]   G. Collier: "E-learning Application Infrastructure", Sun Microsystems, White paper, Jan. 2002. Available at http://www.sun.com/products-n-solutions/edu/whitepapers/index.html

[12]   ISO/IEC 10746-3: "Information Technology. Open Distributed Processing. Reference model: Architecture", 1996.

[13]   Ford P., Goodyear P., Heseltine R., Lewis R., Darby J., Graves J., Sartorius P., Harwood D. and King T.: "*Managing Change in Higher Education: a Learning Environment Architecture*", Open University Press, London, 1996.

[14]   Lindner R.: "Proposals for an Architecture WG and new NPs for this WG - Expertise and Role Identification for Learning Environments (ERILE)", 2001. Available at http:// jtc1sc36.org/

[15]   McConnell D.: "Implementing computer-supported cooperative learning", London: Kogan Page, 1994.

[16]   IEEE Learning Technology Standards Committee, (LTSC), Draft Standard for Learning Object Metadata (LOM), Draft 6.4, 2001. Available at http://ltsc.ieee.org.

[17]   Avgeriou P., Papasalouros A. and Retalis S.: "Web-based Learning Environments: issues, trends, challenges. *Proceedings 1ˢᵗ IOSTE Symposium in Southern Europe, Science and Technology Education,* Paralimni, Cyprus, May 2001.

[18] S. Retalis and P. Avgeriou: "Modeling Web-based Instructional Systems", *Journal of Information Technology Education*, Vol.1, No.1, pp.25-41, 2002.

[19] Kruchten P.: "The Rational Unified Process, an Introduction", Addison-Wesley, 1999.

[20] Booch G., Rumbaugh J. and Jacobson I.: *"The UML User Guide"*, Addison-Wesley, 1999.

[21] Rumbaugh J., Jacobson I. and Booch G.: *"The UML Reference Manual"*, Addison-Wesley, 1999.

[22] Avgeriou P., Retalis S., Papasalouros A. and Skordalakis M.: "Developing an Architecture for the Software Subsystem of a Learning Technology System – an Engineering Approach", *Proceedings Conference of Advanced Learning Technologies*, pp.17-20, 2001.

[23] Shaw M. and Garlan D.: "Software Architecture - Perspectives on an Emerging Discipline", Prentice Hall, 1996.

[24] IEEE Recommended Practice for Architectural Description of Software-Intensive Systems (IEEE std. 1471-2000).

[25] The Rational Unified Process, 2000, v. 2001.03.00.23, Rational Software Corporation, part of the Rational Solutions for Windows suite.

[26] Kruchten P.: "The 4+1 View Model of Architecture", *IEEE Software*, Vol.12, No.6, pp.42-50, 1995.

[27] Buschmann F., Meunier R., Rohnert H., Sommertland P. and Stal M.: *"Pattern-Oriented Software Architecture, Vol.1: a System of Patterns"*, Wiley, 1996.

[28] Bass L., Clements P. and Kazman R.: *"Software Architecture in Practice"*, Addison-Wesley, 1998.

[29] IMS Global Learning Consortium, 2001. IMS Question & Test Interoperability Specification- Best Practice and Implementation Guide, version 1.2.1. Available at http:// www.imsproject.org/

[30] Robbins J.E., Medvidovic N., Redmiles D.F. and Rosenblum D.S.: "Integrating Architecture Description Languages with a Standard Design Method", *Proceedings 1998 Conference on Software Engineering*, 1998.

[31] Medvidovic N. and Taylor R.N.: "A Classification and Comparison Framework for Software Architecture Description Languages. *IEEE Transactions on Software Engineering*, Vol.26, No.1, pp.70-93, 2000.

[32] Medvidovic N.; Rosenblum D.; Redmiles D. and Robbins J.: "Modelling Software Architectures in the Unified Modeling Language", *ACM Transactions on Software Engineering and Methodology*, Vol.11, No.1, pp.2-57, 2002.

[33] Gamma R., Helm R., Johnson and Vlissides J.: *"Design Patterns: Elements of Reusable Object-oriented Software"*, Addison Wesley, 1995.

[34] Rossi G., Schwabe D. and Lyardet F.: "Improving Web Information Systems with Navigational Patterns", *International Journal of Computer Networks and Applications*, May 1999.

[35] Garzotto F., Paolini P., Bolchini D. and Valenti S.: "Modeling-by-patterns of Web Applications", Springer *LNCS* Vol.1727, 1999.

[36] Lyardet F., Rossi G. and Schwabe D.: "Patterns for Dynamic Websites", *Proceedings PloP'98 Conference*, Allerton, GA, 1998.

A Knowledge Based Approach
on Educational Metadata Use

Fotios Kokkoras[1], Dimitrios Sampson[2], and Ioannis Vlahavas[1]

[1] Department of Informatics, Aristotle University
54006 Thessaloniki, Greece
{kokkoras,vlahavas}@csd.auth.gr
[2] Center for Research and Technology - Hellas
Informatics and Telematics Institute, 1 Kyvernidou Str
54639 Thessaloniki, Greece
sampson@ath.forthnet.gr

Abstract. One of the most rapidly evolving e-services is e-Learning, that is, the creation of advanced educational resources that are accessible on-line and, potentially, offer numerous advantages over the traditional ones like intelligent access, interoperability between two or more educational resources and adaptation to the user. The driving force behind these approaches is the definition of the various standards about educational metadata, that is, data describing learning resources, the learner, assessment results, etc. The internal details of systems that utilize these metadata is an open issue since these efforts are primarily dealing with "what" and not "how". Under the light of these emerging efforts, we present CG-PerLS, a knowledge based approach for organizing and accessing educational resources. CG-PerLS is a model of a web portal for learning objects that encodes the educational metadata in the Conceptual Graph knowledge representation formalism, and uses related inference techniques to provide advanced functionality. The model allows learning resource creators to manifest their material and client-side learners to access these resources in a way tailored to their individual profile and educational needs.

1 Introduction

As the World Wide Web matures, an initial vision of using it as a universal medium for educational resources is, day by day, becoming reality. There is already a large amount of instructional material on-line, most of it in the form of multimedia HTML documents, some of which are enriched with Java technologies. Unfortunately, most of these approaches have been built on general purpose standards and fail to utilize Web's potential for distributed educational resources that are easily located and interoperate with each other.

Y. Manolopoulos et al. (Eds.): PCI 2001, LNCS 2563, pp. 201–216, 2003.

Information technology assisted education has reached sophisticated levels during 90's, taking into account issues like pedagogy, individual learner and interface, apart from the basic educational material organization. Following the recent "e-" trend, these approaches are just beginning to appear on the internet. The reason for this late adoption is mainly the substantial effort that is required to bring them on the Web since all of them have been designed without the Web in mind.

On the other hand, it is commonplace that our society has already moved away from the "once for life" educational model. The complexity and continuous evolution of modern enterprises' activities requires continuous training of their personnel. The networked community enables the management and enhancement of knowledge in a centralized - yet personal way, while keeping track and merging new intellectual resources into that process. The above requirements and advances lead us to the "*Lifelong Learning*" concept. The idea is to integrate the WWW technology with a novel, dynamic and adaptive educational model for continuous learning. The result will be a learning environment that will enable the individual learner to acquire knowledge just-in-time, anytime and anywhere, tailored to his/her personal learning needs.

Until recently, the majority of the, so-called, "e-learning" approaches were limited to simple hyperlinks between content pages and "portal pages" organizing a set of related links. The lack of widely adopted methods for searching the Web by content makes difficult for an instructor or learner to find educational material on the Web that addresses particular learning and pedagogical goals. In addition, the lack of standards prevented the interoperability of educational resources.

Towards this direction and under the aegis of the IEEE Learning Technology Standards Committee (LTSC), several groups are developing technical standards, recommended practices and guides for software components, tools, technologies and design methods that facilitate the development, deployment, maintenance and interoperation of computer implementations of educational components and systems. Two of the most important LTSC groups are the Learning Object Metadata group and the Learner Model group. The former is trying [7] to define the metadata required to adequately describe a learning object (LO) while the latter [10] deals with the specification of the syntax and semantics of attributes that will characterize a learner and his/her knowledge abilities.

The above standardization efforts, together with generic and robust knowledge based approaches for problem solving, developed during the last two decades, offer a fertile ground for the development of advanced on-line educational services. In addition, from the educational resources developer point of view, the standardization of all the education related aspects and the transition to more intelligent computer assisted education, will lead to autonomous, on-line educational resources that will be used by multiple tutorials and will operate independently of any single tutorial. Furthermore, the standardization will dramatically improve the reusability of the educational material. This is very important since educational material is expensive to create in terms of cost and time.

The wishful state of the art in e-Learning systems described as "Adaptive and Intelligent Web-based Educational Systems" (AIWES). As the term indicates, such approaches have their roots in the fields of Intelligent Tutoring Systems (ITS) and Adaptive Hypermedia Systems (AHS). The main features of AIWES are [2]:

- *Adaptive Curriculum Sequencing*: the material that will be presented to the learner is selected according to his learning request, which is initially stated to the system, and the learner's model, that is, the perception that the system has about the learner's current knowledge status and goals.
- Problem Solving Support: the system offers Intelligent analysis of learner's solution, Interactive Problem Solving Support and Example based Problem Solving Support.
- *Adaptive Presentation*: that is, the system's ability to adapt the content of the supplied curriculum to the learner's preferences.
- *Student Model Matching*: based on a categorization of the learners to classes with similar educational characteristics, the system will be able to provide collaborative problem solving support and intelligent class monitoring.

Such e-Learning systems will be easier to implement when the standardization efforts come to an end. The internal details of these systems are an open issue since the standardization efforts are primarily dealing with "what" and not "how". However, the IMS Global Learning Consortium has developed a representation of learning object and learner's metadata in XML, namely the IMS-LOM [21] and IMS-LIP [22] specifications (or simply LOM and LIP, respectively).

One of the most ambitious efforts on e-Learning that make use of educational metadata is the Advanced Distributed Learning (ADL) initiative [13]. Recently, ADL released the Sharable Courseware Object Reference Model (SCORM) that attempts to map existing learning models and practices so that common interfaces and data may be defined and standardized across courseware management systems and development tools.

In this paper we present the CG-PerLS, a knowledge based approach on organizing and accessing educational resources. CG-PerLS is a model of a WWW portal for learning resources that is based on a Conceptual Graph binding of educational metadata and related inference techniques. CG-PerLS allows learning resource creators to manifest their educational material, even if this material is not LOM aware, client-side learners to access these educational resources in a way tailored to their individual profile and educational needs, and dynamic course generation based on the user's learning request.

The rest of the paper is organized as follows: Section 2 presents the basic features of Conceptual Graphs (CGs), a formalism for knowledge representation and reasoning. Section 3 describes an integration of the educational metadata and the conceptual graphs technologies, in the form of the CG-PerLS model. Section 4 outlines related work and, finally, section 5 concludes the paper.

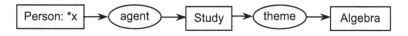

Fig. 1. A Conceptual Graph stating that "there is some person *x* studying Algebra"

2   Conceptual Graphs: Primitives and Definitions

The elements of CG theory [14] are *concept-types*, *concepts*, *relation-types* and *relations*. Concept-types represent classes of entity, attribute, state and event. Concept-types can be merged in a lattice whose partial ordering relation < can be interpreted as a categorical generalization relation. A concept is an instantiation of a concept-type and is usually denoted by a concept-type label inside a box (Fig.1). To refer to specific individuals, a referent field is added to the concept ([book:*] - a book, [book:{*}@3] - three books, etc). Relations are instantiations of relation-types and show the relation between concepts. They are usually denoted as a relation label inside a circle (Fig.1). A relation type (also called the *signature* of the relation) determines the number of arcs allowed on the relation. Each relation has zero or one incoming arcs and one or more outgoing arcs. For example, the signature of the relation *agent* is (*Act, Animate*), which indicates that the type of the concept linked to its first arc must be *Act* or some subtype, such as *Go*, and the type of the concept linked to its second arc must be *Animate* or some subtype, such as *Person*.

A CG (Fig.1) is a finite, connected, bipartite graph consisting of concept and relation nodes. Each relation is linked only to its requisite number of concepts and each concept to zero or more relations. CGs represent information about typical objects or classes of objects in the world and can be used to define new concepts in terms of old ones.

The type hierarchy established for both concepts and relations is based on the intuition that some types subsume other types, for example, every instance of the concept *cat* would also have all the properties of *mammal*.

In the CG formalism, every context (situation, proposition, etc.) is a concept. Thus, contexts are represented as concepts whose referent field contains a nested CG (contextual concepts). With a number of defined operations on CGs (canonical formation rules) one can derive allowable CGs from other CGs. These rules enforce constraints on meaningfulness; they do not allow nonsensical graphs to be created from meaningful ones. The canonical formation rules are:

- *Copy* creates a copy of a CG.
- *Restriction* takes a graph and replaces any of its concept nodes either by changing the concept-type to a subtype or adding a referent where there was none before.
- *Joining* joins two graphs with a common concept over it, to form a single graph. The resulting graph is the common specialization of the two graphs.
- *Simplifying* removes any duplicate relations between two concepts.

Other operations on CGs include:

- *Contraction* tries to replace a sub-graph of a given CG with a single, equivalent concept (or relation), using the CG definition of this concept (or relation).
- *Expansion* is the opposite of the contraction operation.
- *Maximal Join* is a join of two CGs followed by a sequence of restrictions, internal joins and simplifications so that the maximum amount of matching and merging of the original graphs is achieved.

- *Unification* is the complex process of finding the most general subtypes for pairs of types of concepts. The resulting graph of two graphs being unified has exactly the same information as the two individual graphs together.
- *Projection* is an complex operation that projects a CG over another CG. The result is a CG that has the same shape/structure as the projected CG (this is also a requirement to be able to perform projection), but some of its concepts is possible to have been specialized by either specializing the concept type or assigning a value to some generic referent, or both.

Inference rules based on CGs have also been defined. A rule $R:G_1 \Rightarrow G_2$ is composed of two CGs, G_1 and G_2, which are called *hypothesis* and *conclusion*, respectively (Fig.2). There may be coreference links between concepts of G_1 and G_2. These are called connection points and must be of the same type. In more complex and useful situations it is possible to have more CGs in either part of the rule, joined with the logical operators. Furthermore, coreference links might exist between concepts belonging to either part of a rule. For example, the CG-rule in Fig.2 states that "if person x teaches lecture y in university z, then this person x is a member of some faculty w and there is an educational institute z that offers lecture y and its faculty is w. Notice how it is possible (using a concept type hierarchy) to relate the concept "university" in the hypothesis part with the concept "educational institute" in the conclusion part.

The CG model of knowledge representation is a practical way to express a large amount of pragmatic information through assertions. All of the algorithms defined on CGs are domain-independent and every semantic domain can be described through a purely declarative set of CGs. CGs have the same model-theoretic semantics with the Knowledge Interchange Format (KIF) and are currently under a standardization process [4].

A number of CG related software tools have been implemented by various researchers and/or research teams. One such tool is the CoGITaNT (Conceptual Graphs Integrated Tools allowing Nested Typed graphs) [17], a library of C++ classes that allows to design software based on Conceptual Graphs. CoGITaNT is available under a GNU General Public License [18].

3   Conceptual Graphs for Educational Services

Since the use of artificial intelligence methods towards Adaptive and Intelligent Web-based Educational Systems (AIWES) seems inevitable, the seamless integration of educational metadata into a knowledge based framework will offer better possibilities for AIWES. We propose next such an integration approach that binds certain educational metadata onto CGs. We use that binding to establish CG-PerLS, a knowledge based approach (model) for manifesting and accessing educational resources over the Internet.

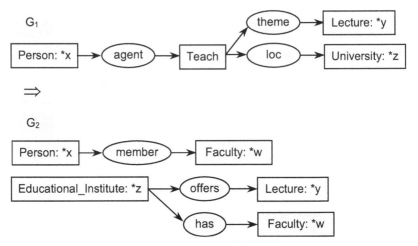

Fig. 2. An example of a CG Rule

3.1   A Conceptual Graph Binding for Educational Metadata

The LOM and LIP standards precisely define data models and their semantics for describing the properties of learning objects and learners, respectively. Any LOM/LIP compliant system is free to internally handle these metadata in any way, but should be able to meaningfully interchange such metadata with other systems without loss of any information.

We selected to map these metadata to CGs in order to seamlessly incorporate them into a knowledge based educational portal. CGs define knowledge both at the type and instance levels. They are particularly well suited to model/organize/implement learning repositories at the knowledge level, since they support [5]:

Classification and partial knowledge: Before gathering and storing information about things, we neither need to define all possible concepts that exist in the application domain, nor need to know all properties of things. Furthermore, we can define different concepts to classify things into (multiple classification), each one corresponding to a different perspective.

Category and/or instance in relationship: It is possible to represent associations between categories and things.

Category or instance in metamodel: Concepts give information about instances, but they may be also seen as instances in a metamodel that gives information about the concepts themselves. This is very important, since an element should allow to be viewed as a concept or an instance. This allows defining categories of categories, i.e. it is possible to integrate higher-order information in the same knowledge base. For example, "Java" can be defined both as a concept and an instance of the concept [programming_language].

In addition, the CG formalism offers a unified and simple representation formalism that covers a wide range of other data and knowledge modeling formalisms, and allows matching, transformation, unification and inference operators to process the knowledge that it describes [20]. CGs and the operations defined over them can be used not only as powerful tools to create ontologies, but also as reasoning tools over ontologies [16]. In that way, the previously static knowledge representation of an ontology is becoming a dynamic, functional reasoning system. This is a very important feature because the educational ontologies that will be required towards AIWES will be better integrated into a knowledge based educational system if both share common representation formalism. Furthermore, the graphical representation of CGs allows easier interpretation of the knowledge that they encode. This is not the fact for XML encoded data, since the XML notation aims at better, general purpose, machine data handling.

Therefore, we suggest that, a metadata binding into a knowledge representation formalism, such as CGs, allows for better integration of metadata into knowledge based e-Learning systems and particularly to systems that built upon the CG formalism.

```
<record>
    <general>
        <identifier>123</identifier>
        ...
    </general>
    ...
    <classification>
        <keyword>
            <langstring xml:lang="en">Kepler's Law</langstring>
        </keyword>
        <keyword>
            <langstring xml:lang="en">simulation</langstring>
        </keyword>
    </ classification>
    ...
    <educational>
        <interactivitytype>
            <source>
                <langstring xml:lang="x-none">LOMv1.0</langstring>
            </source>
            <value>
                <langstring xml:lang="x-none">Active</langstring>
            </value>
        </interactivitytype>
        ...
        <typicalagerange>
            <langstring xml:lang="x-none">16-99</langstring>
        </typicalagerange>
        ...
        <typicallearningtime>
            <datetime>0000-00-00T00:45</datetime>
        </typicallearningtime>
        ...
    </educational>
    ...
<record>
```

Fig. 3. LOM record (partial) in XML binding

We have defined CG templates to capture the semantics of the LOM elements. Fig.3 and 4 display a syntactical comparison between the XML and our proposed, CG-based, LOM binding. Apart from the more compact representation of the CG binding, the resulting CGs have, in some cases, better semantics. This is because LOM is primarily a data model with it's semantics lying into the specification document of the model. For example, the *<typicalagerange>* element of the LOM record do not refer to the learning object itself but to the intended learning object user. This is better depicted into the CG binding of LOM (Fig.4). Similarly, the learner's information is encoded in CGs derived from the XML LIP metadata. Arbitrary level of detail can be gradually asserted into a learner's model as his/her model evolves.

...
[LO:#123] → (classification) → [KEYWORD:%en "Kepler's Law"]
[LO:#123] → (classification) → [KEYWORD:%en "simulation"]
...
[LO:#123] → (interactivity)→[INTERACTIVITY_TYPE:%x-none "Active"]
...
[LO:#123] ← (theme) ← [USE] → (agent) → [Person] → (typ_age) → [AGE_RANGE: :%x-none "16-99"]
...
[LO:#123] → (has_duration) → [DATETIME: 0000-00-00T00:45]
...

Fig. 4. The LOM record of Fig.3, into the CG binding

We use this CG binding of metadata to establish the CG-PerLS, a knowledge based approach (model) for manifesting and accessing educational resources over the Internet.

3.2   The CG-PerLS Model

The CG-PerLS is a web-enabled model of a knowledge-based system that uses the Conceptual Graph knowledge representation formalism and related inference techniques to reason over educational metadata expressed as CGs. The outline of the model is illustrated in Fig.5 where the CG-PerLS plays the role of an application server in a WWW educational portal. CG-PerLS consists of:

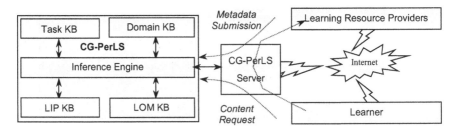

Fig. 5. Abstract diagram of a CG_PerLS based educational portal

- an *inference engine* capable of performing forward and backward reasoning over CGs and CG rules, and having TCP/IP networking capabilities,
- the *lom KB*, which is the knowledge related the learning resources; it is automatically derived from their metadata records as long as these resources are declared to the system,
- the *lip KB*, which is the knowledge related to the learner who is accessing the learning resources. It represents the system's understanding of the student by defining parameters like who is the student (user identification, password, e-mail address, surname etc), what are his/her capabilities, preferences, equipment etc.,
- the *domain KB*, which includes knowledge related to but not explicitly defined in learning objects, such as the concept type hierarchy, concept/relation definitions and the definition of courses. A *course* is described as a set of CGs outlining the structure of the course. For example, a course includes some semester curricula, which consist of modules, each of them having a number of lectures about some theme. There is no direct link to any particular educational material at this point. Since, in the general case, there would be more than one available learning objects aiming at some lecture theme, the selection of the proper learning objects to cover a course (or a part of a course) for a particular learner, would be an inference problem. That is, the application of the axiomatic knowledge presented in the *domain* and *task* KBs to the fact CGs (CGs without generic referents) in the LOM and LIP KBs, in order to arrive to some conclusion. Furthermore, the dependencies between themes are also described. For example, "Linear Algebra" requires "Matrix Calculus".
- the *task KB*, which materializes the services the system is able to offer to the user as well as its internal operations. Such services include, without limited, the binding of learning objects over a course description, the packaging and delivery of all the information describing in detail what the learner should study, bidirectional transformations between LOM/LIP and CG-LOM/CG-LIP bindings, generation of dynamic hyperlinks for the user to traverse and the communication of the CG-PerLS server with other similar servers.

The knowledge derivation process is fully automated for the case of LOM compliant educational resources. This is done by a module that reads the XML LOM metadata that come with the learning resource and converts then to the system's internal CG representation, according to the CG-LOM binding. Otherwise, the resource provider should manually give that information by filling in a form/questionnaire. All the inference is performed by a CG inference engine (Fig.5) implemented using the CoGITaNT library [18].

Forward and backward execution methods of CG rules have been implemented. *Forward Chaining* (or data driven) inference, is typically used in order to explicitly enrich facts with knowledge which is implicitly presented in some knowledge base. If G is a fact and R is a rule, then if G fulfills the hypothesis part of R, then the conclusion of R can be added to G. Forward chaining is primarily used to enrich the learner's model according to his/her progress.

Backward chaining is primarily used when we want to "prove" something. Since this operation requires some splitting and unification operations over CGs it is used mainly in the course generation task, where a course template, which refers to generic (unbound) learning themes, is enriched with specific learning resources.

The CG-PerLS model supports multiple-strategy, knowledge-based educational resource access which includes operator-based queries and dynamic course generation. We describe these access methods in the following sub-sections.

3.3   Operator-Based CG-Queries

An operator-based user query is a set of one or more query CGs connected with logical operators (AND, OR etc). A query CG is a CG that the user wants to match against the KB. It contains concepts with either individual markers (bound referent fields) or generic markers (unbound referent fields). A CG-PerLS query is defined as:

$$Q(QCGs, \; SemanticFlags, \; MaxResults)$$

[LO: x] ⤳ (classification) → [KEYWORD:%en "Kepler's Low"]
        ⤵(interactivity) → [INTERACTIVITY_TYPE:%x-none "Active"]

Fig. 6. A query CG with a transparent AND operator

where *QCGs* is a set of query CGs connected with logical operators, *SemanticFlags* is a set of flags (*true/false*) denoting whether to use semantic match or not on specific concepts of the query CG, and *MaxResults* is the desired maximum number of returned learning objects.

Currently, our inference engine can transparently handle only the AND logical operator. We demonstrate this with the following example: Consider a learner that wants some learning objects related to "Kepler's Low" which are of interactivity type "Active". In terms of elementary CGs (see Fig.4) this request is expressed like:

[LO: x] → (classification) → [KEYWORD:%en "Kepler's Low"]
     AND
[LO: x] → (interactivity) → [INTERACTIVITY_TYPE:%x-none "Active"]

where x is a coreference point between the two CGs. x should be bound to an identification number of some individual learning object. That would require, from the inference engine point of view, to handle the two CGs separately and interpret the logical operator at a later stage. Instead, the inference engine can directly handle the more compact and semantically equivalent representation presented in (Fig.6).

Note that this representation is the exact expression that is given to the inference engine. Other types of logical operators are currently handled outside the CG formalism. That is, the individual CG queries are answered separately and then the operator consistency is checked.

The utilization of the KB is expected to increase the effectiveness of the operator-based learning resource access. This is due to the fact that exact term matching suffers in the following cases:

*   *poor recall*: in this case, useful learning resources are not retrieved because their metadata contain a synonym or a semantically similar term rather than the exact one presented in the CG-PerLS query, and

- *poor precision*: too many learning resources contain the given term(s), but not all the retrieved ones are actually semantically relevant to the query.

The use of the *domain KB* (particularly the concept and relation type hierarchy) alleviates the poor recall problem. For example, an attempt to match the term "Logic Programming" with educational resources containing the term "Prolog" in their meta-data record will succeed as soon as the *domain KB* includes knowledge about Prolog being a programming language for Logic Programming.

The KB can be used to improve precision as well. If a query has produced too many results, it is possible to use this knowledge to construct system queries, that is, queries constructed by the system and presented to the user, to improve the precision of the returned learning objects. For example, if searching for video clips demonstra-ting Kepler's law has returned too many resources, then, the system can ask the learner if he/she is interested in any particular video encoding, given that such infor-mation is not included in the initial query. This system-side behavior is controlled by task knowledge, which defines such response patterns and is currently limited.

The existence of the KB provides two modes of operator-based query evaluation: *raw matching* and *semantic matching*. The mode is determined by the value of the *SemanticFlag* argument (false or true, respectively) in a query expression. The first case is straightforward: a learning resource "answers" a query if its metadata (in the CG form) match with the query CGs posed by the user and all the constraints intro-duced by the operators are satisfied. In the second case, a *similarity measure* (often called *semantic distance*) is required to be able to determine the extent to which two CGs may be considered "similar". Calculation of the similarity of two CGs depends upon the prior identification of appropriate "sources" of similarity. Such sources are the extend of use of the concept-type hierarchy and the ratio of arcs in the maximal join CG to the total number of arcs in the larger of the two CGs that participate in the maximal join operation (a form of unification between CGs). The contribution from any of the above sources of evidence of similarity can be equal or weighted. In gen-eral, the total similarity is defined as:

$$\text{TotalSimilarity} = w_1 \bullet \text{Eviden}_1 + w_2 \bullet \text{Eviden}_2 + \ldots + w_N \bullet \text{Eviden}_N . \qquad (1)$$

where w_i are the weights and $\Sigma w_i = 1$. This combined similarity allows for superior retrieval to that obtained by any individual form of evidence [1]. Currently, we only utilize the concept type hierarchy as a similarity measure.

Let us give an example of how the use of the concept-type hierarchy can be used as a similarity measure. For a semantic match, if two concepts are syntactically different from each other but they belong to the same branch of a concept-type hierarchy, the more specific one can be repeatedly generalized to shorten the semantic distance between them. Between two semantic matches, the one that uses fewer successive generalizations is more important since the semantic distance between this one and the matching concept is shorter. Thus it has higher rank. We restrict to generalization since specialization does not always preserve truth [14]. For example, specializing the concept [*mathematics*] to [*algebra*] is not correct in all contexts. Polysemy cases (ex. bank – financial institute / river) are dissolved based on the different conceptual defi-nitions of the polysemy terms, together with the rest of the metadata elements of the metadata record in which the polysemy term occurs. These elements help to select the right CG definition automatically. If this is not possible, the ambiguity is manually dissolved by the user.

If a part of a query CG does not match some CG-LOM metadata element entry, a try to generalize certain concepts using the concept-type hierarchy is performed. On successful generalization, the matching try is repeated, this time for the term which is the result of the generalization. This is depicted in Fig.7. The system can automatically switch to semantic term match if direct term match produces no result. However, the user decides whether to use semantic term matching or not on some concepts using the semantic flag of each concept.

Notice that the effect of an operator-based query to a CG-PerLS metadata KB is the derivation of a ranked subset of learning resources. This allows users to recursively refine their queries, that is, the query evaluation process is recursive.

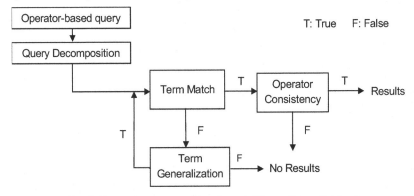

Fig. 7. Semantic term matching through "Term Generalization"

3.4   Dynamic Tutorial Generation

The term Dynamic Tutorial Generation refers to the identification of the learning objects that the learner should successfully attend in some specific order, to improve his/her knowledge, according to his learning request and current knowledge state. At the current state our model does not take into account any assessment results. This would required a CG binding for the related metadata which is, for the moment, not included in the CG-PerLS knowledge base. Therefore, we assume that the learner "gets" the knowledge of a learning object as soon as he/she accesses it.

Given an individual's current knowledge state KS_1 and a target knowledge state KS_2 where $KS_2=KS_1+DKS$, we want to find a way (*learning path*), in terms of proper curricular elements, that will enable the learner to "get" the extra knowledge DKS and evolve from KS_1 to KS_2. At the same time we want to ensure that the suggested curricular elements will not violate any user preferences such as difficulty level, media type, hardware requirements, time constraints etc. As soon as the system locates a learning object that satisfies the user's learning request, it uses appropriate (*record.relation*) metadata elements of this learning object in an attempt to "break" it down into fine-grained learning resources. For example, in order for a learner to successfully "interact" with a learning resource about "Linear Algebra" he should be familiar with "Matrix Calculus".

This process is outlined in Fig.8, where DKS is the knowledge of some learning object, say LO_1, that covers directly the user's learning request, augmented with the knowledge of additional learning objects the user should "attend" to become able to "attend" LO_1. The set of all the required learning objects constitute the Learning Path that will transfer the learner from KS_1 to KS_2.

Two example rules that are used in the dynamic tutorial generation are presented in Fig.9. Rule R_1 augments a learning object x that has as prerequisite the learning object y physically located at URL z, with a dynamic hyperlink to that URL. That is, the conclusion of the rule enriches the [LO:*x] learning object with additional information. Rule R_2 is similar to R_1 in the first part but it creates a system event that forces the CG-PerLS server to communicate with peer servers, instead. The particular rule will force the system to ask some known peer server for the physical location (URL) of the learning object with identifier *id2*.

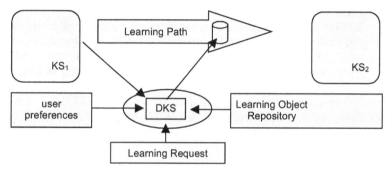

Fig. 8. Abstract definition of Personalized Knowledge Path construction

R1
[LO: *x] → (requires) → [LO: *y] → (phys_loc) → [URL:*z]
⇒
[LO: *x] → (d_link) → [URL:*z]

R2
[LO: *x] → (requires) → [LO: *y] → (phys_loc) → [URL:*z]
⇒
[SYS_EVENT: p2pquery] → (q_params) → [QCG: *ref*]

where *ref* corresponds to:
" [LO: id2] → (phys_loc) → [URL:?] "

Fig. 9. CG rules of the agent's task knowledge base

Communication between peer CG-PerLS servers requires that they share a common identification scheme. Of course this is also true for the domain knowledge.

4   Related Work

A very early adoption of CGs for semantic information retrieval can be found in COMFRESH [6] where the content of nodes in a hypertext network is selectively encoded in CGs and a CG based inference engine provides semantic query and retrieval of hypertext data, as well as dynamic, knowledge based hypertext links.

AI-Trader [12] is a type specification notation based on Conceptual Trees (a special case of CGs) to support service trading in open distributed environments where services are freely offered and requested. Our work resembles AI-Trader in the spirit of trading educational services, and goes one step further introducing the metadata usage.

WebKB [8], is a tool that interprets semantic statements (CGs) stored in Web-accessible documents. WebKB aims towards the semantic Web concept and, from one perspective, can be seen as an elaborated COMFRESH model.

Corby et al [3] describe Corese, a conceptual resource search engine. It enables the processing of RDF Schemas and RDF statements within the CG formalism. Based on the functionality, Corese has some relation to WebKB and mainly to COMFRESH, but goes beyond both of them since it uses the modern RDF/RDFS statements as an information source and presents its results with XSLT style sheets.

Murray [9] describes a framework called Model for Distributed Curriculum (MDC) that uses a topic server architecture to allow a Web-based tutorial to include a specification for another tutorial where the best fit to this specification will automatically be found at run time. A specific reasoning mechanism towards this functionality is not presented though.

DGC [15] is a tool that generates individual courses according to the learner's goals and previous knowledge and dynamically adapts the course according to the learner's success in acquiring knowledge. Unlike CG-PerLS, which is based on the metadata info, DGC uses "concept structures" as a road map to generate the plan of the course.

5   Conclusions - Future Work

We have presented CG-PerLS, a knowledge based approach on organizing and accessing educational resources. CG-PerLS is a model of a web based educational brokerage system which combines the descriptive power of metadata with the inference power of Conceptual Graphs to allow learning resource providers to manifest proprietary or LOM aware educational resources, client-side learners to access these educational resources in a way tailored to their individual profile and educational needs, and dynamic course generation.

A prototype system based on the CG-PerLS model is in development on the wintel platform. Some core ideas of our approach have been already successfully tested in the past, in the prototype of the COMFRESH system [6] using Prolog.

Furthermore we plan to add a cooperating evaluator module, in the form of a client-side agent that will further rank the knowledge transfer of a learning resource according to the assessment results the learner got. This information can be sent back to the CG-PerLS server and used to improve its overall knowledge transfer to the learner by preferring to serve him/her with a specific learning object from a set of similar ones, based on the assessment results obtained by learners with similar profiles. This will require substantial work on aspects related to the learner's model. Some early thoughts on this aspect have been already outlined in [19].

Acknowledgements

The work presented in this paper is partially funded by the European Commission Information Society Technologies (IST) Program through the IST No 12503 KOD "Knowledge on Demand" Project.

References

[1]   Brkich F. and Wilkinson R.: "A Conceptual Graph Matching Algorithm for Information Retrieval", *Proceedings 1st Australian Conceptual Structures Workshop*, University of New England, New South Wales, 1994.

[2]   Brusilovsky P.: "Adaptive and Intelligent Technologies for Web-based Education", In C. Rollinger and C. Peylo (eds.), *"Kunstliche Intelligenz"*, Special Issue on Intelligent Systems and Technology, 1999.

[3]   Corby O., Dieng R. and Hebert C.: "A Conceptual Graph model for W3C Resource Description Framework", *Proceedings 8th Conference on Conceptual Structures (ICCS'2000)*, Springer, 2000.

[4]   "Conceptual Graphs Standard Working Draft". Available at: http://www.jfsowa.com/cg/ cgstand.htm

[5]   Gerbe O.: "Conceptual Graphs for Corporate Knowledge Repositories", *Proceedings 5th Conference on Conceptual Structures (ICCS'97)*, 1997.

[6]   Kokkoras F. and Vlahavas I.: "COMFRESH: a Common Framework for Expert Systems and Hypertext", *Information Processing and Management*, Vol.31, No.4, 1995.

[7]   IEEE P1484.12/D6.0, "Draft Standard for Learning Object Metadata", February 2001.

[8]   Martin P. and Eklund P.: "Embedding Knowledge in Web Documents", *Proceedings 8th WWW Conference*, special issue of *The International Journal of Computer and Telecommunications Networking*, Toronto, Canada, 1999.

[9]   Murray T.: "A Model for Distributed Curriculum on the WWW", *Journal of Interactive Media in Education*, Vol.5, 1998. Available at: www-jime.open.ac.uk/98/5

[10]   IEEE P1484.2/D7, "Draft Standard for Learning Technology - Public and Private Information (PAPI) for Learners (PAPI Learner)", November 2000.

[11]   Petermann H., Euler L. and Bontcheva K.: "CG-Pro: a Prolog Implementation of Conceptual Graphs", Technical Report, Hamburg University, FBI-HH-M-251/95, 1995.

[12] Puder A., Markwitz S. and Gudermann F.: "Service Trading Using Conceptual Graphs", *Proceedings 3ʳᵈ Conference on Conceptual Structures (ICCS'95),* Springer, 1995.

[13] ADL: "Sharable Courseware Object Reference Model (SCORM)", Version 1.1, January 2001. Available at http://www.adlnet.org

[14] Sowa J.: "Conceptual Structures: Information Processing in Mind and Machine", Addison-Wesley Publishing Company, 1984.

[15] Vassileva J.: "Dynamic Course Generation on the WWW", *Proceedings 8ᵗʰ World Conference on AI in Education (AI-ED97),* Knowledge and Media in Learning Systems, Kobe, Japan, 1997.

[16] Corbett D.: "A Method for Reasoning with Ontologies Represented as Conceptual Graphs", In: M. Brooks, D. Corbett and M. Stumptner (Eds.): AI 2001, Springer-Verlag LNAI Vol. 2256, pp.130-141, 2001.

[17] Genest D. and Salvat E.: "A Platform Allowing Typed Nested Graphs: How CoGITo Became CoGITaNT", *Proceedings 6ᵗʰ Conference on Conceptual Structures,* Montpellier, France, pp.154-161, 1998.

[18] The CoGITaNT library. Available at http://cogitant.sourceforge.net/

[19] Kokkoras F. and Vlahavas I.: "eLPA: an e-Learner's Personal Assistant", *Proceedings Workshop on Application of Conceptual Structures,* Bulgaria, 2002. Available electronically only at http://lml.bas.bg/iccs2002/acs/kokkoras.pdf

[20] Gerbe O. and Mineau G.: "The CG Formalism as an Ontolingua for Web-Oriented Representation Languages", *Proceedings 10ᵗʰ Conference on Conceptual Structures (ICCS'02),* pp. 205-219, 2002.

[21] IMS Global Learning Consortium, Learning Resource Metadata (LOM) Specification, Version 1.2.1, Final Specification, September 2001. Available at http://www.imsglobal.org/ metadata/index.html

[22] IMS Global Learning Consortium, Learner Information Package (LIP) Specification, Version 1.0, Final Specification, March 2001. Available at: http://www.imsglobal.org/profiles/index.html

Website Evaluation: A Usability-Based Perspective

Nikolaos Avouris, Nikolaos Tselios, Christos Fidas, and Eleftherios Papachristos

Human-Computer Interaction Group
Electrical & Computer Engineering Department, University of Patras
GR-265 00 Rio-Patras, Greece
{N.Avouris,nitse,fidas,papachristos}@ee.upatras.gr

Abstract. The usability is recognized as an important quality factor of any modern website. In this paper, techniques for usability evaluation of a website are proposed and their use is described. The results of application of these techniques are discussed in the frame of the design and evaluation of a web portal, serving an Academic Department. The applicability of the developed techniques in a wide area of web-based applications and their importance in the context of today's web applications development is also discussed in this paper.

1   Introduction

The evaluation of a website is an important phase of the development cycle, often overlooked during the fast-paced development processes adopted by modern web applications developers. This is more important today when the web becomes gradually a platform for deployment of complex applications of increased interactivity, a front end for databases and corporate information systems. This new use of the medium increases the importance of usability, as the web is used for accomplishment of complex tasks, like learning, retrieving information, interacting and collaborating with peers [1]. The effective accomplishment of such tasks has to be proved during the design of web applications. According to Ivory and Hearst [2], many web sites today are characterized by low usability, while millions of new web sites are expected to become operational during the next years, further intensifying the problem.

Today's highly interactive web applications tend to adopt interaction styles borrowed from traditional software. This is not however always acceptable, since the web poses special requirements that need to be taken in consideration [3]. For instance, the web users' characteristics are often not well known beforehand or can vary considerably. Also the computing platforms, network bandwidth and access devices used can be very different. For example, users can access a certain application through wap-enabled devices using 9,6 kbps connection, through typical modems of 33,6-56 kbps or through high bandwidth connections allowing few hundred kbps or higher. These can affect considerably the user interaction characteristics.

According to Nielsen [4], the highly quoted user-centred design methodology is considered applicable in this new context. The principal characteristics of this ap-

Y. Manolopoulos et al. (Eds.): PCI 2001, LNCS 2563, pp. 217–231, 2003.

proach, as described by Theng et.al [5], are: (i) Interactive systems design should be based on a systematic user requirements capturing and recording of possible ways in which the users interact with the application. (ii) Design of highly interactive applications needs to be an iterative process. This approach, if adopted, brings iterative usability evaluation [6,7] at the center of the design process. However, involvement of users and setting up of usability testing experiments, advocated by user-centered design, is often considered a burden to the design team. Despite this, the need for such design approaches is widely recognized by the research community. Additionally there is an increased need to adapt the established usability testing techniques [6] (application inspection methods [4,8], observation methods [9], questionnaires and interviews [10]) to the requirements of web usability evaluation and to accelerate the often tedious process they propose [11,12].

In this paper, we report our experience with a website usability testing. The case study discussed relates to a web portal that has been designed and is in operation during the last years, to serve the academic community of the Electrical and Computer Engineering Department of the University of Patras in Greece (www.ee.upatras.gr). This application, typical of many similar University Departments, offers information on the activities of the Department to the public and the members of the Department and includes some more interactive components like support to the students for building their personal semester timetable and exams schedule.

A number of usability tests of this application have been contacted recently. These were based on adapted techniques proposed in the literature: (a) an experiment involved on-line questionnaires filled by the users, (b) heuristic evaluation by usability experts in the lab, and (c) user observation techniques and analysis of usage log files. The contacted experiments are presented and discussed. The findings are compared and their usefulness in the design of web applications is discussed. The re-design of the portal following these evaluation studies is also briefly described. Wider implications of the multi-faceted usability evaluation framework described in design of web applications are discussed in the last part of the paper.

2   Case Study: Usability Evaluation of an Academic Website

The web site of the ECE Department of the University of Patras (www.ee.upatras.gr) is a bi-lingual portal (in English and Greek) that has been developed with the objective to promote the Department and to provide information about its research and educational activities while at the same time to serve the Department students and faculty members. This latter use necessitates some interactive components, which need special attention during usability evaluation. The eight areas covered by the portal relate to:

(a) Information on the Department history and structure,
(b) Academic matters (courses offered, curriculum content etc.),
(c) Research activity (laboratories, publications, results),
(d) Personnel (faculty and researchers information, personal web pages etc.),
(e) Additional information (the area, access instructions etc.),

(f) Internal pages (password controlled services) and
(g) Web site information (contact info, sitemap etc.).

One of the provided services, which has been the focus of evaluation, as discussed in the following, is the *search engine* of the site. The user of the search facility can select one of four information areas (faculty, graduate students, personnel, curriculum subjects) and use keywords for searching information in each of these areas. Another service of the site that has been evaluated is the *personal timetable* and *exam schedule*. Users can select, out of a menu, the courses or the exams to which they have been registered for and request their personal course timetable or exams schedule to be shown on the screen. In figure 1 typical interaction screens of the personal exam schedule application are shown. The courses/exams can be selected from an alphabetical list, attached to a combo-box, as shown in Fig. 1.

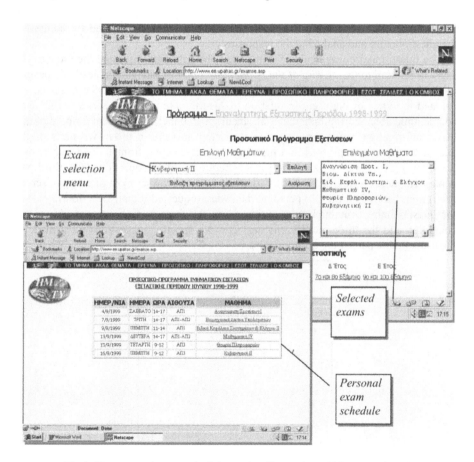

Fig.1. The personal exam schedule service (September 1999 exams shown)

3   Usability Evaluation Experiment

A series of usability evaluation experiments took place, after the web site had been in operation for two years. The experiments are presented in this section. In the final section of the paper a discussion on the findings is included.

3.1   Questionnaire-Based Evaluation Studies

Questionnaires have been extensively applied in usability evaluation experiments [10, 11]. In our case two separate experiments have been contacted using this technique.

On-line questionnaire. The first one involved an on-line questionnaire, particularly useful in web usability evaluation when the users are distant, an extract of which is shown in figure 2. The questionnaire contained a number of simple questions requesting the view of the users on the quality of the provided services and the utility of the web site. The *zoomerang* (www.zoomerang.com) service was used for compiling the questionnaire and analyzing the responses.

The questionnaire was made of four parts. The first part requested the view of the users in relation to the *quality of the application* (ease of navigation, aesthetic design, quality of content and usefulness of services). The second part requested *frequency of use* and the view of the users in relation to specific site parts and services (personal course timetable, curriculum material, faculty/personnel, department info, diploma thesis information, news service). The requested answers in these two parts of the questionnaire were expressed in a multi-point scale ranging from 1 (inadequate) to 5 (excellent). Similar scale was used for the frequency of use questions. The third part contained questions on the *context of use*, like type of browser most often used, screen resolution, bandwidth etc. No personal data were requested. Finally, the fourth part of the questionnaire contained open questions on the three more *serious problems* encountered and the three more *useful services*. No specific suggestions were made to the users in this part of the questionnaire.

Fig. 2. Extract of the on-line questionnaire

Table 1. Evaluation of quality of design through online questionnaire

Site feature	answers					Mean value	Stand. Dev.	Mean error	Confidence limits
	Inadequate	poor	average	good	excellent				
Navigation	3%	6%	35%	44%	10%	3.51 (average/ good)	0.88	0.1121	3.292-3.740
Aesthetic design	11%	14%	40%	29%	5%	2.91 (average)	0.94	0.1201	2.679-3.160
Content	6%	16%	43%	29%	3%	3.06 (average)	0.92	0.1189	2.828-3.303
Services	6%	25%	35%	25%	5%	2.96 (average)	0.99	0.1280	2.711-3.223

For twenty (20) days the questionnaire was linked through a visible button to the home page of the site. During this period sixty five (65) users volunteered a response. An overview of the responses to the first two parts of the questionnaire is shown in Tables 1 and 2. According to these tables, navigation was considered good, while aesthetic design, in-formation content and the quality of the provided services received an average mark.

The Usefulness/frequency of use questionnaire demonstrated the high value of the personal timetable and exam schedule service, while the other services received bellow average marks, probably not considered useful and adequately designed. The third part of the questionnaire revealed useful information about the users of the site, like browsers used and connection bandwidth. For instance from the answers of this part it was deduced that more than 60% of the users connect to the site through modem, thus special attention should be paid not to include heavy web pages in the site, while all the responders used computing equipment with screen resolution equal or higher to 800X600 pixels, suggesting that the web pages design should be adequately adjusted to make for more efficient use of screen space.

Finally the replies to the open questions of the fourth part of the questionnaire, shown in Table 3, identified the need for new services like links to library, course marks on line, student magazine etc, while revealed some usability problems, like the low visibility of the link to web servers of laboratories, a service that despite the fact that it was already provided, it was proposed as a new service in Table 3.

Table 2. Frequency of use according to online questionnaire

Site part	Frequency of use					Mean value	Stand. Dev.	Mean error	Confidence limits
	Never	Rarely	Sometimes	Frequently	Very Frequently				
Personal timetable/ exams schedule	2%	0%	3%	23%	73%	4.64 (frequently/ very frequently)	0.70	0.08	4.466-4.824
Curriculum material	15%	29%	24%	26%	6%	2.80 (sometimes)	1.17	0.14	2.509-3.104
Faculty	21%	39%	19%	13%	8%	2.48 (sometimes)	1.19	0.15	2.180-2.780
Department	18%	39%	24%	15%	3%	2.45 (sometimes)	1.05	0.13	2.188-2.730

Table 3. Proposed new services and identified problems according to the online questionnaire

Proposed new services		Most severe problems	
On line Grades for individual students	35,7%	*Late update*	42,9%
Richer news services including student news	32,1%	*Out of date layout*	23,8%
Electronic delivery of applications to secretary	28,6%	*Lack of detailed news services*	19,0%
Relevant links to library	21,4%	*Small number of services delivered*	9,5%
Links to lab/department web servers	17,9%	*Lack of links to lab/department web servers*	9,5%
Relevant course material download	14,3%	*Greek encoding problems in some pages*	4,8%
Detailed exams material for courses	14,3%	*Slow response*	4,8%
On line student magazine	10,7%	*Problems in search*	4,8%

Table 4. Replies of WAMMI questionnaire in a strongly disagree (1) to strongly agree (5) scale

> *This web site has much that is of interest to me:* 3.83 (agree)
> *It is difficult to move around this web site:* 2.33 (disagree)
> *I can quickly find what I want on this web site:* 3 (neutral)
> *This web site seems logical to me:* 4 (agree)
> *This web site needs more introductory explanations:* 3.16 (neutral)
> *The pages on this web site are very attractive:* 2.83 (neutral)
> *I feel in control when I'm using this web site:* 3 (neutral)
> *This web site is too slow:* 2.16 (disagree)
> *This web site helps me find what I am looking for:* 3.33 (neutral)
> *Learning to find my way around this web site is a problem:* 2.16 (disagree)
> *I don't like using this web site:* 2.66 (neutral)
> *I can easily contact the people I want to on this web site:* 4.33 (agree)
> *I feel efficient when I'm using this web site:* 3 (neutral)
> *It is difficult to tell if this web site has what I want:* 2.83 (neutral)
> *Using this web site for the first time is easy:* 3.33 (neutral)
> *This web site has some annoying features:* 3 (neutral)
> *Remembering where I am on this web site is difficult:* 1.66 (disagree)
> *Using this web site is a waste of time:* 1.83 (disagree)
> *I get what I expect when I click on things on this web site:* 2.83 (neutral)
> *Everything on this web site is easy to understand:* 3.16 (neutral)

The WAMMI questionnaire. A second experiment involving a questionnaire was directed to users who participated in the users observation experiment described in section 3.3. In this case the users (six experienced users of the system) were asked to fill a Wammi inspired questionnaire [13]. The requested replies were in Likert-type scale (strongly agree / agree / neutral / disagree / strongly disagree), though which the users expressed their attitude towards the statements. This kind of questionnaire, filled by users during a usability experiment can be used for checking their attitude and can be complementary to the usability evaluation experiment. The average values of the received responses are shown in Table 4. Comparing this questionnaire with the online one presented above one can verify that the results are not contradictory.

Validation of questionnaires with logfiles. Finally, a cross checking of the findings of the questionnaires with log files collected by the web server was performed. This identified the frequency of use of parts of the site as well as characteristics of accessing equipment (e.g. browser version). Data from a period of two months have been used. The study of the log files confirmed the validity of the filled questionnaires. For instance the browser type data of the log file and the questionnaire were almost identical. However the emphasis is different, the log files do not present the views of the users, while provide some additional information like patterns of use during the day/week/year, referring domains etc, which can be useful complementary material for user profiling ([14],[15]). Development of automatic techniques for analysis of these log files and use of them in a complementary way in the evaluation is a matter of further research.

3.2   Heuristic Evaluation

The second evaluation technique involved eleven (11) evaluators, knowledgeable in user-centered design, with high web usage experience. They applied an inspection technique, called *heuristic evaluation* [4] using heuristic rules that govern good interface design. This is a well-known, highly appraised experts-based evaluation technique, which has been successfully used in many similar experiments [16,8].

Method of the study. During the first phase of the study, the evaluators were encouraged to navigate the application and carefully validate the implementation of each heuristic rule. Evaluators were asked to simulate execution of representative tasks during this phase. When a rule violation was detected, the evaluator identified where the violation occurred, and proposed likely solutions. Each evaluator filled a report describing his/her findings. Evaluators were also provided with an evaluation sheet, in which they could quantify their subjective judgment, by assigning marks expressed in a 5 mark scale, indicating degree of conformance with each particular rule. The range of assigned values was 1 (inadequate) to 5(excellent). A relevance weight (w_i) was also assigned to each rule, according to the expert's opinion. Quantitative results of the evaluation are presented in table 5. Factor-weighted score, u, derives according to

$$u = \frac{\sum_{i=1}^{10} r_i \cdot w_i}{\sum_{i=1}^{10} w_i} \tag{1}$$

where r_i is the rule rating and w_i is weight for each heuristic rule i. The overall usability score was average to good (3.38 excluding rule weight factors, and 3.42 including weight factors). 7 out of 10 heuristic rules ranked with a relative high grade. Rules h7, h9 and h10 received average grade, indicating usability problems related to the specific rules as discussed in the following.

Heuristic Rule h7. (Flexibility and efficiency of use) The system in general does not provide shortcuts to facilitate user's tasks especially in complex processes such as Searching and Personal Timetable. For example, frequently searched terms are not provided in a form of ready-to-select links. Also users cannot make multiple-course selections in Timetable building, such as all the courses of a specific semester. Additionally to this no specific reference to post-graduate courses was allowed.

Table 5. Average subjective score, weight factor, and total errors found for each heuristic rule

Heuristic Rule : [1]	h1	h2	h3	h4	h5	h6	h7	h8	h9	h10
Score (mean value)	3.63	4.45	3.63	4.18	3.27	3.54	2.55	3.72	2.63	2.19
Stand. deviation	0.36	0.28	0.24	0.37	0.38	0.36	0.31	0.19	0.27	0.22
Relevance (mean value)	4.54	4.45	3.45	4.45	4.27	4.18	3.18	3.81	3.81	3.72
Stand. deviation	0.28	0.24	0.34	0.24	0.27	0.35	0.35	0.35	0.40	0.33
Number of detected Errors	4	3	2	3	7	2	3	2	5	2

Heuristic Rule h9. (Support the users to recognize, diagnose, and recover from errors) The most severe problem is that the typical 404 page has not been replaced with a page showing the site map of the site, explaining that a system error occurred (possibly because of wrong URL), and providing a search link. Also some error messages do not constructively suggest solutions or indicate why the problem occurred.

Heuristic Rule h10. (Help and documentation) Even though the system can be used without a lot of online documentation as resulted from the user's observation experiment, at least some help should be provided in high interactivity tasks (search engine and Personal timetable). The help should be easy to search, focused on the user's task and explicitly list the steps to be carried out.

Overall thirty-three (33) usability flaws were unveiled during this study. Many of the usability problems were reported by more than one evaluators, confirming Nielsen's and Landauer's finding that four to five evaluators typically unveil about 80% of the overall usability problems [17].

3.3   User Observation

The third usability evaluation technique used involved observation of typical users, as they interacted with the application, executing typical tasks. The experiment took place in a usability laboratory. The users were six students of the Department, 4 undergraduate and 2 post-graduate, 5 male, 1 female, aged 23-28. They were all experienced users of the Internet, which they use daily in their activities. The equipment used in the study was a Personal Computer (Pentium III, 600 MHz, 128 Ram, 17" monitor, 1024*768 screen resolution) with good connection to the web site through the high band University network.

At the beginning of the experiment, the users were informed that they were not them-selves the subject of evaluation. Five tasks were carefully described to them (table 6), however, while the objective of each task was made clear, no precise instructions on its execution were provided in order not to condition the users' strate-

---

[1] The applied heuristic rules were the following: 1. Visibility of system status, 2. Match between system and the real world, 3. User control and freedom, 4. Consistency and standards, 5. Error prevention, 6. Recognition rather than recall, 7. Flexibility and efficiency of use, 8. Aesthetic and minimalist design, 9. Help users recognize, diagnose, and recover from errors, 10. Help and documentation

gies [9]. The users were provided with sufficient time to complete their tasks. The observers did not provide any additional information or support. Timing of tasks and observations on strategies and patterns of use were made by the evaluation facilitators.

First remark was that Tasks T2, T3 and T5 were completed promptly with no special difficulties by any of the students. This proved that the application was sufficiently well structured to support the users identify specific information items. In contrary tasks T1 and T4, proved to be time-consuming and cognitively demanding.

The developed strategies varied; often multiple browser windows where used in order to accomplish the tasks. Usability problems in the application design clearly emerged. In the T1 the courses were sorted alphabetically in the Personal Timetable page, no provision was made for alternative presentation (e.g. cluster per academic year). Also luck of redo and undo option hindered considerably task execution. A search option was not available in the same page. Availability of a single button for transfer of all courses of an academic year in the timetable would have considerably accelerated the process.

The search engine of the site was hidden behind a relevant icon, as shown in Fig. 3. This icon was not easily identified by the users as a button, since there was no familiar search textbox associated. So many users had difficulties in locating the Search engine of the site.

In order to accomplish task T4 the users needed to use the site Search engine. Some misunderstandings related with the use of this facility were identified during the study. The Search engine requires selection of a search category first, before inserting a keyword. There was no way to make a global search in all categories (course subjects, faculty, undergraduate students, post-graduate students etc.). Also the logic applied by the search engine was not made clear and was not explained. (e.g. Computer Networks searches for Computer OR Networks or the string "Computer Networks"). Finally, a subsequent search was not clear if it was made in the first search results or in the original search space. Some insecurity was observed to some users in relation to the validity of the search results.

Table 6. Description of tasks and time required to complete them

Task description	Average Time (sec)	Stand. Dev	Mean error
T1: To build a personal timetable for a student of the third year who is also registered to a limited number of courses of the 2nd year	266.33	54.58	22.286
T2: For a specific course to search for the course description and relevant handouts and other material	34.83	18.17	7.418
T3: To search for details of the CV of a faculty member (University and year of PhD award)	20.66	6.77	2.765
T4: To find all courses offered in the curriculum that involve computer networks	400.33	158.85	64.851
T5: To find information relating with access by public transport to the Department and the University.	19.16	7.521	3.07
Total	**741.33**	**196.71**	**80.305**

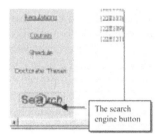

Fig. 3. The search button, through which the search engine of the site is invoked

Fig.4. The home page of : (a) the re-designed portal and (b) the original portal

One user did not manage to complete Task T4 for this reason. In summary 29 out of 30 tasks were successfully accomplished, however the difficulties encountered in tasks T1 and T4, as discussed here and the unexpected long times required for accomplishing the tasks, taking into consideration that expert users were involved, unveiled many limitations of the design.

4   Website Re-design

The Academic Department web portal has been recently re-designed, taking in consideration the results of the usability evaluation studies described in the previous section. The new design is characterized by improved aesthetic appearance of the site, lower download times due to reduced multimedia content, following the user access data, more compact layout and more information content per webpage. At the same time the original structure and the content of the website were maintained.

A considerable modification was made to the *search facility* and the *personal timetable* and *exams schedule* services, following the remarks of the users and the observed difficulties in particular during the user observation experiments. For instance the selection screen for courses in the personal timetable service, in the new portal is done through a list of all available courses, grouped by year, as shown in figure 5, instead of an alphabetic list through a combo-box in the original design. This screen provides an overview of all courses. The user is provided with the possibility to select or deselect the courses from this view and then proceed with the timetable. This new design tackles the observed problems in the course selection task, discussed in section 3.

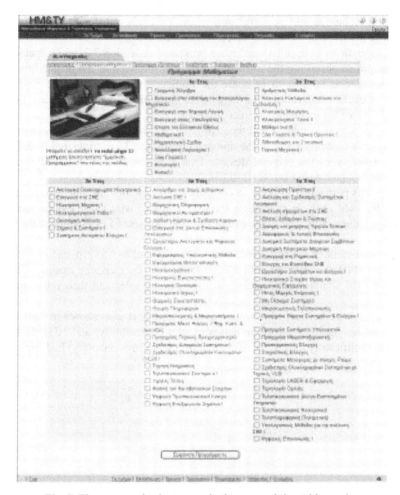

Fig. 5. The course selection screen in the personal timetable service

Table 7. Heuristic evaluation of the updated portal design

Heuristic rule	h1	h2	h3	h4	h5	h6	h7	h8	h9	h10
Score r_i (mean value)	4,22	4,33	3,83	4,50	3,28	4,11	3,12	3,94	2,61	3,89
Relevance w_i (mean value)	4,22	4,56	3,39	4,06	3,78	4,11	3,06	3,94	4,06	3,56

4.1 Heuristic Evaluation of the New Portal Design

The new portal design has been recently evaluated, using the adapted heuristic evaluation approach discussed in section 3.2, in order to compare the findings of the evaluation with the evaluation study of the original design, discussed in section 3. The evaluators in this experiment were seventeen (17), all experienced in using the evaluation technique and powerful web users. This was a different set of evaluators than those involved in the studies discussed in section 3.

The heuristic rules applied were those presented in section 3.2, while special attention was put in observing the evaluation protocol followed in the original evaluation study in order to be able to compare the findings of the two evaluation studies. A number of useful observations and suggestions were made by the evaluators. In table 7 the overview of the evaluation results is shown.

From the scores in table 7 and those of table 5, it was deduced that the mean value of the overall usability score of the updated design was 3.78, compared to 3.38 of the overall usability of the original design. This difference was considered significant, according to a pair wise t test ($P(t)=0.036$).

A test was performed in order to compare the evaluators' attitude towards the heuristic rules used in these evaluation studies. So a pair wise t test was performed between the values of w_i (relevance of rule) for the two sets of evaluators of the specific website.

The mean value of the rules relevance in the two studies was proven not statistically significant ($P(t)=0.1649$), an indication that the two independent groups of heuristic evaluators had similar attitudes towards the heuristic rules and their relevance to the specific site.

The difference between the two evaluation studies is also shown in figure 6. According to this figure, the score in heuristic rules 7 (flexibility) and 10 (help and support) has significantly improved, while that of rule 9 (error recovery) had similar value in both studies.

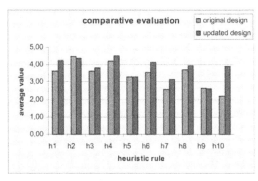

Fig. 6. Comparison of heuristic usability evaluation scores in the two portal designs

5   Discussion – Conclusions

Three complementary usability evaluation techniques were presented and their application in the usability evaluation of a web portal was described in this paper. All three presented approaches provided the design team with useful insight into the application and revealed many usability problems not previously detected.

The *on-line* and *Wammi* questionnaires helped us collect information relating to the users view on the supplied services and content of the site. The questionnaires are techniques easy to implement, however the findings are mostly useful for identifying problem areas without suggesting solutions. Also crosschecking of the findings should be performed. The usage log files of the website can be valuable complementary information. Additionally, control questions incorporated in the questionnaire can be used for quality control of the supplied answers.

In addition, it should be observed that the questionnaires sometimes are not filled by representative part of the user population and can provide a distorted view of use. For instance, in our case the questionnaire was mostly filled by students and not faculty members, something reflected in the provided suggestions.

The second technique used was heuristic evaluation by experts. This technique requires more effort, since experts have to be engaged in experimentation. However the number of problems identified by this experiment, as presented in section 3.2, was impressive. A limitation was however that the identified problems were not deduced from realistic interaction patterns, but from dialogue flow analysis. This was due to the fact that this technique does not involve real users, but experts making hypotheses on user attitude.

The third experiment, involving real users closely observed as they executed typical tasks, revealed additional problems often overlooked by the designers and not identified by the previous two experiments. Typical examples of analysis of the observations made during this experiment were included in section 3.3. However this, technique requires additional effort, as typical users have to be identified and actively engaged in the experiment, not an easy task in commercial and general-purpose applications. Also the experiment has to be made in adequately equipped environment and has to be well designed. Finally the effort required for analysis of the findings and their interrelation to design decisions is not trivial. So it is questionable if this technique can be fully implemented as part of the typical fast web application development process.

The findings of all three evaluation studies were transformed in new design requirements and were fed in the development team who recently updated the portal. This is the case with most web sites of this nature who need to go through a major redesign phase every two to three years. The new design was recently evaluated, by a new group of evaluators, using heuristic evaluation in the same way as in the evaluation study of the original design. The number of observations was in this case as high as in the original evaluation. By comparing the usability score of the two studies, the improvement in usability was considered statistically significant.

In conclusion, this study has shown us that by incorporating systematic usability evaluation studies in the development of the web portal, a significant improvement of the web site usability was achieved. We feel that an approach similar to the one described in this paper is indispensable part of a user-centered design and it should be followed in a rigorous way in websites where the customer's needs and desires need to be taken in consideration in great extend, like for instance portals of commercial nature.

In addition, the reported study showed that alternative usability evaluation techniques put different emphasis and provide the designer with different findings. So preferably a combination of them should be used in web application development. Given the importance of usability evaluation for development of this kind of applications and the effort required for most of usability analysis tests, it is worth investigating further techniques and supporting tools that automate parts of the described usability evaluation process.

Acknowledgements

The web site described in this paper has been developed by a group of volunteers, members of the ECE Department. Financial support by the EPEAEK/ECE Department Curriculum Development Project and the PENED 99ED234 Project is acknowledged. Also the free service of Zoomerang of Market Tools Inc., used in the frame of the reported study, is also acknowledged.

References

[1] Shum S. B.: "The Missing Link: Hypermedia Usability Research & the Web", *ACM SIG-CHI Bulletin*, Vol.28, No.4, pp.68-75, 1996.
[2] Ivory M.Y., Sinha R. and Hearst. M.A.: "Improving Web Site Design", *IEEE Internet Computing*, pp.56-63, March-April 2002.
[3] Bevan N.: "Usability Issues in Web Site Design", *Proceedings UPA'98 Conference*, Washington DC, 1998.
[4] Nielsen J.: "*Usability Engineering*", Academic Press, London, 1993.
[5] Theng Y.-L., Jones M. and Thimbleby H.: "Lost in Hyperspace, Psychological Problem or Bad Design", *Proceedings 1st AsiaPacific Conference on HCI*, pp.387-396, 1996.
[6] Avouris N.M.: "Introduction to Software Usability", *Proceedings 8th Panhellenic Conference on Informatics (Workshop on Software Usability)*, Vol.II, pp.514-522, Nicosia, November 2001.
[7] Fitzpatrick R. and Higgins C.: "Usability Software and its Attributes: a Synthesis of Software Quality", European Community Law and HCI, People and Computers XIII, pp.3-22, Springer, London, 1998.
[8] Levi D.M. and Conrad F.G.: "Usability Testing of World Wide Web Sites", Research Papers of Bureau of Labor Statistics, 1998. Available at http://www.bls.gov
[9] Rubin J.: "*Handbook of Usability Testing*", Wiley, New York, 1994.
[10] Feinberg S. and Johnson P.Y: "Designing and Developing Surveys on WWW Sites Getting Feedback on your Web Site", *Proceedings 16th ACM Conference on Systems Documentation*, pp.38-42, 1998.
[11] Kantner L. and Rosenbaum S.: "Usability Studies of WWW Sites: Heuristic Evaluation vs. Laboratory Testing", *Proceedings 15th ACM Conference on Systems Documentation*, pp. 153-160, 1997.
[12] Keevil B.: "Measuring the Usability Index of your Web Site", *Proceedings ACM Con-ference on Human Factors in Computing Systems (CHI)*, pp.271-277, 1998.

[13] Management N. and Kirakowski J.: "Web Usability Questionnaire", 2000. Available at http://www.nomos.se/wammi

[14] Hochheiser H. and Shneiderman. B.: "Understanding Patterns of User Visits to Web Sites: Interactive Starfield Visualizations of WWW Log Data", *Proceedings ASIS'99 Conference*, 1999.

[15] Pirolli P. and Pitkow J.E.: "Distributions of Surfers' Paths Through the World Wide Web: Empirical Characterization", *World Wide Web*, Vol.2, No.1-2, pp.29-45, 1999.

[16] Avouris N.M., Tselios N.K. and Tatakis E.C.: "Development and Evaluation of a Computer-based Laboratory Teaching Tool", *J Comp. Applications in Eng. Education*, Vol.9, No.1, pp.8-19, 2001.

[17] Nielsen J. and Landauer T.K.: "A Mathematical Model of the Finding of Usability Problems", *Proceedings ACM/IFIP INTERCHI'93 Conference*, pp.206-213, Amsterdam, The Netherlands, April 1993.

Concepts to Consider when Studying Computer-Mediated Communication and Online Learning

Charalambos Vrasidas

School of Education, Intercollege, 46, Makedonitissas Ave.
P.O. Box. 24005, Nicosia 1700, Cyprus
cvrasidas@cait.org

Abstract. This paper presents a conceptual framework for studying interaction in online environments. The theoretical underpinnings of the framework will be presented as well as the results from studies that led to the development and refinement of the framework will be discussed. This framework is based on symbolic interactionist ideas and extensive research in the areas of computer-mediated communication and distance education. The framework consists of the following categories: context, learner control, social presence, structure, feedback, dialogue, and interaction. The categories of the conceptual framework are characterized by a reciprocal determinism, and they are all parts of a broader system. The implications of this framework and the research that will be presented will be discussed in detail as they relate to the design and study of online learning environments.

1 Introduction

Telecommunications are changing education and are blurring the boundaries between traditional and distance education. Several university courses are offered completely online, or they require a combination of face-to-face and online meetings. Distance education, in the form of virtual universities and online learning environments, has become a major venue for delivering education and training. During the last few years, one of the most popular technologies employed in distance education has been computer-mediated communication (CMC).

CMC refers to the use of networked computers for communication, interaction, and exchanging of information [1]. Examples of CMC include electronic mail, bulletin boards, newsgroups, and computer conferencing. As a result of the rapid growth of computer networks and the Internet, CMC is used extensively for delivering education and training worldwide [2, 3]. This paper will discuss the research behind a conceptual framework developed for studying human-human interaction in computer-mediated online environments. This framework was based on symbolic interactionist

Y. Manolopoulos et al. (Eds.): PCI 2001, LNCS 2563, pp. 232–247, 2003.

ideas and consists of some of the most important theoretical constructs identified in distance education research [4].

Some of the issues that face CMC and online education are: the need for solid theoretical foundation on which to build and expand the field of distance education; the lack of empirical studies that identify effective models for the design and evaluation of CMC and online learning environments; the need to understand interaction in technology mediated situations and how it affects learning [5, 6, 7]. The proposed framework allows researchers to examine Human Computer Interaction (HCI) as it applies in the design and implementation of online learning environments.

2   Symbolic Interactionism

Our research is based on symbolic interactionism, a social-psychological approach used for the study of human affairs. This approach places a great emphasis on interaction, meaning, and interpretation. As a school of thought, it has guided research in the social sciences for decades. Although the theoretical foundations of this school are decades old, it is regarded as one of the most important approaches in studying interaction, social phenomena, and education [8, 9, 10, 11]. The particular emphasis that symbolic interactionism places on interaction, makes it very appropriate for the study of interaction in technology-mediated situations. We have been using interpretive research methods in our work since they are based on symbolic interactionist ideas [12]. Erickson argues that interpretive approaches to inquiry place an emphasis on the meanings-in-action of the actors involved and rely heavily on the interpretation of the phenomena under study, as the researcher provides it [9].

According to Blumer, there are three basic premises posed for symbolic interactionism [4]. First, human beings act upon the world on the basis of the meanings that the world has for them. Second, the meaning of the world is socially constructed through one's interactions with members of the community. And third, the meaning of the world is processed again through interpretation. Under a symbolic interactionist conceptual framework, interaction can be defined as the process consisting of the reciprocal actions of two or more actors within a given context. Blumer argued that interaction is actors engaged in joint action. The minimum interactional sequence consists of at least two reciprocal actions [4]. There is reciprocity with the sense that each actor has to indicate, interpret, and act upon objects on the basis of the meanings that the objects have for her or him. Interaction always takes place in response to others' actions or in relation to others' actions. Under a symbolic interactionist conceptual framework, interaction is not a variable that you take out from a broad context and you examine on its own. Interaction is an ongoing process that resides in a context and also creates context. Context is provided by the history of the situation, past interactional sequences, and future interactional sequences. There is a reflexive relationship between context and interaction that prevents us from isolating interaction from its context. To examine human action and interaction, it is important to examine carefully the context and the moment-to-moment events that lead to further interaction among people. An important component of the interlinkage of action is that any joint action always arises from the past actions of participants.

How others act with regards to the world, influences the meanings of the world for the individual. Meanings are used to form action through the process of interpretation. Human beings are active organisms. They make indications to themselves, act upon objects, interpret their environment, and engage in action. Social interaction is an ongoing process, which shapes human conduct as actors fit their actions with one another and form a continuous flow of interaction. In an online learning environment, when participants fit their actions to each other's actions, they constantly make choices. In an online discussion, they can respond to each other's messages or they can ignore them. Participants have intentions that influence interaction. However, participants always take into account other's actions, and in light of those actions they revise, abandon, replace, or follow their initial intention [13, 14, 15, 16].

3   Theoretical and Methodological Framework

During the last five years we have been conducting research to examine the nature of interaction in computer-mediated online environments and try to understand the complexities of such environments, particularly as they are developed and used for education and training [14, 15]. In our work, we have studied a variety of contexts, programs, and settings including online classes (undergraduate, graduate, and high-school level), complete online degrees, virtual highs school projects, and online professional development programs [14, 15, 16, 17]. It is not the purpose of this article to describe in detail every setting we examined but to rather present the framework and major findings of our work.

Interaction is one of the most important components of any learning experience [18, 19] and it has been identified as one of the major constructs in distance education research [2, 20, 21]. Researchers identified four kinds of interaction in distance education: learner-content, learner-teacher, learner-learner, and learner-interface [20, 22].

From our studies we have gradually developed a framework (see Figure 1) that consisted of the following categories: interaction, learner control, social presence, structure, dialogue, and feedback. The broader category within which all categories reside is the context of interaction. Context is defined by the content of the course, the technology via which communication is mediated, the teaching philosophy of the teacher, and departmental and institutional policies. Learner control consists of the learner's competency to take control of his/her learning, the support and resources provided to him/her, and learner independence [23]. The amount of dialogue that takes place among learners and between teacher and learners will also influence interaction and the feeling of social presence. These categories were fine-tuned by conducting an extensive literature review of research on distance education and computer-mediated online environments.

Samples of research questions addressed in research studies conducted using this framework include the following:

1.   What kinds of interaction take place in an online environment?
2.   What is the meaning of interaction for those involved?
3.   What factors influence interaction in computer-mediated online environments?

4. How can we best utilize technology to promote interaction and learning?
5. How does structure influence interaction?
6. What are the differences between online interactions and face-to-face interactions?
7. What are the power relationships like and how do they relate to the nature of interaction?

For studies to address the complexity of social life in an online environment, their design has to be evolving and allowing for new relationships to emerge from the data. The conceptual framework of a study guides the process of inquiry, provides a rough guide-map for the study, and communicates the purpose of the study to the researcher's audience. The categories of the framework are not fixed, but instead are changing and evolving during the course of the study [8, 9, 11]. In our studies, which followed interpretive methods, the conceptual framework is neither fixed, nor sequential. It is rather fluid and it evolves as the study proceeds. In fact, the conceptual framework changed several times. For example, the category of feedback falls within the interaction category. However, by carefully examining the data from pilot studies, feedback emerged as a strong category by itself. Therefore, feedback was added as a separate category in the conceptual framework.

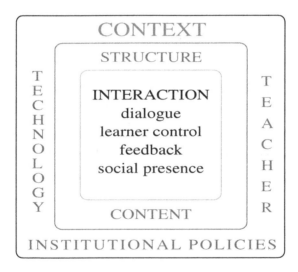

Fig. 1. Conceptual framework for studying interaction in computer-mediated online environments

4 Discussion of the Framework

In the following sections, I will discuss in detail the conceptual framework developed for studying interaction in computer-mediated online environments. I will be referring to studies that we conducted with colleagues at Arizona State University, at the Center for the Application of Information Technologies at Western Illinois University, and at Intercollege, Cyprus. I will also be referring to studies conducted by others, which relate to the major categories of the framework. It is not the purpose of this paper to discuss in detail the context and method of our research, but to present some of the findings of our work and discuss its implications.

4.1   The Context of Interaction in Online Environments

In order to examine a complex construct such as interaction, researchers should carefully examine the context within which interaction is taking place. Learning, knowledge, and human activity are situated within specific contexts [24, 25]. As Dewey put it, "experience does not occur in a vacuum"(p. 40) [18]. In an online course, the context of interaction consists of institutional and departmental policies, technologies employed, teacher philosophy, and course content [16]. Policies and curricula will influence the teacher's approach and the content of the course. The content of an online course is an important component of the educational context.

One of the major factors of context category is the teacher. His/her philosophy about education and his/her epistemological beliefs will be reflected in his/her approach to teaching and structuring the online environment. What strategies he/she employs, how enthusiastic he/she is about the subject matter, and what his/her attitude is about the mediating technology, will also have an impact on interaction [26]. The impact that the teacher's philosophy has on interaction is mainly reflected by the structure of the learning environment, which consists of strategies employed, assignments, selection of content, and other requirements specified by the teacher [14, 15, 16].

One of the most important components of the context of interaction is the mediating technology. Different media allows for different cues to be communicated. Technologies used in distance education include books and other print material, broadcast television, video, audio, telephones, and computers. Various technologies allow for different cues to be communicated and different communication strategies. Print material used in correspondence education was limited in the kinds of interactions allowed, and was more appropriate for one-way communication [27]. Affordances of telecommunication technologies such as computer conferencing, interactive video, and audiographics, allow for two-way communication and interaction [28]. The nature of these technologies and the role that educationists play in their development is a topic, often ignored.

4.2   Interaction

In traditional face-to-face learning environments and classrooms, interaction is often limited to the teacher lecturing which leads to the teacher dominating the discourse [29]. Even though the learner-learner interaction was found to be a critical factor in cognitive development [19, 30], learner participation in classroom discourse is limited in the traditional classroom [29]. Computer-mediated online environments have been proven to be a viable way for promoting learner-learner interaction and learner engagement [28, 31].

Moore made the distinction between three types of interaction in distance education: learner-content, learner-teacher, and learner-learner [20]. For Moore, learner-content interaction is the fundamental form of interaction on which all education is based. Learning will occur when learners interact with some content. Content is found, among others, in books, objects from the environment, abstract ideas, problems to be solved, videotapes, computer programs, and websites. The learner-teacher interaction can take the form of the teacher delivering instruction, lecturing, and providing support, encouragement, and feedback to each learner. The learner might be interacting with the instructor by asking questions, submitting homework, and discussing a problem. The learner-learner interaction is a challenge to our thinking and practice in the 1990s"(p. 4). Learners collaborate with peers on projects and discuss exchange ideas on topics that relate to the course. Furthermore, learners might be interacting among themselves for reasons that do not relate to the course and engage in informal conversations and chats.

Some researchers have argued that past discussions of interaction failed to acknowledge the fact that for any of the three types of interaction to take place, the learner has to interact with the medium [22]. They based their argument on Salomon's symbol attributes theory according to which each medium employs different symbol systems to convey a message [32]. The message conveyed is colored by the medium's attributes. The learner needs to be able to comprehend the message coming from that medium. Communication will be successful when both the sender and receiver of a message are confident in coding and decoding messages transmitted via that medium. Therefore, the learner's skill to engage in technology-mediated communication is an important factor that will influence success in distance education. In addition, teacher-interface interaction is rarely examined or discussed in distance education literature. However, problems of teacher-interface may have more to do with the success or failure of distance education than any other kind of interaction. Furthermore, the interface may not be simply a medium"but may be content in its own right. Just as McLuhan argued that the medium is the message,"in the age of cheap, personal telecommunications the medium may become an essential part of the content.

Several studies were conducted to examine the learner-interface interaction and the impact of technology on communication. One study examined the impact of an interactive network on classroom communication and learning [33]. The findings showed that awareness of technology hampered interaction. Ross found that learners, who do not have the skills to communicate with computers, are more aware of technology rather than the content of communication during interaction [34].

Some researchers have examined the impact of telecommunication technologies on learning outcomes by comparing face-to-face instruction with instruction delivered via telecommunications [35]. The findings showed no significant differences in learning outcomes, which is in agreement with several studies that indicated no difference between delivery media [36]. They also found that in the face-to-face setting students interacted more often with the teacher, whereas off-campus students interacted more often among themselves.

Others have examined the characteristics of conference interactions in an electronic network over a period of sixteen months [37]. This network was formed for the professional development of ESL teachers in Hong-Kong. It was found that the frequency of interaction increased over time, as teachers became more comfortable using technology. Factors they identified that might have influenced interaction included computer skills, access to the network, perceptions of the nature of the network, perceptions of relationship with other users, and perceptions of self as it was manifested through the network.

A study was conducted to compare face-to-face and online discussions [38]. It was found that online discussions had multiple threads, were slower, and there were longer delays between the exchange of two messages. In addition, the back channeling associated with face-to-face interaction was minimal in the online environment. Back channeling refers to the process during which participants constantly reinforce each other's contribution in a conversation with simple gestures such as eye contact, nodding of a person's head, and short verbal exchanges such as "yeah" and "umm" [39].

In studies we conducted [14, 15, 16], we found that human-human interaction in computer-mediated environments is slower and lacks in continuity, richness, and immediacy, as it is compared with face-to-face interaction. Because of the text nature of online interaction, it is easier to get confused and misunderstood in an online than in a face-to-face situation. Furthermore, we found that interaction was influenced by the structure of the course, feedback provided to participants, prior experience with computer-mediated communication, and the number of participants in the online environment or course.

4.3   Learner Control

Learner control is a very important construct in distance education. Some scholars have argued that the concept of control consists of three major components: independence, power, and support [40]. Therefore, control should be examined as the balancing result among these three factors. Independence is defined as the degree to which the learner is free to make choices. Power refers to the abilities and competencies of the learner to engage in a learning experience. Support refers to the resources available that will enable the learner to successfully participate in the distance education course. In a later study, Baynton found that there are other factors that might influence control such as institutional context, administrative policies, course design, and economic issues [23].

Studies showed that certain learner characteristics are more likely to be identified in successful distance learners [41, 42]. Such characteristics include internal locus of control, self-motivation, and independence. Those learners that perceive their accomplishments as a result of their own efforts have an internal locus of control and are more likely to be successful as distance learners [2]. Parker conducted a study to examine the degree to which locus of control, financial support, and number of previously attended distance education courses could predict course completion among college student populations [43]. She found that learners that have an external locus of control are more likely to dropout than learners with an internal locus of control.

The learner's competency to participate in an online course is an important factor that will determine the degree to which he/she will engage in interaction with the instructor and peers. In order to interact with the instructor, the content, and peers in an online course, the learner must have the necessary technology and computer communication skills [44]. Ross found that when learners do not have the skills to communicate using computers, they are more aware of technology rather than the content of communication during interaction [34]. In addition, students that are self-motivated and provided with the resources to use technology are more likely to engage in interaction. Vrasidas and McIsaac found that experience with CMC was an important factor that influenced interaction in an online environment [14]. Participants that had more experience participated more often in online discussions and felt less intimidated by the technology.

4.4   Dialogue and Structure

The constructs of dialogue and structure will be examined together since they are the two components of transactional distance [35]. Moore postulated that transactional distance is the psychological and communication gap that results from the geographical separation between the learners and the teacher [45]. Structure refers to the overall design of the course, which is a reflection of the broader context, that influences interaction. The teacher's philosophy, content of the course, institutional policies, and technology that mediates communication will shape the overall design of the course. Dialogue refers to the learner-teacher interaction. A program is effective when it provides sufficient dialogue opportunities between learner and teacher and enough structure that provides sufficient guidance to students. How much dialogue takes place in an educational setting depends on factors such as teacher and learner characteristics, teacher philosophy, strategies employed, the medium via which interaction takes place, and the content of instruction.

Saba and Shearer conducted a study to empirically verify the concepts of transactional distance, dialogue, and structure [46]. Their study was based on a causal interpretation of the construct of transactional distance. Their approach derived from a model based on systems dynamics that Saba developed in an earlier study [47]. The authors constructed a model based on mathematical formulas that would predict the amount of transactional distance depending on a set of variables. The variables used in this formula were learner control, teacher control, dialogue, and structure. The results indicated that transactional distance depends on the rate of dialogue and structure. When dialogue increases and structure decreases, then transactional distance decreases. When the structure of an educational program increases, transactional distance increases, and dialogue decreases. Therefore, increased structure will result in the decrease of dialogue.

Vrasidas and McIsaac found that structure influenced interaction in several ways [14]. Parts of structure, such as required participation in online activities, led to more interactions and increased dialogue among participants. This finding is in contradiction with the hypothesis that increasing structure decreases dialogue and increases transactional distance [45, 46]. Requiring students to engage in discussions and collaborate on projects can increase interaction in an online course. In other programs we evaluated, we found that if participants are not required to engage in online discussions, they rarely do so [13, 17]. Therefore, increased structure can lead to more dialogue and interaction. In another study that examined transactional distance, it was found that the use of email in a distance education course increased dialogue and decreased transactional distance [48].

The original definition of transactional distance was based on the idea that dialogue and transactional distance can only be influenced by the teacher-learner interaction. New media such as computer conferencing allow for increased learner-learner inter-action, which can influence transactional distance in the online classroom. In addition, Saba and Shearer attempted to empirically verify transactional distance by following a model based on a mathematical formula, thus ignoring the reciprocal nature of human-human interaction and the importance of context [46]. Cookson and Chang also criti-cized Saba and Shearer's analysis of interaction because they focused more on the teacher and they excluded learner-learner and group interactions [49]. Recent studies showed that educators can structure for dialogue and interaction and that learner-learner interaction is also an important component of dialogue [14]. In light of the new developments in technology and pedagogy, transactional distance theory fails to cap-ture the essence of teaching and learning when students and teacher are separated.

4.5   Social Presence

The term social presence derived from research in the field of social psychology of telecommunications. According to Short, Williams, and Christie who coined the term, social presence is a quality of the medium itself [50]. Different media have different degrees of social presence. Social presence can be defined as the degree to which a medium allows the user to feel socially present in a mediated situation. It is hypothe-sized that the more cues transmissible by a medium, the more social presence charac-terizes the medium. Therefore, media such as interactive video, and multimedia com-puter conferencing carry with them higher degrees of social presence than text-based computer-conferencing systems.

Gunawardena conducted a study to examine the construct of social presence and its implications for text-based CMC [51]. She examined whether social presence is a characteristic of the medium itself or if it is an attribute of the user's perception of the medium. The findings of her study showed that social presence could be promoted in a CMC setting by employing strategies that encourage interaction. In addition, she found that the lack of audio-visual cues led CMC users to invent other means of com-pensating for the lack of those cues. These findings are in agreement with other stud-ies that showed that the temporal, spatial, and contextual limitations of online interac-tion lead to the development of strategies that compensate for the lack of visual and aural cues present in face-to-face interaction [52, 53, 54]. Such strategies include the use of capitalization, abbreviating the message, and use emoticons.

4.6   Feedback

Feedback has been associated with kinds of responses that provide information to students about the correctness of their assignments, homework, and class contribu-tions. In computer-mediated online environments and distance education, feedback is more important than just a mechanism of informing the student on how well she did on an assignment. In face-to-face situations nonverbal gestures are constantly exchanged thus providing both the teacher and learners with feedback [55]. A verbal comment by the teacher, a smile, a facial expression, and a gesture, are all ways with which students can receive feedback on their work and ideas. A confused face can indicate to the teacher that she needs to elaborate more on a topic. In the online environment, however, you loose all the contextual cues of communication, which are important in creating the feeling of social presence. Some researchers found that one of the most important things, associated with learner satisfaction in a course, was timely and encouraging feedback on their assignments [56]. Several other researchers [51, 57, 58] supported the importance of feedback in distance education.

Vrasidas and McIsaac found that in online environments the lack of immediate feedback contributed to the feeling of isolation among students and reduced levels of social presence [14]. Increased interaction in a computer-mediated environment is more likely to increase the feelings of social presence among participants. Thus, interaction, social presence, and feedback, are interrelated and influence each other.

5   Findings and Discussion

The major findings of our research include the following:

-    Meanings of interaction could be classified according to the intentions of the participants and what they were trying to accomplish [16].
-    The structure of the course, class size, feedback, and prior experience with computer-mediated communication influenced interaction [14, 15].
-    Online interaction was found to be slower and lack in continuity, richness, and immediacy, as it was compared with face-to-face interaction [59].
-    Because of the text nature of online interaction, it was easier to get confused and misunderstood in an online than in a face-to-face situation. Confusions and misunderstandings were easier to resolve face-to-face rather than online [59].

The conceptual framework followed and results of the study reconceptualize interaction as a theoretical construct and emphasize the importance of socially constructed meanings from the participants' perspectives. Based on our work, as well the work of others, some practical implications for the design and evaluation of online environments include the following:

-    Structure for interaction. CMC allows multiple kinds of interactions. However, interaction will not take place unless it is required and contributes to the overall goals of the course. Structuring collaborative projects is a good way to promote interaction among students. Assigning students to moderate online discussions, engage in debates, summarize results, and reflect on their postings, are also strategies that promote interaction.
-    Provide immediate feedback. During face-to-face situations nonverbal gestures and other cues are constantly exchanged thus providing both the teacher and learners with feedback. A teacher's smile, verbal comment, and a facial expression are all ways students can get feedback from. Students' confused faces can indicate to the teacher that she needs to elaborate more on a topic. Online you loose all the contextual cues of communication and therefore, frequent feedback is very

important. Students need many opportunities for feedback on their assignments, discussion participation, and overall progress. Feedback needs to be personalized and addressed to the individual student's work. Feedback addressed to the class as a group is also helpful, but it is individual feedback that touches the student. In text-based CMC settings, users invent other means for compensating for the lack of visual and audible cues. Instructors can create an environment within which learners can interact with peers and feel socially present. In addition, it is important to contact the students on a regular basis to check if they are having any problems with the course, assignments, use of technology, and get their continuous feedback. Some institutions have a policy according to which instructors have to acknowledge receipt of an email within 24 hours.

- Provide for opportunities for practice with technology. An important component of online interaction is that it is mediated with technology. It is important that both teacher and students have the skills necessary to engage in technology-mediated interaction. Teacher professional development before developing and teaching an online course is essential. Without the necessary skills, the teacher will not be able to utilize the medium for more effective instruction and provide the best learning experience for the students. Furthermore, the teacher will not be able to model expert behavior, unless he/she him/herself is an expert. Students without the necessary skills will get disappointed, not be able to participate, and more likely to drop out.

- Assessment of online learning. Online learning environments require a variety of methods for evaluating and assessing student learning [15, 42, 60]. Traditional face-to-face classrooms provide teachers with several ways to assess student learning. For example, non-verbal communication is a big part of the evaluation process of the traditional face-to-face classroom. However, the online teacher does not have access to facial expressions, voice intonation, or body language. Therefore, a variety of methods are essential for evaluating students and educational programs offered online. Such methods include information gathered from students' weekly assignments, students' moderations of online discussions, students' postings in online conferences, students' final papers and presentations, and midterm evaluations.

6   Conclusion

Computer-mediated interaction is a complex construct and it is influenced by several factors. The framework discussed in this paper ties together research conducted in distance education and online environments and provides an integrated look at computer-mediated interaction. It examines interaction following symbolic interactionist ideas and focuses on how the interplay of context, social presence, dialogues, structure, learner control, and feedback, influence interaction. The theoretical underpinnings of this framework, as well as the research behind it, can help guide future researchers and practitioners alike, as they design and study interaction in computer-mediated environments.

The conceptual framework discussed in this chapter can be used to:

- Describe and classify distance education programs.
- Help educators, policy makers, developers, and administrators better understand what influences students, teachers, and distance education programs.
- Study distance education programs and how the various categories included in the framework influence each other and student learning.
- Examine the importance of technology affordances for the design of successful online learning environments.
- Ask questions about possible relationships among constructs in distance education courses as well as hybrid courses offered via a variety of technologies.

As we continue to study online programs we will be looking at several issues involved in the design and successful implementation of online learning environments. Future questions to be addressed include:

- How do technology affordances permit and constrain certain kinds of interactions?
- What does it mean to be a teacher and learner in today's heavily technology-mediated educational environments?
- How does technology-mediated interaction shape structure, learning, learner control, and social presence?
- What combination of technologies, content, context, and instructional methods are appropriate for what kinds of instructional goals, teachers, and learners?

References

[1]   Kerr E. B. and Hiltz S.R.: "*Computer-mediated Communication Systems: Status and Evaluation*", Academic Press, New York, 1992.

[2]   McIsaac M.S. and Gunawardena C.N.: "Distance Education", in "*Handbook of Research for Educational Communications and Technology*", by D.H. Jonassen (ed.), Simon & Shuster Macmillan, New York, pp.403-437, 1996.

[3]   Owston R.D.: "The World-Wide-Web: a Technology to Enhance Teaching and Learning?, *Educational Researcher*, Vol.26, No.2, pp.27-32, 1997.

[4]   Blumer H.: "*Symbolic Interactionism: Perspective and Method*", Prentice Hall, Englewood Cliffs, NJ, 1969.

[5]   Collis B. and Moonen J.: "*Flexible Learning in a Digital World*", Kogan Page, London, 2001.

[6]   Garrison R.: "Theoretical Challenges for Distance Education in the 21st Century: a Shift from Structural to Transactional Issues", *International Review of Research in Open and Distance Learning*, Vol.1, No.1, 2000.

[7]   Vrasidas C. and Glass G.V.: "A Conceptual Framework for Studying Distance Education", In "*Current Perspectives in Applied Information Technologies: Distance Education and Distributed Learning*", by C. Vrasidas and G. V. Glass (eds.), pp.31-56, Information Age Publishing, Greenwich, CT, 2002.

[8] Stake R.E.: *"The Art of Case Study Research"*, SAGE, Thousand Oaks, CA, 1995.

[9] Erickson F.: "Qualitative Methods in Research on Teaching", In *"Handbook of Research on Teaching"* by M. C. Wittrock (ed.), pp.119-161, Macmillan, New York, 1986.

[10] Schwandt T.A. "Constructivist, Interpretivist Approaches to Human Inquiry", In *"The Landscape of Qualitative Research: Theories and Issues"*, by N.K. Denzin and Y.S. Lincoln (eds.), SAGE, Thousand Oaks, CA, pp.221-259, 1998.

[11] Patton M.Q.: *"Qualitative Research and Evaluation Methods"*, 3rd edition, SAGE, Thousand Oaks, CA, 2002.

[12] Vrasidas C.: "Interpretivism and Symbolic Interactionism: Making the Familiar Strange and Interesting Again" in *"Educational Technology Research - Research Methods in Educational Technology"*, by W. Heinecke and J. Willis (eds.), Information Age, Greenwich, CT, pp.81-99, 2001.

[13] Vrasidas C. Zembylas M. and Chamberlain R.: "Evaluation of Distance Education and Virtual Schooling", Paper presented at the Annual Meeting of the International Council of Educational Media, Granada, Spain, October, 2002.

[14] Vrasidas C. and McIsaac S.M.: "Factors Influencing Interaction in an Online Course", *The American Journal of Distance Education*, Vol.13, No.3, pp.2-36, 1999.

[15] Vrasidas C. and McIsaac M.: "Principles of Pedagogy and Evaluation of Web-based Learning", *Educational Media International*, Vol.37, No.2, pp.105-111, 2000.

[16] Vrasidas C.: "A Working Typology of Intentions Driving Face-to-face and Online Interaction in a Graduate Teacher Education Course", *Journal of Technology and Teacher Education*, Vol.10, No.2, pp.273-296, 2002.

[17] Vrasidas C.: "The Design, Development, and Implementation of the LUDA Virtual High School", *Computers in the Schools*, Vol.20, No.1, 2002.

[18] Dewey J.: *"Experience and Education"*, Collier Macmillan, New York, 1938.

[19] Vygotsky L.S.: *"Mind in Society"*, Harvard University Press, Cambridge, MA, 1978.

[20] Moore M.G.: "Three Types of Interaction", *The American Journal of Distance Education*, Vol.3, No.2, pp.1-6, 1989.

[21] Wagner E.D.: "In Support of a Functional Definition of Interaction", *The American Journal of Distance Education*, Vol.8, No.2, pp.6-29, 1994.

[22] Hillman D.C., Willis D.J. and Gunawardena C.N.: "Learner Interface Interaction in Distance Education - an Extension of Contemporary Models and Strategies for Practitioners", *The American Journal of Distance Education*, Vol.8, No.2, pp.30-42, 1994.

[23] Baynton M.: "Dimensions of 'control' in Distance Education: a Factor Analysis", *The American Journal of Distance Education*, Vol.6, No.2, pp.17-31, 1992.

[24] Brown J.S., Collins A. and Duguid P.: "Situated Cognition and the Culture of Learning", *Educational Researcher*, Vol.18, No.1, pp.32-42, 1989.

[25] Suchman L.A.: *"Plans and Situated Actions. The Problem of Human Machine communication"*, Cambridge University Press, Cambridge, MA, 1987.

[26] Vrasidas C.: "Constructivism vs. Objectivism: Implications for Interaction, Course Design, and Evaluation in Distance Education", *International Journal of Educational Telecommunications*, Vol.6, pp.339-362, 2000.

[27] Garrison D.R.: "A Cognitive Constructivist View of Distance Education: an Analysis of Teaching-learning Assumptions", *Distance Education*, Vol.14, pp.199-211, 1993.

[28] Dede C.: "The Evolution of Distance Education: Emerging Technologies and Distributed Learning", *The American Journal of Distance Education*, Vol.10, No.2, pp.4-36, 1996.

[29] Mehan H.: "*Learning Lessons: Social Organization in the Classroom*", Harvard University Press, Cambridge, MA, 1979.

[30] Johnson D.W.: "Student-student Interaction: the Neglected Variable in Education", *Educational Researcher*, Vol.10, No.1, pp.5-10, 1981.

[31] Harasim L., Hiltz S.R., Teles L. and Turoff M.: "*Learning Networks: a Field Guide to Teaching and Learning Online*", The MIT Press, Cambridge, MA, 1995.

[32] Salomon G.: "What is Learned and How it is Taught: the Interaction between Media, Message, Task, and Learner", in "*Media and Symbols*" by D.R. Olson (ed.), The University of Chicago Press, Chicago, pp.383-406, 1974.

[33] Comeaux P.: "The Impact of an Interactive Distance Learning Network on Classroom Communication", *Communication Education*, Vol.44, pp.353-361, 1995.

[34] Ross A.R.: "The Influence of Computer Communication Skills on Participation in a Computer Conferencing Course", *Journal of Educational Computing Research*, Vol.15, No.1, pp.37-52, 1996.

[35] Haynes K.J.M. and Dillon C.; "Distance Education: Learning Outcomes, Interaction, and Attitudes", *Journal of Education for Library and Information Science*, Vol.33, No.1, pp.35-45, 1992.

[36] Clark R.E.: "Reconsidering Research on Learning from Media", *Review of Educational Research*, Vol.53, pp.445-460, 1983.

[37] Tsui A.B.M. and Ki W.W.: "An Analysis of Conference Interactions on Telenex - a Computer Network for ESL Teachers", *Educational Technology Research and Development*, Vol.44, No.4, pp.23-44, 1996.

[38] Black S.D., Levin J.A., Mehan H. and Quinn C.N.: "Real and Non-real Time Interaction: Unraveling Multiple Threads of Discourse", *Discourse Processes*, Vol.6, No.1, pp.59-75, 1983.

[39] Duncan S.J.; "Some Signals and Rules for Taking Speaking Turns in Conversation", *Journal of Personality and Social Psychology*, Vol.23, pp.283-292, 1972.

[40] Garrison D.R. and Baynton M.: "Beyond Independence in Distance Education: the Concept of Control", *The American Journal of Distance Education*, Vol.1, No.3, pp.3-15, 1987.

[41] Dille B. and Mezack M.: "Identifying Predictors of High Risk Among Community College Telecourse Students", *The American Journal of Distance Education*, Vol.5, No.1, pp.24-35, 1991.

[42] Hiltz S.R.: "Evaluating the Virtual Classroom", in *"Online Education: Perspectives on a New Environment"*, by L.M. Harasim (ed.), Praeger, New York, pp.133-184, 1990.

[43] Parker A.: "Distance Education Attrition", *International Journal of Educational Telecommunications*, Vol.1, pp.389-406, 1995.

[44] Ellsworth J.H.: "Using Computer-mediated Communication in Teaching University Courses", in *"Computer Mediated Communication and the Online Classroom"*, by Z.L. Berge and M.P. Collins (eds.), Hampton Press, Cresskill, NJ, pp.29-36, 1996.

[45] Moore M.G.: "Distance Education Theory", *The American Journal of Distance Education*, Vol.5, No.3, pp.1-6, 1991.

[46] Saba F. and Shearer R.L.: "Verifying Key Theoretical Concepts in a Dynamic Model of Distance Education", *The American Journal of Distance Education*, Vol.8, No.1, pp.36-57, 1994.

[47] Saba F.: "Integrated Telecommunications Systems and Instructional Transaction", *The American Journal of Distance Education*, Vol.2, No.3, pp.17-24, 1988.

[48] Bischoff W.R., Bisconer, Kooker B.M. and Woods L.C.: "Transactional Distance and Interactive Television in the Distance Education of Health Professionals", *The American Journal of Distance Education*, Vol.10, No.3, pp.4-19, 1996.

[49] Cookson P.S. and Chang Y.: "The Multidimensional Audio Conferencing Classification System", *The American Journal of Distance Education*, Vol.9, No.3, pp.18-36, 1995.

[50] Short J., Williams E. and Christie B.: *"The Social Psychology of Telecommunications"*, John Wiley, London, 1976.

[51] Gunawardena C.N.: "Social Presence Theory and Implications for Interaction and Collaborative Learning in Computer Conferences", *International Journal of Educational Telecommunications*, Vol.1, No.2/3, pp.147-166, 1995.

[52] Gunawardena C. N. and Zittle F.J.: "Social Presence as a Predictor of Satisfaction Within a Computer-mediated Conferencing Environment", *The American Journal of Distance Education*, Vol.11, No.3, pp.8-26, 1997.

[53] Rezabek L.L. and Cochenour J.J.: "Visual Cues in Computer-mediated Communication: Supplementing Text with Emotions", *Journal of Visual Literacy*, Vol.18, No.2, pp.201-216, 1998.

[54] Werry C.C.: "Linguistic and Interactional Features of Internet Relay Chat", in *"Computer-mediated Communication: Linguistic, Social, and Cross-cultural Perspectives"*, by S.C. Herring (ed.), John Benjamin, Philadelphia, PA, pp.47-63, 1996.

[55] Wolcott L.L.: "The Distance Teacher as Reflective Practitioner", *Educational Technology*, Vol.35, No.1, pp.39-43, 1995.

[56] Stevenson K., Sander P. and Naylor P.: "Student Perceptions of the Tutor's Role in Distance Learning", *Open Learning*, Vol.11, No.1, pp.22-30, 1996.

[57] Roman N.J.: "Mentoring the Distance Learner", *Open Learning*, Vol.12, No.3, pp.62-64, 1997.

[58] Wagner E.D. and McCombs B.L.: "Learner Centered Psychological Principles in Practice: Design for Distance Education", *Educational Technology*, Vol.35, No.2, pp.32-35, 1995.

[59] Vrasidas C. and Chamberlain R.: "The Differences Between Face-to-face and Computer-mediated Interactions", Paper presented at the Annual Meeting of the American Educational Research Association, New Orleans, April, 2002.

[60] Mason R.: "Rethinking Assessment in the Online Environment", in "*Current Perspectives on Applied Information Technologies: Distance Education and Distributed Learning*", by Vrasidas C. and Glass G.V. (eds.), Information Age, Greenwich, CT, pp.57-74, 2002.

Website Content Accessibility of the Cyprus Domain

Panayiotis Zaphiris[1] and Giorgos Zacharia[2]

[1]The Center for Human Computer Interaction Design
City University, London, UK
zaphiri@soi.city.ac.uk
[2] Artificial Intelligence Lab, Center of Biological and Computational Learning
Massachusetts Institute of Technology, Cambridge, MA 02139, USA
lysi@ai.mit.edu

Abstract. This paper extends previous studies that investigated the accessibility of different web sites of specific content, to an analysis of the whole web of a specific country (Cyprus). To our knowledge no previous study has analyzed such a big number of web sites for accessibility in a single study. More specifically this paper evaluates the compliance of 30,000 Cyprus related websites spidered by Arachne search engine. The 30,000 Cyprus related websites where evaluated for accessibility using the Bobby accessibility tool. Statistical analysis and comparison of the accessibility ratings for the different main domain categories (commercial, academic, governmental, and organizational) of the Cypriot web are also provided.

1   Introduction

Currently millions worldwide have physical, sensory or cognitive limitations that make interacting with traditional monitor, keyboard and mouse configurations difficult [1]. The number of people with disabilities is expected to increase significantly in the next decade as the world's population is rapidly growing older, and the number of World Wide Web (WWW) users of old age also increases exponentially [2, 3].

To make computer technology accessible to people with disabilities, companies provide specialized human computer interface devices (e.g. special mouse for people of age that have difficulty in motor movements, special magnification for monitors, special keyboards). However, although being able to interact with a computer is a necessary prerequisite to using the WWW, the web provides unique features (dynamic content, heavily graphical user interfaces, complicated navigation structures) that often make accessibility of the web an even more complicated challenge. More specifically Laux [1] lists three basic types of problems associated with making the information in web sites accessible. These include making printed text and graphic information available to users with vision problems, making audio information available to users with hearing impairments, and providing an interaction method for users with visual or motor problems that affect their ability to use a mouse or keyboard.

Y. Manolopoulos et al. (Eds.): PCI 2001, LNCS 2563, pp. 248-261, 2003.

More specifically, people with visual disabilities use screen readers to access information on the web and use keyboard command keys to navigate through the site. Unfortunately a lot of the currently designed web sites are not screen reader friendly.

1.1   Definition of Web Accessibility and Universal Design

Researchers have been advocating a universal design strategy when designing web interfaces. Universal design refers to the design of products and environments that are usable by all people, to the greatest extent possible, without the need for case-by-case accommodation. If you adopt universal design when developing WWW pages, your pages will be more readily accessible to most people with disabilities who are already using computers [1].

Chuck Letoumeau [4] defines web accessibility to mean that "anyone using any kind of web browsing technology must be able to visit any site and get a full and complete understanding of the information as well as have the full and complete ability to interact with the site if that is necessary".

There are three different levels of approaches to the provision of accessibility to web-based applications [5].

1.   Use of alternative access systems.
2.   Adaptive information content and structure.
3.   Adaptive user interface.

This paper is primarily concerned with the second of the above three adaptation levels. Adaptation concerning content and structure focuses on the provision of guidelines for web authors, allowing them to produce more accessible web documents [6-8]. These efforts have become increasingly unified into the world wide web accessibility initiative (WAI 3) which has important implications on the use of the web by people with special needs [9].

1.2   Accessibility Mandates, Guidelines and Tools

In recent years the importance of providing mechanisms for delivering information for all potential users of the emerging Information Society has increased significantly [10].

There are some encouraging signs that the accessibility of the Internet is taken into account by mainstream society [11]. Accessibility for information on the Web has been well regulated in the U.S. Some legal mandates regarding accessibility are Section 255 of the Telecommunications Act 1996 [12], which regulates the accessibility of Internet Telephony, and Section 508 of the Rehabilitation Act Amendments of 1998 [13], which requires that when Federal departments or agencies develop, procure, maintain, or use electronic and information technology, they shall ensure that the technology is accessible to people with disabilities, unless an undue burden would be imposed on the department or agency.

Similarly, the European Commission [14] through an action plan recognizes the importance of making the information highway accessible to people with disabilities by pointing out that "special attention should be given to disabled people and the fight against info-exclusion". Furthermore the commission points out that:

"as government services and important public information become increasingly available on-line, ensuring access to government web sites for all citizens becomes as important as ensuring access to public buildings. In the context of citizens with special needs, the challenge consists of ensuring the widest possible accessibility to information technologies in general as well as their compatibility with assistive technologies" [14]

The commission points out that public sector web sites and their content in member states and in the European Institutions must be designed to be accessible to ensure that citizens with disabilities can access information and take full advantage of the potential for e-government. More specifically, among other things, the eEurope action plan advocates that member states should share information in order to enforce policies to avoid info-exclusion (deadline - end of 2001), work for the publication of "Design for all" standards for accessibility of information technology products (deadline – end of 2002), adopt the Web Accessibility Initiative (WAI) guidelines for public websites (deadline – end of 2001).

Various institutions also compiled accessibility guidelines for information on the Web. Those resources are well documented and available for public viewing on the Internet. Some examples of those guidelines are:

- W3C Web Content Accessibility Guidelines (WCAG) [15]
- WAI Quick Tips Reference Card [16]
- Penn State University's Center for Academic Computing Web Accessibility Check-List [17]
- Public Service Commission of Canada: Designing Universal Web Pages [18]
- Captioning and Audio Description on the Web - The National Center for Accessible Media [19]

Apart from the many social and economic motivations for addressing Web accessibility, regulatory compliance is becoming an important factor. More specifically [1]:

1. When a web site is used in a job or in schools or universities, accessibility becomes an issue that may be addressed by the Americans with Disabilities Act of 1990 (ADA) [20].
2. If employees need to use an outside Web site for a critical job function, the employer or institution may be responsible for providing adequate access.
3. If web sites are designed so that current adaptive equipment cannot make the pages accessible, employers and educational institutions may have difficulty providing acceptable accommodation (e.g. heavily graphic oriented web pages).
4. A service provided to the public via a web site or page that is not accessible to users with disabilities may be subject to an ADA claim; and more important, the service provider may loose market share because many potential customers are unable to access the service.

Others [21] advocate that inaccessible web pages are also in violation of Title III of ADA since the internet is a public space.

The following suggestions [22] are based on the WAI guidelines and Section 508 standards for Web Content:

1. General Page Design
   - Maintain a simple, consistent page layout throughout your site.
   - Keep background simple. Make sure there is enough contrast.
   - Use standard HTML.
   - Design large buttons.
   - Caption video and transcribe other audio.
   - Make links descriptive so that they are understood out of context.
   - Include a note about accessibility.
2. Graphical Features
   - Include appropriate ALT/LONGDESC attributes for graphical elements on your page.
   - Include menu alternatives for image maps to ensure that the embedded links are accessible.
   - Include descriptive captions for pictures and transcriptions of manuscript images.
   - Use a NULL value for unimportant graphics.
   - Provide audio descriptions and transcripts of video.
   - Consider other options for making graphical features accessible.
3. Special Features
   - Use tables and frames sparingly and consider alternatives.
   - Provide alternatives for forms and databases.
   - Provide alternatives for content in applets and plug-ins.

Unfortunately the Cypriot legislature is not yet in line with the European action plan on the issue of web accessibility. To our knowledge, the only accessibility related Cypriot legislature available (which is very narrowly related to web accessibility) is the regulations relating to the accessibility of public buildings and highways [23]. These regulations:

1. Defines the term "disabled" as anyone who due to physical disability or limitation is faced with permanent or temporary difficulty in accessing buildings or roads.
2. Lists the categories of buildings (public buildings, shopping centers, apartment complexes and educational institutions) to which these regulations are applicable.
3. Provides a set of requirements that need to be satisfied (accessible entrance, corridor and pathway dimensions, safety requirements etc) before a building license can be issued.

Unfortunately, although this legislature provides the required legal framework for the protection of the right of access for the people with disabilities to the road highways of Cyprus, no similar legislature is available to protect their right of access to the information highway.

To demonstrate the importance of the topic of web accessibility let us for example consider the following hypothetical (but very likely) scenario:

We are at 2004, Cyprus is now a full member of the European Union. Andreas (hypothetical name) is a blind student of a Cypriot college/university. The tremendous increase of academic information (conference/journal papers, data) becomes available (and often *only* available) on the web. Andreas is highly required to access the web for his research. His academic performance is highly influenced by how accessible the web is. Furthermore, let us assume that his department has recently shifted to a "paperless" system where it requires its students to perform all registration and grade enquires online. This puts Andreas' into an inferior position compared to his classmates. Andreas' after complaining to his department about it, and his calls being ignored decides to seek legal advice. Although there is still no Cypriot legislature to protect his right for access to the information highway, he decides to use his legal right as a European citizen to seek help from the European bodies.

Apart from the ethical dimension of the scenario above, there is also an important legal/economic dimension that primarily the Cyprus government and its educational institutions need to seriously consider.

1.3   Research Motivation

Sullivan and Matson [24] compared 50 most popular web sites in terms of their usability and content accessibility and found a marginal correlation ($\rho=0.23$) between manually analyzed content accessibility in conformance to the Priority 1 of the WCAG and overall automated usability testing result provided by LIFT [25]. Other studies [26, 27] applied this methodology to other domains (educational and health related websites) and found similar results. Table 1 presents a summary of these studies.

The present study tries to take the issue of accessibility evaluation a step further, by analyzing the accessibility of a whole country's (Cyprus') web. To our knowledge no previous study has analyzed such a big number of web sites for accessibility in a single study. The authors believe that analysis of the whole Cyprus domain is a better reflection of the nature of the whole World Wide Web than a thematic analysis of selective small number of web sites.

Apart from the academic interest in such an analysis of the Cyprus domain, we believe that there is also an ethical and social importance to the data reported in this study.

In particular, with the current negotiations for Cyprus entry to the European Union and the attempts for harmonization of the Cyprus legislature with the European Unions' one we believe such a study will give valuable data to the groups that push for a more user-friendly information society in Cyprus. This will hopefully lead to the adoption of the relevant laws that will prevent info-exclusion of the disabled people in Cyprus.

More specifically this paper aims to answer two main research questions:

1. To what extend is the Cyprus web accessible?
2. Are there significant differences between the accessibility rating of different categories (governmental, commercial, educational, organizational) of Cyprus websites?

Table 1. Previous Web Accessibility research (N = number of sites analyzed)

Authors	Topic of websites evaluated	N	% Accessible
Sullivan and Matson [24]	Most popular web sites	50	18%
Zaphiris and Ellis [27]	Top USA universities	50	30%
Zaphiris and Kurniawan [26]	Health & Aging Websites	89	28%

The automatic evaluation tool used in this study is Bobby [28]. Bobby is the most widely used automatic accessibility evaluation tool. To become Bobby approved, a Web site must:

1. Provide text equivalents for all images and multimedia such as animations, audio, and video.
2. Ensure that all information conveyed with color is also available without color.
3. Identify headers for data tables and make line-by-line reading sensible for layout tables.
4. Provide summaries of graphs and charts.
5. Identify document language and any changes of the language.
6. Organize content logically and clearly, such as with headings, list elements, meaningful links, and navigation bars.
7. Provide alternative content for features (e.g., applets or plug-ins) that may not be supported.

Bobby also analyzes Web pages for compatibility with various browsers and automatically checks sites for compatibility with HTML 4.0 [28]. Bobby recommends effective Web page authoring for special Web browsers (e.g. the one which reads text out loud using a speech synthesizer for blind users). Bobby divides the accessibility errors into 4 sections to be tested:

1. *Priority 1 Errors* are problems that seriously affect the page's usability by people with disabilities, in accordance with Priority 1 of WCAG. A Bobby Approved rating can only be granted to a site with no Priority 1 errors. Bobby Approved status is equivalent to Conformance Level A (i.e. Priority 1 checkpoints are satisfied) for the WCAG.
2. *Priority 2 Errors* are secondary access problems. If all items in this section including relevant User Checks passed the test, it meets Conformance Level AA (i.e. Priority 1 and 2 checkpoints are satisfied) for the WCAG.
3. *Priority 3 Errors* are third-tier access problems. If all items in this section including relevant User Checks passed the test, it meets Conformance Level AAA (i.e. Priority 1, 2 and 3 checkpoints are satisfied) for the WCAG.

The Browser Compatibility Errors are HTML elements and element attributes that are used on the page which are not valid for particular browsers. These elements do not necessarily cause accessibility problems, but users should be aware that the page may not be rendered as expected which may impact usability and accessibility.

As a general rating, Bobby gives the rating with the picture of "Bobby-hats". Hats with wheelchairs indicate Priority 1 accessibility errors that are automatically detectable. A question mark identifies a possible Priority 1 error that cannot be fully automatically checked, indicating that the user will need to address that question manually.

2   Methodology

2.1   Data Collection Method

In order to collect as many URLs on Cyprus as possible, we deployed a recursive multithreaded spider, which we bootstrapped by collecting as many Cypriot URLs as possible. We collected the URLs through a combination of heuristics:

1. We collected all the registered .cy domains, as of Spring 2000, by listing all the database of the primary Domain Name Servers (DNS) of Cyprus.
2. We also collected several hundreds of Top Level Domain (TLD) URLs (.com, .net, .org as opposed to .com.cy, net.cy and .org.cy) that were hosted by the four major ISPs of Cyprus. We collected those domain names by listing the domain name tables of the primary DNS servers of the 4 major Internet Service Providers (ISP) of Cyprus (Cytanet, Spidernet, Logosnet and Cylink).
3. Finally, in order to include as many Cypriot websites hosted outside Cyprus, we spidered major Cypriot indexers, like Eureka [29] and Yiasou [30] and collected all the URLs listed on those indexes.

We merged the several lists we collected, eliminated the duplicate entries and fed them to a spidering product we had developed in order to create Arachne [31] a search engine that indexes Cypriot sites.

We ran Arachne's spider with 256 concurrent threads, half of which searched for new URL's in a Breadth First Search manner, and the other half in a Depth First Search manner. The spider filtered out all URLs that were not sub-WebPages of the initial bootstrapping set, or did not include stemmed names of Cypriot geography.

The spider collected 96,000 URLs of which only 30,000 represented html files. The 30,000 html files included almost 12,000 placeholder, under construction or dead pages. We identified the dead pages, by recording the status responses of the http requests to the collected URLs, and eliminated all URLs that did not return a status of '200 OK'. Many pages were personal WebPages, which had only the default boilerplate file provided by their ISP for personal pages. After we eliminated the pages without content, we were left with 18,096 URLs to analyze for accessibility.

These 18,096 were then analyzed for accessibility using Bobby (Figure 1) automatic accessibility tool.

2.2   Analysis

To answer the aforementioned two research questions, several statistical analysis techniques were employed. For the first research question, the means and standard deviations of the accessibility of the whole Cyprus domain is calculated. To investigate whether there were significant differences between the accessibility rating of different categories (governmental, commercial, educational, organizational) of Cyprus websites separate analysis for each group of domain extensions (.gov.cy, .com and .com.cy, .ac.cy, .org and .org.cy respectively) were performed and finally an analysis of variance was carried out to notice any significant differences.

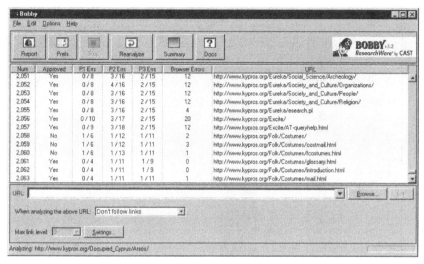

Fig. 1. Screenshot of Bobby Interface

3   Results and Discussions

Table 2 lists the mean and standard deviation of the accessibility ratings for the whole Cyprus related websites analyzed in this study. Bobby's approval rating is converted into a binary variable with '0' representing 'Not Approved' and '1' representing 'Approved' status. From Table 2 it is apparent that the Cyprus web sites analyzed are ranked very low in terms of accessibility (only 20% of them are bobby approved). Table 2 also shows high browser compatibility errors (average=6.5, maximum = 50) for these websites.

One possible reason for this high number of browser incompatibilities might be the fact that most web site designers tend to rely commercial web design tools that are very often only compatible with one or a few particular type of browser.

Table 2. Bobby approval results for the complete set of pages analyzed

	N	Minimum	Maximum	Mean	Std. Deviation
APPROVAL	18096	0	1	.20	.40
Priority 1	18096	.00	4.00	.9907	.6296
Priority 2	18096	.00	7.00	2.2371	1.0619
Priority 3	18096	.00	4.00	1.7512	.4490
Browser Incom.	18096	.00	50.00	6.5115	5.1789
Valid N (listwise)	18096				

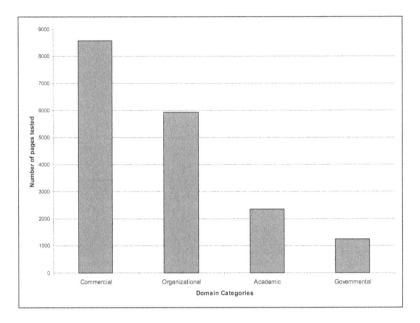

Fig. 2. Number of web pages tested per domain category

To answer the second research question, the 18,096 pages analyzed where divided into four groups:

1. Commercial (8, 566 pages with a .com and .com.cy domain extension)
2. Academic (2,360 pages with a .ac.cy domain extension)
3. Governmental (1,242 under the pio.gov.cy domain)
4. Organizational (5,933 with an .org and .org.cy domain extension)

These data are presented graphically in Fig 2.

Specific accessibility results for each of the four cases above are presented in tables 3 to 6. Figure 3 shows the above results in a graphical representation.

Table 3. Bobby approval results for the Cyprus commercial web sites analyzed

	N	Minimum	Maximum	Mean	Std. Deviation
APPROVAL	8555	0	1	.18	.39
Priority 1	8555	.00	4.00	.9873	.6004
Priority 2	8555	.00	7.00	2.4866	1.1049
Priority 3	8555	.00	4.00	1.8428	.3813
Browser Incom.	8555	.00	50.00	7.6638	6.1132
Valid N (listwise)	8555				

Table 4. Bobby approval results for the Cyprus academic web sites analyzed

	N	Minimum	Maximum	Mean	Std. Deviation
APPROVAL	2360	0	1	.25	.43
Priority 1	2360	.00	2.00	.9123	.6322
Priority 2	2360	.00	5.00	1.7309	.9139
Priority 3	2360	.00	2.00	1.6013	.5216
Browser Incom.	2360	.00	20.00	4.9288	3.2879
Valid N (listwise)	2360				

Table 5. Bobby approval results for the Cyprus governmental web sites analyzed

	N	Minimum	Maximum	Mean	Std. Deviation
APPROVAL	1242	0	1	8.00E-03	8.94E-02
Priority 1	1242	.00	2.00	1.8776	.3516
Priority 2	1242	.00	4.00	2.2697	.4704
Priority 3	1242	1.00	2.00	1.9968	5.668E-02
Browser Incom.	1242	2.00	13.00	8.8953	1.1047
Valid N (listwise)	1242				

Table 6. Bobby approval results for the Cyprus organizational web sites analyzed

	N	Minimum	Maximum	Mean	Std. Deviation
APPROVAL	5933	0	1	.25	.43
Priority 1	5933	.00	2.00	.8411	.5604
Priority 2	5933	.00	7.00	2.0720	1.0400
Priority 3	5933	.00	2.00	1.6270	.4974
Browser Incom.	5933	.00	36.00	4.9771	4.1112
Valid N (listwise)	5933				

As a follow up analysis we conducted an analysis of variance (ANOVA) to see if there are any significant differences in terms of accessibility among the four different domain category groups. The ANOVA results show a significant main effect ($F_{(3, 18086)} = 144.485$, $p < 0.05$). Since one of the four groups (governmental) is way below the other groups in terms of accessibility a pair-wise post-hoc analysis (bonferroni) was performed. The pair wise analysis shows a significant difference among all of the pairs (at $p < 0.05$) except for the organization and academic pair.

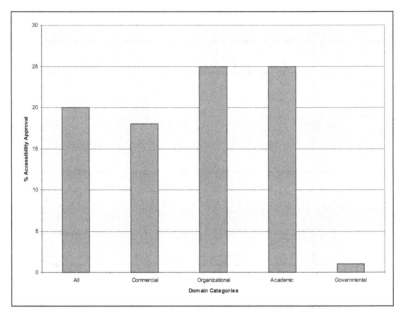

Fig. 3. Graphical representation of the Accessibility Results per Domain Category

The results show a clear weakness in accessibility in all four categories. Even though academic and organization websites are ranked top among the four categories only one quarter (25%) of Cypriot academic and organizational websites are accessible. Furthermore from Table 5 it has to be noticed that the governmental websites (in year 2000 for which data was used in this paper, Arachne contained only all the websites under the .pio.gov.cy) are basically in total inaccessible (a merely 1% of them is accessible).

4   Conclusions

This study aimed to answer two research questions:

1. To what extend is the Cyprus web accessible?
2. Are there significant differences between the accessibility rating of different categories (governmental, commercial, educational, organizational) of Cyprus websites ?

The analysis revealed that the Cyprus websites analyzed are ranked very low in terms of accessibility (only 20% of them are Bobby approved). Even though academic and organization websites were found to be rated significantly better than the governmental and commercial websites still only 25% of them were accessible.

The legal dimension of making websites accessible to people with disabilities is clearly specified by bodies like the European council and thus especially the governmental but also the academic community should develop a policy that pays more careful attention in incorporating accessibility guidelines in the web site development of their websites.

Further research could be conducted in several directions. First, in this study, only simple descriptive statistics were employed. Advanced statistical analysis such as structural equation modeling would be fruitful to explore the underlying relationship between different measures of accessibility evaluation. Secondly, the authors plan to extend the present study into a longitudinal research project that will evaluate the accessibility of the Cyprus web domain on a regular basis. Finally, this study can be extended in analyzing the web domain of other countries providing a geographic comparison of web accessibility.

In this study, an automatic evaluation tool (Bobby) was used. Although Bobby can be used as a first step in an accessibility evaluation, some limitations of using automatic evaluation tools need to be recognized:

1. There are important elements (such as the web navigation structure, the information's layout, the value of information, or various aesthetic aspects) which are not evaluated by the automatic tools.
2. The meaning/significance/appearance of graphics is not evaluated, only the inclusion of ALT tags are taken into consideration by Bobby.
3. Text-only web sites will get high ranking with both tools regardless of the quality of information or the readability of the fonts.

These limitations might imply that, although automatic evaluation tools provide a quick reference and a first step analysis of the web site's accessibility and usability, formal usability and accessibility evaluation involving user testing combined with a series of other non-empirical methods (such as cognitive walkthroughs or GOMS [32]) still hold a major importance in the thoroughness of web site evaluation.

References

[1]   Laux L.: "Designing Web Pages and Applications for People with Disabilities", in Grose, E. and Forsythe, C. (eds.): "*Human Factors and Web Development*", Erlbaum Associates, Mahwah, NJ, pp.87-95, 1998.

[2]   USA Census Bureau: "Projections of the Total Resident Population by 5 Year Age Groups, and Sex with Special Age Categories: Middle Series, 2025 to 2045". Available at: http://www.census.gov/population/projections/nation/ summary/np-t3-f.txt

[3]   Curry J.O.: "Young at Heart, and Online: the over-50 Crowd Finds Empowerment Community and New Friends on the Web. Available at: http://www.buyingarizona.com/ Senior_Source/senior_source.html

[4]   Letourneau C.: "Accessible Web Design - a Definition". Available at: http:// www.starlingweb.com/webac.htm

[5]   Treviranas J. and Serflek C.: "Alternative Access to the World Wide Web". Available at: http://www.utoronto.ca/atrc/rd/library/papers/WWW.html

[6]   Vanderheiden G., Chisholm W. and Ewers N.: "Design of HTML Pages to Increase their Accessibility to Users with Disabilities", University of Wisconsin at Madison, 1996.

[7]   Richards J.: "Guide to Writing Accessible HTML". Available at: http://www.utoronto.ca/ atrc/rd/html/html.html

[8]   Gunderson J.: "World Wide Web Browser Access Recommendations". Available at: http://www.staff.uiuc.edu/~jongund/access-browsers.html

[9]   Brown D., Evett L. and Lawton J.: "Accessible Web Based Multimedia for Use by People with Learning Disabilities", *Proceedings Conference on Assistive Technology*, Derby, UK, 2002.

[10]   Stephanidis C., Savidis A. and Akoumianakis D.: "Unified User Interface Development: Tools for Constructing Accessible and Usable User", *Proceedings HCI'99 Conference*, San Francisco, CA, 1997.

[11]   Newell A.F. and Gregor P.: "Human Computer Interfaces for People with Disabilities", in: Helander M., Landauer T.K. and Prabhu P. (eds.): "*Handbook of Human-Computer Interaction*". Elsevier, 1997.

[12]   Federal Communications Commission: Section 255. Available at: http://www.fcc.gov/cab/ dro/section255.html

[13]   The National Institute on Disability and Rehabilitation Research: Legislation and Policy. Available at: http://www.ed.gov/offices/OSERS/NIDRR/Policy/

[14]   European Commission: Participation for all in the knowledge-based economy. Available at: http://europa.eu.int/comm/information_society/eeurope/ actionplan/actline2c_en.htm

[15]   W3C: Web Content Accessibility Guidelines 1.0. Available at: http://www.w3.org/TR/ WAI-WEBCONTENT/

[16]   W3C: WAI Quick Tips Reference Card. Available at: http://www.w3.org/WAI/ References/QuickTips/

[17]   Penn State University: Education Technology Services Web Accessibility Guidelines. Available at: http://tlt.its.psu.edu/suggestions/accessibility/

[18]   Public Services Commission of Canada: Designing Universal Web Pages. Available at: http://www.psc-cfp.gc.ca/eemp-pmpee/access/welcome1-e.htm

[19]   The National Center for Accessible Media: A Resource Center for Developers of Rich Media. Available at: http://ncam/wgbh.org/richmedia/

[20]   Department of Justice: ADA standards for Accessible Design. Available at: http:// www.usdoj.gov/crt/ada/adastd94.pf

[21]   Margolin M.: "The Web Isn't for Everyone Yet". Available at: http://www.hotwired.com/ webmonkey/98/21/index2a.html

[22]   Do-It: World Wide Access: Accessible Web Design, University of Washington, Seattle, 2001.

[23]   Cyprus Parliament: "Regulation for Access to Public Buildings and Roads", *Cyprus Gazette*, 1999.

[24]   Sullivan T. and Matson R.: "Barriers to Use: Usability and Content Accessibility on the Web's Most Popular Sites", *Proceedings Conference of Universal Usability*, Arlington, VA, 2000.

[25]   UsableNet: LIFT Website Testing System. Available at: http://www.usablenet.com

[26] Zaphiris P. and Kurniawan S.: "Usability and Accessibility of Aging/Health-Related Web Sites", *Proceedings HCI'01 Conference*, New Orleans, LA, 2001.

[27] Zaphiris P. and Ellis R.D.: "Website Usability and Content Accessibility of the top USA Universities", *Proceedings WebNet'01 Conference*, Orlando, FL, 2001.

[28] Center for Applied Special Technology: Bobby. Available at: http://bobby.cast.org/

[29] Kypros-Net: Eureka - The Indexer of Cyprus. Available at: http://www.kypros.org/Eureka/

[30] Yiasou: Yiasou Cyprus Web Index. Available at: http://www.yiasou.com.cy/

[31] Kypros-Net: Arachne Search Engine. Available at: http://www.arachne.org/

[32] Nielsen J.: "*Designing Web Usability*", New Riders, Indianapolis, IN, 1999.

An Information Hiding Method Based on Computational Intractable Problems

Spyridoula M. Armeni[1], Dimitris N. Christodoulakis[1,2],
Ioannis Kostopoulos[1,2], Polychronis D. Kountrias[1],
Yannis C. Stamatiou[1,2], and Michalis Xenos[2,3]

[1] University of Patras, Computer Engineering & Informatics Dept.
Rio 26500, Patras, Greece
{armeni,kostopul,pkount}@ceid.upatras.gr
[2] Computer Technology Institute
61 Riga Ferraiou Str., 261 10 Patras, Greece
{dxri,stamatiu}@cti.gr
[3] Hellenic Open University
16 Sachtouri Str., 262 23, Patras, Greece
m.xenos@eap.gr

Abstract. This paper presents an information hiding method that can be used for proving copyright ownership of a digital object. In contrast with other methods, the identity of the owner of the object is proved by the owner's ability to demonstrate *knowledge* of a certain property of the signature. The method utilizes *Zero Knowledge Interactive Proof (ZKIP)* protocols for computationally intractable, or NP-complete, problems and in particular for the 3-coloring problem. This problem requires an assignment of a color out of three available colors to the vertices of a graph so that no two adjacent vertices have the same color. The method prescribes the construction of signatures that represent *adjacency matrices* of graphs while proof of ownership is effected by knowledge of a 3-coloring by an individual. The computational intractability of the 3-coloring problem implies that knowledge of a coloring of the graph/signature presents sufficient evidence of ownership of any digital file containing this signature. The method has the additional advantage that the disclosure of the signature is of no consequence, since it is essentially the knowledge of the property of the signature (the 3-coloring of the graph it represents) that enables one to use it as proof of ownership of the cover data. The paper focuses on the design of the method and presents experiments from its application on high quality color images. From the experiments it is derived that it is feasible to add the 3-colored graph into color images without affecting image quality (PSNR measurements and HVS examples are presented). More importantly, experiments prove the signature tolerance against various attacks even against attacks that significantly reduce image quality.

Y. Manolopoulos et al. (Eds.): PCI 2001, LNCS 2563, pp. 262–278, 2003.

1   Introduction

It is a fact that, nowadays, digital information is more and more exposed to various acts of unauthorized modification, duplication and redistribution, not only due to the widespread use of the Internet where it appears, but also due to the invention of inexpensive data reproduction means. This has determined the emergence of a variety of signature-based protection methods (see [4, 12]) for protecting copyrighted digital material such as audio, still images, and video ensuring that the owner of the material can be identified.

The majority of these methods face two major difficulties: a) the fact that anyone can use the digital signature to claim that he is the rightful owner of the data (provided that the signature is stolen), and b) the fact that increasing the signature size either makes the method less tolerant to attacks (in case of a large non-repeatable volume of signature data), or makes the unauthorized detection and extraction of the signature easier (in case of multiple signatures). Most methods are using an embedded, user-specific bit-sequence in the material to be protected that, when detected, uniquely identifies the legal owner in cases of copyright related disputes. However, given the fact that the identification of the legal owner is effected by simply presenting the signature string, if the signature is stolen, it can be subsequently used by anyone to claim data ownership ("inversion" attacks). Additionally, most methods use a large signature consisting of repetitions of a fixed, small string consisting of different bits, usually produced randomly. In the former case, because of data repetition, the signature is easy to detect statistically. In the latter case, the unique large signature is very fragile as minor alterations of the cover data may render the signature unusable. In both cases the capacity (i.e. the ability to embed in the target image a large quantity of data) of the target image [26] is always an obstacle, since adding a large volume of data as signature may significantly decrease the quality of the image.

The method proposed in this paper, addresses both problems mentioned above. It is based on a well-known Zero Knowledge Interactive Proof (ZKIP) protocol (see Papadimitriou [24], page 291, for example) for the computationally intractable, or NP-complete, *3-coloring* problem (see [13]). The main advantage of the proposed method lies in the fact that the signature represents a graph. The legal owner of the protected data knows a 3-coloring of this graph and, thus, user identification is effected not by showing the signature/graph itself but by displaying knowledge of this 3-coloring. What is important is that such a 3-coloring is not easy to find due to the computational intractability of the 3-coloring problem. In other words, the possibility of a string to identify a person stems from its interpretation as an instance of computationally intractable problem. This has the effect that even if one steals the string, it will not be possible for him to impersonate the rightful owner of the data since a 3-coloring is needed to perform the identification.

More specifically, a user's signature represents the adjacency matrix of a random 3-colorable graph with edges to vertices ratio within a region that, experimentally, is known to produce instances that are most hard to color as shown in

Section 2. In a copyright dispute, the rightful owner will be the only one able to efficiently exhibit a 3-coloring for the graph representing his signature, while the computational difficulty of producing a 3-coloring for such instances can be considered as a strong evidence in favor of him. It is for this reason that the method described here also constitutes a way for performing an alternative characterization of a strong signature. Unlike other methods, the proposed method does not focus on certain statistical signature properties (e.g. being random), or signatures representing a company logo, but on the proper representation of a combinatorial object (graph) with a hard to compute characteristic (3-coloring). In this way, digital data copyright protection is enforced, since revealing a person's digital signature (which is by itself a difficult task requiring knowledge of a, perhaps, complex embedding process) is not enough to impersonate the rightful owner; only the latter will be able to readily exhibit the 3-coloring, which is hard to compute if not already known. Such a signature, a characterization and uniqueness of which is based on a computationally intractable problem, provides an example of a cryptographically secure signature in analogy to the cryptographically secure pseudorandom number generators.

Furthermore, the proposed method uses the *wavelet transform* (see, for example, [21]), which is a transform that provides a simultaneous time-frequency representation of a given signal. Using this representation, it is possible to insert a large volume of data (a large 3-colored graph) into cover data without affecting image quality. The experiments presented in Section 5 demonstrate that the PSNR remains higher than 39dB. The Discrete Wavelet Transform is used in order to accumulate the energy of the image into the LL band. By embedding the graph information into the LL band, the algorithm achieves robustness to several image alterations since it modifies the most significant part of the image data. Considering the security of the method, two points should be considered: the robustness of the method and the security of the graph. The proposed algorithm is indeed robust to some image alterations but it cannot provide robustness against strong benchmarking tools like Stirmark or Checkmark. This does not come as a surprise since the size of information that is embedded to the image is much larger than the size of a typical watermark used for copyright purposes in most of the watermarking methods. However, even a relatively small portion of this information that remains into the cover data is still useful to the legal owner: the information bits that survive the attack define a sub-graph of the original graph and a 3-coloring of the original graph is also a 3-coloring of this sub-graph. Thus, the remaining bits still have the property that they can be used by the legal owner in order to prove ownership of the image file that contain the surviving bits.

A number of variants of the concept of Zero Knowledge authentication has been presented in the past. Namely, in [10], Craver attempts to protect the digital data by producing a scrambling that is difficult to reproduce. His scheme is based on the Hamiltonian Path problem, which is computationally intractable. Data copyright is protected by a protocol that proves ownership and at the same time avoids revealing the signature string. In another scheme proposed by Hirotsugu in [16], the topology of the signature graphs depends on (is related to) the properties of the image in which the signature graphs will be used. Hirotsugu manages to protect the copyright of an image without revealing the signature graph by taking advantage of the fact that the graph isomorphism problem is computationally intractable and by using a ZKIP protocol for it.

The approach presented in this paper differs significantly from both aforementioned approaches: even if the signature string is successfully extracted, it cannot be used unless its 3-coloring is known in advance when interpreted as a graph. The proposed Zero Knowledge variation is applicable at a second level, and is based on knowledge of a 3-coloring of a bit-string (signature) when interpreted as an instance of the 3-coloring problem. The strength of embedding instances of computationally intractable problems as watermarks in a digital image lies in the fact that even if the attacker steals the signature, he cannot use the watermark in order to impersonate the legal owner of the file. In other words, revealing the signature is of no consequences to the legal owner as a potential attacker will be in difficulty in obtaining a 3-coloring of the vertices of the graph represented by the signature. Thus, we have at the same time copyright protection due to the embedded string (watermark) and user authentication due to the knowledge of the 3-coloring of the graph represented by the string. Another difference between this approach and Hirogutsu's is that in this case the embedded graph does not depend on the cover data; this fact enables the use of the theory of threshold phenomena of hard combinatorial problems in order to construct a signature of adequate hardness.

The method described in this paper can be applied to any cover data (image, sound, video) in need of protection, although the presented experiments were conducted with still images [3]. This paper presents experiments that prove the applicability of the proposed method to high quality still color images, the ability to embed a large graph using wavelets without affecting the quality of cover data and the robustness of the method against various attacks. It should be stressed that in this case the signature's resistance against attacks does not only lie in the embedding process, but also within the properties of the graph; for this reason copyright ownership can be determined even if only a small fraction of the graph survives from the attacks (since as previously mentioned 3-coloring of it still constitutes a hard combinatorial problem).

The paper is organized as follows: Section 2 describes a method for producing random 3-colorable graphs, along with a 3-coloring of their vertices. Section 3 discusses the concept of protecting the ownership of an image by proving knowledge of the 3-coloring without revealing it, while Section 4 presents capacity issues, as well as the embedding and extracting process of the 3-colored graph. Section 5 presents results from the experiments conducted during the application of the method. Finally, in Section 6 the focal points of the paper as well as some thoughts for future investigations are discussed.

2   Producing Random Hard Instances of the 3-Coloring Problem

A graph $G = (V, E)$, where V is the set of vertices and E is the set of edges of G, is 3-colorable if its vertices can be colored using at most three colors so that no two adjacent vertices are assigned the same color. A color assignment that respects this constraint is called a 3-coloring of G.

While it is difficult to color a given graph using three colors, as this problem is *computationally intractable* or *NP-complete* (see Papadimitriou [24] and Garey and Johnson [13]), it is nevertheless easy to *construct* a 3-colorable graph randomly along with a 3-coloring of its vertices. An algorithm that achieves this is the following:

1. Let p_1, p_2, and p_3 be real numbers such that $p_1 + p_2 + p_3 = 1$ and $p_1 p_2 p_3 \neq 0$.
2. Generate a random permutation $i_1, i_2, \ldots, i_n$ of the numbers $1, 2, \ldots, n$.
3. For each $j = 1, \ldots n$, vertex v_j is assigned to color class C_k with probability p_k, $k = 1, 2, 3$.
4. For each pair u, v of vertices that do not belong to the same color class, introduce the undirected edge (u, v) with probability p.

For *any* value of p, the above algorithm is guaranteed to produce a *solved* instance of the 3-coloring problem with expected color class sizes $|C_1| = p_1 n$, $|C_2| = p_2 n$ and $|C_3| = p_3 n$. The algorithm provides both a 3-colorable graph along with a coloring of its vertices. However this does not suffice. What is actually needed, is a 3-colorable graph for which it is also hard to find a 3-coloring. In other words, a hard instance of the 3-coloring problem is sought. In general, the problem of characterizing hard instances of computationally intractable problems has led to the development of a rich theory, the theory of *instance complexity*, which is, in turn intimately related to the theory of *descriptional* or *Kolmogorov* complexity. Although the current theory does not offer an effective way to generate directly or, at least, recognize a hard instance of a computationally intractable problem, there is a number of heuristic approaches that one may follow in order to produce an instance that has some increased probability of being hard. An interesting possibility for creating such instances comes from the area of threshold phenomena in combinatorial problems.

Let G be a random graph with m edges and n vertices and r the ratio m/n. In 1991, Cheeseman, Kanefsky, and Taylor ([6]) demonstrated experimentally that for values of r that cluster around the value 2.3, randomly generated graphs with rn edges were either almost all 3-colorable or almost none 3-colorable depending on whether $r < 2.3$ or $r > 2.3$ respectively. This suggested that there is some value r_0 for r around which an abrupt transition can be observed from almost certain 3-colorability to almost certain non 3-colorability of the random graphs. However, from a complexity-theoretic perspective, their crucial observation was that graphs with edges to vertices ratio around r_0 caused the greatest difficulty to the most efficient graph coloring algorithms.

To return to the algorithm that produces solved instances of 3-colorability, it seems that the edge probability p should be selected so that the *expected* ratio

$\mathbf{E}[r] = \mathbf{E}[m]/n$ is around r_0. Thus p is obtained from the following, assuming that $|C_k| = p_i n$, $k = 1, 2, 3$ (i.e. they contain exactly the expected number of vertices):

$$r_0 = \mathbf{E}[r] = \frac{\mathbf{E}[m]}{n} = p(p_1 p_2 + p_1 p_3 + p_2 p_3)n.$$

Solving for p, gives $p = \frac{r_0}{(p_1 p_2 + p_1 p_3 + p_2 p_3)n}$. It has also been experimentally observed that instances are more difficult to solve when all color classes are of about equal size so setting $p_1 = p_2 = p_3 = 1/3$ results to $p = 3r_0/n$. In this way, the "hard-instances" region is sampled.

What is not, however, clear is whether this sampling is biased towards instances that may contain many colorings besides the one produced by the proposed algorithm. This may have the undesirable effect of an opponent stealing the graph and discovering one of these colorings, thus using the graph as his own signature. A similar concern about the satisfiability problem with clauses of 3 literals (3-SAT) is expressed in [1]. The problem considered there is the generation of random formulas with clauses to variables ratio around the threshold value that are, however, constructed so as to satisfy a given truth assignment (similar to the construction of a 3-colorable graph). The problem is that the obvious methods to achieve this seem to produce formulas that, apart from the desired assignment, also satisfy many more assignments. This again might have the averse effect that when such formulas are given as inputs to randomized algorithms such as *Walksat*, they may be easier to solve than the satisfiable formulas that are sieved out of the formulas produced uniformly around the threshold value by a 3-SAT formula generator.

Another heuristic approach that can be adopted to "fortify" the instances against this deficiency is to ensure that, except for the solution which the instance is forced to have, no other solution (or, at least, a few of them) exists. Such an approach was followed in [23] for the 3-SAT problem, where it is shown that if sufficiently many clauses are chosen at random from the clauses satisfying a given truth assignment, then the formula that results possess a single solution with probability $1 - o(1)$ (see [23]). Due to the increased number of possible values per variable for 3-coloring (3 values versus 2 for 2-SAT), the technique of [23] cannot be directly generalized in the presented case. However, it can be still claimed that a number of special colorings are excluded from being legal colorings for this instance after it is constructed (with the algorithm given before): these are the colorings that result from the prescribed coloring with the change of a single color to a "higher numbered" color. Therefore, assuming that colors are numbered as 0, 1, and 2, the colorings that are excluded (see below) are the ones resulting from the initial coloring by changing the colors of single vertices to a "higher" color. More formally, a coloring P is a partition of the vertex set V into three vertex sets V_0, V_1, and V_2 so that no edge connects two vertices belonging to the same partition. A vertex u of color i is *unmovable* if every change to a higher indexed color j invalidates the coloring P. Thus, u of color i is unmovable if it is adjacent with at least one vertex of every cell V_j, such that $j > i$. A coloring P is *rigid* if all its vertices are unmovable. A good thought would, then, be to start with initial coloring that has high probability of being rigid. In [17] the probability of rigidity is computed for a given coloring P given (i) the fractions x, y, z of the chosen edges connecting vertices from $V_0 V_1$, $V_0 V_2$ and $V_1 V_2$ respectively and (ii) the fractions α, β, γ of the vertices assigned color 0, 1, and 2 respectively.

$$\mathbf{P}[P \text{ is rigid given } x, y, z, \alpha, \beta, \gamma] \asymp$$

$$\left[e^{-\alpha(\int_0^1 \ln(\frac{u_{12}-x}{1-x})dx - c_{12}\ln u_{12}) - \alpha(\int_0^1 \ln(\frac{u_{13}-x}{1-x})dx - c_{13}\ln u_{13}) - \beta(\int_0^1 \ln(\frac{u_{23}-x}{1-x})dx - c_{23}\ln u_{23})} \right]^n$$

with

$$u_{12} = \frac{1}{1 - e^{-c_{12}}\phi_2(c_{12}e^{-c_{12}})}, \quad c_{12} = \frac{xr}{\alpha}$$

$$u_{13} = \frac{1}{1 - e^{-c_{13}}\phi_2(c_{13}e^{-c_{13}})}, \quad c_{13} = \frac{yr}{\alpha}$$

$$u_{23} = \frac{1}{1 - e^{-c_{23}}\phi_2(c_{23}e^{-c_{23}})}, \quad c_{23} = \frac{(1-x-y)r}{\beta}$$

and $\phi_2(t)$ the smallest root of the equation $\phi_2(t) = e^{t\phi_2(t)}$. This root can be expressed using the *Lambert W function* (see [8]). The "$\asymp$" symbol means that a polynomially large factor is neglected (that can be, however, easily computed from Stirling's approximation to the factorial function obtaining an asymptotically sharp expression). As a heuristic, the values of $x, y, z, \alpha, \beta, \gamma$ can be adjusted so as to increase the estimate given above. Note that the fact that α, β, and γ enter in the probability estimate leads to the conclusion that the form of the initial coloring has an effect on how probable it is for other "neighboring" colorings to be illegal.

On the other hand, there is a trivial way to exclude many possible solutions by simply adding a large number of edges to the graph produced by the algorithm above (even making it a complete 3-partite graph). The drawback of this approach is that instances with *too few* (i.e. $o(n)$ or *too many* (i.e. $\omega(n)$) edges are easy to solve. Without delving into rigorous arguments, the former simply possess too many possible colorings. As for the latter, there is a simple randomized algorithm based on random sampling that colors a class of such graphs, called "dense" graphs, which are characterized by each vertex having $\Theta(n)$ neighbours.

Another, more rigorous and interesting approach is to construct a *certain* random class of solved 3-coloring instances with the following property: if an algorithm can be found capable of solving an instance of the class with positive (no matter how small) probability, then there is also an algorithm solving one of the NP-complete problems *in the worst case*, which would be most surprising. In [2], this goal was accomplished for a special class of *lattice problem*. We are currently trying to apply this approach for the 3-coloring problem.

What should be born in mind is that the area of hard *solved* instance generation is a very active one and there is much ongoing research aimed at building instances with a *limited* number of solutions.

3   Identification of Image Ownership

The application of the well known zero-knowledge interactive protocol for 3-coloring (see, e.g., [24] for details on this protocol) to signature creation and verification involves three parties:

- The owner A of the original image.
- The person B who attempts to, wrongfully, claim the image as his own.
- The referee, C.

The interactive protocol described in this paper is zero-knowledge, as far as revealing the signature to the referee is concerned, and provides a proof image ownership. The owner, A, embeds a sufficiently large, *hard to solve*, 3-colorable graph (that was produced using the procedure outlined in Section 2) in the original image I using techniques described in Section 4. What A actually embeds, is the graph's adjacency matrix which for an undirected graph without loop edges requires $n(n-1)/2$ bits. Let I' be the resulting image. This is the image that the owner A will publish (say on the Web). Suppose now that B downloads I' and claims ownership. Then A may convince the referee C that A is the owner as follows:

1. A says to C that there is a set of bits in B's image (the image I'), that represent the adjacency matrix of a graph of which we know a 3-coloring.
2. A gives to C the method to extract the positions of the bits of the adjacency matrix and A and C start executing the zero knowledge protocol for 3-coloring.

Now if B claims that he owns the image too, A challenges him to show his signature in I by telling to the referee the coordinates of the bits of his signature (I is not revealed to B). I is the *original* image which only A may possess since he only publishes the marked image I'. However, this will be impossible for him and he can only claim that A has completely removed his signature.

Therefore the referee can conclude one of the following:

1. B tells the truth and A, apart from having supposedly destroyed B's signature in I, has also managed to luckily discover some string in I' (B's "original") and then interpret it as the adjacency matrix of a graph of which A, subsequently, discovered a 3-coloring before the execution of the protocol.
2. A tells the truth, having shown a hard to compute property of a string that was embedded in I' and B has not managed to destroy this signature.

The first conclusion, if true, would lead the referee to attribute the ability to exhibit a three coloring in a graph to pure luck. However, due to the intractability of the 3-coloring problem, pure luck can be excluded with high probability. Therefore, the second conclusion is more credible than the first.

4   Data Hiding Process

4.1   Data Hiding Feasibility

There are three factors that are customarily considered in any information hiding system design: the *capacity* of the image as mentioned before, the *quality* of the new image produced after the insertion of the signature (also called watermarked image) and the *robustness* of the method. These factors are related to each other in the way shown in Figure 1 that appears in [20]. Keeping fixed one of the three factors, a trade-off relationship between the other two factors appears.

An information hiding process, generally, causes visual quality degradation, as it changes the actual values of the host data. Thus, it is important that a minimum tolerance value for a quality measure is set that will be used to evaluate the method. The proposed method has been designed so as to maintain a Peak Signal to Noise Ratio (PSNR) between the original and the watermarked image larger than 39dB. That value is considered as very high assuming the size of the signature which in this case could reach 500 Kbits (depending on the 3-colored graph and the size of the cover image).

Since the quality of the watermarked image can be controlled to be over the tolerance value, the capacity of the image and the robustness of the method are the other two interacting factors. In the proposed method, *perceptual* evaluation criteria were chosen to evaluate the quality of the embedding of large amounts of data in digital images as well as the robustness against some of the most common attacks.

As host signals in the experiments of this work, high resolution color images with dimensions equal or larger than 1024×1024 pixels were used. The signature size for such volumes of cover data was approximately 500 Kbits, which is almost a whole bit plane after the first decomposition of the image. The embedding of the signature made use of the *discrete wavelet transform*. The wavelet transform

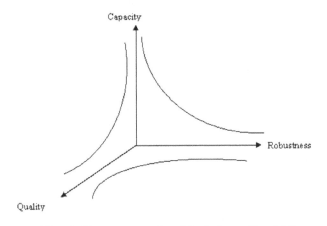

Fig. 1. Factors considered in information hiding

has an advantage over other transformations, due to its ability to represent the signal in the time and frequency domain simultaneously. The signal is passed through a series of high-pass filters to analyze the high frequencies, and through a series of low-pass filters to analyze the low frequencies. In this paper, the signal is an image which can be considered as a two-dimensional signal. By applying the discrete wavelet transform in the original image, the latter is decomposed into 4 sub-images, as follows. The columns are passed through the smoothing (L) and highpass (H) filters, and the rows of each of these resultant images are passed again through L and H, this results in 4 new images. Three of them, LH, HL, and HH correspond to the highest resolution wavelet coefficients. Whereas the LL band is a smoothed version of the original and can be further decomposed in exactly the same way as the original image [25]. It should also be noted that the size of signature in this case depends on the size of the graph which is, in turn, chosen according to the size of the cover image. As a rule, for smaller cover images smaller signatures will be used and for larger images proportionately larger signatures are utilized.

The main requirement of the method is to embed the signature so that it stays intact after several attacks that could possibly applied to the watermarked image. As a consequence, the places where the signature will be embedded in the host image should be selected carefully, from the data where the most significant information of the image appears. This constraint is generally required for the design of any robust information hiding system and it is satisfied by applying a *transformation* from the spatial domain to the frequency domain (example transforms are the Discrete Cosine Transform (DCT), the Fast Fourier Transform (FFT), the Discrete Wavelet Transform (DWT) etc.).

The signature information is embedded in the LL band of the image after the first level decomposition with the discrete wavelet transform which is the most significant band. The dimensions of this band correspond to one fourth of the cover image dimensions. If, for example, a a 1024×1024 image is used, then the LL band will have 512×512 pixels. The embedding process that is described in the following section shows that hiding one bit of information in every value of the LL band is effective for embedding a large 3-colorable graph in a digital image.

4.2 Embedding the 3-Colorable Graph

The technique for embedding the 3-colorable graph is based on concepts presented in [5] and can, also, be applied to other kinds of digital objects such as video.

The wavelet transform is used in this technique, as it is capable of providing the time and frequency information simultaneously, giving a time-frequency representation of the signal. This kind of transform provides the opportunity to embed a large volume of data imperceptibly in the watermarked image and at the same time achieves robustness against various image filtering operations used as attacks.

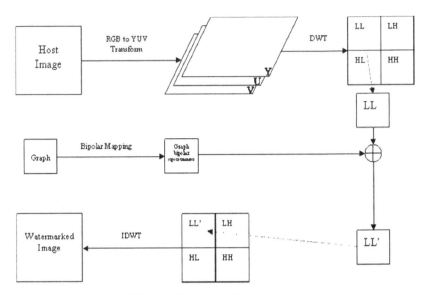

Fig. 2. The embedding process

A 3-colorable graph can be described by its *adjacency matrix*. Such a matrix contains zeros and ones, which represent the non-existence or existence, respectively, of edges between vertices and can be viewed as a binary (black and white) image.

The graph information is embedded into color images and its size can be the one fourth of the host image size (see Figure 2). First of all, the host image is transformed from the RGB color model into the YUV color model. The embedding process takes place in the Y component, but it can be extended using the two components U and V. Then, the 1-level discrete wavelet transform (DWT) is applied to the host image, resulting in the four sub-images LL, LH, HL and HH of the host image. The 3-colorable graph adjacency matrix bits are mapped (by means of a simple bipolar transform) from $\{0, 1\}$ to $\{-1, 1\}$. In addition, extra strength is given to the bipolar information by multiplying it with a factor equal to 25 that gives a good compromise between the image quality of the watermarked image and the robustness of the watermark. The graph is embedded in the LL band of the host image, using the formula $I' = I + W$, where I is the initial host image, W is the graph and I' is the final watermarked image.

When the embedding procedure in the LL band of the host image is completed the inverse discrete wavelet transform (IDWT) is applied and the final watermarked image is produced. Finally, this image is transformed from the YUV color model to the RGB color model.

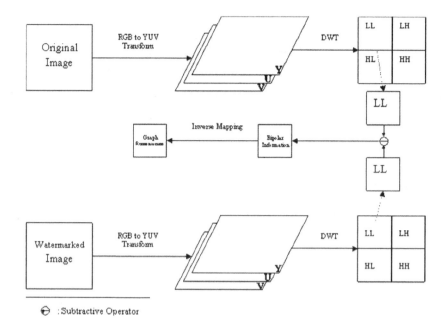

Fig. 3. The extracting process

4.3   Extracting the 3-Colorable Graph

In order to extract the graph, both the host and the watermarked image are needed, as shown in Figure 3. These images are, first, transformed from the RGB color model to the YUV color model. The graph information exists in the Y component of the watermarked image. Then, the 1-level discrete wavelet transform (DWT) is applied both to the Y component of the host and watermarked image. The four bands LL, LH, HL and HH are then obtained from the host and the watermarked images respectively. As mentioned before, the graph is placed in the LL band of the watermarked image. For this reason, the wavelet coefficients of the LL band of the host image are subtracted from the respective coefficients of LL band of the watermarked image to obtain the graph. If this difference is positive then the extracted graph value is equal to one. If it is negative then the extracted graph value is equal to zero.

5   Quality Issues and Method Tolerance

Any information hiding technique inserts a volume of data into the cover data (e.g. an image). The quality of the method depends on the extent to which the original image remains unchanged which, as discussed in Section 4.1, is usually in a trade off relationship with robustness. Successful methods are those that result in the minimum possible changes to the original image. The extent to which the

Table 1. PSNR-based image quality measurements

Image name	PSNR measurements
House	39.64
Train	39.75
Bridge	39.73
Rose	39.50
Swing	39.51
Saturn V	39.84

cover data is modified can be measured using an objective measure such as the PSNR or, subjectively, by means of the Human Visual System (HVS). The latter quality measure is based on the principle that the watermarked image should look similar to the original one to the average observer. Obviously, embedding large graphs in the original image results in small PSNR measurements while embedding smaller graphs results in higher PSNR measurements. In the method presented in this paper, the goal was to achieve a PSNR higher than 39dB. This goal is difficult to achieve as even a Jpeg Medium compression operation usually results in a PSNR measurement approximately equal to 33dB. Therefore, in order to achieve a 39dB measurement, the embedding process was designed to minimize image modifications and the size of the graph was chosen to match the size of the cover data. For an image of 1024×1024 pixels, it was observed that embedding a graph with over 500 vertices could result in PSNR higher than 39dB. Table 1 shows the PSNR measurements for the 6 images used in the experiments.

As far as the HVS criterion is concerned, no differences between the original and the watermarked images were noticeable by human observers, in any of the experiments. In Figure 4, the original image is shown on the left and the watermarked on the right.

Fig. 4. Original (left) and watermarked (right) image

Table 2. PSNR measurements after various attacks

Attacked Images	Blurring	Sharpen	JPEG medium	JPEG high	Uniform noise
House	36.04	31.31	33.29	38.50	26.57
Train	37.25	32.24	34.47	38.18	26.46
Bridge	36.95	32.32	36.44	39.26	26.49
Rose	36.78	32.09	33.93	38.63	26.54
Swing	36.36	31.63	33.88	38.63	26.41
Saturn V	37.07	32.30	35.51	39.19	26.59

Table 3. Percentage of adjacency matrix that survived after attacks

Image Name	Blurring	Sharpen	JPEG medium	JPEG high	Uniform noise
House	84.12%	85.62%	71.46%	90.02%	65.71%
Train	85.11%	85.77%	79.64%	91.26%	62.92%
Bridge	92.12%	92.76%	78.04%	94.15%	65.26%
Rose	86.76%	88.10%	72.22%	90.20%	65.29%
Swing	85.67%	87.93%	74.60%	90.86%	66.39%
Saturn V	88.49%	90.03%	76.43%	91.42%	63.76%

The effectiveness of an information hiding method is also related to its robustness against modifications of the watermarked image. Such modifications, called *attacks*, can be either intentional (also called malicious, aiming at removing the embedded signature), or unintentional (i.e. a lossy compression such as Jpeg). It is obvious that the stronger the attacks are, the less tolerant a signature remains. Usually, a signature is expected to be tolerant at least to attacks affecting the watermarked image quality to a degree similar to the information hiding technique. However, the objective of the proposed method was to be tolerant to attacks that result in PSRN measurements even lower than 30dB. In order to test the robustness of the method, the following attacks were used: blurring (for evaluating robustness against attacks that amplify low frequencies), sharpening (for evaluating robustnass against attacks that amplify high frequencies), Jpeg compression using different rates (50% and 80%) and noise (adding 20% uniform noise to the watermarked image). As shown in the 6 examples of Table 2, the PSNR measurements of the watermarked images after the attacks are quite low. Blurring was always measured lower than 38dB, sharpen lower than 33dB, Jpeg-medium lower than 37dB, Jpeg-high lower than 39dB and noise lower than 27dB. As far as the 20% uniform noise is concerned, an attack that significantly affects the quality of the images, a signature is expected to have low tolerance.

A method is normally characterized as robust against attacks, if the embedded signature can be used to prove ownership of the cover data when extracted from an image altered by attacks. Table 3 illustrates the percentage of the 3-colored graph recovered for each attack case against the 6 test images.

It must be noted that in the cases of blurring, sharpening and Jpeg compression (high and medium), more than 70% of the graph was recovered in all cases (namely, in cases of blurring, sharpening and Jpeg high compression this percentage was over 80%), while in the case of noise this percentage was over

60%. As already remarked, this method is not based on the signature bits themselves to prove cover data ownership, but on the *knowledge* of a 3-coloring of the graph or sub-graphs that survived (expected to be hard themselves). Note that a 3-coloring of the original graph is also a 3-coloring for any of its subgraphs.

6   Conclusions and Future Work

Due to the advent of technological means that are able to copy and transmit information fast and at a very low cost, the need for effective methods that are able to protect copyrighted work stored in a digital form is today more apparent than ever. This need calls for solutions that are able to protect this work by identifying the legal owner in cases of copyright disputes. In this paper, a new method of protecting copyrighted work was proposed with main features (a) the shift of interest from *how user signatures look like*, as bit sequences, to *what the user signatures represent*, and (b) the use of the *wavelet transform* in order to embed signatures in the least disturbing, for the quality of the target file, way.

Regarding feature (a), the signature string is constructed so as to represent instances of hard combinatorial problems. The problem that was chosen to demonstrate the feasibility of the method was the 3-coloring problem and the signatures are adjacency matrix representations of graphs produced to possess a specific coloring that is used as a proof of identity of the legal owner. Constructing a 3-colorable random graph along with a 3-coloring of its vertices is easy while *discovering* such a coloring is hard. In addition, if these graphs are constructed within a specific region defined by a control parameter (edges to vertices ratio), the instances are expected to be considerably more difficult to solve than equal sized graphs defined outside this region. Thus, knowledge of a coloring can be used as evidence of ownership.

A major question for future research, that is also an open question in Computational Complexity Theory, is the *characterization* of hard instances. Until now, all such characterizations are either of a heuristic nature or too theoretical to be used in practice. In addition, it would be good to relate the hardness of subgraphs of a given graph to the hardness of the graph.

References

[1] D. Achlioptas, C. Gomez, H. Kautz and B. Selman: "Generating Satisfiable Problem Instances", *Proceedings AAAI'2000 Conference*, 2000. 267

[2] M. Ajtai: "Generating Hard Instances of Lattice Problems", Electronic Colloquium on Computational Complexity, ECCC Report TR96-007, 1996. 268

[3] S. Armeni, D. Christodoulakis, I. Kostopoulos, Y. C. Stamatiou and M. Xenos: "Proving Copyright Ownership Using Hard Instances of Combinatorial Intractable Problems", *Proceedings 8th Panhellenic Conference in Informatics*, pp.137-145, Nicosia, 2002. 265

[4] W. Bender, D. Grul, N. Morimoto and A. Lu: "Techniques for Data Hiding", *IBM Systems Journal*, Vol.35, No.3-4, 1996. 263

[5] J. J. Chae, D. Mukherjee and B. S. Manjunath: "Color Image Embedding Using Multidimensional Lattice Structures", *Proceedings IEEE International Conference on Image Processing (ICIP'98)*, Vol.1, pp.460-464, Chicago, IL, October 1998. 271

[6] P. Cheeseman, B. Kanefsky and W. M. Taylor: "Where the Really Hard Problems Are", *Proceedings IJCAI'91 Conference*, Vol.1, pp.331-337, 1991. 266

[7] S. Cook and D. Mitchel: "Finding Hard Instances of the Satisfiability Problem: a Survey", *Satisfiability Problem: Theory and Applications*, DIMACS series in Discrete Mathematics and Theoretical Computer Science, Vol.25, pp.1-17, 1997.

[8] R. M. Corless, G. H. Gonnet, D. E. G. Hare, D. J. Jeffrey and D. E. Knuth: "On the Lambert W function", manuscript, Department of Computer Science, University of Waterloo. 268

[9] S. Craver, N. Memon, B.-L. Yeo and M. Yeung: "Can Invisible Watermarks Resolve Rightful Ownerships?", *IBM Research Report*, RC 20509, 1996.

[10] S. Craver: "Zero Knowledge Watermark Detection", *Proceedings 3rd International Workshop on Information Hiding (IHW'99)*, 1999. 264

[11] E. R. Dougherty: "Random Processes for Images and Signal Processing", *SPIE/IEEE Series on Imaging Science & Engineering*, 1999.

[12] A. Fabien, P. Peticolas, R. J. Anderson and M. G. Kuhn: "Information Hiding - a Survey, *IEEE special issue on Protection of Multimedia Content*, Vol.87, No.7, pp.1062-1078, July 1999. 263

[13] M. R. Garey and D. S. Johnson: *"Computers and Intractability - a Guide to the Theory of NP-Completeness"*, W. H. Freeman, 1979. 263, 266

[14] R. Gonzalez and R. Woods: *"Digital Image Processing"*, Addison Wesley, 1992.

[15] B. Hayes: "Computing Science: Can't Get no Satisfaction", *American Scientist*, March-April, 1997.

[16] K. Hirotsugu: "An Image Digital Signature System with ZKIP for the Graph Isomorphism", *Proceedings ICIP'96 Conference*, 1996. 265

[17] A. C. Kaporis, L. M. Kirousis and Y. C. Stamatiou: "A Note on the Non-colorability Threshold of a Random Graph", *Electronic Journal of Combinatorics*, Vol.7, #R29, 2000. 268

[18] S. Katzenbeisser, A. Fabien and P. Petitcolas: *"Information Hiding Techniques for Steganography and Digital Watermarking"*, Artech House Books, 1999.

[19] S. Kirkpatrick and B. Selman: "Critical Behavior in the Satisfiability of Random Boolean Expressions", *Science*, Vol.264, pp.1297-1301, 1994.

[20] C.-Y. Lin: "Watermarking and Digital Signature Techniques for Multimedia Authentication and Copyright Protection", PhD Thesis, Columbia University, 2000. 270

[21] S. Mallat: *"A Wavelet Tour of Signal Processing*, 2nd Edition, Academic Press, 1999. 264

[22] F. Massacci and L. Marraro: "Logical Cryptanalysis as a SAT problem: the Encoding of the Data Encryption Standard", manuscript, 1999.

[23] M. Motoki and R. Uehara: "Unique Solution Instance Generation for the 3-Satisfiability (3SAT) Problem", Technical Report C-129, Department of Mathematics and Computer Sciences, Tokyo Institute of Technology, 1999. 267

[24] C. H. Papadimitriou: *"Computational Complexity"*, Addison-Wesley, 1994. 263, 266, 269

[25] R. Polikar: "The Wavelet Tutorial". Available at:
     http:// www.polikar.iastate.edu/ rpolikar/WAVELETS/Wttutorial.html   271
[26] K. Solanski, N. Jacobsen, S. Chandrasekaran, U. Madhow and B.S. Manjunath:
     "Introducing Perceptual Criteria into Quantization Based Embedding", *Proceedings ASSP'2002 Conference*, 2002.   263
[27] R.B. Wolfgang and E.J. Delp: "Overview of Image Security Techniques with Applications in Multimedia Systems", *Proceedings SPIE Conference on Multimedia Networks: Security, Displays, Terminals, and Gateways*, Vol.3228, pp.297-308, Dallas TX, 1997.

An Experimental Evaluation of a Monte-Carlo Algorithm for Singular Value Decomposition*

Petros Drineas[1], Eleni Drinea[2], and Patrick S. Huggins[1]

[1] Yale University, Computer Science Department
New Haven, CT 06520, USA
{drineas,huggins}@cs.yale.edu
[2] Harvard University, Division of Engineering and Applied Sciences
Cambridge, MA 02138, USA
edrinea@deas.harvard.edu

Abstract. We demonstrate that an algorithm proposed by Drineas *et. al.* in [7] to approximate the singular vectors/values of a matrix A, is not only of theoretical interest but also a fast, viable alternative to traditional algorithms. The algorithm samples a small number of rows (or columns) of the matrix, scales them appropriately to form a small matrix S and computes the singular value decomposition (SVD) of S, which is a good approximation to the SVD of the original matrix. We experimentally evaluate the accuracy and speed of this randomized algorithm using image matrices and three different sampling schemes. Our results show that our approximations of the singular vectors of A span almost the same space as the corresponding exact singular vectors of A.

1   Introduction

In many applications we are given an $m \times n$ matrix A and we want to compute a few of its left (or right) singular vectors. Such applications include data clustering [1], information retrieval [13], property testing of graphs, image processing, etc. Singular vectors are usually computed via the Singular Value Decomposition (SVD) of A (see section 2).

There are many algorithms that either exactly compute the SVD of a matrix in $O(mn^2 + m^2n)$ time (an excellent reference is [11]) or approximate it faster (e.g. Lanczos methods [17]). In [10] and [7] randomized SVD algorithms were proposed: instead of computing the SVD of the entire matrix, pick a subset of its rows or columns (or both), compute the SVD of this smaller matrix and show that it is a good approximation to the SVD of the initial matrix; theoretical error bounds for these Monte-Carlo algorithms were presented. In this paper we experimentally evaluate the performance of the algorithm proposed in [7] (which is better suited for practical applications) by demonstrating its accuracy and speedup over traditional SVD algorithms. Our test set consists of image

---

* A preliminary version of this work appeared in the 2001 Panhellenic Conference on Informatics [5].

Y. Manolopoulos et al. (Eds.): PCI 2001, LNCS 2563, pp. 279–296, 2003.
© Springer-Verlag Berlin Heidelberg 2003

matrices; we explain our choice below. This randomized SVD algorithm returns approximations to the top k right (or left) singular vectors of the image matrix. Our goal is to compare these approximations to the exact singular vectors; we measure the accuracy of our approximations by computing rank k approximations to the matrices of our test set, using both sets of vectors, and comparing the results. We will explore three different schemes for sampling rows (columns) of the input matrix: uniform sampling with replacement, uniform sampling without replacement and weighted sampling; in this latter case, "heavier" rows/columns are included in the sample with higher probability. The most encouraging result is that the experimental performance of the algorithm is *much better* than its theoretical error bounds.

A general family of applications for this algorithm is Principal Component Analysis applications (e.g. eigenfaces [14] or Latent Semantic Indexing in information retrieval), where a database (of documents, images etc.) that exists in a high dimensional space is projected to a lower dimensional space using SVD. Then, answering a query (that is searching for an instance in the database that is close to the query) amounts to projecting the query to the same low-dimensional space and then finding the nearest neighbor. The projections need not be exact for two reasons: the values of the elements of the database are usually determined using inexact methods *and* the exact projection to the lower dimensional space is not necessary, since we are only interested in a nearest neighbor search.

The main reason behind picking image matrices in order to demonstrate the accuracy and speed of our algorithm is that beyond evaluating numerical results (i.e. the relative error of the approximation), we can also estimate the accuracy of the approximation visually. Also, by experimenting with image matrices, we can demonstrate that our methods work well even for relatively small and very dense matrices (up to 1000 rows and columns, density in general close to 1). We will see that for these matrices, uniform sampling performs equally well to our more sophisticated sampling methods. The performance of our algorithm has also been examined in [13] using a matrix from information retrieval datasets, but the matrix there was very large (more than 10^5 rows and columns) and less than 10% dense. Finally, singular vectors of image matrices are quite useful in image processing (e.g. eigenfaces, image compression, image restoration, etc. for details see [19, 15, 2, 20, 4, 3, 12, 16]). With images getting larger and larger, certain applications might not be able to afford the computational time needed for computing the SVD. Next we describe just such an application in medical imaging.

In dynamic Magnetic Resonance Imaging (MRI) a series of time ordered images is obtained by continually updating image data as changes occur (e.g. monitoring of surgical procedures). In [23, 22] Zientara *et. al.* investigated the use of SVD for creating and encoding these images. Their technique approximates the top few left or right singular vectors of an initial image and uses them to define "excitation profiles". These profiles are in turn used to create SVD encoded data for the next image in the series. The authors argue that this process is much faster than fully generating the image using state of the art

MRI equipment. Recreating the image (that is "decoding" SVD) amounts to a multiplication with the computed singular vectors. One major constraint is the time required by the SVD computation, which can now be reduced using our algorithm.

The paper is organized as follows: in section 2 we state some basic Linear Algebra definitions and theorems related to SVD. In section 3 we present the algorithm in a different way than it was presented in [7], more suitable for implementation purposes. In section 4.1 we describe our experimental dataset and in section 4.2 we demonstrate that although the theoretical error bounds are very weak for relatively small matrices (such as image matrices), in practice the algorithm is very efficient and accurate. Finally, in section 4.3 we experimentally compare the speed of our algorithm vs. Lanczos/Arnoldi techniques.

2   Background on SVD

Any $m \times n$ matrix A can be expressed as

$$A = \sum_{t=1}^{r} \sigma_t u^{(t)} v^{(t)^T}$$

where r is the rank of A, $\sigma_1 \geq \sigma_2 \geq \ldots \geq \sigma_r$ are its singular values and $u^{(t)} \in \mathcal{R}^m, v^{(t)} \in \mathcal{R}^n, t = 1, \ldots, r$ are its left and right singular vectors respectively. The $u^{(t)}$'s and the $v^{(t)}$'s are orthonormal sets of vectors; namely, $u^{(i)^T} \cdot u^{(j)}$ is one if $i = j$ and zero otherwise. We also remind the reader that

$$\|A\|_F = \sqrt{\sum_{i,j} A_{ij}^2} \quad \text{and} \quad |A|_2 = \max_{x \in \mathcal{R}^n : |x|_2 = 1} |Ax|_2 = \sigma_1$$

In matrix notation, SVD is defined as $A = U \Sigma V^T$ where U and V are orthonormal matrices, containing the left and right singular vectors of A. $\Sigma = \mathbf{diag}(\sigma_1, \ldots, \sigma_r)$ contains the singular values of A; we remind the reader that $U^T U = I$ and $V^T V = I$.

If we define $A_k = \sum_{t=1}^{k} \sigma_t u^{(t)} v^{(t)^T}$, then A_k is the best rank k approximation to A with respect to the 2-norm and the Frobenius norm. Thus, for any matrix D of rank at most k, $|A - A_k|_2 \leq |A - D|_2$ and $\|A - A_k\|_F \leq \|A - D\|_F$. A matrix A has a "good" rank k approximation if $A - A_k$ is small with respect to the 2-norm and the Frobenius norm. It is well known that

$$\|A - A_k\|_F = \sqrt{\sum_{t=k+1}^{r} \sigma_t^2(A)} \quad \text{and} \quad |A - A_k|_2 = \sigma_{k+1}(A)$$

Finally, from basic Linear Algebra, $A_k = U_k \Sigma_k V_k^T = A V_k V_k^T = U_k U_k^T A$, where U_k and V_k are sub-matrices of U, V containing only the top k left or right singular vectors respectively; for a detailed treatment of Singular Value

Decomposition see [11]. In the following, $A_{(i)}$ denotes the i-th row of A as a row vector and $A^{(i)}$ denotes the i-th column of A as a column vector. The length of a column (or row) will be denoted by $|A^{(i)}|$ (or $|A_{(i)}|$) and is equal to the square root of the sum of the squares of its elements.

3   The Randomized SVD Algorithm

In this section we discuss the SVD algorithm of [7] and, more specifically, an efficient implementation of the algorithm. We also present theoretical error bounds for three sampling schemes (weighted sampling, uniform sampling with replacement, uniform sampling without replacement) and we comment on the quality of the bounds in practice.

3.1   The Algorithm

Given an $m \times n$ matrix A we seek to approximate its top k right singular values/vectors. Intuitively, our algorithm picks s rows of A, forms an $s \times n$ matrix S and computes its right singular vectors. Assume that we are given a set of probabilities $p_1, \ldots, p_m$ such that $\sum_{i=1}^{m} p_i = 1$.

FastSVD Algorithm

Input: $m \times n$ matrix A, integers $s \le m$, $k \le s$.
Output: $n \times k$ matrix H, $\lambda_1, \ldots, \lambda_k \in \mathcal{R}^+$.

1. **for** $t = 1$ **to** s
   - Pick an integer from $\{1 \ldots m\}$, where $\mathbf{Pr}(\text{pick } i) = p_i$.
   - Include $A_{(i)}/\sqrt{sp_i}$ as a row of S.
2. Compute $S \cdot S^T$ and its singular value decomposition. Say

$$SS^T = \sum_{t=1}^{s} \lambda_t^2 w^{(t)} w^{(t)^T}$$

3. Compute $h^{(t)} = S^T w^{(t)}/|S^T w^{(t)}|, t = 1 \ldots k$. Return H, a matrix whose columns are the $h^{(t)}$ and $\lambda_1, \ldots, \lambda_k$ (our approximations to the top k singular values of A).

In step 2, λ_t^2 are the singular values of SS^T and $w^{(t)}, t = 1 \ldots s$ its left (and right[1]) singular vectors. In step 3, the $h^{(t)}$'s are the right singular vectors of S (and our approximations to the right singular vectors of A). It should be obvious that the SVD of S is $S = \sum_{t=1}^{s} \lambda_t w^{(t)} h^{(t)^T}$. We emphasize here that if we were

---

[1] We remind the reader that for symmetric matrices the left and right singular vectors are equal.

computing the right singular vectors of S directly after step 1, the running time would be $O(n^2)$, while now it is $O(n)$ (see section 3.3). The algorithm is simple and intuitive; the only part that requires further attention is the sampling process (see section 3.3).

3.2 Theoretical Analysis

How does one evaluate how close H is to V_k (the top k right singular vectors of A)? We are usually interested in the space spanned by V_k; this space is *invariant* for A: $\mathbf{span}\,(AV_k) \subset \mathbf{span}\,(V_k)$. A consequence of this property is that $A_k = AV_k V_k^T$ is the "best" rank k approximation to A. Thus, to evaluate the quality of H as an approximation to V_k, we will show that $P = AHH^T$ (a rank k matrix) is *almost* as "close" to A as A_k is. The "closeness" will be measured using the standard unitarily invariant norms: the Frobenius norm and the 2-norm (see section 2). More specifically, our analysis guarantees that $\|A - P\|_{F,2}$ is at most $\|A - A_k\|_{F,2}$ plus some additional error, which is inversely proportional to the number of rows that we included in our sample. As the "quality" of H increases, H and V_k span *almost* the same space and P is *almost* the optimal rank k approximation to A.

In the following theorem $\mathbf{E}\,(X)$ denotes the expectation of X. For detailed proofs of the theorem see [7, 6].

Theorem 1. *If $P = AHH^T$ is a rank (at most) k approximation to A, constructed using the algorithm of section 3, then, for any $s \le m$,*

1. If $p_i = |A^{(i)}|^2/\|A\|_F^2$ and sampling is done with replacement,

$$\mathbf{E}\left(\|A - P\|_F^2\right) \le \|A - A_k\|_F^2 + 2\sqrt{\frac{k}{s}}\|A\|_F^2$$

$$\mathbf{E}\left(|A - P|_2^2\right) \le |A - A_k|_2^2 + \frac{2}{\sqrt{s}}\|A\|_F^2$$

This sampling minimizes the variance for the error of the approximation.

2. If $p_i = 1/m$ and sampling is done with replacement,

$$\mathbf{E}\left(\|A - P\|_F^2\right) \le \|A - A_k\|_F^2 + 2\sqrt{k\frac{m}{s}\sum_{t=1}^{m}|A^{(t)}|^4}$$

$$\mathbf{E}\left(|A - P|_2^2\right) \le |A - A_k|_2^2 + 2\sqrt{\frac{m}{s}\sum_{t=1}^{m}|A^{(t)}|^4}$$

3. If $p_i = 1/m$ and sampling is done without replacement,

$$\mathbf{E}\left(\|A - P\|_F^2\right) \le \|A - A_k\|_F^2 + 2\sqrt{\left(\frac{km}{m-1}\right)\left(\frac{m}{s}-1\right)\sum_{t=1}^{m}|A^{(t)}|^4}$$

$$\mathbf{E}\left(|A - P|_2^2\right) \le |A - A_k|_2^2 + 2\sqrt{\left(\frac{m}{m-1}\right)\left(\frac{m}{s}-1\right)\sum_{t=1}^{m}|A^{(t)}|^4}$$

The first bound is clearly a relative error bound; the relative error of our approximation is at most the relative error of the optimal rank k approximation plus an additional error, inversely proportional to the number of rows that we include in our sample. The other two bounds imply weaker relative error bounds, depending on how close $\|A\|_F^2$ is to $\sqrt{m \sum_{t=1}^m |A^{(t)}|^4}$. Intuitively, these two quantities are close if the Frobenius norm of A is distributed evenly among its rows. Indeed, if $|A_{(i)}|^2 \geq (\gamma/m)\|A\|_F^2$ for some $\gamma \leq 1$, it is easy to show that

$$\sqrt{m \sum_{t=1}^m |A^{(t)}|^4} \geq \gamma \|A\|_F^2$$

Comparing the above bounds, we see that the first one is, generally, the tightest. The third one is tighter than the second, since a row can not be included in the sample twice[2] (thus our sample has more useful information). Finally, we note that weighted sampling without replacement is very difficult to analyze; indeed, it is not even clear that we can perform such sampling and compute the scaling factors efficiently.

Theoretically, the above algorithm necessitates the sampling of a significant number of rows of A in order to achieve reasonable error guarantees. As an example, if we seek to approximate the top 50 right singular vectors, in order to achieve 2% expected relative error with respect to the Frobenius norm, we need to pick at least $5 \cdot 10^5$ rows! The situation is even worse if we seek a probabilistic statement[3] instead of the *expected* error. Thus, an experimental evaluation of the algorithm is imperative; indeed, in practice (see section 4.2), the algorithm achieves small relative errors by sampling only a constant fraction of the rows of A.

3.3   Implementation Details and Running Time

An important property of our algorithm is that it can be easily implemented. Its heart is an SVD computation of an $s \times s$ matrix (SS^T). Any fast algorithm computing the top k right singular vectors of such a matrix could be used to speed up our algorithm (e.g. Lanczos methods). One should be cautious though; since s is usually of $O(k)$, we might end up seeking approximations to almost all singular vectors of SS^T. It is well known that in this scenario full SVD of SS^T is much more efficient than approximation techniques. Indeed, in our experiments, we observed that full SVD of SS^T was faster than Lanczos methods.

The other interesting part of the algorithm is the sampling process. Uniform sampling ($p_1 = \ldots = p_m = 1/m$), with or without replacement, is trivial to implement and can be done in constant time. Sampling with respect to row (or column) lengths is more interesting; we describe a way of implementing it when $p_i = |A_{(i)}|^2/\|A\|_F^2, i = 1 \ldots m$.

---

[2] Observe that if $s = m$, the error in this case is zero, unlike 1 and 2.

[3] We can use martingale arguments to show that $\|A - P\|_{F,2}$ is tightly concentrated around its mean, see [8, 9, 6].

Preprocessing step:

1. **For** $i = 1$ **to** m compute $|A_{(i)}|^2$.
2. Compute $\|A\|_F^2 = \sum_{i=1}^m |A_{(i)}|^2$.
3. Compute $z_i = \sum_{j=1}^i |A_{(j)}|^2, i = 1 \ldots m$.

Sampling step:

1. Pick a real number r, uniformly at random from $(0, \|A\|_F^2]$.
2. Find i such that $z_i < r \le z_{i+1}$ and include row i in the sample.

It is easy to see that $\mathbf{Pr}(\text{pick } i) = |A_{(i)}|^2/\|A\|_F^2$. We can repeat the sampling step s times to form S. The total running time of the preprocessing step is mn and of the sampling steps $s \log m$; we use binary search to implement the latter.

We emphasize that our sampling can be viewed as a two-pass algorithm: it reads the input matrix once to form the z_i's, decides which rows to include in the sample and, in a second pass, extracts these rows. Observe that once S is formed, A can be discarded. Thus, we only need $O(sn)$ RAM space to store S and not $O(mn)$ RAM space to store A.

Theorem 2. *After the preprocessing step, the algorithm runs in $O(n)$ time.*

Proof: The sampling step needs $s \log m$ operations; the scaling of the rows prior to including them in S needs sn operations. Computing SS^T takes $O(s^2n)$ time and computing its SVD $O(s^3)$ time. Finally, we need to compute H, which can be done in $O(nsk)$ operations. Thus, the overall running time (excluding the preprocessing step) is $O(s \log m + s^2n + s^3 + nsk)$. Since s and k are constants, the total running time of the algorithm is $O(n)$. However, the constant hidden in this big-Oh notation is large, since it is proportional to the square of the number of rows that are included in our sample.

$\diamond$

Finally, we note that we could modify the algorithm to pick columns of A instead of rows and compute approximations to the *left* singular vectors. The bounds in Theorem 1 remain essentially the same (rows become columns and m becomes n). P is now equal to RR^TA, where R is an $m \times k$ matrix containing our approximations to the top k *left* singular vectors. The analysis of Theorem 2 holds and the running time of the algorithm is $O(m)$.

4   Experiments

4.1   Setup

We implemented our randomized SVD algorithm using weighted sampling with replacement, uniform sampling with replacement and uniform sampling without replacement. We did not use weighted sampling without replacement, since we have no theoretical bounds for it. These experiments returned approximations to the top k right singular vectors; we also implemented the same experiments sampling columns instead of rows, thus approximating the top k left singular vectors. We ran every experiment 20 times for each image-matrix.

We fixed k for each image so that $\|A - A_k\|_F^2/\|A\|_F^2$ is small ($\leq 1\%$). We varied s (the number of rows or columns that are included in our sample) between k and $k + 160$ (in increments of 8). We ran our experiments on all images of the MatLab ImDemos [21] directory (more than 40 images of different characteristics). We present a variety of results, both with respect to accuracy and running time.

To measure the error of our approximations to the top k right (or left) singular vectors, we compute the rank k approximation P to A using H (or R, see section 3.3) and the relative error of the approximation, namely $\|A - P\|_{F,2}^2/\|A\|_{F,2}^2$. We also compute (for each image) the relative error of the optimal rank k approximation to A, namely $\|A - A_k\|_{F,2}^2/\|A\|_{F,2}^2$.

The speedup is measured as the ratio of the time spent by the deterministic SVD algorithm to compute the right singular vectors (which are used to compute A_k) over the time needed by our randomized SVD algorithm to compute H or R (which is used to compute P). In section 4.3 we compare the running time of our approach with the running time of Lanczos/Arnoldi techniques.

4.2   Accuracy

General Observations Our first goal is to demonstrate the accuracy of our algorithm. In figures 1 through 4 we plot the average loss in accuracy for different values of s (number of rows sampled) over all images. The loss in accuracy for a particular image and a specific s is defined as the relative error of our approximation *minus* the relative error of the optimal rank k approximation, namely

$$\|A - P\|_{F,2}/\|A\|_{F,2}^2 - \|A - A_k\|_{F,2}^2/\|A\|_{F,2}^2 \geq 0$$

We average the above error over all images (for the same value of s) and plot the results. It should be obvious from the plots that as the number of rows included in our sample increases the accuracy increases as well.

The most important observation is that our methods seem to return very reasonable relative error bounds, much better than the ones guaranteed by Theorem 1. The second observation is that uniform sampling without replacement -usually- returns the best results! The reason for this phenomenon is twofold: sampling without replacement guarantees that more rows are included in the sample (while weighted sampling is biased towards including heavier rows, even more than once[4]) *and* the lengths of the rows in our matrices are -more or less- in the same range (see section 3.2). We also observe that uniform sampling with replacement and weighted sampling return almost the same relative error in all

---

[4] This feature of weighted sampling is very useful when dealing with large, sparse matrices (see i.e. [13]).

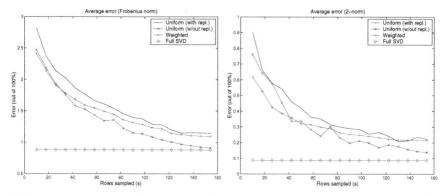

Fig. 1. F-norm error (row sampling)   **Fig. 2.** 2-norm error (row sampling)

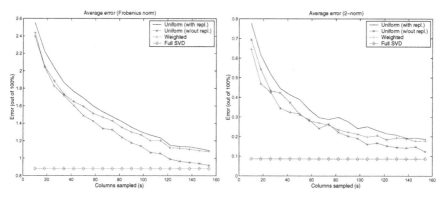

Fig. 3. F-norm error (column sampling)   **Fig. 4.** 2-norm error (column sampling)

cases (the distance between the 2 curves is within the standard deviation of the experiments).

We now examine the speedup of our technique, for various values of s, over full SVD. The speedups (assuming uniform sampling w/out replacement) are: 827, 230, 95, 70, 56, 45, 35, 30, 25, 21, 18, 15, 13, 11, 10, 8, 7, 6, 6, where each value corresponds to a sample of size $s = k+8\cdot i$, $i = 1, \ldots, 19$. The corresponding values for approximating the left singular vectors (column sampling) are: 643, 341, 170, 104, 76, 54, 44, 37, 29, 25, 21, 18, 15, 13, 11, 9, 8, 7, 6 (again using uniform sampling w/out replacement). We should emphasize here that the above comparison is not fair; full SVD returns *all* singular vectors of a matrix, while our technique approximates the top k singular vectors. We present a fair running time comparison in section 4.3; still, we believe that the above numbers illustrate the power of our technique.

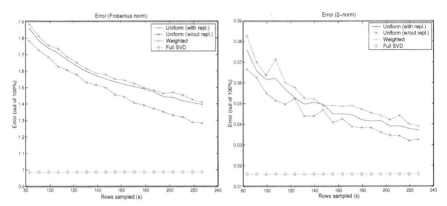

Fig. 5. Baboon (F-norm error, row sampling)

Fig. 6. Baboon (2-norm error, row sampling)

Case-Studies on 2 Images We present results on 2 images: the well-known `baboon` image and a large and more complicated image, the `hand_with_sphere` image[5]. In figures 5 through 8 we plot the error of our approximation with respect to the 2-norm and the Frobenius norm as a function of s. All relative error values are out of 100%. For the `baboon` image we set $k = 73$, thus seeking approximations to the top 73 right singular vectors, while for the `hand_with_sphere` image we set $k = 191$.

Figures 9-12 show the optimal rank k approximation to the image and our randomized rank k approximation to the image. One can easily observe that our approximation is quite accurate, even though most of the original image was discarded while computing the singular vectors!

4.3   Running Time

In this section we compare the running times of our algorithms vs. the running time of the well-known Lanczos/Arnoldi methods. The latter are the dominant techniques used to approximate singular vectors of matrices. There is an extensive literature exploring the power of Lanczos/Arnoldi methods (see e.g. [17]); we give a brief, high-level presentation of Lanczos/Arnoldi methods.

Lanczos/Arnoldi Methods Consider a symmetric $n \times n$ matrix A. The heart of these techniques is the ℓ-dimensional Krylov subspace of A, defined as

$$\mathcal{K}_\ell(x) = \mathbf{span}\left(x, Ax, A^2x, A^3x, \ldots, A^\ell x\right)$$

where x is a -usually random- vector in $\mathcal{R}^n$. Assume that Q is an $n \times \ell$ orthogonal matrix, such that the columns of Q form an orthogonal basis for $\mathcal{K}_\ell(x)$;

---

[5] Hand with Reflecting Sphere image (1935), copyright by M.C. Escher, Cordon Art, Baarn, Netherlands.

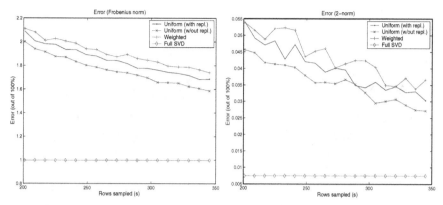

Fig. 7. Hand with sphere (F-norm error, row sampling)

Fig. 8. Hand with sphere (2-norm error, row sampling)

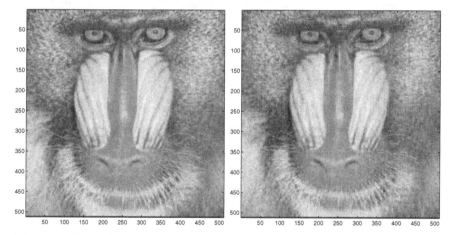

Fig. 9. Baboon (rank 73 approxima-tion, error=0.99%)

Fig. 10. Baboon (uniform sampling w/out repl. 203 rows, error=1.33%)

then, $Q^T A Q$ is an $\ell \times \ell$ matrix whose singular values are "close" to the singular values of A. Similarly, if $\tilde{v}^{(i)}$ is the i-th right singular vector of $Q^T A Q$, then $Q\tilde{v}^{(i)}$ approximates the i-th right singular vector of A. We note that $Q^T A Q$ is an $\ell \times \ell$ matrix, thus its SVD can be computed in $O(\ell^3) = O(1)$ time. As ℓ increases, the accuracy of the approximations increases as well; for theoretical error bounds see [17].

In practice, computing Q after $\mathcal{K}_\ell(x)$ has been formed is very unstable; there are huge losses in accuracy due to numerical errors. Instead, the following incremental, iterative algorithm is employed.

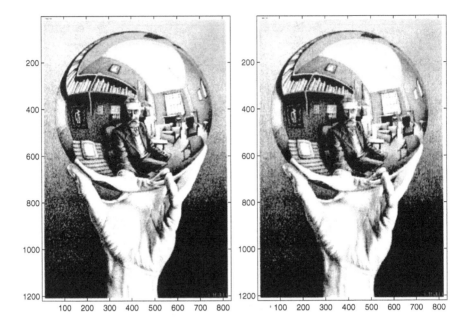

Fig. 11. Hand with sphere (rank 191 approximation, error=1%)

Fig. 12. Hand with sphere (uniform sampling w/out repl. 321 rows, error=1.65%)

Basic Lanczos/Arnoldi

1. Pick $x \in \mathcal{R}^n$ such that $|x|_2 = 1$.
2. Set $q^{(1)} = x$.
3. **For** $i = 1$ **to** ℓ
   - Set $t = A \cdot q^{(i)}$.
   - Orthonormalize t with respect to $q^{(1)}, \ldots, q^{(i-1)}$.
   - Set $q^{(i+1)} = t$.

Now, $q^{(1)}, \ldots, q^{(\ell)}$ form an orthogonal basis for $\mathcal{K}_\ell(x)$; in practice, it is easy to modify the above algorithm to compute $H_\ell = Q_\ell^T A Q_\ell$ as well. There are various modifications of the above algorithm to increase its stability, i.e. a second orthogonalization step might be added etc.

It should be obvious that as ℓ increases, the above procedure becomes very expensive; a remedy was suggested by Sorensen [18]: at some point, *restart* the algorithm with a starting vector x which is "rich" in the subspace spanned by the top k eigenvectors. Since we already have some information on the top k eigenvectors of A (from the iterations done thus far) we can compute such a starting vector; Sorensen described an elegant solution to this problem. Indeed, most Lanczos/Arnoldi codes incorporate restarting to reduce their running time/memory requirements.

Finally, even though the above description was focused on symmetric matrices, one should note that given an arbitrary $m \times n$ matrix B, $A = \begin{bmatrix} \mathbf{0} & B^T \\ B & \mathbf{0} \end{bmatrix}$ is an $(m + n) \times (m + n)$ symmetric matrix.

Comparing Lanczos to Our Technique We remind the reader that, from Theorem 2, the running time of our algorithm using uniform sampling without replacement is $O(n)$. The running time required for *convergence* of Lanczos/Arnoldi techniques to machine precision accuracy is usually $O(n^2k^2)$ for $n \times n$ symmetric matrices (see e.g. [11]). It should be obvious that step 3 of the Lanczos/Arnoldi algorithm described above takes at least $O(n^2)$ time; as more and more vectors are added in $\mathcal{K}_\ell(x)$, the orthogonalization becomes more and more expensive. Implicit restarting can reduce these costs, by guaranteeing that a bounded number of orthogonalizations will be performed; still, in order to create a Krylov subspace of dimension ℓ we need at least $O(\ell n^2)$ time.

By construction, our algorithm seems faster than Lanczos/Arnoldi techniques; for a fair comparison, we are interested in the accuracy vs. running time performance of the two approaches; a theoretical comparison of such performances is difficult. Thus, we resort to an experimental evaluation in the next section.

Finally, we emphasize that our approach works by keeping only a few rows of the original matrix in RAM; in the case of uniform sampling without replacement, one pass through A is all we need. On the other hand, the Lanczos/Arnoldi algorithm requires multiple accesses to A; one could easily see that if A were a large matrix stored in secondary devices the performance penalty would be significant.

Comparing the Accuracy Experimentally We used a widely available implementation of the Lanczos/Arnoldi algorithm, the svds command of MatLab. svds is an interface, calling eigs, which computes the top few eigenvalues/eigenvectors of a matrix. eigs is also an interface, calling routines from ARPACK iteratively to perform the computations.

We ran svds in our image-matrices; we forced an upper bound on the dimension (denoted by ℓ) of the Krylov subspace computed by svds. Indeed, we tried different values for ℓ, starting at $\ell = k$; since we seek to approximate the top k singular vectors, it should be obvious that a Krylov subspace of lesser dimension could not return approximations to the top k singular vectors.

We emphasize that svds does implement restarting to achieve maximum speedup and minimize memory usage. svds also offers timing results, which essentially bypass the inherent inefficiencies of MatLab; e.g. it does not time for loops. Thus, we believe that the running time that we measured for svds

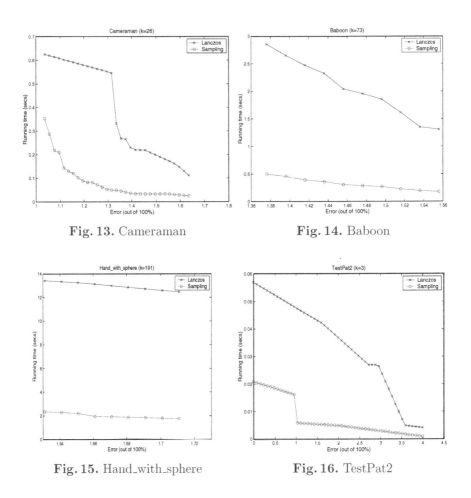

Fig. 13. Cameraman

Fig. 14. Baboon

Fig. 15. Hand_with_sphere

Fig. 16. TestPat2

accurately reflects running time spent in actual computations; we remind that `ARPACK` is built in `C/Fortran`.

Experiments We now present running time vs. accuracy curves on a few images for `svds` and our algorithm. In all cases, our technique was faster, usually significantly so, regardless of the number of vectors (k) that we seek to approximate. In the figures 13–18 we present results on a few images; we chose these images to represent different values of k.

We present two tables for the `baboon` image (a 512×512 image). Table 1 shows how the accuracy of the approximation increases as the dimension (ℓ) of the Krylov subspace increases. We also give an estimate of the number of operations needed to construct $\mathcal{K}_\ell(x)$ ($512^2 \cdot \ell$) as well as the actual running time of `svds` in every instance. We note that this running time includes the orthogonalization steps as well, which are not included in our estimate since restarting makes such

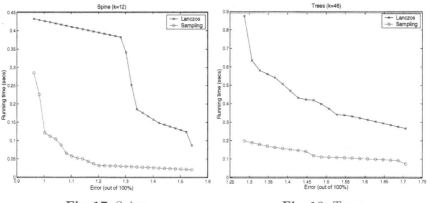

Fig. 17. Spine

Fig. 18. Trees

Table 1. Statistics for *svds* for the *baboon* image

Dimension (ℓ)	Computing $\mathcal{K}_\ell(x)$ ($\times 10^6$)	Running time (in seconds)	Error (out of 100%)
73	19.1365	1.2980	1.5586
77	20.1851	1.3610	1.5299
81	21.2337	1.4580	1.5255
85	22.2822	1.5090	1.5212
89	23.3308	1.5600	1.5198
93	24.3794	1.6350	1.5144
97	25.4280	1.6800	1.5029
101	26.4765	1.7740	1.4990
105	27.5251	1.8520	1.4965
109	28.5737	1.9430	1.4791
113	29.6223	2.0220	1.4570
117	30.6708	2.1260	1.4518
121	31.7194	2.2200	1.4517
125	32.7680	2.3120	1.4381
129	33.8166	2.3940	1.4233
133	34.8652	2.4360	1.4226
137	35.9137	2.5370	1.4036
141	36.9623	2.6300	1.4000
145	38.0109	2.7090	1.3823
149	39.0595	2.8010	1.3764
153	40.1080	2.9040	1.3756

a prediction impossible. In table 2, we present similar results for our approach; namely, how the accuracy increases as a function of s, as well as the number of operations required by our approach to compute the small matrix (see section 3) and its SVD ($512 \cdot s^2 + s^3$). Finally, in figures 19 and 20 we show low rank approximations of the **baboon** and **hand_with_sphere** image, by approximating the top few right singular vectors using Lanczos/Arnoldi techniques.

Table 2. Statistics for uniform sampling w/out replacement for the *baboon* image

Rows (s)	Computing svd$(S \cdot S^T)$ $(\times 10^6)$	Running time (in seconds)	Error (out of 100%)
81	3.8907	0.0640	1.7846
89	4.7605	0.0770	1.7279
97	5.7301	0.1000	1.6844
105	6.8024	0.1270	1.6289
113	7.9806	0.1390	1.6062
121	9.2678	0.1540	1.5785
129	10.6669	0.1970	1.5325
137	12.1811	0.2200	1.5171
145	13.8134	0.2600	1.5020
153	15.5670	0.2970	1.4580
161	17.4448	0.3460	1.4446
169	19.4500	0.4000	1.4076
177	21.5857	0.4690	1.3931
185	23.8548	0.5070	1.3724
193	26.2605	0.5660	1.3538
201	28.8059	0.6040	1.3326
209	31.4940	0.6880	1.3224
217	34.3279	0.8420	1.2864

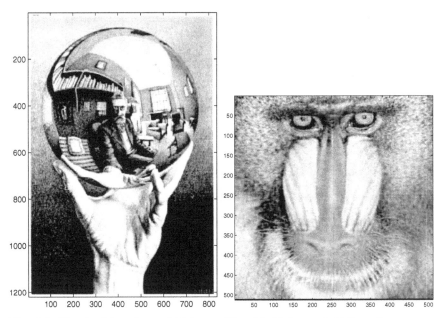

Fig. 19. Hand with sphere. 199 iterations, error =1.67%

Fig. 20. Baboon. 149 iterations, error = 1.38%

5   Open Problems

The most interesting open problem is to combine our sampling technique with Lanczos/Arnoldi methods. It is well-known that the speed of convergence of the Lanczos/Arndoldi algorithm crucially depends on the starting vector (see section 4.3). Our sampling technique could be used to create starting vectors for Lanczos/Arnoldi iterations; more specifically, we could use our randomized SVD algorithm to generate vectors that are rich in the directions of the singular vectors that we seek to approximate. We experimented with the above idea in our test set but we did not achieve significant gains; we were only able to save a few iterations. This essentially means that random starting vectors are actually quite good for our test set. On the other hand, this hybrid scheme might be useful for matrices with poorly separated singular values, where random vectors might be almost orthogonal to the singular vectors that we seek to approximate with high probability.

A second problem is to theoretically analyze and compare the accuracy vs. running time tradeoff of Lanczos/Arnoldi techniques and our algorithm; such analysis seems quite challenging.

Acknowledgments

We wish to thank Ravi Kannan for many helpful discussions. The first author was supported by NSF grant CCR-9820850 and the second author by NSF grants CCR-9983832 and ITR/SY-0121154.

References

[1] http://cluster.cs.yale.edu/. 279
[2] P. Anandan and M. Irani. Factorization with uncertainty. *International Journal on Computer Vision*, 49(2-3):101–116, September 2002. 280
[3] H. C. Andrews and C. L. Patterson. Singular value decomposition image coding. *IEEE Transactions on Communications*, pages 425–432, April 1976. 280
[4] H. C. Andrews and C. L. Patterson. Singular value decompositions and digital image processing. *IEEE Transactions on ASSP*, pages 26–53, February 1976. 280
[5] E. Drinea, P. Drineas, and P. Huggins. A randomized singular value decomposition algorithm for image processing. *Proceedings 8th Panhellenic Conference on Informatics*, 2001. 279
[6] P. Drineas. *Fast Monte-Carlo algorithms for Approximate matrix operations and applications*. PhD thesis, Yale University, 2002. 283, 284
[7] P. Drineas, A. Frieze, R. Kannan, S. Vempala, and V. Vinay. Clustering in large graphs and matrices. *Proceedings 10th SODA Symposium*, pages 291–299, 1999. 279, 281, 282, 283
[8] P. Drineas and R. Kannan. Fast Monte-Carlo algorithm for approximate matrix multiplication. *Proceedings 10th IEEE FOCS Symposium*, pages 452–459, 2001. 284
[9] P. Drineas and R. Kannan. Fast Monte-Carlo algorithms for approximating the product of matrices. under submission, 2002. 284
[10] A. Frieze, R. Kannan, and S. Vempala. Fast Monte-Carlo algorithms for finding low rank approximations. *Proceedings 39th IEEE FOCS Symposium*, pages 370–378, 1998. 279

[11] G. Golub and C. Van Loan. *Matrix Computations*. Johns Hopkins University Press, 1989. 279, 282, 291

[12] T. Huang and P. Narendra. Image restoration by singular value decomposition. *Applied Optics*, 14(9):2213–2216, September 1974. 280

[13] F. Jiang, R. Kannan, M. Littman, and S. Vempala. Efficient singular value decomposition via improved document sampling. Technical Report CS-99-5, Duke University, February 1999. 279, 280, 286

[14] B. Moghaddam and A. Pentland. Probabilistic visual learning for object representation. *IEEE Transactions on Pattern Analysis and Machine Intelligence*, 19(7):696–710, 1997. 280

[15] H. Murase and S. K. Nayar. Visual learning and recognition of 3-d objects from appearance. *International Journal on Computer Vision*, 14(1):5–24, January 1995. 280

[16] M. Murphy. Comparison of transform image coding techniques for compression of tactical imagery. *SPIE*, 309:212–219, 1981. 280

[17] B. Parlett. *The Symmetric Eigenvalue Problem*. Classics in Applied Mathematics. SIAM, 1997. 279, 288, 289

[18] D. Sorensen. Implicit application of polynomial filters in a k-step arnoldi method. *SIAM Journal Matrix Analysis and Applications*, 13:357–375, 1992. 290

[19] M. Turk and A. P. Pentland. Face recognition using eigenfaces. In *Proceedings CVPR'91 Conference*, pages 586–591, 1991. 280

[20] P. Wu, B. S. Manjunath, and H. D. Shin. Dimensionality reduction for image retrieval. In *Proceedings ICIP'00 Conference*, page WP07.03, 2000. 280

[21] www.MathWorks.com. 286

[22] G. Zientara, L. Panych, and F. Jolesz. Dynamic adaptive MRI using multiresolution SVD encoding incorporating optical flow-based predictions. Technical report, National Academy of Sciences Committee on the "Mathematics and Physics of Emerging Dynamic Biomedical Imaging", November 1993. 280

[23] G. Zientara, L. Panych, and F. Jolesz. Dynamically adaptive MRI with encoding by singular value decomposition. *MRM*, 32:268–274, 1994. 280

PROSOPO – A Face Image Synthesis System

Andreas Lanitis

Department of Computer Science and Engineering
Cyprus College, P.O Box 260002, Nicosia, Cyprus
alanitis@cycollege.ac.cy

Abstract. In this paper we address the problem of synthesizing face images displaying predefined facial attributes, such as the shape and color of the overall face, the shape and color of individual facial features and the age of the subject shown in the synthesized image. The face image synthesis method is based on a statistical face model that enables the reversible representation of face images using a small number of parameters. By manipulating the parameters of the face model it is possible to generate different instances of faces. We describe how the mathematical relationship between the model-based representation of faces and facial attributes of interest can be defined and used for transforming a set of facial attributes to model parameters, so that a face image consistent with the description provided can be synthesized. Our methodology can be applied to the problem of generating facial images of suspects based on witness's descriptions.

1 Introduction

In numerous occasions police authorities utilize handcrafted facial drawings, in an attempt to locate suspects. During the process of generating such drawings, eyewitnesses provide a description of the facial appearance of suspects and artists produce facial drawings consistent with the description provided. The facial description provided by eyewitnesses contains information about various facial characteristics, such as gender, age , hairstyles, ethnic origin of the suspect, the overall shape of the face, the shape of individual facial features, the color of the skin and the presence of mustaches, beards, scars and spectacles. The procedure of generating a facial drawing based on witness's descriptions requires a considerable amount of effort and effective co-operation between artists and eyewitnesses.

In this paper, we describe an attempt for automating the process of generating a face image, based on a text-based description provided by eyewitnesses. The basis of our approach is a statistical model of facial appearance, which is generated using a set of training face images. The model can be used for compact and reversible representation of face images using a small number of model parameters. We demonstrate how the model parameters in the low dimensional space can be adjusted, in an attempt to generate face images consistent with a given description defined interactively by the user of the system. In this pilot

Y. Manolopoulos et al. (Eds.): PCI 2001, LNCS 2563, pp. 297–315, 2003.

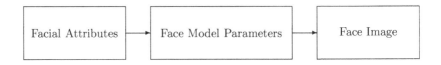

Fig. 1. Block diagram of the proposed methodology

study we mainly focus on facial attributes which can be quantified and take values within some limits - a brief description of the way we deal with other types of facial attributes is also included.

In order to enable the reconstruction of face images based on a quantified description of certain facial attributes, we establish transformation functions that can be used for mapping facial attributes to the model-based parametric description of face images. Once the values of certain facial attributes are defined, we transform them to the corresponding model parameters, which can subsequently be used for generating a face image displaying the attributes defined earlier. This process is illustrated in the block diagram in Figure 1. Our approach has many advantages over the traditional ways in which images of suspects are generated. A discussion of the applicability of our methodology in real applications and a comparison with existing systems are presented in Section 2 and Section 6.

In the remainder of the paper we present a brief literature review and we then outline our previous work on building a statistical face model. The methods for determining the transformation functions, required for transforming a quantified facial attribute to a set of face model parameters, are presented in Section 4. In Section 5 we describe our pilot face image generation system. Conclusions related to our work and our plans for future work in this area are described in Section 6.

2   Literature Review

Our work is influenced by work in the area of automatic face interpretation - an area that attracted a large number of researchers in recent years [5, 15, 20]. Researchers working in the area aim to produce a low-bit representation of face images, which can be used as the feature vector in automatic face interpretation systems. One of the most widely used face coding scheme is based on face models generated by applying Principal Component Analysis (PCA) [22] on an ensemble of faces. In this context Kirby and Sirovich [16] first proposed the decomposition of the intensities of face images into a weighted sum of basis images (or eigenfaces) using a Karhumen-Loeve expansion. Based on this methodology Turk and Pentland [23] describe an automatic face identification system that uses the weights of the basis face images as the feature vector during the classification procedure. As an extension to this technique Craw et al [8] suggest that before the PCA decomposition is applied the shape of faces should be normalized so that eigenfaces capture only variation in the intensities of face images. A complete representation of face images can be obtained by applying PCA based decomposition on shape and texture facial information independently [17, 24]. In this context the shape and intensity of a face are coded in terms of the parameters of a shape model and an intensity model respectively. As an extension to this technique Edwards et al [9] describe how a shape model and an intensity model can be combined in order to produce a combined shape-intensity face model capable of modeling effectively both shape and intensity variation - the model used in our work is based on the work reported by Edwards et al [9]. Models based on principal component decomposition have two major disadvantages:

- Since they are based on a linear formulation, they are not cabable of modeling non-linear variation in the data thus they are not suitable for modeling extreme changes in the orientation of faces in images.
- The model-based representation of face images obtained, is sensitive to facial occlusion.

Several improvements to the basic method have been proposed in order to deal with the issues raised above. New proposed methods include the use of 3D models [21] in order to deal effectively with changes in viewpoint and the use of a bank of local models instead of using a single model. In this context local models can be generated based on the partition of the eigenface space into several local clusters [4], the partition of the training set to local sets displaying limited range of viewpoints [7], the geometric partition of the facial region into smaller areas [19] and the formation of clusters of pixels within the facial area based on the pixel intensities [1].

Once a face model is build, the exploitation of the coded representation of faces allows the isolation of various sources of variation in face images, such as inter-individual appearance variation [2], variation due to changes in expression [17], 3D orientation and lighting [11], resulting in robust face interpretation systems.

In our work we address the reverse problem, i.e. we aim to define the relationship between certain facial attributes and the low dimensional representation of face images, so that we will be able to generate faces with predefined facial attributes. Our work bears similarities with the work reported by Blanz and Vetter [3]. They use a training algorithm for learning the relationship between certain facial features and the shape and texture of a 3D face model. Once they do so it is possible to deform the shape and the texture of the 3D model so that generated faces display certain attributes. The use of a 3D model is restrictive, in terms of computational complexity and in the terms of flexibility of the system. The system proposed by Blanz and Vetter was not intended to be used for generating face images based on witness's descriptions.

Commercial systems [13, 14] used for generating face images of suspects based on descriptions provided by witnesses, rely on the composition of faces by merging individual facial features, chosen from databases containing samples of all

features (i.e samples of eyes, mouths, noses etc). Users of such systems interactively select and replace individual facial features on generated images until
they obtain the closest match between a suspect's face and the generated face
image. Since individual facial features are fixed independently it is possible to
generate faces with illegal combinations of facial features. Also correlations in
the appearance of facial characteristics are not utilized for predicting the appearance of facial features which could not be defined by witnesses. We believe
that it is beneficial to generate facial images by treating a face as a single entity,
rather than building a face by selecting individual facial features.

In our work the generation of faces is done through a statistical face model,
which ensures that all generated images show faces consistent with the training
set, thus less probable combinations of facial features are avoided. Also our approach deals effectively with facial attributes that cause global modifications to
all facial features (i.e changing the perceived age of faces in synthesized images).

3   Generating a Face Model

The basis of our approach is a statistical face model similar to the one described
by Edwards et al [9, 10]. Statistical models [6] are generated from a set of training
examples. We perform Principal Component Analysis (PCA) on the deviations
of each example from the mean example. As a result of the analysis training
examples can be reconstructed/ parametrized using:

$$\mathbf{X} = \overline{\mathbf{X}} + \mathbf{Pb} \tag{1}$$

where $\mathbf{X}$ is a vector describing the shape or color intensity pattern of a face
image, $\overline{\mathbf{X}}$ is the mean example, $\mathbf{P}$ is the matrix of eigenvectors and $\mathbf{b}$ is a vector
of weights, or model parameters. In the case of modeling shape variation $\mathbf{X}$
contains the x and y coordinates of a number of landmarks located on all training
samples (see Figure 2). When dealing with color variation $\mathbf{X}$ contains the red,
green and blue intensities of all pixels within the shape normalized facial region -
i.e prior to the collection of the color information, faces are warped to the mean
shape, as defined form the training set.

Edwards et al [9] describe in detail how this type of model can be used for
modeling combined shape and color variation [10] in face images. In this case
a shape model and a color model are trained independently and each training
example is coded in terms of a set of shape and a set of color parameters. For
each sample the shape and the weighted color parameters are concatenated in
a single vector and based on the resulting representation of training examples,
a new combined shape and color model is generated. In order to ensure that the
resulting combined model deals effectively both with shape and color variation,
we weight the color parameters so that the total variation in color and shape
parameters is equal. Models based on this methodology can be used as the basis
for coding the overall facial appearance to a small number of model parameters
(the $\mathbf{b}$ vector) and for reconstructing faces from a set of model parameters.
During the reconstruction process a set of model parameters is transformed to

a vector containing the corresponding set of shape parameters and the set of weighted color parameters. These parameters are used in conjunction with the shape and color model respectively in order to construct the shape and the color pattern of the face to be synthesized. The final image is generated by warping the synthesized color patch to the shape defined by the shape parameters.

Based on the methodology outlined above we have trained a statistical color face model, using the training images from a face database of 500 images. The database contains images showing approximately 40 individuals at different ages and different viewing conditions. Based on the resulting model, 22 model parameters are required for explaining 95% of the total variance within our training set i.e. face images similar to the ones in the training set can be coded/reconstructed based on 22 model parameters. It should be noted that the process of generating a face model implies that a set of landmark points are already located on all training images. For our model we used 50 landmarks - the positions of those landmarks are shown in Figure 2.

Since the relationship between model parameters and the training examples is linear, such models are not suitable in the cases that we wish to model extreme variations in the 3D orientation of faces. However, models based on this methodology deal effectively with minor modifications in the 3D pose (approximately +/-15 degrees rotation in any axis) since in those cases the anticipated variation in facial appearance is approximated adequately by linear functions. In our work the 3D orientation of the generated facial drawings is strictly limited (usually frontal images are generated in this application) hence a linear model is suitable for our proposed framework.

Model parameters account for many types of appearance variation in face images, as shown in Figure 3. For example they account for changes in skin color/lighting (1st parameter), 3D pose (2nd and 3rd parameters) and changes in expression (fourth and fifth parameter). In order to produce the animations shown in Figure 3, we vary one element of the vector **b** and at each step we use

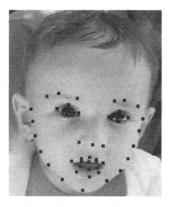

Fig. 2. The location of the landmarks used for training the face model

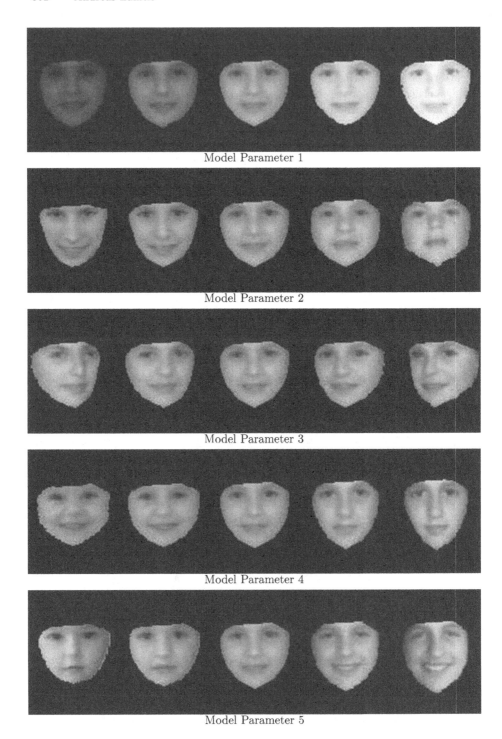

Model Parameter 1

Model Parameter 2

Model Parameter 3

Model Parameter 4

Model Parameter 5

Fig. 3. The main modes of variation within the training set. Each row shows the variation explained by the corresponding model parameter

Equation 1 to calculate the shape and intensity pattern of the corresponding face image, so that the actual image can be reconstructed.

4 Isolating Sources of Variation

Model parameters explain the most distinct types of facial appearance variation in the training set, such as changes in expression, rotation and inter-individual facial variation. These types of variation are not necessarily associated with the facial attributes used for describing the appearance of a human face. Our work aims to establish functions defining the mathematical relationships between the model-based parametric representation of face images and facial attributes which are usefull for describing the facial appearance of any individual. We are primarily interested in facial attributes which are provided by eyewitnesses during the process of generating facial drawings of suspects. Once the appropriate transformation functions are formulated it is possible to transform the information provided by eyewitnesses to model parameters and subsequently reconstruct the corresponding face image. The process of generating such transformation functions is presented in this section. In particular we describe how a mapping function relating model parameters and a certain facial attribute is defined and present how the functions in question can be used for deforming existing face images. Finally we present an extension of our method, which can be used to model cross-population appearance variation in facial attributes using a bank of transformation functions.

4.1 Defining the Transformation Functions

Given a set of training images we aim to model the relationship between model parameters and a specific facial attribute. This can be achieved by using a function of the form:

$$q = \mathbf{f}(\mathbf{b}) \tag{2}$$

where q is a scalar containing the numerical value of a quantified facial attribute, $\mathbf{b}$ is a vector containing 22 raw model parameters and $\mathbf{f}$ is the mapping function. The mapping function defines the relationship between the facial characteristic in question and the parametric description of the corresponding face images. In our experiments we have adopted a quadratic formulation for the mapping function of the form:

$$q = c + \mathbf{w_1}\mathbf{b} + \mathbf{w_2}\mathbf{b^2} \tag{3}$$

where $\mathbf{b}$ and $\mathbf{b^2}$ are vectors containing the raw model parameters and the squares of the raw model parameters respectively, $\mathbf{w_1}$ and $\mathbf{w_2}$ are vectors containing weights for each element of $\mathbf{b}$ and $\mathbf{b^2}$ respectively and c is the offset required.

We calculate the weights ($\mathbf{w_1}$, and $\mathbf{w_2}$) and offset (c), using an optimization method, where we seek to minimize the difference between the actual values of the quantified facial attribute (q) among all face images in the training set, and the q estimated using Equation 3. For the experiments described in this paper our experiments, genetic algorithms [12] were used for calculating the optimum values for the weights and offset. It is possible to use other optimization algorithms for this task; currently we are in the process of assessing the performance of different optimization algorithms for this application.

Once the required mapping function is established we use Equation 3 for converting a set of raw model parameters to the estimated value of a facial attribute, displayed in the corresponding face image. However, for our application we are primarily interested in solving Equation 3 with respect to **b** (see Equation 4) in order to be able to derive a vector of model parameters **b** for a given value of the facial attribute in question.

$$\mathbf{b} = \mathbf{f}^{-1}(q) \tag{4}$$

Instead of solving Equation 4 with respect to the vector **b** directly, we adopted a simulation approach, where we generate a large number of plausible combinations of the elements of **b**. For each combination we estimate q using Equation 3. As a result we generate a number of **b** vectors corresponding to each value of the facial attribute q among the range of values we are interested in. By averaging the elements of all **b** vectors corresponding to a certain value of the facial attribute we generate a look up table showing the most typical set of **b** parameters for each q within the range of values of interest.

4.2 Examples of Transformation Functions

In this section we present some examples in order to demonstrate the applicability of our approach in generating transformation functions, suitable for mapping a quantified facial attribute to a corresponding face image. The examples presented deal both with facial attributes mainly associated with the geometric structure of a face and attributes primarily associated with changes in texture. In most cases the calculation of the actual values of quantified facial attributes of training images is done by making use of the landmarks already located on all training images (see Figure 2. Examples of some features and the quantification methods used are as follows:

Aspect Ratio: The aspect ratio of a face image is defined as the height of the face over the width of the face. The aspect ratio for all images in the training set was calculated and used for training a transformation function which can be used for defining a set of model parameters for a given value of the aspect ratio.

Age: The age of each subject shown in our images, was quoted during the collection of the images. Based on the age of the subjects and the corresponding model parameters, we establish a function which allows the derivation of a set of **b** parameters corresponding to a face at a certain age. Since the ages of the subjects in the training set ranges from 0 to 35 years old, the corresponding transformation function is suitable only for this age range.

Distance between the Eyes: We have defined a transformation function which can be used for generating face images with a pre-specified distance between the eyes. For our experiments the distance between the eyes was calculated as the distance between the two eyes, over the width of the face at the height of the eyes.

Blinking/Shape of the Eyes: By considering the height of the eyes in the training set, it is possible to quantify the the action of blinking and/or the shape of the eyes.

Shape of the Nose: The shape of the nose is quantified by considering the aspect ratio of the three points located on the nose (see Figure 2).

Color of Eyebrows: The color of the eyebrows is quantified by sampling the training images at the six points located on the eyebrows (see Figure 2).

Width of the Mouth: The width of the mouth is quantified by considering the width of the mouth normalized by the width of the face.

Examples of face images, generated by manipulating the numeric values of the aspect ratio, age, distance between the eyes, blinking, shape of the nose, eyebrow color and width of the mouth are shown in Figure 4. The illustrations shown in Figure 4 demonstrate that the transformation functions can be used for primarily altering certain facial attributes. Since the appearance of various facial attributes is correlated, in most cases a change in a single attribute causes a change in other facial attributes in a way consistent with the training set. For example when we modify the "blinking" parameter the shape of the mouth is also modified, since in many cases when we blink we also tend to adopt a facial gesture that affects the shape of the mouth. Another obvious example is the significant change in the skin color during the manipulation of the parameter controlling the color of the eyebrows; usually subjects with dark skin tend to have dark colored eyebrows - an observation learned by the corresponding transformation function.

The global modification of a face, when a single attribute is modified is an advantage of the system since it ensures that only faces constistent with the normal facial appearance are generated.

4.3   Generating Multiple Transformation Functions for a Certain Attribute

In Section 4.1 we presented how the relationship between a quantified facial attribute and model parameters can be defined. In effect the process of generating such transformation functions is the process of defining a trajectory in the multi-dimensional face space, that best explains facial appearance variation caused by a modification of the facial attribute in question.

However, due to the uniqueness of the facial appearance and behavior of different individuals, it is possible that a change in a facial attribute may cause different types of variation to different individuals. For example different individuals may smile in a different way hence it is not possible to model the smiling action in faces using a single function. Another obvious example is the process of

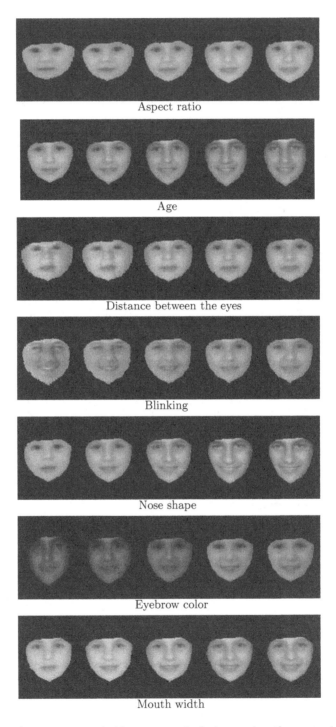

Aspect ratio

Age

Distance between the eyes

Blinking

Nose shape

Eyebrow color

Mouth width

Fig. 4. Face images, generated by progressively increasing the numeric values of different facial attributes

aging, where different individuals may undergo aging deformations of facial appearance which may vary both in the type of aging deformation and the rate of aging [18]. In order to face this problem we adopted a training procedure where we iteratively establish transformation functions based on the training data until all training examples are modelled adequately by a bank of transformation functions. The training algorithm is as follows:

  I Use the training set for training a transformation function using the method described in Section 4.1

 II For each training example calculate the error between the actual and estimated attribute value. All examples for which the error is smaller than a threshold are eliminated from the training set.

III Go back to step I. The procedure terminates until most (usually 95%) of the training examples are explained properly by the transformation functions.

As far as the error threshold used in step II, is within reasonable limits, the method is not sensitive to the exact value. For our experiments the error threshold was set to 5% of the total variation of the quantified facial attribute in question.

Examples of multiple transformation functions for the age, shape of the nose and width of the mouth are shown in Figure 5. Multiple transformation functions modify the appearance of the corresponding features in different ways. For example the first age transformation function (first row of Figure 5 imposes a male-type aging variation where as a more female-type aging deformation is explained by the second age transformation function (second row of Figure 5). Typically about five to ten transformation functions are required to fully explain the training data.

4.4   Modifying Facial Attributes on Existing Images

The method described in the previous sections allows the generation of a new face image displaying a pre-specified facial attribute. Modification of facial attributes of existing face images can be achieved by modifying the model-based representation of the face using Equation 5.

$$\mathbf{b_{new}} = \mathbf{b_{now}} + [\mathbf{f}^{-1}(q_{new}) - \mathbf{f}^{-1}(q_{now})] \tag{5}$$

where $\mathbf{b_{now}}$ are the face model parameters for the existing face image, q_{now} is the estimated value of the attribute in the existing face image (calculated using Equation 2), q_{new} is the new value of the attribute, specified by the user of the system, $\mathbf{b_{new}}$ is the vector containing the estimated face parameters for the new attribute and $\mathbf{f}$ is the transformation function for the attribute in question.

In effect Equation 5 modifies the current set of model parameters of an existing face, in order to accommodate a change in a certain facial attribute. The new set of model parameters ($\mathbf{b_{new}}$) and Equation 1 can be used for synthesizing a face with a pre-specified attribute. Examples of using this method for changing various facial attributes on existing face images are shown in Figure 6.

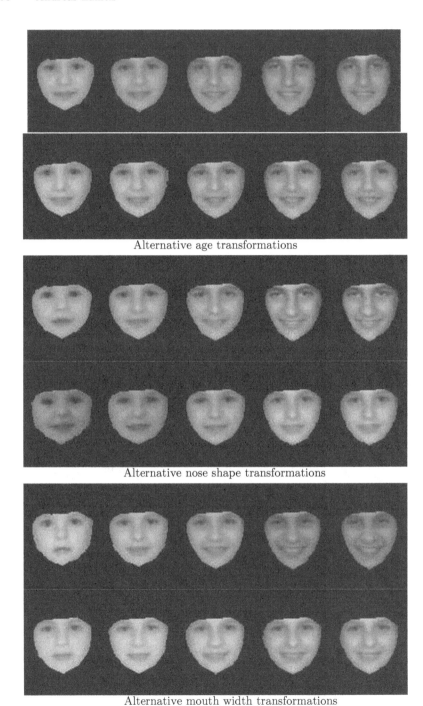

Alternative age transformations

Alternative nose shape transformations

Alternative mouth width transformations

Fig. 5. Examples of multiple transformation functions for different facial attributes

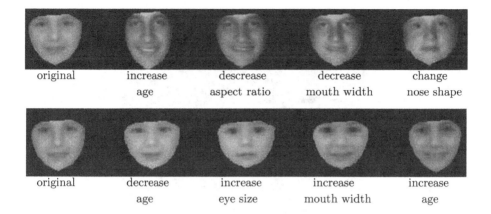

| original | increase age | descrease aspect ratio | decrease mouth width | change nose shape |
| original | decrease age | increase eye size | increase mouth width | increase age |

Fig. 6. Modifying facial attributes on existing images

In the case of using multiple transformation functions for a specific facial attribute, it is possible to generate several variations of an existing image, depending on the choice of transformation function among the bank of transformation functions for each attribute. The user of the system is probed with deformations of the existing image based on different transformation functions for the attribute in question and the most appropriate deformation can be chosen.

5   A System for Generating Face Images

In this section we describe the features of our pilot system for generating face images based on descriptions provided by eyewitnesses.

5.1   Generating Face Images

The methodology described in the previous section was used as the basis for building the experimental face image generation system, where face images are generated by iteratively modifying various facial attributes including the aspect ratio, age, distance between the eyes, blinking, shape of the nose, eyebrow color and width of the mouth. In addition we implemented alternative methods for dealing with other facial attributes for which the method proposed in Section 4 is not applicable. In summary those attributes include:

Size of the Face: Standard Computer graphics techniques were used for scaling the face image.

Applying Random Modifications: The system allows the user to apply random modifications to a face image. This is accomplished by modifying the face

Fig. 7. Examples of random deformations of an existing face image. The initial image is shown in the center of the figure

model parameters randomly, withing a predefined range, in order to impose random modifications on the current image. If we keep the range of possible modifications of model parameters within certain limits (about one standard deviation from the current values), randomly generated face images display minor modifications of the existing image. This feature can be usefull for probing the user of system for the possible close alternatives to a suspect's appearance. Examples of randomly generated face images are shown in Figure 7.

Lighting, 3D Orientation and Expression: The 3D orientation and expression of a face in an image are modeled directly in the face model (see Figure 3) thus there is no need to establish transformation functions for this type of facial appearance variation. By manipulating the corresponding entries in the model parameter vector we inflict modifications in 3D orientation and expression of the generated face images in order to simulate the exact conditions under which the face of the suspect was observed. Examples of varying the 3D orientation on a synthesized image are shown in Figure 8.

Gender: Face images from the training set are used for calculating the mean model parameters corresponding to the male and female subjects within our training set. In that way the user of the system may initiate the process of

Fig. 8. Manipulation of the 3D pose of an existing face image

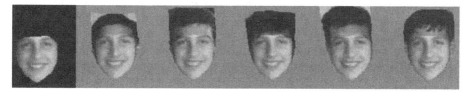

Fig. 9. Overlaying hairstyles on a synthesized image

generating a face image of a suspect, by starting with the most typical face image of a male or a female suspect accordingly.

Hairstyles: Although it is possible to generate a face model that includes the hairline, we avoided to do so, since the increased variability in the shape and texture of hairstyles dominates the principal modes of variation of the model. As a result the ability of the model to model subtle, but important for our application, sources of variability decreases. Also due to the increased and highly non-linear variability in hairlines, the model will not be specific enough, resulting in increased possibility of tolerating illegal faces. In order to overcome this problem we use standard computer graphics techniques for overlaying hairstyles on synthesized images. The hairstyles used were segmented from our training examples, and present a large variety of possible hairstyles. A similar technique is employed for adding mustaches and spectacles to the synthesized images. Examples of hairstyles overlaid on facial images are shown in Figure 9.

5.2   Additional Functionality of the Face Generation System

Apart from the face image generation engine, our experimental system includes an embedded on-line face recognition system and the ability to generate facial animations of subjects. A brief description of those features follows:

On-line Face Recognition: The model-based representation of the facial appearance (**b** vector) is also used as a feature vector in an on-line face recognition system, linked with the proposed face synthesis system. In this context the vector of model parameters used for generating a face (at any instance during the process of generating the facial appearance of a suspect) is compared with the vector of model parameters corresponding to each subject from our database. In this context the most similar database entries are defined as the ones for which the Mahalanopis distance [22] between the two vectors is minimized. Based on this methodology each time a face image is generated the most similar database entries are also indexed. The details concerning the implementation of a face recognition system based on this methodology have been reported elsewhere [17]. In real applications the face generation system will be connected to a database containing all individuals with criminal record, so that during the process of generating the face image of a subject, witnesses will also be shown images of criminals who look most similar to the current appearance of the face image that is being synthesized. This feature can prove usefull both for determining the identity of a suspect and for prompting witnesses with possible close alternatives to a suspect's appearance.

Generating Facial Animations of Suspects: Once the facial appearance of a face is generated, it is possible to vary the expression and 3D orientation parameters in order to generate animations of the suspect's face. Such animations can offer better visual stimuli for identifying the suspect.

5.3   Using the Face Generation System

The face generation system is intended to be used by the witnesses directly so that misunderstandings between witnesses and artists are minimized. Typically the procedure for generating an image showing a suspect includes the following steps:

  I The user specifies the gender of the suspect, so that the most typical male or female faces are generated.
 II The user specifies the age of the suspect so that typical face images showing faces at the specified age are generated.
III The user specifies which facial attribute to change. Once a facial attribute is defined, the user is probed with new images on which the facial attribute in question was modified.
IV In the case that the user is not sure how to proceed to get a closer match between the generated face and the suspect's face, it is possible to use the option for generating random modifications of the existing face.
 V The user adds hairstyles selected from the database of hairstyles.

The process mentioned above, is iterative - at each step the user can either go back to undo changes or follow a different order of the steps.

6   Conclusions

We have presented a preliminary investigation into the design of a face generation system based on the transformation of quantified descriptions of facial attributes to a low dimensional parametric face representation, so that a face image consistent with a set of pre-specified attributes is synthesized. Our methodology can form the basis of face image generation systems that can be used by the Police Authorities for generating face images of suspects based on witnesses' descriptions. A system based on the proposed methodology could provide numerous advantages when compared with existing computer-based systems or the traditional ways of drawing facial images of subjects. In summary those advantages are:

- Eyewitnesses are given the opportunity to generate the required face image themselves, rather than providing a description. Inaccuracies due to misunderstandings between eyewitnesses and artists will be eliminated.
- Computer generated drawings can be more realistic than hand-drawn facial drawings.
- The use of a statistical face model for generating images ensures that the resulting images are consistent with the rules describing the normal appearance of a face. In this way inconsistencies in the description of eyewitnesses do not result roach deals effectively with the issue of uniqueness in facial appearance - i.e the fact that different individuals undergo different types of variations when a particular facial attribute is modified.
- Face images are generated in real time, enabling the generation of a large number of trial images, until the best match is found.
- Face images generated, are fed directly to automatic face recognition systems, used for indexing all subjects from a database whose face image is similar to the face shown in the generated image.
- Once a suspect's face is generated, it is possible to view different instances of the same face (i.e. simulate changes in viewing angle, expression, lighting conditions etc) so that the real conditions under which the face is observed can be simulated. As an extension to this feature, a sequence showing facial movements of the suspect's face can be generated.
- Most commercial face synthesis systems currently available, can only be used for generating gray level images. In our work we generate color images - according to conversations with eyewitnesses and artists responsible for drawing facial images, color information can be important for describing the facial appearance of a suspect. Also once a facial drawing is generated its more likely to identify the suspect if color information is included.
- The methodology presented can be used in other related face processing applications. For example a similar approach has been used for designing an automatic age progression system [18].

We plan to build on our early work in this area in order to design a system, which can be used in real applications. The main issues to be addressed in our future work include the following:

Use an Improved Face Model: The model used in our initial investigation was trained using only 500 images. Such a model is not general enough to cope with all possible modifications in facial appearance. There is need to train the model on a large number of images, including face images of subjects of different ethnic origin, so that the model will be able to cope with all possible sources of variability.

Training a Model with Hairstyles: Currently we add hairstyles to synthesized images by selecting a hairstyles from a database. This procedure is not ideal, since the possible correlation in the appearance of the internal face and hairstyles, is not exploited. We are in the process of investigating ways in which hairstyle information can be embedded in our face model, so that the overall facial appearance can be generated by manipulating the model parameters.

Assessing the System in Real Applications: Currently we work in close cooperation with officials from the Police Authorities, in an attempt to improve the functionality and interaction of our system. In particular we are in the process of assessing the system and identifying areas that need improvement.

Acknowledgements

Our research was carried out as part of the projects PROFONA (Project 33/1997) and PROSOPO (Project 26/2001) funded by the Research Promotion Foundation of the Republic of Cyprus. We gratefully acknowledge the help and co-operation provided by the Cyprus Police Authorities and especially Sergeant S. Pericleous.

References

[1] S. Avidan: "EigenSegments: a Spatio-Temoral Decomposition of an Ensemble of Images", *Proceedings 7th European Conference on Computer Vision*, Springer LNCS Vol2352, pp.747-758, 2002. 299

[2] P. N. Belhumeur, J. P. Hespanha and D. J. Kriegman: "Eigenfaces vs. Fisherfaces: Recognition Using Class Specific Linear Projection", *IEEE Transactions of Pattern Analysis and Machine Intelligence*, Vol.19, No.7, pp.711-720, 1997. 299

[3] V. Blanz and T. Vetter: "A Morphable Model for the Synthesis of 3D Faces", *Proceedings Computer Graphics*, pp.187-194, 1999. 299

[4] R. Cappelli, D. Maio and D. Maltoni: "Multi-Space KL for Pattern Representation and Classification", *IEEE Transactions of Pattern Analysis and Machine Intelligence*, Vol.23, No.9, pp.977-996, 2001. 299

[5] R. Chellapa, C. L. Wilson and S. Sirohey: "Human and Machine Recognition of Faces: a Survey", *Proceedings of the IEEE*, Vol.83, No.5, 1995. 298

[6] T. F. Cootes, C. J. Taylor, D. H. Cooper and J. Graham: "Active Shape Models - their Training and Application", *Computer Vision Graphics and Image Understanding*, Vl.61, No.1, pp.38-59, 1995. 300

[7] T. F. Cootes, G. V. Wheeler, K. N. Walker and C. J. Taylor: "View Based Appearance Models", *Image and Vision Computing*, Vol.20, No.9, pp.658-664, 2002. 299

[8] I. Craw and P. Cameron: "Face Recognition by Computer", *Proceedings 1992 British Machine Vision Conference*, pp.489-507, Springer, 1992. 298

[9] G. J. Edwards, A. Lanitis, C. J. Taylor and T. F.Cootes: "Statistical Face Models: Improving Specificity", *Image and Vision Computing*, Vol.16, No.3, pp.203-211, 1998. 299, 300

[10] G. J. Edwards, T. F.Cootes C. J. Taylor: "Advances in Active Appearance Models", *Proceedings 7th International Conference on Computer Vision*, Vol.1, pp.137-141, 1999. 300

[11] A.S Georgiades, P. N. Belhumeur and D. J. Kriegman: "From Few to Many: Generative Models for Recognition Under Variable Pose and Illumination", *Proceedings 4th International Conference on Face and Gesture Recognition*, pp.277-284, 2000. 299

[12] D. E. Goldberg: "*Genetic Algorithms in Search Optimization and Machine Learning*", Addison Wesley, 1989. 304

[13] http://www.iwsinc.com/crimes/suspectid.html, 2002. 299

[14] http://www.efitforwindows.com, 2002. 299

[15] IEEE Transactions of Pattern Analysis and Machine Intelligence. Special issue on Face and Gesture Recognition, Vol.19, No.7, 1997. 298

[16] M. Kirby and L. Sirovich: "Application of the Karhumen-Loeve Procedure for the Characterization of Human Faces", *IEEE Transactions on Pattern Analysis and Machine Intelligence*, Vol.12, No.1, pp.103-108, 1990. 298

[17] A. Lanitis, C. J. Taylor and T. F. Cootes: "Automatic Identification and Coding of Human Faces Using Flexible Models", *IEEE Transactions of Pattern Analysis and Machine Intelligence*, Vol.19, No.7, pp.743-756, 1997. 299, 312

[18] A. Lanitis, C. J. Taylor and T. F. Cootes: "Toward Automatic Simulation of Aging Effects on Face Images", *IEEE Transactions of Pattern Analysis and Machine Intelligence*, Vol.22, No.4, pp.442-455, 2002. 307, 313

[19] A. M. Martinez: "Recognizing Imprecisely Localized, Partially Occluded, and Expression Variant Faces from a Single Sample per Class", *IEEE Transactions of Pattern Analysis and Machine Intelligence*, Vol.24, No.6, pp.748-763, 2002. 299

[20] Proceedings 1st , 2nd, 3rd and 4th International Conference on Face and Gesture Recognition, 1995, 1996, 1998, 2000. 298

[21] S. Romdhani, V. Blanz and T. Vetter: "Face Identification by Fitting a 3D Morphable Model Using Linear Shape and Texture Error Functions", *Proceedings 7th European Conference on Computer Vision*, Springer LNCS Vol.2353, pp.3-19, 2002. 299

[22] B. G. Tabachnick and L. S. Fidell: "*Using Multivariate Statistics*", Harper Collins Press, 1996. 298, 312

[23] M. Turk and A. Pentland: "Eigenfaces for Recognition", *Journal of Cognitive Neuroscience*, Vol.3, No.1, pp.71-86, 1991. 298

[24] T. Vetter and T. Poggio: "Linear Object Classes and Image Synthesis from a Single Example Image", *IEEE Transactions of Pattern Analysis and Machine Intelligence*, Vol.19, No.7, pp.733-742, 1997. 299

Communicating X-Machines:
From Theory to Practice

Petros Kefalas, George Eleftherakis, and Evangelos Kehris

Computer Science Department
City Liberal Studies
Affiliated College of the University of Sheffield
13 Tsimiski Str., 54624 Thessaloniki, Greece
{eleftherakis,kefalas,kehris}@city.academic.gr

Abstract. Formal modeling of complex systems is a non-trivial task, especially if a formal method does not facilitate separate development of the components of a system. This paper describes a methodology of building communicating X-machines from existing stand-alone X-machine models and presents the theory that drives this methodology. An X-machine is a formal method that resembles a finite state machine but can model non-trivial data structures. This is accomplished by incorporating a typed memory tuple into the model as well as transitions labeled with functions that operate on inputs and memory values. A set of X-machines can exchange messages with each other, thus building a communicating system model. However, existing communicating X-machines theories imply that the components of a communicating system should be built from scratch. We suggest that modeling of complex systems can be split into two separate and distinct activities: (a) the modeling of standalone X-machine components and (b) the description of the communication between these components. This approach is based on a different view of the theory of communicating X-machines and it leads towards disciplined, practical, and modular development. The proposed methodology is accompanied by an example, which demonstrates the use of communicating X-machines towards the modeling of large-scale systems.

1 Introduction

Formal modeling of complex systems can be a non-trivial task if the formal method used does not provide the appropriate means of abstraction or does not facilitate gradual development of the system model. In addition, as the complexity of the system increases, it eventually becomes clear that it is necessary to break down the system model into several components that need to communicate with each other. There are mainly two ways to accomplish this: either (a) to built a communicating system from scratch in which models and communication between them will be inseparable, or (b) to model (or even to use off-the-shelf) separate components and then establish the communication between them. We believe that the latter is a more disciplined approach since modeling of components and modeling of communication are viewed as two distinct activities.

Y. Manolopoulos et al. (Eds.): PCI 2001, LNCS 2563, pp. 316–335, 2003.

1.1   Motivation and Contribution

In this paper, we use a methodology built around X-machines as a means for modular modeling communicating systems. The communicating X-machines is a formal method that facilitates a disciplined development of large scale systems. Unlike similar theoretical approaches, we are motivated by the practical use of communicating X-machines for system development. Our intention is to demonstrate that incremental development can be achieved without destroying the fundamental properties of stand-alone X-machine components, namely the ability of complete testing and model-checking. The contribution of this work is:

- a sound and general theoretical framework: the theory developed is not only equivalent but also subsumes the existing theoretical approaches.
- a theoretical framework which will lead towards a practical methodology: one does not need different modeling languages or tools for stand-alone as well as communicating systems.
- a modular development methodology: communicating systems are built from stand-alone X-machines, while parts of communicating systems can be reused by simply changing the description of the communication between components.
- an asynchronous mode of communication: components are independent of each other, read and write messages in a asynchronous way, while synchronization, if required can be achieved through generic components.
- a disciplined development: modeling of components and communication between them are regarded as two separate activities.

1.2   Definition of X-Machine

An X-machine is a general computational machine introduced by Eilenberg [1] and extended by Holcombe [2], that resembles a Finite State Machine (FSM) but with two significant differences: (a) there is an underlying data set attached to the machine, and (b) the transitions are not labeled with simple inputs but with functions that operate on inputs and underlying data set values. These differences allow the X-machines to be more expressive and flexible than the FSM. An extremely useful in practice is the class of so called stream X-machines, defined by the restrictions on the underlying data set, involving input symbols, memory values and output symbols.

The majority of formal languages facilitate the modeling of either the data processing or the control of a system [3]. Stream X-machines can model nontrivial data structures as a typed memory tuple. X-machines employ a diagrammatic approach of modeling the control by extending the expressive power of the FSM. Therefore, X-machines are capable of modeling both the data and the control by integrating methods, which describe each of these aspects in the most appropriate way. Transitions between states are performed through the application of functions, which are written in a formal notation and model the processing of the data. Data is held in memory, which is attached to the

X-machine. Functions receive input symbols and memory values, and produce output while modifying the memory values (Fig. 1). The machine, depending on the current state of control and the current values of the memory, consumes an input symbol from the input stream and determines the next state, the new memory state and the output symbol, which will be part of the output stream. The formal definition of a deterministic stream X-machine [4] is an 8-tuple:

$$\mathcal{M} = (\Sigma, \Gamma, Q, M, \Phi, F, q_0, m_0) \text{ where:}$$

- Σ, Γ is the input and output finite alphabet respectively,
- Q is the finite set of states,
- M is the (possibly) infinite set called memory,
- Φ is the type of the machine $\mathcal{M}$, a finite set of partial functions ϕ that map an input and a memory state to an output and a new memory state, $\phi : \Sigma \times M \to \Gamma \times M$
- F is the next state partial function that given a state and a function from the type Φ, denotes the next state. F is often described as a transition state diagram. $F : Q \times \Phi \to Q$
- q_0 and m_0 are the initial state and memory respectively.

Starting from the initial state q_0 with the initial memory m_0, an input symbol $\sigma \in \Sigma$ triggers a function $\phi \in \Phi$ which in turn causes a transition to a new state $q \in Q$ and a new memory state $m \in M$. The sequence of transitions caused by the stream of input symbols is called a computation. The computation halts when all input symbols are consumed. The result of a computation is the sequence of outputs produced by the sequence of transitions.

X-Machines are more general than Turing Machines. They possess the computing power of Turing machines and, since they are more abstract, they are expressive enough to be closer to the implementation of a system. This feature makes them particularly useful for modeling and also facilitates the implementation of various tools, which makes the development methodology built around

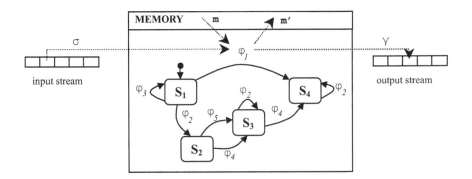

Fig. 1. An abstract example of an X-machine; ϕ_i: functions operating on inputs and memory, S_i: states

X-machines more practical. In addition, X-machines not only provide a modeling formalism for a system but also offer a strategy to test the implementation against the model [5]. Ipate and Holcombe [4] presented a testing method, which is proved that it finds all faults in an implementation [6]. Furthermore, X-machines can be used as a core notation around which an integrated formal methodology of developing correct systems is built, ranging from model checking to testing [7].

1.3   Definition of Communicating X-Machines

A Communicating X-machine model consists of several X-machines, which are able to exchange messages. These are normally viewed as inputs to some functions of an X-machine model, which in turn may affect the memory structure. A Communicating X-machine model can be generally defined as a tuple:

$$((M_i)_{i=1..n}, R), \text{ where}$$

- M_i is the i−th X-machine that participates in the system, and
- R is a communication relation between the n X-machines.

There are several approaches in order to formally define a communicating X-machine [8, 9, 10, 11]. Some of them deviate from the original definition of the X-machine M_i, which has the effect of not being able to reuse existing models. Also, different approaches define R in a different way, with the effect of achieving either synchronous or asynchronous communication.

In section 2, a review of the communicating X-machine theoretical approaches is presented together with the motivation and the theoretical background of our work. The practical contribution of this paper to communicating system modeling is analytically discussed in section 3 where our methodology as well as the appropriate notation is described. A concrete case study is presented in order to demonstrate the applicability of the methodology in section 4. Finally, in the last section the current approach is discussed and ideas for further work are given.

2   Theory of Communicating X-Machines

2.1   The Standard Theoretical Approach

A number of communicating X-machine approaches has been proposed [8, 9, 10]. A communicating stream X-machine with n components is a tuple [8]:

$$((XM_i)_{i=1..n}, C, C_0) \text{ where:}$$

- XM_i is the i−th X-machine of the system,
- C is a $n \times n$ matrix, namely the Communication Matrix,
- C_0 is the initial communication matrix.

In this approach, an XM_i is different from a stand-alone X-machine definition M_i, since it utilizes an IN and an OUT port for communication (Fig. 2).
Both ports are linked to C, which acts as the communication means between
XMs. The C cells contain "messages", i.e. the cell (i,j) contains a "message"
from XM_i to XM_j. The special value λ stands for "no message". The "messages" can be of any type defined in all XM memories. In addition, there exist
special kind of states and functions. The communicating functions emerge only
from communication states, accept the empty symbol ϵ as input, and produce ϵ
as output, while not affecting the memory. The communicating functions either
read an element from CM and put it in the IN port, or write an element from
the OUT port to the C:

$$cf(\epsilon, m, in, out, c) = (\epsilon, m, in', out', c') \text{ where:}$$
$$m \in M, \, in, in' \in IN, \, out, out' \in OUT, \, c, \, c' \in C$$

The communicating functions can write to the matrix only if the cell contains
the special value λ. After the communicating functions read from C, the cell is
assigned the value λ. If a communication function is not applicable, it "waits"
until it becomes applicable. The processing functions affect the contents of IN
and OUT ports, emerge from processing states, and do not affect the communication matrix:

$$pf(\sigma, m, in, out) = (\gamma, m', in', out') \text{ where:}$$
$$\sigma \in \Sigma, m, m' \in M, in, in' \in IN, out, out' \in OUT, \gamma \in \Gamma$$

The above approach is sound and preserves the ability to generate a complete
test set for the system, thus guarantying its correctness. A different methodology,
namely COMX, of constructing communicating X-machines [10] also utilizes IN
and OUT ports, which are described as a separate diagram. The methodology
follows a top-down approach and the intention is to verify that certain properties of the communicating system are satisfied, such as reachability, boundness,
deadlocks etc. A complex formal notation is used, which however is far from

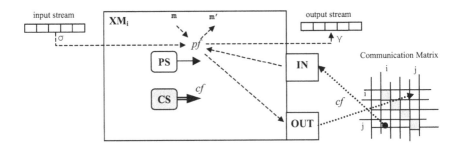

Fig. 2. An abstract example of an XM_i with IN and OUT ports and the Communication Matrix

being standard in order to lead to the construction of appropriate tools. In addition, no effort is made to preserve the semantics of stand-alone X-machines, and therefore existing techniques for testing are unusable.

2.2   An Alternative Theoretical Approach Leading to Practical Development

The above approaches towards building communicating systems suffer one major drawback, i.e. a system should be conceived as a whole and not as a set of independent components. As a consequence, one should start from scratch in order to specify a new component as part of the large system. In addition, specified components cannot be re-used as stand-alone X-machines or as components of other systems, since the formal definition of an X-machine $\mathcal{M}$ differs significantly from the definition of an XM. Moreover, the semantics of the functions affecting the communication matrix impose a limited asynchronous operation of an XM.

The alternative approach that we propose in this paper preserves to a great extend the standard theory described earlier. The only major difference is to abolish the communicating states and communicating functions and use an equivalent way to establish communication. In addition, the new proposal views the communicating system as a result of a sequence of operations that gradually transform a set of X-machines to a system model. Three operators will be defined, namely OP_{inst}, OP_{comm} and OP_{sys}, which will be used for the incremental development of X-machine components of a communicating system. In practice, these operators map conveniently to the tools used and the practical development methodology described in the following section.

Firstly, the stream X-machine Type $(\mathcal{MT})$ is defined as an X-machine without an initial state and initial memory as the tuple:

$$\mathcal{MT} = (\Sigma, \Gamma, Q, M, \Phi, F)$$

An X-machine can be constructed through the application of the operator OP_{inst}, $OP_{inst}: \mathcal{MT}_i \times (q_{0i}, m_{0i}) \rightarrow \mathcal{M}_i, \forall q_{0i} \in Q, m_{0i} \in M$, which results in an instance of a $\mathcal{MT}$:

$$\mathcal{M} = \mathcal{MT} \; OP_{inst} \; (q_0, m_0)$$

A communicating X-machine component $(\mathcal{XMC})$ is defined as the result of the following composition:

$$\mathcal{XMC}_i = (\Sigma_i, \Gamma_i, Q_i, M_i, \Phi_i, F_i) OP_{inst}(q_{0i}, m_{0i}) OP_{comm}(IS_i, OS_i, \Phi IS_i, \Phi OS_i)$$

where:

- IS_i is a $n-$tuple that corresponds to n input streams, representing the input sources used for receiving messages from other $\mathcal{XMC}$ (in_i is the standard input source of $\mathcal{CXMC}_i$):
  $IS_i = (is_1, is_2, ...is_i, ..., is_n)$, and $is_j = \epsilon$ (if no communication is required) or $is_j \subseteq \Sigma_i$

- OS_i is a tuple that corresponds to n output streams, representing the n output destinations used to send messages to n other $\mathcal{XMC}$ (os_i is the standard output destination of $\mathcal{XMC}_i$):
$OS_i = (os_1, os_2, ..., os_i, ..., os_n)$, and $os_j = \epsilon$ (if no communication is required) or $os_j \subseteq \Sigma_j$
- ΦIS_i is an association of function $\phi_i \in \Phi_i$ and the input stream IS_i, $\Phi IS_i : \phi \leftrightarrow IS_i$
- ΦOS_i is an association of function $\phi_i \in \Phi_i$ and the output stream OS_i, $\Phi OS_i : \phi \leftrightarrow OS_i$

The application of the operator

$$OP_{comm} : \mathcal{M}_i \times (IS_i, OS_i, \Phi IS_i, \Phi OS_i) \to \mathcal{CXMC}_i$$

has as a result a communicating X-machine component $\mathcal{CXMC}_i$ as a tuple:

$$\mathcal{XMC}_i = (\Sigma_i, \Gamma_i, Q_i, M_i, \Phi C_i, F_i, q_0, m_0, IS_i, OS_i), \text{ where:}$$

- ΦC_i is the new set of partial functions that read from either standard input or any other input stream and write to either the standard output or any other output stream.

Thus, the set consists of four different sets of functions, which combine any of the above possibilities:

$$\Phi C_i = SISO_i \cup SIOS_i \cup ISSO_i \cup ISOS_i$$

- $SISO_i$ is the set of functions ϕ that read from standard input stream (is_i) and write to standard output stream (os_i):
$SISO_i = \{(is_i, m) \to (os_i, m) | \phi_i = (\sigma, m) \to (\gamma, m) \in \Phi_i \wedge \phi_i \notin dom(IS_i) \wedge \phi_i \notin dom(OS_i)\}$
- $SIOS_i$ is the set of functions ϕ that read from standard input stream (is_i) and write to the j-th output stream (os_j): $SIOS_i = \{(is_i, m) \to (os_j, m) | \phi_i = (\sigma, m) \to (\gamma, m) \in \Phi_i \wedge \phi_i \notin dom(IS_i) \wedge (\phi_i \to os_j) \in OS_i\}$
- $ISSO_i$ is the set of functions ϕ that read from the j-th input stream (is_j) and write to the standard output stream (os_i) $ISSO_i = \{(is_j, m) \to (os_i, m) | \phi_i = (\sigma, m) \to (\gamma, m) \in \Phi_i \wedge (\phi_i \to is_j) \in IS_i \wedge \phi_i \notin dom(OS_i)\}$
- $ISOS_i$ is the set of functions ϕ that read from the j-th input stream (is_j) and write to the k-th output stream (os_k): $ISOS_i = \{(is_j, m) \to (os_k, m) | \phi_i = (\sigma, m) \to (\gamma, m) \in \Phi_i \wedge (\phi_i \to is_j) \in IS_i \wedge (\phi_i \to os_k) \in OS_i\}$

Finally, the communicating X-machine is defined as a tuple of n $\mathcal{XMC}$ as follows:

$$\mathcal{CXM} = (\mathcal{XMC}_1, \mathcal{XMC}_2, ..., \mathcal{XMC}_n), \text{ with}$$

- $\Sigma_1 \cup \Sigma_2 \cup ... \cup \Sigma_n = (os_{11} \cup os_{12} \cup ... \cup os_{1n}) \cup ... \cup (os_{n1} \cup os_{n2} \cup .... \cup os_{nn})$, and
- $\Gamma_1 \cup \Gamma_2 \cup ... \cup \Gamma_n = (is_{11} \cup is_{12} \cup ... \cup is_{1n}) \cup ... \cup (is_{n1} \cup is_{n2} \cup ... \cup is_{nn})$

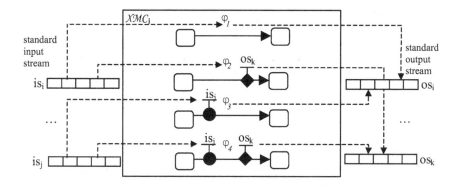

Fig. 3. An abstract example of a $\mathcal{XMC}_i$ with input and output streams and functions that receive input and produce output in any possible combination of sources and destinations

which can be constructed through the application of the operator:

$$OP_{sys} : \mathcal{XMC}_1 \times ... \times \mathcal{XMC}_n \to \mathcal{CXM}.$$

Fig. 3 depicts the four different kinds of functions that may exist in a communicating X-machine component. For exposition reasons, we use a special graphical notation, namely the *solid circle* and the *solid diamond*. If a solid circle appears on a transition function, this function accepts input from the communicating steam instead of the standard input stream. If a solid diamond appears on a transition function, this function may write to a communicating input stream of another X-machine.

In our approach, we have replaced the communication matrix by several input streams associated with each X-machine component. Although, this may look only as a different conceptual view of the same entity, it will serve both exposition purposes as well as asynchronous operation of the individual machines. X-machines have their own standard input stream but when they are used as components of a large-scale system more streams may be added whenever it is necessary. The number of streams associated with one $\mathcal{XMC}$ depends on the number of other $\mathcal{XMC}$s, from which it receives messages (Fig. 4).

The way of describing the communication with annotations does not retract anything from the theoretical model containing processing as well as communicating functions and states. In fact, the X-machine models annotated in the way described above can be transformed into X-machines containing the two kinds of functions and states. A function that reads input from its own communication input stream, can be viewed as a communicating state followed by a communication function that reads the matrix and changes the IN port. If the function writes a message to another machines communication input stream, can be viewed as a processing state that writes to the OUT port, followed by a communicating state which in turn is followed by a communication function that

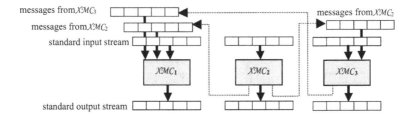

messages from $\mathcal{XMC}_3$

messages from $\mathcal{XMC}_2$

standard input stream

$\mathcal{XMC}_1$ $\mathcal{XMC}_2$ $\mathcal{XMC}_3$

messages from $\mathcal{XMC}_2$

standard output stream

Fig. 4. Three communicating X-machine components $\mathcal{XMC}_1$, $\mathcal{XMC}_2$, and $\mathcal{XMC}_3$ and the resulting communicating system where $\mathcal{XMC}_2$ communicates with $\mathcal{XMC}_1$ and $\mathcal{XMC}_3$, while $\mathcal{XMC}_3$ communicates with $\mathcal{XMC}_1$

writes to the matrix. This subsumption guarantees that the properties proved in [8] are also valid for the current approach.

The replacement of the communicating states and communicating functions with the same functions that belong to the type Φ but with the option to read and write to different input and output streams, facilitate the practical development of communicating X-machine models.

3   Practical Modeling of Communicating X-Machines

The alternative theoretical approach presented earlier leads towards a methodology of developing large-scale communicating systems. Since the communicating X-machine model is viewed as the composition of X-machine type with the initial memory and an initial state as well as with a set of input/output streams and associations of these streams to functions, the development of a model can be mapped into three distinct actions: (a) develop X-machine type models independently of the target system, or use existing models as they are, as components, (b) create X-machine instances of those types and (c) determine the way in which the independent instance models communicate. Optionally, a fourth step may follow, which extends the model of a communicating system in order to provide additional functionality.

The approach has several advantages for the developer who: (a) does not need to model a communicating system from scratch, (b) can re-use existing models, (c) can consider modeling and communication as two separate distinct activities in the development of a communicating system, and (d) can use existing tools for both stand-alone and communicating X-machines.

In addition, for a formal method to be practical, it needs certain tools that will facilitate modeling. A prerequisite for those tools is to use a standard notation to describe models in that formal language, other than any ad-hoc mathematical notation. The formal definitions of the X-machines can be presented using the notation of X-machine Description Language [12], which is intended to be an ASCII-based interchange language between X-machine tools [13, 14].

Briefly, XMDL is a non-positional notation based on tags, used for the declaration of X-machine parts, e.g. types, set of states, memory, input and output symbols, functions etc. The functions take two parameter tuples, i.e. an input symbol and a memory value, and return two new parameter tuples, i.e. an output and a new memory value. A function may be applicable under conditions (*if-then*) or unconditionally. Variables are denoted by the prefix ?. The informative *where* in combination with the operator <- is used to describe operations on memory values. The functions are of the form:

```
#fun <function name> ( <input tuple> , <memory tuple> ) =
if <condition expression> then
   ( <output tuple>, <memory tuple> )
where <informative expression>.
```

XMDL has been enriched with syntax that provide the ability to define instances of X-machine types. The syntax is the following:

```
#model <instance name> instance_of <model name>
[with:
#init_state = <instance initial state>.
#init_memory = <instance initial memory tuple>].
```

Finally, XMDL provides syntax to express the solid circle and the solid diamond that are attached to the functions of the communicating machine and denote input and output streams respectively. In order to incorporate the above semantics of communication, the syntax of XMDL is enhanced by the following annotation:

```
#communication of <model name>:
[<function name> reads from <model name>
where <expression> from (memory|input|output) <tuple>]+

[<function name> writes <message> to <model name>
where <expression> from (memory|input|output) <tuple>]+.
```

One can imagine that XMDL code for X-machine types are kept in different files from XMDL code for X-machine instances and communication definitions. All these files may be compiled into one in order to produce the communicating X-machine model in XMDL which can then be used for various reasons, e.g. testing, model checking etc. by other tools (Fig. 5).

4   Case Study: Building a Communicating System

This section presents a case study of developing a communicating system based on the methodology described above. The notation used to define X-machine components is XMDL. The description of the system to be modeled as a communicating system is as follows: a lift with a finite capacity operates in a five-floor

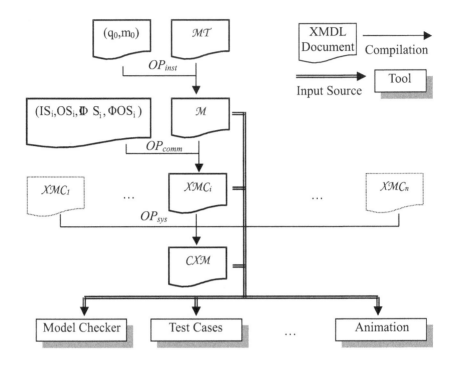

Fig. 5. Incremental practical development of Communicating X-machine systems

building by serving people that want to move from one floor of the building to another. The lift records and satisfies all the requests generated by people who are either inside the lift, or outside it: people outside the lift waiting on a floor call the lift by pressing the call button that is located at their floor, while people inside the lift determine their destination floor e.g. by pressing the appropriate button. The lift is moving among the floors to satisfy the generated requests. When the lift reaches a floor for which a request has been generated, it stops so that people may enter or leave the lift: people in the lift destined to that floor exit the lift while people waiting on that floor for the lift to arrive may enter the lift (provided the lift capacity is respected). When all possible loading and unloading of the lift is over, the lift may start moving to a new floor (if it carries people) or it may remain idle (if it is empty). It is assumed that people waiting for the lift to arrive on a floor, form a queue.

Clearly this scenario is a case that implies a communicating system because if one chooses to build a monolithic model, then this will be complex and rigid, i.e. not susceptible to future extensions.

4.1   Modeling of X-Machine Type

In the above system, there are three types of X-machines to be modeled: the queue of people waiting at a floor, a call button in front of the lift door at each floor and the lift itself. Assuming that there is no limit in the number of people waiting at a floor, the queue is modeled as an X-machine with two states: empty and filling (Fig. 6). The memory of the X-machine holds the actual sequence of persons waiting at a floor. Functions are activated by input tuples of the form (event, person), where event is the arrival or departure of a person in the queue. In this case, $PERSON$ is a basic type, i.e. anything, without any further reference to its implementation.

The following is the XMDL listing for the specification of queue:

```
#model queue.
#basic_types = [PERSON].
#type messages = {FirstPersonInQueue, PersonInQueue, PersonLeft,
                  LastPersonLeft}.
#type event = {arrival, departure}.
#states = {empty, filling}.
#input (event,PERSON).
#output (messages,PERSON).
#memory (sequence_of PERSON).
#fun first_person_arrives((arrival, ?p), (nil)) =
if ?p belongs PERSON then
   ((FirstPersonInQueue, ?p), (<?p>)).
#fun person_arrives((arrival, ?p), (?queue)) =
if ?p belongs PERSON then
   ((PersonInQueue, ?p), (<?new_queue>))
where
   ?new_queue <- ?p addatendof ?queue.
#fun person_leaves((departure,?p), (<?p::?queue>)) =
if ?queue =/= nil then
   ((PersonLeft, ?p), (<?queue>)).
#fun last_person_leaves((departure,?p), (<?p>)) =
   ((LastPersonLeft, ?p), (nil)).
#transition(empty,first_person_arrives)=filling.
#transition(filling,person_arrives)=filling.
#transition(filling,person_leaves)=filling.
#transition(filling,last_person_leaves)=empty.
```

Accordingly, the button is an X-machine with no memory, i.e. a finite state machine, with two states off and on (Fig. 6):

```
#model button.
#type messages = {Pressed, NotPressed, AlreadyPressed,
                  AlreadyNotPressed}.
#type action = {press, unpress}.
```

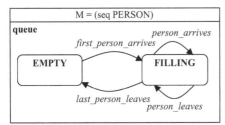 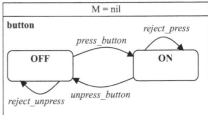

Fig. 6. The state transition diagrams of the queue and button X-machines

```
#states = {on, off}.
#memory nil.
#input (action).
#output (messages).
#fun press_button((press), nil) = ((Pressed),nil).
#fun unpress_button((unpress),nil)=((NotPressed),nil).
#fun reject_press((press),nil)=((AlreadyPressed),nil).
#fun reject_unpress((unpress),nil)=((AlreadyNotPressed), nil).
```

Finally, the model lift is slightly more complicated (Fig. 7). The memory of the X-machine consists of the floor at which the lift is currently at, the set of floors, which are recorded as destinations following requests, the set of people that are in it, the maximum floor number that the lift can serve and the total capacity in persons that the lift can bear:

```
#basic_types = [INDIVIDUAL].
#type floor = natural0.
#type capacity = natural.
#type destinations = set_of floor.
#type people = set_of INDIVIDUAL.
#memory (floor, destinations, people, floor, capacity).
```

The lift can exist in four states:

```
#states = {moving, idle, loading, unloading}.
```

The input that the functions receive are defined as tuples in which the first element denotes the action to be performed while the second element is either a floor or a person making a request. The output is defined accordingly:

```
#type messages = {CallRequested, LiftAtFloor, LiftMoving,
                  LoadingPeople, UnloadingPeople,
                  LiftPassedFloor, LiftFull}.
#type action = {get_in, get_out, request, continue}.
#input (action, floor union INDIVIDUAL).
#output (messages, floor union INDIVIDUAL).
```

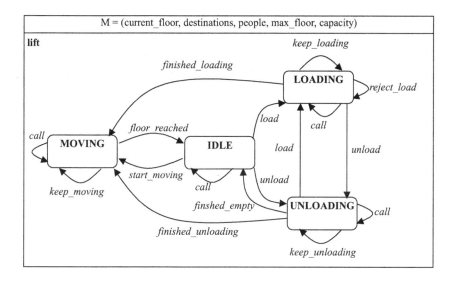

Fig. 7. The state transition diagram of the lift X-machine

While in any state, the lift can accept a request, either from a person within the lift or a person in any floor. The request triggers the function call, which is responsible to update the memory:

```
#fun call( (request, ?f), (?cf, ?d, ?p, ?mf, ?c)) =
if ?f belongs floor and ?f =< ?mf then
    ((CallRequested,?f), (?cf, ?nd, ?p, ?mf, ?c))
where
    ?nd <- ?f addsetelement ?d.
```

The rest of the functions are defined accordingly. Briefly, `keep_loading` and `load` are triggered when an individual enters the lift, while `reject_load` is triggered when the maximum capacity is reached. The functions `unload` and `keep_unloading` are counterparts of the above when individuals exit the lift. `Finished_loading` and `finished_unloading` mark the start of the lift's move to its recorded destinations. When a floor that is in its destinations is reached the lift becomes stationary (`idle`) in this floor:

```
#fun floor_reached( (continue, ?f), (?cf, ?d, ?p, ?mf, ?c)) =
if ?f belongs floor and ?f belongs ?d and ?f =< ?mf then
    ((LiftAtFloor, ?f), (?f, ?nd, ?p, ?mf, ?c))
where
    ?nd <- ?f delsetelement ?d.
```

At this stage, the three independent models of the components of the systems are developed as if they were stand-alone X-machines, without initial state and initial memory.

4.2   Creation of X-Machine Instances

The system would require components, which are X-machine instances of the previously defined X-machine types. Assuming that the overall system consists of 5 floors and one lift that serves all five plus the ground floor (number 0), this is achieved through the following declarations:

```
#model queue0 instance_of queue with:
#init_state = {empty}
#init_memory = (nil).
#model queue1 instance_of queue with:
. . .
#model button_floor0 instance_of button with:
#init_state = {off}
#model button_floor1 instance_of button with:
. . .
#model my_lift instance_of lift with:
#init_state = {idle}
#init_memory = (0,nil,nil,10,5).
```

4.3   Modeling of the Communicating System

The communicating system consists of six queues (one for each floor), six buttons (one for each floor) and one lift (Fig. 8). The communication between the components should be established so that when any person who arrives in the queue presses the button, which in turn causes a request to be recorded in the lift destinations. For example, the communication of the queue and the button at ground floor is established as follows (Fig. 9):

```
#communication of queue0:
first_person_arrives writes (press) to button_floor0.
person_arrives writes (press) to button_floor0.

#communication of button_floor0:
press_button reads from queue0.
reject_press reads from queue0.
```

In addition, the communication of the button at ground floor and the lift is established with the following XMDL code:

```
#communication of button_floor0:
press_button writes (request,0) to my_lift.

#communication of my_lift:
call reads from button_floor0.
```

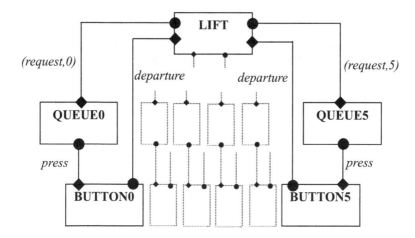

Fig. 8. The overall communicating X-machine system with the messages exchanged. The solid circle should be read as "from" while the solid diamond as "to"

On the other hand, when an individual enters the lift, in order to remove the persons from the waiting queue, the function `load` and `keep_loading` should notify the functions `person_leaves` and `last_person_leaves` of the model queue. For example, this communication between the lift and the queue at the fifth floor is decoded as follows:

```
#communication of my_lift:
load writes (departure) to queue5
where ?f==5 from memory (?f,_,_,_,_).
keep_loading writes (departure) to queue5
where ?f==5 from memory (?f,_,_,_,_).

#communication of queue5:
person_leaves reads from my_lift.
last_person_leaves reads from my_lift.
```

Finally, the functions `finish_loading` and `finish_unloading` that are triggered in order to move the lift to the rest of the destinations, should notify the button of the specific floor to turn off:

```
#communication of my_lift:
finish_loading write (unpress) to button_floor4
where ?f==5 from memory (?f,_,_,_,_).
finish_unloading write (unpress) to button_floor4
where ?f==5 from memory (?f,_,_,_,_).
start_moving write (unpress) to button_floor4
where ?f==5 from memory (?f,_,_,_,_).
```

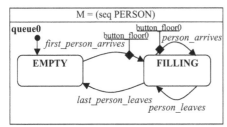 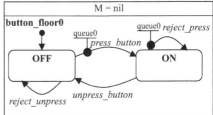

Fig. 9. The state transition diagrams for the communication between a queue and its related button

```
#communication of button_floor5:
unpress_button reads from my_lift.
reject_unpress reads from my_lift.
```

The communication, which is declared separately from the X-machine types and the X-machine instances, completes the overall description of the communicating system.

4.4   Extending the Communicating System

Developing larger models as communicating systems from existing building blocks implies the need for some more features, which can be included in communicating X-machines. For example, if there are two lifts that serve the five-floor building, then there must be an X-machine created as an instance of the model lift and an additional X-machine that performs the scheduling (Fig. 10). In the approaches presented by other researchers [8, 9, 10], this is not easily done. In the current approach, re-building the system includes only the modification of the communication part and the new specification of the scheduler. The simple scheduler that is presented below allocates a task to a device with the fewer tasks, only if the task is not recorded to any of the two devices (Fig. 11).

The complete model of the scheduler in XMDL can be found in [15]. The model can either be created from scratch, or it may already exist as a component of some other system. The scheduler is general and does not refer to any of the other two X-machines. However, the communication part is system specific:

```
#communication of scheduler:
reject_task reads from button_floor0.
 . . .
assign_device1 reads from button_floor0.
 . . .
assign_device2 reads from button_floor0.
 . . .
```

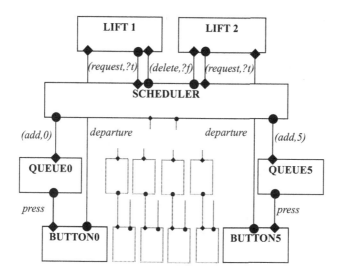

Fig. 10. The overall communicating X-machine system

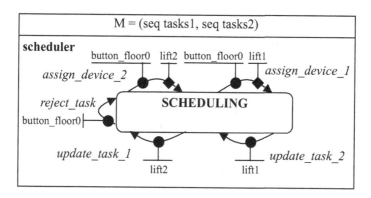

Fig. 11. The transition diagram of the scheduler specification as a part of a communicating system

```
update_task1 reads from lift1.
update_task2 reads from lift2.
assign_device1 writes (request,?t) to lift1
where ?t from input (_,?t)
assign_device2 writes (request,?t) to lift2.
where ?t from input (_,?t).
```

The communication part of the queues and the buttons should change accordingly. The kind of synchronization described above, also appears when buffering or synchronization is required. For example, if a function requires a n-tuple as input, then, assuming that every element of the n-tuple is produced by other machines, a new buffer X-machine should be specified in order to construct the n-tuple and then pass for consumption. In such cases, one can imagine "ready-made" generic X-machines that would act as synchronization interfaces or buffers between other machines in a communicating system.

5   Conclusions

We have presented a theoretical framework that leads towards a methodology for building communicating systems out of existing stand-alone X-machines. This framework facilitates the practical development of communicating X-machine models. This is because the software engineer can separately specify the components and then describe the way in which these components communicate. This allows a disciplined development of large-scale systems. Also, X-machine models can be re-used in other systems, since one needs to change only the communication part. The major advantage is that the methodology also lends itself to modular testing and model checking strategies in which X-machines are individually tested and verified as components while communication is tested and verified separately.

We have applied the methodology in order to develop formal models of multi-agent systems [16, 17, 18]. It is found that by using communicating X-machines, we can formally model the behaviour of reactive agents as well as their cooperation. Future work will include the implementation of communicating systems on top of the already existing tools [13, 14] and an enhanced theoretical framework that will provide the ability to describe types of communication in accordance to types of models. We are also looking for a more effective way to adapt off-the-shelf X-machine models that require minor changes in their specifications, i.e. inherit several elements of the X-machine 8-tuple while being able to override or modify some of them, as well as dynamic adaptation of communication. Finally, a methodology for deriving a complete test set for communicating systems as well as a model checking strategy will be further investigated [7].

References

[1] Eilenberg S.: "*Automata Machines and Languages*", Vol.A, Academic Press, 1974. 317

[2] Holcombe M.: "X-machines as a Basis for Dynamic System Specification", *Software Engineering Journal*, Vol.3, No.2, pp.69-76, 1988.   317

[3] Clarke E. and Wing J. M.: "Formal Methods: State of the Art and Future Directions", *ACM Computing Surveys*, Vol.28, No.4, pp.626-643, 1996.   317

[4] Ipate F. and Holcombe M.: "Specification and Testing using Generalised Machines: a Presentation and a Case Study", *Software Testing, Verification and Reliability*, Vol.8, pp.61-81, 1998.   318, 319

[5] Kehris E., Eleftherakis G. and Kefalas P.: "Using X-machines to Model and Test Discrete Event Simulation Programs", In *Systems and Control: Theory and Applications* by N. Mastorakis (ed.), World Scientific, pp.163-168, 2000. 319

[6] Holcombe M. and Ipate F.: "*Correct Systems: Building a Business Process Solution*", Springer Verlag, London, 1998. 319

[7] Eleftherakis G., Kefalas P. and Sotiriadou A.: "XmCTL: Extending Temporal Logic to Facilitate Formal Verification of X-Machines Models", *Annales Univerisitate Bucurest Matematica Informatica*, Annul L, pp.79-95, 2002. 319, 334

[8] Balanescu T., Cowling A. J., Gheorgescu H., Gheorghe M., Holcombe M. and Vertan C.: "Communicating Stream X-machines Systems are no Mmore than X-machines", *Journal of Universal Computer Science*, Vol.5, No.9, pp.494-507, 1999. 319, 324, 332

[9] Gheorgescu H. and Vertan C.: "A New Approach to Communicating X-machines Systems", *Journal of Universal Computer Science*, Vol.6, No.5, pp.490-502, 2000. 319, 332

[10] Barnard J.: "COMX: a Design Methodology using Communicating X-machines", *Information and Software Technology*, Vol.40, pp.271-280, 1998. 319, 320, 332

[11] Kefalas P., Eleftherakis G., Holcombe M. and Gheorghe M.: "Simulation and Verification of P Systems using Communicating X-Machines", *Biosystems*, to appear. 319

[12] Kefalas P. and Kapeti E.: "A Design Language and Tool for X-machines Specification", In *"Advances in Informatics"* by D. I. Fotiadis and S. D. Nikolopoulos (eds.), World Scientific, pp.134-145, 2000. 324

[13] Kefalas P.: "Automatic Translation from X-machines to Prolog", TR-CS01/00, Dept. of Computer Science, CITY Liberal Studies, 2000. 324, 334

[14] Kefalas P. and Sotiriadou A.: "A Complier that Transforms X-machines Specification to Z", TR-CS06/00, Dept. of Computer Science, CITY Liberal Studies, 2000. 324, 334

[15] Kefalas P., Eleftherakis G. and Kehris E.: "Modular Modelling of Large Scale Systems using Communicating X-Machines", *Proceedings 8th Panhellenic Conference in Informatics*, pp.20-29, 2001 332

[16] Georghe M., Holcombe M. and Kefalas P.: "Computational Models for Collective Foraging", *BioSystems*, Vol.61, pp.133-141, 2001. 334

[17] Kefalas P.: "Formal Modelling of Reactive Agents as an Aggregation of Simple Behaviours", *Proceedings 2nd Hellenic Conference on AI (SETN-02)*, pp.461-472, 2002. 334

[18] Kefalas P., Holcombe M., Eleftherakis G. and Gheorghe M.: "A Formal Method for the Development of Agent-Based Systems", In *"Intelligent Agent Software Engineering"*, by V.Plekhavona (ed.), Idea Group Publishing, pp.68-98, 2003. 334

TOPPER: An Integrated Environment for Task Allocation and Execution of MPI Applications onto Parallel Architectures

Dimitris Konstantinou and Nectarios Koziris

Computing Systems Lab, Computer Science Division
Department of Electrical & Computer Engineering
National Technical University of Athens
Zografou Campus, Zografou 15773, Greece
{dkonst,nkoziris}@cslab.ntua.gr

Abstract. Although the use of parallel computing systems has significantly expanded in the last years, the existence of many processing elements is not fully exploited, due to the interprocessor communication overhead. In this paper we present an integrated software environment for optimizing the performance of parallel programs on multiprocessor architectures. TOPPER can efficiently allocate the tasks of a parallel application on the various nodes of a multiprocessing machine, using several algorithms for task clustering, cluster merging and physical mapping. The programmer outlines the application's task computation and communication requirements along with the multiprocessor network available in two similar graphs. TOPPER aims to minimize the application's overall execution time, proposing an efficient task allocation. In the case of MPI programs, TOPPER proves more powerful, since the application is automatically executed on the target machine with the provided task mapping.

1 Introduction

The general scheduling problem of an arbitrary task graph with communication delays onto an architecture with fixed size and interconnection topology is NP-Complete. El-Rewini et H. Ali in [10] and [11] proved this NP completeness by representing the problem of task allocation on a multiprocessor system with a split graph. The task allocation is, therefore, equivalent to a weighted clique graph partitioning, which is NP-Complete, thus proving inherent intractability.

Even though a large body of literature exists in the area of scheduling and mapping, it is only partially exploited. While some have proposed software tools that support automatic scheduling and mapping [8, 7, 9], the main functionality of these tools is to provide a simulation environment. They can help us understand how scheduling and mapping algorithms behave, but they are inadequate for practical purposes. On the other hand, there are numerous parallelizing tools, but they do not integrate well with scheduling algorithms.

Y. Manolopoulos et al. (Eds.): PCI 2001, LNCS 2563, pp. 336–350, 2003.

We have developed an integrated software tool, called TOPPER, designed to help the programmers of parallel applications to efficiently execute such programs. Initially, TOPPER's user constructs a directed graph to describe the parallel application, where the computational work is depicted by the graph's nodes, while the data exchange is represented by the edges of the graph. Additionally, the tool's user forms another similar graph to describe the available multiprocessor system. After these initial steps, TOPPER copes with the task-scheduling problem, performing a series of appropriate functions for mapping the given task graph onto the target processor graph. Moreover, TOPPER's assorted methods for task allocation can perform an effective mapping, regardless of the task or the processor topology, guaranteeing portability and substantial speedup for most parallel programs. The paper is structured as follows: Chapter 2 examines the Multi-Step approach to the scheduling problem of parallel applications. In Chap. 3 we present a detailed description of TOPPER's functions. Finally, in Chap. 4 the experimental results are presented, illustrating TOPPER's high performance.

2   The Multi-step Approach Overview

The task allocation problem can be optimally solved in special cases such as two-processor distributed systems, or linear array of any number of processors. More specifically, if the target architecture contains two processors the task allocation problem is stated as a maximum flow minimum cut problem [1] that can be polynomially solved using, for example, the Ford-Fulkerson algorithm. There also exists a heuristic presented in [3], which addresses the general m-processor problem using the 2-way min cut algorithm m times. Most of the theoretical work on mappings considers structured graphs like grids, hypercubes, trees, etc [5]. An increasing number of applications demand methods dealing with irregular graphs. The general mapping problem is unfortunately NP-complete, thus allowing only for efficient heuristics.

In order to find efficient methods to enhance parallel programs' performance, researchers have followed a multistep approach, addressing separately each step of the general scheduling problem. These successive steps are outlined as follows: *task clustering, cluster merging* and *physical mapping*.

2.1   Task Clustering - Scheduling a Task Graph with Communication Delays onto a Bounded/Unbounded Clique of Processors

In this first step, as stated also in [13, 15], the task graph with computation and communication costs and precedence constraints is scheduled onto a fully connected network of processors. This classical clique architecture is, therefore, used as a target with either limited or unlimited number of processors. In this first step, researchers propose algorithms that minimize the maximum makespan, disregarding the actual processor's topology. The scheduling problem is NP-Complete in the majority of general cases. Papadimitriou et Yannakakis in [6] have proved that the classical scheduling problem of a task graph with arbitrary communication and computation times is NP-Complete and proposed an approximation algorithm that approaches the optimal solution within a factor of two. In addition to this, Sarkar in [4] and Gerasoulis in [12] proposed faster heuristics with efficient performance. All of these algorithms perform the same initial step: Cluster the tasks into large nodes, so that the grain of the parallelism increases and the use of distributed processors minimizes the task graph makespan. This initial step generates a graph of clusters, encapsulating several tasks in each cluster, the ones scheduled in the same processor and, therefore, having zero intracommunication overhead. As far as cluster intracommunication is concerned, it equals to the aggregate intercommunication cost between all the tasks of the various clusters.

2.2   Cluster Merging into p Physical Clusters

In this step, the set of clustered tasks is mapped onto a clique of bounded number of processors. Assuming that the set of clusters exceeds the number of available processors, two or more clusters end up being assigned to the same processor, reducing the number of clusters to the exact number of processors. Sarkar in [4] has proposed a scheduling heuristic with $O(|V|(|V| + |E|))$ complexity, where $|V|$ stands for the number of nodes and $|E|$ for the number of edges. A lower complexity heuristic, used in PYRROS [8], is the work profiling method, which merges clusters offsetting their diverging arithmetic load. Liou et Palis in [14] have demonstrated that, when task clustering is performed prior to scheduling, load balancing is the preferred approach for cluster merging, producing better final schedules than other methods such as minimizing communication traffic.

2.3   Physical Mapping of p Physical Clusters onto p Network Connected Processors

The final stage of the multi-step approach consists of the physical mapping of clustered task graph onto the processor graph. As shown in the two previous stages, the number of clusters is now equal or smaller than the number of processors. Therefore, it is feasible to assign to each processor a single cluster.

On the whole, the physical mapping problem is NP-Complete. The sole known algorithm that can provide optimal mapping is the exhaustive one, which selects the most efficient mapping combination, after having tested all the possible ones. The extremely high complexity of this algorithm $O(V!)$ necessitated the elaboration of heuristic methods to tackle the problem of physical mapping. Many scheduling tools, such as Oregami, PYRROS and Parallax, use occasionally efficient heuristics or approximation algorithms. More specifically, Gerasoulis et Yang in PYRROS [8] have used Bokhari's heuristic, based on simulated annealing. Furthermore, OREGAMI's MAPPER [7], a tool for task allocation on distributed architectures, uses a greedy heuristic, called the NN-Embed, a rather simple method, that lists all edges in ascending order of their weights and assigns them to the processor's network edges. However, MAPPER currently supports only mesh and hypercube processor networks, limiting its potential use. Finally, the PMAP algorithm, proposed by Koziris et al in [15] has proven to be efficient regardless of the processor topology. More specifically, this heuristic detects the most communication-intensive clusters, mapping them along with their neighboring ones on the closest possible processor-nodes.

3   Developping TOPPER

The emerging demand for the optimization of parallel applications generated the need for the development of a software environment, which could incorporate all the above-mentioned methods. More specifically, TOPPER integrates the operations of task clustering, cluster merging and physical mapping, allowing its users to make full benefit of the resources of a multiprocessor architecture.

3.1   Graph Model Assumptions

Each of the three graph models, on which all of TOPPER's functions are based on, is used in every stage of the multi-step approach. Let us closely examine these models:

A. Let $V_T = \{t_0, t_1, \ldots, t_n\}$ be a set of tasks, whose precedence constraints form a directed acyclic graph G_T. In a precedence graph for a set of tasks the weight of a task-node depicts the time needed for a processor to perform all the computations involved in this task, apart from the necessary communication with its neighboring tasks. Additionally, the weight on a directed edge (t_i, t_j) represents the communication time needed for t_i to send a certain amount of data to t_j, supposing the two tasks are located on two neighboring processors.

In the above-described model, all the processors are considered to be identical, thus the execution time of each task does not depend on the processor on which this task is allocated. Furthermore, this model of directed acyclic task graphs, combined with the general form of implemented tasks, guarantees that deadlocks are avoided during the execution of a parallel application. The tasks follow the *atomic task execution model* and block their operation until they receive all the incoming messages. Next, the computations are carried out, and finally all the resulting data is sent to the neighboring tasks.

B. The next graph model concerns the processor network. Let us denote $V_P = \{p_0, p_1, \ldots, p_m\}$ as the set of available processors that will be used to execute a parallel application. This set of processor-nodes, along with the actual interprocessor links, is depicted with the help of an undirected graph G_P, whose edges represent the physical connection of two neighboring processors.

C. The third graph model that has to be clarified is the cluster graph model G_C. This graph's nodes constitute a set $V_C = \{c_1, c_2, \ldots, c_k\}$, while each c_i contains a set of tasks that are to be executed in the same processor. Therefore these

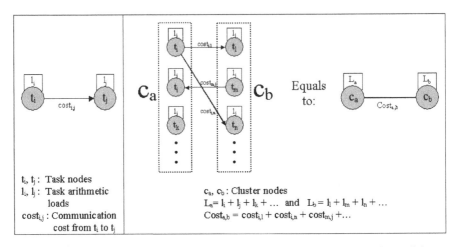

Fig. 1. Left: instance of a task graph. Right: the cluster graph model

clusters are often referred to as *virtual processors*. An arbitrary edge of $G_C(c_a, c_b)$ represents the communication between all tasks that belong to c_a and all tasks that belong to c_b, thus the edge's cost is the aggregate of those task-related edge weights Fig. 1. Finally, it should be noted that the cluster graph is non-directed due to the various direction of task-edges between clusters c_a and c_b.

The description of the first two graphs is essential for TOPPER's functionality, a feature strongly related with the optimal performance of a parallel application. As far as the cluster graph is concerned, it is generated in the task clustering stage and is taken into account during the following steps of the multistep approach, without the interference of the tool's user. Consequently, users are required to form only the task and processor graphs in a plain ASCII form by declaring nodes and edges with the help of a set of simple syntax rules.

Additionally, these rules provide the users with the ability to exploit loop or flow-control syntax structures and predefined procedures (i.e. the definition of a function "`torus(4, 3, ...)`" for the construction of a 3x4 toroidal mesh), as they may provide valuable help with large and complicated graphs. A detailed description of these syntactic rules can be found in [16]. The two graph definitions are stored in two separate ASCII files and are inserted as the input in TOPPER.

After the forming of the task and processor graph has been completed, TOPPER proceeds in the elaboration of the two graphs in order to discover the most suitable task allocation.

3.2   Task Clustering

The selected algorithm for task clustering, proposed by Yang et Gerasoulis in [12], is based on the existence of a Dominant Sequence (DS) in a directed, acyclic, scheduled task graph. This sequence represents the longest path that can be traversed in such a graph. Obviously, parallel execution time (PT) is strongly related with the DS.

Dominant Sequence Clustering (DSC) algorithm performs a series of edge eliminations, placing the two endpoint-tasks of the zeroed edge in the same cluster as follows:

1. Initially set each task to form a single cluster.
2. Compute the initial DS.
3. Mark all edges as unexamined.
4. While there are still unexamined edges do:
   (a) Zero an edge in DS if PT does not increase.
   (b) Mark this edge as examined.
   (c) Find the new DS.

This algorithm's time complexity is sufficiently low: $O((|V_C| + |E_C|)log|V_C|)$. Additionally, DSC's performance, as outlined in [12] and also tested in practice in [2], is a guaranty of the tool's total effectiveness in optimizing parallel applications.

Clearly, DSC groups the tasks into clusters, supposing an infinite number of processors are available. The processor graph size and connection network is actually taken into account during the next steps of the multi-step approach.

3.3   Cluster Merging

The method used for cluster merging, which is developed and applied in TOPPER, is called the work profiling method proposed in [2], and is based on the balancing of the arithmetic load of the processors involved. Based on this method, Konstantinou in [16] developed the load-balancing algorithm, which is implemented in TOPPER. Let $|V_C|$ be the number of resulting clusters from the previous step and $|V_P|$ the number of actual processors available for the execution of the parallel application, with $|V_P| < |V_C|$. The arithmetic load of each cluster is the aggregate of the load of all tasks belonging to this cluster, as shown in the cluster graph model in Sect. 3.1. The algorithm used for cluster merging is described as follows:

1. Compute the arithmetic load of each cluster.
2. Sort the $|V_C|$ clusters in decreasing order of their loads.
3. Assign the first $|V_P|$ clusters to the $|V_P|$ free processors.
4. While there are still clusters not assigned to any processor do:
   (a) Find the physical processor with the minimum arithmetic load
   (b) Assign the next cluster to this processor.

The algorithm's complexity is $O(|V_C|log|V_C|)$ for the necessary sorting of the clusters and $O((|V_C| - |V_P|)|V_P|)$ for the rest of the procedure, concluding in $O(|V_C|(log|V_C| + |V_P|))$. In terms of load balancing, this algorithm can easily be proved to be *optimal*.

3.4 Physical Mapping

The next and final step of the multi-step approach is the efficient allocation of the clusters on the processor network. The efficiency of a certain heuristic, when elaborating assorted types of cluster and processor graphs cannot be guaranteed. Additionally, an exhaustive search for the best suitable mapping cannot always be conducted, due to the high complexity of the physical mapping problem. Consequently, TOPPER consists not only of the exhaustive algorithm, but also of three heuristics, which are proven to be quite competent in solving the physical mapping problem. However, the final choice of a certain mapping is made with the help of a cost function, which objectively computes the theoretical execution time of a parallel application mapped on the available processor network.

Definition 1. *Let us consider two graphs $G_C(V_C, E_C)$ and $G_P(V_P, E_P)$, where V is the set of nodes and E is the set of edges, with $|V_C| = |V_P|$. We define the following function $Fm : V_C \rightarrow V_P$ as the* physical mapping function*:*

$$\forall v, u \in V_C with \quad (v, u) \in E_C, \exists (F_m(v), F_m(u)) \in E_P \qquad (1)$$

Definition 2. *Let (v, u) an edge in G_C, having weight $comm(v, u)$. Additionally, hop is the* unit *distance between any two directly connected processors in the G_P and, finally, $dist(v', u')$ represents the number of hops in the shortest path that connects vertices v' and u' in G_P. The following formula defines CF, the* objective cost function *used by TOPPER to evaluate the cost of a specific mapping F_m:*

$$CF(F_m) = \sum_{\forall (v,u) \in E_C} dist(F_m(v), F_m(u)) \cdot comm(v, u) \qquad (2)$$

Definition 3. *An optimal mapping F_m^{opt} with respect to the CF is the one with*

$$CF(F_m^{opt}) = min\{CF(F_m) \quad | \quad F_m \in MAP\} \qquad (3)$$

where MAP is the set of all possible mappings.

In detail, in the physical mapping step a selective execution of the provided mapping algorithms is being performed, according to the following guidelines. If the number of clusters or processors is small enough (usually less than 16), the exhaustive algorithm takes over the search for the optimal solution. On the contrary, if the number of clusters/processors exceeds 16, some heuristics are executed, generating different mapping results. The best mapping is finally selected from these results with the help of the CF. Let us briefly examine each algorithm.

A. The *Exhaustive* one, after having tested all the possible mapping combinations, selects the most efficient one, with the use of the CF function, and therefore, generates the optimal solution. Nevertheless, this algorithm's high complexity $O(p!)$ makes it suitable only for processor networks with a small number of nodes.

B. The *NN-Embed* [7], although mostly applied in hypercube and mesh processor topologies, can be used in all other cases, but with a poor performance. This drawback is based on the algorithm's focus on a single-edge adjacency, omitting any set of adjacent nodes. Nevertheless, the simplicity of the algorithm consist the main advantage of NN-Embed. Originally, the algorithm constructs a list of all the edges in the given task graph, in a descending order of weight. The heuristic traverses this list in linear time and for each edge, assigns endpoints as follows:

1. If both nodes have already been assigned, do nothing
2. If only one node has been assigned, then assign the other node to the closest free processor
3. If neither node has been assigned, randomly choose a free processor and assign one node to it and the other to its closest free neighbor.

The necessary time is $O(|E|log|E|)$ for the sorting part, and $O(|E|)$ for the rest of the procedure.

C. PMAP is a heuristic, which efficiently maps a task graph on processor graph, regardless of the processor topology [15]. This heuristic tries to find the most communication intensive task-nodes and map them and their neighbors into neighboring processing nodes on the processor graph. In the beginning, TOPPER calculates the number of adjacent nodes of every node. Subsequently, the nodes of the task graph are sorted by ascending order of their total communication weight and number of neighbors. The heuristic then places the most demanding, in terms of total communication cost, task-nodes to the respective nodes of the processor graph. Once these core task nodes are placed, there is no backtracking. Next, the heuristic places the adjacent of the core nodes to adjacent cells of the processor graph by making locally best-fit comparisons. The algorithm performs the following steps:

1. Phase 1
   (a) 1st step: Adjust the maximum number of neighboring clusters to the maximum number of neighboring processors in the processor graph, by removing the less communication cost edges for each cluster-node.
   (b) 2nd step: Sort the nodes of the processor graph by ascending order of their neighboring links and the nodes in the cluster graph by the number of communication links they need.
   (c) 3rd step: Assign the most demanding cluster-node to the best suitable node of the processor graph, and then assign its neighboring nodes to the best suitable neighboring nodes of the processor graph.
2. Phase 2
   (a) 4th step: Place back the edges removed at the first step.

(b) 5th step: Examine the processors that are not assigned any cluster to find the one who neighbors with the most occupied processors.

(c) 6th step: Find a cluster that is distanced by at most i (at the beginning $i = 1$) from all the clusters that are mapped to the neighboring processors of the processor found on the previous step. If found assign this cluster to the processor of the 5th step.

(d) 7th step: Repeat steps 5-6 until no more assignments can be made. If there are more processors to be allocated, increase i by one and go back to the 5th step.

The complexity of the PMAP is $O(|V|log|V|+|E|)$ for the first phase, due to the sorting of nodes and the removing of edges, and $O(|V|^2)$ for the second phase, due to the necessary $O(|V|)$ cycles.

D. The last algorithm for physical mapping used in this tool is an alternative version of PMAP, called the *PMAP-Exhaustive*, and combines both PMAP and the exhaustive algorithm. This algorithm differs from the plain PMAP in the following sense: Firstly, a limit k is set, up to which the plain PMAP is applied. After the allocation of k clusters on processors with the use of PMAP, the Exhaustive algorithm is applied for the mapping of the remaining $p - k$ clusters. Obviously, PMAP-Exhaustive outperforms plain PMAP, yet with a complexity that approaches PMAP's complexity for small values of k. In practice, this algorithm applies only when a small number of clusters remain to be allocated after the heuristic stage, thus allowing the use of the exhaustive procedure.

In order to familiarize with the terms of the algorithm, an example of physical mapping is presented. The G_C shown in Fig. 2 is mapped on a 3-cube processor network. The cluster allocation is performed using the PMAP algorithm.

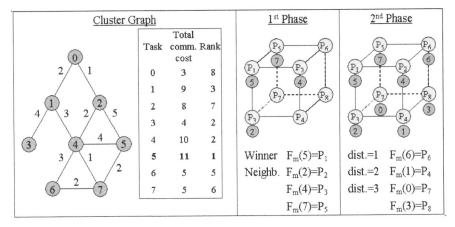

Fig. 2. An example of PMAP illustrating the heuristic's methods for successfully allocating the cluster graph shown on the left onto a 3-cube processor network

During the first phase the clusters are sorted, as it is described in steps one and two of the algorithm. The cluster with the lower ranking (Cluster 1) is assigned to P_1 and its three neighbors are allocated on the near by processors. In the second phase the candidate processors are P_4, P_6 and P_7, as they neighbor with the most already occupied processors. The remaining clusters are examined, in order to select a suitable assignment. Cluster 6 is assigned to P_6, and the criteria introduced in the 5th step are satisfied, because this particular cluster is allocated next to its cluster-graph neighbors (Clusters 3 and 7). During the next cycle of the second phase no other assignments can be made when the distance offset is set to 1, so the next cycle begins with distance offset increasing by one. During this cycle Cluster 1 is allocated on P_4 and the distance is again increased by one. Finally clusters 0 and 3 are assigned to P_7 and P_8 and the mapping is completed. The cost of this mapping according to equation (2) is $CF(F_m) = 34$, which is sufficiently low, as only three out of eleven messages require two hops to reach their destination (edges $(0 \rightarrow 1)$, $(2 \rightarrow 4)$ and $(4 \rightarrow 7)$), and the aggregate of total messages transferred through the processor network increases only by 5 units.

3.5   Single Shell Command Execution

TOPPER can automatically execute all the above-mentioned operations allow-ing its users to be exclusively involved with the drawing of the task and pro-cessor graph. From this point onwards, only a single command issued in the command line is sufficient for the execution of the necessary operations of the multi-step approach. Before executing a certain parallel program, TOPPER's users can consult the efficient task allocation results specified by the tool. The left hand path in Fig. 3 is followed, and the application is programmed according to these task specifications. Furthermore, users can even execute automatically, with the appropriate command switches, a parallel application whose communi-cation primitives are provided by MPI (Message Passing Interface). In this case,

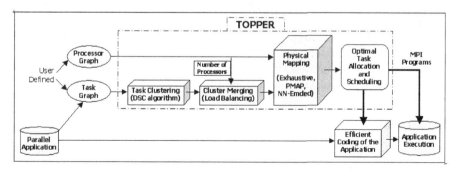

Fig. 3. Outline of TOPPER's flow chart. The bold arrows on the right hand-side demonstrate the two alternative paths that can be followed towards the application's execution on the target multiprocessing machine

the right hand path towards the application execution is followed, and the user is certain that the application's tasks will be properly allocated on the multiprocessor system. Obviously, this facilitates the optimization of parallel applications, requiring a minimal effort by the programmer.

4 Experimental Results

In order to verify TOPPER's efficiency, two parallel applications have been developed and executed in a processor cluster of 16 Pentium III processors, working on 500 MHz and having 128 MB RAM each. The cluster works under LINUX 2.2.17 and supports MPICH (MPI CHameleon). These processors are connected on a Fast Ethernet network (100 Mbps).

The applications consist of several tasks, which follow the task graph model exhibited in Sect. 3.1. More specifically, every task is blocked until all messages are received and, after executing its computational load, sends sequentially the respective messages to its neighboring tasks. Serializing all sends is a reasonable assumption, as in most cases the network interface card operates in a similar fashion. Message passing between tasks was implemented using MPI primitives and several Mbytes of data were transferred through the processor network.

The only problem arising during the execution of the applications, was the inability of MPI to exchange faster messages between tasks running on the same processor. In fact, not only was the transmission of these messages slower, but it was measured to have no relevance whatsoever with the size of the message. This drawback can be alleviated with the use of other type of communication, such as semaphores, which are quite sufficient for simulation applications, but unsuitable for actual parallel programs. As a result of this problem, the programming of simulation applications became a strenuous procedure, degrading the tools most functional feature: the automated execution of these applications. Every application had to be reprogrammed, its tasks were reallocated on the processor network, and semaphore-oriented communication had to be established between tasks executed on the same processor However, the potential elimination of this drawback in future versions of MPI will allow the development of an example generator and the thorough examination-evaluation of the tool's efficiency. In this way, the testing of all of the multi-step procedures that is now hindered by the small sized task and processor graphs, will become a feasible operation.

Let us now demonstrate the generated results during the programming and execution of two simulation parallel applications.

4.1 Example 1

The first application is a fork-join graph, with slight variations, that consists of 10 tasks, and is mapped on a 4-ring processor network. Presenting the application's task graph, Fig. 4 shows an intensive communication path $\{0 \rightarrow 1 \rightarrow 5 \rightarrow 9\}$ on the left hand side of the task graph. The task and the processor graph were given to TOPPER, and the result was the task allocations defined as "MAP"

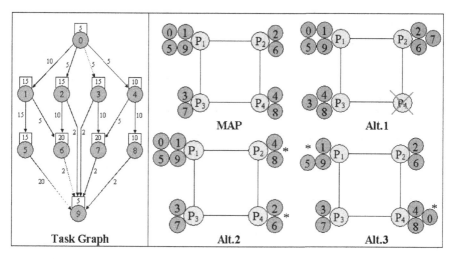

Fig. 4. The first example's task graph is presented, along with the different mapping implementations. The node tags and the figures beside the links of the task graph represent respectively the computational load and the communication cost between the tasks. The tasks are executed on the attached processors. The asterisks in Alt.2 mapping indicate the swapped clusters while the asterisk in Alt.3 shows that task 0 is moved from P_1 to P_4

implementation, as shown in Fig. 4. The finding of an optimal physical mapping was not a very complicated procedure, as less than 4! different mappings could be made. It should be noted that all the heavy-weighted edges are zeroed, and that 30% acceleration was achieved, compared to the serial execution time Fig. 6. Next, three alternative ways of task allocation were implemented, which will be called Alt.1, 2 and 3.

In Alt.1 only three out of the four available processors are used. It is easy to observe that P_2 and P_3 exchange data only with P_1, and thus an optimal mapping of these three clusters is easy to find. As Fig. 6 indicates, the acceleration achieved with Alt.1 is approximately 20%, significantly lower than MAP's acceleration.

In Alt.2 the synthesis of the clusters was the same as he ones in MAP, and a different mapping was chosen, in order to demonstrate the importance of physical mapping. Indeed Alt.2 demonstrated lower acceleration, due to several two hop-needing messages but it still remains the best possible alternative implementation, achieving sufficient acceleration approximately 25%, even though the clusters are not allocated on processors the optimal way. This fact is a strong indication of the high efficiency of the DSC algorithm in decreasing the parallel execution time.

In Alt.3 the arithmetic load of the clusters is being equalized, by moving task 0 from P_1 to P_4, and the physical mapping is the same as in MAP. Although the new clusters dispose a better-balanced load, the edge $(0 \rightarrow 1)$ is no longer a zero-valued edge. This feature renders Alt.3 inferior to all other implementations, exhibiting the worst execution time, speeding up the application only by 9%.

4.2   Example 2

The graph of the second application is more complicated, consisting of 11 tasks (Fig. 5), and is mapped on a hypercube of 8 processors. Once again the task and processor graph were given to TOPPER, and the results were 5 clusters, an indication that after task clustering the merging step was not necessary, as $8(> 5)$ processors are available. The synthesis of these clusters is shown on the left hand-side of Fig. 5. The optimal physical mapping was obtained with an exhaustive search and is also presented in the same figure and is denoted by "MAP". As a result of the DSC algorithm, P_2 is assigned a significantly overweighed cluster with an aggregate arithmetic load of 100 units, which is more than $1/3$ of the total arithmetic load of all the tasks. Nevertheless, the elimination of edges $(1 \rightarrow 4)$, $(4 \rightarrow 9)$ and $(9 \rightarrow 10)$ offers a parallel time speedup of 20% that cannot be achieved otherwise (Fig. 6).

Similarly to the previous example, three alternative task allocations were implemented. First, in Alt.1 the clusters dispose a more balanced computational load, while task 1 was moved from P_2 to P_4. All clusters possess an arithmetic

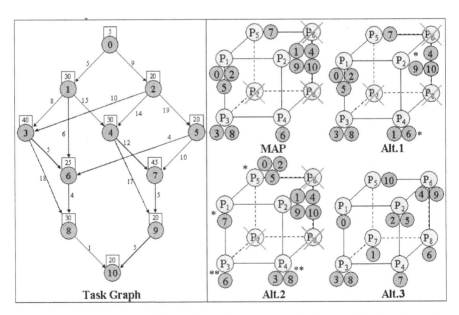

Fig. 5. The second example's task graph is presented, along with the alternative mapping implementations. The asterisk in Alt.1 shows that task 1 was moved from P_2 to P_4 and the asterisks in Alt.2 indicate the swapped clusters

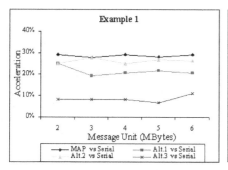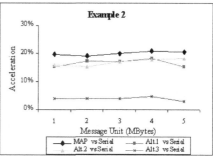

Fig. 6. Acceleration of the two applications' execution time achieved for every one of the four implementations, relatively to the message unit size. This increase of send/receive unit was, of course, followed by a proportional increase of computation unit, maintaining the task model's consistency

load between 45 and 70, though the general scheme of the previous implementation has not been altered. The resulting execution time speedup is quite reasonable, remaining though lower than TOPPER's mapping.

In Alt.2, although the clusters used are identical to those in the MAP implementation, their allocation on the processor network is altered, with clusters P_1 and P_3 swapping places correspondingly with P_5 and P_4. As a result of this "misplacement" the parallel execution time increases Fig. 6.

In Alt.3 all eight processors are used. Firstly, the three most demanding communication edges are zeroed by the formation of three clusters $\{2, 5\}$, $\{4, 9\}$ and $\{3, 8\}$. Then, every one of the remaining tasks is assigned to a free processor, forming the remaining clusters. Finally the clusters are allocated on the processor network trying to avoid multiple hops for large messages. The result constitutes a quite well "handmade" implementation, in practice, however, its acceleration is minimal, and the parallel time almost equals to the serial time.

5   Conclusion – Acknowledgements

Summarizing we should mention that TOPPER is an integrated software tool that can contribute to the improvement of parallel applications' effectiveness, thus taking one more step towards the expansion of parallel and distributed programming as a solution to computational need. TOPPER manages to overcome the task allocation problem, one of the main handicaps of parallel programming. The tool offers its users an easy yet successful way to make use of the benefits of the modern highly sophisticated multiprocessing systems, without getting trapped in the intensive communication needs between the tasks of a parallel program. Additionally, TOPPER is portable, as it is not specifically designed for a certain type of architecture, but it can be useful for executing parallel applications over all types of processor networks.

This research was supported in part by the Greek Secretariat of Research and Technology (GSRT) under a PENED 99/308 Project.

References

[1] Stone H.: "Multiprocessor Scheduling with the Aid of Network Flow Algorithms", *IEEE Transactions on Software Engineering*, Vol.3, No.1, pp.85-93, 1997. 337

[2] George A., Heath M. T. and Liu J.: "Parallel Cholesky Factorization on a Shared Memory Processor", *Linear Algebra and Applications*, Vol.77, pp.165-187, 1986. 341

[3] Lo V.: "Heuristic Algorithms for Task Assignment in Distributed Systems", *IEEE Transactions on Computers*, Vol.37, No.11, pp.1384-1397, 1988. 337

[4] Sarkar V.: "Partitioning and Scheduling Parallel Programs for Execution on Multiprocessors", Cambridge, MA, MIT Press, 1989. 338

[5] Monien B. and Sudborough H.: "Embedding one Interconnection Network in Another", *Computational Graph Theory*, Springer-Verlag, Computing Supplement, Vol.7, pp.257-282, 1990. 337

[6] Papadimitriou C. H. and Yannakakis M.: "Toward an Architecture-independent Analysis of Parallel Algorithms", *SIAM J. Computing*, Vol.19, pp.322-328, 1990. 337

[7] Lo V., Rajopadhye S., Gupta S., Keldsen D., Mohamed M., Nitzberg B., Telle J. And Zhong X.: "OREGAMI: Tools for Mapping Parallel Computations to Parallel Architectures", *International Journal of Parallel Programming*, Vol.20, No.3, pp.237-270, 1991. 336, 338, 343

[8] Yang T. and Gerasoulis A.: "PYRROS: Static Task Scheduling and Code Generation for Message Passing Multiprocessors", *Proceedings 6th Conference on Supercomputing (ICS92)*, pp.428-437, New York, NY, 1992. 336, 338

[9] Lewis T. and El-Rewini H.: "Parallax: a Tool for Parallel Program Scheduling", *IEEE Parallel and Distributed Technology*, Vol.1, No.2, pp.62-72, 1993. 336

[10] Ali H. and El-Rewini H.: "Task Allocation in Distributed Systems: a Split Graph Model", *Journal of Combinatorial Mathematics and Combinatorial Computing*, Vol.14, pp.15-32, 1993. 336

[11] El-Rewini H., Lewis T. G. and Ali H.: "*Task Scheduling in Parallel and Distributed Systems*", Prentice Hall, 1994. 336

[12] Yang T. and Gerasoulis A.: "DSC: Scheduling Parallel Tasks on an Unbounded Number of Processors", *IEEE Transactions on Parallel and Distributed Systems*, Vol.5, No.9, pp.951-967, 1994. 338, 340, 341

[13] Koziris N., Papakonstantinou G. and Tsanakas P.: "Optimal Time and Efficient Space Free Scheduling for Nested Loops", *The Computer Journal*, Vol.39, No.5, pp.439-448, 1996. 337

[14] Liou J. C., Palis. M. A.: "A Comparison of General Approaches to Multiprocessor Scheduling", *Proceedings 11th Parallel Processing Symposium (IPPS'97)*, pp.152-156, Geneva, Switzerland, 1997. 338

[15] Koziris N., Romesis M., Papakonstantinou G. and Tsanakas P.: "An Efficient Algorithm for the Physical Mapping of Clustered Task Graphs onto Multiprocessor Architectures", *Proceedings PDP'2000 Conference*, pp.406-413, Rhodes, 2000. 337, 339, 343

[16] Konstantinou D. and Panagiotopoulos A.: Thesis, Department of Electrical & Computer Engineering, NTUA, Athens, 2000. 340, 341

Communication Assist
for Data Driven Multithreading

Costas Kyriacou[1] and Paraskevas Evripidou[2]

[1] Computer Engineering Depart., Frederick Institute of Technology
P.O. Box 24729, 1303 Nicosia, CYPRUS
[2] Department of Computer Science, University of Cyprus
P.O. Box 20537, 1678 Nicosia, CYPRUS

Abstract. Latency tolerance is one of the main concerns in parallel processing. Data Driven Multithreading, a technique that uses extra hardware to schedule threads for execution based on data availability, allows for better performance, through latency tolerance. With Data Driven Multithreading a thread is scheduled for execution only if all of its inputs have been produced and placed in the processor's local memory. Communication and synchronization are decoupled from the computation portions of a program, i.e. they execute asynchronously. Thus, no synchronization or communication latencies will be experienced. The processor can, though be idle when there are no threads ready for execution, Thus, communication latencies are difficult to hide completely in applications with high communication-to-computation characteristics.

This paper presents three mechanisms for the implementation of the communication assist of a Data Driven Multithreaded architecture. The first mechanism relies only on fine grain communication, where each packet can transfer a single value. With the second mechanism, the communication assist is modified to support block data communication through the same fine grain interconnection network of the first configuration. The third mechanism employs a broadcast network such as Ethernet to transfer blocks of data, while fine grain communication is handled the same way as with the other two mechanisms.

1 Introduction

Memory and communication latency is one of the main bottlenecks that greatly affects the performance of a parallel machine [1]. Various techniques are used to reduce or avoid latency. The remaining latencies can be tolerated by using latency hiding techniques that allow the processor do other useful work while a long latency event is in progress. Such a technique is Multithreading [9, 3, 11, 10, 12]. The effectiveness of such techniques is greatly affected by the communication/computation patterns of applications. In algorithms where there is a need for distribution of large blocks of data it is possible that there is limited computation available while the communication is in progress, hence communication latency will be experienced. The degree of involvement of the computation

Y. Manolopoulos et al. (Eds.): PCI 2001, LNCS 2563, pp. 351–367, 2003.
© Springer-Verlag Berlin Heidelberg 2003

processor in the communication also affects the ability of an architecture to hide communication latency. In architectures with implicit communication there is a limited or no participation of the computation processor in the communication. In such architectures all communication is handled by the communication assist. This does not apply to architecture that employ explicit communication, where the computation processor initiates the communication.

Multithreading is a technique used to tolerate latency by allowing the processor to perform useful work, while a long latency event such as synchronization or communication is in progress. In blocking multithreading a thread may begin execution before all of its operands are available. A thread suspends whenever a missing operand is needed or synchronization is required. In such a case the processor switches to another thread ready for execution. Thus, these long latency events are tolerated by switching to other threads. The processor though, should provide hardware support for more than one concurrent program counter and register file and have the ability to switch among threads efficiently [2]. Blocking multithreaded architectures have been traditionally implemented as tightly coupled multiprocessors. In non-blocking multithreading, a thread is scheduled for execution only if all of its input operands are available in the local memory, thus no synchronization nor communication nor remote memory latencies will be experienced. Hence there is no need for thread suspension and switching to other threads, eliminating the need for multiple program counters and register files.

The communication assist plays a significant role in the ability of a Data Driven Multithreaded architecture in tolerating communication latencies. Communication can be classified according to the amount of data needed to be transferred per packet or communication session. In this sense, communication can be either fine grain (one value per session), medium grained (up to few tens of values per session) or coarse grained (hundreds or thousands of values per session). For optimal operation, the communication assist must process fine grained communication efficiently with minimal overheads due to system calls. This is achieved by allowing the hardware carrying out most of the operations required for the data transfer. Medium and coarse grain communication are more efficiently carried out with data block transfers. Applications with bursty communication patterns, characterized by large blocks of data that need to be distributed by a single processing node, will suffer from a speedup reduction if only fine grain communication is supported.

In this paper we examine three mechanisms for the implementation of the communication assist of a Data Driven Multithreaded architecture. The first one supports only fine grain communication. With the second mechanism, modifications are made on the communication assist to enable the transfer of blocks of data through a fine grain interconnection network. With the third mechanism, blocks of data are transferred though an Ethernet network, while single value information is transferred through the fine grain interconnection network.

An implementation of of a Data Driven Multithreaded architecture is the Data-Driven Network of Workstations (D^2NOW). It utilizes conventional control-flow workstations, augmented with an add-on card called the Thread Synchronization Unit (TSU), to support data driven sequencing of threads.

2   The D²NOW Architecture

Data Driven Multithreading is a non-blocking multithreaded model of execution evolved from the dataflow model of computation. An implementation of a Data Driven Multithreaded architecture is the Data-Driven Network of Workstations (D²NOW). It utilizes conventional control-flow workstations, augmented with an add-on unit called the Thread Synchronization Unit (TSU), to support data driven sequencing based on the Decoupled Data-Driven (D³-model) [7] model of execution. However, D²NOW differs from other data driven machines in that instructions are not synchronized and scheduled individually, but are combined into larger blocks of instructions, called threads. A key feature of the D³-model of execution is that the synchronization part of a program is separated from the computation part. The computation part represents the actual instructions of the program. The synchronization part contains information about data dependencies among instructions and it is used for instruction scheduling. The processor executes instructions using control flow sequencing, and is not aware of the existence of the TSU. The application activates the run time system that initializes the TSU to implement data driven sequencing between threads. Thus, the same hardware can execute multithreading as well as sequential control flow applications.

A D²NOW processing node is shown in Figure 1. The TSU is made out of three units: the Thread Issue Unit (TIU), the Post Processing Unit (PPU) and the Network Interface Unit (NIU). The Synchronization Engine (SE) acts as the control unit of the TSU. The function of the TIU is to schedule threads deemed executable. The PPU processes information about completed threads, and determines which threads are ready for execution. The NIU is responsible for the communication between the TSU and the interconnection network. A detailed description of the TSU is presented in [4].

In D²NOW a thread is a sequence of instructions that is executed sequentially. A producer/consumer relation exists among threads. The data needed by a thread is produced by other threads, called the producers. The data produced by a thread might be needed by other threads, called the consumers. The consumers of each thread are stored in the Graph Cache (GC). The GC contains also a pointer to the first instruction of each thread (Instruction Frame Pointer - IFP).

Synchronization occurs only at the top of a thread, i.e. before the thread is fired for execution. Each thread is associated with a synchronizing parameter, called the Ready Count, that indicates the number of inputs still needed to be produced before the thread is ready for execution. The Ready Count of each thread is stored in the Synchronization Memory (SM). This count is decremented whenever an input value of the thread is produced. A thread is enabled, that is, ready for execution, when its Ready Count reaches zero. In such a case the IFP

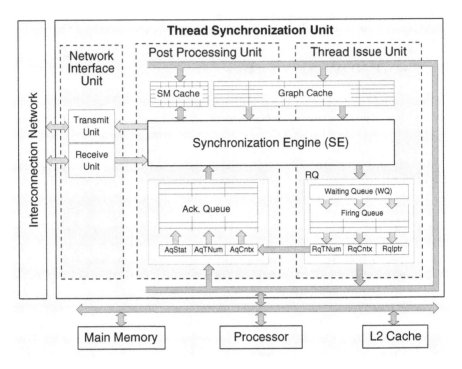

Fig. 1. A D^2NOW processing node with the Thread Synchronization Unit

of the thread is placed in the Ready Queue (RQ) of the TIU and waits for is turn to be executed.

The processor reads the address (IFP) of the next thread to be executed from the Ready Queue (RQ). After the processor completes the execution of a thread, it stores in the Acknowledge Queue (AQ) of the PPU the status and identification number of the completed thread and then reads the next thread to be executed from the RQ. The PPU fetches the completed threads from the AQ, reads their consumers from the Graph Cache and updates their Ready Count of the consumer threads in the Synchronization memory. If the consumer of a completed thread belongs to a remote node, then the PPU passes all necessary information to the NIU for further processing.

A number of features of D^2NOW enable the tolerance of communication latency. Thread synchronization and communication are handled by the TSU, while thread execution is handled by the processor. The two run asynchronously, i.e. they operate on different threads at a given instance. Thus thread synchronization and communication is carried out in parallel with the execution of other threads. Furthermore, whenever a thread produces data for a remote workstation, the producer workstation is responsible for transferring the data to the remote workstation. Since thread scheduling is based on data availability, there is no need for remote read operations. This reduces the overall communication cost, since remote read operations are usually more expensive than remote write operations. Finally, the TSU communicates with the interconnection network via queues. A packet transfer is initiated whenever a packet is placed in the transmit queue. At the receiving workstation, the TSU stores the received data in the memory without interrupting the processor. Communication is carried out solely by the hardware, thus the communication system is free from any system call overheads.

3   The Communication Assist

One of the main aims of Data Driven Multithreading is to tolerate communication latency by allowing the computation processor do other useful work while a communication event is in progress. This is obtained by hiding communication from the computation processor. The computation processor, is though involved in many cases in the initiation of a message transfer. The overhead associated with initiating a message transfer can be reduced by reducing the number of messages, by grouping messages, thus increasing their size. Making messages larger is easy in applications where block data transfer is inherent or in applications that have regular and predicted communication patterns. It is, though difficult in applications with irregular communication patterns. Furthermore, in Data Driven Multithreading, it is impossible to determine when a thread will cause a remote memory operation, since threads are scheduled for execution at run time, according to data availability. Thus, in Data Driven Multithreading, it is essential to use a fast communication system that does not relay on complex communication protocols and system calls, so that communication can be tolerated as much as possible.

When designing the communication assist of a parallel machine, it is essential to identify the nature of communication required. Communication can be classified according to the amount of data needed to be transferred as fine grain, medium grain and course grain.

- **Fine grain communication** refers to cases where single values need to be transferred from one node to another. Fined grain communication requires simple communication mechanisms with a minimal communication overhead.
- **Medium grain communication** refers to cases where small blocks of data need to be transferred from one node to another. Medium grain communication requires communication mechanisms capable of block data transfers.
- **Coarse grain communication** refers to cases where large blocks of data need to be transferred from one node to another. Course grain communication requires communication mechanisms capable of block data transfers.

D^{2}NOW utilizes the Telegraphos switch [5, 6] to implement its interconnection network. Telegraphos is a project carried out at ICS-FORTH, that investigates network interfaces for efficient parallel processing on networks of workstations (NOWs). The Telegraphos switch is a high performance switch that can be used in high speed networks, NOWs, and multiprocessor networks. Telegraphos is a low latency, fixed size packet switch based on virtual circuit, hop by hop credit-based flow control. Telegraphos is a 4 channel switch, with each channel carrying in parallel 8 data bits and a flag bit. Each packet consists of 17 bytes: one byte for the header and 16 bytes for the payload. A flag bit is used to identify the header of each packet, which identifies the virtual circuit number. Each link can support up to 256 virtual circuits. The clock cycle time is 40ns, giving a 400Mbps throughput. The selection of the Telegraphos switch to implement the interconnection network was primarily based on the need of a fine grain communication mechanism that does not rely on complex protocols. Communication is completely handled in hardware without the need for any system calls.

In this paper we examine three mechanisms for the implementation of the communication assist. The first one relies on a fine grain interconnection network based on the Telegraphos switch, and communication mechanisms that handle only fine grain communication. In the second mechanism, the TSU is modified to support medium and course grain communication. The third mechanism utilizes an Ethernet network to support block data transfers while fine grain communication is handled by the interconnection network.

3.1   Fine Grain Communication Support

With this mechanism, all communication is handled by the TSU and the interconnection network without any support for block data transfer. Whenever data needs to be transferred to a remote workstation, the computation processor executes a sequence of instructions to initiate the data transfer. These instructions store in the Ack. Queue the Thread ID, its context and a special code that specifies a remote write operation. The Post Processing Unit uses the Consumers of the thread specified in the Graph Cache to determine the destination processor and the data to be transferred. If these instructions are part of a thread that performs some computation, then they do not add any significant overheads to the computation processor. These overheads are though more important in applications where blocks of data need to be transferred, reducing significantly the overall speedup.

The block diagram of the NIU unit that supports only fine grain communication is depicted in Figure 2. The NIU is made out of two units: the Transmit Unit and the Receive Unit. Both units have their own controller and their operation is independent from each other.

The transmitter unit performs two functions. The first one is to monitor the state of the interconnection network, by keeping a record of the credits for each virtual circuit. The second is to assemble and transmit packets of data to the interconnection network. Information needed to be send to other processors is first stored in the Xmit Queue, in the form of a packet. Each packet contains the receiving processors ID number, the base and context values of the receiving thread, as well as the data. The first entry of each packet is always the receiving processor ID number. The Transmit Control Unit monitors the 'Empty' signal of the Send Queue to check if a packet waits to be transmitted. In such a case the

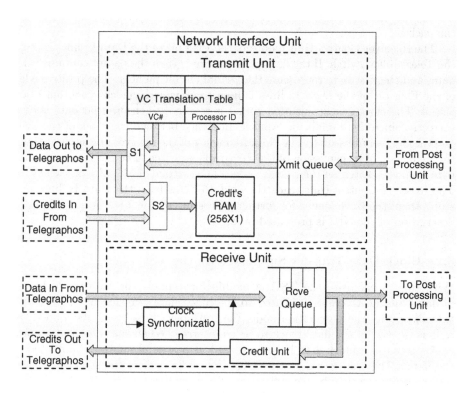

Fig. 2. The Network Interface Unit with fine grain communication support

first entry in the queue is used as the address for the Virtual Circuit Translation Table. The function of this look-up table is to determine the virtual circuit number of the destination processor. This table is static, i.e. its entries do not change, since the Telegraphos switch uses static (hardwired) virtual circuits. After finding the virtual circuit number (VC#), the Transmit Control Unit reads the corresponding entry in the Credits RAM. Each entry in this RAM indicates whether there is an empty slot in the Telegraphos switch for a specific virtual circuit. This is a 256X1 RAM, since the Telegraphos switch can support up to 256 virtual circuits per link. If there is an empty slot, i.e. the credit for that virtual circuit is one, the Transmit Control Unit sends first, the virtual circuit number to the Telegraphos switch through the Data Out lines. The rest of the packet is then transmitted, one byte per cycle. After sending a packet to the switch, the Transmit Control Unit resets the content of the credit RAM for that virtual circuit. This is required because only one slot is allocated for each virtual circuit in the Telegraphos switch. If a packet is to be sent through a virtual circuit that has no empty slot, i.e. its credit is zero, then that packet has to wait until the corresponding slot is empty. In this case, the Transmit Control Unit has to wait until it receives a credit for that virtual circuit, and then transmit the packet.

The Receiver Control Unit monitors the Flag bit of the Data In lines sent by the Telegraphos switch. If the flag bit is at logic 1, then the packet contains valid data, and the first byte represents the virtual circuit number. The positive edge of the Flag bit of the Data In lines is used to trigger the clock synchronization circuit. The clock synchronization circuit is required to ensure that data is read correctly, since there might be a phase difference between the clock of the TSU and the clock of the switch. The clock frequency of the receiver unit is three times the frequency of transmission of the Telegraphos switch. The receiver reads each byte from the switch on the positive edge of the second clock pulse of each cycle. The Receiver Control Unit reads the next 16 bytes from the Data In lines and stores them the Rcve Queue for further processing by the TSU. A more detailed description of the NIU is presented in [8].

3.2   Block Data Transfer Supported by the TSU

With this mechanism, the TSU is modified to enable the transfer of blocks of data. Special threads, dedicated to the block data transfer are used. These threads specify the destination node, the consumer thread with its context, as well as the size of the data block to be transferred. When the computation processor executes a block data transfer thread, it passes all information related to the data to be transferred to the TSU. Figure 3a depicts the structure of the information needed to be passed to the TSU to enable the transfer of a block of data. Figure 3b shows a typical thread that initiates the transfer of a block of data. The overheads introduced by a block data transfer thread is ten instructions for one consumer. Three instructions are added for each extra consumer. These overheads are insignificant for medium grain and course grain block data transfers.

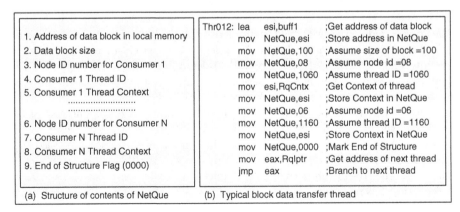

(a) Structure of contents of NetQue   (b) Typical block data transfer thread

Fig. 3. Thread structure to support block data transfer using a modified TSU

The modifications needed to be made on the TSU to support the transfer of blocks of data are shown in figure 4. A queue, called the NetQue, is placed in the NIU to hold the information related to the data block to be transfer. This queue is visible to the computation processor. A communication processor is embedded in the NIU to control its operation. If the NetQue is not empty, the communication processor fetches all necessary data from the main memory, via a DMA engine. It then, sends to the Transmit Buffer (Xmit Queue) of the Transmit Unit, all data values by forming one packet per value. The first packet in each block identifies the beginning of a block data transfer and specifies the size of the block. At the receiving end, the communication processor checks all packets received. Ordinary fine grain packets are sent directly to the Post Processing Unit (PPU) for further processing. If the received packet is a block data transfer packet, it is intercepted by the communication processor. When all packets of a block are received, the processor copies the data in the main memory via a DMA engine, and then signals the PPU to decrement the Ready Count of the consumer thread.

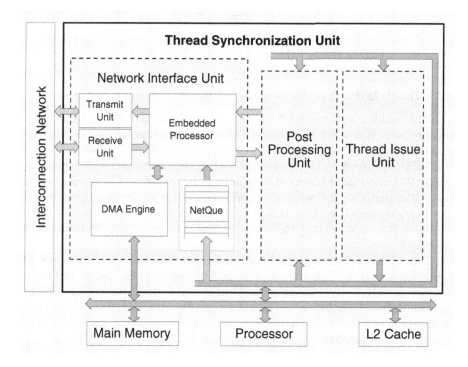

Fig. 4. Modified TSU to support block data transfer

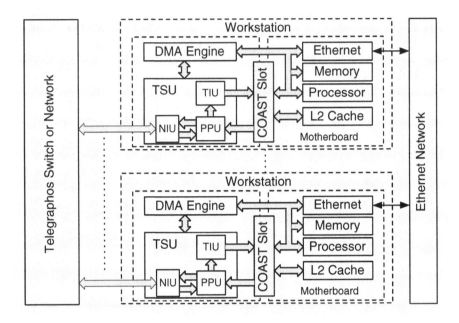

Fig. 5. Use of Ethernet to transfer large blocks of data

3.3 Block Data Transfer Supported by an Ethernet Network

D^2NOW utilizes an Ethernet LAN that runs in parallel with a dedicated fast interconnection network as shown in Figure 5. Parallel processing data is transferred through the interconnection network, while Ethernet is used to copy the code of the program to be executed to each node, as well as for debugging purposes. Whenever large blocks of data need to be transferred, a special thread is used, that performs the necessary operation to transfer the data block through the Ethernet network. This thread must also send a message to the TSU of the receiving node, so that the receiving TSU can update its Synchronization Memory.

The overheads introduced by this mechanism are relatively high, since Ethernet is accessed through system calls and interrupts. Thus, the use of Ethernet is efficient only for course grain block data transfers. This mechanism can be used only when large blocks of input data must be distributed to the processing nodes, or when the output data is to be collected from the processing nodes. Fine grain and medium grain communication is handled by the TSU.

4   Evaluation Methodology

In order to evaluate the ability of D^2NOW in tolerating latency, we have used a combination of analytical modeling and an execution driven simulator. Analytical modeling is used to verify the functionality of the TSU, and to provide the simulator with the timing characteristics of the TSU and the interconnection network. All applications used are hand coded directly in assembly language. The partition to threads and the development of thread templates is also done manually.

Simulations were carried out for systems with 2, 4, 8 and 16 processors. To investigate the capability of D^2NOW to hide communication latency, simulations were carried out for various communication clock cycle times, ranging from 0 ns to 100 ns. A byte is transferred on every clock with a 4-clock cycle node-to-node delay. Simulations were carried out for the three communication assist mechanisms, for 0 ns, 20 ns, 40 ns and 100 ns interconnection network clock cycle times.

4.1 Hardware Implementation

The three units of the TSU (PPU,TIU and NIU) have been coded in VHDL, and simulated separately. Each unit has been downloaded to a Xilinx XC4005E FPGA for functional and timing verification. The TSU can be implemented using the Xilinx FPGAs as well as standard components like SRAM and FIFO chips. It is estimated that nine XC4005E FPGAs are needed for the implementation of the TSU. These FPGAs are not fully utilized. This is done in order to reduce the routing delays in the FPGAs and thus obtain higher speeds.

The cycle time for all units of the TSU is 20 ns. The minimum time needed by the TIU to process one thread is 120 ns. This is the case of threads that have only one input data. The minimum time needed by the PPU to process one thread is 100 ns. This is the case of threads that have only one consumer that refers to local memory. At least 20 ns must be added for any extra consumer. We choose these low speeds for the implementation of the TSU because of the routing delays encountered on the FPGAs. These speeds are though, compatible with the speed of the pentium processors used (166MHz).

4.2 Simulation Facility

The D^2NOW simulator is an execution driven simulator that uses native execution. Both the host and the target processor is a Pentium processor. The instructions of the simulated program are executed directly by the host. Calls to functions that simulate the TSU and the interconnection network are interleaved with the execution of threads on the host processor. In order to accurately simulate the behaviour of the TSU, the simulator uses the timings produced by the actual implementation of the TSU. The time needed to execute each thread is derived using the processor's time stamp counter. At the end of each simulation phase, the simulator produces results showing the time needed to execute a thread, as well as the state of each TSU unit, so that buffer occupancy can be investigated.

The simulation of the TSU must not affect the state of the target machine. Since the machine used as the host is also the target, the state of the cache of the simulated application is affected by the simulation process. To ensure that the state of the cache of the target processor is not affected by the operation of the simulator, a buffer that contains the last 1K data memory references generated by the target processor is maintained. Before branching to the execution of a thread, the simulator reads the data from the memory locations stored in this buffer, thus the contents of the cache will be closed to the contents of the cache on the real system. A similar approach is used for the code of the simulated program, that is the starting addresses of the last threads executed are read from the memory, so that the code of these threads is placed in the cache.

4.3 Benchmark Suite

The applications used to evaluate the three communication assist mechanisms are listed in Figure 6. These applications have different communication characteristics, in terms of volume and distribution. These applications are the matrix multiplication (**Mult**), LU decomposition **LU**, the trapezoital method of integration (**Trapez**) and the Fast Fourier Transform (**FFT1**, **FFT2** and **FFT3**). For all applications the typical thread size is equivalent to the instructions needed to perform the necessary computation for one point (10 to 15 instructions).

Mult is a block oriented matrix multiplication algorithm. One of the two matrices is assumed to hold constant coefficients that are preloaded on the local memory of each node. The second matrix is partitioned into smaller square matrices by one node and distributed to the rest. Each node is responsible for generating complete sub-matrices of the result matrix. Computed sub-matrices are finally collected by a single node. **LU** is the LU decomposition Gaussian elimination method for solving a linear system. **Trapez** is the trapezoital rule for numerical estimation of a definite integral. As an example integrand we have used a third degree polynomial.

In order to get more conclusive results on the ability of D^2NOW to tolerate communication latency, we used algorithms that have different communication

Application	Data Size	Communication		
		Fine Grain	Medium Grain	Course Grain
Mult	256X256	Low	No	High/Bursty
LU	256X256	Low	Low	High/Bursty
Trapez	1000000 points	Low	No	No
FFT1	256X256	Low	Average	No
FFT2	256X256	Average	Average/Bursty	Average/Bursty
FFT3	256X256	Average	Average	Average

Fig. 6. Communication characteristics of benchmark suite

characteristics for the FFT application. **FFT1** is the Binary Exchange algorithm. The input values are assumed to be distributed among the processing nodes. At the end of the computation, each processing node holds a contiguous set of transformed values. The twiddle factors (W-terms) of the FFT algorithm are preloaded in the local memory of each processing node. **FFT2** is the same as the **FFT1** application, with the difference that the input values are distributed by one processing node to the rest. At the end of the computation the transformed values are collected by a single processing node. **FFT3** is the Transpose FFT algorithm. The input values are distributed by one processing node to the rest. At the end of the computation the transformed values are collected by a single processing node.

4.4   Results

The speedup, compared to single processor execution, for varying number of nodes and varying communication clock cycles for the three communication assist mechanisms is depicted in Figure 7. Column A shows the speedups obtained when only fine grain communication is supported. Column B shows the speedups obtained when block data transfer is supported by the TSU. Column C shows the speedups obtained when block data transfer is supported by an Ethernet network.

- **Effect of Communication Latency on Performance**
  The speedup, compared to single processor execution, for 2, 4, 8 and 16 nodes with varying communication clock cycles, for all applications is depicted in Figure 8. These results were obtained using block data transfer supported by the TSU. The effect of the speed of the interconnection network on speedup is indicated by the distance between the speedup lines for each communication clock cycle. The denser these lines are, the less the effect on speedup.
  Table in Figure 9 shows the effect of the communication clock cycle on speedup. This tables shows the percentage reduction in speedup, with 16 processors, when the communication clock cycle is increased from 20ns to 100ns (400% increase). The reduction in speedup is lower for the **Trapez** and **FFT1** applications since the communication needed by these applications is very low. The rest of the applications have a slightly higher reduction in speedup (around 20%). This is still very low compared to the 400% increase in the communication clock cycle. Thus, communication latencies can indeed be tolerated.
- **Effect of Communication Assist Mechanism on Performance**
  The percentage speedup improvement obtained when block data transfer is supported by the TSU or an Ethernet network, compared to the speedup obtained when only fine grained communication is supported, is depicted in the table in Figure 10. Most of the applications, (**Mult, LU, FFT2** and **FFT3**) have a significant speedup improvement ranging from 28% to 60% when block data transfer is supported by the TSU, and 18% to 50% when

	Number of Processors	n=2			n=4			n=8			n=16		
Comm. Clock Cycle		A	B	C	A	B	C	A	B	C	A	B	C
Mult	0 ns	1.45	1.81	1.68	2.77	3.51	3.36	5.44	6.83	6.42	10.48	13.43	12.38
	20 ns	1.30	1.70	1.66	2.48	3.08	3.20	4.82	6.34	6.18	9.05	12.31	12.14
	40 ns	1.19	1.56	1.61	2.28	2.92	2.96	4.42	5.78	5.89	8.15	11.42	11.72
	100 ns	1.04	1.47	1.48	1.92	2.76	2.79	3.91	5.42	5.48	6.97	10.49	10.36
LU	0 ns	1.32	1.81	1.70	2.45	3.68	3.42	5.02	7.01	6.73	9.91	13.20	12.82
	20 ns	1.24	1.68	1.66	2.38	3.29	3.20	4.71	6.41	6.17	9.12	12.16	12.12
	40 ns	1.14	1.56	1.61	2.21	2.98	2.98	4.36	5.92	6.01	8.43	11.38	11.41
	100 ns	1.06	1.35	1.54	2.12	2.68	2.88	4.11	5.29	5.83	7.51	10.84	10.56
Trapez	0 ns	1.82	1.86	1.83	3.42	3.54	3.45	6.57	6.71	6.63	12.51	12.62	12.58
	20 ns	1.76	1.80	1.78	3.25	3.32	3.29	6.41	6.63	6.49	12.03	12.16	12.13
	40 ns	1.71	1.74	1.72	3.12	3.31	3.19	6.02	6.24	6.13	11.57	11.76	11.65
	100 ns	1.64	1.68	1.67	2.95	3.20	3.17	5.78	5.96	5.85	11.06	11.38	11.26
FFT1	0 ns	1.72	1.83	1.82	3.38	3.53	3.49	6.46	6.85	6.73	11.53	11.92	11.83
	20 ns	1.64	1.76	1.73	3.23	3.43	3.39	6.08	6.41	6.37	10.92	11.31	11.29
	40 ns	1.52	1.63	1.62	2.99	3.12	3.07	5.72	6.09	5.99	10.15	10.58	10.51
	100 ns	1.47	1.59	1.56	2.78	2.91	2.87	5.45	5.85	5.73	9.79	10.28	10.23
FFT2	0 ns	1.41	1.90	1.78	2.41	3.38	3.12	4.65	6.23	5.98	8.02	11.15	10.31
	20 ns	1.35	1.82	1.72	2.28	3.19	2.87	4.23	6.01	5.44	6.95	10.04	9.22
	40 ns	1.25	1.76	1.66	2.09	2.95	2.77	3.95	5.33	5.12	6.42	9.42	9.01
	100 ns	1.14	1.61	1.54	1.96	2.76	2.61	3.37	5.12	4.65	5.41	8.67	8.14
FFT3	0 ns	1.50	1.91	1.81	3.08	3.61	3.37	5.53	6.62	6.44	9.03	11.52	11.06
	20 ns	1.43	1.84	1.61	2.76	3.42	3.10	5.05	6.25	6.05	8.21	10.63	10.21
	40 ns	1.32	1.72	1.53	2.51	3.15	2.81	4.52	6.01	5.42	7.33	10.02	9.23
	100 ns	1.17	1.55	1.40	2.28	2.95	2.63	4.12	5.56	4.98	6.72	9.41	9.06

Fig. 7. Speedup for fine grain communication support (Column A), block data transfer support by the TSU (Column B) and block data transfer support by an Ethernet network (Column C) with varying communication clock cycles and number of nodes.

block data transfer is supported by an Ethernet network. Two of the applications, (**Trapez** and **FFT1**), have a low speedup improvement (less than 5%). This is due the low communication requirements of these applications. The speedups obtained when Ethernet is used, is in always less than the speedup obtained when block data transfer is supported by the TSU. This is because medium grained communication is not efficient on Ethernet. In many cases, especially in the FFT applications, there is a need to transfer

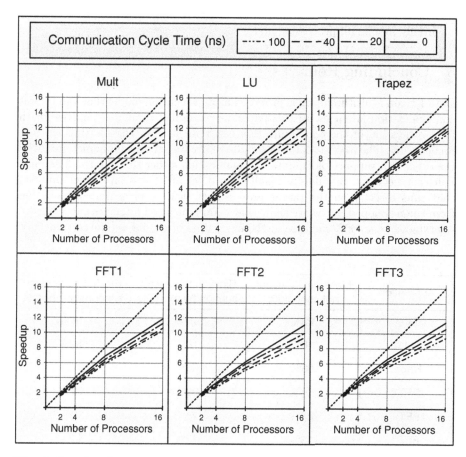

Fig. 8. Speedup for varying communication clock cycles, with block data transfer supported by the TSU

few tens of bytes between nodes (all-to-all communication). This can not be handled efficiently by Ethernet due to communication overheads.

The three FFT applications have different communication characteristics in terms of volume and intensity, while they carry out the same amount of computation. Thus more conclusive observations can be derived from the results of these three versions of the FFT algorithm. For **FFT1** there is a very low effect of the speed of the interconnection network on the speedup. This is because the input data is assumed to be distributed among the processors in advance. Hence there is a very low improvement in the speedup when block data transfer is used. A bigger decrease in speedup is observed in **FFT2** due to the high volume communication needed for the distribution of the sample values at the beginning of each FFT, and the collection of computed values at the end of each FFT. Moderate results are obtained for **FFT3** because communication incurs at almost all stages of the algorithm, and is spread evenly among all processing nodes.

5   Concluding Remarks

Data Driven Multithreading is proposed as an execution model that can tolerate communication latencies. In this paper we examined three mechanisms for the implementation of the communication assist for a Data Driven Multithreaded architecture. The first mechanism supports only fine grain communication, while the other two support block data communication either through the TSU or an Ethernet network. Simulation results based on an execution driven simulator that runs directly on the target processor as well as measurements obtained from the developed hardware show that communication latencies can indeed be tolerated. For a 400% increase in the cycle time of the interconnection network

Application	Block data transfer not supported	Block data transfer support by the TSU	Block data transfer support by Ethernet
Mult	23%	15%	14%
LU	18%	14%	14%
Trapez	08%	06%	07%
FFT1	10%	09%	09%
FFT2	22%	14%	12%
FFT3	18%	12%	11%

Fig. 9. Speedup reduction for a 400% increase in the communication clock cycle

Application	Block data transfer support by the TSU	Block data transfer support by Ethernet
Mult	28% - 51%	18% - 48%
LU	32% - 44%	29% - 41%
Trapez	01% - 03%	00% - 02%
FFT1	03% - 05%	03% - 04%
FFT2	39% - 60%	29% - 50%
FFT3	27% - 40%	22% - 35%

Fig. 10. Speedup improvement when block data transfer is supported compared to the speedup obtained when only fine grain communication is supported

the maximum speedup reduction among all applications is only 23% when block data transfer is not supported. This effect is reduced further when block data transfer is supported. Applications that need block data transfer have shown a significant improvement in the speedup when block data transfer is supported by the TSU, ranging from 28% to 60%, while the improvement in speedup when Ethernet is used for block data transfer is slightly less, ranging from 18% to 50%.

References

[1] Arvind and R. A. Iannucci. Two Fundamental Issues in Multiprocessors: the Data-Flow Solutions. Technical Report LCS/TM-241, Laboratory for Computer Science, Massachusetts Institute of Technology, Cambridge, Massachusetts, September 1983. 351

[2] Panel Discussion. Architectural Implementation Issues for Multithreading. R. Iannucci et al. (eds), *Mutlithreaded Computer Architecture a Summary of the State of the Art.* Kluwer Academic Publishers, 1994. 352

[3] Herbet Hum et al. A Design Study of the EARTH Multiprocessor. *Proceedings International Conference on Parallel Architectures and Compilation Techniques (PACT95)*, Limassol, Cyprus, June 1995. 351

[4] P. Evripidou, C. Kyriacou, Data Driven Network of Workstations (D^2NOW), *Journal of Universal Computer Science (JUCS)*, Vol.6, No.10, Oct. 2000. 353

[5] M. Katevenis, P. Votsalaki, A. Efthymiou and M. Stratakis. Vc-level Flow Control and Shared Buffering in the Telegraphos Switch. *Proceedings IEEE Hot Interconnects III Symposium*, 1995. 355

[6] E. Markatos and M. Katevenis. Telegraphos: High-performance Networking for Parallel Processing on Workstation Clusters. *Proceedings Symposium on High Performance Computer Architectures*, 1996. 355

[7] P. Evripidou. D^3-machine: a Decoupled Data-Driven Multithreaded Architecture with Variable Resolution Support. *Parallel Computing*, Vol.27, No.9 pp.1197-1225, 2001. 353

[8] C. Kyriacou and P. Evripidou. Network Interface for a Data Driven Network of Workstations (D^2NOW), In *Proceedings International Symposium on High Performance Computing (ISHPC-99)*, Kyoto, Japan, May 1999. 358

[9] J. Sile, B. Robic and T. Ungerer. Asynchrony in Parallel Computing: From Dataflow to Multithreading. *Parallel and Distributed Computing Practices*, Vol.1, No.1, March 1998. 351

[10] Boon S. Ang, Derek Chiou, Larry Rudolph and Arvind. The StarT Voyager Parallel System. *Proceedings International Conference on Parallel Architectures and Compilation Techniques (PACT98)*, Paris, France, October 1998. 351

[11] Eggers et al. Simultaneous Multithreading: a Platform for Next Generation Processors. *IEEE Micro*, pp.12-18, September/October 1997. 351

[12] D. Culler et al. Tam: a Compiler Controlled Threaded Abstract Machine. *Journal of Parallel and Distributed Computing*, June 1993. 351

A Framework for Mobility and QoS Provisioning in IPv6 DECT Networks

Sarantis Paskalis[1], Georgios Lampropoulos[1],
Dimitris Skyrianoglou[1], and Evangelos Zervas[2]

[1] Communication Networks Laboratory
Department of Informatics and Telecommunications
University of Athens, Greece
{paskalis,glambr,dimiski}@di.uoa.gr
[2] Department of Electronics, TEI of Athens, Athens, Greece
zervas@ee.teiath.gr

Abstract. The Internet Protocol suite is emerging as the ubiquitous communication platform for almost every conceivable information exchange. Hence, a worldwide effort to support IP functionality over any existing link technology has started, including the booming wireless industry. DECT is a well-standardized wireless access network technology, supporting high bitrate digital communications. Moreover, IPv6, the emerging Internet Protocol version, extends support for mobility, QoS, wireless nodes and addressing issues. We propose a framework for mobility and QoS provisioning in IPv6 DECT networks. Mobile IPv6 is deployed, in conjunction with standard DECT mobility procedures to provide a suitable environment for Internet users on the move. Furthermore, RSVP is utilized to handle QoS signaling.

1 Introduction

Wireless devices are constantly enhanced with new capabilities that open up a great window of opportunity for their exploitation. Whereas the size of the handheld terminals continues to shrink, their processing power continues to increase. Nowadays, handheld devices posses more computing power than many workstations some years ago. Since the mobile devices are serving well to many of everyday productivity tasks, they are posed with more challenging missions.

The most important feature of any mobile device is a generic communication capability. The devices should be able to connect to other networks wherever they are. DECT is a well-standardized wireless access network specification with an extensive user base in residential and business wireless telephony. It can provide a flexible and adjustable bearer support for the information transmission of various applications. Since the Internet Protocol suite is the dominant network architecture, a wireless device should exhibit an IP stack in order to be able to communicate globally. The IPv6 standard supports mobile devices through

Y. Manolopoulos et al. (Eds.): PCI 2001, LNCS 2563, pp. 368–385, 2003.

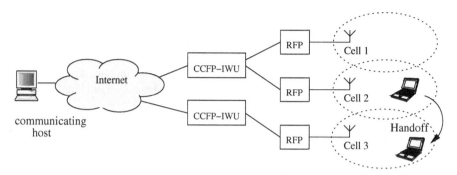

Fig. 1. Network topology

its extensive addressing and mobility extensions, while QoS guarantees can be satisfied through the use of the well established RSVP protocol.

The combination of the aforementioned technologies, however, is a difficult task, given the different focus points. An overview of the involved technologies is given in Section 2. The proposed system architecture is analyzed in Section 3 defining the basic mobility management infrastructure, interconnecting IP and DECT. Section 4 examines the interworking between RSVP and our framework and points out some possible approaches for their integration, while Section 5 concludes this work.

2   Overview

2.1   DECT

DECT (Digital Enhanced Cordless Telecommunications) [8] denotes a radio technology suited for voice data and networking applications with range requirements up to a few hundred meters. DECT mobility entities are separated into Portable Parts (PPs) and Fixed Parts (FPs). A DECT access network consists of an FP with one or more PPs attached to it. The FP encompasses three functional entities: the Radio Fixed Part (RFP), the Common Control Fixed Part (CCFP) and the Inter-Working Unit (IWU) as shown in Fig. 1.

The RFP controls the radio interface to the PPs. It contains all the radio endpoints that are connected to a single system of antennas and its coverage area represents a single cell in a cellular system. Concerning the protocol stack functionality, the RFP implements the Physical (PHY) and the Medium Access Control (MAC) layer procedures of DECT, while a Data Link Control (DLC) relay capability is included in order to make the exchange of DLC frames between the CCFP and the PP feasible.

CCFP is in a higher hierarchical position compared to the RFP. It is the core of the FP functionality and only one CCFP can be present in each FP. It supports both the DLC and Network (NWK) layers for communication with several RFPs. Each DECT network is supervised by a CCFP and consists of a number of RFPs, each responsible for a single cell.

The IWU is directly connected to the CCFP, and its role is mainly to transform any kind of control or data information in a proper format for transmission over different types of networks and vice-versa. A direct interworking of DECT with Ethernet, Token Ring, PPP and IP has already been specified by ETSI [12].

DECT Connectivity Modes DECT supports three modes of connection, Call Control (CC), Connection Oriented Message Service (COMS), and Connection-Less Message Service (CLMS) [10]. Call Control is the main service instance. It provides a set of procedures that allow the establishment, maintenance and release of switched services, as well as support for call related signaling. COMS offers a point-to-point protocol oriented packet service. On the contrary, CLMS offers a connectionless point-to-point or point-to-multipoint service.

DECT Location Management Three location tracking mechanisms have been specified in DECT: Location Registration, Location Update and Detach [10].

The Location Registration mechanism is used by the PP to indicate to the FP its current location in terms of Location Areas (LAs). The LA usually consists of one or several DECT systems and may cover several RFPs. The PP initiates the registration mechanism after it figures out that it has moved to a new LA. The RFP in each cell broadcasts periodically the cell identity to its associated PPs. This is a Radio Fixed Part Identifier (RFPI). It consists of a Primary Access Right Identity (PARI) field and a Radio Fixed Part Number (RPN) field. A default Location Area is defined as the PARI field of the RFPI, but it is also possible to define Location Areas by a fraction of the RFPI identity using the Location Area Level (LAL) indicator. In order to initiate the registration process, the PP compares the LA field of the last RFPI kept in its buffer with the LA field of the current RFPI. If these are different, the PP sends a Location Request message to the FP including its IPUI. The FP responds with a Location Accept message in case of successful registration or with a Location Reject message otherwise. If the LA values are the same, the PP remains in the same LA, and the registration procedure is similar and named "attach".

Location Update is used by the FP to inform the PP of a modification of the LAs. Detach is the process whereby a PP informs the FP that it is not ready to receive incoming calls.

2.2 IPv6

IP version 6 (IPv6) [6] is the new version of the Internet Protocol, which contains many enhancements over the current version (IPv4) that is deployed in today's Internet. A communication protocol that was designed a few decades ago could not foresee all the needs for the highly evolving computer industry. In that respect, IPv6 offers improvements in those areas that exhibited scalability or other types of problems. Some of these are:

- Enhanced addressing scheme. The most visible and needed feature of IPv6 is the expansion of the address space from 32 to 128 bits, that provides support for a huge number of hosts, most of which are expected to be mobile. It also simplifies the address self configuration task for those devices. Multicast is improved and the "anycast" address is specified to send a packet to any one of a group of nodes.
- Header simplification. Although the header size increases significantly (128 from 32 bits), the default header fields are reduced in number, resulting to more flexible processing in the intermediate routers.
- Extensibility. The header fields restructuring has resulted in a more flexible header option processing manner. New header fields can be added without causing significant processing overhead.
- Discrimination of packet flows. The Flow Label field added in the IPv6 header allows the distinction of packets according to their traffic "flows" and their potential preferential treatment.

Mobile IPv6 is a solid migration path from today's Internet to next generation networks, where mobile nodes and terminals need to be always on-line.

2.3   IPv6 Addressing Issues

In IPv6 environments, a node may communicate through several interfaces. All interfaces are required to have at least one IPv6 address, their link-local address. Link-local addresses are used for communication between nodes in the same link (subnet), are unique for that link, and should be assigned prior to any other IPv6 address [16]. A link-local address is constructed by a specific prefix indicating local use only (FE80::/64), and an interface identifier that could be based on the EUI-64 [17]. In order to avoid any duplicate addresses, the "Duplicate Address Detection" mechanism is performed on all addresses before assignment. After a node is assigned a link-local address, it can proceed with stateful (DHCPv6) or stateless (IPv6 Stateless Auto-configuration) mechanisms to obtain a global IPv6 address.

DHCPv6 In DHCPv6 [7], the allocation of addresses to nodes follows the client-server paradigm. The mobile node acts as a DHCP client requesting an address (or other configuration parameters) from a DHCP server. The client sends a solicitation message to the multicast address of all DHCP agents (FF02::1:2) in order to find a DHCP server that could provide the requested configuration parameters.

Each server identifies the client by a DHCP Unique Identifier (client DUID) contained in the solicitation message and replies with an advertisement message including the server DUID. The DUID (both client and server) is of variable length and constructed into one of four possible formats: Link-layer address plus time, Vendor-assigned unique ID based on domain name, Vendor-assigned unique ID based on Enterprise Number or Link-layer address.

The solicitation and the advertisement messages also contain an option field called Identity Association (IA), which is a construct for identification, grouping and management of addresses assigned to a client interface. It is characterized by an IA identifier (IAID), chosen by the client to be unique among the IAIDs for the particular client. According to the suitability of the advertisement messages received regarding the IAs, the client choses the fittest server. DHCP servers may not be located on the client's physical link for scalability and economy reasons. In such cases, a DHCPv6 relay agent is placed in the client's subnet and is responsible for forwarding messages from client to server and vice versa.

After a specific server is chosen, the communication between the client and the particular server continues with the exchange of request-reply messages. The client sends a request message to the server, asking for resources. The request message includes the client identifier (DUID), the server identifier (DUID) and one or several IAs. The server, upon reception of a request message, examines an internal table, where the configuration parameters for each interface are kept, and allocates IPv6 addresses to the client. The allocation procedure is based on the link to which the client is attached, the DUID supplied by the client and other information supplied by the client or the relay agent. During this process, a binding between each interface of the client and the allocated IPv6 addresses for that interface is built. This binding is indexed by the tuple <DUID, IA-type, IAID>, where the DUID is the client DUID, the IA-type is the address type of the IA (for example temporary) and the IAID is the identifier for the IA that requests DHCP resources from the server. After the allocation mechanism is completed, a reply is sent back to the client, indicating successful or unsuccessful binding, i.e IPv6 addresses are allocated or not to the requesting interface. Each IPv6 address assigned to an IA has a specific expiration time (lease), which is included in the reply message and may be renewed later.

IPv6 Stateless Auto-Configuration IPv6 provides a stateless configuration mode [27] for IPv6 nodes. In this mode, the assignment of IPv6 addresses is simplified and there is no need for servers. After an interface is assigned a link-local address, the node tries to construct a global IPv6 address. The global address is formed by substituting the link-local prefix with the subnet prefix in the link-local address. In other words, the IPv6 address is formed with the addition of the advertised subnet prefix to the interface identifier.

The powered-on node discovers the subnet prefix, by means of Router Advertisements (broadcast periodically) or by sending a Router Solicitation to the all-routers multicast group [20]. The Router Advertisements contain the subnet prefix and additional information, such as the lifetime values which indicate how long the addresses remain valid. Since the delay for a Router Advertisement is critical for the performance of stateless configuration, the node may generate a link-local address and send a Router Solicitation in parallel in order to speed

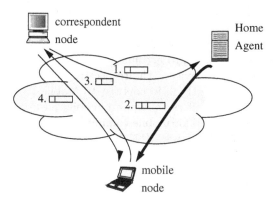

Fig. 2. Mobile IPv6 functionality

the process. This procedure may save time when the Router Advertisement is not received a short time after the assignment of the link-local address.

Addressing Schemes Assessment The two ways of IPv6 addressing configuration offer different advantages according to the configuration needs.

The use of stateless auto-configuration minimizes the signaling required before an address is assigned to an interface. Thus, stateless auto-configuration is attractive in cases where the need for extra configuration parameters is legible and the domain is not particularly concerned with the exact addresses used by hosts.

DHCPv6 instead, is not only a "stateful" version of stateless auto-configuration, but it extends the configuration parameters supported. With DHCPv6, the administration of IPv6 addresses is very flexible. The use of Dynamic Updates to Domain Name Servers (DNS) for auto-registration is also possible. DHCPv6 capabilities move beyond the usual addressing issues and may include load balancing mechanisms between DHCP servers [28] or security enhancements [13]. The drawback of the DHCPv6 approach is the accurate addressing issues, the necessity to keep several identifiers on persistent storage and the increased signaling exchanged. This implies the presence of servers with certain hardware capabilities.

2.4   Mobile IPv6

Mobile IPv4 [23] was developed as a mobility extension for IPv4 [24]. It introduced the concept that a mobile node should be always reachable through a single IP address, independently of its actual location. To achieve this goal, new entities and terms were introduced and existing components were enhanced. The main concept is that any mobile node should always be reachable by means of a single IP address, its Home Address.

Since the Internet Protocol was not designed for mobile hosts, Mobile IPv4 had to work around many problems in suboptimal manners. Triangular routing, extensive tunneling and firewall problems are but a few. IPv6, on the other hand, is a new protocol that takes into account the expected growth in the number and capabilities of mobile devices. The respective mobility extension for IPv6 is Mobile IPv6 [18]. Mobile IPv6, in contrast to Mobile IPv4, takes advantage of the infrastructure IPv6 offers to support mobile hosts and enables a more efficient communication path for mobile computers.

The philosophy behind Mobile IPv6 has remained the same as in Mobile IPv4. Each mobile node is always identified by its Home Address, regardless of its current point of attachment to the Internet. When it is located away from its home network, the mobile node has also a Care-of Address indicating its current location. Any packets destined to the Home Address are rerouted to its Care-of Address. IPv6 supports bindings between the Home Address of the PP and its respective Care-of Address in any other IPv6 host that communicates with that mobile. An analytical signaling exchange is illustrated in Fig. 2.

The mobile node is roaming in a foreign network and has informed its Home Agent with a Binding Update about its current Care-of Address previous to the presented packet exchange. In the first step, an IPv6 capable host across the Internet is sending a packet destined to the mobile node's IPv6 Home Address. The Home Agent intercepts it by means of IPv6 Network Discovery [20]. It figures out that the mobile node is not attached to its home link, but it roams in a foreign network and has acquired the Care-of Address. The second step is the transmission from the Home Agent to the Care-of Address of the mobile node of an encapsulated packet, that contains the original packet as payload and an additional header consisting of the current Care-of Address. The mobile node decapsulates it and, wishing to establish a direct communication to the correspondent host, transmits to the correspondent host a Binding Update, that informs it about the <Home Address, Care-of Address> binding (packet 3). The correspondent host, on the reception of the Binding Update, creates a cache binding for the Home and Care-of Address of the mobile host and transmits any remaining packets directly to the Care-of Address (packet 4) bypassing the home network altogether. The procedure is transparent to the higher layers (above IPv6) and the application need not know that the communicating node is not attached to its home network.

2.5   Quality of Service

Quality of Service (QoS) is an ambiguous concept with different interpretations. In the Internet community, two schools of thought have gained ground for the provision of QoS: the Integrated Services Architecture [4] and the Differentiated Services Architecture [3]. The common aspect in both architectures is the effort undertaken to treat certain packets preferentially, so as to "guarantee" their on-time delivery. They are mainly targeted to real-time applications such as Voice-over-IP or streaming video.

RSVP [5] is a protocol implementation of the Integrated Services Architecture. It provides a well defined means to specify a data flow and to reserve resources in the communication path of the flow. It is designed to deal end-to-end with unidirectional flows, facilitating QoS requests throughout the communication route. Its flexibility stems from the fact that it does not deal directly with QoS service details or flow specification, but merely interacts with the respective "packet scheduler" and "packet classifier" at each node to ensure provision of the necessary QoS and flow identification. In our study, we will use the Fixed Filter reservation style, suitable for unicast applications. The two fundamental RSVP message types are Resv and Path.

Each RSVP sender host transmits RSVP "Path" messages downstream along the route provided by the routing protocol, following the paths of the data. These Path messages store "path state" in each node along the way. This path state includes at least the unicast IP address of the previous hop node, which is used to route the Resv messages hop-by-hop in the reverse direction.

Each receiver host sends RSVP reservation request (Resv) messages upstream toward the senders. These messages must follow exactly the reverse of the path(s) the data packets will use, upstream to the sender host. They create and maintain "reservation state" in each node along the path(s). Resv messages must finally be delivered to the sender host, so that the host can set up appropriate traffic control parameters for the first hop.

The Integrated Services architecture is best applied to access networks due to its fine-grained classification, whereas core networks can scale better when the Differentiated Services architecture is applied. In our study, we assume that QoS reservations are performed with RSVP in the access network. The core network can support either kind of QoS architecture. If it only supports Differentiated Services, then some interworking scheme can be employed [1]. If the core network supports RSVP, then no extra components need to be added.

2.6 Related Work

IP transportation over DECT is an issue that is generally covered by the DPRS specification [12]. The provision, however, of efficiency and flexibility is the goal of ongoing research work. Mobility between different DECT access networks and DECT interworking with Mobile IP is dealt with in [19]. The efficiency of IP transportation over DECT is examined in [30]. QoS in the light of interworking with the service classes of 3G networks is approached in [15]. Our work aims to provide an integrated framework, in which DECT terminals can be used as fully fledged QoS-aware IPv6 terminals.

3 Proposed Framework

3.1 System Architecture

The system architecture for the integration of DECT with Mobile IPv6 and RSVP is based on the standard functionality of DECT mobility procedures. As

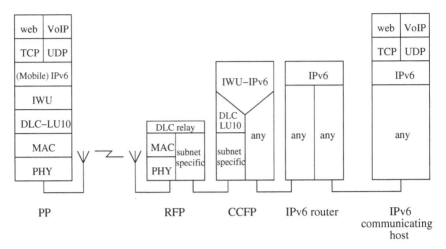

Fig. 3. System Protocol Stack – User Plane

shown in Fig. 1, the DECT access network is considered as the subnet link in the DECT/Mobile IPv6 architecture. Each DECT network (subnet) is supervised by a CCFP and consists of a number of RFPs, each responsible for a single cell. The CCFP is directly connected to the IWU in order to provide Internet connectivity. The PP is always identified by two unique addresses: the IPv6 Home Address in the IPv6 network and the DECT International Portable User Identity (IPUI) in the DECT access network

The overall architecture is divided into two planes: The Control Plane (C-Plane) and the User Plane (U-Plane). The U-Plane includes the PHY, MAC and DLC layers. It is used for transmission of IP packets over the DECT links using the LU10 frame format service [9] of the DLC layer [12]. The essential entity for the data transfer is the IWU, placed between the DLC and IPv6 layers. The set of IWU functions is realized as a separate sublayer which is already defined in [12]. The CCFP-IWU is the border between DECT and IPv6 procedures, as illustrated in Fig. 3.

Regarding the signaling information transfer, the Control Plane is extended with the NWK layer functionality compared to the User Plane as illustrated in Fig. 4. The use of the PHY, MAC, DLC layers and IWU is similar to that in the U-plane. In order to establish, negotiate, modify and release a connection, the Call Control (CC) entity procedures are used, while the Mobility Management (MM) entity describes the steps needed for the treatment of each type of location tracking and handoff.

3.2   IP Transportation over DECT Connections

After careful analysis of the functionality provided by the DECT connection modes in Section 2.1, CC seems to be more suitable to support IP traffic with

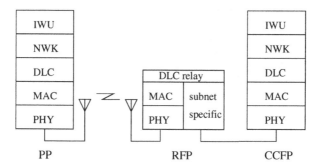

Fig. 4. DECT Protocol Stack – Control Plane

QoS provisioning. Specifically, CLMS is not quite suitable due to its limitation in supporting bandwidth demanding applications. COMS does not offer advanced connection modes which allow negotiation of the bandwidth allocated for the specific instance. Therefore, the remaining approach was to utilize the CC service that supports an extended functionality for service negotiation.

In CC procedures, each independent service is a "call" and is controlled by an independent instance of the CC. CC represents a group of procedures covering all aspects of call establishment, modification and release. In our proposed framework, the procedure of initiating a CC connection executes upon the terminal's power-on. Following this initiation sequence, the DECT enabled device has a setup IP communication route as soon as possible after the power-on.

3.3   DECT–Mobile IPv6 Location Management – Registration

In every mobile environment, it is important for the network to keep track of the position of each terminal, in order to set up and route properly incoming calls, connections or packets. Issues of determining and finding the mobile hosts are covered through the Location Management procedures.

The mobility management procedures in DECT and Mobile IPv6 described earlier point out that the interworking between DECT and Mobile IPv6 has to be very efficient so as not to affect the current functionality of the two technologies. The efficiency can be accomplished by considering two levels of mobility: A DECT mobility level and a Mobile IPv6 mobility level. The former is responsible for any movement inside a single DECT network, whereas the latter deals with cases where mobility is extended beyond the boundaries of a single DECT island.

Based on the architecture presented in Fig. 1, the CCFP can be considered as an edge router related to the DECT network. It is responsible for forwarding messages outside the DECT boundaries and generating proper Router Advertisement messages. The advertisements are used to determine the address configuration policy for a non-configured host [20]. In our proposed system, advanced configuration and security features are desirable and, thus, DHCPv6 is deemed

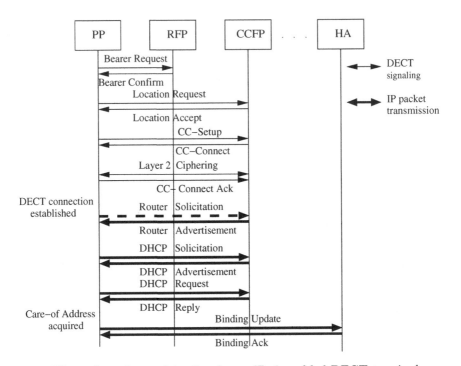

Fig. 5. Location registration for an IPv6 enabled DECT terminal

appropriate. The DHCPv6 server can be included in the CCFP functionality, whereas the PP can act as a DHCPv6 client. The necessary signaling flow for the location registration case is illustrated in Fig. 5.

After the PP determines a change regarding the LA, it tries to establish a physical connection with the RFP in its current area. This is accomplished by the Bearer Request and Bearer Confirm messages. Since the PP has recently moved to the new location area, it is important to register its position. This is done with the exchange of DECT Location Registration messages. A Location Request message is sent from the PP to the CCFP, including the IPUI of the PP. A Location Accept message is returned from the CCFP. At this point the DECT mobility functionality stops and IPv6 procedures take over in order to establish a communication path for IPv6 packets to be received from and transmitted outside the DECT network. Afterward, a NWK layer set-up process is initiated between the PP and the CCFP. A CC-Setup message is sent to the CCFP indicating a new connection and a response is sent back from the CCFP through the CC-Connect message. The communication between the two entities can be ciphered (Layer 2 Ciphering messages) for enhanced security. The new connection establishment is finished with a CC-Connect Ack sent from the PP to the CCFP.

Before acquiring a global IPv6 address, the PP must have a link-local address for communication inside the subnet (a single interface per IPv6 node is assumed). The interface identifier for a link-local address can be for example the 40-bit type N IPUI, which is the residential default IPUI. It is a unique type, as mandated by [11]. The IPUI is zero-padded in order to build a 64-bit interface identifier [17]. After acquiring a link-local address, the PP must get a global address. The PP may optionally generate a Router Solicitation message in order to check the presence of a router. If a Router Advertisement is received, the PP can decide for the use of DHCPv6 or the Stateless Autoconfiguration based on the contents of the message. If no Router Advertisement is received, the absence of a router is assumed and DHCPv6 is used. If DHCPv6 is the preferred configuration protocol, the PP will send a Solicitation message to the multicast address of all DHCP Agents in order to discover a proper DHCPv6 server. The Solicitation message should contain a Link-layer type DUID and particularly the 40-bit type N IPUI in the place of the client DUID for unique identification. DHCPv6 servers (CCFP) reply with Advertisement messages containing the offered resources (addresses or other parameters) and the server DUID. In order to avoid any conflict between clients' and servers' DUIDs, the servers' DUIDs are selected to be different than any DECT IPUI. After receiving Advertisement messages, the PP selects a DHCPv6 server (the server located on the CCFP is recommended for minimum signaling traffic) and sends a Request message to the selected server (CCFP). The DHCPv6 server (CCFP) updates its internal resource tables, selects an IPv6 address and sends a Reply message to the PP. After the PP receives the Reply, it may immediately use an IPv6 address and Mobile IPv6 Registration procedures follow.

The PP will send a Binding Update to its Home Agent (HA) indicating its new Care-of-Address. The Home Agent checks the credentials of the mobile and if the authentication is successful, it replies with a Binding Ack. After that message exchange, the mobile is globally reachable through its Home Address.

3.4   Handoff

A handoff occurs when the PP switches to a different point of attachment (RFP). Two handoff cases exist, the internal and the external handoff. In the former case the two successive RFPs, onto which the PP attaches, are controlled by the same CCFP (Cells 1 and 2). In the latter case, the PP switches to an RFP that is controlled by a different CCFP.

The internal handoff case is handled exclusively through DECT mobility procedures [10]. Hence, no interaction with IP takes place when a PP is moving solely inside a DECT access network that is controlled by a single CCFP.

The interesting case is the external handoff. When the PP switches to an RFP that is controlled by a different CCFP, it can no longer maintain the same address for roaming in that network. For illustration purposes, we assume the generic case, where the PP is already roaming in a foreign network, has acquired a Care-of Address, and is communicating with another host on the Internet.

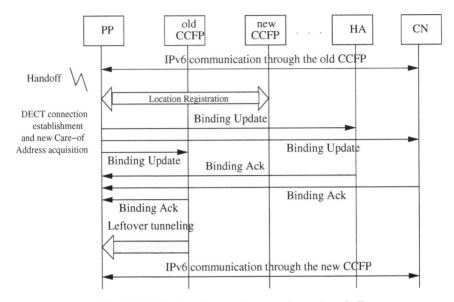

Fig. 6. IPv6 signaling exchange after a handoff

When the PP detects that a neighboring cell offers better communication conditions, the PP hands off to the new RFP. The new RFP is assumed to be controlled by a different CCFP. Since no communication mechanisms are defined in DECT for CCFP–CCFP interaction and we are dealing with IPv6 enabled devices, Mobile IPv6 is activated and its mobility procedures are applied.

Figure 6 illustrates the signaling exchange for a handed off PP. The RFP entities are omitted, since they just relay the data to the respective CCFPs. When the PP hands off, it begins the location registration procedure detailed in Fig. 5. After the DECT location registration procedure, and the Care-of Address configuration is completed, the PP sends a Binding Update to its Home Agent to inform it about the Care-of Address modification. Since it is already engaged in an IPv6 communication with a correspondent node (CN), it issues a Binding Update to it as well. Additionally, the PP may send a Binding Update to the previous CCFP. The old CCFP acts as a Home Agent for the previous Care-of Address and forwards any incoming packets toward the new Care-of Address.

Any entity that received a Binding Update (Home Agent, Correspondent Node, old CCFP) should respond with a a Binding Ack to indicate the reception and successful processing of the Binding Update. After this mobility signaling, the communication with the correspondent node can continue through the new Care-of Address.

4 QoS Provisioning

A DECT network constituted by portable parts and fixed parts, comprises a characteristic example of access network. Due to the rather limited available bandwidth and the foreseen demand for QoS with strict requirements, the Integrated Services architecture and the RSVP signaling protocol form the basis for the preferred QoS framework.

4.1 DECT–RSVP Interworking

The Integrated Services Architecture supports the following QoS traffic classes:

- Controlled Load Service Class [29]. Controlled-load service provides a data flow with a quality of service closely approximating the QoS that the same flow would receive from an unloaded network element. It uses admission control to assure that this service is received even when the network element is overloaded.
- Guaranteed Service Class [25]. Guaranteed service provides firm (mathematically provable) bounds on end-to-end datagram queuing delays. This service makes it possible to provide a service that guarantees both delay and bandwidth.
- Null Service Class [2]. Null service is intended for applications that require some form of prioritized service, but cannot quantify their resource requirements. The requirements specification is left to the network administrator.

These classes along with the Best Effort service class should be supported by DECT. One method is to use the different DECT Layer 3 services such as Call Control (CC), Connection Oriented Message Service (COMS) and Connection-Less Message Service (CLMS) to support the QoS classes as suggested in [15]. A more efficient method is to explore the extended functionality offered by CC, to accommodate the IP service requirements.

To this end, we assume that the PP has already established a connection with CCFP, using the CC service. A DECT connection is setup at power-on so that the portable can configure an IP address and various other network characteristics as described in the previous section. This connection is used by the portable as a default route for its IP traffic from and to the outside IP networks. It should be always up, although it may be configured to reduce its bandwidth in idle periods. This is the route for all the non-QoS traffic for the Portable Part, i.e. its best-effort connection. The actual QoS provisioning procedures depend on whether the DECT terminal includes RSVP functionality or not, as will be described in the following sections.

4.2 DECT Terminals with RSVP Functionality

If an application, running at the mobile terminal with RSVP functionality, wishes to establish a QoS connection with the outside IP network, it will issue a Path message toward the CCFP. This RSVP message will reach CCFP through the established best effort connection and it will be forwarded to the outside IP network. On the return path, the CCFP receives a corresponding Resv message, with parameters denoting the availability of the outside routers to support the requested QoS reservation. This Resv message has to be forwarded to the mobile terminal, which is unaware of the available radio resources, which are generally known at the fixed terminal side. Hence, the CCFP may alter the Resv parameters in such a way, that traffic requirements can be met. The modified Resv message is forwarded to the mobile terminal, through the established best effort CC connection. A new CC instance is initiated for the aforementioned QoS demanding flow.

Alternatively, the CCFP upon reception of the Resv message from the outside IP network, may issue a CC-setup toward the PP, with attributes denoting the supporting capabilities, before forwarding the Resv message to the mobile terminal. The Resv message can be delivered to the PP either through the newly established connection or, through the default best effort route. Both alternatives require a proactive behavior of the RSVP entity at the CCFP.

In the case that an IP node wishes to establish a QoS connection with the PP, the RSVP message Path will reach the PP through the best effort connection. Upon reception of this message, the PP may negotiate the connection characteristics with the CCFP through a CC-setup message and standard DECT procedures. A successfully established connection may generate a local Resv message at the CCFP, which proceeds as usual by issuing a Resv message toward the requested IP node. Alternatively, the Resv message can be sent by the PP through the newly established connection.

4.3 DECT Terminals without RSVP Functionality

The DECT terminals are widely deployed as simple telephone devices and may not possess a fully operational IP stack, not to mention RSVP capabilities. Hence, for the low end of the DECT terminal capabilities spectrum, we propose that the CCFP-IWU can take over the role of a RSVP Proxy [14].

In the case of incoming flows (toward the DECT network), the CCFP acts as a RSVP Receiver Proxy. The CCFP intercepts incoming Path messages and originates Resv messages in response to them. It also performs all the necessary state keeping as if the CCFP were the endpoint of the reservation request. Furthermore, it establishes internal DECT connections to the PP that is the destination of the data flow as bearers for the data flow. Alternatively, the CCFP may re-configure the existing CC-instance, adjust its bandwidth allocation and perform scheduling to the incoming data packets to ensure QoS guarantees for the particular data flow to the PP, while leaving some space for the default best effort traffic.

In the case of outgoing flows, the CCFP should possess the functionality of a RSVP Sender Proxy. The Sender Proxy could be triggered by external filters that examine the outgoing IP packets and determine whether the identified flows need any kind of resource reservation. Obviously, the decision for flow classification and reservation for the respective flows is a matter of policy and, therefore, it is possible that a policy server be contacted before any reservation request is made. In every case, if the RSVP reservation succeeds in the external IP network, the CCFP should provide the necessary QoS guarantees inside the DECT access network. The CCFP might install a new CC-instance for the new flow, but this approach requires extra signaling to indicate to the PP the reason for this DECT connection setup, i.e. that the newly discovered data flow from the PP should be transmitted over the new instance.

In that case, the preferable solution is the adjustment of the existing CC-instance provided to serve best-effort traffic from the PP. Thus, the PP will be able to transmit the data flow with QoS guarantees through its default route (the adjusted default CC-instance) in the DECT network and with RSVP signaled guarantees through the outside IP networks.

4.4   Clustering DECT–IPv6 Access Networks

Through our analysis in the previous sections, we have proposed some methods to provide QoS support through RSVP signaling in DECT access networks. Whereas RSVP-enabled QoS could be considered adequate for such an access network, it falls short in cases where multiple DECT networks are located in a greater domain, that handles mobility through Mobile IPv6. In such cases, interworking problems arise between Mobile IP and RSVP [26]. The core of the problem lies in the observation that RSVP marks each QoS "session" by the triplet <Destination Address, Destination Port (or Flowlabel in IPv6), Protocol Type>. If a mobile moves within the area controlled by the same CCFP, only DECT mobility procedures will apply and its IP address will remain the same.

If the DECT terminal moves to an area controlled by a different CCFP, it will perform the procedures described in Section 3.4. In that case, through Mobile IPv6 procedures, a new Care-of Address will be assigned to the terminal and the RSVP session will be incorrect (or at least unusable) in the new context. One possible solution would be to enhance the edge IP router with some extra functionality. Bearing in mind, that the edge router already deal with Mobile IPv6 and RSVP, an interworking between the mobility and QoS functionalities could be deployed to eliminate the incompatibilities. Such a solution is proposed with the RSVP Mobility Proxy concept in [21] and [22].

5   Conclusions

A DECT/IPv6 interworking framework was presented, that overcomes the limited mobility and QoS capabilities DECT offers. The extended features were realized through the exploitation of Mobile IPv6 and RSVP QoS signaling protocol respectively.

In order to specify the exact interaction between DECT and Mobile IPv6 location management procedures, the system architecture for the DECT/IPv6 interworking was analyzed and the necessary protocol stacks were defined. The location management procedures were pointed out for DECT as well as for the IPv6 domain, while mobility was demonstrated by means of Mobile IPv6. Moreover, guidelines were set for the interworking between the RSVP QoS signaling protocol and DECT procedures for allocating resources in the wireless medium. The Interworking Unit, located on the border between the DECT access network and the IP layer was identified as the essential communication entity that deals with any interaction between DECT and IPv6.

Finally, the enhanced functionality placed on the DECT controller is justified by the seamless, QoS enabled, wireless Internet access for DECT/IPv6 terminals.

References

[1] Y. Bernet. RFC 2996: Format of the RSVP DCLASS object, November 2000. 375

[2] Y. Bernet, A. Smith, and B. Davie. RFC 2997: Specification of the Null Service Type, November 2000. 381

[3] S. Blake, D. Black, M. Carlson, E. Davies, Z. Wang, and W. Weiss. RFC 2475: An architecture for differentiated services, December 1998. 374

[4] R. Braden, D. Clark, and S. Shenker. RFC 1633: Integrated services in the Internet architecture: an overview, June 1994. 374

[5] R. Braden, Ed., L. Zhang, S. Berson, S. Herzog, and S. Jamin. RFC 2205: Resource ReSerVation Protocol (RSVP) — version 1 functional specification, September 1997. 375

[6] S. Deering and R. Hinden. RFC 2460: Internet Protocol, Version 6 (IPv6) specification, December 1998. 370

[7] R. Droms (ed.), J. Bound, M. Carney, C. Perkins, T. Lemon, and B. Volz. Dynamic Host Configuration Protocol for IPv6 (DHCPv6). Internet Draft, October 2002. Work in Progress. 371

[8] ETSI. Digital Enhanced Cordless Telecommunications (DECT); Common Interface (CI); part 1: Overview. ETSI EN 300 175-1, January 2002. 369

[9] ETSI. Digital Enhanced Cordless Telecommunications (DECT); Common Interface (CI); part 4: Data link control (DLC) layer. ETSI EN 300 175-4, January 2002. 376

[10] ETSI. Digital Enhanced Cordless Telecommunications (DECT); Common Interface (CI); part 5: Network (NWK) layer. ETSI EN 300 175-5, February 2002. 370, 379

[11] ETSI. Digital Enhanced Cordless Telecommunications (DECT); Common Interface (CI); part 6: Identities and addressing. ETSI EN 300 175-6, January 2002. 379

[12] ETSI. Digital Enhanced Cordless Telecommunications (DECT); DECT Packet Radio Service (DPRS). ETSI EN 301 649, October 2002. 370, 375, 376

[13] P. Flykt, C. Perkins, and T. Eklund. AAA for IPv6 Network Access. Internet Draft, March 2002. Work in Progress. 373

[14] S. Gai, D. G. Dutt, N. Elfassy, and Y. Bernet. RSVP Proxy. Internet Draft, March 2002. Work in Progress. 382

[15] A. Gyasi-Agyei. Mobile IP–DECT Internetworking Architecture Supporting IMT-2000 Applications. *IEEE Network*, pages 10–22, November 2001. 375, 381

[16] R. Hinden and S. Deering. RFC 2373: IP version 6 addressing architecture, July 1998. 371

[17] IEEE. Guidelines for 64-bit global identifier (EUI-64) registration authority, March 1997. 371, 379

[18] D. Johnson, C. Perkins, and J. Arkko. Mobility Support in IPv6. Internet Draft, June 2002. Work in Progress. 374

[19] A. Lo, W. Seah, and E. Schreuder. An efficient DECT-Mobile IP interworking for mobile computing. In *IEEE Vehicular Technology Conference*, Tokyo, Japan, May 2000. 375

[20] T. Narten, E. Nordmark, and W. Simpson. RFC 2461: Neighbor discovery for IP Version 6 (IPv6), December 1998. 372, 374, 377

[21] S. Paskalis, A. Kaloxylos, E. Zervas, and L. Merakos. RSVP Mobility Proxy. Internet Draft, December 2001. Work in Progress. 383

[22] S. Paskalis, A. Kaloxylos, E. Zervas, and L. Merakos. An Efficient RSVP–Mobile IP Interworking Scheme. *Journal on Special Topics in Mobile Networking and Applications (MONET)*, 8(3), June 2003. 383

[23] C. Perkins. RFC 2002: IP mobility support, October 1996. 373

[24] J. Postel. RFC 791: Internet Protocol, September 1981. 373

[25] S. Shenker, C. Partridge, and R. Guerin. RFC 2212: Specification of guaranteed quality of service, September 1997. 381

[26] M. Thomas. Analysis of Mobile IP and RSVP interactions. Internet Draft, February 2001. Work in Progress. 383

[27] S. Thomson and T. Narten. RFC 2462: IPv6 stateless address autoconfiguration, December 1998. 372

[28] B. Volz. Load balancing for DHCPv6. Internet Draft, July 2002. Work in Progress. 373

[29] J. Wroclawski. RFC 2211: Specification of the controlled-load network element service, September 1997. 381

[30] D. Ziotopoulou, D. Skyrianoglou, K. Orfanakos, and E. Zervas. A DECT-IP interworking for quality of service support. In *8th Panhellenic Conference on Informatics*, Nicosia, Cyprus, November 2001. 375

High Level Timed Petri Net Templates for the Temporal Verification of Real-Time Multiprocessor Applications

Dimitra Ananidou[2], George Hassapis[1], and Dimitrios Kleftouris[2]

[1]Aristotle University of Thessaloniki
540 06 Thessaloniki, Greece
chasapis@eng.auth.gr
[2]Technological Educational Institute of Thessaloniki
P.O. Box 14561, 541 01 Thessaloniki, Greece
klefturi@it.teithe.gr

Abstract. In this work templates for modeling the execution of application software on a shared memory real-time multiprocessor system are presented. These templates are parameterized High Level Timed Petri Nets which can be adapted to the design specifications of a specific application software design by customizing their token data structures. Simulating the solution of the derived Petri net models, the satisfaction of timing characteristics of the application software design, such as response time to external stimuli, can be studied. Each model describes with the same degree of detail the execution of application software running on the specific computer platform. Three different application programs were modeled by each template and a comparative evaluation of the ability of the three templates to predict timing characteristics of these programs was performed. On the basis of the results of this study the model that predicts the timing characteristics of the software execution with the best computation cost, is identified.

1 Introduction

A special class of shared memory multiprocessors consisting of a set of processors connected to a set of memory and interface modules by means of a common bus are used extensively in industrial monitoring and automation applications. A real-time multitasking operating system residing on every processor controls the running of the application software. These computer platforms are usually called by their manufacturers as real-time multiprocessors. The application software is decomposed into concurrent and dependable tasks, each one coded in a high level language and its running scheduled and synchronized by the services of the real-time operating system. Methods and software tools able to model the way application software is executed on these platforms with the purpose of analyzing the functional and timing behavior of the programs at the design level are of great importance to the system developers.

Y. Manolopoulos et al. (Eds.): PCI 2001, LNCS 2563, pp. 386-400, 2003.

Some of these methods are those proposed by Jrjung et al [17] for the performance modeling of client-server systems , by Koriem [18] for the performance evaluation of hard real-time systems and by Zuberek [19] et al for modeling distributed memory multithreaded multiprocessors.

In this work, *template models* related with the operation of the previously ·described specific class of multiprocessors are considered. A template model can be used as a systematic tool for the automated construction of a model of the application software describing its structure and its dynamic execution behavior.

Based on well-known Petri Net types [9], such as High Level Timed PN [2,8], Colored PN [4,5] and Extended High Level Timed PN [3,13], three different template models were constructed. Each one has a fixed and steady topology, with specified token data structures in every place and with a set of either logical or algebraic conditions for the activation of every transition. A comparative study of the three templates was conducted with the purpose of identifying the one that can be used in evaluating functional and temporal behavior of the application software with the least complexity. Complexity is defined in terms of the numbers of the places and the transitions required to model the running of the application software, the number of tokens in each place and finally the size of the state space that must be searched in order to find states that validate the functional and temporal behavior of application software.

It is shown that the third template model, with its particular characteristics such as sorting algorithms in the places, temporal attributes in the tokens and priorities associated with the transitions, is more suitable to describe the dynamic behavior of the specific class of application software and presents less complexity.

The paper is organized as follows. In section 2 the computer platform is briefly introduced and in section 3 the way application software is executed on this computer platform is described. In section 4 the specifications for a framework, the template model, to simulate the execution of application software for the specified class of systems are defined. Moreover three Petri Net realizations of the template model are developed .In section 5 a demonstration example is given to show how the EHLTPN template can model and verify temporal characteristics of the execution of the control program of a real-life application. In section 6 comparisons from the use of the templates to model the execution of three different programs and evaluate their performance are given. Finally, the main points of this study are discussed in the conclusions section.

2   The Real-Time Multiprocessor

The computer platform which we usually call real-time multiprocessor [10] consists of the hardware part and the real-time operating system. A brief description of each one of these two major components of the platform is given in the following sections.

2.1   The Computer Hardware

The architecture of the computer hardware may be seen as a collection of functional units communicating between each other over a common set of back-plane buses satisfying open bus standards. VME-bus and Microbus [10] are typical standards, which define the electrical specifications, the data exchange protocols and bus arbitration rules, which the common bus of an industrial computer should be built upon. According to this architecture the set consists of three buses, that is the data bus, the arbitration bus and the interrupt bus. The functional units are distinguished to data transfer units and to priority interrupt units. The data transfer units process and exchange data. Based on their functions, they are further divided into masters and slaves. In Figure 1 a schematic diagram of the computer hardware architecture is presented. Each one of the master units is a Central Processing Unit (CPU), able to initiate data transfers between itself and a slave. A slave may also be a CPU or a passive unit, such as a memory shared by all masters or an I/O interfacing card. However, functionally it is different from the master because it is able only to detect a data transfer request issued by the master and provide or accept data. The priority interrupt units (i.e. I/O modules in Figure 1) place interrupt requests to a master by driving one of the lines of the interrupt bus.

2.2   The OS-9 Real-Time Kernel

The nucleus of the OS-9 [6] real-time multitasking operating system is a kernel that is loaded on each master CPU. It facilitates platform initialisation after hardware reset, the handling of exceptions, system security, offers a number of system calls that alleviate the need for users to write redundant routines for memory and I/O management and allow task synchronization and communication.

However, the most important feature of this kernel is the concurrent execution of many tasks that can take place after initialization. In fact tasks appear to run concurrently but the CPU executes one task at a time.

Once a set of tasks is created, the kernel determines those tasks that will run on the computer and the duration of their run. This is achieved by interrupting with a clock pulse, called a 'tick', the CPU at regular timing instants. At any occurrence of a tick, the routine that services the interrupts is triggered. This may suspend the currently executing task and start the execution of another. Apart from being suspended, an executing task can be pre-empted by an external interrupt. Such an interrupt may be triggered by an I/O module and is considered to be of higher priority than the interrupt of the clock tick.

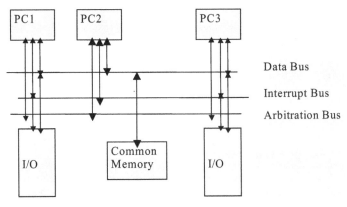

Fig. 1. Computer Hardware

For synchronization and task communication the kernel offers different software routines with varying sizes of internal data sets/structures that can be created, deleted and updated by the tasks.

3   Execution of Application Software

Application software is made up of tasks the execution of which is practically carried out between successive ticks of the kernel. This constitutes the normal mode of operation of the system whereas the creation of tasks may be assumed to be part of the initialization phase of the computer system.

The actual running of application software on the computer platform is performed as follows. Each task is assigned to a processor for execution and may resume any of the states 'idle', 'ready', 'requesting a bus', 'executing', 'waiting Semaphore' and 'interrupted'. A task may enter the 'idle' state when resources required for its execution have not become available yet. When these resources become available it enters the 'ready' state and in the waiting list of the tasks to be scheduled for execution. Once the scheduler selects a task, this task enters the 'executing' state. Depending on the task functions, the task can complete its execution and return to the 'idle' state releasing at the same time the resources assigned to it, or it may enter in a 'requesting-a-bus' state when it competes with other tasks for accessing the data bus. An interrupted task is assumed to retain the resources required by the routine that services the interrupt for the continuation of its critical part and for this reason it is placed in the scheduler list of the other ready and interrupted tasks. However, its position in the list is determined by the interrupt priority that is associated with the specific task.

4   Template Models

Separating the functions that application software must perform into different tasks and working out their communication and synchronization are the major parts of the basic design [15]. This separation is based on an educated guess of the worst-case execution time of each considered task, which is believed to lead to an overall software response time that meets requirements. Because of the importance of these decisions and the consequences they might have in the development of the complete software application, designers wish to have a generalized model of the way their design will execute on the specific platform. They can use this model to run different cases, predict timing and functional behaviour of each case and evaluate alternative design decisions [1].

In order to formalise the description of the execution of application software on such a computer system, generalized modeling frameworks, based on the High Level Timed Petri net, Colored Petri net and Environment/Relationship Petri net formalisms have been devised. These frameworks were called *template models*. It is argued that the selected types of Petri Nets have the descriptive power to create models of complex real-time systems that can be analysed with reasonable effort.

Each one of these template models has a fixed and steady topology with specific but different token data types in each place and with a set of either logical or algebraic conditions for the firing of every transition. The different token types represent the different compositional elements of the real-time system such as Tasks, Processors, Semaphores, Bus, Interrupts and other computer resources. Tokens of any type contain number of attributes, each one expressing a property of the element of the real-time system or a timing consideration. The values of the attributes can be modified by the transitions corresponding to different system behaviour. System behaviour can be charted with one or more of its state spaces. Furthermore, algorithms [13] and tools [14] generating efficiently all the possible states the net might undergo have been developed and are available to the designer. Therefore the template model can provide a design framework, which if a modeler follows it can lead to a design specification that can be verified for inconsistencies and ambiguities automatically and validated against application requirements. The description of the design of an application program running on the computer platform already considered, merely ends up in defining the number of tokens in each place, valuating the attributes of each token and specifying the firing rules of each transition.

4.1   The HLTPN Template Model

High-Level Timed Petri nets enrich the original Petri net model by attaching information and timestamps to the tokens, thus integrating the representation of both the functional and timing aspects of a system in full detail. Using HLTPN the net in Figure 2 representing the template for modeling the application software execution on the considered real-time multiprocessor is constructed. In this template there are places which host tokens that represent the program tasks in the idle state (Place P1), the tasks that are ready and wait for their assignment to a processor (place P2), the executing and bus requesting tasks (Places P3 and P4). Also processors, suspended tasks waiting for semaphores to be enabled, semaphores and the bus are represented by appropriate tokens in places P5, P6, P7 and P8 respectively. Tasks that are holding the bus and a processor are represented by tokens in place P12. Similarly, places are provided to hold tokens that represent the lists of tasks that request the use of the bus (P15 for ordinary tasks, P21 for interrupt routines) or a processor (P16) and those that are selected by the scheduler to run first (P19). Tasks serving interrupts are modeled by places P9 to P14. Tokens representing the sources of interrupts and the enabled interrupts are stored in places P10, P9 respectively. The tasks that have been suspended by the enabled interrupts are represented by tokens in P11. The executing interrupt servicing routines and the processors that have been assigned to these routines are represented by tokens in P13. The remaining places P17 up to P20 include tokens that represent the functions of the scheduling algorithm. Places 21 to 24 are used to simulate the arbitration mechanism. Depending on the place that a token resides, the associated token attributes provide information regarding the execution time of the task, its deadline, and its precedence constraints or if the token represents processors or the bus the state of the processor or the bus, and the interrupt resources that the processor can serve. The transition relationships are logical propositions or algebraic functions on the token attributes of the input place of the transition and express the conditions of transferring tokens to the output places with simultaneous modifications on the number, type and data of the attributes. For example transition t_2 expresses the application of the scheduling algorithm on the selection of the next executing task, whereas transition t12 expresses the bus arbitration algorithm.

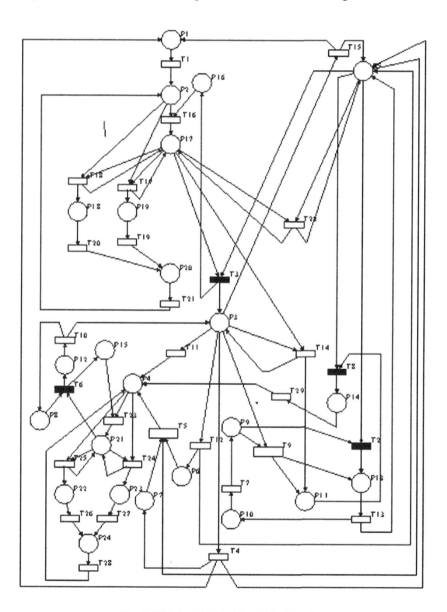

Fig. 2. High Level Timed Petri Net Template

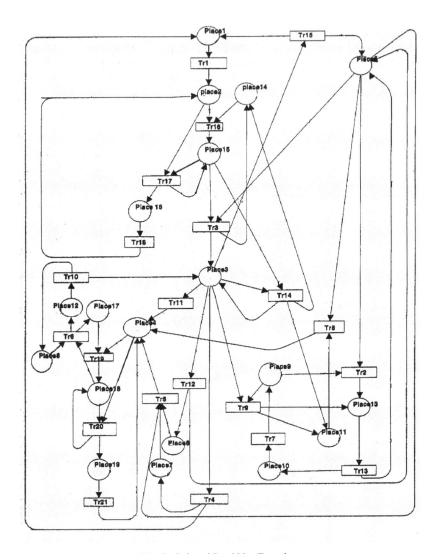

Fig. 3. Colored Petri Net Template

4.2   The Colored Petri Net (CPN) Template Model

Colored Petri nets are characterized by places that have a common property (color) and tokens with data structures that can be manipulated by a programming language. On the basis of the Colored Petri Net formalism the template in Figure 3 has been produced. It presents a similar topology with that of the HLTPN template. There are places for tasks that are in one of the states idle (P1), ready (P2), executing (P3), requesting a bus (P4), interrupted (P11) and waiting synchronization data (P6). Also there are places for lists of ready (P14), requesting the bus (P17) and interrupted tasks (P19) prepared by the scheduling and bus arbitration policies of the computer platform. Available hardware components such as the processors and the bus are represented by tokens in places P5 and P8 respectively. Presence of tokens in these places allows the satisfaction of conditions for the transfer of task tokens from a ready to executing state. Similarly, tokens representing synchronization primitives of the operating system in place P7 provide the data needed for enabling or disabling the transfer of tasks from the waiting to the ready or executing state. In contrast with the HLTPN where the tokens include in their data structure information regarding their state, in this net the state is determined by the color of the place the token is moved into. Depending on the color of the place that is related with tasks, the data structures of the tokens in such a place may consist of data for the task execution time, the deadline of the task, its precedence constraints, the processor it is assigned to, a flag for holding the bus, its priority of execution and a timestamp indicating the time that the token was entered in the place. In the same way as in HLTPN, the transition conditions are logic and algebraic functions of token data and when they are fired, they transfer tokens from one place to another or split one token to a number of others and transfer them to the appropriate places.

4.3   The Extended High-Level Timed Petri Net (EHLTPN) Template Model

The Extended High-Level Timed Petri Net enriches the original High-Level Petri net model by attaching

- Sorting algorithms to places, in order to create ordered lists of tokens according to the value of a certain attribute (i.e. priority of a task execution).
- Attributes to tokens that represent tasks for storing the run time of each task as this is obtained by model execution.
- Priorities to transitions for defining the order of transition firing in case two or more transitions are enabled at the same time.

Using EHLTPN the Template in Figure 4 has been produced. In this template all the places of the net (P1 to P13) play the same role with that described for the places with the same identification number in the HLTPN template. However, because of the ability provided in this new type of net to assign at a place a sorting algorithm and transition priorities the need to insert additional places and token types that will allow the description of the scheduling and arbitration policies of task execution and bus assignment to tasks is eliminated.

5   Demonstration Example

An automatic pot filling system [11] is used to demonstrate the application of the EHLTPN template for modeling the running of the system over a specified period of time and verifying that over that period there is no danger of pot overfilling. In this system a conveyor belt moves pots, positioned at equal distances the one from the other, under a tap (see Figure 5). Once a pot arrives under the tap, the belt stops for a time period equal to the time required to fill the pot. As long as the tap remains on water is poured into the pot. Initially, the pots are placed on the belt in such a way that the distance of the first pot from the tap is equal to half of the distance between two successive pots. The control of the belt movement and the opening and closing of the tap is carried out by a real-time multiprocessing system having a single processor, a memory module and an I/O module, all communicating over a common VME bus [7]. The application software consists of two periodic tasks with the same period. The first one controls the belt movement and the other the tap flow. The function of the task that controls the belt movement is to move the belt for a distance equal to the distance between two successive pots. Upon system start-up the task that controls the belt movement is initiated. After the elapse of the time required for the first pot to be placed under the tap, the task that controls the opening of the tap gains the use of the CPU because a higher priority is granted to it. Then, the execution of the belt movement task is suspended and the tap opening task starts executing and keeps the tap open for a time period equal to that required for filling the pot. Next, the execution of the suspended belt movement task is resumed and moves the pot at a distance equal to the half of the distance between two pots. Then, the whole process of pot moving and filling is repeated.

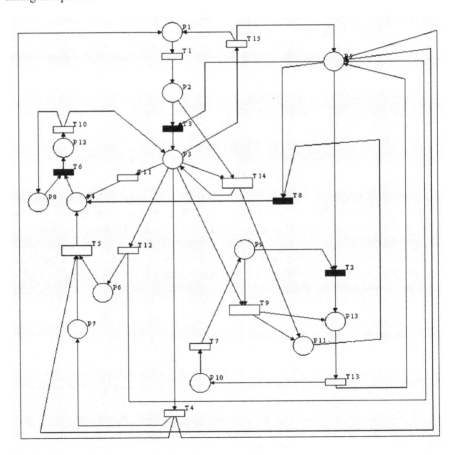

Fig. 4. The EHLTPN Template

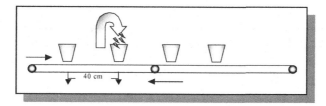

Fig 5. Automatic pot filling system

Based on the EHLTPN the modeler considers two tokens in Place 1 to represent the two application tasks. Also the modeler considers a token in place P5 to represent the processor of the system and a token in place P8 to represent the single bus. At system initialization there are not any tokens in the other places. Defining as marking of the net the set that has as elements the number of tokens in each place, the above initial state of the net will be represented by the set :

$$M_0=\{2(Ts1,Ts2), 0, 0, 0, 1(C), 0, 0, 1(B), 0, 0, 0, 0, 0\}$$

The notation 2(Ts1,Ts2) denotes that in place P1 there are two tokens with ids Ts1 and Ts2 respectively, representing the two tasks in idle state, in place P5 there is a token 1(C) to represent the processor nad in P8 a token 1(B) to represent the single bus. Assume now, the distance between two pots is 40 cm and the speed of the movement of the belt is 10 cm/sec . One would expect that at the time instant of 2 sec task Ts1 must be suspended and task Ts2 must be executing. If the time to fill a pot is 5 sec, then after the elapse of this time the system is expected to be found at a state where Ts1 is executing and Ts2 has returned in the idle state.

Executing the model on the template, the markings in table 1 were obtained. They include markings that can be directly associated to physical system states and markings that represent the way that tasks are handled by the computer, as mentioned in section 3. Task handling by the computer takes some time which is taken into consideration in system modeling by the template. In table 1 the markings M_4 and M_8 correspond to the two considered system states, that is when the system is at the state of staring the pot filling and the state of having the pot filled.

Table 1. Markings produced by the template during the model execution

Time (sec)	Marking
0	M_0={2(Ts1,Ts2), 0, 0, 0, 1(C),0,0, 1(B),0, 0, 0, 0, 0}
0.001	M_1={1(Ts2), 1(Ts1), 0, 0, 1(C),0,0, 1(B),0, 0, 0, 0, 0}
0.002	M_2={1(Ts2), 0, 1(Ts1-C), 0, 0, 0,0, 1(B),0, 0, 0, 0, 0}
0.003	M_3={0, 1(Ts2),1(Ts1-C), 0, 0, 0,0, 1(B),0, 0, 0, 0, 0}
2.004	M_4={0, 0, 1(Ts2-C), 0 , 0, 0,0, 1(B),0, 0, 1(Ts1), 0, 0}
7.005	M_5={1(Ts2), 0, 0, 0, 1(C),0,0, 1(B), 0, 0, 1(Ts1), 0, 0}
7.006	M_6={1(Ts2), 0, 0, 1(Ts1-C), 0, 0,0,0, 1(B), 0,0, 0, 0, 0}
7.007	M_7={1(Ts2) 0, 0, 0, 0, 0,0, 0, 0,0, 0,1(Ts1-C-B),0}
7.009	M_8={1(Ts2), 0, 1(Ts1-C), 0, 0, 0,0, 1(B),0, 0, 0, 0, 0}
9.010	M_9={2(Ts2,Ts1),0, 0, 0, 1(C),0, 0, 1(B),0, 0, 0, 0, 0}

Table 2. Number of states in the state space of each case

Template	Places	Transitions	Case 1	Case 2	Case 3
HLTPN	24	29	13	701	194
CPN	19	21	12	581	182
EHLTPN	13	15	9	354	110

One observes that the times of occurrence of these markings, are respectively 2.004 sec and 7.009 whereas the expected times of the equivalent system states are 2 and 7 sec. This leads us to the conclusion that the prediction of the specific template model has an accuracy of 1,1%. Note that marking M_9 is exactly the same as marking M_0 denoting that the process has been completed and another cycle is due to start.

6   Template Evaluation

Looking at the three template models, one observes that the HLTPN and CPN ones present a more complex topology than the EHLTPN. The reason is that HLTPN and CPN templates include some places and transitions with no physical meaning but used to perform basic functions such as sorting. EHLTPN Template associates sorting algorithms with places P2 and P4 and therefore there is no need of extra subnets for token sorting. Its number of places and transitions is kept considerably small and all the states in the state space represent real physical system states.

To evaluate the accuracy of each Template Model in predicting the timing behavior of application software, and the complexity of each net with which this prediction is achieved, three case studies were modeled. The number of states in the resulting state space of each case is shown in Table 2.

The first case study has been already described in section 5. The second case study refers to a chemical reactor system [12]. This system consists of a tank in which two chemical ingredients are poured into the tank at volumes determined by the position of level switches in the tank. These switches provide the signals for shutting down the valves that control the flow of the two ingredients. When the tank is filled up, the temperature of the mixture is raised to 300^0C, the mixture is stirred for a 20 minutes period and is retrieved by opening a solenoid valve at the bottom of the tank. When a new cart is placed under the tank, the mixing procedure is repeated. The automation of the just described procedure is carried out by a real-time multiprocessing computer with a single processor, a memory module and two I/O modules, one sampling the level switches and issuing the commands to the valves for opening and closing and the other monitoring the temperature and commanding the on/off control of the heater. The application software consists of 11 periodic intertwined tasks with differing periods, which are synchronized by semaphores.

The third case study refers to an industrial controller [13] of general use, performing the model predictive control [16] of a 2-analogue input, 2-analogue output interactive process. The control algorithm is implemented on a real-time multiprocessing computer consisting of two processors, a common data bus and two interrupt modules. External clocks trigger interrupts to one of the processors at intervals equal to the sampling intervals required for the control of each output variable. The application software consists of 12 periodic intertwined tasks with different periods.

It is obvious that the execution of the same application software on each of the three templates produces a different number of states, and as seen from Table 2, this number of states heavily depends on:

- the complexity of the topology of the used template,
- the complexity of the physical system.

Owing to the definition of the HLTPN and CPN nets, the respective template models possess a serious deficiency regarding the sequences of firing of simultaneously enabled transitions. So the firing of one transition may exclude another one from firing and thus exclude certain states from being created. This may result to different state spaces at consecutive runs of the same application software on the same template and with the same attributes of the tokens. However this is not permissible since real software systems with steady temporal and functional parameters always pass from the same states when they run repeatedly. The EHLTPN Template model does not suffer from this deficiency since the underlying net allows a priority index to be assigned to every transition, based on the operating characteristics of the system to be modeled and therefore application programs can pass always from the same states when they run repeatedly. This priority index is not meant to model any scheduling of tasks based on priorities.

The predicted values of the completion time of each task of the application software in all the three studied cases are shown in Tables 3, 4 and 5. In addition, in Table 3 desired dead-times for the tasks of case 1 are also given in order to verify whether predicted completion times are within or outside the required limits. The observed differences on the predicted completion times by the three templates is attributed to the different level of the accuracy that each model predicts the actual timing figures. This is due to the fact that each templates describes the operation of the software application with a differing level of detail, i.e number of states each task can enter.

Table 3. Timing Parameters for case 1

Templates	Task 1			Task 2		
	HLTPN	CPN	EHLTPN	HLTPN	CPN	EHLTPN
Completion Time	9.01	9.01	9.01	5.001	5.001	5.001
Dead Time	10	10	10	10	10	10

7   Conclusions

With the purpose of assisting the software developer of industrial automation applications with real-time multiprocessing computers in the verification of the timing specifications of his or her design, template models were devised by using three different types of Petri Nets. These types are the High-Level Timed Petri nets (HLTPN), the

Colored Petri nets (CPN), and the Extended High level Timed Petri Nets (EHLTPN). The execution of the software that implements the three automation applications was modeled and simulated using these templates.

Table 4. Timing parameters for case 2

Completion Time	Template		
	HLTPN	**CPN**	**EHLTPN**
1	20	21	20
2	152	156	153
3	144	150	144
4	642	658	643
5	636	642	636
6	3053	3073	3050
7	3047	3067	3048
8	2442	2460	2442
9	3114	3136	1243
10	1242	1259	1243
11	11	2	1

Table 5. Timing parameters for case 3

	HLTPN		CPN		EHLTPN	
	Completion time		Completion time		Completion time	
Process	Min	Max	min	max	min	max
111	25	28	21	25	21	25
112	42	47	37	44	37	43
113	35	42	30	35	31	36
121	14	16	10	14	10	14
131	11	11	10	10	10	10
211	23	27	23	26	22	24
212	12	16	10	11	10	11
213	23	28	23	25	21	23
221	32	36	21	50	21	36
222	34	41	34	38	33	38
231	11	19	32	10	10	49
311	43	49	40	46	38	44

It was found that the complexity of the EHLTPN template, expressed by the number of places, transitions and size of state space is the minimum when it is compared with that of the HLTPN and CPN ones. Furthermore, it was made possible to predict the timing performance of the application software, expressed as the satisfaction of constraints on the completion time of the tasks. A comparison of these predictions with actual software execution data has indicated that the use of the EHLTPN template provides a more accurate prediction.

References

[1]   Clarke E., Wing J. et al.: "Formal Methods : State of the Art and Future Directions", *ACM Computing Surveys*, Vol.28, 1996.

[2]   Genrich H.: "Predicate/transition nets", In W. Brauer, W. Reisig, G. Rozenberg (eds) *Advances in Petri Nets 1986*". Springer LNCS Vol.254, 1987.

[3]   Ghezzi C., Mandrioli D., Morasca S. and Pezze M.: "A Unified High-level Petri Net Formalism for Time-Critical Systems", *IEEE Transactions on Software Engineering*, Vol.17, pp.160-171, 1991.

[4]   Jensen K.: "An Introduction to the Theoretical Aspects of Colored Petri Nets", Springer, pp.230-272, 1994.

[5]   Jensen K.: "Colored Petri Nets – Basic Concepts, Analysis Methods and Practical Use", Vol.2, Springer, 1994.

[6]   Microwave Systems Corp.: "OS-9 Operating Systems Manuals Version 2.4", Product Number UPR-68-NA-68-MO, Des Moines, Iowa, 1991.

[7]   ANSI/IEEE STF 1014 : "The VMEbus Specification", VITA Zaltommel, The Netherlands, 1987.

[8]   Morasca S., Pezze M. and Trubian M.: "Timed High-level Nets", *Real Time Systems*, Vol.3, pp.165-189, 1991.

[9]   Peterson J.: "Petri Net Theory and the Modeling of Systems", Prentice Hall, 1981.

[10]   Ripps L.D.: "An Implementation Guide to Real-Time Programming", Yourdon Press, 1989.

[11]   Ananidou D., Hassapis G. and Kleftouris D.: "Evaluation of Real_time Software Design with the Aid of a Petri Net Template Model", *Proceedings 7th Panhellenic Conference on Informatics*, pp.310-319, Ioannina, 1999.

[12]   Hassapis G., Ananidou D. and Kleftouris D.: "A Timed High Level Petri Net Model of the Automation Scheme of a Chemical Process", *Proceedings IEEE International Conference on Electronics, Circuits and Systems (ICECS'99)*, Vol.2, pp.897-882, Paphos, 1999.

[13]   Ananidou D.: "Modeling and Analysing of Real-Time Systems using High-Level Timed Petri Nets", Ph.D. Thesis, Electrical & Computer Engineering, Aristotle University, 1999.

[14]   Pezze M.: "CABERNET: a Customizable Environment for the Specification and Analysis of Real-Time Systems", *Proceedings DECUS Europe Symposium*, Cannes, France, 1992.

[15]   Ward P.T. and Mellor S.J.: "*Structured Development for Real-time Systems*", Vol.1, Introduction and Tools, Prentice Hall, 1985.

[16]   Maciejowski J.M.: "Predictive Control with Constraints", Prentice Hall, 2002.

[17]   Jrjung L., Jyh-Hong D. and Hsing L.: "Petri Nets for Performance Modeling Study of Client-Server Systems", *International J. of Systems Science*, Vol.29, pp.565-571, 1998.

[18]   Koriem M.S.: "R-nets for the Performance Evaluation of Hard Real-Time Systems", *The Journal of Systems and Software*, Vol.46, pp.41-58, 1999.

[19]   Zuberek W.M., Govindarajan R. and Suciu, F.: "Timed Colored Petri Net Models of Distributed Memory Multithreaded Multiprocessors", *Proceedings Workshop on Practical Use of Colored Petri Nets and Design (CPN)*, pp.253-270, 1998.

A Greek Morphological Lexicon and Its Exploitation by Natural Language Processing Applications

Georgios Petasis, Vangelis Karkaletsis, Dimitra Farmakiotou,
Ion Androutsopoulos*, and Constantine D. Spyropoulo

Software and Knowledge Engineering Laboratory
Institute of Informatics and Telecommunications
National Centre for Scientific Research "Demokritos"
Aghia Paraskevi, Athens, 153 10 Greece
{petasis,vangelis,dfarmak,ionandr,costass}@iit.demokritos.gr

Abstract. This paper presents a large-scale Greek morphological lexicon, developed at the Software & Knowledge Engineering Laboratory (SKEL) of NCSR "Demokritos". The paper describes the lexicon architecture and the procedure to develop and update it. The morphological lexicon was used to develop a lemmatiser and a morphological analyser that were exploited in various natural language processing applications for Greek. The paper presents these applications (controlled language checker, information extraction, information filtering) and discusses further research issues and how we plan to address them.

1   Introduction

During the last decade, we have witnessed a remarkable acceleration in the growth of Internet, communication networks, multimedia, etc. In this new era, the main vehicle for digital content products and services is natural language, increasing the need for robust language engineering systems. Language resources, such as lexicons and grammars, constitute the main ingredient of such systems. For this reason, there is a strong need for development of language resources that can be exploited by various natural language processing applications. For instance, lexicons with morphological and syntactic information are needed for the development of tools such as spelling and syntax checkers that can be integrated in word processors, as well as for the development of morphological and syntactic analysers that can be exploited by more complex natural language processing applications (search engines, information filtering and extraction systems, machine translation systems, etc.).

The Greek institutions involved in language engineering have paid special attention to the development of Greek language resources. During the last few

---

* Now with the Department of Informatics, Athens University of Economics and Business, Greece. E-mail: ion@aueb.gr

Y. Manolopoulos et al. (Eds.): PCI 2001, LNCS 2563, pp. 401–419, 2003.

years, computational lexicons for Modern Greek have been developed by the
Computer Technology Institute, the Institute for Language & Speech Processing, the Wire Communications Laboratory at the University of Patras, and the
Software & Knowledge Engineering Laboratory at NCSR "Demokritos". The
development of computational lexicons (i.e. lexicons that can be exploited by
natural language processing applications) is a difficult task and becomes even
more difficult due to the characteristics of the Modern Greek language. The complexity of the Modern Greek inflectional system, the existence of marked stress,
free-word-order, the parallel use of Ancient Greek word forms and inflections
along with Modern Greek word forms and inflections, as well as use of foreign
words that have been partly incorporated or have not been incorporated in the
Modern Greek language system are the main characteristics of Modern Greek
that affect the computational treatment of its morphology.

The lexicon of the Computer Technology Institute (CTI) contains ~80.000
lemmas (~1.000.000 word-forms) [7]. Given a word-form, the CTI lexicon returns the corresponding lemma (or lemmas in case of lexical ambiguity) along
with morphosyntactic and semantic information, i.e. part of speech, number,
gender, case, person, tense, voice, mood, etc. The CTI lexicon is based on the
CTI lexicon formalism for the description of inflected words. The CTI formalism
treats each stem as a lexicon entry, embodies rules for inflectional morphology
and marked stress, and denotes morphosyntactic or semantic attributes of mor-
phemes and syntactic or semantic relations involving lemmas. The CTI lexicon
has been used as the basis for the Greek spelling checker adopted by Microsoft
for its word-processor MS Word. This lexicon has also been used recently for the
development of the Greek WordNet, a semantic network that includes for every lemma not only morphosyntactic but also semantic information (synonyms,
semantic groups-synsets, etc.) based on the EuroWordnet formalism (project
EPET-II DIALEXICO).

The lexicon of the Institute of Language & Speech Processing (ILSP) has
been developed in the context of the EC project LE-PAROLE, aiming at natural language processing applications. It contains ~20.000 lemmas encoded at
the morphological and the syntactic level according to the PAROLE/SIMPLE
schema. Each lemma is represented as a Morphological Unit, which may correspond to more than one Graphical Morphological Units expressing in this manner
alternative spellings of same lemma and is linked to Combinations of Morphological Features (number, gender etc.). Each Graphical Morphological Unit is
linked to a Graphical Inflectional Paradigm, which expresses how different word
forms are generated from the lemma. The initial ILSP lexicon has been extended
in the context of the EPET-II project LEXIS. The new version of the lexicon
is comprised of ~65.000 lemmas containing morphological information of which
a subset also contains syntactic and semantic information [1].

The lexicon of the Wire Communications Laboratory (WCL) contains
~35.000 lemmas along with the inflected forms of the words and their grammatical features stored in a Directed Acyclic Word Graph (DAWG). This lexicon
was exploited in the context of the EPET-II project MITOS for the development

of a fast morphological analyser [9]. The morphological analyser results are used by the MITOS[1] information extraction system.

The lexicon presented in this paper has been developed at the Software & Knowledge Engineering Laboratory (SKEL) of NCSR "Demokritos". The SKEL lexicon consists of ~60.000 lemmas that correspond to ~710.000 different word forms. The SKEL lexicon has been developed in parallel with *Ellogon* [8], a general-purpose text-engineering platform which facilitates the development of new tools as well as their integration in different applications. Thus the SKEL lexicon or its components can be easily embedded in different applications taking advantage of the facilities provided by *Ellogon*.

The SKEL lexicon architecture, the procedure to create it, and the provided functionalities for updating it, are presented in Section 2. The morphological lexicon has been exploited in the development a lemmatiser and a morphological analyser, which have been integrated in a controlled language checker for Greek, in Greek information extraction systems, as well as in a Greek information filtering system. Sections 3, 4 and 5 discuss the lexicon exploitation in the context of these natural language processing applications. Finally, section 6 presents further research issues and how we plan to address them. Our goal is to produce a wide-coverage morphological lexicon of Modern Greek that can be easily maintained and that can be easily exploited in new natural language processing applications.

2   The SKEL Lexicon for Modern Greek

In this section we describe the lexicon architecture and organisation, the way it was originally created and the infrastructure provided for accessing and maintaining its morphological database.

2.1   Lexicon Organisation

The lexicon consists of two independent components, the *query component* and the *generation component*. The query component is responsible for querying the lexicon about a specific word form and retrieving the associated linguistic information of a word form (Fig. 1). The query component is organised around a morphological database, which associates word forms with sets of morphological entries. Morphological entries are the basic elements for storing morphological information. Each morphological entry contains a fixed number of fields describing a specific word form, where each field represents a morphological feature, such as the lemma or the part of speech of the word form. A complete list of available fields as well as all their corresponding values is presented in Table 1.

In Greek it is often the case that the same word form may be found in text associated with different sets of morphological features. Thus, more than one morphological entry may be associated with a single word form. Figure 2

---

[1] http://www.iit.demokritos.gr/skel/mitos/

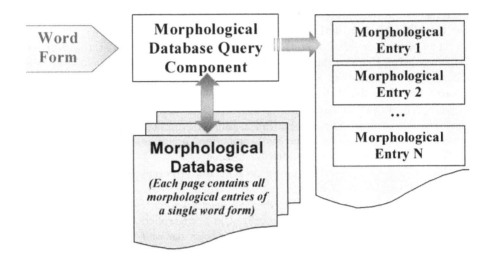

Fig. 1. The lexicon Query Component

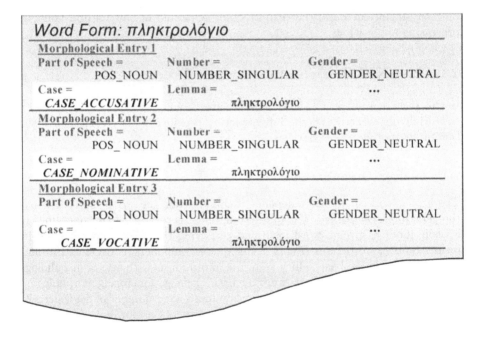

Fig. 2. A page from the morphological database, describing the word form "πληκτρολόγιο"

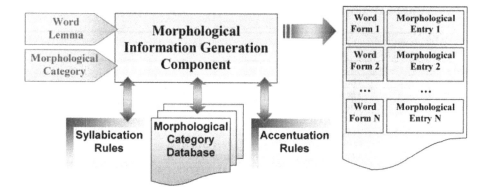

Fig. 3. The lexicon Generation Component

for example, presents all the morphological entries associated with the word form "πληκτρολόγιο" (keyboard): all three morphological entries share the same values for all features (i.e. the same lemma, part-of-speech, number, etc.), except the case feature, as the same word form can appear in texts having three different case values. All morphological entries associated with the same word form are regarded as entries belonging to the same *page*.

The morphological database comprises of a fixed number of *pages*. As each page is associated with a unique word form, there are as many pages as the number of different word forms the lexicon can recognise. The number of morphological entries in each page is equal to the number of all the different instantiations of a word form the lexicon is aware of. During a word form search, the query component locates the page that describes the requested word form. If such a page is located (i.e. if the word form is contained in the database), all its morphological entries are returned (Fig. 2).

The generation lexicon component is responsible for generating all the possible word forms as well as all the morphological entries of each word form for a given lemma. Apart from the lemma, this component also requires classification of the given lemma in one of the predefined morphological categories contained in the morphological categories database (Fig. 3). Each morphological category contains instructions describing how the various word forms can be generated from the word lemma and what morphological feature values must be associated with it. An example is presented in Table 2: this category can be used to create the instantiations of male proper names ending in "ός", like the name "Ασκληπιός". Given the word lemma and an appropriate morphological category, the generation component also utilises language specific rules regarding syllabication and accentuation in order to produce all possible word forms. During the creation process, each generated word form is represented with one morphological entry. As a result, a word form can be generated more than once if ambiguity exists, but each instance will be represented by a different morpho-

Table 1. Morphological Entry fields and their permissible values

Morphological Entry Field	Available Field Values
Word Form	The word form
Lemma	The word lemma
Stem	The word stem
Suffix	The word suffix
Part of Speech	POS_ARTICLE, POS_NOUN, POS_ADJECTIVE, POS_PRONOUN, POS_VERB, POS_PARTICIPLE, POS_ADVERB, POS_PREPOSITION, POS_CONJUNCTION, POS_PARTICLE
Number	NUMBER_SINGULAR, NUMBER_PLURAL
Case	CASE_NOMINATIVE, CASE_GENITIVE, CASE_DATIVE, CASE_ACCUSATIVE, CASE_VOCATIVE
Tense	TENSE_PRESENT, TENSE_PAST_CONTINUOUS, TENSE_FUTURE_CONTINUOUS, TENSE_FUTURE, TENSE_PAST, TENSE_PRESENT_PERFECT, TENSE_PAST_PERFECT, TENSE_FUTURE_PERFECT
Translation	An English translation, if available
Other Fields	Info, Mood, Mode, Voice, Person, Syllabication, Part of Speech Detail, Inflectional Type, Accented Syllable, Gender, Inflection, Explanation, Examples, Synonyms

Table 2. A Morphological category example

Category Type	PNM_1		
Suffix	ός		
Part of speech	Noun		
Inflectional type	ACCENT_OXYTONO		
Inflection	INFLECTION_EQSYL		
Info	Proper Noun		
Generative Suffix	**Case**	**Number**	**Accented Syllable**
-ός	CASE_ACCUSATIVE	NUMBER_SINGULAR	1
-ού	CASE_GENITIVE	NUMBER_SINGULAR	1
-ό	CASE_NOMINATIVE	NUMBER_SINGULAR	1
-έ	CASE_VOCATIVE	NUMBER_SINGULAR	1

logical entry. For example, if we had the word lemma "πληκτρολόγιο" the word form "πληκτρολόγιο" would be generated three times (Fig. 2). However, if all morphological entries for a generated word form are collected, the resulting set may not in general be a page, as a specific word form may also be generated by other lemmas that may even belong to different parts of speech. For example many articles (e.g. "του") share the same word forms with pronouns. If the generation component is used on the article lemma ("o") the returned morphological entries for the word form "του" will not be a page, as the morphological entries regarding its instantiations as a personal pronoun will be missing.

2.2 Lexicon Creation

Once the infrastructure described above was available, an initial version of the lexicon was created. Initially, a list of word lemmas was constructed. In order to collect as many word lemmas as possible, various textual corpora have been used, as well as freely available lists of words intended to be used by Greek versions of open source spell checkers (like "ispell" and "aspell"). The list of word forms collected from all these sources contain approximately 260.000 unique word forms. These word forms were examined in order to identify and fix errors as well as to extract the corresponding word lemmas. Finally, the list of word lemmas was enriched with proper names (names of persons and locations) that were extracted from the various lists of proper names (gazetteers) developed at our laboratory. Currently, the list of word lemmas contains approximately 60.000 unique lemmas.

As a next step, the listed lemmas were classified in categories using simple heuristics. Word forms that shared the same stems with a lemma (based on heuristics to remove prefixes) were considered different instantiations of the lemma. Lemmas that share the same suffix and also their associated instantiations share common suffixes were classified in common categories. Finally, the morphological categories created with the automatic classification were reviewed by human experts and generation instructions were added for each category. This simple approach worked remarkably well for some parts of speech, like adjectives and nouns. However, it has not managed to generate categories for verbs, articles, pronouns and all the other parts of speech. The main reason for this was either the fact that these parts of speech are not inflected, or the fact that their inflected word forms were very diverse from the lemma or other word forms associated to the lemma. However, lemmas that belong to closed categories like articles or pronouns can be classified fast. On the other hand, lemmas for verbs are more difficult to classify into categories. For instance, past tenses are mostly characterised by prefixes or infixes added to the stem, besides the inflectional suffixes for different tenses. For example, the past form of "κάν-ω" (do) is "έ-καν-α". At the same time, the various participles are quite similar, even for verbs that belong to different declension categories, making their classification to different categories impossible with our simple heuristics, as the evidence is limited.

After the morphological categories had been manually corrected, word lemmas were manually classified according to their part of speech and morphological category. Approximately 350 morphological categories were created, covering mainly nouns, adjectives, verbs and pronouns. The number of morphological categories is not fixed since new categories may be added to cover new words. The process of manual classification of a word lemma into a morphological category is partially supported by a specialised tool that is able to propose possible morphological categories (Fig. 4). With this tool, the user can select any of the proposed categories and see all the word forms that can be generated if the word lemma is classified into the selected inflectional category. In case all proposed

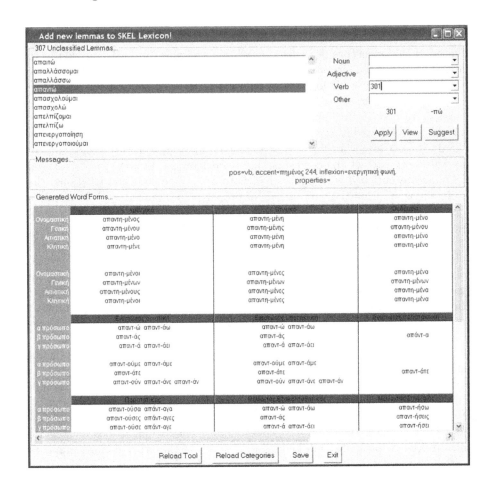

Fig. 4. A tool for updating the lexicon with new words

morphological categories are inadequate, the user can create a new category and classify the word lemma in it.

The last step of the process was to process the morphologically classified word lemmas with the lexicon generation component. The generation component created all word forms as well as all relevant morphological entries for each word form and filled the morphological database of the lexicon. From the initial list of approximately 60.000 unique word lemmas, 710.000 different word forms were generated, leading to ~2.500.000 morphological entries in the morphological database. Approximately 3.000 word lemmas were not processed by the generation component due to various errors (including errors in morphological category classifications detected by the generation component). In Table 3 the distribution of lemmas over parts of speech is shown, as well as the number of currently defined morphological categories.

Table 3. The distribution of lemmas to the various parts of speech

Part of Speech	Lemma Number	Percentage (%)	Morphological Categories Number
Noun	29744	50,82	201
Adjective	13203	22,56	107
Verb	5850	10,00	48
Adverb	234	0,40	–
Other	9495	16,22	–

2.3 Lexicon Access and Maintenance

Both the query and the generation components as well as the whole software infrastructure of the lexicon have been developed in the C++ programming language, as our main concern was to build a portable and efficient system that could be easily embedded inside other applications that need to access the lexicon. This infrastructure offers an object-oriented environment that facilitates memory management and allows the insertion of an abstraction layer between the lexicon functionality and the specific internal details of the lexicon implementation. Through the provided programming interface (API) the caller can access both the query and generation components. Additionally, the software offers direct access to the morphological database by offering the ability to insert new morphological entries as well as to retrieve, modify or delete existing ones. Having direct access to the morphological entries of the database, the caller can extract part of the information contained in a morphological entry and create a separate, specialised database to satisfy specific needs. For example, one may extract a lemmatiser for specific purposes from the lexicon, e.g. a lemmatiser that associates word forms with the corresponding lemmas, ignoring all other pieces of information, resulting in a specialised tool that can be used independently of the lexicon.

The modularity and the provided API of the lexicon infrastructure have permitted the embedding of the lexicon infrastructure under the Tcl programming language. Tcl is an easy to learn, high level scripting language that provides features like Unicode support, portability and a cross-platform graphical user interface. All functionality provided by the C++ API is also available from Tcl, thus easing the process of writing applications that access or modify the lexicon. Additionally, the fact that the lexicon is accessible from Tcl enables the incorporation of the lexicon in various Tcl-based text engineering platforms like *Ellogon* [8] or GATE [3]. An application is illustrated in figure 5, where a tool for querying a word form in the lexicon is presented. The user is also able to browse among all morphological entries associated with a specific word form and examine or modify the contained morphological information.

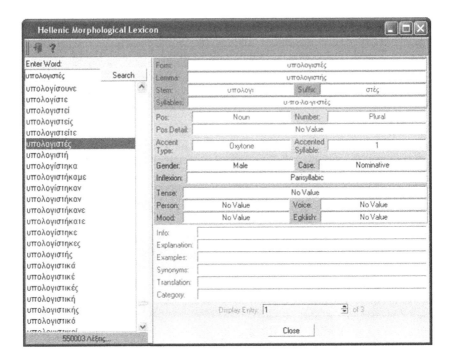

Fig. 5. A tool for querying the lexicon

2.4 Lemmatisation and Morphological Analysis

The lexicon infrastructure forms a strong basis upon which various task-oriented tools can be easily constructed. In this section we describe two such examples: a lemmatiser and a morphological analyser. Both tools have been developed as components of the *Ellogon* platform but each of them exploits the lexicon in a different way: the lemmatiser extracts and utilises a specialised database from the lexicon, while the morphological analyser accesses the lexicon's database in order to annotate words with all available linguistic information.

The process followed for the creation of the lemmatiser was fairly simple. Initially, a specialised database, that associated word forms with lemmas, was created. A module was also developed that queries all the word forms contained in the lexicon, retrieves the lemma for each word form and fills the specialised database. The lemmatiser requires about 25 MB of memory and it processes ~2.000 words/sec on a PIII/500 PC with 256 MB RAM.

The development of the morphological analyser was also straightforward, as it simply interfaces the lexicon infrastructure with the *Ellogon* platform. The analyser utilises the provided API to query the lexicon about word forms, retrieve the associated morphological entries and pass all the morphological information contained in each entry to the *Ellogon* platform. The component requires about 45 MB of memory, and is able to process ∼500 words/sec on the same PC.

3 Lexicon Exploitation
by a Greek Controlled Language Checker

A controlled language is a language with a restricted syntax, vocabulary and terminology that is typically applied to technical documents. The aim of using controlled languages in technical documentation is the production of texts with simple structure and restricted vocabulary that can be read and translated more easily [4]. Several software companies (e.g. Bull, IBM) as well as other companies (e.g. Caterpillar, General Motors, Boeing) have been using controlled languages during technical writing of their products documentation. The restrictions imposed by the use of a controlled language preserve uniformity in the writing style, especially in cases where authors tend to follow diverse writing approaches. Additionally, these restrictions reduce ambiguities in the resulting text. The use of a controlled language makes translation faster and of higher quality. A controlled language may also facilitate machine translation, since its resources (vocabulary, terminology and syntax rules) can be exploited by a machine translation system, improving its performance.

In the context of the Greek R&D project SCHEMATOPOIESIS[2], we developed a controlled language checker for the Greek language to assist Greek technical writers as well as to facilitate translation from Greek to other languages [6]. The lexical and grammatical resources of this controlled language cover technical documents from the domain of computational equipment. Technical writers are able to call the checker through their word processor (MS Word is used in the current implementation) as well as through a Web-based application. This allows users to check the format and language of their documents in a similar way as a spelling/syntax checker. The technical document is first converted into an XML format in order to be processed by the checker (Fig. 6). The checker outputs the identified errors in a format "understandable" by the word-processor in order to let users see their errors. The checker checks both text language (correct application of controlled language grammar and vocabulary) and text format (e.g. line spacing, font style and size). The XML text is first processed using linguistic resources (restricted terminology, vocabulary, grammar) and tools (tokeniser, sentence splitter, part of speech tagger, case tagger, morphological analyser, lexical analyser) in order to apply the language checker. Language checking involves lookup of a terminological database (termbase) and a restricted vocabulary as well as checking for paragraph and sentence size, number of sentence clauses, correct appearance of terms, application of syntax

---

[2] SCHEMATOPOIESIS is an R&D project funded partially by the Greek General Secretariat of Research & Technology (GSRT) and the EC. The project partners include the Institute for Language & Speech Processing (coordinator), the National Technical University of Athens, NCSR "Demokritos", ALTEC, UNISOFT.

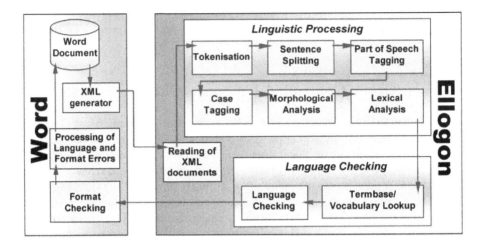

Fig. 6. Architecture of the controlled language checker

restrictions, etc. The text is also checked using a format DTD (Document Type Definition) in order to locate possible errors in format.

At the first stage of the checker's development, we decided to exploit the morphological lexicon as a lemmatiser in order to enrich the output of the part of speech and case tagger with the word lemmas taking into account the lookup module requirements. The lookup module locates those words, phrases or terms that exist in pre-stored lists (in our case the termbase and vocabulary lists). However, in order to reduce the lists size, we maintain only the lemmatised forms of the words appearing there. For instance, there is one entry in the termbase for the term "τελικός χρήστης" (end-user) that covers the phrases "τελικός χρήστης" (nominative-singular), "τελικού χρήστη" (genitive-singular), "τελικό χρήστη" (accusative-singular), "τελικοί χρήστες" (nominative-plural), "τελικών χρηστών" (genitive-plural), "τελικούς χρήστες" (accusative-plural). This in turn requires the lemmatisation of the text, since the lookup module attempts to match only the lemmatised forms.

During the evaluation of this version of the checker, we realised that we had to improve the results of linguistic processing in order to improve language checking. This was mainly related to the results of the part of speech and case taggers. Both taggers are based on a machine learning technique, Transformation-Based Error-Driven learning with performance of around 95%. Although this is a good performance for several language engineering tasks (named entity recognition, information extraction), it is not good enough for a task such as controlled language checking. Let's take for instance, one of the rules of the controlled language in the project SCHEMATOPOIESIS that issues an upper limit in the number of consecutive adjectives occurring in a sentence (no more than three). A common mistake of our Greek part of speech tagger concerns the tagging of adjectives as nouns and vice versa due to the morphological similarity of these part of speech categories. Although the tagger is not based only on the morphological form of a word (this is the same for nouns and adjectives) but also on their context, there are several cases where the tagger recognises mistakenly a noun as an adjective. Thus, the technical writer may receive by mistake error messages concerning the number of consecutive adjectives. However, this affects negatively the general impression that the users have for the checker. This is also the case for the case tagger, which may mistakenly characterise a noun in nominative case although it is in accusative, due to their morphological similarity (the accuracy of the case tagger is ~93%). Another issue concerns the need to enrich the results of the taggers in order to cover more requirements issued by the controlled language rules. The part of speech tagger is able to identify the following information: part of speech, number and gender for nouns, adjectives and pronouns as well as the tense for verbs. However, the controlled language issues rules concerning the voice and person for verbs, two features that cannot be handled by the part of speech tagger.

The problems mentioned above motivated us to exploit more features of the morphological lexicon apart from the lemma. We had to improve the accuracy of the part of speech and case taggers as well as to enrich their results with more features, such as voice and person for verbs. For this purpose, we developed a morphological analyser as well as a lexical analyser (see Fig. 6). The morphological analyser extracts from the lexicon the required morphological features for those words in the text for which a lexicon entry exists. The lexical analyser, on the other hand, combines the results of both taggers with the results of the morphological analyser. For those words that cannot be analysed by the morphological analyser, we keep the results of the taggers. Concerning those words for which the morphological analyser provides more than one results (e.g. three morphological entries for a noun form that differ in the case: nominative, accusative, vocative) the lexical analyser checks if the tagger agrees with one of these results. If it does agree, this result is kept, otherwise some heuristics are used to select one of the morphological analyser results.

Table 4. Lexicon coverage evaluation

Tokens	Words	Greek			
		Symbols, punctuation marks, digits		2.505 – 15,7%	
		Foreign		359 – 2,2%	
		Greek	Analysed	11.351 – 86,5%	15990
				13.126 – 82,1%	
			Not Analysed	1.775 – 13,5%	

We evaluated the lexicon coverage as well as the lexical analysis. The lexicon coverage in a corpus of 15.990 tokens is shown in table 4. From these tokens, 15,7% corresponds to symbols, punctuation marks and digits and 2,2% to foreign words (in total 17,9%). From the remaining tokens (Greek words), 86,5% were analysed with the morphological analyser (there was at least one entry for them in the morphological lexicon) whereas 13,5% were unknown (no entry for them was found in the lexicon).

Concerning the lexical analyser results, compared to the results obtained for the tagger there was a considerable improvement in part of speech (accuracy 97,8%), reducing errors such as the adjective-noun confusion. However, the results were about the same in case identification (accuracy 92,5%), a fact that shows the difficulty of the task for the Greek language. Concerning those features not covered by the taggers (person and voice for verbs) it must be noted that for those verbs that are not known to the lexicon there is no person and voice information.

4   Lexicon Exploitation by an Information Extraction System

Information Extraction (IE) systems fill in predefined data structures with information they extract from unstructured natural language texts that refer to a particular domain. The main processing tasks of an IE system are the following: *Named Entity, Coreference, Template Element, Template Relations and Scenario Template*. The Named Entity task involves the detection and categorization of proper names into predefined domain-dependent semantic categories (e.g. person, location, date). The Coreference task unifies expressions (e.g. proper names, pronouns, definite noun phrases) that refer to identical entities. For each entity, the Template Element task collects particular types of descriptions from the texts, typically pre- and post-modifiers of proper names, like job titles and company descriptions (e.g. "Newton, *a start-up electronics manufacturer*"). The Template Relations task then identifies particular domain-specific semantic relations between template elements; for example, a PRODUCT_OF relation may show a relation between a product and its manufacturer. Finally, the Scenario Template task builds upon the results of the previous tasks to fill an overall template that describes an entire event. For example, the creation of a new joint venture may be seen as an event, that involves PARTICIPANT relations between the new company and each one of the companies that participate in the joint venture, a PRODUCT_OF relation between the new company and a product it will be producing, etc.

In the context of the European R&D project CROSSMARC[3], the SKEL lexicon has been exploited in the construction of a Hellenic Information Extraction system. CROSSMARC applies state-of-the-art language engineering tools and techniques to achieve commercial strength technology for information extraction from web pages, which is applied for e-retail product comparison. The core components of CROSSMARC technology are the following:

- A Web page collection component, which involves a mechanism for identifying domain-specific e-retailers Web sites and navigating through these sites in order to identify and collect Web pages that describe relevant products.
- A high-quality Information Extraction component for several languages (this is demonstrated in the project's four languages: English, Greek, French and Italian), which locates product descriptions in the collected web pages and extracts important information from them so as to populate a database with information about vendors' offers. The IE component can be adapted semi-automatically to new domains, reducing drastically programming effort and cost.
- A web-based user interface, which processes the user's query, performs user modelling, accesses the databases and presents product information back to the user.

CROSSMARC's technology is demonstrated and evaluated through a prototype e-retail comparison system, based on multi-agent technology, for two different product types (laptops in e-retailers sites, job adverts on companies' sites).

So far, we have used the morphological lexicon in the 1st processing stage of the Hellenic IE system, the Named Entity Recognition and Classification (NERC) task, applied in the 1st domain of the project, that is laptops descriptions in e-retailers web pages [5]. Among different types of information NERC systems utilise information offered by Gazetteers, i.e. tools that identify known entity names in the text and lexical information such as lemmas or stems, which combined with other types of information are the components of rules for NERC grammars. More specifically, the Hellenic NERC (HNERC) module involves three processing stages (Fig. 7):

- Lexical Pre-processing, which includes tokenisation, sentence splitting, lexical analysis (part of speech tagging and lemmatisation).
- Gazetteer lookup, which involves the recognition of known entity names in the text.
- Application of rules for identification and classification of named entities.

The SKEL morphological lexicon has been used as a lemmatiser in the context of lexical analysis (Fig. 7) in order to enrich the output of the part-of-speech

---

[3] CROSSMARC (IST 2000 – 25366) is a R&D project on cross-lingual information extraction applied in e-retail product comparison, funded partially by the EC. CROSSMARC partners include NCSR "Demokritos" (coordinator), University of Edinburgh (UK), University of Roma Tor Vergata (Italy), Informatique CDC (France), VeltiNet (Greece). http://www.iit.demokritos.gr/skel/crossmarc/.

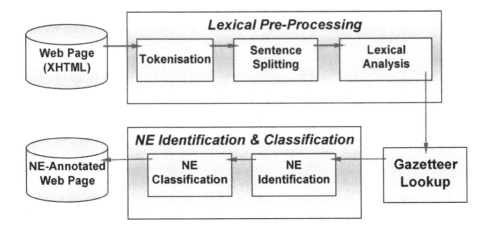

Fig. 7. Architecture of the Hellenic NERC system

tagger with the lemma. More specifically, the lemmatiser produces the lemmas for Greek words found in the pages leaving non-Greek words intact.

Lemmas are used in the rules of the HNERC grammars along with other information from lexical pre-processing, e.g. capitalisation, part-of-speech. The use of a lemma instead of all the different forms of an inflected word reduces the size of the rules. For the same reason of economy, the Gazetteer lookup tool uses the output of the lemmatiser and matches lemmatised lists of known names to the lemmas of the words found in the text.

We recently started the development of the subsequent modules of the IE systems in CROSSMARC, the so-called Fact Extraction (FE) modules. An FE module takes as input the results of the corresponding NERC module (i.e. named entities found in a web pages containing one or more product description) aiming to fill the fields of a pre-defined template with the corresponding information found in a product description (e.g. that a numeric expression of MONEY type identified by the NERC module is the price of the specific laptop offer). We are going to exploit the SKEL lexicon in the hand-written grammars of the Hellenic FE (HFE) module in order to reduce the size of the rules (as we did in the HNERC grammar case). We will also exploit the lexicon in the training of the machine-learning based HFE, using the lemmas of the Greek words occurring in the web pages instead of the exact word forms.

5   Lexicon Exploitation by an Information Filtering System

Information Filtering (IF) systems are used for managing large information flows, presenting users information related to their interests. Many IF systems have been developed in recent years for various applications: news filtering, e-mail messages filtering, web pages filtering, etc. We used information filtering techniques in the context of the R&D project ADIET[4].

The objective of ADIET was the development of a decision support system to analyse share-holdings between companies, exploiting the relevant expertise in the area of the French partner Informatique-CDC. This system visualises the companies' stock connections as a network, the nodes of which are the companies and the links between them represent the percentage of equity capital owned. The ADIET system consists of:

- a text categorisation module for detecting interesting news from the Greek Stock market announcements (Kapa-TEL provides these announcements to their clients),
- a named entity recognition module for detecting the entities involved in the interesting news, and
- a Web-based interface that enables the user to update the network of Greek companies stocks connections, taking into account the categorised announcements and the names of companies identified in them.

In ADIET we exploited information filtering techniques in the text categorisation module in order to identify interesting stock-market announcements. The information filtering system that we developed was based on a machine learning technique that we used originally for the filtering of unwanted e-mails (spam e-mails) [2].

More specifically, a Naïve Bayes learner was developed which was trained on a training corpus of manually classified documents. For each document of the training corpus, a vector representation of the form $\vec{x} = \langle x_1, x_2, x_3, \ldots, x_n \rangle$ was computed, where $x_1, \ldots, x_n$ are the values of the features $X_1, \ldots, X_n$. All features are binary: $X_i = 1$ if feature X_i is present in the document; otherwise $X_i = 0$. Features correspond to words, pairs or triplets of words (1-grams, 2-grams, 3-grams). Therefore, each feature indicates whether or not a certain word (e.g. "συγχώνευση", the Greek word for "merge") or a sequence of 2 or 3 words (e.g. "μετοχικό κεφάλαιο" which means "capital stock", or "αύξηση μετοχικού κεφαλαίου" which means "capital stock growth") occurs in the current document. In order to select the appropriate features (words or sequences of words) for each text category, we calculated the Information Gain (IG) of every candidate feature. For each event type, the features with the highest IG scores were selected.

During training, each Greek word in the training corpus was replaced by its lemma. Consider for example that the four different forms of the lemma "κεφάλαιο" (κεφάλαιο, κεφαλαίου, κεφάλαια, κεφαλαίων) occur once within a document. During training, each of the four word forms will be treated as the same word (the lemma), increasing in turn the IG for the corresponding feature.

---

[4] ADIET is a bilateral (Greek-French) R&D project funded partially by the Greek General Secretariat of Research & Technology (GSRT) and the French government. ADIET partners include NCSR, Informatique CDC and Kapa-TEL.

A separate Boolean classifier was constructed for each text category, using the features that were selected for that category. Incoming documents are first processed by a tokeniser and a lemmatiser and then they are classified into one or more categories, based on the results of the corresponding classifiers.

We conducted two sets of experiments. In the first one, features corresponded to single words, while in the second one features correspond to words, pairs of words and triplets of consecutive words. There was no significant difference in the results, which indicates that adding features for two or three consecutive words has no significant effect. Results were very good for all the text categories (F-measure > 90%).

6   Conclusions and Future Work

In this paper, we presented the main characteristics of the SKEL morphological lexicon and described its exploitation by three different natural language applications (controlled language checking, information extraction, information filtering).

Efficient access to the lexicon was one of our main objectives in order to facilitate its exploitation. The integration of the lexicon in the *Ellogon* text engineering platform has facilitated the development of the necessary tools that use the content of the morphological lexicon (lemmatiser, morphological analyser). The efficient update of the lexicon was another issue we focused on. For this reason, we developed a user-friendly interface for adding new lexicon entries.

During the first stages of the lexicon development, we focused on nouns and adjectives since our objective was to improve the accuracy of the lookup modules we used in text processing applications. For instance, in the controlled language checker the lookup module uses lists of terms that are mainly comprised of nouns and adjectives. This is also the case in the gazetteer lookup module and the grammar of the named entity recogniser in the CROSSMARC information extraction system, as well as in the classifiers of the ADIET information filtering system. We plan to update the lexicon with the addition of new entries for verbs. We will also improve the lexicon structure concerning verb entries since in its current state it cannot handle all verb types.

In the context of the CROSSMARC project, we will exploit the lexicon in the development of the Hellenic Fact Extraction module for both domains examined (laptops and job offers).

Finally, we are also examining the use of the lexicon by a natural language generator for Greek. In the context of the M-PIRO[5] project we are developing natural language generation technology that allows personalized descriptions of

---

[5] M-PIRO (Multilingual Personalised Information Objects) is a project of the Information Societies Programme of the European Union, running from February 2000 to January 2003. The project's consortium consists of the University of Edinburgh (UK, coordinator), ITC-irst (Italy), NCSR "Demokritos" (Greece), the University of Athens (Greece), the Foundation of the Hellenic World (Greece), and System Simulation Ltd (UK).

museum exhibits to be generated in several languages (English, Greek and Italian in the current implementation), starting from symbolic, language-independent information stored in a database, and small fragments of text. In the context of M-PIRO we have developed a Greek lexicon for morphological generation according to the formalism imposed for all languages by the ILEX natural language generation system. We would like to examine the merging of the 2 lexicons, the SKEL lexicon used so far for morphological analysis and the M-PIRO Greek lexicon used for morphological generation in order to have a common resource for both types of morphological processing.

References

[1]   Anagnostopoulou D., Desipri E., Labropoulou P., Mantzari E. and Gavrilidou M.: "LEXIS–Lexicographical Infrastructure: Systematizing the Data", *Proceedings Workshop on Computational Lexicography and Multimedia Dictionaries (COM-LEX 2000)*, pp.63-66, Greece, September 2000. 402

[2]   Androutsopoulos I., Paliouras G., Karkaletsis V., Sakkis G., Spyropoulos C. D. and Stamatopoulos P.: "Learning to Filter Spam E-Mail: a Comparison of a Naive Bayesian and a Memory-Based Approach", *Proceedings Workshop Machine Learning and Textual Information Access, European Conference on Principles and Practice of Knowledge Discovery in Databases (PKDD)*, pp.1-13, Lyon, France, 2000. 417

[3]   Cunningham H., Humphreys K., Gaizauskas R. and Wilks Y.: "GATE - a TIPSTER-based General Architecture for Text Engineering", *Proceedings TIPSTER Text Program (Phase III) 6 Month Workshop*, DARPA, Morgan Kaufmann, CA, 1997. 409

[4]   Eijk P.: "Controlled Languages in Technical Documentation", *Elsnews, the Newsletter of the European Network in Language and Speech*, pp.4-5, February 1998. 411

[5]   Farmakiotou D., Karkaletsis V., Samaritakis G., Petasis G. and Spyropoulos C. D.: "Named Entity Recognition from Greek Web Pages", *Proceedings 2nd Hellenic Conference on AI (SETN-02)*, Companion Volume, pp.91-102, Thessaloniki, Greece, April 2002. 415

[6]   Markantonatou S., Karkaletsis V. and Maistros Y.: "An Authoring Tool for Controlled Modern Greek", *Proceedings 2nd Hellenic Conference on AI (SETN-02)*, Companion Volume, pp.165-176, Thessaloniki, Greece, April 2002. 411

[7]   Ntoulas A., Stamou S., Tsakou I., Tsalidis Ch., Tzagarakis M. and Vagelatos A.: "Use of a Morphosyntactic Lexicon as the Basis for the Implementation of the Greek Wordnet", *Proceedings 2nd Conference on Natural Language Processing (NLP 2000)*, pp.49-58, Patras, Greece, 2000. 402

[8]   Petasis G., Karkaletsis V., Paliouras G., Androutsopoulos I. and Spyropoulos C. D.: "Ellogon: a Text Engineering Platform", *Proceedings 3rd Language Resources and Evaluation Conference (LREC 2002)*, pp.72-78, Las Palmas, Spain, May 2002. 403, 409

[9]   Sgarbas K., Fakotakis N. and Kokkinakis G.: "A Straightforward Approach to Morphological Analysis and Synthesis", *Proceedings Workshop on Computational Lexicography and Multimedia Dictionaries (COMLEX 2000)*, pp.31-34, Greece, September 2000. 403

A Comparison of Design Patterns and Roles in the Context of Behavioural Evolution

Dimitrios Theotokis, Anya Sotiropoulou,
George Gyftodimos, and Panagiotis Georgiadis

Department of Informatics and Telecommunications
University of Athens, 157 84 Athens, Greece
{dtheo,anya}@mm.di.uoa.gr
{geogyf,georgiad}@di.uoa.gr

Abstract. Component-based software development focuses on building software systems by integrating existing software components. Central to component-based software development are the notions of reusability, extensibility and adaptability. Components as well as their composition must be easily reused and extended to meet new requirements. Variation-oriented programming is concerned with the incorporation of context-dependent variations in existing object-oriented systems. Based on the principle of separation of concerns, variation-oriented programming addresses - amongst other issues - behavioural evolution and behaviour composition, at runtime. We identify the limitations imposed by the use of design patterns when used for behavioural evolution, in terms of behaviour composition, while at the same time satisfying reusability and extensibility. Then we proceed to present the ATOMA framework as an architecture and a means for achieving behaviour composition, as this is guided by the incorporation of context-dependent behavioural variations based on the concept of roles. Roles are considered, in this light, as pluggable behavioural adjustments of an existing object-oriented system.

1   Introduction

Decoupling behaviour modelling from a specific inheritance hierarchy has become one of the challenges for object-oriented software engineering and software composition. The goal is to encapsulate behaviour on its own, and yet be able to freely apply it to a given class or component structure, thus resulting in composable behavioural units.

If we were to take a bird's eye view of any given software system, we would find that its sole purpose is to perform a function for its user. The "black-box" metaphor attests exactly this fact. A given software application has a set of inputs and produces a set of outputs, via a transformation known as the behavioural characteristics of the function, which is expressed in terms of algorithms. A more in-depth inspection shows that a large system may be decomposed into smaller functions that collaborate to produce the desired behaviour, when recomposed for that purpose. This strict functional decomposition fuelled

Y. Manolopoulos et al. (Eds.): PCI 2001, LNCS 2563, pp. 420–439, 2003.

the structured programming approach to software development. Key to structured programming is the decomposition of a system's entire functionality into many functions smaller in scope, and with clear interfaces.

However, strict functional decomposition raises a considerable problem: The data over which the functions operate are usually spread throughout the program with no explicitly guaranteed integrity, as well as its inability to cater for functional evolution. This is known as *scattering*. Object-oriented programming emerged as a solution to this problem. In addition to decomposing a system into functions, classes are used to group data that share the same characteristics so that categorisation, classification and subsumption may be established. The functions are then mapped onto these classes. Encapsulating data and functions into classes guarantees the integrity of the data an object contains.

Once initial analysis is performed, data and functional decomposition is what is deduced from the problem space. Functional decomposition establishes the roles and responsibilities. Object-oriented methodologies either explicitly or implicitly identify the roles of a system being modelled.

Classes can be then reused and extended to meet new requirements and take part in the development of software systems that require already established functionality. Hence, classes can be seen as software components whose composition can result in the development of a new system. However, since any system is prone to changes, due to changes in the context in which it operates, components, as well as classes, must be able to incorporate context-dependent behavioural variations, in order to guarantee reusability and extensibility.

2   Context-Dependent Behavioural Variations

The behaviour of the components of a software system may be qualitatively different depending on (a) their internal state, (b) the perspective from which one part of the system is regarded by other parts or aspects of the system, (c) the computing environment that the software realising the system is operating in, and (d) the usage patterns exhibited by applications built on top of the system.

We use the term context-dependent behaviour variations to encapsulate all these aspects of behavioural characteristics that qualitatively differentiate between the behavioural parts of a software system. Based on the conditions that trigger their occurrence we divide context-dependent variations into four categories: state-dependent behaviour variations, perspective-dependent behaviour variations, application-dependent behaviour variations and environment-dependent behaviour variations. A detailed examination of context dependent behaviour variations is beyond the scope of this paper and can be found in [14].

2.1   Modelling and Composing Behavioural Variations with Design Patterns

The introduction of highly reusable software components is a fundamental goal of software engineering in light of the needs for software composition. Besides code reuse, the need for design reuse has been recognised, particularly through the work on design patterns proposed in [2]. A design pattern focuses on a particular object-oriented design problem: it names, abstracts, and identifies the key aspects of a common design structure useful for creating reusable and extensible object-oriented software. The design pattern identifies the participating classes and instances, their roles and collaborations, and the distribution of responsibilities. Furthermore, it describes when the design structure can be applied, whether it can be applied in the presence of other design constraints, and the consequences and tradeoffs of its use. In this way, design patterns are playing an important role in establishing a clear notion of reusable design constructs and means for software composition.

In addition to introducing the notion of a design pattern, Gamma et al. [2] have also compiled a first catalogue of design patterns useful for everyday programming practice. The patterns contained in this catalogue are based on practical solutions that have been implemented in mainstream object-oriented programming languages, such as Smalltalk, C++ and Java, i.e., not only the design structure is described, but also a typical implementation in one of the above languages is presented along with a motivation for preferring the presented implementation to other possible alternatives.

From the perspective of this paper, design patterns are important because they have helped the software engineering community to recognise forms of behaviour variations in an application domain [8] and a way of incorporating them in a existing system. Several design patterns, collectively called behavioural patterns in [2], identify an aspect of a system that may vary, and propose a way of writing programs such that the variation becomes possible. Despite the differences in the design issues they deal with, two main techniques are uniformly used to model these patterns, based on a combination of aggregation and parameterisation with inheritance.

The basic idea behind these two techniques is that the varying aspect is separated from the other aspects of a certain design by encapsulating them in two separate objects, which we call the *variation object* and the *base object*, respectively. In order to (loosely) couple the varying aspects to the rest of the design, the varying object is either made as an attribute of the base object, or it is passed as a parameter to the base object. Thus, their relationship is expressed by aggregation or parameterisation, respectively. In the remainder of this paper we refer to this technique as the aggregation/parameterisation-plus-inheritance technique (APPI).

Having discussed the drawbacks of inheritance, Gamma et al. [2] argue that APPI is the technique that solves the problems associated with inheritance with respect to behavioural evolution and therefore should be employed as an alternative to inheritance. The aim of this section is to determine whether APPI is really suitable for incremental behaviour variations and composition. For this purpose we briefly consider the implementation of two of the behavioural patterns, the Strategy and the Visitor pattern. The Strategy pattern is representative of a set of patterns, such as State, Bridge, etc., for expressing behaviour variation of

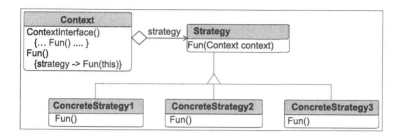

Fig. 1. Strategy pattern

a single object. On the other hand, the Visitor pattern proposes a design for expressing the behaviour variations presented in the previous section.

The Strategy Pattern The Strategy pattern allows multiple algorithms for the same functionality to co-exist and to be interchanged depending on application requirements without affecting the client that uses the functionality. Thus, the aim of the Strategy pattern is to provide a design for modelling application-dependent behaviour variations. Figure 1 describes the Strategy pattern by means of the aggregation and inheritance relations.

The main aim of the strategy pattern is to circumnavigate the flexibility problems of inheritance with regard to modelling dynamic variation by making use of aggregation. However, this solution exhibits several drawbacks, as outlined in the following.

Drawbacks of the Strategy pattern Modelling the relation between the Context and the corresponding Strategy by means of aggregation implies explicitly delegating the responsibility for the Fun request to the Strategy object via the aggregation relationship (with the Context object as an argument). The Strategy object then executes the appropriate behaviour on behalf of the Context object. The message Fun implemented in any of the Strategy classes should actually be executed on an instance of the class Context, i.e., the self-reference within Fun's implementation in Strategy should denote the receiver Context interface.

There are two main problems with this delegation-based solution. First, most of class-based-languages, such as Smalltalk or Java, do not support passing the self-reference implicitly as part of a message delegation. However, the Strategy object defines behaviour on behalf of the Context object and might need to reference data fields of the base object. The solution is to send messages back to the Context object.

Second, there will be an increased number of objects in the application, as well as a communication overhead between Strategy and Context. Furthermore, an extra class, the abstract Strategy class, is needed merely to represent the common interface shared by its concrete subclasses. In Java this class could of course be substituted by an interface implemented by all concrete classes. Nonetheless, the interface of the Strategy class is often a duplication of the interface of the Context class. Strategy's interface is shared by all concrete strategy classes, independently of whether the algorithms they implement are trivial or complex. Hence, it is likely that some concrete strategy classes will not use all the information passed to them through this interface by the context object; simple concrete strategies may even use none! This means that there will be times when the Context creates and initialises parameters that never get used.

Other drawbacks are related to the use of the inheritance hierarchy to represent the different Strategy implementations. While the inheritance relationship may be useful for defining different implementations of a method in subclasses (overriding or incremental modification), it is not appropriate for defining different implementations of a method for a single object, as it is the case in the Strategy hierarchy. Thus, the first argument given by Gamma et al. [2] against using inheritance does also apply to the solution provided by the pattern. The Strategy hierarchy suffers from the drawbacks imposed by the inheritance relationship. If the Strategy hierarchy gets complicated, it will be difficult to extend it incrementally and to reuse it and may lead to combinatorial class explosion. To summarise, the use of delegation does not provide a principal solution. For complex applications with a multiplicity of possibly complex strategy implementation, the use of delegation simply postpones the problem to another level - the modelling of the Strategy hierarchy - but does not solve it in a satisfactory way.

Other Similar Behavioural Patterns Other behavioural patterns, such as Adapter, Bridge and State [2] are closely related to the Strategy pattern: they differ from each other in their intention, but are very similar from the perspective of their structure and implementation. In particular, Strategy, Bridge and State can be considered as being concerned with (different forms of) application-, environment-, and/or state-dependent variations.

The Visitor Pattern The Visitor pattern is used to specify operations, which are performed on (during an iteration over) the elements of an object structure [2] as independently of the concrete structure as possible. The aim is to allow behaviour to be added - in fact to be composed - to a composite structure, without changing the existing class definitions of the structure. Visitors reduce the number of operations embedded within a class, thus preventing class definitions from being cluttered. Visitors avoid this dispersion by grouping operations performed on multiple classes (related via inheritance or associations) together into one program unit. In our terminology, the Visitor pattern can be considered as an attempt to remedy some of the problems of object-oriented programming with properly modelling perspective-dependent behaviour and making use of component software. A visitor object encapsulates a perspective-dependent sub-definition of a group of objects. The Visitor object model is depicted in Figure 3.

New functionality can be added to the computer's object structure (shown in Figure 3) by adding new concrete subclasses of EquipmentVisitor. This is the benefit of the visitor pattern. Let us now consider some of its drawbacks.

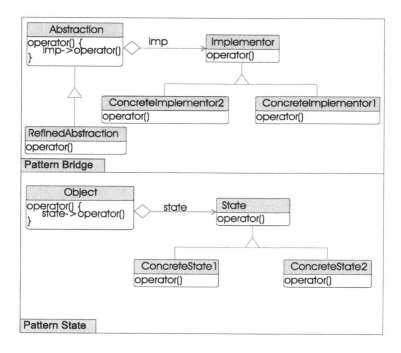

Fig. 2. Bridge and State pattern

Drawback of the Visitor pattern In this way, concrete visitor classes are unnecessarily coupled to each other. As pointed out by Vlissides [17, 16], this has drawbacks with respect to extensibility. Suppose that a new class has to be added to the equipment hierarchy. To perform this conceptually additive variation - a new abstraction is being added. The base class of the visitor hierarchy must also be changed. Hence, although being proposed to overcome the problems of class-based inheritance for modelling behaviour variations (of a whole structure of collaborating objects), the Visitor pattern forces us to perform editing even for a conceptually additive variation! The essence of the Visitor pattern, namely to dynamically alter the implementation of one or more classes for the duration of some task, is lost.

To summarise the discussion on design patterns, two further notes that hold for all behavioural patterns are made in the following. The first issue concerns the scope of the implementations in the variation hierarchies. The methods in the variation hierarchies have a distinct purpose: they implement behaviour for the base object. Second, it should be emphasized that design patterns do not provide a principal solution to modelling context-dependent variations nor their composition into existing software. As discussed in [6] patterns represent idioms to be used to resolve certain non-functional forces. As such, to a certain degree they also testify the shortcomings of object-oriented programming languages.

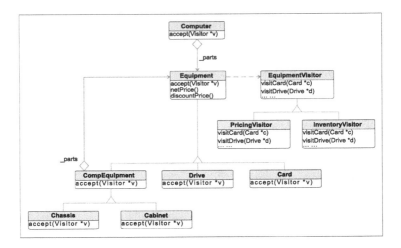

Fig. 3. Visitor Object Model

Patterns and idioms are cover-ups and not principal solutions to the problems they cover. The principal solution implies turning idioms into language features.

3   The ATOMA Framework in a Nutshell

The main motivation for designing a new language model is to allow context-dependent behaviour variations to be modelled properly, meaning that software that involves context-dependent behaviour can be easily extended in an incremental way. The design of this model is governed by several conflicting issues: dynamic behaviour, mutation versus encapsulation of the client interface, and incremental modification versus internal encapsulation, as well as the dynamic composition of behaviour. The ATOMA framework [12, 13, 15] is based on the idea of introducing additional abstractions - the explicit composition layer and managers for structuring the definition layer - for the orthogonalisation of the conflicting issues. Its main features are the following:

– First, the atom mechanism allows to quite naturally dynamically modify an object's behaviour definition by sending an insert/remove request to the object's atom.
– By allowing both the insertion and cancellation of roles [10], the solution enables behaviour alterations that may remain valid under certain conditions.
– Due to the fact that the dispatching functionality operates on the basis of the information encapsulated by atoms, modifications can be performed transparently, but nevertheless they immediately affect an object's future behaviour.

- Despite object modification, the encapsulation of the client interface is preserved in the framework. In [11], Steyaert et al. have formulated the immaculate client interface design principle, which states that an object should expose only the client interface to its message passing clients, and hide knowledge about how the object can be modified from them. Objects in the ATOMA framework follow the immaculate client interface principle. They remain records just like in the class-based model and expose only the client interface to their clients. The modification of the behaviour definition of an object does not happen in conjunction with message passing. Modifications of the object's method environment happen in conjunction with the creation of the object and role activation/removal. In contrast to object-based inheritance, message passing does not involve a re-interpretation of the self-environment.
- In the ATOMA composition model, incremental modification and internal encapsulation are treated separately. While internal encapsulation is realised by means of visibility scopes, incremental modification happens independently of these scopes, individually for each method. Roles are separated in visibility scopes according to their replica definitions. This ensures that a module in one scope of a replicated message cannot invoke the definition valid in another scope. Nevertheless, definitions from roles in different scopes can be flexibly arranged in an incremental modification relationship by means of their individual execution ordering or they can invoke shared attributes from each other by means of self-calls. The impossibility to treat these two cases separately is made responsible for the flexibility problems of the other approaches to name collisions. In the ATOMA framework it is made possible due to the additional abstraction level provided by atoms separating the inheritance structure from behaviour definition.

Thus the model the ATOMA framework represents provides the expressiveness required to model and compose context-dependent behaviour variations. In a following section we will show how this model ensures for good extensibility and reusability, as well.

3.1 ATOMA's Underlying Philosophy

The basic philosophy behind ATOMA is to support the separation of concerns that distinguishes basic behaviour and its context-dependent variations. This separation is explicitly supported at the syntactic level through the provision of dedicated constructs for separately describing basic and context-dependent sub-definitions of objects, namely classes and roles respectively. The separation is maintained at the semantic level by providing appropriate mechanisms for structuring and composing the separated behaviour definitions in a way that guarantees loose coupling.

In the ATOMA framework the programmer models basic behaviour of an abstraction defined in terms of classes. Variations of a basic behaviour are specified/defined in roles. A role defines a single behaviour variation separately from the basic functionality and from other variations. In this respect it resembles, to some extend, mixins and mixin-layers [9], but unlike mixins roles can also be removed from a behavioural definition dynamically. Such behaviour variations can be "enforced" on another behaviour specification either dynamically or statically. The key idea behind roles in the ATOMA framework is that a given basic behaviour can be enhanced in functionality for a given purpose and a given time by the addition of a role that specifies this specific behaviour and will be removed when no longer applicable. Thus behaviour is composed out of basic behaviour specification and context-dependent behaviour specification. Key to the ATOMA framework is its composition layer which is described in detail in the following section. The ATOMA framework is implemented in the Java programming language [14]. Implementations in other programming languages are also possible and are not restricted only to object-oriented languages.

The Composition Layer As already indicated, despite the similarity between roles and subclasses at the syntactic level, there is an important semantic difference in the way the behaviour they define is bound to that of their "parent". In contrast to class entities created by the Java compiler and manipulated by the Java VM, which embody the inheritance relationships in their structure, their counterpart entities created by the ATOMA engine do not embody any composition structure. Class and role entities in the ATOMA framework are only behaviour repositories and managers are used simply to maintain the specific modification relationships amongst them without implying any actual composition structure.

In other words, there is no "physical" composition relationship between the class of an object and the roles that may get involved in its behaviour definition over time. Dynamically "assembling" together default and special behaviour is the responsibility of the atoms which belong to the composition layer. An atom is associated to each object at instantiation time, taking responsibility for the compositional aspects of the object's behaviour. Placed between an object and its dispersed behaviour definition, an atom realises some kind of a connecting bridge between both.

An atom encapsulates the information about how behaviour definitions from different modules cooperate to yield a full behaviour in a way that provides internal encapsulation between different definitions. From this information it derives the environment where to evaluate the messages sent to the object. Modifying the behaviour of the object is a matter of requesting its atom to update the information it encapsulates, and can thus be performed dynamically. The main responsibilities an atom has, are to:

- integrate the behavioural definitions provided by a role into the behavioural environment that a specific atom represents,
- integrate the state specific definition provided by a role into the state environment that a specific atom represents,

- integrate the definitions (behaviour and state specific) as specialisations or replacements of another role that has already been integrated into the behaviour and state environments,
- remove the definitions (behaviour and state specific) from both the behaviour and state environments,
- evaluate a request in the current behaviour environment,
- retrieve the roles participating in the composition, represented by an atom,
- determine whether a specific role is participating in the composition, represented by an atom,
- add a role after an existing one (both roles must be of the same property), and
- add a role before an existing one (both roles must be of the same property).

Note that we use object-oriented terminology to outline the functionality of atoms. This suggests that atoms are first-class entities, which are "requested" to provide a service instead of just being operated upon.

Let us now consider the way atoms realise the composition semantics of the ATOMA framework.

We start the discussion with the structure of the method environment. As it is the case with many object-oriented languages which use method-lookup tables an atom's method environment has the structure of a table, in fact more likely a hash-table, in which each message supported by the object occupies an entry indexed by its signature. However, and in contrast to method-lookup tables and classes an atom does not contain any behaviour definition itself. Instead of containing the code corresponding to a message name, the method environment of an atom simply contains information about the behavioural structure of the message as follows:

In order to support internal encapsulation, the modules involved in the definition of an object are virtually - through the information stored in the method environment - grouped in visibility scopes individually for each message. Each replica definition of a message has its own visibility scope. The visibility scope of a given replica definition is the set of modules for which a given message has the replica definition as specified in the following: Let m be a message of an object o. Let s be the set of different replica definitions currently available for m, that is, the definitions that are currently managed by the atom responsible for object o. Let d be the set of behaviour definition modules currently involved in the behaviour definition of o, i.e. those already activated for o. Let $def(replica\_definition)$ be a set of definition modules that jointly contribute to the definition of the replica definition. Then a replica definition is visible within the modules that jointly contribute to its implementation as well as in other modules specified to modify or connect the replica definition itself. Each scope has a unique identifier that is constructed successively along the alterations of the object's behaviour. This identifier encodes the set of modules in the scope.

For messages with several scope-specific definitions, the corresponding entry in the method environment contains one sub-entry for each scope-specific definition. This sub-entry is indexed by the corresponding scope identifier. The structure stored in the entry encodes the set of modules jointly contributing to this scope-specific definitions and the order in which these contributions should be executed. Messages with a single definition are a special case of those with multiple scope-specific definitions: their corresponding entry in the method environment has a single sub-entry.

Consider, for illustration, the definition of an object which consists of the composition of its basic behaviour plus that of a number of roles attached to it in Figure 4. Let us assume that the behaviour of object o is specified in **A**, **B**, **C**, **D**, **E**, which are roles attached to object's o class. As illustrated in Figure 4 there are two sub-entries for the *meth2* message. This is the case because the implementations of *meth2* are replica definitions. The definition structures (the definition chain column in the method environment in Figure 4 associated with each of these sub-entries point to roles **B** and **C** respectively. This means that each (replica) definition of *meth2* consists of a single implementation provided by roles **B** and **C**, respectively.

These sub-entries are indexed by the visibility identifiers **B** and **C**, respectively. In contrast to *meth2*, entries for *meth1* and *meth3* have only one sub-entry in the method environment, i.e. for both of them there is a unique definition with the respective visibility scopes as encoded by the corresponding scope identifiers. The implementation in the method environment is exploited by the dispatcher used in the ATOMA framework represented by the execute method. According to the definition structure of the *meth1* entry the execution of the information provided by the visibility chain starts in **D** with the execution of *meth1*, then proceeds with the execution of *meth1* in **C**, then with the execution of *meth1* in **B**, and finally with the execution of *meth1* in **A**.

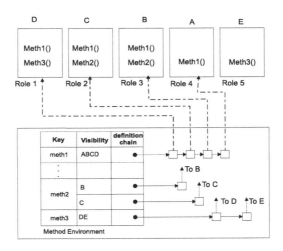

Fig. 4. Atom and its Method environment

Let us now consider the initialisation and maintenance of the method environment information. It is initialised when an object is created. Initially, all entries have a single scope identifier: a special label marking class definitions, and all definition structures have a single element pointing to the object's class. This initialisation corresponds to the inclusion of the class into the behaviour definition of the object being executed. As already mentioned, in addition to the class, several other roles may be included in the initial definition of an object. However, including these roles is equivalent to the general case of modifying a previous behaviour definition of an object, as discussed below.

Changing an object's behaviour takes place as the result of invoking a *raise/undo* message on the object for which the behaviour modification will take place. As a result of this invocation, the module corresponding to the raised event is searched in the definition layer. The second environment of the object's atom is the property updated in order to integrate or cancel the definition in the role. This is represented by the *addRole, addRoleBeforeRole, addRoleAfterRole* and *removeRole* methods, which appropriately update the method environment. Based on the modification relationships, the atom successively constructs the visibility scope identifiers, such that the internal encapsulation of the replica definitions is ensured, as described in the following summary of the functionality of the *addRole* method:

– First, the role to be inserted is marked with a label. A role that is inserted more than once will have as many different labels as the number of its insertions. This allows to achieve a similar effect as the so-called repeated inheritance [4]. A new element of the definition structure is created for the role. Labels are released by the functionality supplied by the *removeRole* method.
– For each message with a replica definition in the role to be inserted, a new scope is created with the label of the role as its identifier. A new sub-entry is created for the message in the method environment, mapping the new scope identifier to the new definition structure element. A message implemented by the role to be inserted is given the attribute "replica", if there are already other implementations for the message managed by the atom and the role is not a modification of any of the modules that contribute to these implementations.
– For each non-replica definition of a message that already exists in the method environment, the label assigned to the role is added into all currently existing identifiers, which makes the method visible within all currently existing scopes. In this way, the late binding of self is emulated. The new definition structure element is added at the beginning of the definition structure, thus incrementally modifying the current composed definition of the message.
– For each new method definition, i.e. a definition for a message that did not exist in the method environment, a new scope identifier is created, containing the label of the role. A new entry is added into the method environment for the new message mapping the creating identifier to its definition.

– Finally, the role's label is added to all scopes in the method environment that contains a module of which the role is specified to be a specialisation or connection role. This ensures that the role gains visibility for the definitions of the roles it modifies.

The *addRole* operation represents the modification of the entire composed behaviour of an object; method definitions of the role to be inserted are added at the end of the corresponding definition structures. The *addRoleAfterRole* operation serves to modify a sub-part of the composed behaviour. This is necessary when roles are inserted that modify or connect roles which have already been inserted or in general when the predefined order among the composition categories imposes inserting a role into a certain position in the existing composition. Similar is the use of the *addRoleBeforeRole* functionality. This functionality as well as the cancelling functionality supported by the *removeRole* operation are similar to *addRole* and therefore not described further. In any case, after a modification has taken place, the evaluation of future messages to the underlying object, accomplished by the dispatching functionality, will happen in the context of the updated method environment.

Finally, let us consider instance variable (data members) declared in roles. The implementation of a method in a role is executed in the environment of the receiver as well as the additional environment consisting of the instance variables declared by the role. This simulates dynamic extension of the instance variable of the receiver. In the current realisation of the model, the "basic" object and the "add-on-objects" are kept separate from each other.

Again, atoms emulate their common self, by managing the relationship between roles and their corresponding "sub-objects" in order to know in which "sub-object" environment a certain method implementation should be evaluated. This solution has been preferred to the alternative of eagerly extending objects by allocating new memory and copying the values of the old object into the new (extended) allocation. This choice is made because it is better suited when state may not only be extended but also restricted (roles get inserted and removed). Additionally, it enables a natural solution to internally controlling the scope of instance variables.

4   Comparison

4.1   The ATOMA Framework versus Design Patterns

In section 2.1 the State, Strategy and Visitor patterns we considered as representatives for state-, application-, and perspective-dependent behaviour respectively. In this section we will address the implementation of the Visitor pattern under the ATOMA framework.

The Visitor pattern can be considered as an attempt to model a perspective-dependent behaviour variation in a flexible way, allowing new functionality to be added to an existing object structure with little changes. The implementation technique proposed to achieve this goal was the combination of inheritance and parameterisation. Several drawbacks of this technique, in terms of extensibility and reusability, were discussed. These drawbacks are due to the need to hard-code information about the type of the objects included in the structure to be visited in the implementation of the visitors. In this section, the example (see [2]) used to illustrate the Visitor pattern in figure 3 is revisited, in order to illustrate how the same functionality would be implemented in the ATOMA framework and to demonstrate the advantages of this implementation.

A possible ATOMA-based implementation of the Computer class and the Equipment hierarchy are given in Figure 5.(a). Computer defines an attribute,

```
class Computer {
        Vector parts;
        public void accept() {
                Enumeration e = parts.elements();
                while( e.hasMoreElements() {
                        Equipment eq = (Equipment) e.nextElements();
                        eq.accept();
                }
        }
}

class Equipment {
        String name;
        public void accept() {...}
        public Cost getNetPrice() {...}
        public Cost getDiscountPrice() {...}
        public Cost powerConsumption() {...}
        ...
}

class CompositeEquipment extends Equipment {
        Vector parts;
        public void accept() {
                Enumeration e = parts.elemenst();
                while( e.hasMoreElements()) {
                        Equipment eq = (Equipment) eq.nextElements();
                        eq.accept();
                }
        }
}
```

(a)

```
Role Visitor {
        public void accept() {
                initMyObject();
                super.accept();
                undoMe();
        }
        public Object printResults() {
                return myObject.toString();
        }
}

RoleSet PricingRoleSet {
        Cost total = new Cost(0);
        Role PricingEntry {
                public void initMyObject() {
                        Enumeration e = parts.elemenst();
                        while (e.hasMoreElements()) {
                                Equipment eq = (Equipment) e.nextElement();
                                eq.raise(new PricingEvent());
                        }
                }
                public void undoMe() {
                        Enumeration e = parts.elemenst();
                        while (e.hasMoreElements()) {
                                Equipment eq = (Equipment) e.nextElement();
                                Eq.undo(new PricingEvent());
                        }
                }
                Boolean expensive() {
                        return (myObject() > 1000000);
                }
```

```
                Cost myObject() {
                        return total;
                }

        Role PricingEquipment {
                public void accept() {
                        total.add(this.getNetPrice());
                        super.accept();
                }
        } alters Equipment when PricingEvent

        Role PricingCompositeEquipment {
                public void accept() {
                        total.add(this.getDiscountPrice());
                        super.accept();
                }
        } alters CompositeEquipment when PricingEvent
}

Visitor connects {Computer,PricingEntry} when PricingEvent
```

(b)

Fig. 5. (a) Computer Equipment Classes, (b) Pricing Functionality

parts, which is a set of Equipment objects. Additionally, in the same vein with the implementation of the Visitor pattern, we assume that Computer and all classes in the Equipment hierarchy implement an accept method - the entry point for injecting new functionality into the computer structure. The implementation of accept in Computer and CompositeEquipment iterates over the corresponding parts by sending the accept message to each Equipment object included in parts. In the simple equipment classes, accept is an empty method. Other methods implemented in Equipment return the attributes of a piece of equipment, such as, its power consumption and cost. Subclasses only redefine their operations for specific types of equipments (e.g. chassis, drives, buses etc).

Suppose we would like to add pricing functionality to the computer structure in Figure 5.(a). A possible ATOMA-based implementation of this functionality is given in Figure 5.(b).

Amongst the roles defined in Figure 5.(b), Visitor plays a special role. It provides a very abstract specification of a "visitor-functionality", i.e., of a piece of functionality that is composed to an existing object structure after this structure has already been implemented. The only assumption made by this specification about the object structure to be visited is that any element in this structure understands the method *accept*. No assumptions are made about the concrete visiting functionality.

The pricing functionality is implemented by the *role set* including *PricingEntry*, *PricingEquipment* and *PricingCompositeEquipment*. The *role set* construct is syntactic sugar for a set of roles which share some data structures (working space) in defining a behaviour variation that affects several classes. In the code for the pricing functionality in Figure 5.(b), all involved roles share a common attribute, *total*, in which the price to be computed will be stored. Among these roles, *PricingEntry* is responsible for initialising the common attribute (the *initMyObject* method). The two other roles are specified to modify the behaviour of the *Equipment* and *CompositeEquipment*, respectively, when the pricing functionality has to be performed. They are activated from the *initMyObject* method in *PricingEntry*.

Attaching a piece of functionality depicted in Figure 5.(b) to the concrete computer structure illustrated in Figure 5.(a) is accomplished by the separate role *Visitor* which is specified to connect *Computer* with *PricingEntry* when the event *PricingEvent* is raised. Notice that in the code relationships between behaviour definition modules are specified in two different ways. The *alters* specification is directly attached to the pricing specific roles: *PricingEquipment* and *PricingCompositeEquipment* roles. Hence, there is little evidence why the specifications of their modification-relationships should be kept separate from their implementation.

However, the situation is different for the Visitor role. As already indicated, its implementation is generic - the role can be used in different scenarios. Hence, the specification of its role as a connection between Computer and PricingEntry is done from its implementation. After having made the above specifications, the piece of code in Figure 6 will create a computer object, initialise it together with

```
Computer comp = new Computer(somePartsSet);
comp.raise(new PricingEvent());
comp.accept();
comp.printResult();
comp.undo(PricingEvent.class);
```

Fig. 6. Invoking the pricing functionality

the equipment objects it is composed of, then perform the pricing functionality and finally re-establish the initial situation.

When *raise(PricingEvent)* is sent to *comp* in the second line in Figure 6 the role associated to the event *PricingEvent* in the manager of the objects' class will be inserted into the object's atom. Consequently, the behaviour definition of the created computer object, *comp*, will be composed of the class *Computer*, the role *PricingEntry*, and the connection role *Visitor*. Hence, *comp* can now understand the additional messages: *initMyObject*, *undoMe*, *myObject*, *printResult* and *expensive*. Additionally, the *accept* method of *comp* will be the old one incrementally modified by the implementation in Visitor, i.e. when *accept* is sent to *comp* it will first invoke *initMyObject* to create and initialise *total*, raise the *PricingEvent* on all equipment objects included in its parts, and then invoke the super call to execute the original implementation of *accept* as provided in Computer.

The execution of the original implementation of *accept* will send accept to the equipment of *comp*. The implementations of accept in Equipment and CompositeEquipment have been incrementally modified by the time this message's delivery takes place: *initMyObject* has already raised *PricingEvent* on all equipment objects in *comp*. Thus when *accept* is sent to a simple equipment, the *total* attribute will be increased with the result of *getNetPrice*. In a similar way, when *accept* is sent to a composite equipment, *total* will be increased with the result of invoking *discountPrice*; additionally super invocation will cause *accept* to be sent to the simple equipments the composite object consists of. After *accept* sent to *comp* returns, the result will be printed. Finally, the roles implementing pricing functionality will be removed leaving comp in its original status.

4.2   Comparing ATOMA and APPI for Behavioural Composition

After having explained how the ATOMA based implementation of the pricing functionality works, let us now compare it with the implementation based on the Visitor pattern presented in section 2.1. First, there is a drastic reduction of the number of methods required to be implemented. This is demonstrated clearly by comparing both techniques in the case of the containment hierarchy represented in the upper part of Figure 7.

The *accept* methods that need to be implemented when using the Visitor pattern technique are written on the left side of each class, while those needed in the ATOMA-based implementation are written on the right side. Other methods

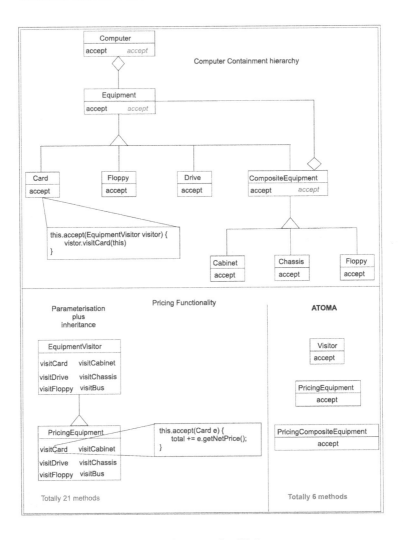

Fig. 7. Two techniques for Visitor pattern

of the containment hierarchy, such as *netPrice*, or *discountPrice* must be implemented in both alternatives and are therefore omitted in Figure 7. Additionally, the implementations of the pricing functionality using each technique are shown at the bottom of the figure together with the names of the additional methods required to be implemented.

The result of this simple evaluation shows very clearly the superiority of the ATOMA-based implementation. Instead of 21 methods required to be implemented when using the APPI, only 6 (more than three times less!) methods are needed in the ATOMA-based implementation. The relation gets even worse for a larger number of classes in the containment hierarchy: for n different visitor classes, each new kind of equipment would require n+1 methods to be implemented in order to establish the connection between the new equipment class and the existing visitors.

The increased number of methods is strongly related to the extensibility problems exhibited by the APPI. The reason for the high number of methods is that by encapsulating the behaviour variation (pricing functionality) in a separate object, the information about the concrete kind of the equipment object for which the pricing object should perform the pricing functionality needs somehow to be transmitted from the equipment to the visitor objects. This is realised by using different method names as the transmission medium.

With respect to using method names as the means to distinguish (dispatch) kind-specific behaviour, the APPI implementation strongly reminds us of an implementation in a procedural language.

In Section 2.1 we showed that several existing classes must be edited in order to support a new type of equipment. In contrast, none of the existing classes needs to be modified in the ATOMA-based implementation when a new class is added into the containment hierarchy. It is not even necessary to add anything into the existing implementation of the pricing functionality. Hence, better reuse is achieved. The reason for this gain in extensibility is that the philosophy underlying the ATOMA framework is much more "object-oriented", as well as component-based!

The advantages become even more clear when new visiting functionality needs to be added. Only one new *accept* method needs to be implemented. If we had used the APPI technique instead, 6 new *visitXXX* methods must be implemented in the new class *InventoryVisitor*. Furthermore, with the ATOMA-based implementation it is possible to execute simultaneously multiple number of visiting operations.

Besides the advantages discussed above, the ATOMA framework is superior also with respect to another aspect. In the comparison in this section we assumed the existence of the *accept* methods in the base object structure, in a similar way the implementation based on the visitor pattern does. However, while the existence of these operations is a must for the visitor pattern, under the ATOMA framework it is possible to add visiting functionality to an existing class structure that does not have *accept* methods.

5   Related Work

Apart from design patterns the realisation of behavioural variations through behavioural composition is also addressed by other approaches such as composition filters [1], aspect-oriented programming [6], adaptive programming [7] and subject-oriented programming [5].

Compared to theses approaches the ATOMA framework differs in that the composition of new behaviour with existing one can be performed dynamically, thus not requiring enhancement of the dispatch filter and recompilation in the case of composition filters, reweaving in the case of aspect-oriented programming, or restructuring and redefining composition rules in the case of subject-oriented programming.

6 Conclusions

In this paper we have shown the limitations imposed by behavioural design patterns that employ the APPI technique when used for composing functional/ behavioural aspects that stem from context-dependent behaviour variations.

To complement for these limitations the ATOMA framework was presented and used for modelling and implementing the very same examples that stressed the limitations of behavioural design patterns. The advantage of the ATOMA framework with respect to extensibility, reusability, and incremental variation was clearly demonstrated, as it is solely based on dynamic behaviour composition.

References

[1] M. Aksit, K. Wakita, J. Bosch, L. Bergmans and A. Yokezawa: "Abstracting User Interactions using composition filters", In R. Guerraoui, O. Nierstratz and M. Riveill (eds.), *"Object-Based Distributed Processing"*, Springer LNCS Vol.791, pp.152-184, 1993. 437

[2] E. Gamma, R. Helm, R. Johnson and J. Vlissides: *"Design Patterns – Elements of Reusable Object-Oriented Software"*, Addison-Wesley, 1994. 422, 424, 433

[3] J. Gill and D. Lorenz: "Design Patterns and Language Design", *IEEE Computer*, pp.118-120, March 1998. 425

[4] G. Gottlob, M. Schefl and B. Roeck: "Extending Object-Oriented Systems With Roles", *ACM Transactions on Information Systems*, Vol.14, No.3, pp.268-296, 1996. 431

[5] W. Harrison and H. Ossher: "Subject-oriented Programming (a Critique of Pure Objects)", *Proceedings 8th Conference on Object-Oriented Programming, Systems, Languages, and Applications (OOPSLA'93)*, pp.411-428, 1993. 437

[6] G. Kiczales, J. Lamping, A. Mendhekar, C. Maeda, C. V. Lopes, J. M. Loingtier and J. Irwin: "Aspect-oriented Programming", Invited talk in M. Aksit and S. Matsuoka (eds.), *Proceedings 11th European Conference on Object-Oriented Programming (ECOOP'97)*, Springer LNCS Vol.1241, pp.220-243, 1997. 437

[7] K. Lieberherr: *"Adaptive Object-Oriented Software. The Demeter Method with Propagation Patterns"*, PWS Publishing Company, 1996. 437

[8] M. Shaw: "Abstraction Techniques in Modern Programming Languages", *IEEE Software*, Vol.1, No.4, pp.10, 1984. 422

[9] Y. Smaragdakis and D. Batory: "Mixin Layers: an Object-oriented Implementation Technique for Refinements and Collaboration-based Designs", *ACM Transactions on Software Engineering and Methodology*, Vol.11, No.2, April 2002. 428

[10] F. Steimann: "On the Representation of Roles in Object-oriented and Conceptual Modelling", *Data and Knowledge Engineering*, Vol.35, pp.83-106, 2000. 426

[11] P. Steyaert and W. de Meuter: "A Marriage of Class-based and Object-based Inheritance without Unwanted Children", *Proceedings 9th European Conference on Object-Oriented Programming (ECOOP'95)*, pp.127-145, 1995. 427

[12] D. Theotokis, G. Gyftodimos and P. Georgiadis: "Atoms: a Methodology for Component Object-oriented Software Development", *Proceedings Conference on Object Oriented Information Systems (OOIS'96)*, pp.226-242, London UK, December 1996. 426

[13] D. Theotokis, G.-D. Kapos, C. Vassilakis, A. Sotiropoulou and G. Gyftodimos: "Distributed Information Systems Tailorability: a Component Approach", *Proceedings 7th IEEE Workshop on Future Trends of Distributed Computing Systems (FTDCS'99)*, pp.95-101, Cape Town, South Africa, December 1999. 426

[14] D. Theotokis, A. Sotiropoulou, G. Gyftodimos and P. Georgiadis: "Are Behavioural Design Patterns Enough for Behavioural Evolution in Object-Oriented Systems?" *Proceedings 8th Panhellenic Conference in Informatics*, Vol.1, pp.90-99, Nicosia, Cyprus, November 2001. 421, 428

[15] D. Theotokis, A. Sotiropoulou and G. Gyftodimos: "Complementing Inheritance to Model Bbehavioural Variation Using Roles", *Proceedings JCKBSE 2002 Conference*, Maribor, Slovenia, September 2002. 426

[16] J. Vlissides: "Visiting Rights", *C++ Report*, September 1995. 425

[17] J. Vlissides: "The Trouble with Observer", *C++ Report*, September 1996. 425

A New Randomized Data Structure for the 1 1/2-dimensional Range Query Problem

Panayiotis Bozanis

Department of Computer and Communication Engineering
University of Thessaly, Volos 38221, Greece
pbozanis@inf.uth.gr

Abstract. We propose RPST, a randomized data structure for the 1 1/2-dimensional range query problem, based on a version of Skip Lists, as an alternative to solutions that use deterministic height balanced trees. Our scheme exhibits, with high probability, logarithmic, output-sensitive search time, expected logarithmic update time, expected constant reconstruction time and linear space overhead with high probability.

1 Introduction

In the 1 1/2-query problem, we are given a set of points $S = \{(x, y)|x, y \in \mathbb{R}\}$ in the plane, and we are asked to find all points $p \in S$ contained in a semi-infinite strip-query region $Q = [x', x''] \times (-\infty, y']$ or $Q = [x', x''] \times [y', +\infty)$, $x', x'', y' \in \mathbb{R}$. This kind of problem has applications in Database Systems, e.g. report all employees with wages between $2,000$ and $2,500$ euros and with at most 15 years of employment, or find all intervals on the real line stabbed by a point (*point stabbing query*) or an interval (*interval stabbing*). The interested reader can find more information in [2, 7].

McCreight [6] gave an elegant solution to this problem, introducing the *Priority Search Tree* (PST)—a mixture of search tree on **x**-axis and a heap structure on **y**-axis—achieving $O(\log n + t)$, $O(n)$ time-space complexity respectively (t the output size). The difficulty one confronts with the PST is its dynamization, i.e. the adjustment of the data structure to changes of the underlying set S without loss of the query efficiency. The solutions reported in [7] vary from $O(\log^2 n)$ in the worst case to $O(\log n)$ in the worst case. This "variance" follows from the choice of the underlying binary search tree, and the primitive *reconstruction* operations that employ—single or double rotations.

That intrinsic weakness of PST was a motive for the IS-List scheme [4], which only solves the point stabbing problem in expected $O(n \log n)$ space, expected $O(\log n + t)$ query time and expected $O(\log^2 n)$ update time. In this paper we propose a scheme that achieves logarithmic output-sensitive query time with high probability, expected logarithmic update time with expected constant reconstruction time using linear space with high probability. Additionally, all presented algorithms are developed in a top-down fashion. In Section 2 we briefly describe PST and Skip Lists. Section 3 introduces RPST and discusses its performance, while Section 4 concludes our work.

Y. Manolopoulos et al. (Eds.): PCI 2001, LNCS 2563, pp. 440–452, 2003.

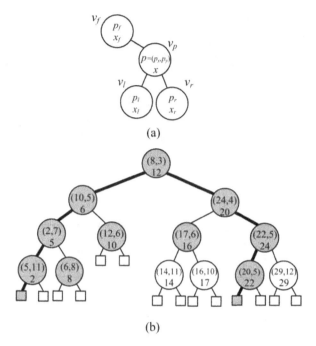

Fig. 1. (a) Instance of a Priority Search Tree node v_p carrying point p and x-coordinate x, with father node v_f and children nodes v_l, v_r, (b) An instance of a priority search tree. With grey color are denoted nodes that are visited for the query region $[1, 22] \times (-\infty, 5]$

2   Overview of Data Structures

Priority Search Trees. Let $S = \{(x, y)|x, y \in \mathbb{R}\}$ be a set of points in the plane. In the discussion that follows we assume that the points in S have distinct x-coordinates. This assumption can be removed with some extra effort, see for example [2, 7]. We would like to build a dynamic search structure $\mathcal{T}$ on S with operations range_search$([x', x''] \times (-\infty, y'])$, insert$(p)$ and delete(p). Priority search trees (PST), as their name denotes, are a mixture of search trees and priority queues. They are defined as follows:

Definition 1. *Let $\mathcal{T}$ be a binary search tree on $S_{\mathbf{x}} = \{x|(x, y) \in S\}$, i.e. on the $\mathbf{x}$-coordinates of the input point set. Each $p = (p_{\mathbf{x}}, p_{\mathbf{y}}) \in S$ is stored in exactly one node v_p of $\mathcal{T}$, so that (a) v_p lies on the search path $\mathcal{P}_{p_{\mathbf{x}}}$ of $p_{\mathbf{x}}$; and (b) the heap (priority queue) invariant is imposed: if p^f, p^l, p^r are respectively the points stored in the father, the left and the right child of v, then $p^f_{\mathbf{y}} \leq p_{\mathbf{y}}$ and $p^l_{\mathbf{y}}, p^r_{\mathbf{y}} \geq p_{\mathbf{y}}$.*

Figure 1.(a) gives an example of a typical Priority Search Tree node v_p while Fig. 1.(b) presents an instance of a Priority Search Tree. The search operation

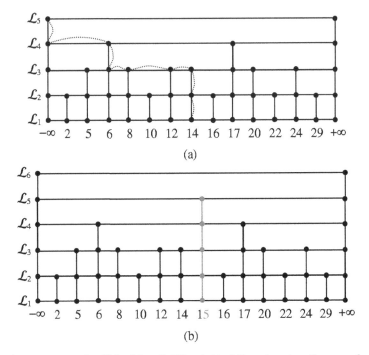

Fig. 2. An instance of a Skip List S. The dotted line denotes the search path of search(15). Scheme (b) shows the effect of insert(15)

range_search($[x', x''] \times (-\infty, y']$) goes as follows: Let $P = P_{x'} \cup P_{x''}$ be the set of nodes of the two search paths of x', x'', and F be the forest of subtrees having as roots nodes with parents belonging to P. Then the algorithm (i) examines all nodes in P, and (ii) explores each subtree in F top-down while the query condition on **y**-coordinate is satisfied.

The underlying binary search tree is responsible for the logarithmic term in the query time, while the heap invariant guarantees its output sensitive character. On the other hand, with some extra care and programming effort, update time varies ([7]) from $O(\log^2 n)$ in the worst case, if AVL Trees are used, or $O(\log n)$ in the worst case if red-black or half-balanced trees are employed.

Skip Lists. In this section we briefly discuss Skip Lists [9, 10, 11]. More details can be found in the cited references. Let Σ be a set of n elements $s_1 < s_2 < \cdots < s_n$ drawn from a totally ordered universe U. Let also $\mp\infty$ denote the smallest and biggest elements of U, respectively. We would like to build a dynamic search structure S on Σ with operations search(x), range_search($[x, x']$), insert(x) and delete(x). Assume we are given a biased coin with probability of success—the bias—$p \in (0, 1)$. Starting with Σ, we form a sequence σ of subsets of Σ, of level l:

$$\Sigma = \Sigma_1 \supseteq \Sigma_2 \supseteq \cdots \supseteq \Sigma_{l-1} \supset \Sigma_l = \emptyset$$

Each Σ_i is derived from Σ_{i-1} by flipping the coin independently for each $s \in \Sigma_{i-1}$ and collecting all those elements with a success outcome. Then $\mathcal{S}$ is built as following (see Fig. 2). We store each Σ_i in a sorted linked list $\mathcal{L}_i$. Each s in $\mathcal{L}_i$ stores a descent pointer to its occurrence in $\mathcal{L}_{i-1}$. Search(x) proceeds like this: Commencing with level l, in each $\mathcal{L}_i$ we locate the maximum element $s \leq x$. We follow the associated descent pointer to level $i{-}1$ and so on, until we reach level 1. In case of range_search($[x, x']$) after we search(x), we move to the right until we find some element bigger than x'.

When we want to insert(x), we toss the biased coin until we fail. Let k be the number of successes. After we search(x) (see Fig. 2), we know the element $s_{\mathcal{L}_i}$ that precedes x in every ordered list $\mathcal{L}_i$. So we add x to $\mathcal{L}_1, \mathcal{L}_2, \ldots, \mathcal{L}_{k+1}$ after $s_{\mathcal{L}_1}, s_{\mathcal{L}_2}, \ldots, s_{\mathcal{L}_{k+1}}$ respectively. The case of delete(x) is quite simple; we just remove x from every list $\mathcal{L}_i$ containing it.

Besides their simplicity, Skip Lists are popular since they exhibit very good performance. That is, the number of levels l and the search cost is $O(\log_{1/p} n)$ with high probability, the occupied space is $O(n)$ also with high probability, whereas, if s_j, s_{j+1} are two consecutive elements in $\mathcal{L}_i$, then the expected number of elements between them in $\mathcal{L}_{i-1}$ is $O(1)$. Finally, each element is stored in expected $O(1)$ levels.

3   Randomized Priority Search Tree (RPST)

3.1   Motivation

The main motivation was the "weakness" of the underlying deterministic binary search tree of the PST solution: the logarithmic height is achieved using (a) rotations, i.e. operations that are a bit complex to implement and (b) auxiliary balance information in nodes that is costly to maintain.

There is another view of Skip Lists which we will use throughout this paper, and it is mentioned in [8, 12] without any explicit use. This "dual" view was capitalized on in [3] in order to accommodate skip lists in the SDDS model. Sets Σ_i partition U in $|\Sigma_i| + 1$ intervals I_{i_j} (consult Fig. 3). Every such interval I_{i_j} belonging to a level i is divided into a number of child subintervals in level $i{-}1$. If we associate with each interval a node, connect with an arc each node to its child nodes, and relate with each arc the upper bound of the child interval to which it points, then a leaf-oriented search tree $\mathcal{T}$ on Σ results. $\mathcal{T}$ has the following:

Properties *(a) All leaves are at the same depth; (b) Height and storage are $O(\log_{1/p} n)$ and $O(n)$ respectively with high probability; (c) Every node has expected $O(1)$ number of children; (d) An insertion (deletion) causes expected $O(1)$ number of reconstruction operations, that is, splits (merges) of nodes along the insertion (deletion) path.*

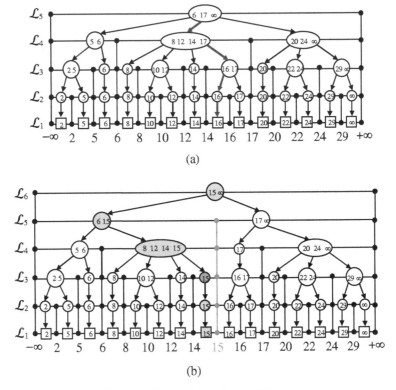

(a)

(b)

Fig. 3. Alternative view of Fig. 2

Properties (a)–(d) suggest that the resulting tree is a randomized version of $(1, c)$-Trees, with c being a constant (cf. [5] for a thorough discussion on (a, b)-Trees.)

3.2 Description

We use the equivalent tree representation of skip lists as the underlying search structure on the **x**-axis. The points of S are distributed to the tree nodes so that (i) the heap invariant holds, and (ii) only one point is allocated to a node. We could also store multiple points—one per subtree—on each node; this depends on whether one can afford the storage requirements of such a decision. More typically

Definition 2. *Let $S = \{(x, y)|x, y \in \mathbb{R}\}$ be a set of points in the plane, $\mathcal{SL}$ be a skip list on $S_{\mathbf{x}} = \{x|(x, y) \in S\}$, i.e. on the **x**-coordinates of the input point set, and $\mathcal{T}$ be the equivalent search tree of $\mathcal{SL}$. Each $p = (p_{\mathbf{x}}, p_{\mathbf{y}}) \in S$ is stored in exactly one node v_p of $\mathcal{T}$, so that (a) v_p lies on the search path $\mathcal{P}_{p_{\mathbf{x}}}$ of $p_{\mathbf{x}}$; and (b) the heap (priority queue) invariant is imposed: if p^f, Π are respectively*

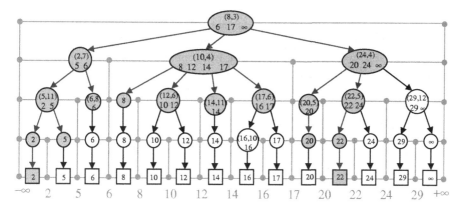

Fig. 4. An instance of RPST. With grey color are denoted nodes that are visited for the query region $[1, 22] \times (-\infty, 5]$

the point stored in the father and the set of points stored in the chlidren of v, then $p_{\mathbf{y}}^f \leq p_{\mathbf{y}}$ and $\pi_{\mathbf{y}} \geq p_{\mathbf{y}}, \forall \pi \in \Pi$.

Figure 4 illustrates an instance of RPST. In the next paragraphs we describe the search and update algorithms in a C-like pseudo-code. We assume that each tree node v has

a. an array $v.Children$, storing pointers to children nodes;
b. an array $v.Keys$ of auxiliary values for the branching during the search operation; and
c. an entry $v.point$ for placing exactly one input point $p \in S$.

Searching The search operation **range_search**$([x', x''] \times (-\infty, y'])$ takes into consideration the multiple children of each node: Let $\mathcal{P} = \mathcal{P}_{x'} \cup \mathcal{P}_{x''}$ be the nodes of the two search paths of x', x'', and $\mathcal{F}$ be the forest of subtrees $\mathcal{T}_v$, each having as root a tree node v with a sibling node w, such that $w \in \mathcal{P}_{x'}$ and lies to the left of v or $w \in \mathcal{P}_{x''}$ and lies to the right of v. Then the algorithm, first, examines all nodes in $\mathcal{P}$, and, second, explores each subtree in $\mathcal{F}$ top-down while the query condition on **y**-coordinate is satisfied.

Algorithm RANGE_SEARCH$(x', x'', y', \mathcal{T})$
Input. The boundaries of the query strip and an instance $\mathcal{T}$ of a RPST
Output. All points of $\mathcal{T}$ lying into $[x', x''] \times (-\infty, y']$

1. $v = root(\mathcal{T})$;
2. $A = \{\ \}$; //*the initially empty answer set*
3. **while** $((v \neq \textbf{null}) \&\& (\exists$ only one $j : v.Keys[j] \in [x', x'']))$ {
4.   **if** $(v.point.y \leq y')$
5. $A = A \cup \{v.point\}$;
6. $v = v.Children[j] : v.Keys[j] \in [x', x'']$;

7. }
8. $splitnode = v;$ //we reach the node where $\mathcal{P}_{x'}, \mathcal{P}_{x''}$ split
9. $v =$ the leftmost child of $splitnode$ lying into $[x', x'']$;
10. $w =$ the rightmost child of $splitnode$ lying into $[x', x'']$;
11. **for each** (child $u \neq v, w$ of $splitnode$ lying into $[x', x'']$) **do**
12. $A = A \cup$ EXPLORE-SUBTREE(x', x'', y', u);
13. **while** $((v \neq$**null**$))$ {
14.   **if** $(v.point \in [x', x''] \times (-\infty, y'])$
15. $A = A \cup \{v.point\}$;
16.   **for each** $(j : (v.Keys[j] \geq x')$ min value excluded) **do**
17. $A = A \cup$ EXPLORE-SUBTREE$(x', x'', y', v.Children[j])$;
18. $v = v.Children[k] : (\min k) \wedge (v.Keys[k] \geq x')$;
19. }
20. **while** $((w \neq$**null**$))$ {
21.   **if** $(w.point \in [x', x''] \times (-\infty, y'])$
22. $A = A \cup \{w.point\}$;
23.   **for each** $(j : (w.Keys[j] \leq x''))$ **do**
24. $A = A \cup$ EXPLORE-SUBTREE$(x', x'', y', w.Children[j])$;
25. $v = v.Children[k] : (\min k) \wedge (w.Keys[k] \geq x'')$;
26. }
27. **if** $(splitnode.point.y \leq y')$
28. $A = A \cup \{splitnode.point\}$;
End of RANGE_SEARCH

The auxiliary EXPLORE-SUBTREE algorithm recursively explores the input subtree $\mathcal{T}_v$ until it discovers all points lying into the query strip:

Algorithm EXPLORE-SUBTREE(x', x'', y', v)
Input. The boundaries of the query strip and a tree node v
Output. All points of $\mathcal{T}_v$ lying into $[x', x''] \times (-\infty, y']$

1. **if** $(v.point ==$**null**$)$ {
2.   **return**;
3. **if** $(v.point \in [x', x''] \times (-\infty, y'])$ {
4. $A = \{v.point\}$;
5.   **for each** $(j < $#children of $v)$ **do**
6. $A = A \cup$ EXPLORE-SUBTREE$(x', x'', y', v.Children[j])$;
7.   **return** A;
8. }
End of EXPLORE-SUBTREE

Update Operations In the description that follows, we will employ four auxiliary procedures: SHIFT-UP(v), SHIFT-DOWN(p, v), SPLIT&SHIFT-UP(v) and MERGE&SHIFT-DOWN(v). For the sake of space, we only describe the first two;

the other two are combinations of two elementary operations, as their name denotes, and they are illustrated by inline figures.

SHIFT-UP operation takes as argument a node v of the tree structure. Then, it removes and returns the accommodated point p, if any exists. The created gap is filled properly in a recursive manner:

Algorithm SHIFT-UP(v)

Input. A node v of an instance of a RPST

Output. Removes the point p stored in v, filling the gap according to
         the heap invariant

1. **if** ($v.point$ ==**null**)
2.   **return null**;
3. $w = (w$ is a child of $v) \wedge (w.point$ has the min **y**-value among its siblings);
4. $p = v.point$;
5. $v.point =$ SHIFT-UP(w);
6. **return** p;

End of SHIFT-UP

The SHIFT-DOWN procedure inserts the input point p into node v, creating recursively the necessary space. More specifically:

Algorithm SHIFT-DOWN(p, v)

Input. A node v of an instance of a RPST and a point p

Output. Stores the point p in v, making a gap according to the heap invariant

1. **if** (p==**null**)
2.   **return**;
3. $p' = v.point$;
4. $v.point = p$;
5. $w = v.Children[j] : (\min j) \wedge (v.Keys[j] \geq p'_\mathbf{x})$; // *the leftmost w.r.t.* $p'_\mathbf{x}$
6. SHIFT-DOWN(p', w);

End of SHIFT-DOWN

Insertion. We use a top-down approach for point insertion, which is illustrated in Fig. 5: After we randomly decide the number of levels l that $p_\mathbf{x}$ must be inserted, we descend the tree towards $p_\mathbf{x}$. When we find the node v into which, according to the heap invariant, we must store p, we place p creating the necessary gap by a SHIFT-DOWN operation. When we reach level l, we start splitting the nodes on the search path towards the leaf-level and filling the gaps by SPLIT&SHIFT-UP operations.

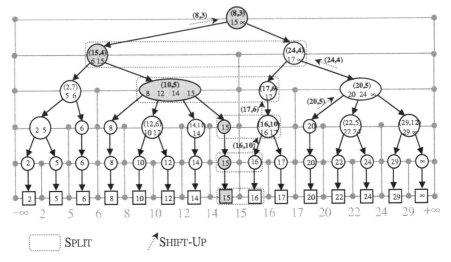

Fig. 5. The effect of `insert((15,4))`

Algorithm INSERT$(p, \mathcal{T})$
Input. A point p and an instance $\mathcal{T}$ of a RPST
Output. The updated version $\mathcal{T}'$

1. We toss the coin to find the level l of $\mathcal{T}$ at which we start inserting p_x;
2. **if** $(l > height(\mathcal{T}))$ {
3. $root(\mathcal{T}) =$ **new** root-node w with $w.Keys[0] == p_x$;
4. $root(\mathcal{T}).point =$ SHIFT-UP(old $root(\mathcal{T})$);
5. }
6. $v = root(\mathcal{T})$;
7. **while** $(v \neq$ **null**) {
8.   **if** $(v.point.y > p_y)$ { // *accommodate* p
9. $p' = v.point$;
10. $v.point = p$;
11. $w = v.Children[j] : (\min j) \wedge (v.Keys[j] \geq p'_x)$;
12.   SHIFT-DOWN(p', w);
13.   }
14.   **if** $(level(v) \leq l)$
15.   SPLIT&SHIFT-UP(v); //
16. $v = v.Children[j] : (\min j) \wedge (v.Keys[j] \geq p_x)$;
17. }
End of INSERT

Deletion. We descend the tree towards $p_\mathbf{x}$. When we meet p, we delete it and fill the created gap by a SHIFT-UP operation. When, for the first time, we find $p_\mathbf{x}$ in a node v, we start merging the nodes on the search path towards the leaf-level with their appropriate siblings. Whenever the two nodes v, w under merging store both a point, the "excess" point p' is the one with the maximum $\mathbf{y}$-value; p' is accommodated by a SHIFT-DOWN operation on the path towards the leaf hosting $p'_\mathbf{x}$.

Algorithm DELETE($p, \mathcal{T}$)
Input. A point p and an instance $\mathcal{T}$ of a RPST
Output. The updated version $\mathcal{T}'$
1. $v = root(\mathcal{T})$;
2.   **if** ($v.point == p$)
3. $v.point =$SHIFT-UP($v.Children[j] : (\min v.Children[j].point.y)$);
4.   **if** ($\exists j : p_\mathbf{x} == v.Keys[j]$) {   //

5.   MERGE&SHIFT-DOWN($v.Children[j]$);
6.   **if** ($|v.Children| == 1$) //*we must delete the root*
7. $root(\mathcal{T}) = v.Children[0]$;
8.   }
9. $v = v.Children[j] : (\min j) \wedge (v.Keys[j] \geq p_\mathbf{x})$;
10. **while** ($v \neq$**null**) {
11.   **if** ($v.point == p$)
12. $v.point =$SHIFT-UP($v.Children[j] : (\min v.Children[j].point.y)$);
13.   **if** ($\exists j : p_\mathbf{x} == v.Keys[j]$)
14.   MERGE&SHIFT-DOWN($v.Children[j]$);
15. $v = v.Children[j] : (\min j) \wedge (v.Keys[j] \geq p_\mathbf{x})$;
16. }
End of DELETE

Extensions. Firstly, we will drop the assumption of distinct $\mathbf{x}$-values. This can be achieved if we associate with each leaf l of x_l $\mathbf{x}$-value a list, sorted on non-decreasing $\mathbf{y}$-values, accommodating the "excess" points that cannot be stored in non-leaf nodes and have the same x_l $\mathbf{x}$-value.

Secondly, in case that multiple points are stored into each node, then—more or less—the same rationale about the search and update operations holds. This extension could be used when S is too big to be accommodated in main memory and it must reside in secondary storage. We leave this as an open issue for future research.

3.3   Performance Analysis

Lemma 1. *A RPST structure needs $O(n)$ space with high probability for storing a set of n points in the plane.*

Proof. Each point $p \in S$ is stored in exactly one tree node v_p. From property (b) of the underlying search tree $\mathcal{T}$ the lemma follows.   □

Lemma 2. *A search operation in a RPST of n points costs $O(\log_{1/p} n + t)$ time with high probability.*

Proof. The search cost consists of two parts: (i) the cost of checking the nodes of the two search paths $\mathcal{P}_{x'}, \mathcal{P}_{x''}$ of x', x'' respectively, and (ii) the cost of exploring top-down the forest $\mathcal{F}$ of relevant subtrees $\mathcal{T}_v$.

Cost (i) is logarithmic with high probability from property (a). Cost (ii) is responsible for the output-sensitive—the $O(t)$—part. It is derived by the observation that each node v, that EXPLORE-SUBTREE visits and $v.point$ does not belong to the answer, has a parent w whose point is a part of the answer. So, we can charge the cost of visiting v to w.

Therefore, we have maximum t nodes $v_1, v_2, \ldots, v_t$ carrying the points $p_1, p_2, \ldots, p_t$ of the answer. Let $\mathbf{X}_i$ be the random variable denoting the number of children of v_i that are visited during the search and have no useful information. Then, the random variable

$$\mathbf{X} = \mathbf{X}_1 + \cdots + \mathbf{X}_t \tag{1}$$

corresponds to the number of nodes that are visited in vain. It is known ([8]) that $\mathbf{X}_i$'s follow independent geometric distributions with parameter p. Then, the expected value of $\mathbf{X}$ is

$$\mathbf{E}[\mathbf{X}] = \frac{t}{p} = O(t) \tag{2}$$

As a matter of fact, one applying the Chernoff technique to sums of independent geometric distributions can show that (2) holds with high probability. The interested reader is referred to [8] for further details on Chernoff bounds.   □

Lemma 3. *An update operation costs expected $O(\log_{1/p} n)$ time.*

Proof. We only discuss insertion since the case of a deletion operation is symmetrical. There are three costs during inserting a point p: (i) the "descending" cost $T_d(n)$ towards $p_{\mathbf{x}}$; (ii) the cost $T_a(n)$ of accommodating p in a tree node at level k; and (iii) the expected cost $T_s(n)$ of inserting $p_{\mathbf{x}}$. The latter cost represents the *reconstruction* time complexity of our scheme.

$T_d(n)$ is clearly analogous to the height h of the auxiliary search tree $\mathcal{T}$, that is

$$O(\log_{1/p} n) \tag{3}$$

with high probability from property (b). $T_a(n)$ equals with the expected cost of a SHIFT-DOWN operation at level k plus the expected cost of a SHIFT-UP operation at the highest level h with probability p^{h-1}:

$$
\begin{aligned}
T_a(n) &= T_{\text{SHIFT-DOWN}}(n, k) + p^{h-1} T_{\text{SHIFT-UP}}(n, h) \tag{4} \\
&= \sum_{j=2}^{k} O(\text{expected \# children at level } j - 1) +
\end{aligned}
$$

$$p^{h-1} \sum_{j=2}^{h} O(\text{expected \# children at level } j-1) \tag{5}$$

$$\leq \quad 2 \sum_{j=2}^{h} O(\text{expected \# children at level } j-1) \tag{6}$$

$$\overset{\text{property(c)}}{=} 2 \sum_{j=2}^{h} O(1) = O(h) = O(\log_{1/p} n) \tag{7}$$

$T_s(n)$ equals with the time needed for performing the necessary SPLIT&SHIFT-DOWN operations. Let $\mathbf{X}$ be the random variable denoting the number of levels where we insert $p_{\mathbf{x}}$. Then

$$T_s(n) = \sum_{j=1}^{\infty} \mathbf{Prob}[\mathbf{X} = j] \, O\left(\sum_{k=1}^{j} T_{\text{SHIFT-DOWN}}(n, k) \right) \tag{8}$$

$$= \sum_{j=1}^{\infty} p^{j-1}(1-p) O(j^2) \tag{9}$$

$$= O(1) \tag{10}$$

The result follows from equations (3)–(10).   □

4   Conclusion

In this paper we proposed RPST, a randomized data structure for the the 1 1/2-dimensional Range Query Problem, based on a version of Skip Lists, as an alternative to deterministic solutions. We feel that its logarithmic height, kept with highly local criteria without dependence on data distribution, makes our treatment quite appealing. Our future plans include experimental evaluation of our approach and application to other geometric searching problems (e.g. extension to d dimensions or treatment of the range searching problem) employing the decomposition paradigm (see, for example, [7]).

References

[1] Bentley J. L., Wood D.: "An Optimal Worst-Case Algorithm for Reporting Intersections of Rectangles", *IEEE Transactions on Computers*, Vol.29, No.7, pp.571-577, 1980.

[2] de Berg M., van Kreveld M., Overmars M. and Schwarzkopf O.: "*Computational Geometry: Algorithms and Applications*", Springer, Berlin, 2000. 440, 441

[3] Bozanis P. and Manolopoulos Y.: "DSL: Accommodating Skip Lists in the SDDS Model", *Proceedings 3rd Workshop on Distributed Data and Structures (WDAS'2000)*, pp.1-9, L'Aquila, Italy, July 2000. 443

[4] Hanson E. N. and Johnson, T.: "The Interval Skip List: a Data Structure for Finding all Intervals that Overlap a Point", *Proceedings 2nd Workshop on Algorithms and Data Structures (WADS'91)*, pp.153-164, Ottawa, Canada, August 1991. 440

[5] Huddleston S. and Mehlhorn K.: "A New Representation for Linear Lists", *Acta Informatica*, Vol.17, pp.157-184, 1982. 444

[6] McCreight E. M.: "Priority Search Trees", *SIAM Journal on Computing*, Vol.14, pp.257-276, 1985. 440

[7] Mehlhorn K.: "*Data Structures & Algorithms, Vol. 3: Multidimensional Searching and Computational Geometry*", Springer, Berlin, 1984. 440, 441, 442, 451

[8] Mulmuley K.: "*Computational Geometry: an introduction Through Randomized Algorithms*", Prentice-Hall, Englewood Cliffs, NJ, 1994. 443, 450

[9] Papadakis T.: "Skip Lists and Probabilistic Analysis of Algorithms", Ph.D. Thesis, University of Waterloo, May 1993. 442

[10] Pugh W.: "A Skip List CookBook", Technical Report CS-TR-2286, Department of Computer Science, University of Maryland at College Park, July 1989. 442

[11] Pugh W.: "Skip Lists: a Probabilistic Alternative to Balanced Trees", *Communications of the ACM*, Vol.33, pp.668-676, 1990. 442

[12] Seidel R. and Aragon C. R.: "Randomized Search Trees", *Algorithmica*, Vol.16, pp.464-497, 1996. 443

Acceptor-Definable Counting Classes

Aggelos Kiayias[1], Aris Pagourtzis[2,3], Kiron Sharma[4], and Stathis Zachos[1,3]

[1] Department of CIS, Brooklyn College, CUNY, NY, USA
akiayias@csp.gc.cuny.edu
[2] Institute of Theoretical Computer Science, ETH Zürich, Switzerland
pagour@inf.ethz.ch
[3] Computer Science Dept., National Technical University of Athens, Greece
zachos@cs.ece.ntua.gr
[4] Department of Computer Science, Fairleigh Dickinson University, NJ, USA
sharma@alpha.fdu.edu

Abstract. Counting functions that can be defined on non-deterministic *acceptors* (Turing machines without output), as opposed to those defined by *transducers* (Turing machines with output), have attracted much interest since 1979, when Valiant introduced the important class #P [19]. Apart from #P, several such classes have been defined in the literature [2, 5, 3, 12, 6]. Here we study the path-order complexity classes RAP, LAP and MAP, introduced in [6], which consist of functions that output the order of the rightmost, leftmost and middle accepting computation path (respectively) of a polynomial-time non-deterministic Turing acceptor (PNTM). We also consider TotP [6], the class of functions that output the total number of paths of a PNTM. We show several properties of these classes. In particular we prove that RAP and LAP are are equivalent under the Cook[1] sense with #P and TotP. This implies that all these classes are equally powerful when used as oracles to a polynomial computation, even if only one query is allowed. We also show that problems #PERFECT MATCHINGS and #DNF-SAT are complete for RAP and LAP in the Cook[1] sense and for MAP in the Cook sense. Path-order classes give rise to corresponding path-order operators; these operators applied on the class NP provide alternative characterizations for known classes of optimization problems. Using these characterizations, we present natural complete problems for optimization classes.

1 Introduction

Counting functions that can be defined on non-deterministic *acceptors*, as opposed to those defined by *transducers*, have attracted much interest since 1979 when Valiant introduced the important class #P [19].

Computations of polynomial time non-deterministic acceptors (PNTMs) are nicely represented by trees. Classes of functions related to properties of such computational trees were defined and studied in [2, 3, 5, 12, 6].

Here we focus on the function-classes RAP, LAP, MAP [6], which contain functions that count the order of the rightmost, leftmost and middle (respectively) accepting path of a PNTM computation tree. In [6] we also defined the

Y. Manolopoulos et al. (Eds.): PCI 2001, LNCS 2563, pp. 453–463, 2003.

class TotP which contains functions that count the total number of paths of a PNTM computation; among them are several *hard-to-count easy-to-decide* problems like the well-known #PERFECT MATCHINGS, as was shown in [11]. We have shown [6] that all these classes are Cook-interreducible with Valiant's #P: $P^{RAP} = P^{LAP} = P^{MAP} = P^{TotP} = P^{\#P}$.

In this paper we show a stronger result, namely that #P, TotP, RAP and LAP are Cook[1]-interreducible. This means that one query to an oracle from any of these classes can be replaced by one query to some oracle from any other class. A second important consequence is that a very wide class of counting problems, the Counting Polynomial-time Hierarchy (#PH), can be solved by a polynomial time computation with one query to an oracle from RAP or LAP.

Fenner, Fortnow and Kurtz [2] have defined the class GapP, which consists of functions that give the difference between accepting and rejecting paths of a PNTM. Pagourtzis [11] defined the class #PE which contains counting problems with easy decision version. The classes GapP and #PE were shown to be Cook[1]-equivalent with #P in [2] and [11] respectively. Therefore, our present results imply that RAP and LAP are also Cook[1]-equivalent with GapP and #PE. Another implication is that all problems that are TotP-complete under the Cook[1] reducibility, e.g. #PERFECT MATCHINGS and #DNF-SAT, are also RAP-complete and LAP-complete in the Cook[1] sense and MAP-complete in the (weaker) Cook sense.

In [6] they gave an alternative characterization of Krentel's optimization class OptP [7] and Toda's MidP [16] class using a restricted form of path-order operators. Following this relation, complete problems for the class MaxP (a refinement of OptP introduced in [4]) were presented in [12]. In this paper we extend this result by presenting natural complete problems for MinP and MidP under Karp reductions. Note that a problem which is complete for a class under this kind of reductions is considered to be a good representative of the class with respect to computational complexity.

2   Preliminaries

Our model of computation is the polynomial-time non-deterministic Turing acceptor (PNTM). An input of a PNTM computation is a string over an alphabet Σ. The length of a string x is denoted by $|x|$; we also use $|S|$ to denote the cardinality of a set S but this should not cause any confusion. We will consider PNTMs standardized as follows:

- The computation tree of a PNTM M is binary.
- On any input x all paths of the computation tree have the same length.

It is not difficult to see that every polynomial time non-deterministic Turing machine can be standardized as above. For any standardized PNTM M there is a polynomial p_M such that on input x all computation paths have the same length $p_M(|x|)$. At every non-deterministic step there are at most two choices that can be lexicographically ordered: the one is called 'left' or '0'-choice while the other is called 'right' or '1'-choice. Therefore, the sequence of non-deterministic choices along a computation path may be represented by a string of the form $\{0,1\}^{p_M(|x|)}$ which is called *choicestring*. In the rest of the paper we will identify a computation path with its corresponding choicestring. The computation paths are ordered lexicographically. The set of all paths of a PNTM M on input x is denoted by $Paths_M(x)$. The set of all *accepting* paths of a PNTM M on input x is denoted by $AccPaths_M(x)$.

Definition 1 *A binary relation R is called* (polynomial time) tree-constructible *if there exists a PNTM M such that $R(x, y) \Leftrightarrow y \in Paths_M(x)$.*

Given any PNTM M we denote by R_M the associated tree-constructible relation:

$$R_M = \{\langle x, y \rangle \mid y \in Paths_M(x)\}$$

For any PNTM M we define $AccR_M$ to be the relation that relates inputs to accepting paths:

$$AccR_M = \{\langle x, y \rangle \mid y \in AccPaths_M(x)\}$$

Notice that $AccR_M \subseteq R_M$ and that it is unlikely that for every PNTM M the corresponding $AccR_M$ relation is tree-constructible (otherwise we would have $\mathsf{P} = \mathsf{NP}$, as shown—in similar formulation—in [6]).

If S is a family of tree-constructible relations, then every PNTM M such that $R_M \in \mathsf{S}$ will be denoted by S-PNTM.

For any class of languages $\mathcal{C}$ that is defined via PNTMs we may define a subclass with respect to S:

$$\mathsf{S} \diamond \mathcal{C} = \{L \mid L \in \mathcal{C} \text{ and } L \text{ is computed by an } \mathsf{S}\text{-PNTM }\}$$

Analogously, for any class of functions $\mathcal{F}$ computed by or defined via PNTMs,

$$\mathsf{S} \diamond \mathcal{F} = \{f \mid f \in \mathcal{F} \text{ and } f \text{ is computed by an } \mathsf{S}\text{-PNTM }\}$$

An interesting family of tree-constructible relations that we will use in the sequel is CB, the family corresponding to complete binary trees, i.e. $R \in \mathsf{CB}$ iff there exists a polynomial p such that $R(x, y) \Longleftrightarrow |y| = p(|x|)$.

All functions that are considered throughout the paper, unless otherwise stated, have Σ^* as their domain and $\mathbb{N}$ as their range ($\Sigma^* \to \mathbb{N}$).

Definition 2 *The following functions are associated with a PNTM M:*

- $\mathrm{acc}_M(x)$ *gives the number of accepting paths of M on input x.*
- $\mathrm{rej}_M(x)$ *gives the number of rejecting paths of M on input x.*
- $\mathrm{gap}_M(x) = \mathrm{acc}_M(x) - \mathrm{rej}_M(x)$.
- $\mathrm{tot}_M(x)$ *gives the total number of paths of M on input x minus one.*

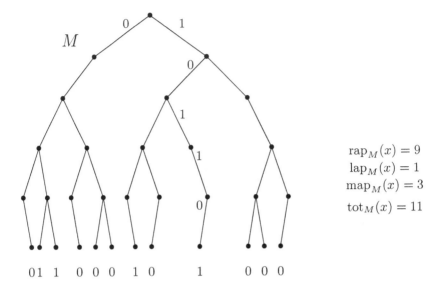

$$\mathrm{rap}_M(x) = 9$$
$$\mathrm{lap}_M(x) = 1$$
$$\mathrm{map}_M(x) = 3$$
$$\mathrm{tot}_M(x) = 11$$

Fig. 1. Path functions defined on a PNTM M

The functions max, min and mid applied to a set of paths of a PNTM result to the maximum, minimum or middle path respectively. The function mid is defined as follows $\mathrm{mid}(\{s_1, s_2, \ldots, s_k\}) = s_{\lceil \frac{k}{2} \rceil}$.

Let V be a totally ordered finite set and $S \subseteq V$. We define the (partial) function $\mathrm{order}_S : V \to \mathbb{N}$ as follows:

$$\mathrm{order}_S(t) = \begin{cases} |\{s \in S \mid s < t\}| + 1 & \text{if } t \in S \\ \bot & \text{otherwise} \end{cases}$$

Notice that the order of the minimum element of S is 1 and the order of the maximum element is $|S|$.

Definition 3 *The following functions are associated with the order of the rightmost, leftmost and middle accepting path of a PNTM (see Figure 1):*

$$\mathrm{rap}_M(x) = \begin{cases} \mathrm{order}_{Paths_M(x)}(\max(AccPaths_M(x))) & \text{if } AccPaths_M(x) \neq \emptyset \\ 0 & \text{otherwise} \end{cases}$$

$$\mathrm{lap}_M(x) = \begin{cases} \mathrm{order}_{Paths_M(x)}(\min(AccPaths_M(x))) - 1 & \text{if } AccPaths_M(x) \neq \emptyset \\ |Paths_M(x)| & \text{otherwise} \end{cases}$$

$$\mathrm{map}_M(x) = \begin{cases} \mathrm{order}_{Paths_M(x)}(\mathrm{mid}(AccPaths_M(x))) & \text{if } AccPaths_M(x) \neq \emptyset \\ 0 & \text{otherwise} \end{cases}$$

The corresponding complexity classes, which are called *path-order complexity classes*, were defined in [6], together with the closely related complexity class TotP.

Definition 4 *[6]*

- RAP = {rap$_M$ | M *is a* PNTM }.
- LAP = {lap$_M$ | M *is a* PNTM }.
- MAP = {map$_M$ | M *is a* PNTM }.
- TotP = {tot$_M$ | M *is a* PNTM }.

The following way of defining operations between complexity classes of functions starting from ordinary arithmetic operations, will be used in the rest of the paper.

Definition 5 *If $\mathcal{F}, \mathcal{G}$ are function classes and $*$ a binary operation on $\mathbb{N}$, we define the function class*
$$\mathcal{F} * \mathcal{G} = \{h \mid \exists f \in \mathcal{F}, g \in \mathcal{G}, \forall x \in \Sigma^* : \quad h(x) = f(x) * g(x)\}$$
Similarly, for $k \in \mathbb{N}$ we define the function class
$$k * \mathcal{F} = \{h \mid \exists f \in \mathcal{F}, \forall x \in \Sigma^* : \quad h(x) = k * f(x)\}$$

3 Properties of Acceptor-Definable Path-Order Classes

In this section we present some properties of path-order classes and their relation to TotP and to Valiant's class #P defined in [19]:

$$\#\text{P} = \{\text{acc}_M \mid M \text{ is a PNTM }\}$$

The following proposition lists some known properties and is given without proof; the reader is referred to the cited papers.

Proposition 6 *[6, 10]*
(1) TotP + RAP $\subseteq$ RAP, TotP + LAP $\subseteq$ LAP, TotP + MAP $\subseteq$ MAP.
(2) LAP + LAP $\subseteq$ LAP.
(3) RAP − RAP = LAP − LAP.
(4) RAP + k $\subseteq$ RAP, LAP + k $\subseteq$ LAP, MAP + k $\subseteq$ MAP, $\forall\, k \in \mathbb{N}$.
(5) $k \cdot$ RAP $\subseteq$ RAP, $k \cdot$ LAP $\subseteq$ LAP, $k \cdot$ MAP $\subseteq$ MAP, $\forall\, k \in \mathbb{N}$.

Proposition 7 *[6] If* P $\neq$ NP *then* RAP $\neq$ LAP.

Proof. Let $L \in$ NP. Then, there exists a PNTM M such that $x \notin L$ iff all paths of M on input x reject. Let M' be a PNTM that first guesses $z \in \{0, 1\}$ and for $z = 0$ it accepts while for $z = 1$ it proceeds by simulating M. Thus $L = \{x \mid \text{rap}_{M'}(x) > 1\}$.

If RAP = LAP then there exists a PNTM N such that $\text{lap}_N(x) = \text{rap}_{M'}(x)$ for all x. Consequently $L = \{x \mid \text{lap}_N(x) > 1\}$. Given any PNTM N we can check in polynomial time whether $\text{lap}_N(x) > 1$ since it suffices to follow deterministically the two leftmost path and check if any of them accepts or not; if not then it is $\text{lap}_N(x) > 1$ (recall that if no paths accept then $\text{lap}_N(x) = |Paths_N(x)| > 1$). Thus $L \in$ P and P = NP − contradiction. □

Proposition 8

1. #P $\subseteq$ TotP $-$ FP.
2. TotP $\subseteq$ RAP, TotP $\subseteq$ LAP, TotP $\subseteq$ MAP.
3. MAP, RAP *and* LAP *are contained in* FP$^{\#P}$.

Proof. (1) Suppose $f \in$ #P, via a PNTM M i.e. $f = \text{acc}_M$. Without loss of generality we may assume that the computation tree of M is complete binary, thus $\text{tot}_M(x) = 2^{p(|x|)}$ for every input x. Let M_d be a PNTM almost identical to M, the only difference being that whenever M accepts M_d branches once generating two accepting leaves. It is easy to check that

$$f(x) = \text{tot}_{M_d}(x) - \text{tot}_M(x) = \text{tot}_{M_d}(x) - 2^{p(|x|)}$$

(2) Let M be a PNTM; Suppose M' is a PNTM that operates like M but all the paths except for the one before the rightmost are rejecting. This path is then the only accepting so it is, at the same time, the leftmost, rightmost and middle accepting path. Therefore:

$$\text{tot}_M = \text{rap}_{M'} = \text{lap}_{M'} + 1 = \text{map}_{M'}$$

This shows directly the first and third inclusions and that TotP $\subseteq$ LAP $+ 1$. For showing TotP $\subseteq$ LAP it suffices to combine with LAP $+ 1 \subseteq$ LAP which is known from Proposition 6.4.

(3) Let $f \in$ MAP via M. In order to find the "middle" accepting path, a binary search on the computation tree of M is performed; two counters are maintained, which count the accepting leaves of the right and the left subtree respectively. Both counters make use of a #P oracle. After finding the middle accepting path, its order can be determined by performing an other #P query to an oracle whose computation tree resembles the computation tree of M with the following modification: all paths to the left of the middle path accept and all others reject. We omit the details. The inclusions involving RAP and LAP can be proved similarly. $\square$

Combining Proposition 8.2 with the fact that #PERFECT MATCHINGS belongs to TotP [11] we get the following:

Corollary 9 #PERFECT MATCHINGS *belongs to the classes* RAP, LAP, *and* MAP.

Further inclusions deduced from the above propositions are summarized in Figure 2. Immediate consequence of these inclusions is the following theorem:

Theorem 10 [6] FP^{TotP} = FP^{RAP} = FP^{LAP} = FP^{MAP} = FP$^{\#P}$.

Therefore classes #P, TotP, RAP, LAP, and MAP are equivalent when used as oracles to polynomial time computations. We will now prove a stronger result for RAP and LAP, namely that #P, TotP, RAP LAP are equivalent relevant to polynomial-time oracle computations that use the oracle *once*.

Fig. 2. Inclusion structure

Theorem 11 $\mathsf{FP}^{\#P[1]} = \mathsf{FP}^{\,\mathsf{TotP}[1]} = \mathsf{FP}^{\,\mathsf{RAP}[1]} = \mathsf{FP}^{\,\mathsf{LAP}[1]}$.

Proof. From proposition 8 we get that:
$$\mathsf{FP}^{\#P[1]} \subseteq \mathsf{FP}^{\,\mathsf{RAP}[1]} \text{ and } \mathsf{FP}^{\#P[1]} \subseteq \mathsf{FP}^{\,\mathsf{LAP}[1]}$$
The reverse can be proved using proposition 13 (below) and the theorem of Toda and Watanabe [17] which states that $\#\,\mathsf{PH} \subseteq \mathsf{FP}^{\#P[1]}$. In particular:

$$\mathsf{RAP} \subseteq \#\cdot\mathsf{NP} \subseteq \#\mathsf{P}^{\,\mathsf{NP}} \subseteq \#\,\mathsf{PH} \subseteq \mathsf{FP}^{\#P[1]} \Rightarrow \mathsf{FP}^{\,\mathsf{RAP}[1]} \subseteq \mathsf{FP}^{\#P[1]}$$
$$\mathsf{LAP} \subseteq \#\cdot co\text{-}\mathsf{NP} \subseteq \#\mathsf{P}^{\,\mathsf{NP}} \subseteq \#\,\mathsf{PH} \subseteq \mathsf{FP}^{\#P[1]} \Rightarrow \mathsf{FP}^{\,\mathsf{LAP}[1]} \subseteq \mathsf{FP}^{\#P[1]}$$

$\square$

Combining Theorems 10 and 11 with the Corollary 9 we get the following interesting result:

Theorem 12 $\#\mathrm{PERFECT\ MATCHINGS}$ *is complete for the classes* RAP, *and* LAP *under the Cook[1] reducibility and for the class* MAP *under the Cook reducibility.*

Note that, by the above, all TotP-complete problems under the Cook[1] reducibility, e.g. $\#\mathrm{DNF\text{-}SAT}$, are also RAP-complete and LAP-complete – and MAP-complete under the Cook reducibility.

Proposition 13 $\mathsf{RAP} \subseteq \#\cdot\mathsf{NP}, \quad \mathsf{LAP} \subseteq \#\cdot co\text{-}\mathsf{NP}, \quad \mathsf{MAP} \subseteq \#\cdot\mathsf{PP}$

Proof. (1) Let M be a PNTM. The order of the rightmost accepting path equals the number of paths that are less or equal to it; this number in turn is equal to the number of paths for which there exists greater or equal accepting path. Hence, for all inputs x:

$$\mathrm{rap}_M(x) = |\{y \mid R_M(x,y) \wedge [\exists y' : R_M(x,y') \wedge y' \geq y \wedge AccR_M(x,y')]\}|$$

where $R_M(x,y)$ means that $y \in Paths_M(x)$, i.e. R_M is a polynomial-time decidable predicate. Also, $AccR_M(x,y)$ means that M on input x following choicestring y accepts, which is also polynomial-time decidable.

Let $Q_M(x,y) = R_M(x,y) \wedge [\exists y' : R_M(x,y') \wedge y' \geq y \wedge AccR_M(x,y')]$. Then Q_M is clearly an NP-predicate, and $\forall x \in \Sigma^*, \mathrm{rap}_M(x) = |\{y \mid Q_M(x,y)\}|$. Therefore the function rap_M belongs to the class $\#\cdot\mathsf{NP}$.

(2) Similarly we can write:

$$\text{lap}_M(x) = |\{y \mid R_M(x,y) \land [\forall y' : (R_M(x,y') \land y' \le y) \Rightarrow \neg AccR_M(x,y')]\}|$$

Hence, $\forall x \in \Sigma^*, \text{lap}_M(x) = |\{y \mid Q'_M(x,y)\}|$, where $Q'_M(x,y) = R_M(x,y) \land [\forall y' : (R_M(x,y') \land y' \le y) \Rightarrow \neg AccR_M(x,y')]$. Since $Q'_M \in$ co-NP we get $\text{lap}_M \in \# \cdot$ co-NP.

(3) Finally, one can describe the order of the middle accepting path as:

$$\begin{aligned}
\text{map}_M(x) = | \{ \, y \mid R_M(x,y) \land \\
[\,|\{y' \mid R_M(x,y') \land y' \ge y \land AccR_M(x,y')\}| > \\
|\{y' \mid R_M(x,y') \land y' < y \land AccR_M(x,y')\}|\,]\,\} |
\end{aligned}$$

The expression $[\dots]$ can be seen as a relation in the class PP (details are omitted) and thus we get $\text{map}_M \in \# \cdot$ PP.   □

Combining the above result with the previously shown inclusions we get altogether:

$$\begin{aligned}
\text{FP}^{\#P[1]} = \text{FP}^{\text{TotP}[1]} = \text{FP}^{\text{RAP}[1]} = \text{FP}^{\text{LAP}[1]} &\subseteq \text{FP}^{\text{MAP}[1]} \\
\subseteq \text{FP}^{\text{MAP}} = \text{FP}^{\#P} = \text{FP}^{\text{TotP}} = \text{FP}^{\text{RAP}} &= \text{FP}^{\text{LAP}}
\end{aligned}$$

4   Path-Order Operators vs. Optimization Problems

An alternative characterization of RAP was given in [6]: $f \in$ RAP iff there exist a tree-constructible relation R and a predicate $Q \in$ P s.t. for all x, $f(x) = \text{order}_{\{y|R(x,y)\}}(\max\{y \mid R(x,y) \land Q(x,y)\})$. It is not difficult to check that this is an equivalent definition.

Using the functions min or mid instead of max we get equivalent descriptions for LAP and MAP respectively. These new descriptions give rise to the definition of path-order operators.

Definition 14 *Let $\mathcal{C}$ be a complexity class of languages. Then* ra·$\mathcal{C}$ *is the class of functions f for which there exist a polynomial-time tree-constructible relation R and a predicate $Q \in \mathcal{C}$ such that for all x,*

$$f(x) = \begin{cases} \text{order}_{\{y|R(x,y)\}}(\max\{y \mid R(x,y) \land Q(x,y)\}) & \text{if } \{y \mid R(x,y) \land Q(x,y)\} \ne \emptyset \\ 0 & \text{otherwise} \end{cases}$$

For a family of tree-constructible relations S we may define ra$_S$·$\mathcal{C}$ as above by adding the restriction $R \in$ S. Operators la·, ma·, la$_S$·, ma$_S$· can be defined analogously using the functions min and mid, respectively, instead of max.

In [6] it was also shown that there is a close relation of classes defined via path-order operators to the well known optimization classes MaxP and MinP (defined by Krentel in [7]) as well as to Toda's MidP([16]). We give now the definitions of these classes using poly-time non-deterministic transducers (PNTs). A PNT is a PNTM with output device. For a PNT T let $\text{Out}_T(x)$ denote the set of different output values of T on input x.

Definition 15

1. $\mathsf{MaxP} = \{f \mid \exists \text{ PNT } T, \forall x \in \Sigma^*, f(x) = \max(\mathrm{Out}_T(x))\}$.
2. $\mathsf{MinP} = \{f \mid \exists \text{ PNT } T, \forall x \in \Sigma^*, f(x) = \min(\mathrm{Out}_T(x))\}$.
3. $\mathsf{MidP} = \{f \mid \exists \text{ PNT } T, \forall x \in \Sigma^*, f(x) = \mathrm{mid}(\mathrm{Out}_T(x))\}$.

In case $\mathrm{Out}_T(x) = \emptyset$ we consider all the above functions equal to $\perp$ (undefined).

Theorem 16 [6] (1) $\mathsf{ra_{CB}} \cdot \mathsf{NP} = \mathsf{MaxP}$ (2) $\mathsf{la_{CB}} \cdot \mathsf{NP} = \mathsf{MinP}$
(3) $\mathsf{ma_{CB}} \cdot \mathsf{NP} = \mathsf{MidP}$.

Let us note here that this alternative characterization of the optimization classes MinP, MaxP and MidP allows us to show several complete problems for these classes under many-one (Karp-like) reductions:

Definition 17 A function f Karp-reduces to a function g $(f \leq_m^p g)$ if

$$\exists h \in \mathsf{FP}, \forall x \, f(x) = g(h(x))$$

We will now define some problems that are complete for MaxP, MinP and MidP under Karp reductions $(\leq_m^p)$.

Definition 18 Let G be a boolean circuit. An m-initial truth assignment for G is an assignment of values "True" or "False" to the first m variable gates of G. A satisfying m-initial truth assignment for G is an m-initial assignment such that, there exists an assignment for the remaining variables which together with the m-initial assignment give a satisfying truth assignment for G. An m-initial (satisfying) truth assignment for a boolean formula ϕ is defined similarly.

Problem CIRMAXINISAT
Input: (G, k) | G boolean circuit, $k \in \mathbb{N}$, $k \leq v(G)$, where $v(G)$ is the number of variable gates of G.
Output: The order of the lexicographically greater k-initial truth assignment for G, if G is satisfiable, 0 otherwise.

Problem MAXINISAT
Input: (ϕ, k) | ϕ boolean formula, $k \in \mathbb{N}$, $k \leq v(G)$, where $v(G)$ is the number of variables of ϕ.
Output: The order of the lexicographically greater k-initial truth assignment for ϕ, if ϕ is satisfiable, 0 otherwise.

It was shown in [12] that CIRMAXINISAT and MAXINISAT are MaxP-complete under $\leq_m^p$. Here we extend this result by defining the problems CIRMININISAT and MININISAT and by showing their completeness for MinP under $\leq_m^p$.

Problem CIRMININISAT
Input: $\langle G, k \rangle$ | G boolean circuit, $k \in \mathbb{N}$, $k \leq v(G)$, where $v(G)$ is the number of variable gates of G.
Output: The order of the lexicographically smaller k-initial truth assignment for G, if G is satisfiable, 0 otherwise.

Problem MinIniSat
Input: $\langle \phi, k \rangle \mid \phi$ boolean formula, $k \in \mathbb{N}$, $k \leq v(G)$, where $v(G)$ is the number of variables of ϕ.
Output: The order of the lexicographically smaller k-initial truth assignment for ϕ, if ϕ is satisfiable, 0 otherwise.

Theorem 19 *The problems* CirMinIniSat *and* MinIniSat *are* MinP-*complete under* $\leq_{\mathrm{m}}^{p}$.

Proof. First we show completeness of CirMinIniSat for the class $\mathsf{la}_{\mathsf{CB}} \cdot \mathsf{NP}$ $(= \mathsf{MaxP})$ under $\leq_{\mathrm{m}}^{p}$.

Membership. The output for an instance $\langle G, k \rangle$ is the order of the leftmost $y \in \Sigma^{k}$ such that y is a satisfying k-initial assignment of G. Clearly, for each candidate y an NP-computation could answer if it is such an assignment by guessing all possible assignments for the $v(G) - k$ remaining variables.

Hardness. Let $f \in \mathsf{la}_{\mathsf{CB}} \cdot \mathsf{NP}$ via some NP-predicate Q and some poly-time tree-constructible relation $R \in \mathsf{CB}$. Consider a PNTM M that on input x first guesses a y according to R; then simulates the PNTM that corresponds to Q on input $\langle x, y \rangle$. Now $f(x)$ is exactly the order of the leftmost interior node v of M's computation tree such that the height of v is $p(|x|)$ and the subtree rooted in v is accepting. Using a reduction of Papadimitriou [14, pp. 171–172], a circuit G can be derived in polynomial time from M such that G has as many variable gates as the number of non-deterministic steps of M along a computation path. Let p be the polynomial corresponding to the relation R. Then $f(x)$ is the order of the smallest $p(|x|)$-initial satisfying assignments of G, which equals the output value for CirMinIniSat on input $\langle G, p(|x|) \rangle$.

Membership of the problem MinIniSat in $\mathsf{la}_{\mathsf{CB}} \cdot \mathsf{NP}$ can be proved in a similar manner as for the problem CirMinIniSat. The hardness part can be proved by a reduction of CirMinIniSat to MinIniSat: given any circuit G one can construct in polynomial time a formula ϕ with the same number of variables and such that the satisfying assignments of G are the same with the satisfying assignments of ϕ. □

In a completely analogous manner we can define CirMidIniSat and MidIniSat and prove that they are complete for MidP under $\leq_{\mathrm{m}}^{p}$:

Theorem 20 *The problems* CirMidIniSat *and* MidIniSat *are* MidP-*complete under* $\leq_{\mathrm{m}}^{p}$.

References

[1] D. P. Bovet, P. Crescenzi and R. Silvestri: "A Uniform Approach to Define Complexity Classes", *Theoretical Computer Science*, Vol.104, pp.263-283, 1992.

[2] S. A. Fenner, L. J. Fortnow and S. A. Kurtz: "Gap-definable Counting Classes", *Proceedings 6th Annual Structure in Complexity Theory Conference*, pp.30-42, Chicago, IL, 1991. 453, 454

[3] U. Hertrampf, H. Vollmer and K. W. Wagner: "On Balanced vs. Unbalanced Computation Trees", *Mathematical Systems Theory*, Vol.29, No.4, pp.411-421, July/August 1996. 453

[4] H. Hempel and G. Wechsung: "The Operators min and max on the Polynomial Hierarchy", Technical Report, TR97-025, ECCC, 1997. 454

[5] B. Jenner, P. McKenzie and D. Thérien: "Logspace and Logtime Leaf Languages", *Proceedings 9th Annual Structure in Complexity Theory Conference*, pp.242-254, Amsterdam, The Netherlands, 1994. 453

[6] A. Kiayias, A. Pagourtzis, K. Sharma and S. Zachos: "The Complexity of Determining the Order of Solutions", *Proceedings 1st Southern Symposium on Computing*, 1998, Hattiesburg, Mississippi, 1998. 453, 454, 455, 456, 457, 458, 460, 461

[7] M. W. Krentel: "The Complexity of Optimization Problems", *Journal of Computer and System Sciences*, Vol.36, No.3, pp.490-509, June 1988. 454, 460

[8] J. Köbler, U. Schöning and J. Torán: "On Counting and Approximation", *Acta Informatica*, Vol.26, No.4, pp.363-379, 1989.

[9] M. Ogiwara and L. A. Hemachandra: "A Complexity Theory for Feasible Closure Properties" *Journal of Computer and System Sciences*, Vol.46, No.3, pp.295-325, June 1993.

[10] A. Pagourtzis: "Trees, Paths, and Leaves in the Forest of Non-Deterministic Algorithms", PhD thesis, National Technical University of Athens, Greece, 1999. 457

[11] A. Pagourtzis: "On the Complexity of Hard Counting Problems with Easy Decision Version", *Proceedings 3rd Panhellenic Logic Symposium*, Anogia, Crete, July 2001. 454, 458

[12] A. Pagourtzis, K. Sharma and S. Zachos: "Computation Trees: the Rightmost Accepting Path", *Proceedings CTS Workshop on Combinatorics and Algorithms*, Academia Sinica, Taipei, Taiwan, 1998. 453, 454, 461

[13] C. H. Papadimitriou and S. Zachos: "Two Remarks on the Power of Counting", *Theoretical Computer Science*, Vol.145, 1983.

[14] C. H. Papadimitriou: "*Computational Complexity*", Springer-Verlag, 1994. 462

[15] S. Toda: "On the Computational Power of PP and $\oplus P$", *Proceedings 30th Annual Symposium on Foundations of Computer Science (FOCS)*, pp.514-519, Research Triangle Park, NC, 1989.

[16] S. Toda: "The Complexity of Finding Medians", *Proceedings 31st Annual Symposium on Foundations of Computer Science (FOCS)*, Vol.II, pp.778-787, St. Louis, Missouri, October 1990. 454, 460

[17] S. Toda and O. Watanabe: "Polynomial-time 1-Turing Reductions from #PH to #P", *Theoretical Computer Science*, Vol.100, No.1, pp.205-221, 1992. 459

[18] J. Torán: "Structural Properties of the Counting Hierarchies", PhD thesis, Facultat d'Informatica de Barcelona, 1988.

[19] L. G. Valiant: "The Complexity of Computing the Permanent", *Theoretical Computer Science*, Vol.8, No.2, pp.189-201, April 1979. 453, 457

[20] H. Vollmer and K. Wagner: "The Complexity of Finding Middle Elements", *International Journal of Foundations of Computer Science*, Vol.4, 1993.

Stability Behavior of FIFO Protocol in the Adversarial Queuing Model

Dimitrios K. Koukopoulos, Sotiris E. Nikoletseas, and Paul G. Spirakis*

Computer Technology Institute (CTI) & University of Patras
61 Riga Feraiou Str., P.O.Box 1122, 26 110 Patras, Greece
{koukopou,nikole,spirakis}@cti.gr

Abstract. Packet-switched networks, where packets arrive dynamically at the nodes and they are routed in discrete time steps across the edges, widely use the FIFO (*First-In-First-Out*) protocol to provide *contention resolution* due to its *simplicity*. In this work, the stability properties of the FIFO protocol are analyzed in depth and new performance bounds are presented. Roughly speaking, *stability* requires that the number of packets in a network remains bounded, as the network runs for an arbitrarily long period of time. We focus on a basic adversarial model for packet arrival and path determination for which packets are injected with predetermined paths, such that the time-averaged arrival rate of packets requiring a single edge is no more than 1. We discover:

- FIFO is stable for any adversary with injection rate r less than or equal to $\frac{1}{9}$ ($r \leq \frac{1}{9}$) for a specific simple network with four queues.
- We present a *general method* that allows the specification of upper bounds on injection rate for FIFO stability on networks with a finite number of queues answering partially an open question raised by Andrews *et al.* [2].
- Through an involved combinatorial construction, we significantly improve the current state-of-the-art record [2, 7, 9] for the adversary's injection rate that implies instability for the FIFO protocol to 0.771.

1 Introduction

1.1 Motivation-Framework

A lot of research has been done in the field of packet-switched communication networks for the specification of their behavior. In such networks, packets arrive dynamically at the nodes and they are routed in discrete time steps across the edges. In this work, we embark on a study of the impact the employed contention resolution protocol on the network queues has on the correctness and performance properties of networks. More specifically, we wish to investigate which (and how) the conditions under which the contention resolution protocol operates affect the correctness and performance properties of networks. We

---

* The work of all the authors was partially supported by the IST Programme of the European Union under contract number IST-1999-14186 (*ALCOM-FT*).

Y. Manolopoulos et al. (Eds.): PCI 2001, LNCS 2563, pp. 464–479, 2003.

study here FIFO protocol that is a popular *greedy contention-resolution* protocol due to its *simplicity* as our test-bed. Such a protocol always advance a packet across a queue (but one packet at each discrete time step) whenever there resides at least one packet in the queue. The protocol specifies which packet will be chosen.

Framework of Adversarial Queuing Theory. We focus on a basic adversarial model for packet arrival and path determination that has been recently introduced in a pioneering work by Borodin *et al.* [3]. It was developed as a robust model of queuing theory in network traffic, and replaces stochastic by worst case inputs. Roughly speaking, this model views the time evolution of a packet-switched communication network as a game between an *adversary* and a *protocol*. At each time step, the adversary may inject a set of packets into some nodes. For each packet, the adversary specifies a simple path (including an *origin* and a *destination*) that the packet must traverse; when the packet arrives to its destination, it is absorbed by the network. When more than one packets wish to cross a queue at a given time step, a *contention-resolution* protocol is employed to resolve the conflict. A crucial parameter of the adversary is its *injection rate r*, where $0 < r < 1$. Among the packets that the adversary injects in any time interval I, at most $\lceil r|I| \rceil$ can have paths that contain any particular edge. Such a model allows for adversarial injection of packets, rather than for injection according to a randomized, oblivious process (cf. [5]).

Stability. One crucial aspect of FIFO performance is that of *stability*. *Stability* requires that the number of packets in the network remains bounded, as the network runs for an arbitrarily long period of time. Naturally, achieving stability in a packet-switched communication network depends on the *rate* at which packets are injected into the network, and on the employed contention-resolution protocol. We say that a protocol P is *stable* [3] on a network G against an adversary $\mathcal{A}$ of rate r if there is a constant C (which may depend on G and $\mathcal{A}$) such that the number of packets in the network at all times is bounded by C. Furthermore, we say that a protocol P is *universally stable* [3] if it is stable against every adversary $\mathcal{A}$ of rate less than 1 on every network. We say that *a network G is universally stable* [3] if every greedy protocol is stable against every adversary of rate less than 1 on G.

1.2   Contribution

Summary of Results. In this work, we analyze the stability properties of FIFO protocol in the Adversarial Queuing model. Our results are three-fold; they are summarized as follows:

1. Firstly, we show that FIFO protocol is stable for the particular network in Fig. 1, for any adversary with injection rate $r \leq \frac{1}{9}$.
2. We present *a method* for the estimation of upper bounds on injection rate for FIFO *stability*. More specifically, we show that for any network N of k queues $\exists r_0 = r_0(k)$, such that N is stable $\forall r \leq r_0$. This result answers partially in the positive the question raised in [2] showing that for any network, FIFO

protocol is stable against any adversary with a small injection rate that depends on the network topology.

3. Through an involved combinatorial construction, we significantly improve the current state-of-the-art record [2, 7, 9] for the adversary's injection rate that implies instability for the FIFO protocol. Our adversarial construction leads the network in Fig. 4 that runs FIFO protocol on its queues to instability for any injection rate $r \geq 0.771$.

Basic Ideas for Establishing Stability of FIFO Protocol. Our method proves a basic property of FIFO, which states that if $L(t_0)$ is the set of packets in the network at time t_0, then there is a time t_1 depending on the $L(t_0)$, the network topology (number of network queues, maximum in-degree, maximum directed path length) and the injection rate of the adversary at which all the $L(t_0)$ packets have arrived to the end of their paths and have been absorbed (removed from the network). Therefore after time t_1, the packets that are queued into the network have been injected after time t_0 and we can estimate them.

Basic Ideas for Establishing Instability of FIFO Protocol. We present involved combinatorial constructions of a network and an associated adversary that leads to instability, which significantly extend ones that appeared before in [2, 9]. More specifically, in order to create instability, we heavily exploit the *fair mixing* property of FIFO stating that if two packet sets arrive at the same queue simultaneously during a time period, they will get mixed according to the initial proportion of their sizes. This property appears to characterize FIFO, and it does not hold for other contention-resolution protocols. Our improvement is based on some new ideas of a) suitably exploiting *initial* paths and b) controlling the injection rounds in the adversarial construction. Moreover, we pursue a tight analysis of the time evolution of the various packet sets by exactly computing the number of packets remaining at various queues of the network, and their corresponding delays.

General Contribution. We feel that our study of the stability and instability properties of FIFO protocol (within the theoretical context of Adversarial Queuing Theory) provides a further insight towards understanding the performance properties of FIFO protocol even under worst-case scenarios.

1.3   Related Work

Studying FIFO Stability under Various Packet Models. Besides the *adversarial queuing model* [3], a lot of packet routing models have been proposed in the international bibliography for the study of the stability properties of FIFO protocol, see for example [1, 4, 6, 8]. Some important results that have been obtained by this study are summarized with respect to the used packet routing model as follows:

i. The *(σ, ρ)-regulated session-model*. This model considers that packets are injected into the network by k sessions. Each session has a fixed path where the adversary injects packets with a specific injection rate (with some bursti-ness allowed). The adversary injections are subject to the constraint that the total injection rate of all sessions using any edge is strictly less than 1 [6]. In this model the FIFO protocol has been shown to be unstable for network loads close to 1 [1]. In particular, Andrews in [1] presented an adversarial construction that leads a specific network that uses the FIFO protocol for contention resolution on the network queues to instability for any injection rate $r \geq 1 - 3 \cdot 10^{-9}$.

ii. The *non-fluid model*. According to this model the injection rate is con-stant [8]. In this model the FIFO protocol has been proved to be stable [8].

iii. The *fluid model*. This model results from the (σ, ρ)-regulated session-model if time is scaled, such that the packet sizes and the burstiness tend to zero [4]. In this model the FIFO protocol has been shown to be stable [4] when the injection rate of the adversary is constant.

iv. The *Kelly network model*. This model considers that the packet sizes and the service times are exponentially distributed. FIFO protocol has been proved to be stable in this model if the service time distribution of any server is independent of sessions [10].

Studying FIFO Stability under Adversarial Queuing Model. The *Ad-versarial Queuing Model* was developed by Borodin *et al.* [3] as a more realistic model that replaces traditional stochastic assumptions made in Queueing Theory (cf. [5]) by more robust, worst-case ones. This model received a lot of interest and attention (see, e.g., [2, 9, 12]) for the study of the stability properties of greedy contention-resolution protocols such as FIFO. As far as it concerns the specification of lower bounds on adversary's injection rate for FIFO instability there is a long history. Lower bounds of 0.85, 0.84 and 0.8357 on the instability threshold of FIFO protocol (in the Adversarial Queuing Model) were presented before in [2, Theorem 2.10], in [9, Section 2] and in [7, Theorem 3]. On the other hand, it remains an open problem the decidability of the following question: *is G stable for the FIFO protocol?* Till now, there was not known if there is an injection rate $r_0 > 0$ such that, even simple networks, are stable for FIFO for any injection rate $r \leq r_0$. Here, we present a method to estimate upper bounds on injection rate for FIFO stability answering partially in the positive the question raised in [2].

1.4   Road Map

The rest of this paper is organized as follows. In Section 2, we discuss the basic points of the model we apply in this work. In Section 3, we show that FIFO protocol is stable on a specific network with four queues for any adversary with injection rate $r \leq \frac{1}{9}$. Then, we generalize this result to present *a method* for the estimation of upper bounds on injection rate for FIFO *stability*. In Section 4, we present our instability result for the FIFO protocol demonstrating an adversarial construction that leads a specific network running FIFO protocol to instability for any injection rate $r \geq 0.771$. We conclude, in Section 5, with a discussion of our results and some open problems.

2   The Model

The definition of a *bounded adversary* $\mathcal{A}$ of rate (r, b) (where $b \geq 1$ is a natural number and $0 < r < 1$) in the Adversarial Queuing model [3] states that of the packets that the adversary injects in any interval I of t time steps, at most $\lceil rt \rceil + b$ may have paths that contain any particular edge. Such a model allows for adversarial injection of packets that are "bursty" using the integer $b > 0$. We say that a packet p *requires* an edge e at time t if the edge e lies on the remaining path that packet p has to traverse at time t to reach its destination.

The main difference of our work with the definition of *bounded adversary* described in [3] is the assumption that the adversary, can select the initial configuration of the system. Without loss of generality, we will also assume that $b = 1$. When we consider adversarial constructions for proving instability lower bounds of FIFO, it is advantageous to have an adversary that is as weak as possible because any bound that will be proved for such a weak adversary will hold for any stronger adversary, too. Thus, in Section 4 we use a different definition of the adversary, which states that an adversary $\mathcal{A}$ may inject in any interval I of t time steps at most $\lceil rt \rceil$ packets that can have paths that contain any particular edge. Also, for simplicity, and in a way similar to that in [2], we omit floors and ceilings and sometimes count time steps and packets roughly. This only results to losing small additive constants while we gain in clarity. Given a network N, and an edge $e \in N$ will denote $Q(e)$ the queue at the tail of the edge e, and $e(t)$ the size of $Q(e)$ at time t.

The adversarial queuing model considers a communication network that is modelled by a directed graph $G = (V, E)$, where $|V| = n, |E| = m$. Each node $u \in V$ represents a communication switch, and each edge $e \in E$ represents a link between two switches. In each node, there is a queue (buffer) associated with each outgoing link. Queues store packets that are injected into the network with a route, which is a simple directed path in G. When a packet is injected, it is placed in the queue of the first link on its route. The system proceeds in global time steps numbered $0, 1, \ldots$. Each time-step is divided into two sub-steps. In the first sub-step, one packet is sent from each non-empty buffer over its corresponding link. In the second sub-step, packets are received by the nodes at the other end of the links; they are absorbed (eliminated) if that node is their destination, and otherwise they are placed in the queue of the next link on their respective routes. In addition, new packets are injected in the second sub-step.

In order to formalize the behavior of a network under the Adversarial Queuing model, we use the notions of *system* and *system configuration*. A triple of the form $(G, \mathcal{A}, \mathsf{P})$ where G is a network, $\mathcal{A}$ is an adversary and P is the used protocol on the network queues is called a system. Furthermore, the configuration C^t of a system $(G, \mathcal{A}, \mathsf{P})$ in every time step t is a collection of sets $\{S_e^t : e \in G\}$, such that S_e^t is the set of packets waiting in the queue of the edge e at the end of step t. If the current system configuration is C^t, then we can go to the system configuration C^{t+1} for the next time step as follows:

i. Addition of new packets to some of the sets S_e^t, each of which has an assigned path in G.

ii. For each non-empty set S_e^t deletion of a single packet $p \in S_e^t$ and its insertion into the set S_f^{t+1} where f is the edge following e on its assigned path (if e is the last edge on the path of p, then p is not inserted into any set.)

The time evolution of the system is a sequence of such configurations C^1, $C^2, \ldots$, such that for all edges e and all time intervals I, no more than $\lceil r|I| \rceil + b$ packets are injected during I with an assigned path containing e. An execution of the adversary's construction on a system $(G, \mathcal{A}, \mathsf{P})$ determines the time evolution of the system configuration.

In the adversarial construction we study here for proving FIFO instability, we divide time into consecutive *phases*. In each phase, we study the evolution of the *system configuration* by considering corresponding *time rounds*. For each phase, we inductively prove that the number of packets of a specific subset of queues in the system increases in order to guarantee FIFO instability. This inductive argument can be applied repeatedly, thus showing instability. In addition, our construction uses a network that can be split into two symmetric parts. Thus, the inductive argument needs to be applied twice to establish increase in the number of packets. Furthermore, in order to make our inductions work, we assume that there is a sufficiently large number of packets s_0 in the initial system configuration. This will imply instability results for networks with an *empty* initial configuration, as established by Andrews *et al.* [2, Lemma 2.9].

3   A Method for Estimating Upper Bounds for FIFO Stability

Let us consider the network N_1 in Fig. 1. We prove here, that given any initial packet configuration for N_1, the number of packets in the system remains bounded for any adversary $\mathcal{A}$ with injection rate $r \leq r_0$, for a given r_0 to be computed. So we can conclude that FIFO is stable for N_1 against any adversary with injection rate $r \leq r_0$.

In the following proofs, it is assumed that time is divided into consecutive time periods. We denote *initial* packets, the packets that are queued in the system at the beginning of each time period. We consider that each time period is further divided into two parts. In the first part of each period, we analyze the evolution of the system from the initial time to the first step in which all the initial packets have arrived to their destination. The second part allows enough time to guarantee that all initial packets have been served and that the system configuration reproduces the initial ones.

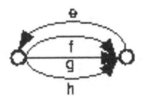

Fig. 1. A simple network N_1 with four queues

Theorem 1. *For the network N_1, given any initial configuration,* FIFO *is stable against any adversary with injection rate $0 < r \leq \frac{1}{9}$.*

Proof. For this proof, we consider the network N_1 in Fig. 1. Notice that the in-degree of edge e is three, therefore this edge can get an input flow bigger than any of the other three edges. So, the largest queue built in N_1 must occur at e. We analyze the flow of initial packets with final destination e. The analysis of edges g, f and h can be done similarly.

Assume that at time 0, the system has a configuration of $f(0)$ packets in $Q(f)$, $g(0)$ packets in $Q(g)$, $h(0)$ packets in $Q(h)$ and $e(0)$ packets in $Q(e)$. Make $M = \max\{f(0), g(0), h(0), e(0)\}$. Let us run the system for M steps, which correspond to the first part of the period.

Let $P(t)$ denote the number of packets in the system at time t. Also, let $P_e(t)$, $f_e(t)$, $g_e(t)$ and $h_e(t)$ denote respectively the number of packets in N_1, $Q(f)$, $Q(g)$ and $Q(h)$ that want to traverse the edge e at time t. Then, it holds $P(0) = f(0) + g(0) + h(0) + e(0)$ and $P_e(0) = f_e(0) + g_e(0) + h_e(0) + e(0)$. As the protocol is FIFO, at time M, the number of packets from $P_e(0)$, which still have not been served by $Q(e)$ is at most $f_e(0) + g_e(0) + h_e(0)$, and they are queued in $Q(e)$. At the same time, the maximum number of new injections of packets targeted with e is at most rM. Thus, $e(M) \leq rM + f_e(0) + g_e(0) + h_e(0)$. Let

$$s = rM + f_e(0) + g_e(0) + h_e(0) \tag{1}$$

Then, at time $M + s$ all the $P_e(0)$ initial packets will have been served by $Q(e)$.

Consider the time intervals with duration: $s, rs, r^2 s, \ldots, r^k s$, where k is such that $r^k s \geq 1$ and $r^{k+1} s < 1$. During these $k + 1$ intervals of time, the total number of packets that have been injected into the system targeted with e is

$$r \sum_{i=0}^{k} r^i s < sr \sum_{i=0}^{\infty} r^i = \frac{rs}{1-r} \tag{2}$$

Let t_1 denote the time at the end of these intervals (which includes the initial time M). Then

$$P_e(t_1) \leq \frac{rs}{1-r} + rM \tag{3}$$

By the previous definitions we take, $f_e(0)+g_e(0)+h_e(0) \le P_e(0) \le P(0)$ and $M \le P(0)$. Substituting in (1) we get $s \le rP(0)+P(0) = (1+r)P(0)$. Plugging this bound for s and M into (3), we get

$$P_e(t_1) \le \frac{r}{1-r}(1+r)P(0) + rP(0) \le (\frac{2r}{1-r})P(0). \tag{4}$$

In order the number of packets in $Q(e)$ not to increase infinitely, the quantity inside the parentheses must be less than or equal to 1, which need a value $r_1 \le 0.3334$.

The constraint $r_1 \le 0.3334$ should hold for $Q(e)$, otherwise the number of packets in this queue can increase infinitely. But, network N_1 has four queues. Therefore, in order to guarantee system stability, we should estimate an upper bound on the injection rate for which the total number of packets in the system at time t_1 is not larger than $P(0)$. As all queues behave in the worst case as $Q(e)$, each queue can get at most one new packet per injection, and N_1 has four queues, we get

$$P(t_1) \le 4rM + \frac{4rs}{1-r}. \tag{5}$$

Substituting the value of s, we get

$$P(t_1) \le 4rP(0) + \frac{4r}{1-r}(1+r)P(0) = (\frac{8r}{1-r})P(0). \tag{6}$$

To guarantee the stability of the system, the quantity inside the parentheses must be less than or equal to 1, which needs an injection rate $r_2 \le \frac{1}{9}$. Taking $r_0 = \min\{r_1, r_2\}$, we have shown that $P(t_1) \le P(0)$ for any value of $r \le r_0$. Repeat the argument, getting an infinite time sequence $t_1, t_2, t_3, \ldots$. In the period between time steps 0 and t_1, the queues of the edges in N_1 are bounded. As at each new period starting at t_{i+1}, the number of packets with a specific target, is a non-increasing function, we have proved the theorem.   □

The previous argument, can be extended to work in full generality, for any network N of k queues, maximum in-degree α, and maximum directed path length β.

Theorem 2. *For any network N that uses FIFO protocol, given any initial configuration, there exist an injection rate $0 < r_N < 1$, such that FIFO is stable with respect to any adversary with injection rate $r \le r_N$, where r_N is independent of the initial system configuration and it is a function of the maximum in-degree α, the maximum directed path length β and the number of network queues k.*

Proof. Assume that N has k queues, maximum in-degree α, and maximum directed path length β and that the injection rate of the adversary $\mathcal{A}$ is r. Notice that if $\alpha = 1$ then we have a tree or a ring, for which it is known that it is universally stable [2], so we assume $\alpha > 1$. Let us denote the queues as $Q_1, Q_2, \ldots, Q_k$

and their loads at time $t \geq 0$ as $q_1(t), q_2(t), \ldots, q_k(t)$. Let $P(0) = \Sigma q_i(0)$ be the initial network load and $P(t) = \Sigma q_i(t)$ be the network load at time t.

We will construct an infinite sequence of consecutive time periods, t_i, at which $P(t_i) \leq P(0)$ thus keeping the network stable. Again, we will refer to the packets at time 0, as the *initial packets*. The fact that we are using a FIFO protocol implies that after a certain time all the initial packets will leave the system. We will compute a bound to this time.

Let's now, consider the worst case of an initial packet being last in a queue Q_j at time 0 and targeted with the largest simple path in the network. Rename the queues in this simple path as $Q_j \equiv Q_{j_0}, \ldots, Q_{j+\beta-1} \equiv Q_{j_{\beta-1}}$ (0). Note that at time $M_1 = q_{j_0}$ all packets of queue Q_{j_0} will have been served and they will have passed to the next queues in their path. There, they can be delayed by at most rM_1 injections of new packets. Therefore, the size of any Q_{j_i} is bounded above by $(\alpha+r)M_1$ as in M_1 time steps the number of packets that arrive in this queue consists of the initial packets that cross the input edges of Q_{j_i} (αM_1 packets) and the packets that can be injected during this period into the queue Q_{j_i} (rM_1).

We repeat the same procedure, each time considering the last queue in the path that still contains initial packets. After $\beta - 2$ additional steps ($M_2, M_3, \ldots, M_{\beta-1}$) all the initial packets would disappear or being in $Q_{j_{\beta-1}}$.

Define $q(t) = \max_{i=0}^{k} \{q_i(t)\}$. Working in the previous way, an absolute bound for the delay of the last initial packet in Q_j is $M = M_1 + \ldots + M_{\beta-1}$, where for every $0 < i < \beta$, we have $M_1 \leq q(\Sigma_{j<i} M_j)$, with $M_0 = 0$. Moreover, during a period of $q(t)$ steps starting at time t, we have $q(t+q(t)) \leq (\alpha+r)q(t)$. Solving the recurrence, we have that the total time is

$$M \leq \Sigma_{i=0}^{\beta-1}(\alpha + r)^i q(0) \tag{7}$$

Consider now, consecutive time periods $M, rM, r^2M, \ldots, r^l M$, where l is such that $r^l M \geq 1$ and $r^{l+1} M < 1$. Let t_1 be the time at which $r^l M$ finishes. The packets in N at time t_1 are all new, therefore the number of packets per queue is at most

$$rM + r^2M + \ldots + r^l M \leq rM + \frac{r}{1-r}M, \tag{8}$$

Therefore, $P(t_1) \leq \frac{2-r}{1-r} rkM$. Substituting the value of M from (7), we have

$$P(t_1) \leq \frac{2 - r}{1 - r} rk(\Sigma_{i=0}^{\beta-1}(\alpha + r)^i)P(0). \tag{9}$$

For the stability condition, we need $P(t_1)$ to be less than $P(0)$, which implies that we must choose an r such that,

$$\frac{2 - r}{1 - r} rk(\Sigma_{i=0}^{\beta-1}(\alpha + r)^i) \leq 1 \tag{10}$$

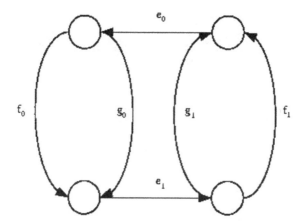

Fig. 2. Network N_2 [2, Theorem 2.10]

which is equivalent to finding in the real interval $(0, 1)$, the root r_N of

$$-2Zk(\alpha + Z)^{(\beta+1)} + 2Zk + Z^2k(\alpha + Z)^{(\beta+1)} - Z^2k + \alpha + 2Z - 1 - \alpha Z - Z^2$$

By the Bolzano's theorem, this polynomial has a root between 0 and 1, which is r_N. □

Using the polynomial obtained in the proof of the previous theorem, we can prove that there is an upper bound on the injection rate of the adversary that is enough to guarantee FIFO stability for any network. For example, if we apply the previous techniques of Theorem 2 (Equation 10) in the network of Fig. 2 that has been used in [2] to prove the instability of the FIFO protocol, we get that this network is stable for $r \leq 0.0026732592$. Moreover, applying the techniques of Theorem 2 (Equation 10) in the network of Fig. 4, we get a value $r \leq 0.0003932323554$ that guarantees FIFO stability. However, if we apply the techniques of Theorem 2 to the network we examine in Theorem 1 we get a value $r \leq 0.0095$ for the upper bound for FIFO stability, while the specific analysis of Theorem 1 gave an upper bound $r \leq \frac{1}{9}$. Therefore, if we do a particular analysis for specific networks, we can get better upper bounds for the values of the injection rate that make the network stable under FIFO protocol. The same holds for the network N_3 in Fig. 3. Applying the techniques of theorem 2 we take for the injection rate an upper bound $r \leq 0.0231$ for FIFO stability, while a more careful analysis [11, Theorem 1] will yield an upper bound on the injection rate $r \leq 0.1428$.

4   An Improved Lower Bound for FIFO Instability

For the network N_2 in Fig. 2, Andrews *et al.* [2] estimated an injection rate lower bound of 0.85, to prove the instability of FIFO. Also, Diaz *et al.* [7] presented an

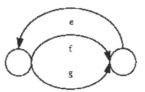

Fig. 3. A simple network N_3 with three queues

adversarial construction that leads the FIFO instability threshold to 0.8357 for a specific network. Here, we significantly lower FIFO instability bound to 0.771, on the network that we consider in Fig. 4.

Theorem 3. *There exists a network N_4 and an adversary $\mathcal{A}$ of injection rate r, such that the (N_4,$\mathcal{A}$,FIFO) system is unstable, starting from a non-empty configuration, for any $r \geq 0.771$.*

Proof. Let us consider the network N_4 in Fig. 4.
Inductive Hypothesis: At the beginning of phase j, there are s_j packets that are queued in the queues e_0, f_2', f_3' (in total) requiring to traverse the edges e_0, g, f_2, all the packets in queue f_3' are of this type, and the number of packets that are queued in queue f_3' is larger than the number of packets that are queued in queue f_2'.
Induction Step: At the beginning of phase $j + 1$, there will be more than s_j packets, s_{j+1} packets, that will be queued in the queues f_2, f_3, e_1, requiring to traverse the edges e_1, g', f_2', all the packets in queue f_3 will be of this type, and the number of packets that will be queued in queue f_3 will be larger than the number of packets that will be queued in queue f_2.

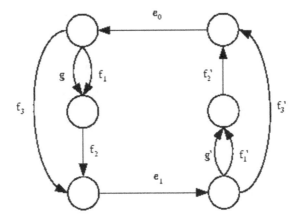

Fig. 4. The network N_4 that is used for FIFO instability

We will construct an adversary $\mathcal{A}$ such that the induction step will hold. Proving that the induction step holds for phase j, we ensure that the inductive hypothesis will hold at the beginning of phase $j+1$ for the symmetric edges with an increased value of s_j packets, $s_{j+1} > s_j$. In order to prove that the induction step works, we should consider that there is a large enough number of packets s_0 in the initial system configuration.

From the inductive hypothesis, initially, there is a packet set S of $|S| = s_j$ packets in the queues e_0, f_2', f_3' requiring to traverse the edges e_0, g, f_2. During phase j the adversary plays three rounds of injections. The sequence of injections is as follows:

Round 1: This round lasts s_j time steps. *Adversary's behavior.* During this round the adversary injects in queue f_3' a packet set X of $|X| = rs_j$ packets wanting to traverse the edges $f_3', e_0, f_1, f_2, e_1, g', f_2'$. Also, the adversary injects in queue g a packet set S_1 of $|S_1| = rs_j$ packets that require to traverse only edge g.

Evolution of the system configuration. The packets of set X are blocked in queue e_0 by the initial set of packets S. Notice that it has been assumed that at the beginning of this round the number of packets belonging to the S packet set that are queued in f_3' is larger than the number of S packets that are queued in f_2'.

At the same time, the s_j packets of packet set S are delayed in queue g by the packets of packet set S_1. The S_1 packets get mixed with the S packets. Notice that due to the FIFO protocol, the packets of S, S_1 sets mix in consecutive blocks according to the initial proportion of their sizes (fair mixing property). Since $|S| = s_j$ and $|S_1| = rs_j$, these proportions are $\frac{1}{r+1}$ and $\frac{r}{r+1}$, respectively. Thus, during the s_j steps of this round, the packets of S, S_1 sets, which traverse edge g are, respectively,

- for S: $s_j \frac{1}{r+1} = \frac{s_j}{r+1}$ packets,
- for S_1: $s_j \frac{r}{r+1} = \frac{rs_j}{r+1}$ packets.

Therefore, the remaining packets of S, S_1 sets in queue g are:

- for S, a packet set S_{rem} of $|S_{rem}| = s_j - \frac{s_j}{r+1} = \frac{rs_j}{r+1}$ packets,
- for S_1, a packet set $S_{1,rem}$ of $|S_{1,rem}| = rs_j - \frac{rs_j}{r+1} = \frac{r^2 s_j}{r+1}$ packets.

Round 2: This round lasts rs_j time steps. *Adversary's behavior.* During this round, the adversary injects in queue f_3' a set Y of $|Y| = r^2 s_j$ packets requiring to traverse the edges $f_3', e_0, f_3, e_1, g', f_2'$. Furthermore, during this round the adversary pushes in queue f_1 a set S_2 of $|S_2| = r^2 s_j$ packets that require to traverse only the edge f_1, and in queue f_2 a set S_3 of $|S_3| = r^2 s_j$ packets that require to traverse only the edge f_2.

Evolution of the system configuration. The packets of set Y are blocked in queue e_0 by the packets of set X. Due to the FIFO protocol, the packets of X, S_2 sets mix in consecutive blocks according to the initial proportion of their sizes. Since $|X| = rs_j$ and $|S_2| = r^2s_j$, these proportions are $\frac{1}{r+1}$ and $\frac{r}{r+1}$, respectively. Thus, during the rs_j steps of this round, the packets of X, S_2 sets that traverse the edge f_1 are, respectively,

- for X, a set X_{pass} of $|X_{pass}| = \frac{rs_j}{r+1}$ packets,
- for S_2, a set $S_{2,pass}$ of $|S_{2,pass}| = \frac{r^2s_j}{r+1}$ packets.

Therefore, the remaining packets of each type in queue f_1 are:

- for X, a set X_{rem} of $|X_{rem}| = rs_j - \frac{rs_j}{r+1} = \frac{r^2s_j}{r+1}$ packets,
- for S_2, a set $S_{2,rem}$ of $|S_{2,rem}| = r^2s_j - \frac{r^2s_j}{r+1} = \frac{r^3s_j}{r+1}$ packets.

Note that in queue g, there are the remaining S packets and the remaining S_1 packets. Since their total number is rs_j (which is equal to the duration of the round), the $S_{1,rem}$ packets do not delay the S_{rem} packets. Note also that, because the $S_{1,rem}$ packets are absorbed after they traverse only the edge g, only the S_{rem} packets require to traverse the edge f_2. Therefore, during round 2, three different flows of packets arrive at queue f_2:

- the X_{pass} packets where $|X_{pass}| = \frac{rs_j}{r+1}$. These packets mix with $S_{2,pass}$ packets. However, since their total number is rs_j (that is equal to the duration of the round), $S_{2,pass}$ packets do not delay the X_{pass} packets. Note also that, because the $S_{2,pass}$ packets are absorbed after they traverse the edge f_1, only the X_{pass} packets require to traverse the edge f_2.
- the S_{rem} packets, where $|S_{rem}| = \frac{rs_j}{r+1}$.
- the S_3 packets, where $|S_3| = r^2s_j$.

Since the total number of packets in the three flows is:

$$T = \frac{r^3s + r^2s + 2rs}{r + 1} \tag{11}$$

the corresponding proportions are:

- for X_{pass}: $\frac{|X_{pass}|}{T} = \frac{1}{r^2+r+2}$
- for S_{rem}: $\frac{|S_{rem}|}{T} = \frac{1}{r^2+r+2}$
- for S_3: $\frac{|S_3|}{T} = \frac{r^2+r}{r^2+r+2}$

Thus, the remaining packets in queue f_2 from each flow at the end of round 2 are:

- for X_{pass}: $\frac{rs_j}{r+1} - \frac{rs_j}{r^2+r+2} = rs_j\frac{r^2+1}{(r+1)(r^2+r+2)}$ packets,
- for S_{rem}: $\frac{rs_j}{r+1} - \frac{rs_j}{r^2+r+2} = rs_j\frac{r^2+1}{(r+1)(r^2+r+2)}$ packets,
- for S_3: $r^2s_j - rs_j\frac{r^2+r}{r^2+r+2} = rs_j\frac{r^3+r}{r^2+r+2}$ packets.

Round 3: This round lasts $r^2 s_j$ time steps. *Adversary's behavior.* During this round, the adversary injects in queue f_3 a set Z of $|Z| = r^3 s_j$ packets requiring to traverse the edges f_3, e_1, g', f_2'.
Evolution of the system configuration. The packets of set Z mix with the packets of set Y in consecutive blocks according to the initial proportion of their sizes. These proportions are $\frac{1}{r+1}$ and $\frac{r}{r+1}$ for Y, Z respectively. Thus, during the $r^2 s_j$ steps of this round, the packets Y, Z that traverse the edge f_3 are:

- for Y, a set Y_{pass} of $|Y_{pass}| = r^2 s_j \frac{1}{r+1} = \frac{r^2 s_j}{r+1}$ packets,
- for Z, a set Z_{pass} of $|Z_{pass}| = r^2 s_j \frac{r}{r+1} = \frac{r^3 s_j}{r+1}$ packets.

Therefore, the remaining packets in queue f_3 are:

- for Y, a set Y_{rem} of $|Y_{rem}| = r^2 s_j - \frac{r^2 s_j}{r+1} = \frac{r^3 s_j}{r+1}$ packets,
- for Z, a set Z_{rem} of $|Z_{rem}| = r^3 s_j - \frac{r^3 s_j}{r+1} = \frac{r^4 s_j}{r+1}$ packets.

During this period the number of X_{pass} packets that traverse the edge f_2 is $r^2 s_j \frac{1}{r^2+r+2}$. Thus, the remaining X_{pass} packets ($X_{pass,rem}$ packets) and S_{rem} packets that are still in queue f_2 at the end of this round are:

$$|S_{rem}| = |X_{pass,rem}| = \frac{rs_j - r^2 s_j}{(r+1)(r^2 + r + 2)}$$

The remaining S_3 packets that remain in queue f_2 at the end of this round are:

$$S_{3,rem} = \frac{r^4 s_j + r^2 s_j}{r^2 + r + 2} - \frac{r^4 s_j + r^3 s_j}{r^2 + r + 2} = \frac{r^2 s_j - r^3 s_j}{r^2 + r + 2}$$

Also, all the X_{rem} packets that are queued in queue f_1 at the beginning of this round traverse the edge f_1 during this round and they are queued in queue f_2 because the total number of packets in queue f_1 ($|X_{rem}| + |S_{2,rem}|$) is equal to the duration of this round as it follows:

$$|X_{rem}| + |S_{2,rem}| = \frac{r^2 s_j}{r+1} + \frac{r^3 s_j}{r+1} = r^2 s_j$$

From the inductive hypothesis, the assumption that the number of packets requiring to traverse the edges f_3, e_1, g', f_2' is larger than the number of packets requiring to traverse the edges f_2, e_1, g', f_2' should be hold.

However in queue f_2, there is a number of S_{rem} and $S_{3,rem}$ packets at the end of this round that mix with the $X_{pass,rem}$ packets, while the X_{rem} packets are queued after the S_{rem}, $S_{3,rem}$ and $X_{pass,rem}$ packets. Because of this mixture the $X_{pass,rem}$ packets are delayed in the next phase. So, we should take them into account for the following comparison, where $Q(f_3)$ and $Q(f_2)$ are the number of packets in queues f_3 and f_2, respectively:

$$Q(f_3) \qquad > Q(f_2)$$
$$\Longrightarrow \frac{r^3 s_j}{r+1} + \frac{r^4 s_j}{r+1} > 2\frac{r s_j - r^2 s_j}{(r+1)(r^2+r+2)} + \frac{r^2 s_j}{r+1} + \frac{r^2 s_j - r^3 s_j}{r^2+r+2}$$
$$\Longrightarrow r \qquad \geq 0.755$$

Thus, for $r \geq 0.755$, we have proved the second part of the *inductive hypothesis*. That is, we have proved that at the end of round 3 the number of packets that are queued in queue f_3 is larger than the number of packets that are queued in queue f_2. Furthermore all the packets that are queued in queue f_3 at the end of round 3 require to traverse the edges f_3, e_1, g', f_2'.

At the end of this round, the number of packets that are in queues f_2, f_3, e_1 requiring to traverse the edges e_1, g', f_2' is:

$$s' = r^3 s_j + r^2 s_j + \frac{r^2 s_j}{r+1} + \frac{r^3 s_j + r s_j}{(r+1)(r^2+r+2)} - r^2 s_j \qquad (12)$$

In order to have instability $s_{j+1} > s_j$ should be hold. This holds for $r \geq 0.771$ as follows:

$$r^3 s_j + \frac{r^2 s_j}{r+1} + \frac{r^3 s_j + r s_j}{(r+1)(r^2+r+2)} > s_j$$
$$\Longrightarrow r^6 + 2r^5 + 4r^4 + 3r^3 > 2r + 2$$
$$\Longrightarrow r \geq 0.771$$

Thus, in order to fulfil the *inductive hypothesis*, we take the maximum of 0.771 and 0755. Therefore, for $r \geq 0.771$ the network in Fig. 4 is unstable. This concludes our proof. □

5   Future Work

In this paper, we investigate the problem of the stability behavior of FIFO protocol and we propose an injection rate lower bound for FIFO instability that improves the best known previous lower bounds [2, 7, 9]. Furthermore, we present an injection rate upper bound for FIFO stability on a specific network along with a general methodology that estimates upper bounds on injection rate for FIFO stability in networks with a finite number of queues.

However, a lot of questions remain open concerning the problem of network stability in adversarial queuing networks. An open issue is the examination of simple protocols with respect to their stability behavior, other than those that have already been studied, as well as the continuity and the further enhancement of the already studied protocols. Another open issue is the investigation of various classes of networks that are universally stable for any adversary. Finally, the issue of adaptive routing where packet injections do not have predetermined paths except their origin and destination should be studied in the context of adversarial queuing theory.

References

[1] M. Andrews: "Instability of FIFO in Session-oriented Networks", *Proceedings 11th ACM-SIAM Symposium on Discrete Algorithms*, pp.440-447, 2000. 466, 467

[2] M. Andrews, B.Awerbuch, A. Fernandez, J. Kleinberg, T. Leighton and Z. Liu: "Universal Stability Results for Greedy Contention-Resolution Protocols", *Journal of the ACM*, Vol.48, No.1, pp.39-69, January 2001. 464, 465, 466, 467, 468, 469, 471, 473, 478

[3] A. Borodin, J. Kleinberg, P. Raghavan, M. Sudan and D. Williamson: "Adversarial Queueing Theory", *Journal of the ACM*, Vol.48, No.1, pp.13-38, January 2001. 465, 466, 467, 468

[4] M. Bramson: "Convergence to Equilibria for Fluid Models of FIFO Queueing Networks", *Queueing Systems*, Vol.22, pp.5-45, 1996. 466, 467

[5] H. Chen and D. D. Yao: *"Fundamentals of Queueing Networks"*, Springer, 2000. 465, 467

[6] R. Cruz: "A Calculus for Network Delay. Part I: Network Elements in Isolation", *IEEE Transactions on Information Theory*, Vol.37, pp.114-131, 1991. 466, 467

[7] J. Diaz, D. Koukopoulos, S. Nikoletseas, M. Serna, P. Spirakis and D. Thilikos: "Stability and Non-Stability of the FIFO Protocol", *Proceedings 13th Annual ACM Symposium on Parallel Algorithms and Architectures*, pp.48-52, 2001. 464, 466, 467, 473, 478

[8] D. Gamarnik: "Stability of Adversarial Queues via Models", *Proceedings 39th IEEE Symposium on Foundations of Computer Science*, pp.60-76, 1998. 466, 467

[9] A. Goel: "Stability of Networks and Protocols in the Adversarial Queueing Model for Packet Routing", *Networks*, Vol.37, No.4, pp.219-224, 2001. 464, 466, 467, 478

[10] F. P. Kelly: *"Reversability and Stochastic Networks"*, Wiley, New York, 1979. 467

[11] D. Koukopoulos, S. Nikoletseas and P. Spirakis: "Stability Results of FIFO Networks in the Adversarial Queueing Model", *Proceedings 8th Panhellenic Conference on Informatics*, Vol.2, pp.30-39, Cyprus, November 2001. 473

[12] P. Tsaparas: "Stability in Adversarial Queueing Theory", M.Sc. Thesis, Department of Computer Science, University of Toronto, 1997. 467

Sphendamnœ: A Proof that k-Splay Fails to Achieve $\log_k N$ Behaviour

D.J. McClurkin and G.F. Georgakopoulos

Department of Computer Science, University of Crete
Heraklion, Greece
{davidmcc,ggeo}@csd.uoc.gr

Abstract. The "splay" technique was introduced to cope with biasedness or changeability in data access frequencies, achieving optimality within a small constant factor w.r.t. static trees, without sacrificing $\log N$ worst-case behaviour, in an amortized sense. It achieves this through a series of local transformations, starting from the search node and propagating upwards along the search path to the root. It seems plausible that a similar policy, suitably adapted to multi-way trees, could achieve $\log_k N$ amortized performance (nodes visited), where k is the degree of the tree. Sherk's k-splay, a generalization of Sleator and Tarjan's splay technique to multi-way trees, proved to exhibit amortized $\log_2 N$ behaviour, could be considered the most likely candidate for a multi-way splay-like self-adjusting policy with $\log_k N$ amortized complexity. We construct a family of k-ary trees having depth k and containing 2^k nodes and we show that Sherk's k-splay applied to the deepest node of any tree in this family always produces another tree in the family. A fractal-like process of replacing leaf-nodes of trees with copies of themselves then allows us to create such trees of arbitrary size for any given k. This provides us with a family of counterexamples for which Sherk's k-splay always visits $\log_2 N$ nodes when applied to the deepest node in the tree.

1 Introduction

For the vast majority of applications requiring a Dictionary structure, a simple balanced binary tree is sufficient, providing a simple implementation of the INSERT, DELETE and FIND operations in worst-case logarithmic time. For data sets, however, in which the access frequencies are non-uniform, the "over-balancedness" of these trees yields sub-optimal performance. In extremely biased data sets, where the optimal static tree's (where the FIND operation does not alter the tree) performance approaches $O(1)$, uniformly balanced trees may be highly sub-optimal.

In [1] Allen and Munro addressed this problem with a simple rotate operation applied upwards along the search path, proving that on average the resulting performance is no worse than $O(1)$ times the optimum static tree with the same data. Their approach, averaging over all possible search keys, while in principle usable under their assumptions, has the drawback that the worst-case performance is $\Omega(N)$.

Y. Manolopoulos et al. (Eds.): PCI 2001, LNCS 2563, pp. 480–496, 2003.

In [6] Sleator and Tarjan defined the splay operation, consisting of a series of double rotations, the so-called "zig-zig" and "zig-zag" operations, which overcomes this drawback, having a worst-case complexity of no more that $O(1)$ times that of the optimum static tree, in an amortized sense. In their paper they ask whether there is a "self-adjusting form of B-tree, namely, a self-adjusting search tree with a most b children per node and an amortized $O(\log_b N)$ access time".

In [5] Sherk defined the k-splay operation for k-ary trees, a generalization of Sleator and Tarjan's original splay operation for binary trees, and proved that the amortized number of node accesses per operation is $O(\log_2 N)$. It seems plausible that k-splay could exhibit an amortized complexity of $O(\log_k N)$, and Sherk himself admits to unsuccessful attempts at eliminating the $\log k$ factor which would prove its $O(\log_k N)$ complexity. In the present article we show that this is not possible, providing a concrete counterexample. This lends credibility to the assertion that no such policy exists.

In section 2 we discuss k-splay operation as defined in [5], its connection with Tarjan and Sleator's original splay operation, and k-splay's conjectured $\log_k N$ performance. In section 3 we present the methodology through which we were able to construct counterexamples to the conjectured $\log_k N$ performance for small values of k. The remaining sections are dedicated to formally defining the classes of ω_k^d-trees, which will provide counterexamples of arbitrary degree, and rigorously proving k-splay's $\log_2 N$ behaviour when applied to these trees.

2   The k-Splay Operation and Sherk's Conjecture

Our work on generalized splay trees [4] lead to an in-depth examination of Sherk's k-splay trees [5], normally applied to k-way search trees where each node has degree k and contains $k-1$ search keys. The k-splay operation is in principle similar to the Tarjan and Sleator's original splay operation: After each INSERT/DELETE/FIND operation, a sequence of local transformations, the k-splay, is applied to the tree, beginning with the final (deepest) node on the search path and leading up to the root of the tree. The number of nodes transformed by each k-splay operation $O(1)$, and so the number of transformations performed in total is proportional to the depth of the node.

The successive application of k-splay to nodes in a tree can be visualized by the concept of a "cursor", which initially points to the deepest accessed node in the tree, e.g., the found node in the case of a successful search. At each stage we consider the cursored node u_0 together with its k ancestral nodes along the path leading towards the root. This provides us with $k+1$ path-nodes $u_0, u_1, \ldots, u_k$ and $k+k(k-1) = k^2$ subtrees $T_1, \ldots, T_{k^2}$. The subtree rooted at u_k is replaced by a 2-level tree with $k+1$ nodes: v_0 (root) and k children $v_1, \ldots, v_k$. There are k^2 leaves to which we attach $T_1, \ldots, T_{k^2}$, according to the original tree-ordering. The $k(k-1)$ search keys from the nodes $u_0, \ldots, u_k$ are likewise redistributed into $v_0, \ldots, v_k$ in the unique way required for the tree to remain a multi-way search tree.

The new cursor position is defined to be the root of this new subtree, v_0, located precisely k levels higher in the initial tree.

Strictly speaking this is not a generalization of Sleator and Tarjan's splay operation, but rather of a variation of it: 2-splay coincides with the "zig-zag" operation but handles differently the "zig-zig" case. See [5], [6].

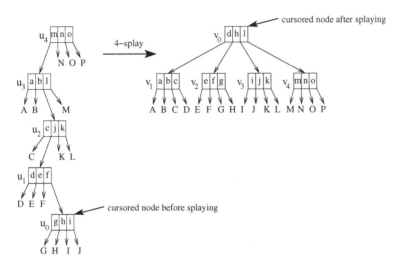

A single k-splay step for $k = 4$. The k-splay operation continues upward towards the root from the new cursor position.

Sherk conjectures that this scheme visits $O(\log_k N)$ nodes per k-splay operation in an amortized sense. We prove on the contrary that k-splay does not combine well the benefits of self-adjustment with those of multi-way structures: There exists a sequence of k-splay operations which visits $\log_2 N$ nodes in every case.

3   Constructing a Counterexample

For the remainder of this paper, we refer only to the structure of k-way trees, providing counterexamples without any node content. The results obtained therefore hold irrespectively of any search keys or other node data, i.e., they hold even when these trees are not used as search trees.

A k-way tree on N nodes may have height as little as $\log_k N$. In order to refute Sherk's conjecture we need a family of k-way trees on N nodes, closed under the k-splay operation, with height $\omega(\log_k N)$. Rather than maximizing the height in a family of trees of fixed size N, we instead try to minimize the size of trees of fixed height h, while maintaining closure w.r.t. k-splay. The simplest such family of trees is a cycle $T_0, T_1, \ldots, T_m = T_0$, where T_{i+1} is obtained by k-splaying T_i at its deepest node, and we insure that all T_i have the same height. As we shall see, we are in fact able to produce families of sparse trees with only 2^h nodes, with the technique described below for $k = 3$ and $h = 3$.

Let us construct a chain of 3-trees T_0, T_1, T_2, ..., whose depth is precisely 3 (so that 3-splay can be applied), keeping their size to the minimum possible. We begin with a template for such a tree, containing a single path of length 3 and "tree-variables" which, when instantiated, will determine the rest of the tree. We now consider the effect of splaying along that path.

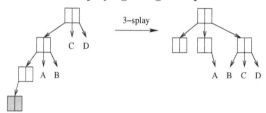

Ideally (for the counterexample) the result will again contain a single path of length 3. We therefore instantiate variable D so as to have a path of length 3 and again splay at the deepest node.

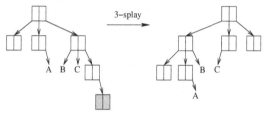

After two more steps, we are also able to instantiate "tree" variables A and C in such a way that the final tree is identical to the initial tree. We finally let B be nil so that all trees are of minimum size. The following pattern emerges: Each tree in the cycle is binomial, and one can verify that the analogous procedure applied to a higher-degree tree produces higher-degree binomial trees. It appears that for any given k we can construct, albeit in an *ad hoc* fashion, a family of k-way trees with depth precisely k and with only 2^k nodes. (In section 8 we show graphically the trees produced.) The k-splay operation applied repetitively to the deepest node produces a periodic sequence of k-trees which cycles after $2^{(k-1)}$ operations. Moreover, the structure of these degree k trees is strongly linked with the structure of the corresponding degree $k-1$ trees in the following way: If we "sever" a degree k tree at the link from its root node to its deepest subtree, the two resulting trees are "augmented" versions of lower-degree trees produced by the same process.

These observations are analysed and proved formally in the following sections.

4   Formalization of the Counterexample

This paper defines for each degree d a class of trees ω_d^d, such that ω_d^d is closed under the application of the d-splay operation, as defined by Sherk. Because of the close relationship between ω_d^d-trees and ω_{d-1}^{d-1}-trees, the trees are defined recursively based on their lower-degree counterparts, which facilitates the exploration and proof of their properties, through a careful inductive process.

Definition 1. *A d-tree is defined recursively as (1) nil (the empty tree), also written as ϕ, or (2) a d-tuple $\langle \tau_1, \tau_2, \ldots, \tau_d \rangle$, each of whose elements τ_i is itself a d-tree.*

If $T = \langle \tau_1, \ldots, \tau_d \rangle$ is a d-tree then the elements $\tau_1, \ldots, \tau_d$ are referred to as T's *subtrees*, where τ_1 is the left-most and τ_d the right-most. Note that in this representation we do not distinguish between a node τ and the subtree rooted at τ, although we may envision such a distinction when dealing with them.

In a d-tree T, it is often convenient to refer to T's d subtrees by $T[1], \ldots, T[d]$. Thus, for example, the right-most subtree of T's left-most subtree would be written $T[1][d]$.

We define recursively the *consecutive-nil* or *cons-nil property* for trees of degree d:

Definition 2. *(1) The empty tree ϕ always satisfies the cons-nil property; (2) a non-empty tree $T = \langle \tau_1, \ldots, \tau_d \rangle$ satisfies the cons-nil property if each τ_i, $1 \leq i \leq d$, satisfies the cons-nil property, and furthermore for some j, $1 \leq j \leq d$, either (i) $\tau_1, \ldots, \tau_j$ are nil and $\tau_{j+1}, \ldots, \tau_d$ are non-nil, or (ii) $\tau_1, \ldots, \tau_j$ are non-nil and $\tau_{j+1}, \ldots, \tau_d$ are nil.*

This says that in each node of T the nil children appear consecutively and the non-nil children appear consecutively. As we shall see, the trees in which we are interested must be reducible in a unique manner, which requires the nils to be placed consecutively within each node.

Definition 3. *A tree T of degree d satisfying the cons-nil property is said to be reducible if (1) $T = \phi$, or (2) $T = \langle \tau_1, \ldots, \tau_d \rangle$ and at least one of $\tau_1, \ldots, \tau_d$ is nil and each of $\tau_1, \ldots, \tau_d$ is reducible.*

This says that each non-nil node in T has at least one nil child. Furthermore, since reducible trees (by definition) satisfy the cons-nil property, in each node the non-nil and nil children appear consecutively.

We define recursively the reduction operator red$(\cdot)$ on reducible trees of degree d, formalizing the relationship between the two "severed" parts of a degree-d tree and trees of degree $d-1$.

Definition 4. *(1) red$(\phi) = \phi$; (2) red$(\langle \tau_1, \ldots, \tau_d \rangle) = \langle red(\tau_1), \ldots, red(\tau_{d-1}) \rangle$ if $\tau_d = \phi$, or red$(\langle \tau_1, \ldots, \tau_d \rangle) = \langle red(\tau_2), \ldots, red(\tau_d) \rangle$ if $\tau_1 = \phi$. [If both are nil then, by the cons-nil property, all children are nil and these amount to the same thing. red$(\cdot)$ is therefore well-defined on such trees.]*

This formalizes the reduction operator as removing a nil from each node in the tree, producing a similar tree of degree one less.

We now recursively define the class of trees w_k^d, which have the basic properties needed for the counter-example.

Definition 5. *A tree of degree d, $T \neq \phi$, is w_d^d if either*

1. *(a) $T[1]$ is w_{d-1}^d, (b) $T[1][d] = \phi$ and (c) $\langle \phi, T[2], \ldots, T[d]\rangle$ is w_{d-1}^d, (in which case we say that T is left-w_d^d), or*
2. *(a) $T[d]$ is w_{d-1}^d, (b) $T[d][1] = \phi$ (c) and (c) $\langle T[1], \ldots, T[d-1], \phi\rangle$ is w_{d-1}^d (in which case we say that T is right-w_d^d).*

T is w_k^d for $k < d$ if T is reducible and $red(T)$ is w_k^{d-1}.
The tree $T = \langle \phi\rangle$ is w_0^1 (base case).

For such trees belonging to class w_r^d, d is their *degree* (number of subtrees at each node) and r their *rank* (depth of the tree, as we shall see below). This formalizes the way a rank-k tree is decomposable into two trees of rank $k-1$. We shall refer to these trees as *sphendamnos* (singular) or *sphendamnœ* (plural)[1].

Finally we define the augmentation operator, the inverse of reduction.

Definition 6. *For a w_k^d-tree T, $k < d$, its augmentation $aug(T)$ is the unique w_k^{d+1}-tree $\overline{T}$ such that $red(\overline{T}) = T$.*

The augmentation operator thus adds a nil to each node of T, producing a similar tree of degree one greater. Because $k < d$, every node contains a nil, and by the cons-nil property, the nil nodes within a node are consecutive, therefore $aug(T)$ is well-defined for such trees. For a w_d^d-tree T, T's root contains no nil child, and therefore there are two choices for where to insert this nil into T's root, as left-most or right-most child. Consequently there are exactly two trees, $\overleftarrow{T}$ and $\overrightarrow{T}$, such that $red(\overleftarrow{T}) = red(\overrightarrow{T}) = T$. These are the so-called left- and right-augmentations of T respectively, denoted by $aug_L(T)$ and $aug_R(T)$, corresponding to inserting ϕ into T's root as left-most or right-most child.

Thus if $T = \langle \tau_1, \ldots, \tau_d\rangle$ is w_k^d for $k < d$ then

$$aug(T) = \begin{cases} \langle aug(\tau_1), \ldots, aug(\tau_k), \underbrace{\phi, \ldots, \phi}_{d-k+1}\rangle & \text{if } \tau_{k+1} = \cdots = \tau_d = \phi \\ \langle \underbrace{\phi, \ldots, \phi}_{d-k+1}, aug(\tau_{d-k+1}), \ldots, aug(\tau_d),\rangle & \text{if } \tau_1 = \cdots = \tau_{d-k} = \phi \end{cases}$$

If T is w_d^d then
$$aug_L(T) = \langle \phi, aug(\tau_1), \ldots, aug(\tau_d)\rangle$$

and
$$aug_R(T) = \langle aug(\tau_1), \ldots, aug(\tau_d), \phi\rangle.$$

---

[1] This is the Greek word for the Canadian flag symbol, a fair choice considering the nationalities of the two authors.

5   Properties of the Sphendamnœ

The first property of the class of trees defined above is that there actually exists such a tree. For this it is sufficient to trace the recursion back from the base case. Various examples can be constructed by choosing either (1) or (2) in definition 5 at each decision-point: To construct a ω_d^d-tree, it suffices to take any two ω_{d-1}^{d-1}-trees, U and V, and combine them according to definition 5, forming either

$$T = \langle \mathrm{aug}_R(U), \mathrm{aug}_L(V)[2], \ldots, \mathrm{aug}_L(V)[d] \rangle$$

or

$$T = \langle \mathrm{aug}_R(U)[1], \ldots, \mathrm{aug}_R(U)[d-1], \mathrm{aug}_L(V) \rangle.$$

The first few ω_d^d-trees are pictured graphically:

If we let both U and V be the first ω_2^2-tree shown above, we can form the following two ω_3^3-trees:

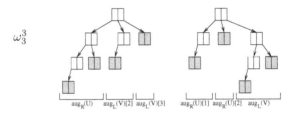

Similarly, if U is the first ω_3^3-tree above and V the second, we can form:

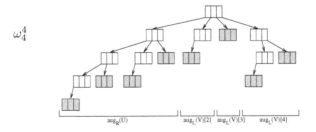

Moreover it is straightforward to compute the number of trees in each class ω_k^d. Two d-trees S and T are identical if and only if $S[i] = T[i]$ for $i = 1, \ldots, d$. To form a ω_d^d-tree we take two ω_{d-1}^{d-1}-trees and combine them according to definition 5, choosing either (1) or (2). Therefore, we have:

$$|\omega_1^1| = 1, \text{ namely, } T = \langle\langle\phi\rangle\rangle$$
$$|\omega_2^2| = 2 \cdot |\omega_1^1|^2 = 2,$$
$$|\omega_3^3| = 2 \cdot |\omega_2^2|^2 = 8,$$
$$|\omega_4^4| = 2 \cdot |\omega_3^3|^2 = 128,$$
$$|\omega_5^5| = 2 \cdot |\omega_4^4|^2 = 32768,$$
$$|\omega_6^6| = 2 \cdot |\omega_5^5|^2 = 2147483648,$$
$$\vdots$$
$$|\omega_d^d| = 2 \cdot |\omega_{d-1}^{d-1}|^2,$$

and in general

$$|\omega_d^d| = 2^{(2^{d-1}-1)}.$$

If T is ω_k^d with $k < d$ then aug(T) is uniquely defined, and therefore $|\omega_k^{d+1}| = |\omega_k^d|$. If T is ω_d^d, there are exactly two trees U such that red$(U) = T$, and therefore $|\omega_d^{d+1}| = 2|\omega_d^d|$.

Binomial trees are ranked trees characterized by the recursive property that a binomial tree of rank k has k subtrees which are binomial of rank $k-1, \ldots, 0$.

Claim. Let T be a ω_k^d-tree. Then T is a binomial tree, i.e., it has k subtrees which are $\omega_{k-1}^d, \ldots, \omega_0^d$.

Proof. A straightforward application of Definitions 3, 4 and 5 suffices.   □

From this it also follows inductively that the depth of a ω_k^d-tree is exactly k, since the depth of a ω_k^d-tree is exactly one greater than the depth of it deepest child, which inductively is a ω_{k-1}^d-tree with depth $k-1$.

6   Producing ω_k^d-Trees from ω_k^d-Trees

We now define the operation σ_k^d on ω_k^d-trees. By carefully following definition 5 and definition 7, it can be seen that an application of σ_k^d to an ω_k^d-tree always produces another ω_k^d-tree.

Definition 7. *Let $T = \langle\tau_1, \ldots, \tau_d\rangle$ be a non-nil ω_d^d-tree. Then one of the following holds (definition of ω_d^d):*

1. *τ_1 is ω_{d-1}^d with $\tau_1[d] = \phi$, and $\langle\phi, \tau_2, \ldots, \tau_d\rangle$ is ω_{d-1}^d (i.e., T is left-ω_d^d and T's deepest node is in its left-most subtree)*
2. *τ_d is ω_{d-1}^d with $\tau_d[1] = \phi$, and $\langle\tau_1, \ldots, \tau_{d-1}, \phi\rangle$ is ω_{d-1}^d (i.e., T is right-ω_d^d and T's deepest node is in its right-most subtree);*

We define $\sigma_d^d(T)$ for the two cases respectively:

1. $\sigma_d^d(T) = \langle U_1, \ldots, U_{d-1}, \langle \phi, \tau_2, \ldots, \tau_d \rangle \rangle$ *where*

$$\langle U_1, \ldots, U_{d-1}, \phi \rangle = aug_R\big(\sigma_{d-1}^{d-1}(red(\tau_1))\big),$$

2. $\sigma_d^d(T) = \langle \langle \tau_1, \ldots, \tau_{d-1}, \phi \rangle, U_2, \ldots, U_d \rangle$ *where*

$$\langle \phi, U_2, \ldots, U_d \rangle = aug_L\big(\sigma_{d-1}^{d-1}(red(\tau_d))\big).$$

Claim. The class of ω_d^d-trees is closed under the application of σ_d^d.

Proof. In the first case, $\langle U_1, \ldots, U_{d-1}, \langle \phi, \tau_2, \ldots, \tau_d \rangle \rangle$ is a ω_d^d-tree because

1. $\langle \phi, \tau_2, \ldots, \tau_d \rangle$ is ω_{d-1}^d (by hypothesis 1 in definition 7), satisfying criteria 2(a) and 2(b) in definition 5, and
2. inductively $\sigma_{d-1}^{d-1}(red(\tau_1))$ produces a ω_{d-1}^{d-1}-tree, and thus its right-augmentation is an ω_{d-1}^d-tree, satisfying criterion 2(c) in definition 5.

In the second case, $\langle \langle \tau_1, \ldots, \tau_{d-1}, \phi \rangle, U_2, \ldots, U_d \rangle$ is a ω_d^d-tree because of the symmetric argument.   □

Although not strictly required for our proof, we define for the sake of completeness the operator σ_k^d for $k < d$:

Definition 8. *Let T be a ω_k^d-tree with $k < d$. Then*

$$\sigma_k^d(T) = aug\big(\sigma_k^{d-1}(red(T))\big)$$

This is not strictly well-defined for the case $k = d-1$, since then $red(T)$ and $\sigma_k^{d-1}(red(T))$ are ω_k^k-trees, and thus have two possible augmentations, aug_L and aug_R. We assume in this case that the root node of $\sigma_k^{d-1}(red(T))$ is augmented so that its nil child is in the same position as in T. This choice is made so that σ_k^d coincides with the way we define splay on similar trees.

7 k-Splay Applied to the Sphendamnœ

The next step is to examine what k-splay does when applied to the lowest node in a ω_d^d-tree. Our immediate goal is to define a generalization of Sherk's k-splay operation, $splay_k^d$, such that $splay_d^d$ is identical to Sherk's k-splay. We then show that σ_k^d and $splay_k^d$ are identical for ω_k^d-trees.

This seemingly awkward approach is necessary because in essence we are not interested in analysing the performance of k-splay on all k-ary trees but rather its restriction to ω_k^d-trees. Furthermore the definition of ω_k^d-trees is inherently recursive whereas k-splay's inherently linear definition does not admit a direct analysis of its behaviour on ω_k^d-trees. For this we need a generalization of k-splay which is defined for ω_k^d-trees where $k < d$. The proof is facilitated by reducing the problem to verifying the identity of two operators, $splay_k^d$ and σ_k^d.

Let $T = (\tau_1, \ldots, \tau_d)$ be a ω_k^d-tree, define recursively $T_k = T$ and T_{i-1} to be the subtree of T_i with greatest rank, for $i = k, k-1, \ldots, 1$. This gives us a sequence of trees $T_k, T_{k-1}, \ldots, T_0$ where T_i is ω_i^d. This sequence corresponds to the search path from the root of T to its deepest element. Each tree T_i has precisely $d-i$ nil children, as follows from Definition 5. We define the *off-path* elements of T_i to be those not equal to T_{i-1}

Definition 9. *For a ω_k^d-tree T, define $T' = \mathrm{splay}_k^d(T)$ as the tree resulting from considering the path leading to T's deepest node together with all off-path pointers, and rearranging them in a 2-level structure, defined as follows: The $d-k$ nil elements at T's root are placed in the root of T' in the same position as they were in T. T' is given k additional children into which are placed the remaining $d + k(d-1) - (d-k) = dk$ off-path elements (nil and non-nil): they are grouped into k d-node groups and hung from T' in their original order.*

Clearly the splay_k^k operation applied to a ω_k^k-tree coincides with Sherk's k-splay operation applied to the deepest node of the same tree. We next prove several lemmata that shed light on the way splay_k^d transforms ω_k^d-trees. These are then used to prove the equivalence of σ_k^d and splay_k^d on ω_k^d-trees.

Lemma 1. *The splay_k^d operation applied to a ω_k^d-tree T is equivalent to the following procedure: We envision splay_k^d as a node-gathering process: The first step consists of taking T's $d-k$ nil children and placing them under T' in the same positions as they were in T. Each subsequent step $i = k, k-1, \ldots, 1$ consists of taking the $i-1$ non-nil (off-path) children of T_i together with the $d-i+1$ nil children of T_{i-1} and placing them together under one of the remaining i nodes in the new framework T'.*

At each stage, before placing these nodes, $T'[a], \ldots, T'[b]$ are still "vacant", where $b - a + 1 = i$. Let $U_1, \ldots, U_{i-1}$ be the non-nil children of T_i and let $V_1, \ldots, V_{d-i+1}$ be the nil children of T_{i-1}. If T_i is left-ω_i^d (i.e., augmented left-ω_i^d) then we set

$$T'[b] = \langle V_1, \ldots, V_{d-i+1}, U_1, \ldots, U_{i-1} \rangle,$$

leaving $T'[a], \ldots, T'[b-1]$ vacant, and we decrement b. If T_i is right-ω_i^d (i.e., augmented right-ω_i^d) then we set

$$T'[a] = \langle U_1, \ldots, U_{i-1}, V_1, \ldots, V_{d-i+1} \rangle,$$

leaving $T'[a+1], \ldots, T'[b]$ vacant, and increment a. The procedure terminates when $a = b$ and we place the children of T_0 (all nil) under $T[a]$.

Proof. The lemma follows in a straightforward fashion by considering the above procedure in conjunction with the definition of splay_k^d for ω_k^d-trees.

More formally, using induction along the search-path, assume that this procedure correctly places all off-path children of $T_k, T_{k-1}, \ldots, T_{i+1}$ and the nil children of T_i. Assume that the nodes $T'[a], \ldots, T'[b]$ are vacant and $b-a+1 = i$.

We are now placing the $i-1$ non-nil children of T_i and the $d-i+1$ nil children of T_{i-1}.

Case 1: T_i is a left-augmented left-ω_i^d-tree. Then T_{i-1} is a right-augmented ω_{i-1}^d-tree. Therefore of the yet-unplaced off-path nodes, the d rightmost are (in order) $T_{i-1}[i], \ldots, T_{i-1}[d]$ (i.e., the $d-i+1$ nil nodes under T_{i-1}) and $T_i[d-i+2], \ldots, T_i[d]$ (i.e., the $i-1$ non-nil nodes under T_i). This node-gathering process correctly places them under $T'[b]$.

The other three cases where T_i is left-augmented right-ω_i^d, right-augmented left-ω_i^d or right-augmented right-ω_i^d are similarly handled correctly.   □

Lemma 2. *Let T be ω_k^d, $k < d$. Then*

$$red\big(splay_k^d(T)\big) = splay_k^{d-1}\big(red(T)\big).$$

This corollary is illustrated in the following figure for $d = 4, k = 3$:

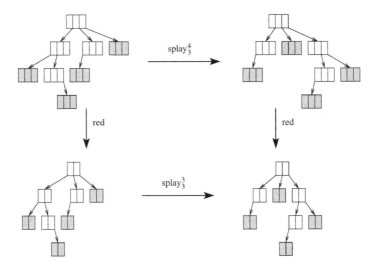

Proof. We compare the splaying operations for an ω_k^d-tree T and its reduction $U = red(T)$, an ω_k^{d-1}-tree, again considering the node-collection as beginning at the root and following the path downwards to T's deepest node. If $T_k, \ldots, T_0$ is the sequence of subtrees leading to T's deepest node, then in U we have the corresponding sequence $U_k = red(T_k), \ldots, U_0 = red(T_k)$.

There is a step-by-step equivalence: $splay_k^d$ applied to T takes $i-1$ non-nil children from each T_i and groups them together with the $d-i+1$ nil children of T_{i-1}, forming in total k nodes of degree d.

Likewise, $splay_k^{d-1}$ applied to U takes $i-1$ non-nil children from each U_i and groups them together with the $d-i$ nil children of U_{i-1}, forming in total k nodes of degree $d-1$.

Run in parallel, these two procedures can be seen never to diverge, the latter producing always the reduction of the former.   □

A *terminal node* in an ω_k^d-tree is a node of the form $\langle \phi, \ldots, \phi \rangle$. These will play a special role in the final section of this work, when we substitute entire trees for terminal nodes in order to construct trees of arbitrary height. They are shaded in our figures.

Lemma 3. *Let Z be a terminal node in an ω_k^d-tree T, and let $T' = \mathrm{splay}_k^d(T)$. Then Z is repositioned atomically, i.e., . More formally, if we substitute for Z an arbitrary tree Z', then an exact copy of Z' will appear in place of Z in T'.*

Proof. If Z is contained within an off-path element E then the lemma clearly holds, since E is repositioned atomically by splay_k^d. If $Z = T_0$ then this is a direct consequence of the proof of lemma 1 when $i = 1$.   □

We now come to the heart of the proof. We first show that the operations σ_d^d and splay_d^d are identical for ω_d^d-trees. Below this is generalized and we treat the case for ω_k^d-trees with $k < d$.

Theorem 1. *If T is ω_d^d then $\sigma_d^d(T) = \mathrm{splay}_d^d(T)$.*

Proof. First we note that for the case $d = 1$ we have only one choice for T, $T = \langle\langle\phi\rangle\rangle$. Then clearly we have $\sigma_1^1(T) = \mathrm{splay}_1^1(T)$.

Next we proceed by induction, assuming that the assertion holds for ω_d^d-trees, and we consider T a ω_{d+1}^{d+1}-tree. Assume T is left-ω_{d+1}^{d+1}. Letting $D = \sigma_{d+1}^{d+1}(T)$ and $U = \mathrm{splay}_{d+1}^{d+1}(T)$, we have

$$\begin{aligned}
D[d+1] &= \langle\phi, T[2], \ldots, T[d+1]\rangle \quad \text{(def. of } \sigma_{d+1}^{d+1} \text{ for left-}\omega_{d+1}^{d+1}\text{-trees)} \\
&= \mathrm{splay}_{d+1}^{d+1}(T)[d+1] \\
&\qquad \text{(since } T\text{'s deepest node is in } T[1] \text{ and } T[1][d] = \phi) \\
&= U[d+1].
\end{aligned}$$

The symmetric argument shows that if T is right-ω_{d+1}^{d+1} then $D[1] = U[1]$.

We now show that the rest of D's children are also identical to U's corresponding children. Again assume T is left-ω_{d+1}^{d+1}. For $i = 1, \ldots, d$ we have

$$\begin{aligned}
D[i] &= \sigma_{d+1}^{d+1}(T)[i] \quad \text{(def of } D) \\
&= \mathrm{aug}_R\Big(\sigma_d^d\big(\mathrm{red}(T[1])\big)\Big)[i] \quad \text{(def of } \sigma_{d+1}^{d+1} \text{ for left-}\omega_{d+1}^{d+1}\text{-trees)} \\
&= \mathrm{aug}_R\Big(\mathrm{splay}_d^d\big(\mathrm{red}(T[1])\big)\Big)[i] \quad \text{(inductive hypothesis)} \\
&= \mathrm{aug}_R\Big(\mathrm{red}\big(\mathrm{splay}_d^{d+1}(T[1])\big)\Big)[i] \quad \text{(lemma 2)} \\
&= \mathrm{aug}_R\Big(\mathrm{red}\big(\langle U[1], \ldots, U[d], \phi\rangle\big)\Big)[i] \\
&\qquad \text{(since } T\text{'s deepest node is in } T[1] \text{ and } T[1][d+1] = \phi) \\
&= \mathrm{aug}_R\big(\langle\mathrm{red}(U[1]), \ldots, \mathrm{red}(U[d])\rangle\big)[i] \\
&= \langle U[1], \ldots, U[d], \phi\rangle[i] \ = \ U[i].
\end{aligned}$$

The symmetric argument shows that if T is right-ω_d^d then $D[i] = U[i]$ for $i = 2, \ldots, d+1$.   □

We now present the full generalized proof for ω_k^d-trees, where possibly $k < d$.

Theorem 2. *If T is ω_k^d then $\sigma_k^d(T) = \text{splay}_k^d(T)$.*

Proof. Our goal is to prove by induction that σ_k^d and splay_k^d yield identical results when applied to a ω_k^d-tree T.

We first note that for a ω_1^d-tree T $\sigma_1^d(T) = \text{splay}_1^d(T) = T$.

Now suppose that T is a ω_{k+1}^d-tree. We assume that it is a left-augmented left-ω_{k+1}^d; the other cases can by handled symmetrically. We proceed by induction, assuming that σ_k^k and splay_k^k are identical for ω_k^k-trees. We examine and compare the effects of the σ_{k+1}^d and splay_{k+1}^d operations. The σ_{k+1}^d operations applied to T can be decomposed as:

$$T \xrightarrow{\text{red}^{(d-k-1)}} B \xrightarrow{\sigma_{k+1}^{k+1}} C \xrightarrow{\text{aug}^{(d-k-1)}} D$$

where

$$B[1] = \text{red}^{(d-k-1)}(T[d-k])$$
$$B[2] = \text{red}^{(d-k-1)}(T[d-k+1])$$
$$\vdots$$
$$B[k+1] = \text{red}^{(d-k-1)}(T[d])$$

and

$$\langle C[1], \ldots, C[k], \phi \rangle = \text{aug}_R \left(\sigma_k^k \big(\text{red}(B[1]) \big) \right)$$
$$C[k+1] = \langle \phi, B[2], \ldots, B[k+1] \rangle$$

and

$$D[1] = \cdots = D[d-k-1] = \phi$$
$$D[d-k] = \text{aug}^{(d-k-1)}(C[1])$$
$$\vdots$$
$$D[d] = \text{aug}^{(d-k-1)}(C[k+1]).$$

We let $U = \text{splay}_{k+1}^d(T)$. Now, since $B = \text{red}^{(d-k-1)}(T)$ we have

$$B[2] = \text{red}^{(d-k-1)}(T[d-k+1])$$
$$\vdots$$
$$B[k+1] = \text{red}(d-k-1)(T[d]).$$

Therefore,

$$C[k+1] = \langle \phi, \text{red}^{(d-k-1)}(T[d-k+1]), \ldots, \text{red}^{d-k-1}(T[d]) \rangle,$$

by the definition of σ_{k+1}^{k+1} for a left-w_{k+1}^{k+1}-tree B. Therefore

$$D[d] = \langle \underbrace{\phi, \ldots \phi}_{d-k}, \mathrm{aug}^{(d-k-1)}\mathrm{red}^{(d-k-1)}T[d-k+1], \ldots, \mathrm{aug}^{(d-k-1)}\mathrm{red}^{(d-k-1)}T[d]\rangle$$

$$= \langle \underbrace{\phi, \ldots \phi}_{d-k}, T[d-k+1], \ldots, T[d]\rangle,$$

since all the trees $T[d-k+1], \ldots, T[d]$ contain $\geq d-k$ nil nodes and are thus left unaffected by $\mathrm{red}^{(d-k-1)}$ followed by $\mathrm{aug}^{(d-k-1)}$.

Furthermore, by the structure of T, a left-w_{k+1}^d-tree, we have that $\mathrm{splay}_{k+1}^d(T) = U$ where

$$U[d] = \langle \underbrace{\phi, \ldots, \phi}_{\text{left-most } d-k \text{ nodes of } T[d-k]}, T[d-k+1], \ldots, T[d]\rangle = D[d].$$

Next we show that the rest of D's children are the same as those of U. By the definition of aug_{k+1}^{k+1} for w_d^d-trees, we have that $D[1] = \cdots = D[d-k-1] = \phi$. This corresponds to U because, by the definition of splay_{k+1}^d, the $d-k-1$ left-most children of U are nil.

Finally we show that the remaining children of D, $D[d-k], \ldots, D[d-1]$ are identical with the corresponding children of U, $U[d-k], \ldots, U[d-1]$. Without loss of generality we consider $D[d-k]$, and the corresponding argument holds for $D[d-k+1], \ldots, D[d-1]$.

$$
\begin{aligned}
D[d-k] &= \mathrm{aug}^{(d-k-1)}(C[1]) \quad \text{(def. of } D) \\
&= \mathrm{aug}^{(d-k-1)}((\sigma_{k+1}^{k+1}(B)[1])) \quad \text{(def. of } C) \\
&= \mathrm{aug}^{(d-k-1)}((\mathrm{aug}_R(\sigma_k^k(\mathrm{red}(B[1]))))[1]) \quad \text{(def. of } \sigma_{k+1}^{k+1}) \\
&= \mathrm{aug}^{(d-k-1)}(\mathrm{aug}((\sigma_k^k(\mathrm{red}(B[1])))[1])) \quad \text{(def. of } \mathrm{aug}_R) \\
&= \mathrm{aug}^{(d-k)}((\sigma_k^k(\mathrm{red}(B[1])))[1]) \quad \text{(collecting augmentation operations)} \\
&= \mathrm{aug}^{(d-k)}((\mathrm{splay}_k^k(\mathrm{red}(B[1])))[1]) \quad \text{(ind. hypothesis)} \\
&= \mathrm{aug}^{(d-k)}((\mathrm{splay}_k^k(\mathrm{red}^{(d-k)}(T[d-k])))[1]) \quad \text{(def. of } B) \\
&= \mathrm{aug}^{(d-k)}((\mathrm{red}^{(d-k)}(\mathrm{splay}_k^d(T[d-k])))[1]) \quad \text{(lemma 2)} \\
&= (\mathrm{aug}^{(d-k)}(\mathrm{red}^{(d-k)}(\mathrm{splay}_k^d(T[d-k]))))[d-k+1] \quad \text{(def. of } \mathrm{aug}) \\
&= (\mathrm{splay}_k^d(T[d-k]))[d-k+1] \quad \text{(collapsing red and aug operations)} \\
&= U[d-k]. \quad \square
\end{aligned}
$$

8 Periodicity of k-Splay

There are exactly two w_2^2-trees, T_0 and T_1, as shown in the following figure. These form an orbit of length 2, since $\mathrm{splay}(T_0) = T_1$ and $\mathrm{splay}(T_1) = T_0$.

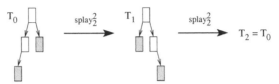

From these two ω_2^2-trees we can construct a variety of ω_3^3-trees, eight in total. We show the result of augmenting and adjoining two copies of the above T_0 and splaying the result.

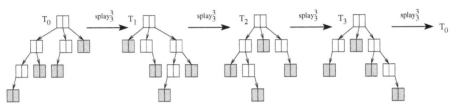

One can construct an arbitrary ω_4^4-tree and verify that it passes through eight unique permutations before cycling.

In general if we have a ω_d^d-tree T constructed by adjoining two ω_{d-1}^{d-1}-trees U and V so that

$$T = \langle \mathrm{aug}_R(U), \mathrm{aug}_L(V)[2], \ldots, \mathrm{aug}_L(V)[d] \rangle$$

or

$$T = \langle \mathrm{aug}_R(U)[1], \ldots, \mathrm{aug}_R(U)[d-1], \mathrm{aug}_L(V) \rangle$$

then we can pinpoint T's orbit, knowing U's and V's orbits: Let T's orbit be $T_0, T_1, T_2, \ldots$ where $T_0 = T$ and $T_{i+1} = \mathrm{splay}_d^d(T_i)$. Denote U's and V's orbits similarly.

In the first case, where T is left-ω_d^d, we have

$$
\begin{aligned}
T_0 &= \langle \mathrm{aug}_R(U_0), \mathrm{aug}_L(V_0)[2], \ldots, \mathrm{aug}_L(V_0)[d] \rangle \\
T_1 &= \langle \mathrm{aug}_R(\sigma_{d-1}^{d-1}(U_0))[1], \ldots, \mathrm{aug}_R(\sigma_{d-1}^{d-1}(U_0))[d-1], \\
&\qquad \langle \phi, \mathrm{aug}_L(V_0)[2], \ldots, \mathrm{aug}_L(V_0)[d] \rangle \rangle \\
&= \langle \mathrm{aug}_R(U_1)[1], \ldots, \mathrm{aug}_R(U_1)[d-1], \mathrm{aug}_L(V_0) \rangle \\
T_2 &= \langle \langle \mathrm{aug}_R(U_1)[1], \ldots, \mathrm{aug}_R(U_1)[d-1] \rangle, \\
&\qquad \mathrm{aug}_L(\sigma_{d-1}^{d-1}(U_1))[2], \ldots, \mathrm{aug}_L(\sigma_{d-1}^{d-1}(U_1))[d] \rangle \\
&= \langle \mathrm{aug}_R(U_1), \mathrm{aug}_L(V_1)[2], \ldots, \mathrm{aug}_L(V_1)[d] \rangle
\end{aligned}
$$

From this it is clear then that if U and V's orbits are of length l then T's orbit is of length $2l$, and in general for ω_d^d-trees the orbit length is 2^{d-1}.

9   From Splay-Steps to Splay-Operations

Thus far we have shown that Sherk's k-splay operation, when applied to a ω_k^k-tree, produces another ω_k^k-tree, in a single splay-step, rearranging precisely k^2

nodes each time. For a given k, each of the ω_k^k-trees contains $N = 2^k$ nodes, and has height exactly k. We now show how to produce a family $\mathcal{S}$ of trees of arbitrary size N, independent of k, such that for any $T \in \mathcal{S}$ the deepest node of T *always* lies at a depth $\log_2 N$, and furthermore splaying at the deepest node of any $T \in \mathcal{S}$ always produces another tree $T' \in \mathcal{S}$.

Refer again to the above figures and consider the terminal (shaded) nodes in the ω_d^d-trees. We have shown that during a splay-operation, these are repositioned atomically in the new structure. This allows us to recursively replace these nodes in a ω_d^d-tree by entire copies of ω_d^d-trees.

More formally, we define the classes $^m\omega_k^d$ as follows:

Definition 10. *A tree is $^1\omega_k^d$ if it is ω_k^d; a tree is $^{(m+1)}\omega_k^d$ if it can be decomposed as a ω_k^d-tree whose terminal nodes have been substituted by entire $^m\omega_k^d$-trees.*

Consider now what happens when we perform a d-splay in a $^m\omega_d^d$-tree T. Beginning from the deepest node in T, the first splay-step essentially "sees" a ω_d^d-tree, ignoring for the present the rest of T above the new cursor position. It transforms this, producing another ω_d^d-tree, and continues on upwards. At each stage of this d-splay operation, the cursor begins at the lowest node of a ω_d^d-tree and finishes at the root of this tree, transformed, which is the lowest node in another ω_d^d-tree.

How many nodes are there in a $^m\omega_d^d$-tree? An ω_d^d-tree contains exactly 2^d nodes, of which exactly half are shaded "socket"-nodes. Therefore $^1\omega_d^d$ trees have height d and size 2^d; $^2\omega_d^d$ trees have height $2d$ and size $2^{d-1} + 2^{d-1}(|\omega_d^d|) < 2^{2d}$; $^3\omega_d^d$ trees have height $3d$ and size $2^{d-1} + 2^{d-1}(|^2\omega_d^d|) < 2^{3d}$; in general an $^m\omega_d^d$-tree has height md and size $N < 2^{md}$. In other words for a given $^m\omega_d^d$-tree, its height is greater than $\log_2 N$.

We have therefore proved the final theorem:

Theorem 3. *Let T be an $^m\omega_d^d$-tree. Then the d-splay operation applied to the deepest node of T visits $\Theta(\log_2 N)$ nodes, independent of the degree d. Furthermore the result is again an $^m\omega_d^d$-tree.*

Corollary 1. *Let k be fixed. For each N there exists a k-tree T with $|T| \geq N$ and a sequence of k-splay operations beginning with T for which the number of nodes visited is $log_2 N$ in every case, independent of k.*

10 Epilogue: Further Work

We are optimistic that this approach could offer similar results for other multiway splay variants, possibly ones without the strong symmetries of k-splay [4]. It would also be nice to examine whether our technique, as explained herein, is capable of finding lower bounds for other tree-based data structures, such as Union-Find, etc.

The reader may easily verify that the elements in our counter-example are accessed in bit-reversal order [8]. We suspect that an analogous phenomenon occurs in ordinary splay trees: Repeatedly accessing the deepest element and splaying produces an access pattern that is essentially a bit-reversal sequence. Our technique may be useful in analysing such access patterns.

Acknowledgements

Many thanks to the anonymous reviewers for their comments and suggestions which helped to improve the structure and readability of this paper.

References

[1] Allen B. and Munro I.: "Self-Organizing Binary Search Trees", *Journal of the ACM*, Vol.25, No.4, pp.526-535, 1978.   480

[2] Cole R., Mishra B., Schmidt J. P. and Siegel A.: "On the Dynamic Finger Conjecture for Splay Trees. Part I: Splay Sorting $\log n$-Block Sequences", *SIAM Journal on Computing*, Vol.30, No.1, pp.1-43, 2000.

[3] Cole R.: "On the Dynamic Finger Conjecture for Splay Trees. Part II: the Proof", *SIAM Journal on Computing*, Vol.30, No.1, pp.44-85, 2000.

[4] Georgakopoulos G. F. and McClurkin D. J.: "General Splay: a Basic Theory and Calculus", *ISAAC*, Vol.10, pp.4-17, 1999.   481, 495

[5] Sherk M.: "Self-Adjusting k-ary Search Trees", *Journal of Algorithms*, Vol.19, pp.25-44, 1995.   481, 482

[6] Sleator D. D. and Tarjan R. E.: "Self-Adjusting Binary Search Trees", *Journal of the ACM*, Vol.32, No.3, pp.652-686, 1985.   481, 482

[7] Subramanian A.: "An Explanation of Splaying", *Journal of Algorithms*, Vol.20, No.3, pp.512-525, 1996.

[8] Wilber R.: "Lower Bounds for Accessing Binary Trees with Rotations", *SIAM Journal on Computing*, Vol.19, No.1, pp.56-67, 1989.   495

Author Index

Lecture Notes in Computer Science

For information about Vols. 1–2552

please contact your bookseller or Springer-Verlag